A Luta Continua

A history of media freedom in South Africa

Lizette Rabe

SUN PRESS

A luta continua: A history of media freedom in South Africa

Published by African Sun Media, Stellenbosch under the SUN PReSS imprint

First edition 2020

ISBN 978-1-928480-80-8
ISBN 978-1-928480-81-5 (e-book)
https://doi.org/10.18820/9781928480815

Set in Amerigo 10/12

Cover design, typesetting and production by African Sun Media
Cover image © streamelements.com/adrianaeliseg
Text editing: Marisa Honey

SUN PReSS is an imprint of African Sun Media. Scholarly, professional and reference works are published under this imprint in print and electronic formats.

This publication can be ordered from:
orders@africansunmedia.co.za
Takealot: bit.ly/2monsfl
Google Books: bit.ly/2k1Uilm
africansunmedia.store.it.si *(e-books)*
Amazon Kindle: amzn.to/2ktL.pkL

Visit africansunmedia.co.za for more information.

Burke said there were three estates in Parliament;
but, in the reporters' gallery yonder
there sat a "fourth estate" more important far than they all.
— *Thomas Carlyle (1795-1881)*

The new press battles which wait are no less important than those fought
by the early pioneers. Their outcome will touch every civilised person. For
whatever its merits as an industry, the press represents a vital but fragile
freedom; a freedom achieved at great cost and, in this country, built on the
courage, tenacity and faith of many men of differing persuasions.
It is a freedom which cannot be taken for granted.
— *Wessel de Kock, A Manner of Speaking, 1982*

A critical, independent and investigative press is the lifeblood of any
democracy … It must enjoy the protection of the Constitution so that
it can protect our rights as citizens. It is only such a free press that can
temper the appetite of any government to amass power at the expense
of the citizen … It is only such a free press that can have the capacity to
relentlessly expose excesses and corruption on the part of the government,
state officials and other institutions that hold power.
— *Nelson Mandela, International Press Institute Congress, 1994*

This publication is dedicated to South Africa's journalists,
who strive to fulfil the public's right to know under difficult circumstances
and uphold the tenets of a free, responsible and independent media as a public trust.

CONTENTS

Abbreviations i

Foreword vii

Preface ix

PART I: Setting the parameters

1. Introduction 3

2. But what, then, is media freedom? 15

PART II: Colonialism's terra incognita

3. Before 1800 31

   The Post Tree, the "discoverers", the Dutch, Adam Tas, a plea letter, the Cape Patriots, and first expressions of freedom of expression

4. The turn of the century and onward 43

   British colonialism, the first fighters for press freedom, the "Magna Carta", and the foundation for South Africa's media industry

5. The second half of the 19th century 89

   The two Colonies, the two Republics, the beginning of media empires, and the Newspaper Press Union

PART III: The unfreedoms of White Unionism and White Nationalism

6. The period 1900 to 1948 127

   The War, Union, Afrikaner Nationalism and partisan journalism on both sides of the language divide

7. The period 1948 to 1990 153

   Media (un)freedom under apartheid

PART IV: The new democracy dawns

8. The period 1990 to 2009 261

   Democracy and its pillar, media freedom

9. The period from 2009 onward 303

   The Tribunal, the Secrecy Bill, Zumacracy, Ramaphoria ... and a pandemic

Addendum 383
   The Press Code of Ethics and Conduct for South African Print and
   Online Media

Selected Sources 391
Index 405
Endnotes 417

ABBREVIATIONS

AB	Afrikaner Broederbond
ABC	African Broadcasting Corporation
ABC	Audit Bureau of Circulation
AI	artificial intelligence
AIP	Association of Independent Publishers
ANC	African National Congress
AP	Afrikaner Party
AP	Associated Press
APAI	African Platform on Access to Information
ASA	Advertising Standards Authority
AU	African Union
B-BBEE	broad-based black economic empowerment
BBC	British Broadcasting Corporation
BC	Black Consciousness
BCCSA	Broadcasting Complaints Commission South Africa
BEE	black economic empowerment, including broad-based BEE
BUSA	Business Unity South Africa
CC	Constitutional Court
CHR	Centre for Humanities Research
ComTask	Communications Task Group
Codesa	Convention for a Democratic South Africa
COM	Campaign for Open Media
COSATU	Congress of South African Trade Unions
CSO	civil society organisations
CP	Conservative Party
CPJ	Committee to Protect Journalists
DA	Democratic Alliance
DIP	Democratic Information Programme
DLF	Democratic Left Front
DM	Daily Maverick
DP	Democratic Party
DPP	Director of Public Prosecutions
DR(C)	Dutch Reformed (Church)
DZA	De Zuid-Afrikaan
EC	Electoral Commission
EFF	Economic Freedom Fighters

EJN	Ethical Journalism Network
FAWO	Film and Allied Workers Organisation
FPA	Films and Publications Act
FPB	Films and Publication Board
FXI	Freedom of Expression Institute
GCIS	Government Communication and Information System
GNU	Government of National Unity
GRA	Genootskap van Regte Afrikaners
HDI	historically disadvantaged individuals
HNZAT	Het Nederduitsch Zuid-Afrikaansch Tydschrift
HRC	Human Rights Commission
IBA	Independent Broadcasting Authority
ICASA	Independent Communications Authority of South Africa
ICFJ	International Center for Journalists
ICT	information and communications technology
ICU	Industrial and Commercial Workers' Union
IFP	Inkatha Freedom Party
IPI	International Press Institute
ISP	internet service provider
ISPA	Internet Service Providers' Association
JCI	Johannesburg Consolidated Investments
JSE	Johannesburg Stock Exchange
KTI	Kagiso Trust Investment
KZN	KwaZulu-Natal
LMS	London Missionary Society
MAT	Media Appeals Tribunal
MDDA	Media Development and Diversity Agency
MG	Mail&Guardian
MISA	Media Institute of Southern Africa
MMA	Media Monitoring Africa
MMP	Media Monitoring Project
MP	Member of Parliament
MPASA	Magazine Publishers' Association of South Africa
MOU	memorandum of understanding
MWASA	Media Workers' Association of South Africa
NAIL	New Africa Investment Limited
NDR	National Democratic Revolution
NEC	National Empowerment Consortium
NEC	National Executive Committee

NKPA	National Key Points Act (of 1980)
NP	National Party
NNP	New National Party
NPA	National Prosecuting Agency
NPU	Newspaper Press Union
NSMS	National Security Management System
NUMSA	National Union of Mineworkers SA
ONO	Organisation of News Ombuds
PAIA	Promotion of Access to Information Act
PBS	public broadcasting service
PCSA	Press Council South Africa
PCS	public commercial service
PDMSA	Print and Digital Media South Africa
PMASA	Print Media Association of South Africa
PFC	Press Freedom Commission
PFP	Progressive Federal Party
PGA	Parliamentary Press Gallery Association
PMSA	Print Media South Africa (PMSA)
PPS	Parliamentary Protection Services
PR	public relations
R2K	Right2Know
RC	Roman Catholic
RDM	Rand Daily Mail
RDP	Reconstruction and Development Programme
RSF	Reporters Without Borders
SA	South Africa(n)
SABC	South African Broadcasting Corporation
SACS	South African Communication Service
SADC	Southern African Development Community
SAHRC	South African Human Rights Commission
SANEF	South African National Editors' Forum
SANNC	South African Native National Congress
SAPS	South African Police Services
SASJ	South African Society of Journalists
SAUJ	South African Union of Journalists
SATU	South African Typographical Union
SAW	South African War (Anglo-Boer War)
SONA	State of the Nation Address
TEC	Transitional Executive Committee

TNU	Transvaal National Union
UBJ	Union of Black Journalists
UN	United Nations
UP	United Party
US(A)	United States (of America)
VOC	Dutch East India Company
VWB	Vrye Weekblad
WAN	World Association of Newspapers
WEF	World Editors' Forum
WASA	Writers Association of South Africa
ZAR	Zuid-Afrikaansche Republiek

Notes

- For the sake of brevity and easier reading, all statements and quotations following a reference are attributed to the *last reference/source*, even when following in a next paragraph or paragraphs. This reference stands until the next source is quoted, unless the author added her own interpretation of history. Therefore, please always refer to the last reference in case of any uncertainty. In some cases, the same reference is repeated to ensure clear attribution.

- It is inevitable that sources will (usually) refer to the male and use the male pronoun as reference. This project attempts to present an inclusive interpretation of the past, and therefore will attempt to rectify this where necessary.

- Where racist descriptions of people and titles of publications appear, they are left as are, as this was the nomenclature of the time. Although historically correct, the author and publisher acknowledge the historic trauma this may trigger.

- Instead of the abbreviations AD (Anno Domini) and BC (Before Christ), CE (Common Era) and BCE (Before Common Era) are used.

- Where quotations were originally in Afrikaans, they were translated.

- As is the case with historical narratives, periods cannot be divided into absolute eras, and although the chapters indicate the various periods, there will be some chronological overlap.

- Spelling follows SA English, except where the source has used US English. The use of lower case and upper case is also left as is in the quotation. The media are referred to as plural, except where in quotations they are referred to as singular.

A Luta Continua

Thank you to the Oppenheimer Memorial Trust Award,
the HB and MJ Thom Award, the Ton Vosloo Journalism Fund and the
LW Hiemstra Trust for making this publication possible.
The latter trust was founded by Riekie Hiemstra in memory of
Ludwig Wybren (Louis) Hiemstra.

THE OPPENHEIMER MEMORIAL TRUST
LW Hiemstra Trust

FOREWORD

One must surely have a deep love and affection for media to tackle such an intimidating self-assignment as the history of media freedom in South Africa. Or one has to be a masochist. Fortunately, for the well-being of the youthful and brittle democracy in South Africa, the task was undertaken by Professor Lizette Rabe. The mind boggles at the demands of such a project. But Rabe is no stranger to vigorous research and sound penmanship of the highest standards. Thus one can state that the result is an incisive, thorough and very readable overview of the trials and tribulations of media in South Africa: in pre-colonial, in colonial, in oppressive centuries, in the modern-day democratic environment, right up to the havoc sown by the arrival of the digital communication era. Rabe has exhaustively mined the information of media history as it unfolded, and constructed it into what to my mind is a very readable and informative tome.

The history is all there, but written in an easy-to-follow style: academic, but well-researched journalism mixed with nuggets of humour on the doings of scalawags, of unsavoury practitioners of the craft of journalism, and of the heroism of many reporters, editors and publishers against the might of the state and governments wishing to act in secrecy, and dictatorially.

There are a plethora of definitions of press or media freedom. One is to publish the truth. But what is the truth? It has many faces. One definition could be the truth based on the human right of freedom of expression. I like the one by John Milton from 1644: The liberty to know, to utter and to argue freely according to one's conscience. Many men and women through the ages took up that challenge to chronicle the unfolding life and times of our society. There were and are white citizens who were punished for their initiatives. There were brown and black fighters for the truth who were ruthlessly victimised, haunted and suppressed. The role of these torchbearers and their work forms the beadwork of this haunting tale of media enterprise in the history of South Africa. For Rabe's book morphs into a history of the unfolding southern Africa: the bumps and grinds, the days of light and darkness, the times of peace and the many times of war, attrition and regression.

What was attained from 1990 onwards is a miracle of sorts. The maltreatment of media was banished and the age of free speech became a cornerstone of the new Constitution. But Rabe, as a seasoned editor and hugely experienced teacher of journalism, retains the wariness of the experienced practitioner by using the well-known struggle phrase as the title of the book, A luta continua. The struggle is unending vigilance. As one steeped in the craft and profession of journalism and publishing, I heartily endorse Rabe's work as a must read, with a suggestion that another sub-title could be added: *Bloodied but unbowed*.

TON VOSLOO
June 2020
*Former editor of Beeld,
former CEO of Naspers and
former chair of the Naspers Board of Directors*

PREFACE

There can be no democracy without media freedom. The notion of media freedom, which encapsulates all types of freedom of expression, is the foundation of any society that calls itself a democracy. In fact, media freedom is the only guarantee of an individual's freedom.

Media freedom concerns every aspect of a citizen's freedom, yet this is something that not all citizens understand. Even the informed are often against the notion of media freedom because they think the media are only there to pry into private lives. But this is not what media freedom entails. The fact that the ordinary South African might oppose media freedom is yet another legacy of South Africa's past – the result of low media literacy in our country, where the citizenry never knew a free media, nor came to the realisation that a free media is their only guarantee of freedom. In the words of Mpumelelo Mkhabela, leading journalist, ex-editor of *Sowetan* and former chair of the South African National Editors' Forum (SANEF): "Media freedom has nothing to do with the media, but with the freedom of citizens."[1]

Media freedom, as in the quote[2] by Nelson Mandela, indeed is the lifeblood of a democracy. In our post-truth age, with fake news of epidemic dimensions – and an American president who goes out of his way to make the news media suspect, declaring them "enemy of the people" – an independent media and media freedom have become more important than ever.

The preamble to the South African Press Code (SAPC) states:

> The media exist to serve society. Their freedom provides for independent scrutiny of the forces that shape society, and is essential to realising the promise of democracy. It enables citizens to make informed judgments on the issues of the day, a role whose centrality is recognised in the South African Constitution.[3]

When the Newspaper Press Union (NPU), which provided the foundation of South Africa's future news industry, was founded in Grahamstown (now Mkhanda) on 27 November 1882, mayor Chas J. Stirk, in welcoming the delegates, said:[4]

> In every free country the Press is held in honour; and we rejoice that your assembling in our midst affords us an opportunity to express recognition of its high value to this Colony, and of the great services it continually renders in the promotion of improvement, the redress of grievances, and the spread of intelligence.

One hundred years later, in 1982, Wessel de Kock wrote on the centenary of the NPU that a free press, in the words of press freedom pioneer John Fairbairn, is not only an "inestimable privilege", but also one about which most people know little. Also, that the history of the press in "this country is turbulent, rich and varied".[5]

This publication is an attempt to portray the development of this cornerstone of democracy from the time that Western communication migrated together with Europeans to what is today South Africa. This is in fact the first comprehensive attempt to compile such a history of media freedom since colonial times in South Africa.

Although the subject matter in this book covers a wide spectrum, it does not pretend to be exhaustive – at all. The topic of press freedom, and in today's language media freedom, is far too complex. As in the words of a scholar as early as 1947: "It is said that South Africa's history, especially history that means something because it is a history of attempts to develop a nation, has few stories more gripping than the struggle for press freedom."[6]

The extent of this struggle is also to be seen in a quote by dictatorial colonial governor Lord Charles Somerset, as recorded by Thomas Pringle, one of the first fighters for press freedom in the early 1800s: "It is my firm determination to put down, by all the means with which the law has entrusted me, such attempts as have recently been made to disturb the public peace, whether by inflammatory or libellous writings, or by any other measures."[7] Somerset went on to describe Pringle's plans for an independent publication to Lord Bathurst, Secretary of State for the Colonies in London, with these words: "I foresee great evil."

**

As some context for the methodology with which the research for this publication has been approached, it should be stated that, in media historiographical research, the two approaches of "deep drilling" and "episodic" methods are useful to mine information. The first approach entails "drilling" deep into one single event in an effort to understand more about that event. The second, the episodic approach, aims to gain a chronological understanding of fact and circumstance. For this publication, the episodic approach was generally applied in an attempt to give an overview of the timeline of the development of South African media freedom.

It is of course no surprise that media freedom developed hand in hand with the complexities of the historical, social, economic and political developments of the various regions that would later become the geopolitical entity of the Republic of South Africa.

Various works on different aspects of South African press and media history have been published over the years, some of them specifically on media freedom. However, none have attempted to provide a chronological overview. Some of these works that have appeared include Bosman's *Hollandse Joernalistiek in Suid-Afrika gedurende die 19de Eeu (Dutch Journalism in South Africa during the 19th Century)*,[8] Nienaber's *Beknopte Geskiedenis (A Brief History)*,[9] Du Plessis's *Die Afrikaanse Pers (The Afrikaans Press)*,[10] Smith's *Behind the Press in South Africa*,[11] Hepple's *Censorship and Press Control in South Africa*,[12] Lewin Robinson's *None Daring to Make Us Afraid*,[13] and Ainslie's *The Press in Africa*.[14] Later publications include Hachten's *Muffled Drums*,[15] Heppel's *Press under Apartheid*,[16] Potter's *The Press as Opposition*,[17] Pollack's *Up Against Apartheid*,[18] Hachten and Giffard's *Total Onslaught: South African Press Under Attack*,[19] Tomaselli, Tomaselli and Muller's *Narrating the Crisis: Hegemony and the South African Press*,[20] Switzer's *South Africa's Alternative Press*,[21] and Switzer and Adhikari's *South Africa's Resistance Press*.[22] De Kock's *A Manner of Speaking*[23] commemorated the NPU's centenary in 1982. To these works can be added Jackson's *Breaking Story. The South African Press*,[24] Reid and Isaac's *Press Regulation in South Africa: An Analysis of the Press Council of South Africa, the Press Freedom Commission and related discourses*,[25] Teer-Tomaselli and McCracken's *Media and the Empire*,[26]

Harmse's *SABC 1936 – 1995*,[27] Kalane's *The Chapter We Wrote*,[28] and Dasnois and Whitfield's *Paper Tiger. Iqbal Survé and the Downfall of Independent Newspapers*.[29]

I gratefully acknowledge the above and all other sources, and it is my wish that this publication does not only add to the literature on what the lifeblood of a democracy should be, but that it will also strengthen the public understanding of why media freedom *must* be the lifeblood of a democracy.

LIZETTE RABE
Stellenbosch University

Part I

Setting the parameters

"Semper aliquid novi Africa affert."

– "Africa always brings forth/contributes something new."

– Thabo Mbeki, 2004

1. Introduction

South Africa has what is probably the most advanced media sector in sub-Saharan Africa.[1] This study on the history of how it all started focuses on the history of media freedom, or, in other nomenclatures, press freedom, freedom of expression, and freedom of opinion. It distinguishes between *communication* and *media*, and in this case the news media, based on the technology of print and the development into radio, television and digital, and not communication *per se*.

The fact that this study regards the first Western modes of communication as the beginning of media communication in this region does not negate pre-colonial ways of communication. This research, however, concerns media, and as media historiographical researcher I cannot write about pre-colonial communication. Still, I would like to point to the vast potential of researching this important aspect of our shared cultural past. One scholar wrote that the media in Africa as a whole can be identified according to three distinct, but overlapping, time periods.[2] They are the colonial, post-colonial and globalisation epochs. Contemporary African media originate in the colonial past, with today's press in Anglophone Africa sprouting from four different kinds of early newspapers. These were official government gazettes, the missionary press, privately owned newspapers, and underground political, anti-colonial publications. In these countries, the development of the media was thus directly or indirectly linked to the British Empire's colonial objectives, with "Africa's modern print and electronic media develop[ing] as the direct or indirect result of contact with Europe". Also, few African societies had a written language, "and in those that did, printing was either unknown or underdeveloped". Although Arab traders brought literacy to West and East Africa, the technology of print came from Europe.

Therefore, a treasure trove of communication information, waiting for new generations of researchers, is still locked up in, e.g., the Bleek Collection, which consists of the papers of W.H.I. Bleek (1827–1875), his sister-in-law Lucy Lloyd (1834–1914), his daughter Dorothea Bleek (1873–1948), and G.W. Stow (1822–1882), containing their research into the San language and folklore. It also contains the stories of specifically one unique individual, //Kabbo. All of these collections will hopefully also be researched from a communication perspective. Fortunately, they are already part of the UNESCO Memory of the World Archive, which can be accessed online.[3]

Out of Africa, always something new

Returning to the focus of this publication, I would nevertheless want to begin with a period long before Western Europeans set foot on the most southern part of Africa.

"Africa is always producing something new," Pliny the Elder (23–79 CE) wrote about 2,000 years ago.[4] However, Aristotle (384–322 BCE) had already formulated the expression three hundred years earlier in his writings on natural history: "There is always something new coming out of Africa."

In Aristotle's Greek, "new" was meant negatively. He referred to the "newness" of some "strange" animals from Africa. His conclusion regarding the "strangeness" of these animals was that, because of Africa's (presumed general) water shortage, animals mated indiscriminately when they met at watering holes, with some "strange" creatures as the result.

When Roman statesman Pliny the Elder used it almost three centuries later in his *Historia Naturalis*, he used the expression that by then had become a proverb: "Africa is always producing something new." In the next decades it became so garbled that, when scribes copied a collection of proverbs by the Greek scholar Zenobius (2nd century CE), they transformed this expression into "Africa is always producing something evil".

Almost twenty centuries later, on the occasion of the forming of the South African Union in 1910, the British banker and politician, R.H. Brand, would write to South African statesman J.C. Smuts: "I wonder why South Africa has the power of being perennially interesting. Something dramatic is always going on there."[5] Brand was a member of what was called "Milner's Kindergarten", a group of young administrators under Alfred Milner, High Commissioner to South Africa, also regarded as the instigator behind the South African War (SAW), or the Anglo Boer War, from 1899 to 1902.

But between those ancient sages and the founding of the South Africa Union in 1910, a totally different "animal" mutated in strange ways in Africa's most southern regions. It resulted in some even stranger creatures. And, to boot, some evil too. Thus the expression, "always something new from Africa" – while being "perennially interesting" – gained a new meaning.

How it all began

This story, literally, begins after Western colonisers set foot on the most southern shores of Africa, after which, with them, the printing presses of the time also arrived. Along with them came the "problem of press freedom", as it was described much later.[6] As the "problem of press freedom" started to develop, it led to all kinds of new, strange, and even evil characters. Of course, this is not unique to our continent. The "problem of press freedom" is universal, but this is the story of those strange and sometimes evil creatures in the evolution of press freedom in the landscape of southern Africa. In later terminology, and during different political ecosystems in what eventually would become South Africa, it mutated into phrases such as freedom of speech and freedom of expression, and today – thanks to technology – into an all-inclusive "media freedom".

As an important first point of departure in this history of media freedom – or to follow in the classical tradition of Aristotle's and Pliny's *Historia Naturalis*, this "Historia Media Libertatum" – the lacunae that exist in scholarship regarding pre-colonial South African communication are acknowledged. Furthermore, this *Historia* will namely also focus only on the evolution of freedom of expression as it occurred after the arrival of the first colonists.

Although the term "media freedom" will be used mostly, it will be used interchangeably with press freedom, and will include the notion of "freedom of the press" as per the predigital age, as well as the notions "freedom of speech" and "freedom of expression". Exactly what this means will be discussed in the next chapter.

Political advocacy equals print media

Political advocacy was a central function of the print media from the beginning of the Western print era, particularly from the time of the Reformation in 1517.[7] By the late 18th and early 19th century, this indeed was its principal function in a number of countries. A new model of political journalism only began to emerge in the late 19th century. A journalist was now regarded as "neutral arbiter" of political communications, "standing apart from particular interests and causes". This was followed by the development of a commercial, profit-driven press, funded by advertisers, rather than one serving a political cause.

Since the first European colonists arrived in southern Africa, all types of freedom, and in this case especially press freedom, have been under pressure, prohibited or censored under different governments, although there were periods of relative calm in between. Under the first democratic[8] government, that of the ANC since 1994, it is ironic that, despite media freedom being entrenched in the Constitution, it still remained under threat.

When South Africa's first independent newspaper was finally published in 1824 – almost two centuries after the first Europeans colonised the Cape – "newspapers the world over were struggling".[9] It was "not so much to print, but to print free from government control" – in other words, to exist free from censorship. In fact, at the time, the word "newspaper" was still new.

Censorship, or the suppression of free expression, thus was imported together with colonialism and, of course, everything else this political construct embodied. It was a repeat of the status quo elsewhere, as, ever since communication has been recorded, censorship has been part of powerful political push-and-pull factors in all regions and in all periods.

Also, the term not only referred to state censorship, but also to church, corporate and self-censorship by the media themselves. The latter might even be a harsher and more crippling type of censorship due to the political-commercial interests of the media that need to be protected – also at the cost of freedom of expression.

But that is exactly why media freedom – the freedom to be informed – is so important. Put simply, "information is power", as phrased by American media mogul Ted Turner, creator of the world's first 24-hour news channel, CNN.[10] And, precisely because information is power, governments and those who control the free flow of information prefer to control that flow, and have tried their utmost to regulate, manage, police and govern that flow. Or fight, resist, combat and censor the flow, as we have also seen in democratic South Africa in ways that are sometimes more pronounced, sometimes more vague, despite media freedom now Constitutionally entrenched.

South Africa's 'unfree free media' and how it all began

It is accepted that one of the most contentious subjects concerning the media, throughout the world, is the right to freedom of expression, and therefore press or media freedom. In South Africa, the freedom of the press, or media freedom, has always been an issue.

After the Dutch colonial period, British colonialism did not imply press freedom. Rather, because press freedom "was achieved in courage and sacrifice and not dribbled from a limp wrist as an official favour, a refreshingly forthright and independent-minded press emerged, remarkable for its articulate sense of professional ethics and integrity".[11] After press freedom was granted in 1829, "literally hundreds of newspapers and journals sprung up and flowered – or withered". By the turn of the century there was scarcely a town not served by at least one newspaper.

Printing in South Africa unfolded in three phases. The first dates from the arrival at the Cape in 1784 of Johann Christian Ritter, a German bookbinder. The second phase was after the granting of press freedom, in 1829, when the press established itself in an arc from Cape Town to the Eastern Province and Natal. The last phase of the first pioneering press was after the discovery of diamonds and gold, when the presses moved northward, to the then Boer Republics.

But press freedom was challenged in every region and under every government. An example: The situation in which the media found themselves under apartheid was referred to as the most "unfree free media" in Africa.[12] Newspapers were "free to publish whatever they wish as long as they do not publish whatever they are told not to publish".

What then is the history of press freedom, or media freedom, or freedom of expression, or freedom of speech, in South Africa? And what about our post-1994 democratic South Africa? Can South African citizens relax, knowing that their freedom – as encapsulated in media freedom and entrenched in the Constitution – is safe?

The answer is that, despite South Africa's so-called liberal Constitution, with media freedom and freedom of expression enshrined in Article 16 of the Bill of Rights, media freedom is continuously under threat. This was illustrated when mobile phone signals were scrambled during the State of the Nation (SONA) address on 12 February 2015. According to several days' news reports, State Security individuals, or the department as a whole, were responsible for this breach of the Constitution.[13] Since then, it was almost as if state officials felt they had a licence not only to violate media freedom, but even to attack journalists. One such incident happened at Parliament on 11 March 2015, when the police assaulted a journalist in what was described as "thuggish" behaviour.[14] Since then there have been numerous attacks on the media, both verbal and physical, such as happened at the 54th ANC Conference at Nasrec, Johannesburg in December 2017, when there was both a verbal attack on the media by outgoing ANC president Jacob Zuma, as well as a physical attack by ANC security staff on a journalist.[15]

There is no law prohibiting media freedom in democratic South Africa. This would be unconstitutional, but apartheid-era laws inhibiting the media are still lurking in existing legislation, as will be described in this publication. These laws are experienced as inhibiting, and therefore constitute a danger to media freedom. The power of intimidation was illustrated with the threats of court cases, e.g., against cartoonist Zapiro, for his portrayal of South Africa's third president.[16]

But what was the situation under previous governments, and in previous eras, since those earliest colonial times? This publication will take a bird's flight over almost four centuries of the history of freedom of expression in South Africa, although the real struggle for press freedom lasted just about two centuries of that period, since no freedom of expression was allowed in the first more than 150 years of colonialism.

1. Introduction

This bird's-eye view will take us over a landscape from the very first Western communication, as per the Post Tree in Mossel Bay, through the era under the Dutch, to the British colonial era and the first attempts to raise voices against the tyranny of a colonial despot, up to the current, post-'94 situation, with constant threats still hanging over the media, such as the Protection of State Information Bill and the proposal of a Media Appeals Tribunal (MAT).

Added to this are issues that developed under the third presidency, still lingering, together with the knowledge that post-democracy South Africa still has many apartheid-era laws in place that can be invoked to keep the media in check ... which means that this bird's-eye view flight might be something of a bumpy ride. But before we can take off, some clarifications are necessary regarding approach and point of departure, as "GPS markers" in terms of the journey and the route to be taken.

A tandem of history and media historiography

The history of censorship – or lack of media freedom – developed in tandem with the history of South Africa from colonial times, as media freedom (or not) is a reflection of the political situation of any given era.

The history of the media in South Africa is therefore also a political history of censorship, repression and oppression. It reflects every government system of its time, since the first colonisation of the Cape under the Dutch East India Company (VOC) in 1652. The first South African publication came off the presses under British colonial rule in the early 1800s. Before this, no freedom of expression was permitted at the Cape. Indeed, there was not even a printing press. This publication therefore begins the story of censorship in those pre-press and pre-newspaper eras.

As the story unfolds from the first Western communication in this region, beginning with the first "hub" of communication, namely the "Post Tree", it is acknowledged once again that the mostly oral and petroglyphic communication of pre-colonial times will not be included in this historiography. It is hoped that studies specifically on the communication aspect of those pre-colonial rock gravures, such as in the following photograph, will be undertaken.

Rock art in the Cederberg Mountains.
Photo: L Rabe

The original inhabitants of the Cape constituted an oral society, one "filled with the excitement of sound but with no written language among the indigenous people".[17] As Wessel de Kock wrote: "[S]ome men relayed meaning through pictures on cave walls, and just a few stories cried out mutely." On the "barren west coast" Portuguese seafarers left inscribed crosses facing "the dun coloured dunes and the sighing wind", as did "the post office stones in the lee of Table Bay close to the thundering surf and, hopefully, passing vessels". Eventually, the missionaries came, "listened to Africa's human sounds", and reduced "to form and rule this language which hitherto floated in the wind".[18]

But "two of the countries in Europe where printing and newspapers made the biggest strides in a relatively short time", Holland and England, "as a matter of policy flatly rejected this privilege for their vassal, the Cape Colony". For almost 150 years after Jan van Riebeeck's arrival there was no printing press at the Cape, with the first press only permitted when the VOC allowed governor Joachim van Plettenberg "some printing type" in 1782 to produce emergency currency when the war with England had caused a delay in the normal consignment from Holland. Requests for a printing press were consistently turned down, with all books and tracts, mostly of a religious nature, imported. In a 1779 "memorial" the burghers fruitlessly petitioned for a press and a printer "to relieve the burden of official paper work and to enable placaaten to be distributed more speedily to outlying districts". Governor Cornelis van de Graaff also added his voice to secure a press, but in vain. In another Dutch colony, Ceylon, it had already been permitted in 1743. To the Dutch and British authorities, "colonies were outposts run mostly at a loss to secure the interests of the home country and not to provide the finer things of life – or risk the discontent inherent in a free press".

Approach clarified

The historical research method is the obvious approach in an attempt to understand a so-called "past reality", such as the focus of this publication. Simultaneously, it needs to be said that no history can ever be complete. Any history can merely suggest "this is what the researcher came across", and that is always determined by a specific point of departure.

South Africa's history, firstly of colonialism (1652 to the early 1900s), through unionism (1910 to 1948, as part of the British Commonwealth) and apartheid (1948 to 1994, including a republic separate from the Commonwealth since 1961), followed by a democratic dispensation since 1994, is a history that was recorded mainly from a male, Western, colonial, racialised point of departure. As described by one scholar, historians were "unavoidably influenced by personal background and social experiences", with mainstream history the "fragile expressions of white male historians' limited perspectives".[19] This is acknowledged, and this history therefore will endeavour to allow the "voiceless" during these eras to be heard as far as is possible, to record an inclusive history of South Africa's press freedom.

As media history is an understudied field in South African media studies, also pointed out by Wigston[20] and Sonderling,[21] it goes without saying that a lacuna exists regarding comprehensive overview studies concerning the history of press freedom in South Africa. The lacuna in the field as a whole is stressed by Teer-Tomaselli,[22] writing that "Media history is a relatively new area in media studies worldwide," and that in South Africa, "it has not made significant inroads onto the agendas of conference programmes, academic journal articles or student syllabi". McCracken[23] emphasised that the "status of Media

History is less defined", and, being "a relatively new discipline", it has been spared much" of "educational baggage". Therefore, as context, a brief discussion follows regarding the position of journalism studies/media studies, and that of history, leading to the concept of media history and the concept of press freedom, or media freedom.

Firstly, history and historiography are two concepts understood as per Canadian historian Daniel Woolf's definitions, namely that *history* is the discipline of history as it has developed as the "accumulated events of the past", consisting of many genres.[24] *Historiography* is understood as the writing of history, including the meta-level of historical thinking – in other words, a study of how history has been written. Closer to home, historian Johan de Villiers's definition of historiography is that it attempts to mine accessible sources, report on, and analyse, events of the past.[25]

It also needs to be stressed that those who govern are the writers of history. Or, as Woolf formulated it: "A new religion, like a new state, will cement its triumph over the old through its control of the past, writing history into a new 'master-narrative' with itself as the inevitable and logical outcome of events."[26] In such an understanding, media history, in effect, also becomes part of a master (political) narrative in any given history or country.

For the purposes of an overview of the history of press freedom, it is also useful to refer briefly to the binary qualities shared by journalism and history. In fact, one scholar wrote that the relationship between journalism and history stretches "at least as far back … as the Greek philosophers".[27]

Journalism has also been described as "history in a hurry", and journalists as "historians in a hurry". Hence this description from 1949 is also apt, namely that "the journalist is himself the historian of the present, and the record which he puts together will, when used with critical discretion, furnish valuable source material for the scholar of the future who delves into the history of our times".[28] In the idiom of 1949 it was an exclusively male phrasing, which emphasises the subjectivity of history as the expression of a certain male perspective. This also explains how different histories can exist, and why histories are constantly rewritten.

For this media history focus, however, let's return to the continuum between journalism and history, as it should be noted that, in fact, the origins of "journalism lie in exactly the same place as the origins of history". The Athenian Thucydides (455–400 BCE) is regarded as the first true historian as well as the first journalist because of his *The History of the Peloponnesian War*.[29] Others regard Herodotus (484–425 BCE) as *pater historiae* because of his account of the Persian Wars,[30] while still others regard the two as the "twin founders" of "approaches to the past".[31] In the Hellenistic era, these two were even portrayed together as a double-headed bust, as in the following picture.

The double-headed bust of Thucydides and Herodotus.
Photo: Freeware Internet

In terms of an "academic pedigree", both journalism and history have been viewed as a "hybrid, interdisciplinary mix of the humanities and the social sciences".[32] Journalism was regarded as lacking a formal academic methodology, and was even described as "a bastard orphan discipline". Today it is accepted that journalism, and therefore journalism and media studies, must be, by nature, trans-, inter- and multi-disciplinary. One scholar felt so strongly about the position of journalism that she claimed "journalism itself is the study and synthesis of everything else, of all disciplines".[33] Added to this, it is interesting to note that the word *history*, as derived from its Greek root, also means to *investigate*, to *inquire*, and even to *discover*,[34] all of which are the tenets of journalism. In other words, history can almost serve as synonym for journalism and its task to investigate, inquire and discover.

A history of media freedom in South Africa can also be regarded as a perfect example of a fusion between what could be found through empirical research, and what can be interpreted according to what played out in terms of "ideology and power". Along with this it needs to be emphasised that history contains only "part truths", as a complete version of a "past reality" is unattainable.[35]

In other words, there cannot be any "objective" narrative. A researcher's own "blind spots" may come into effect unintentionally – a significant caveat. This formulation sums it up: In historical research the researcher's "beliefs, attitudes, assumptions and values" will always influence the interpretation and analysis of historical data and the writing of the research product.[36] As all information studied by a historical researcher is indirect, and mostly only available "through a reconstructed account of past events", it means a historical researcher has the responsibility to cover the subject, event or idea in as much detail, and as accurately and comprehensively as possible in order not to let any bias dictate the findings. Despite these shortcomings, historical research can "shine a light" on past events, why they happened in a certain way, and why we are still influenced by them in our time.

It is especially the temporal divide – including the danger of applying presentism to the past – that needs to be taken into account in any historical study. The challenge for the researcher is to "bridge" the divide between the past and the present.[37] The fact that "all individuals (including social researchers) are shaped by the social and intellectual contexts of their own time", and that researchers must "divest themselves of the limiting biases and preconceptions of the present in order to engage the past openly", means that history has, mostly, reflected the perspectives of white males up to a certain point. Such limitations must be overcome, otherwise historical analysis rests "upon myth, prejudice and misrepresentation". Researchers therefore need to understand their own limitations in terms of how "to understand and translate" historical data to ensure the final product will be, as far as is possible, accurate in relation to the original historical context. And then, of course, one needs to be "acutely aware" of "the naïve assumption that history, as documented, necessarily coincides with what actually happened", as is often warned in historical research.[38]

History as 'record of progress' and 'webs of significance'

If one accepts that an "organising principle" of historiography is a "record of progress",[39] the question is how has press freedom as "record of progress" developed in South Africa? How should one try to understand the Why's and How's of the Who, What, Where and When of press freedom – in other words, applying the 5 Ws and 1 H of journalism?

This is also why history is "more than a list of dates, names and places or facts that speak for themselves".[40] Through analyses, a deeper meaning of past events and perceptions can be found. This involves studying the records of the past, with researchers "selecting, analysing and writing about the past", thus completing the "historical research circle". In doing so, one should re-emphasise that it is about "a reconstructed account of past events" and that researchers themselves need to understand their own possible biases.

On a more philosophical note, to concur with German sociologist Max Weber that "man is an animal suspended in webs of significance he himself spun", culture is "those webs and the analysis of it", and "not an experimental science in search of law, but an interpretive one in search of meaning".[41] What then are the webs of culture and society that were spun around different freedoms in South Africa through the different eras, and what meaning can be gathered from them? In the classic Weberian phrase: What is the "verstehen" (understanding) regarding the facts (and possibly fables) around media freedom and its development in southern Africa?

The answer to this question is something that you, the reader, will have to decide after you have visited the different eras, their socio-cultural histories, and the factors implicated in those eras and cultures. Because how, indeed, can one person attempt to revisit previous eras – maybe even arrogantly: almost four centuries – and attempt to understand those socio-cultural facts and factors, especially in a country as complex as South Africa?

Again, one needs to take into account that everything is just a certain interpretation of a "past reality". This is especially so as there were no newspapers in the beginning, which means that that so important "first draft of history"[42] could not encapsulate the "story of the day". Therefore, one should be aware of "the naïve assumption that history, as documented, necessarily coincides with what actually happened".[43]

Thus, not being naïve about a complex issue such as media freedom in different eras, I, as both media historian and journalist, am cognisant of the fact that, as far as facts can be ascertained, they should speak for themselves in this narrative of media freedom in South Africa.

In 2003, a cabinet minister said in his speech at a media freedom celebration that "[n]o reasonable person can deny that the South African media today enjoy far greater freedom than any other time in history in this country".[44] He continued:

> Though there will continue to be that creative tension between the rights of a free media and the powers of government, it will only be under exceptional circumstances that any future government can curtail the freedom of the media. But can we with confidence say that we have removed everything that restricts the free flow of information in our society?

One year later, in 2004, South Africa's second president, Thabo Mbeki, felt he had to refer to the quote about Africa referred to earlier in this chapter.[45] In an address to the European Parliament in Strasbourg, Mbeki referred to two derogatory remarks about Africa. The first critic referred to the fact that "[d]espite the small flashes of good news, Africa remains in a horrible mess". This critic then referred to Pliny's "Ex Africa semper aliquid novi", or "out of Africa there is always something new", with the meaning that the news from Africa is always depressing. The second person co-incidentally also used Pliny's expression and asked in a rhetorical way what could be "more new" than Africa "pleading for aid".

Mbeki, the "African Renaissance president", then quoted the motto of the South African Museum, the country's premier museum. It reads "Semper aliquid novi Africa affert" – "Africa always brings forth/contributes something new". Mbeki explained that the museum used this particular rendition of the famous expression by Pliny the Elder as this is what was meant originally. As proud Africanist, Mbeki added that the museum's motto means, "Africa always contributes something new to human knowledge". He ended his speech by saying that, regardless of what sceptics might say, the expression must have a positive interpretation.

Thus, for the purposes of this publication, the question is how (South) Africa can contribute something new to human knowledge and our "verstehen" regarding the thorny issue of freedom of expression, or media freedom, from a historical context. What new understandings can we arrive at by looking at the history of the basic human right of freedom of expression?

So let the journey begin ...

According to one scholar, five themes run through the history of the press in South Africa:

- tension and conflict between government and the press;
- divisions in the press based on language;
- further divisions in the press based on race;
- the state viewing the press as a threat to peace and security; and
- efforts by journalists to circumvent undemocratic laws.[46]

It is inevitable that there will always be tensions between the media and the government. In fact, this should be the expected result of the nature of both institutions. Thus: What tensions since colonial times will be revealed, and what "new", even "strange", creatures have developed regarding the tenet of media freedom on South African soil since the arrival of the first European colonists? In terms of this "strangeness", one can include the description of South Africa in 1984, at the height of apartheid, as being "a very strange society".[47]

This narrative of the history of media freedom in South Africa begins with colonialism's first struggles for freedom of expression, through the vice-like grip of censorship during apartheid, up to the new democracy's rainbow nation idealism, almost destroyed by a president who ruled South Africa as his personal fiefdom ... and ends on World Press Freedom Day on 3 May 2020, with our country and our planet in the grip of a viral pandemic that threatened media freedom on all fronts, not only to fight an infodemic of fake news, but also to find post-Covid-19 viable business models to ensure the Fourth Estate survives to continue to serve the public trust.

And maybe then this underlines the theory that media history, as all other histories, is simply about the fact that names and dates, and actors and events, may change, but that the narrative, essentially, remains the same. In this case, that the struggle for freedom of expression or media freedom is a case of "a luta continua". But can one hope for "vitória é certa"?

So, dear reader, fasten your seatbelt for this flight over the most southern part of the subcontinent of Africa, giving you a bird's-eye view of a stormy history, from colonial times to the present era.

Everyone has the right to freedom of opinion and expression;
this right includes freedom to hold opinions without interference and to
seek, receive and impart information and ideas through any media
and regardless of frontiers.
– ARTICLE 19, UN Universal Declaration of Human Rights[1]

2. BUT WHAT, THEN, IS MEDIA FREEDOM?

Introduction

It is not easy to pin down the notion of media freedom in one concept, as there is no easy, single definition. This begs the questions: Why can such a vital aspect of society not be defined? How can something that is so important – regarded as the last freedom of an individual – not have a single, unanimous definition? Especially as it is regarded as a basic human right, or, in SANEF's slogan a number of years ago as on the poster on the following page: "Press freedom is **your** freedom." The SANEF campaign also resonates with this formulation by Reporters Without Borders (RSF): "Freedom of information is the freedom that allows you to verify the existence of all the other freedoms."[2]

Of course, the foundation of press freedom lies in the basic human right of freedom of expression as the basis of a democracy. But how did it originate, and how has it changed over time?

The first deliberation on the principle of freedom of expression as applied to the press was on 4 August, 1735, when a *New York Weekly Journal* writer, John Peter Zenger, was "acquitted of seditious libel against the royal governor of New York on the basis that what he published was true".[3]

Since then, there have been many debates on exactly what press freedom means, and many more struggles about the right to press freedom and how it should be applied – as this publication will illustrate regarding the development of press freedom since the Cape was colonised in 1652.

Deliberations around what press or media freedom means are closely related to what a democracy means. Just as there is no single definition of freedom of expression, there is also no single definition of democracy.

According to James Madison, one of the US's "Founding Fathers", also regarded as the "Father of the [US] Constitution",[4] freedom of expression was "the only effectual guardian of every other right" – "without it, tyranny can advance in silence".[5]

Moving to more recent times, the United Nations (UN) has promoted a free press for decades, though it acknowledges that there is no universal definition, as even among Western democracies there is no agreement about what press freedom entails.[6] In the UN's Article 19 of its Universal Declaration of Human Rights of 1946, it asserts the rights of each individual as including "the right to freedom of opinion and expression; this right includes freedom to hold opinions without interference and to seek, receive and impart information and ideas through any media and regardless of frontiers".

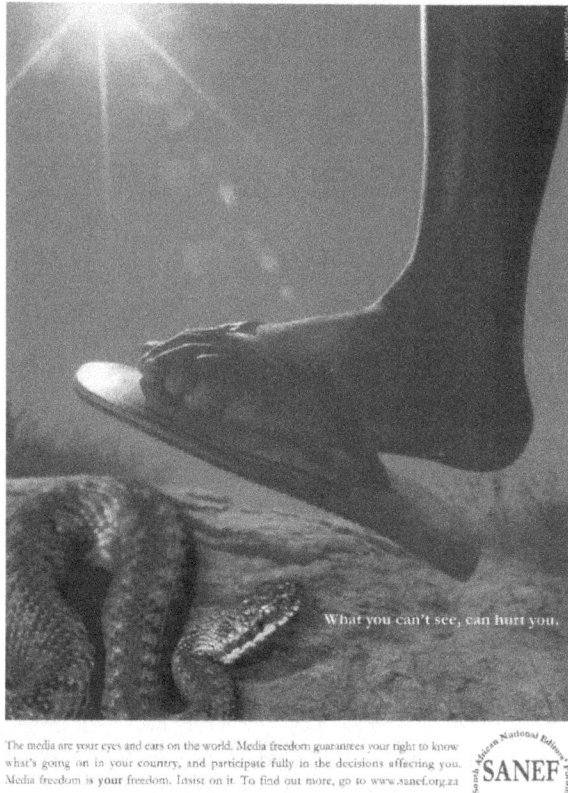

The media are your eyes and ears on the world. Media freedom guarantees your right to know what's going on in your country, and participate fully in the decisions affecting you. Media freedom is **your** freedom. Insist on it. To find out more, go to www.sanef.org.za

SANEF

One of the posters in a SANEF campaign some years ago to educate the public about one of their basic human rights.
Source: SANEF

According to one definition

> [f]reedom of the press is the guarantee by a government of free public speech, often through a state constitution for its citizens, and associations of individuals extended to members of news gathering organizations, and their published reporting. It also extends to news gathering, and processes involved in obtaining information for the public consumption.[7]

The African Union (AU) also stresses the importance of freedom of information, including media freedom.[8] The AU's Commission on Human and People's Rights' Declaration of Principles of Freedom of Expression in Africa, compiled in 2002, stressed freedom of expression and access to information. The declaration was adopted as an official AU document.

When attempting to define press freedom one should also take the notions of propaganda and censorship into account. The first is regarded as the "deliberate influencing and changing of the way people think".[9] A propagandist is "intentionally persuasive". The "manipulation of words and word substitutes" tries "to control the attitudes and consequently the behaviour of ... individuals concerning a controversial matter". One characteristic is to influence audiences by "substituting favourable or unfavourable terms, with an emotional connotation, for neutral ones". In apartheid South Africa, the use of words such as "Reds" or the "Rooi gevaar" ("Red danger") instead of "Communist" or "Russia" springs to mind.

Censorship, in turn, is described as a process "whereby certain elements are withheld in a situation either by the propagandist or someone under his influence who can control a medium of communication".[10] Censorship implies restricting the content of any means of communication. It can even "delet[e] or limit the content", as the public is supposed to be

> protected from "subversive minorities" (majority in the case of South Africa); from alien influences; from their own fears in wartime (e.g., the Angolan War); from morally debasing and obscene material; from intrusion into the personal lives of others; and in general from their own fallible thinking in whatever field authority decrees them to be peculiarly subject to error. Authority assumes a greater wisdom.

Freedom of speech in Africa

As Africa's liberation from her colonial masters progressed, the colonial "dominoes" fell closer and closer to Southern Africa; eventually also for Africa's "white tribe", the Afrikaners, although the National Party (NP) government "used desperate means to counter the impression that white rule could be coming to an end".[11] This was done through censorship and other means of manipulating public opinion. Denying a "right to information" is a feature of all "autocratic, authoritarian or totalitarian" systems,[12] although "a free and responsible press was one of the greatest assets of any society",[13] with the press "the artery through which the lifeblood of democracy flows".

During the transition period from an autocratic regime to a democracy between 1990 and 1994, discussions around media freedom, freedom of expression and freedom of speech were based on various global and local events.

The milestone 1991 Windhoek "Statement of principles" called for a free, independent and pluralistic media on the continent and globally. The "Windhoek Declaration" was regarded as a benchmark for the UN "and for all organisations in the media field".[14] It referred in its preamble to Article 19 of the UN's Declaration of Human Rights and the already referred to statement that freedom of information is a fundamental human right. It also referred to UNESCO's Resolution on the Free Flow of Ideas of 1989.

The Windhoek Declaration focused specifically on print media. In 1992, the Free, Fair and Open Media Conference in Cape Town "tied many of the loose threads of progressive media policy discussions together", but focused mainly on broadcast media. The proposal resulting from this conference was also tabled at the multiparty negotiations, known as the Convention for a Democratic South Africa (Codesa), at Kempton Park. This proposal argued for

- the establishment of an interim independent communications authority to regulate broadcasting during the transition period;

- a new, diverse SABC board; and the

- appointment of a task force to examine obstacles to diversity in the print media.

In September 1993, the Transitional Executive Committee (TEC), effectively ruling South Africa at the time, approved the creation of the Independent Broadcasting Authority (IBA). The IBA (today ICASA)[15] was established in 1994 by an Act of Parliament. Within this Act, "much of the preceding media policy debate was encapsulated", with "definitions and roles ... spelled out in law for the first time". This only applied to the national public broadcaster, as print media, as private companies, were excluded from such legislation.

Other initiatives focusing on the development of "a new progressive media policy", such as the task force on diversity, failed to materialise.[16] However, in the first decade of democracy, from 1994 to 2004, "a network of policies, laws and regulations" unfolded. These included "a raft of new labour relations, freedom of information and monopoly laws that would all have some impact on the media industry at large".

A long way …

These developments could be regarded as "revolutionary", as only in March 1983 had the minister of foreign affairs, R.F. (Pik) Botha, told a nationwide TV audience that "freedom of speech in the West means the right to lie, deceive, and distort".[17] But while South Africa was moving towards democracy, so also did its media industry. The four most important components of the new policy network concerning a free media developed from the 1990s.[18] They were

- the ANC's "Democratic Information Programme", published in 1994;

- the South African Constitution, finalised in 1996;

- the work of ICASA, established in 2000, and the IBA Act, which underpinned it; and

- the 2002 Media Development and Diversity Agency (MDDA).

This "represented the bedrock of South African media policy and its implementation" for the following period and formed "the measure by which the balance of power between the media and the state can be ascertained".

By 1994, the Democratic Information Programme (DIP) formed part of the "heavily influential" Reconstruction and Development Programme (RDP). The RDP was the "policy clarion call" of the first democratic government. It gained "rapid public acceptance", with the "frequently fulsome support" of the South African media. In the first democratic cabinet, Nelson Mandela created a cabinet post to oversee the RDP, with the "charismatic and widely respected unionist" Jay Naidoo as minister. The DIP set out the new government's attitude and expectations regarding the South African media, calling for "the active exchange of information and opinion among all members of society, within and among communities and also between government and society". Besides affirmative action it also asked for resources to be set aside "to set up broadcasting and print enterprises at a range of levels". These included addressing the lack of media literacy in South Africa, and training and educating communities to help them recognise and exercise their media rights. To limit monopolies there were also strict limitations on cross-media ownership. Allowance was made for funds to train journalists and community-based media, and it encouraged media institutions to do the same. The DIP also "served notice" that freedom-of-information legislation would be broadened, and recommended the restructuring of the government's information arm, then called the South African Communications Service.

Mainstream print media, as private companies, were mostly unaffected by these recommendations, as "calls for open debate and the exchange of opinion and information" could be "easily enough accounted for in newspapers' usual *modus operandi*". The much needed diversification of the media was matched by the "rapid expansion of the mainstream media's community newspaper divisions". Affirmative action and equity were enforced by laws such as the Labour Relations Act (1995), the Employment Equity Act (1998), the Skills Development Act (1998) and the Broad-based Black Economic Empowerment Act (2003). In the media industry, though, they "were implemented unevenly ... at best". As foundation for all these policies was the Constitution, accepted in 1996.[19]

Global and local declarations on freedom of speech

Various declarations define and protect freedom of speech. Globally, Reporters Without Borders (RSF), and locally, the Freedom of Expression Institute (FXI), as well as the Right2Know (R2K) campaign, are bodies that watch over the important issue of freedom of expression, including media freedom.

RSF is globally the biggest NGO defending media freedom. It defines media freedom simply "as the basic human right to be informed".[20] According to RSF, almost half of the world population still lacked access to information at the beginning of the 21st century. This meant that individuals were "deprived of knowledge that is essential for managing their lives", effectively "den[ying] their very existence". People are also "prevented from living in pluralist political systems in which factual truth serves as the basis for individual and collective choices".

RSF encapsulates freedom of expression in various values and principles. The first states that there "can be no freedom of thought without knowledge of reality". Also referring to the UN's Article 19, it states that "freedom of opinion and expression" implies the right to "seek, receive and impart information and ideas through any media and regardless of frontiers".

The next value guarantees human dignity. It refers to UNESCO's Constitution, which states that "the unrestricted pursuit of objective truth is indispensable to human dignity and freedom". Simultaneously, it should be accepted that "the truth can take different forms and yield different and even contradictory results because no one is keeper of the sole truth".

RSF also defends journalists, "both professional and non-professional", who may hold opposing views, "as long as they are committed to reporting reality as they see it, and in an independent manner".

Another value is democracy:

> Whatever the political system, it cannot reflect divergent interests and internal contradictions without independent watchdogs [meaning journalists] capable of challenging established authority. In dictatorial regimes, the state apparatus is able to dominate and a few monopolize most of the wealth because journalists are

neutralized. ... Independent journalism is therefore crucial for a "high intensity" democracy.

Another concept, especially for developing countries, is that "the value of development" needs to be promoted, and therefore served, through media freedom:

> Regardless of the economic doctrine we use to analyze human choices, it is clear that the choices made by state and private-sector actors should be based on accurately-reported facts. Freedom of information is a force for transparency and efficiency in state and private-sector procurement and state assistance for development. It is essential for the coherence of public policies, the prosperity of private enterprises, and sustainable growth that respects the balances in nature and human society.

Another principle is to guarantee "individual capacities", with freedom of information "unquestionably one of the freedoms that help to develop the capacities of individuals". This includes "successfully us[ing] public health and education systems and public debate, in short, to have control over their lives". Freedom of information "is a *sine qua non* of growth in all the social, economic and political possibilities available to the individual".

Another definition of media freedom defines it as the "right to speak, print, or broadcast with no prior restraint and minimum legal accountability".[21] There must be "limited legal accountability after publication for violations of law". There must also be legal guarantees of

- reasonable access to information about government, business, and people;
- a right of reply or correction;
- a limited right of access to the media; and
- some special protections for journalists.[22]

South African organisations

The FXI was formed in 1994 and watches over various aspects of freedom of expression, including opposing censorship, promoting access to information and knowledge, and promoting media diversity.[23] It was formed when the Anti-Censorship Action Group and the Campaign for Open Media merged to oppose censorship in South Africa. It "contribute[d] to the creation of a society where everyone enjoys freedom of expression and the right of access to, and dissemination of, information and knowledge". The organisation also engages in litigation, research and education to promote and protect the right to freedom of expression, including public education about the dangers of censorship. It also networks with groups opposing censorship locally and internationally.

R2K was founded in Cape Town's St. George's Cathedral on 31 August 2010 in reaction to the proposed Protection of Information Bill, or, as it was immediately called, the Secrecy Bill. R2K seeks "a country and a world where we all have the right to know – that is to be free to access and to share information".[24] This right is fundamental to a democracy that is "open, accountable, participatory and responsive" to deliver "the social, economic and environmental justice we need". Only on such a foundation can a society be built "in which we all live free from want, in equality and in dignity". As part of its goals, R2K

- co-ordinates, unifies, organises and activates those who share its principles to defend and advance the right to know;

- struggles for the widest possible recognition in law and policy of the right to know and for its implementation and practice in daily life; and

- roots for the struggle for the right to know in the struggles of communities demanding political, social, economic and environmental justice.

R2K subscribes "to the right to know, which is founded in the right to dignity and is realised through rights freely to access and share information" as constituent rights, as affirmed in the SA Constitution, the African Charter on Human and Peoples' Rights, and the Universal Declaration of Human Rights. Among R2K's ten principles are access to information and the free flow of information. For a free and diverse media, R2K states that "the media have rights and corresponding duties to access and disseminate information, including opinion, freely and fairly, without fear or favour". These rights and duties "are vital to the public's exercise of many other democratic rights".

Media (political) ecosystems

As some further context regarding what media freedom entails and how the media function under various government systems, the original "Four Theories of the Press", published by Siebert, Peterson and Schramm in 1956[25] and expanded later, are also relevant. Today they are not so much regarded as media theories, but as different media systems within specific political ecosystems.

Since the first academic reflections on the role of the media in society, mass communication (or mass media) has been described from within its social function.[26] Sociologists such as Durkheim defined it from sociological paradigms, such as functionalism or structural functionalism. This implies that all parts of society maintain a certain equilibrium, consensus and social order, including certain political functions of the media.

In terms of normative functions of the media, the focus is on the freedom – or unfreedom – of the media, the point of departure for the original Four Theories, as it tried to categorise global media systems. This later developed into Five Theories, and eventually into a plethora of theoretical reflections on mass media and their role in society.

Two of the original four models, the libertarian and social responsibility theory, are still applicable to media in democratic societies, and can collectively be regarded as the basis for the role of a free media in a free society.[27]

Although the original Four Theories can be described as prehistoric in comparison with the current flood of theories, especially the more abstract metatheories fashionable in a postmodern society, the libertarian and social responsibility approaches still embody the foundation for media freedom, especially amidst the Fourth Industrial Revolution in which the so-called Fourth Estate, as traditional news media, is being challenged by the "Fifth Estate", namely social media and the digisphere. Regarding the libertarian model, it means everyone has the right to information and the media must present a variety of opinions and serve as watchdogs,[28] and from the social responsibility model the media must maintain professional standards according to a code of conduct, with certain accountabilities and responsibilities, but free from government control.[29] All of these form a confluence of reasons why the media should be free.

Watching the watchdogs

But while a free media is foundational in a democracy, the rights of the individual, religious freedom and economic freedom are also relevant. This stems from the general philosophical climate of the Enlightenment, which undermined authoritarianism, also leading to the development of the press as mass media.[30]

In the quest for what the truth might be as "inalienable natural right", the media are therefore not only a source of information, but also a platform for "expressing different opinions, informing people about government and other matters, and helping them to monitor government, eventually forming their own ideas about policy". It is important that the media are free of government control and influence, with "a free market of ideas and information".[31] The classic assumptions for a free media can be summarised as:[32]

- the media must be free from external censorship;
- publication and distribution must be accessible to any group or individual without a permit or licence;
- criticism of governments or political parties may not be punishable;
- there should be no compulsion to publish anything;
- there may be no restriction on the acquisition of information through legal channels;
- there may be no restriction on the free flow of information across borders;
- the media must support democratic political principles;
- the media must comply with certain standards;
- there must be regulatory bodies independent of government; and
- the media must reflect the diversity of society and offer a voice to everyone.

Within this approach, the concept of self-regulation is the ideal model for guarding the "watchdog", as expressed in the classic expression by Juvenal (late 1st to early 2nd CE) of "Qui custodiet ipsos custodes?" or "Who guard the guards?"

Self-regulation – in other words, through the media by the media – is an essential element of a libertarian/social responsibility model as measure to keep a government from restricting media freedom.

The media as part and parcel of the society they serve was also underlined in one of the first studies of South African press history, namely that the press is "not a single institution", but "functions within the broad social context".[33] The media cannot be isolated, "but must be seen against the backdrop of a larger whole of which it forms such an inseparable part".

Simultaneously, independent mass media within a democratic order cannot be an "organ" of a particular government (or group), but must serve the public interest, and thus pursue objectivity. The notion of objectivity is naturally a highly contested notion, but in brief it can be defined as that personal convictions or opinions may not influence the consideration and representation of facts.[34]

The press and its role in society

The 1947, the US Commission on the Freedom of the Press, titled "A Free and Responsible Press", investigated the "failings" of the American press.[35] The report highlighted the social responsibility of the media and probably led to the Siebert, Peterson and Schramm study. Besides the already mentioned libertarian and social responsibility roles of the press, the study also identified the authoritarian and Soviet communist model. In terms of the history of South Africa's media freedom, the irony surrounding the latter is clear: The more and more the apartheid government tried to combat media freedom, the more and more they resembled the authoritarian and Soviet system – the latter a system they so vehemently condemned.

Under the authoritarian model, the press could not undermine the state's authority and, indeed, was subordinated by authority.[36] The press had to avoid "caus[ing] offence" to the dominant moral and political values, with censorship enforcing these principles. "Unacceptable attacks on authority, deviations from official policy or offences against moral codes could be considered criminal acts." Though the state might not own or control the press, "it does have a clear say about or input into the way it functions".

The social responsibility model was preferred in what can be termed Anglo-American countries. Voluntary "directives" were that the press should accept and fulfil certain obligations to society, "including setting high professional standards of informativeness, truth, accuracy and balance". It should also self-regulate and avoid what "may lead to crime, violence or civil disorder or what may give offence to ethnic or religious minorities". The media should be "a pluralist institution" and reflect the diversity of its society, ensuring access to different points of view and the right to reply. In turn, society and the public have a right to expect high standards, with intervention justified "to secure the public good". This implies "a highly sophisticated system in which consensus has to be reached on extremely subjective concepts, such as high professional standards, self-regulation, the public good and civil disorder". Consequently, a "free" or libertarian system is the ideal model, in which "[p]ublication and distribution should be free from prior censorship or restriction by any third party", and accessible to anyone "without a permit or licence".

More definitions and declarations

South African media expert David Yutar defines media freedom simply as "the right to publish without government interference or fear of punishment", to which he adds the "freedom to publish without the fear of intimidation from *any* other source".[37]

William Hachten and Anthony Giffard's simple definition of press freedom is "the right to talk serious politics and to report and criticize government with impunity".[38] In terms of this, by the mid-1980s it was non-existent for South Africa's black population, and declined steadily for the white population. In the mid-1980s, the battle between the two Nationalisms in South Africa, namely that of African and Afrikaner, was at its zenith. For the latter, survival was "first and foremost", with the state evolving "into a militaristic one, with totalitarian overtones". As already averred, the irony was that the desperate

NP government, in its attempt to counter what it believed to be the "Total Onslaught", positioned itself with its "Total Strategy" squarely inside the Soviet and totalitarian system. For that, it required a "supporting and conforming press".[39]

Several declarations protect freedom of expression in African countries. The one drawn up by delegates to the first All Africa Editors' Conference in April 2003 stated, inter alia:[40]

- that state-owned media be transformed to serve a public service agenda free from political and commercial interference. To do so, independent regulatory bodies to safeguard the independence of state-owned media had to be established;

- that the status and role of independent media require appropriate legal mechanisms. To achieve this, it is necessary to monitor attacks on and harassment of journalists; and

- that it was necessary to conduct a thorough study to write an "African media charter".

Another key document for African media is the already mentioned Windhoek Declaration.[41] This eventually led UNESCO, in 1993, to declare 3 May, the day on which the Declaration was drawn up two years before, as World Press Freedom Day. Calling for press freedom, independence and pluralism, it has been described as the "grand-daddy declaration" on press freedom, leading to the annual world-wide observance of the day.[42] Its limitations were that it was newspaper-centric, ignoring broadcast and new media, audiences and economics. Still, its principles were not limited to the press, and even though it is still called "World Press Freedom Day", it includes all news media platforms, also digital.

The Windhoek Declaration sought to establish, maintain and foster an independent, pluralistic and free press, "essential to the development and maintenance of democracy, and for economic development". This meant independence from governments, politicians and economic control. A "pluralistic press" also implies the end of monopolies and the existence of "the greatest possible number of outlets reflecting the widest possible range of opinion". Funding should ensure the development and establishment of non-government publications to reflect society as a whole, and it should support pluralism as well as independence.[43]

This declaration was also regarded as the first stage of "media liberalisation" in Africa.[44] The journalists and press freedom organisations who drafted it said "a press independent from governmental, political or economic control" was meant, also "from control of materials and infrastructure essential for the production and dissemination of newspapers, magazines and periodicals". The declaration "arguably contains the most precise and simply formulated definitions on media freedom and pluralism to be found among the plethora of international press freedom declarations".

Other declarations include:

- A declaration specifically aimed at broadcasting, namely the Windhoek+10: African Charter on Broadcasting of 2001. It focuses on radio and TV and calls for public, commercial and community broadcasting as well as independent licensing authorities.[45]

- The SADC Protocol on Culture, Information and Sport, also in 2001, according to which SADC countries wanted to create "an environment conducive to pluralistic media, to a code of ethics, and to adopt measures to ensure the freedom and independence of the media".[46]

- Another SADC declaration, also in 2001, on Information and Communications Technology, focusing on "a favourable environment for ICT growth".[47]

- The Highway Africa Charter on the Digital Divide of 2002, stressing the fact that governments need to promote freedom of expression, diversity and affordable access for new media to grow.[48]

- The African Platform on Access to Information (APAI),[49] which was formed in 2011 as part of AU initiatives. The Windhoek Declaration was seen as the "seed" for this initiative, sprouting after a 2009 meeting in Windhoek where "like-minded organisations" and "[a]dvocates passionate about media freedom and democratic development in Africa" came together. The APAI was adopted on 28 September 2011 as "a regional instrument elaborating the right of access to information within a regional context". As was the case with the Windhoek Declaration, also this day was declared by UNESCO as a day of commemoration: In November 2015, UNESCO namely adopted a resolution declaring 28 September as International Day on Universal Access to Information.

- Also in 2015, the African Declaration on Internet Rights and Freedoms[50] was accepted. As a Pan-African initiative it promotes "human rights standards and principles of openness in internet policy formulation and implementation" on the continent. The declaration was intended "to elaborate on the principles which are necessary to uphold human and people's rights on the Internet, and to cultivate an Internet environment that can best meet Africa's social and economic development needs and goals". This declaration built on previously mentioned declarations, such as the 1981 African Charter on Human and Peoples' Rights, the 1991 Windhoek Declaration, the 2001 African Charter on Broadcasting, the 2002 Declaration of Principles on Freedom of Expression in Africa, and the APAI in 2011. It was hoped that the declaration would be "widely endorsed" by all those with a stake in the internet in Africa and that it would help shape approaches to internet policy-making and governance across the continent.

Self-regulation

In South Africa, following several press boards, media councils and other self-regulatory bodies in reaction to the NP government's threats to muzzle the media since 1948, the media have organised themselves into the Press Council (PCSA). Since coming into power, even the ANC government has threatened to silence the media, amongst others through the Media Appeals Tribunal (MAT), first raised at the 2007 Polokwane ANC conference.

Self-censorship is consequently also an issue. It can take many forms and "is not easily identified".[51] Failure to report certain news is "the usual manifestation" of why a particular story was not used, but it "is often difficult to determine".

Thus, together with the notion of media freedom, the term "responsibility", often framed in terms of the "watchdog function" of the media, is often heard.[52] With South Africa's past, its democracy remains fragile, meaning media freedom also is fragile. In "immature democracies" there is also an expectation that the media should be in support of its government's goals – "a guide dog rather than a watchdog" – even if this infringes on media freedom in the process.[53]

Still, self-regulation, within a social responsibility approach – as is also the case in South Africa – is seen "to enjoy global acceptance".[54] But also regarding this, significant differences in the meaning of central normative concepts "have been noted in the Global South".[55] Importantly, "responsibility" is sometimes also used as "a pretext for the protection of powerful interests", as in the case of the so-called "dignity laws" in several African countries that do not allow the media "to insult" political leaders.[56]

What then is media freedom?

What can ultimately stand as a definition of media freedom? If there is no universal definition, and it is accepted that media freedom is "balanced against other social values, such as the citizen's right to privacy and justice and the nation's' security",[57] one can also conclude that there is no universal form of media freedom. All factors contributing to such a freedom – or lack of it – will therefore make up media freedom (or unfreedom) in any particular environment.

Thus, one may safely state that total or absolute media freedom in a libertarian sense does not exist. At most, one can say there are levels of media freedom, brought about by various checks and balances, either of society at large or those acting on behalf of society.[58]

Media freedom therefore remains a relative concept, as even in established democracies it is subject to certain restraints. A moot point was the state of the media in the US after 9/11 in 2001, when media freedom seemed to be a synonym for patriotism. At the time, journalist and ex-editor Mathatha Tsedu, chair of SANEF in 2002, referred to the tension between the public interest and the national interest, saying: "We as the media hold the view that national interest is encapsulated in the Constitution and anyone abiding by that Constitution is at the same time adhering to the national interest." He then referred to the tension between the media and governments:

> However, Government seems to believe that national interest is something else, something beyond the Constitution. We maintain the position of watchdogs of the society and for the society, and we operate in the interest of the greater public. For instance, we are witnessing how a government imposes its own defined national interest on the media in the United States after the September 11 attacks. The American media sold out their own independence and are going along with the State Department's view of events.[59]

Almost two decades later, the explosion of fake news as a result of the digital revolution – and controversies created especially by a post-fact fake era – can also be regarded as a threat to media freedom, not only in the US, but globally.

In essence, one can state that media freedom is about the tug of war between governments that want a pro-government media and the media that want to be subject only to the freedoms and responsibilities of independent journalism.

The matter that then arises is what constitutes independent journalism. Such a definition is easy enough, as in the clichéd "without fear or favour" – or unbiased, independent, verified information. But what about commercial interests? Can media really be free? Media companies should ask themselves in whose interest they practise their "freedom". Is the "deadline", as metaphor for journalism, subject to the "bottom line", as metaphor for business?

Whereas the previous print era depended on circulation to ensure advertising support to feed the "bottom line", in the digital era it is "eyeballs" that are chased through clickbait journalism in a desperate attempt to get users to convince advertisers to spend their advertising rand on that particular website. But how is the public good served through a never-ending stream of sensational journalism (in the interest of commercial journalism), and how does that serve journalism or democracy?

In the 1980s, two foremost scholars on freedom of the press defined it as "the right to report and criticize government without recrimination or retaliation from that government".[60]

Finally, for the purpose of this publication, then, the following is suggested as a definition of media freedom, specifically for our country:

> That the news media are free to report on any event, on any media platform, in a way that is unbiased and verified, independent, honest, neutral, balanced, and fair, without fear or favour, in the interest of the publics they serve, subject to Article 16 of the Bill of Rights, and in doing so, not only acting in a responsible way according to the law, but also upholding standards of ethics, respect and dignity the South African society deserves.

PART II

Colonialism's terra incognita

Although there was no official press at the time, Adam Tas's "chronicles"
is an example of how the word is mightier than the sword.
Through his actions, Tas laid the foundations for press freedom.

3. BEFORE 1800

The Post Tree, the "discoverers", the Dutch, Adam Tas, a plea letter, the Cape Patriots, and first expressions of freedom of expression

Introduction

This chapter gives an overview of how Western modes of communication began with the first Westerners arriving at the shores of what would become South Africa, from the so-called "Post Tree", the Dutch colonisation and the burghers trying to establish their right to freedom of expression, up to the annexation of the Cape by the British in the late 18th century.

First encounters

The colonisation of Southern Africa began with what can be called the first wave of globalisation when ships from Europe set sail to "discover" the "new world". Portuguese navigators, searching for the route to the East's sought-after spices, arrived decades before the Dutch VOC, which, as a company, occupied the Cape from 1652 to 1797, and briefly again from 1803 to 1806.

The first Western "discoverers" set foot ashore in 1497 on what is today the West Coast of South Africa when Vasco da Gama tried to find a route to the East via the Cape.[1] Despite stubborn Western terminology, Da Gama of course was not a "discoverer" of the Cape. The Cape was inhabited by her first nations, namely the Khoikhoi and the San.

Da Gama led two such "expeditions", the first in 1497 and the second in 1502. For the first, he set sail in July 1497 with a crew of 148 in a squadron of three square-riggers and reached the East via the Cape in 1498. They sailed for almost four months without sight of land, until, in early November 1497, they reached a bay named by Da Gama the Bahai da Santa Elena (today's St. Helena Bay), after the mother of Constantine the Great.

The fleet needed fresh water and other supplies, leading to the first violent encounter between the region's original inhabitants and the sailors. After a misunderstanding, the Khoikhoi, fearing an attack, threw spears at them, one which wounded Da Gama in the thigh.

On 22 November the squadron, in the "teeth of a gale", reached what today is Table Bay, leading to the name Cape of Storms. Three days later, Da Gama entered Sao, or Santa,

Bras, today's Mossel Bay. Again there was a misunderstanding, with Da Gama offending the Khoikhoi "when they took fresh water without asking the chief's permission" and the Khoikhoi assembled "in an armed mass". The sailors "hurriedly took to their boats while a couple of cannon blasts dispersed the Khoikhoi".

Thus, these first encounters between the original inhabitants and the eventual European colonisers, in the first wave of globalisation and on the cusp of what would evolve as a global capitalism and imperialism, set the stage for further encounters between South Africa's First Nations and their eventual colonisers – and, with them, the arrival of Western-style communication.

Earliest communications

The Portuguese sailed around the Cape at the end of the 15th century, as well as during the 16th century and up to the middle of the 17th century, but it was the Dutch who colonised the Cape in 1652 *en route* to the East. The VOC's mercantile fleet needed the Cape as a "halfway station" on what became known as the Spice Route.[2]

The first written communication in a Western language can be traced to 1500, when, on the return journey of the Portuguese fleet, a sailor left a message under a milkwood tree in today's Mossel Bay.

This first Western communication was a note by Pedro de Ataide, commander of one of the ships of Portuguese navigator Pedro Álvares de Cabral.[3] On their return journey from the East, Ataide left his letter "in a shoe or iron pot under or near a large tree". Ataide's note was found in 1501 by Joao da Nova, commander of the next Portuguese fleet on its way to India, and this is how the first "Post Office", as Western type of communication, was established.[4]

Today, this milkwood tree (*Sideroxylon inerme*) – according to one source the tree is certainly more than 500 years old[5] – is a national monument known as the "Post Office Tree". It is still in use, with the South African Post Office providing a special post box in the form of a sailor's boot where mail can be posted with a special stamp.

An example of the stamp.

The Post Tree Shoe with a museum guide.

The Post Tree.
All images: http://www.diasmuseum.co.za/index.php/attractions/post-office-tree

The message that Nova read on his journey to India warned him of "problems near Calcutta". He was so grateful for this that he erected a "small stone hermitage to be used for religious purposes". This is regarded as the first Western religious construction in South Africa. The Dias cross is said to be erected where the hermitage was built.[6] Sailors continued to hang old shoes on the milkwood with notes inside "for safe delivery". This can be regarded as the first development of an official Western postal and communication system. Today, post from the letterbox in the form of a sailor's boot carries "a special stamp to commemorate the importance of this tree as the first Post Office of South Africa".[7]

But whence 'mass media'?

For the purposes of this narrative, a brief bird's-eye view in terms of the development of news might give some context:

The first "newspaper" in the West was the Roman Empire's *Acta Diurna*, or Daily Acts, of 59 BCE.[8] As daily "bulletin" of Julius Caesar's Senate it was available in the Roman Forum. The words *journal*, *journalist* and *journalism* have as their root word *diurna*, or *diurnalis*, or "business of the day". Only centuries later could "mass media" evolve after the breakthrough in technology with Gutenberg's press in the 1400s.[9]

Jumping to 17th century Netherlands, before the VOC annexed the Cape for its mercantile reasons, "corantos" were already printed as proto-newspapers. Yet, through the "entire period of Company rule", in other words for about 150 years from 1652 to around 1800 during which the VOC controlled the Cape, the Dutch burghers had to forego an own printing press. They were not even allowed to order a single newspaper from the Netherlands, let alone permitted to own a printing press.[10] Thus, under Dutch rule, no periodical publication was allowed at the Cape, while on French-occupied islands in the Indian Ocean a weekly newspaper was already published in 1773.

The "discoverers"

After the first Europeans set foot on South African shores about 150 years before the Dutch arrived in 1652, a steady stream of "discoverers" followed. A book with a record of some of these travels to the southernmost tip of Africa, *The Wind Makes Dust*, is an anthology reflecting the journals of these first so-called "discoverers" of the sub-continent.[11] The writers are in a sense the first "journalists", as they journaled what they found, saw, heard, tasted and smelled. The book can be regarded as compulsory reading in today's post-colonial era. Also, the media from the Global North, which still struggle with how they tell stereotyped stories of Africa from their "Western gaze" and still mainly colonialist perspective, will find that this publication challenges their biases about a continent that they might even still call "dark".[12]

The selections in the anthology can be regarded as the first expressions of "free speech" in the sense that no one, of course, regulated what they wrote about their expeditions to and "discoveries" in the interior of the Cape and deeper into its hinterland.

The traditional five Ws and one H of news – who, what, where, when, why and how – are clearly present in the about three hundred entries from journals from 1479 to the beginning of the 1900s, spanning the entire colonial era to just before unification in 1910.

The title of the book, *The Wind Makes Dust*, comes from the San belief that the soul possesses wind:

> The wind does thus when we die, our own wind blows; for we, who are human beings, we possess wind; we make clouds, when we die. Therefore, the wind does thus when we die, the wind makes dust, because it intends to blow, taking away our footprints, with which we had walked about while we still had nothing the matter with us; and our footprints, which the wind intends to blow away, would otherwise still lie plainly visible.[13]

The journal excerpts take the reader on the wings of the wind into previous eras and makes for fascinating reading on how the African continent was literally hunted and haunted by "explorers". Here and there one gets a sense of empathy and sympathy from these early observers of a virgin land and virgin peoples, exploited for their treasures by an exploding imperialist and capitalist era. But imagine what we could have learnt could we have heard the tales from the perspectives of those who witnessed the invasion of their land – those who were there all along, yet who were "discovered". There is a glimpse of admission of what the Europeans were actually doing by the wife of a British colonial officer known only as Mrs Hutchinson – maybe she might even have been the first person to have witnessed the events with a deep sense of irony:

> One must hope ... that the Kafirs will accept our apparently violent methods of civilizing them in the spirit in which they are meant, and will cheerfully suffer themselves to be missionized, shot, and bayoneted into tail-coats, monogamy, and trial by jury. They must see – that is, they must be made to see – that it is better to be improved, even if needs be off the face of the earth, than to remain in their present condition of barbarous, if blissful, ignorance.[14]

Besides journaling the awkward, the tragic, the gruesome, the greedy and the eccentric – with instructions along the way on how to cook an elephant's foot – this book opens one's eyes to how an "exotic" Africa was experienced, described and judged through and by Western eyes.

This was the land "discovered" by Europeans, bringing Western modes of communication with them. Eventually two colonial powers ruled over the sub-region, namely the Dutch and the British. They not only suppressed the indigenous peoples, but also successfully established themselves as suppressors of freedom of speech.

The first European colonists were employees of the mighty VOC, possibly the first multinational company in the first wave of globalisation that our planet experienced.

The Cape's indigenous peoples at the time were various Khoikhoi tribes; in total twelve, of which the Goringhaicona, Goringhaiqua and Gourachouqua lived in the Peninsula, with the Cochoqua, Guriqua, Hessequa, Gouriqua and Damsqua further along the coast and inland, up to the Kei River.[15] Across the Kei was Xhosa territory, settled by the ethnic black tribes migrating along the east coast of Africa. Inland, San groups either lived in harmony with the Khoikhoi, or attacked them, with the differences between the two groups "later disappearing".

The European colonisers who migrated to the Cape brought with them their Western culture. However, freedom of expression was not part of this. From the first settlement of the Cape by the VOC, and for its entire rule, the Cape would not see any newspaper of its own.

Why was press freedom, or freedom of expression, suppressed?

The Dutch era

During the Dutch occupation from 1652 to more or less 1800, the Cape was governed by the seventeen VOC directors, the Here XVII (the Lords XVII). The occupation was purely for mercantile reasons, namely to supply the VOC's fleets with fresh produce. During this period there was no press freedom at the Cape. In fact, there literally was no press up to the last few years under the VOC. Cape burghers were not even allowed to order "a single daily paper" from the Netherlands themselves.[16]

When the first five Dutch ships landed in Table Bay on 6 April 1652 to occupy the Cape, this was not done in the name of a state, but of a company. All settlers were in the employ of the company, and the reason for the settlement was to be a refreshment post for ships *en route* to the East to obtain fresh provisions to counter illnesses such as scurvy.

Yet, once the Dutch arrived at the Cape, it inevitably became "home" for the next generation born here, with Europe becoming a distant abstraction. A system of "Free Burghers" was implemented after some time. According to VOC policy, these "burghers" were "set free" from company employ to farm for their own pockets, but had to sell their goods to the company for fixed prices. The company did not invest in cultural matters such as providing education, which meant that the Dutch colonists' offspring had no formal schooling.

One can imagine to what kinds of corruption the system of no free enterprise lent itself, as the governor of the Cape was also allowed to farm. He, together with his VOC officials, were also given first option to sell their produce to their own company. And that is how the first chapter in media freedom – literally in the form of freedom of speech in the face of no free enterprise – was written in South Africa's history.

The historian George McCall Theal described the inhabitants at the Cape in this era – a mixture of Dutch, German and French colonists, slaves and indigenous Khoi – as that their mixture of blood had helped to wean the colonists from attachment to the parent state ... an individual living beyond the Cape Peninsula was cut off from communication with distant lands, and his children, knowing nothing of relatives abroad, did not concern themselves with the home of their ancestors. To this must be added the fact that many of them could not have written a letter if there had been a post with which to send it away.[17]

They soon called themselves "an original nation", "Africaanders" or "Africaners"[18] – a group from Africa, formed by Africa, with blood from Africa. After the Cape was occupied by the British, these descendants of mostly Dutch, French and German migrants, slaves and indigenous peoples were referred to as "Afrikanders" or "Afrikaners".[19] Their bond with Africa was clear: "[A]ll their attachment and all their interests were centred in South Africa, and ... every one of them had a strong affection for the country as a whole. They called themselves Afrikaanders, a term in common use at least as early as 1735."

The independent nature of this mixed-race group was also discernible early on. Their "yearning for freedom", and thus self-governance, was namely also already present. The historian H.B. Thom found "the first elements of this yearning for freedom" in a "plea letter" by the colonists written in 1656. Called a "smeekskrif", a petition, it was against economic suppression as a result of the VOC's corruption in applying its trading policy.[20] This can be regarded as the very first example of the expression of free speech at the Cape.

The VOC also did not recognise the right to religious freedom. Because there were so many Germans in the service of the Cape Regiment as mercenaries, they were not allowed the right to have sermons in German. The Cape government feared that it would show them their real strength in numbers and that, realising their majority, they might mobilise to overthrow the government.[21] Freedom of religion was eventually granted to the Cape German community in 1780.

The first 'official' expression of freedom of speech at the Cape

Exerting strict regulations, VOC officials ruled to serve their own pockets. Governor Simon van der Stel, as well as his son and successor, Willem Adriaan, established a monopoly in trading their produce.

As already referred to, Cape citizens did not have their own publications during all of the Dutch period, from 1652 to 1795, and again from 1803 to 1806.[22] "They had to read about the turmoil of the French Revolution and the American War of Independence in newspapers and magazines brought to the Cape from Europe." News and articles about the Cape itself were rare.

But even before the eventual beginning of the first newspapers, the diaries of Adam Tas, someone who today can be called a pioneer "freedom fighter", caused an uproar because of his "chronicles" of the unjust policies of the colonial rulers.[23]

Van der Stel Snr., of mixed race – his mother was the daughter of a freed slave – was the last commander, but first governor, of the Cape.[24] His father was also in the employ of the VOC. Van der Stel, born in Mauritius in 1639, was appointed commander in 1679. He expanded the colony, also naming Stellenbosch after him. In 1691 he was promoted from commander to governor of the Cape. In 1699 he was succeeded by his son Willem Adriaan, who governed until 1707, when he was recalled.

In 1657, when the first burghers were freed from company employ to produce fresh goods on their allotted grounds, it was declared that no VOC official would be allowed to trade to ensure the livelihood of the Free Burghers. Yet, over time, the officials acquired land, leading to twenty of them forming a monopoly to provide wine, meat, fish and wheat to passing ships.[25]

Adam Tas, a Free Burgher from Stellenbosch, was the first to exert his right to freedom of expression and laid the foundation for the principle of free speech in what would become South Africa. This happened almost half a century after the first settlement, and one century before the first newspaper made its brief appearance.

This milestone in South Africa's history took place under the rule of Willem Adriaan van der Stel. The Free Burghers protested in 1706 against the corrupt and unjust policy of the Cape Dutch colonial elite through Tas's famous "chronicles", co-signed by fellow-Free Burghers.

Tas's petition against the corruption at the Cape was sent via Batavia to the Here XVII in Amsterdam. After this body demanded that the Cape officials explain their position and actions, the reaction at the Cape was to throw Tas and several of his accomplices in the notorious "Swart Gat", or "Black Hole", an underground hole in the Castle which served as jail. Tas paid for exercising his right to freedom of expression with damaged eyesight – he was freed during broad daylight after his incarceration in the pitch dark underground jail.

This caused a further uproar. In 1707 it was announced that the Here XVII was recalling Willem Adriaan and several other officials, among them Johannes Starrenburg, magistrate of Stellenbosch. They also prohibited all officials from any further trading. Moreover, they had to sell all their land.

This victory for the burghers showed that by standing together they could defeat the colonial government. It was the victory celebration in Stellenbosch in front of the Magistrate's Court in 1707 that led to the now famous words of the young Hendrik Biebouw, of mixed descent, to publicly declare "Ik ben een Africaander". This was at least eighty years before the term was used as a reference to Afrikaners, the new indigenous African tribe of mixed descent that was taking root as natives from Africa.

Thus, just more than fifty years after colonisation, Tas was the first exponent of the concept of freedom of expression or freedom of speech. After he was released from the Castle, his property on the outskirts of Stellenbosch was renamed "Libertas", meaning Free Tas. In much later years it also served for some time as a centre for arts and culture. South Africa can celebrate Tas as the first activist for freedom of speech, and even though there was no official press at the time, his "chronicles" provide an example of how the word is mightier than the sword.

It should also be noted that when Tas drew up his petition against the "dwingelandy" (tyranny) of governor Van der Stel and magistrate Starrenburg in 1706, women's voices were also heard. Starrenburg reported to Van der Stel how "verbal" the women were: "Maar Edele Gestrenge Heer, de wyven syn alsoo gevaarlyk als de mans; en zyn niet stil (But, Your Honour, the women are as dangerous as the men, and do not keep quiet)."[26] This was underlined by historian Theal: "The spirit of the women of the country districts was thoroughly roused, and their opposition was as formidable as that of their husbands."

The 2017 exhibition on the Cape Dutch colonial history, titled "Goede Hoop" (Good Hope), in the Rijksmuseum in Amsterdam, with the famous words of Hendrik Biebouw as part of the exhibition.
Photos: L. Rabe

As an aside, during this time 17th-century Dutch creolised into Cape-Dutch, then Dutch-Afrikaans, and eventually Afrikaans, named after Africa, as a language that developed in the soil of Africa. One factor leading to its creolisation was that the "cultural centre" of 17th-century Dutch was almost 10,000 km away. According to pioneer lexicographer D.B. Bosman, linguistic changes were already clear within the first fifty years after the Dutch settlement.[27]

The history of South Africa's struggle for press freedom thus began with this example, and stresses the fact that it takes only one individual to make a difference.

The Cape Patriots

One form of "news" that could not be suppressed and that was sent from the Cape on a regular basis was letters, such as those of Hendrik Cloete. He called his letters "Caabsche Nouvelles" ("Cape Novels") and they were addressed to Hendrik Swellengrebel, Jr., near Utrecht in the Netherlands.[28] Although there was no freedom of expression, interaction, and therefore an exchange of news, between the Netherlands and the Cape could not be suppressed. This contributed to the formation of the "Kaapssche Patriotte", the Cape Patriots, a movement at the end of the eighteenth century that drew its inspiration from the Patriot movement in the Netherlands.[29]

The Cape movement lasted from 1778 to 1787 and consisted of prominent burghers who crossed swords with the Cape government regarding local political representation and economic opportunities for the burghers.

The Cape Patriots disseminated, and quoted from, documents by thinkers from the Enlightenment, but focused on local issues. Despite the Cape government officials being prohibited by the Here XVII from pursuing commercial activities from 1707 onwards, burghers and officials were still at loggerheads. By the 1770s, the Dutch officials at the Cape would work in a more covert way and became much more ingenious in hiding their unlawful commercial activities. The Cape Patriots, in reaction, demanded more representation in government and demanded certain laws to allow for this, as local officials banned and deported burghers at their own whim. Although there still was no press at the Cape, the formation of the Patriot movement can be described as the second utterance of freedom of expression by inhabitants of the Cape.

At the end of the 18th century, the Cape Afrikaner was described as someone with a strong sense of freedom who would act against the arbitrary actions of government.[30] In the interior, in fact, there was already activism to form own republics, like that of Swellendam. The Afrikaners were proud of the name "Afrikaan", and "Kaapsch Burger" was regarded as a "groots" (proud) title.

Up to this point, all "journals, letters, laws and proclamations" at the Cape had to be hand copied with a pen,[31] as a printing press was still not allowed because the authorities believed it would be an "instrument of revolution". Therefore, the Patriots' 1779 request in relation to their "democratic ideal" to have a printing press for laws, regulations and other government notices to be duplicated was something the VOC would not even consider. Official documents and forms were printed in the Netherlands, brought by sailing ship to the Cape, and then hand copied.[32] Hence Cape burghers started to write letters to newspapers in the Netherlands to have their objections heard.[33] The two newspapers that published these grievances were the *Post van den Neder-Rhijn* and the *Zuid-Hollandsche Courant*.

While a press or newspaper was still not allowed at the Cape, a Cape-born "revolutionary ex-teacher", Johannes Henricus Redelinghuijs, baptised at the Cape in 1756, became the Cape's first editor – although in the Netherlands.[34] He travelled to the Netherlands as a representative of the complainants. In Amsterdam he became editor of the *Nationale Courant* as well as of the partisan Jacobean *Oprechte Bataafsche Courant*. He called himself an "Afrikaan" and referred to the Cape as his "fatherland", but remained as editor in the Netherlands, where he died in 1802. The Cape's first editor could proclaim his "freedom, equality and fraternity" only in the Netherlands; at the Cape he was never allowed to do so.

The Cape Patriots' first application for an own Cape press, even though meant only for documents, was finally turned down in 1783 after being submitted in 1779.[35] A second attempt followed in 1786. Dutch governor Baron Joachim van Plettenberg supported this request, even though he was accused by the burghers of injustice; but this appeal also was turned down.[36]

When the next governor, Lieutenant Colonel C.J. van de Graaff, also requested a printing press, as by now there already were printing presses owned by the Company in both Batavia and Ceylon, the matter was "under consideration". However, another reason for the hesitance now was that, in the early 1790s, "serious saving measures" had to be implemented at the Cape. This meant that expenses regarding a printing press were seen as increased costs, rather than bringing about savings.

The Cape Patriot movement was not really successful. Although some of their demands were met, the biggest – to have more representatives in the Political Council – was rejected. In the Netherlands, the Patriot movement was successfully suppressed in 1787, and this also led to the demise of the Cape movement.

Meanwhile, huge strides had been made up to that point regarding freedom of the press globally. This happened because of John Milton's criticism of the licensing system in Britain, which led to his "Aeropagitica" in 1644, regarded as a "source of inspiration" from the Age of Enlightenment.[37] Milton, criticising the system of licensing all publications in Britain, regarded freedom of the press as "the liberty to know, to utter and to argue freely according to conscience".[38] This inspired many countries to table laws safeguarding freedom of expression. Sweden was the first, in 1766, followed by Norway and Denmark in 1770, and the US's First Amendment of the Constitution in 1778.[39]

The Cape's first printer

With Dutch official documents, including "diaries, letters, laws and proclamations", duplicated by hand[40] and the burghers sending their letters to newspapers in the Netherlands,[41] requests for an own Cape press, as mentioned, were twice rejected towards the end of the 18th century.[42] Yet, in 1793, the Company's Political Council at last decided to establish a government press, with the German Johann Christian Ritter (1755–1810) as its first printer.

Ritter arrived at the Cape in 1784 and is credited not only as the person who would introduce the art of printing to South Africa, but also to the Southern Hemisphere.[43] He was the son of a bookbinder from Bayreuth, Germany, and was brought to the Cape as bookbinder in the Company's service. Following him, another German, Valentin Alexis Schönberg (1751–1825), is acknowledged as being the second printer at the Cape.[44]

Ritter was 29 years old when he arrived as a VOC employee in 1784.[45] Although born into a bookbinding family, as the second son he would not inherit the business.

In 1792, the VOC authorities were forced, through escalating costs, to cut down on the number of copyists at the Cape, and in 1794 a printing press was finally granted. Ritter was the designated official printer. He produced handbills, advertisements and almanacs for the years 1795, 1796 and 1797. The title page of the almanac for 1796 has survived and is the oldest example of printing in South Africa. While the origin of the press he used remains a mystery, as bookbinder he had knowledge of the technicalities of printing. Some speculate that he constructed an elementary press at the Cape or may have received a small hand press from his father to bring along. As bookbinder, Ritter also had to stamp letters and official documents and, in addition, was employed as seal-engraver. His workload increased to such an extent that at times he employed two or three part-time assistants besides a permanent one – all at his own expense. In 1795 he approached the government to pay his assistants' wages and to refund him for the past years, otherwise, Ritter said, he would be totally ruined – but with no success.

The first printed matter at the Cape: the surviving 1796 almanac cover.
Source: Bosman, *Hollandse Joernalistiek in Suid-Afrika*

And then the British occupied the Cape and Ritter's dreams were shattered anyway. Still, in partnership with Harry Harwood Smith, a British master printer who arrived together with the British, he petitioned anew to be allowed to work as printer.

In 1800, the now British governor, Sir George Yonge, issued a proclamation banning all private printing, although a "government gazette" was started that year. When, in 1803, the Batavian Republic "took transfer" of the Cape, the new government stuck to the ban and Ritter was again listed in their employ as bookbinder. He also kept a stationery shop and sometimes acted as an agent for books. He died in 1810, never having realised his ambition, although the first printing apprentice had been indentured at the Cape a year before his death, "and the foundations of a great industry laid". This apprentice, Bernardus Josephus van de Sandt, went on to become a top printer, and in 1832 was appointed superintendent of government printing. The irony was that it was he who later, in the name of the government, confiscated the hand press from Robert Godlonton, one of the four master printers among the British Settlers who arrived in 1820.

The oldest trade union

Although Ritter is credited as the person who established the first press at the Cape and was allowed to print nothing more than "almanacs, handbills and advertising leaflets",[46] his work can still be regarded as the foundation of the printing industry at the Cape.

This foundation was probably the reason why South Africa's very first union, namely the Printers' Union, was formed to support the printing industry. Following this first union, the Cape of Good Hope Printers' Protection Society was founded in 1841, and the Cape of Good Hope Printers' and Bookbinders' Society in 1857.

In the early 1880s, a number of printers' unions were established in bigger cities in the various geopolitical areas of today's South Africa. They amalgamated in 1898 to form the South African Typographical Union, at one stage the most efficient and best organised union in the country.[47] Sadly, it goes without saying that this union was a victim of the 21st century's disruptive digital economy.

But back to the late 18th century. As said, Ritter's "monopoly" as sole printer in the Cape was short-lived. When the Cape was occupied by Britain in 1795 and master printer Harry Harwood Smith also arrived,[48] Ritter and Smith – although seemingly opponents – made it their "common cause" to be appointed official government printers.[49] They succeeded, yet were allowed to print only government documents.

And this led to the next phase in the struggle for freedom of expression – and eventually press freedom – at the Cape. But when Ritter's press was finally allowed it was too late for the burghers to benefit from the beginnings of a first press at the Cape, as the new British occupiers also did not allow a free press.

Five years on, on 1 February 1800 and under English colonial rule, Ritter and Smith suddenly found they had competition in the form of two "influential traders", amongst others also traders of slaves.[50] They were Alexander Walker and John Robertson. These two founded, with the blessings of the British colonial government, their own printing works. It consisted of a press, three "tradesmen" and a Dutch translator. Ritter and Smith objected, but by July 1800 Walker and Robertson were proclaimed sole government printers. A warning of a huge fine as well as forfeiture of equipment, should anyone else do any printing, was also issued.

Thus, literally just before the turn of the century, after the first 150 years of mostly Dutch colonial rule, the Cape experienced the benefits of a small press, although only for almanacs and other official documents, followed by the first official printing press, albeit a government one.

A People without a Press cannot be regarded as civilised
— THOMAS PRINGLE AND JOHN FAIRBAIRN, 1824

4. THE TURN OF THE CENTURY AND ONWARD

British colonialism, the first fighters for press freedom, the "Magna Carta", and the foundation for South Africa's media industry

Introduction - A global liberalism

At the beginning of the nineteenth century, a wave of liberalism was sweeping over the West. Rousseau's "Contrat Social" for freedom, equality and fraternity was published in Amsterdam in 1762, Britain's parliamentarianism was established, a new order developed in France thanks to philosophers such as Rousseau, Voltaire and Montesquieu, and in America the colonists revolted against the English.[1]

All of this brought about three political revolutions: the development of British Constitutionalism, the French Revolution and the American War of Independence. Liberalism and democracy were born, while "across the world, at the forefront of the new urge for freedom, was the free press. In countries where the press was not free, liberalism took longer to develop than where a free press could act as mouthpiece for the people. This would also transpire in the first decades of colonisation at the Cape. By the 1800s, the press could eventually act on behalf of both Dutch and English colonists to get a stronger say in government. True to the nature of colonialism, however, it excluded indigenous peoples. Still, liberalism at the Cape developed much slower, with so-called "responsible government" (in which local white men would participate) only from 1872. The proclamation of the so-called 1829 "Magna Carta" for press freedom at the Cape, meant, however, that the authorities could no longer limit the development of the press. The original "Magna Carta", or "Magna Carta Libertatum", meaning the Great Charter of Freedoms, was a royal charter of rights between the unpopular King John of England and a number of rebel barons in 1215, after which it became in general use for any fundamental document guaranteeing rights and liberties.[2]

Those championing a free press at the Cape in the first half of the 19th century "were very much children of their time".[3] As press pioneer John Fairbairn wrote in September 1825:

> We are indebted to two of the most illustrious Inventions with which God has been pleased to reward the ingenuity and perseverance of man, and for which our gratitude should only be second in degree to our thankfulness for the Revelation of Christ and the hopes of immortality. They are – the Invention of Printing, and the Liberty of the Press. By the first the general diffusion of Education was rendered practicable through the multiplication and cheapness of books; and the second enables men

of virtue and ability to render those books worthy of being read and taught. The existence of the first, without the second, would be a pernicious mockery.

It should be noted again that the nature of colonialism excluded indigenous peoples from these ideals. In fact, the press, as Western concept, contributed to their suppression and the denial of their rights. Colonists' minds and attitudes were blueprinted by their countries of origin, and also shaped their mind-set towards indigenous peoples. For the Dutch colonists, as for other European nations at the time, this would include the "stereotyping of blacks as barbarians", together with the 16th-century "theology of Africa and Ham, and thus the notion of Africa as subservient continent".[4] The British brought with them a rigid class system, which translated into a strict class- and race-based society.

New government, same censorship

South Africa's history, "especially history that means something because it is a history of attempts to develop a nation", has few stories "more gripping" than the struggle for press freedom.[5] This certainly played out in events at the Cape in the early 1800s.

Although the colonists protested against their corrupt Dutch colonial government, it did not mean the English were welcome when they annexed the Cape in their first occupation, from 1795 to 1803.[6] In 1806, with the second occupation, England ensured that it would not lose its strategic position again. The Treaty of London meant the Cape became a "permanent" British territory.

This also meant that the Cape would anglicise, even though the majority of colonists were Cape-Dutch. Also, British colonialism followed a strict class differentiation, consisting of "autocratic governors, rich property owners, entrepreneurial businesspeople, free workers, poor 'bywoners' (peasants), contracted workers, and slaves".[7] In this strict hierarchy, indigenous peoples were not even mentioned. The class system led to a growing recognition of race, not only in terms of skin colour, but also of the Dutch colonists being regarded as a different race and inferior to the British. All these factors determined the status of individuals and groups, as it also implied power versus no power, rich versus poor, and elites versus commoners.

As some context, the Cape's total population of European descent numbered 26,000 in 1806, with 30,000 slaves and almost 20,000 Khoikhoi and persons of mixed descent who worked for the white population.[8] By 1814, there were 35,000 inhabitants of European descent.[9]

The printing tradition begins

The history of print only began with the arrival of British colonialism, with the earliest newspapers serving white people only.[10] The English and Dutch press developed almost in tandem, but the "Colonial divide" between them resulted in a press serving "the different linguistic and ethnic divisions, as well as white domination". The different ethnic groups later used the press to advance their own interests:

Historically, various groups in South Africa – mainly English-speaking whites, the defeated Afrikaners after the Boer War, the urban Africans, and, to a lesser extent, the coloured and Asians – have utilized newspapers and the printed word to express their political aspirations and to contest at times either English or Afrikaans domination.

When the British replaced the 150 years of VOC rule, the immediate fortunes of the press did not change dramatically.[11] Looking back,

> [t]he further one goes back in South African press history, the clearer it becomes that little has changed. From the earliest days of the colonial press, newspapers in South Africa have been identified with one or other of the dominant white language groups, with their very different cultures, political philosophies, and economic interests.[12]

The British had qualms similar to those of the Dutch. The British Lieutenant-Governor stated that the editors of the first publication, when it was eventually permitted, should offer "no personal comment on political subjects".[13] The Cape publications therefore "were totally devoid of critical comments, personal style and views".[14] The constant struggle for power between the two white groups became the foundation for the development of the South African press as a whole. When African Nationalism later started to manifest itself among black South Africans, it led to the development of more power blocs inside the media sector. This resulted in a highly partisan press right up to the first democratic elections in 1994 – the seeds of which were sown in the 1800s. It also led to what was called South Africa's "three distinct concepts or theories of the press" up to the 1990s, namely an Afrikaner, English, and African press – "coexisting uncomfortably".[15] The English press developed thanks to imperial and capitalist interests, regarded as part of the "white power structure"; the Dutch-Afrikaans press developed as mouthpiece of Dutch-Afrikaner interests, leading to Afrikaner Nationalism after the South African War (SAW), with the Afrikaans press itself part of a white Afrikaner Nationalist power structure; and the black press developed from its missionary station origins into African Nationalism.

Through the decades, "newspaper owners and editors – British, Afrikaners, and blacks" – were far more than "passive chroniclers of events; they were politically engaged and used their presses to pursue their own economic and political goals". Various rulers, "whether British colonial governors, presidents of Boer republics, or Afrikaner prime ministers, provided ample precedents for the official suppression of expression".

However, the foundations of the origins of the seemingly eternal dispute between press and government were laid in those first beginnings of the South African press around 1800.

When the first printing presses arrived at the Cape, the first conflict under British colonial rule was between the English immigrants and their own colonial government over press freedom.[16] Cape Town, the only area with a denser population than elsewhere in the colony, "was a natural communications centre". News arrived via sea, from the interior via travellers, and from farmers coming to market. As a trading centre, it had a merchant class that could sustain a newspaper with advertisements.

In South Africa, as in Canada and Australia, the press initially had to "do battle with the colonial authorities".[17] In other colonies, "a truly indigenous Press" developed, emphasising regional and local interests. South African newspapers took a more "imperialistic line". They modelled themselves on Fleet Street and "right up until the 1920s imported most of their journalists to ensure that the model closely resembled the original". Although the English-language press had to overcome the hostility of the colonial authorities, it "was not born out of a struggle for freedom, nor to meet the needs of immigrant masses". Rather, indicating its capitalist roots, it "asserted itself on the grounds of the right to run a business for profit". In the Cape, the English press "spoke for commercial and financial interests", as later, in the then Transvaal, it spoke for White "uitlander" mining interests. In contrast, the Dutch-Afrikaans press, developing a bit later than the English press, "was filled with evangelical zeal and kindled the flame of a cause". While English newspapers were "dominated by commercial and managerial demands and where printers were sovereign", the Afrikaans press was "always subservient to the cause 'taal' (language) and 'Volk' (people)". Only in the second half of the 19th century was the English press "particularly ... affected by the climate of the international Press [which] had established Press freedom as one of its basic tenets". In turn, the Afrikaans press, "like the Afrikaner, was never touched by the liberalism sweeping Europe" in the 19th century.

The Cape's first publication

But back to 1800 and the Cape's first publication. As said, the existing two printers, Ritter and Smith, together sent a petition to the new British governor with a reminder of the promise made to them. Their only consolation: The assurance that the government would buy Ritter's new press, which he expected from Europe any moment, and Smith had to hand over his printing equipment to the government.[18]

When, in 1800, the government "authorised"[19] the firm of two businessmen and, inter alia, slave dealers,[20] Alexander Walker and John Robertson, to operate as government printer, it was not meant as a licence to "run a proper newspaper". The government proclamation forbade any private printing emanating from the press, with the warning of a penalty and confiscation. The Walker/Robertson business had a dubious record. Called "ambitious entrepreneurs", they settled at the Cape specifically because it was a "strategic commercial point". Under patronage of the mighty British fleet, they sent out privateers as well as a commercial fleet to the East and West from Cape Town, apparently sharing "profits" with governor Sir George Yonge.[21] One of their ships was even named after his wife, the "Lady Yonge". With their printing monopoly, they could "react swiftly to important events" and print all kinds of general information in a lucrative way.[22]

Thus, South Africa's first newspaper was established as "an astonishing twist of graft and intrigue".[23] Its founding by the "corrupt firm of slave dealers and privateers", the said "Messrs Walker and Robertson of 35, Plein Street", provides "a fascinating glimpse into the inept and freebooting reign of Sir George Yonge".

Yonge governed the Cape from 1799 until April 1801. Business morality was low, with Yonge "heavily involved in shady deals" with Walker and Robertson. Their "bustling wholesale firm had a finger in every available pie in and around the colony". They dealt with as many as six hundred slaves in a single consignment and had "letters of marque" enabling them to prey on "enemy" French and Spanish shipping "in southern waters", where pirates "were still common". Walker held numerous dinner parties at his Newlands home. Among the "rich and powerful" entertained there was the Duke of Wellington.

When Yonge proclaimed Walker and Robertson as sole printers, it meant a monopoly on all printing in the Colony and heavy punishment for anyone who dared to compete. His grant included permission for a weekly newspaper, seemingly part of an earlier promise. In February 1800, Walker and Robertson, "acting with the confidence of foreknowledge", set up a printing plant after Robertson went to London to buy a press and types. They appointed three printers as well as a Dutch translator. The publication was preceded on 1 August by "a lofty announcement" declaring that the paper hopes to draw together "the Natives", "meaning the Dutch colonists", and the English, a "Consummation most devoutly" wished.

So it happened that barely after they had established their printing firm, Walker and Robertson printed South Africa's first publication, albeit under government control. Titled *The Cape Town Gazette, and African Advertiser/Het Kaapsche Stads Courant, en Afrikaansche Berichter*, the first edition was on 16 August 1800. A bilingual weekly, it appeared every Saturday, alternatively in English and Dutch, and was printed by the "Government Press, No 35, Plein Street".

The first edition of *The Cape Town Gazette, and African Advertiser.*
Source: www.sahistory.org.za

One of the main aims of the Cape's first paper, as published in its first edition, was the ideal to consolidate the colonist population by trying, in "drawing more closely together, in Bonds of mutual Harmony and good Understanding", the Dutch and the English.[24] But despite its entrepreneurial owners, it remained nothing more than a government gazette.

Although Walker and Robertson undertook to "make it their particular and anxious study to collect the most authentic materials, and lay before the public the information thus obtained, in the fair Simplicity of Truth", the government, barely two months later, announced on 10 October 1800 that "it was improper and irregular ... to allow the editing of a public newspaper from a press in the hands of private individuals".[25]

The *Gazette*, "born from the press of slave dealers", thus eventually had been "banished to the Castle" by October one year later.[26] From then on it was "Published by Authority", with only "harmless titbits" of news and the "occasional instructive contribution from the pen of an official", "squeezed between the tortuous official announcements". About 1,600 copies were printed weekly; 600 went to the country districts, the rest assigned to officials or sold to the public. Over the years, several "specials" or *Gazettes Extraordinary* were printed, "mostly about British prowess", as with Trafalgar.

In the leading article of the first "Castle" edition, the government secretary explained that news, if any, would be given "without offering an opinion of our own". The principal aim was "to render the paper as far as possible a register of facts".

Although this first paper was started with commercial intentions by Walker and Robertson, the blessings of government meant politics played a major role.[27] Following the government's announcement, there were no attempts to protect it as a proper newspaper and it officially became a government paper.

When the "dubious" friendship between the two entrepreneurs and the government soured and the governor withdrew the printing monopoly, the first Castle edition was printed every Friday.[28] This followed after local companies, critical of the printing monopoly, put so much pressure on the British government that the monopoly was not only ended, but the governor also was recalled in 1801.[29] Government bought the press for £2,000. Importantly, however, the first Cape newspaper had by now established itself and had to be continued by government, as it was realised that "the suppression of the Press, having been once established, would be attended with many inconveniencies". Besides official notices, it also carried advertisements for farmers and, being in both English and Dutch, carried reports under headings such as Baptised/Gedoopt and Passed Away/Overleden – and for that reason was "popular in the platteland (country districts)".[30]

The paper lasted in "private" hands for little more than thirteen months.[31] During this time, the public complained about its price and claimed that Walker and Robertson overcharged for advertisements. When the British government had also had enough of Yonge and he was "ordered" out of Government House, the "old man went to stay with Walker and Robertson and when the navy refused him passage in one of the Navy's man-of-war ships, he returned to Britain" in, of all vessels, the "Lady Yonge".

For the next 22 years, the Castle press did all the printing in Cape Town. Walker and Robertson claimed 17,000 rix-dollars compensation, but received 12,000 (the equivalent of £2,000); their firm was later declared bankrupt in London.

During the brief reoccupation of the Cape by Dutch-Batavian rule from 1803 until 1806, the paper was published in Dutch as the *Kaapsche Courant*, still from the Castle.[32] At the beginning of 1803, the paper was still bilingual, but from March it was in Dutch only. Notices could be placed in French, English and German.[33] The *Kaapsche Courant* now appeared every Saturday from the "Gouvernement Drukkerij in Het Kasteel" (Government's Printers in the Castle). Although it carried news, advertisements and notices, it was "not yet a newspaper". A Batavian government memorandum stated that, to prevent abuse, it had to be under direct government control. It saw in it an ally against "rebellion and ignorance" – if edited by a "loyal and efficient editor". This loyal and efficient person was medical doctor Reinier de Klerk Dibbetz, the Cape's first editor.

After the 1806 British occupation, the paper continued throughout the 19th century, mainly in English, and it formally became *The Cape of Good Hope Government Gazette*.[34] After 1806 it became bilingual again[35] and became more popular in the platteland because it also carried market reports. By 1822, it was even more popular because it was still published partly in Dutch, despite English declared as the Cape's only official language. Until 1824 it remained the only publication at the Cape.[36]

As some context: In 1797, the Cape population, in all of the "big Cape district", consisted of 1,566 male Free Burghers.[37] By 1814, there were 35,000 white people in the area known as the Cape Colony.[38] The number of indigenous people is unknown. The Cape's first paper had "very limited" readership, as Cape Town consisted of only 1,145 homes. By 1806, there were 29,000 slaves and, when slavery was abolished in all British colonies on 1 December 1834, there were 39,000 registered slaves.[39]

Up to the founding of *The South African Commercial Advertiser*, the first independent newspaper, in 1924, *The Cape of Good Hope Government Gazette* was the only paper in the Cape.[40] It was the founding of the *Advertiser* that led to an "extended and acrimonious" first battle between the press and government.[41]

The beginnings

Thus the South African press was born in August 1800 as a state-licensed monopoly in the form of *The Cape Town Gazette, and African Advertiser/Het Kaapsche Stads Courant, en Afrikaansche Berigter*.[42] Thereafter it became the *Gazette*, surviving to this day as the *Government Gazette*.

The press situation at the Cape changed dramatically with the British government's huge immigration project. When the British Settlers, according to one source 4,000 individuals,[43] and another 5,000,[44] arrived in the Eastern Cape in 1820, a new era regarding media freedom arrived with them.

Apparently 90,000 people "clamoured" to join the government-sponsored settlement on the Colony's eastern frontier.[45] Among them was Thomas Pringle. Although not a "civilian agriculturalist", his party of 24 Scots sailed for their new home on the "Brilliant" in February 1820. He would become one of South Africa's press pioneers.

The migration, described as "one of the largest settler movements by English speakers in colonial-era Africa", "strongly influenced" the development of the press in South Africa.[46] The immigrants brought both technology in the form of printing presses, as well as expertise. By the end of the 19th century "there was hardly a town of any size that did not have its own newspaper". The "wave of publishers" championed the cause of the British settler and Dutch farmer alike. Cape Town-based press pioneer, John Fairbairn, would later, with Pringle, "explore more philosophical issues of press freedom".[47] Together, the "English left an indelible stamp on the development of the press in South Africa in their efforts to establish press freedom".[48]

The "principle and practice of free expression were firmly rooted" in Britain.[49] Among the British immigrants also were Robert Godlonton and Thomas Stringfellow. Both worked as printers in England and, on their departure, were given a complete printing press. When their ship, the "Chapman", docked at the Cape, the authorities learnt of the press on board – and Godlonton "discovered that the conditions in the Colony were less permissive than in the mother country". Only Stringfellow was called before Sir Rufane Donkin, acting governor in the absence of Lord Charles Somerset, who was on leave in England. Stringfellow was told that allowing them to proceed to the Eastern Cape with their press "would be equal to scattering firebrand along the Eastern Frontier". The press was seized and, "to keep it out of harm's way", sent to Graaff-Reinet to print government forms.

It was during this time that a Cape customs official, William Wilberforce Bird, wrote in his *State of the Cape of Good Hope in 1822*, published in London in 1823, that

> the liberty of the press is a feeling so congenial to the heart of a British subject,
> that it is mortifying to describe such a degraded establishment as the Government

Printing Office at the Cape of Good Hope. The annual circle of its duties consists in printing the Cape Calendar and Almanac, and a weekly newspaper called the *Cape Gazette*, which is in fact a mere list of proclamations, of civil and military appointments and promotions, marriages, births, christenings, deaths, the price of articles of produce, and advertisements of sales ... The public is rarely indulged with a scrap of European intelligence; and when such a circumstance does take place, it consists of matter suited to the submissive state of the colony ... here are no extracts from Parliamentary debates, nothing breathing opposition or leading to discussion for this might create the habit of thinking; nothing scientific, for this might enlighten; but the whole is a mass of uninteresting, tasteless stupidity.

According to Bird, of the 1,600 copies printed every Friday, 600 were sent gratis to government officials. The rest were bought by merchants and dealers "to guide them in their attendance upon the daily sales, and to inform them of the government regulations". Bird felt that "a free press, bearing hard upon the vices and absurdities of mankind, is the grand corrective of the present times". As there was little hope of such a press in Cape Town, Bird hoped the Eastern Cape immigrants would make a difference, as they would not be "content to bear their fanciful and real grievances without the English luxury of grumbling in print ... it is therefore to the east that the Cape must look for liberty of the press".

Pringle, the stubborn Scotsman

The first independent newspaper did not emanate from the Eastern Cape, however, but from Cape Town itself – but not without a fight.

Somerset had returned from his leave in England. He ruled the Cape "as a despot, tolerating no dissent, and ruthlessly persecuting those who dared inquire into his sometimes dubious dealings".[50] On 24 May 1822, Somerset issued a proclamation that prohibited freedom of expression.[51] This proclamation also prohibited public meetings held without permission "for the discussion of public measures and political subjects". He declared that it was his "firm determination to put down, by all the means with which the law has entrusted me", any attempts to disturb the public peace, whether "by inflammatory or libellous writings, or by any other measures".[52]

But a few newcomers who "challenged the media silence of the colony" started a chain of events that would "rouse a dormant community to awareness and debate".[53]

Foremost was "settler-journalist" Pringle, who had since moved to the Cape. By May 1824, he was ordered to Somerset's offices because of his decision to close the Colony's first, and only, English-language periodical, *The South African Journal*, rather than submit to what he regarded as official censorship.

But what were the events that led to this moment?

Pringle was described as a poet and assistant librarian working in Cape Town after the failure of his farming enterprise in the Eastern Cape.[54] He was a "crippled poet and journalist, doe-eyed and deceptively mild in appearance, an idealist drenched in the reformist passions of the age".[55] To Somerset, however, he was an "arrant dissenter" who "scribbled" for magazines. Pringle himself wrote that he found Somerset on that day in May with "a storm on his brow, and it burst forth at once upon me like a long-gathered south-easter from Table Mountain".

All of this because Pringle, within a "relatively short time", initiated the beginning of the colony's first independent publication.

In Edinburgh, Pringle was involved in "literary circles that included the fiercely critical *Edinburgh Review*". As the leader of the 1820 Scottish immigrant party,[56] he settled on the Baviaans River in the Eastern Cape. But the "lure of a literary career became too strong" and, with his wife, he travelled via ox wagon to the Cape, arriving in September 1822 after leaving in July.[57] He found work as "sub-librarian" at the public library, and also launched an academy for English-speaking pupils.[58] Already in November 1822 he wrote to his college friend John Fairbairn in Scotland to help him run the academy. He also suggested they begin a journal, "[a]s there is not even a decent newspaper in the Colony". Fairbairn, along with Pringle and George Greig, who together are regarded as South Africa's press pioneers, later stated that Somerset treated the colonists as if they were inferior and backward.[59]

Thus, thirty months after Pringle's arrival in the colony, his "old intellectual instincts" surfaced and he wrote to Fairbairn that, tired "of herding nowt [cattle or oxen] and hunting lions and Bushmen", he had accepted the sub-librarian post.[60] His offer to Fairbairn was that of assistant master at his academy. And then, as far as can be established, he also made his first mention of starting a publication.

Things then started to happen at the Cape. If Fairbairn was the "mind" behind the eventual press agitation, Pringle was its "heart". The "popular" Pringle learnt to speak Cape-Dutch in only a few months. Words "like roers, brandewijn, zeekoegat or trektouw [guns, brandy, hippopotamus pool or cattle rope]" appeared early on in his writings". He was "more forbearing" than Fairbairn, who never mastered an indigenous language and appeared "remote and pedantic". When Fairbairn would later "explode" at the founding of their opposition *De Zuid-Afrikaan* (DZA), Pringle "counselled a live and let live attitude".

Pringle's "historical value" lies in the "uncompromising spirit of independence" he voiced at a time when Afrikaners "seemed withdrawn", "always aware of living under a foreign government, and when most of the handful of English-speakers willingly paid lip service to the current ruler". Being "incurably lame" from the age of three, the result of an accident which dislocated his hip and a nursemaid who concealed it until it was too late, it is thought that this handicap "no doubt had much to do with his feeling for the underdog".[61]

John Fairbairn and Thomas Pringle
Source: www.sahistory.org.za

The development of the black press

When the British again occupied the Cape in 1806, politics were barred from the existing *Gazette* and little news of general interest "managed to squeeze in between the official notices".[62] Yet the arrival of the missionaries meant the printed word also arrived. Missionaries regarded literacy as the basis of all education, and print was part of their mission "to educate and to tell people of their beliefs". The history of the earliest printing in South Africa is therefore "the history of these selfless men" who put the various black languages into writing and nurtured a generation of African writers.

Mission stations where printers and presses for mission purposes already operated were at Graaff-Reinet in 1801, Bethelsdorp in 1805 (or 1815, the date is uncertain), Griquatown in 1821, Chumie in 1823, Lovedale in 1826 and, "in the barren northern Cape", at Kuruman in 1830. In the second half of the 19th century, some mission presses became major press concerns in their own right, producing magazines and newspapers. In 1946, the South African Library in Cape Town obtained a small, eight-page pamphlet that proved to be the third earliest example of Cape printing known to exist, also being the first book to be produced in South Africa. Described as "[r]oughly done on hand-made paper", it was a Dutch translation of a letter from the London Missionary Society (LMS) to Christians at the Cape in 1799. Four LMS missionaries, including J.T. van der Kemp, arrived that year in a convict ship bound for Australia. The translation was done in Cape Town and thought to be printed on Ritter's hand press by Valentinus Alexius Schoonberg (according to this source's spelling), the compositor son of a fellow Bavarian.

It is also possible that Ritter's confiscated "humble hand press" was the first to be used at Graaff-Reinet. In 1821, the young Scott John Bennie settled at Chumie mission station, east of Graaff-Reinet, where he was joined in 1823 by the Rev. John Ross, who had with him a small Ruthven press. "They set up and readied the press in two days and started printing literature in Xhosa." This press was lost in the frontier war of 1834. A second, larger, one was destroyed in the War of the Axe in 1846, its type converted into bullets for the military. Ross saw his mission station burnt down five times in his lifetime.

Nevertheless, the black press originated in these mission stations in the Eastern Cape from 1830 onwards, with a "new black intelligentsia" emerging from them, among them names such as Sol Plaatje, John Tengu Jabavu, John Dube, Selope Thema, Rolfes Dhlomo and Pixley Seme.[63] They were not only community leaders, but also journalists and writers. And, while the government confined all printing at the Cape "to a press kept behind the thick walls of the Castle", missionaries and "their black apprentices kept the flame of independent printing alive at distant mission stations".[64]

Fittingly enough, it was a printing press intended for a mission station that would later break the government's monopoly and produce South Africa's first independent newspaper when the LMS made a press intended for a mission station available to Greig.

'I foresee great evil'

But back to the first yearnings for a free press at the Cape. Following Somerset's proclamation in 1822, of English as the only official language,[65] the bilingual government gazette officially changed in 1828 into an English weekly, *The Cape of Good Hope Government Gazette*.[66] Although "a little bit of Dutch" was still allowed since the 1822 proclamation, it became more and more unilingual, and also more and more a government gazette. Not only the Dutch were complaining, but also the English – an indication of the colonists' criticism of the governor's meddling in and suppression of public opinion.

Because of the above, Somerset "reacted with alarm" to Pringle's initial plans for an independent publication in 1823. He wrote to Lord Bathurst, secretary of state for the colonies in England: "I foresee great evil."

The struggle against Somerset intensified. Although Somerset already went as far as suppressing press freedom with his proclamations, neither freedom of speech, nor a free press, can be suppressed. The proof lies in the story of how another printing press arrived at the Cape.

At the time, "government" was vested in one man: Somerset, sole representative of the British sovereign.[67] His power "inside the colony was absolute and his resentment ruin". Most colonists, as did his administration, "bent to his whims" as "to the fuming moods of the immense mountain which dwarfed the settlement". As a closed society, "the civil liberties of the home country" were irrelevant. In accordance with the spirit of the age, press and protest were strictly regulated.

Private presses were prohibited, except for those "distant" missionaries "who with their black helpers produced educational aids and booklets for their illiterate flocks". The only press with official sanction to print "lurked" behind the walls of the Castle, printing a government gazette "filled mostly with sonorous official and civil notices and declamations".

The stage is set

Meanwhile, printer George Greig arrived at the Cape in March 1823. He "rallied" the support of Pringle, as well as Fairbairn, and also the Dutch Reformed (DR) clergyman Abraham Faure, to set up the bilingual *The South African Journal*, while he himself tried to establish a newspaper.[68] In his initial prospectus for the paper, directed to Somerset, Greig "promised an apolitical uncritical, uncontentious medium of communication". For Greig, "its primary task was to supply news of trade and commerce, to act as an advertising medium and to publish literary material".

Pringle, while waiting for Fairbairn, together with Faure attempted to establish a monthly periodical, *The South African Journal*, along with its alternate Dutch edition, *Het Nederlandsch Zuid-Afrikaansch Tijdschrift*. In February 1823, Pringle and Faure had submitted a prospectus to Somerset to publish the monthly. They argued that there was a strong sentiment that, even if only a literary and religious periodical, the colonists had to have their own publication.[69]

Interestingly, Pringle's partner in the first move towards an independent press was not Fairbairn, but an Afrikaner predikant (reverend), Dr Abraham Faure.[70] On 3 February 1823, the Scottish poet-journalist and the 29-year-old theologian jointly approached Somerset for permission to publish the monthly. It is from this "seemingly innocuous step" that flowed a series of events that would erupt in "an acrimonious press battle with overtones of spying, conspiracy and intrigue which rocked the staid Cape society".

Faure, responsible for the magazine's Dutch version, took no part in the press freedom struggle, although the other "actors in the drama soon joined the rest on the stage". Pringle was supported by Greig, as printer, who arrived in March 1823, and Fairbairn, "successful teacher" from Newcastle-on-Tyne, who arrived in October 1823.

'The Battle of the Freedom of the Press'

Just one year before, in 1822, Louis Meurant Snr. bought a set of printing type from a ship *en route* to India for £300. The company that originally ordered it had gone bankrupt. The next year, Meurant offered the set to Greig. As former printer in the "King's Printing Office" in England, it was on condition that Greig train Meurant Jnr. as apprentice.[71]

Thus, in July 1823, Greig applied for permission to publish his paper. Somerset, as "despotic Governor",[72] answered on 14 August that there were "numerous applications" and that "His Excellency will feel himself bound to consider the interests of prior applicants whenever a Printing Press shall be established in the Colony". Meurant Jnr. later would write that it was general knowledge that there were no "prior applicants", and that "the Battle of the Freedom of the Press" commenced on that day.

It was also during this time that Somerset wrote to England: "I foresee so much evil from an independent Press that I have shelved the matter so as to give time, but ... it is one of the subjects which a person in office finds it difficult to word a refusal to that can meet the public eye."[73]

Meurant Jnr. later also wrote that he often asked himself why press freedom was suppressed at the Cape, given that both the English and the Dutch colonists came from "liberty-loving countries".[74] To him there was a logical explanation to be found in the history of both countries regarding freedom of expression. In pre-Protestant Britain, the press first was under censorship of the Roman Catholic Church, and then under the British royal house. The British struggle for freedom of the press was entwined with their constitutional struggle, with censorship only abolished in 1696. In the words of Lord Russell: The press was the "guardian and guide of all other liberties". As for the Netherlands, there was no press freedom until the Dutch Constitution of 1815, after the fall of Napoleon.[75]

When Somerset returned from London in 1821, he was determined not to tolerate any signs of "radicalism". When he pondered Pringle and Faure's application for the magazine, he wrote to London about his concern finding a refusal "that can meet the public eye".[76] It was in this message that he referred to "much evil" and "improper hands". Also: The Cape was different from England; there, "the poison disseminated by one paper today meets its antidote in another tomorrow".

By 1823, the British government was pursuing a "softer line in an attempt to accommodate popular sentiment". This could partly explain Somerset's initial passivity in the face of Greig's "bold step" to start his publication without official permission. Somerset understood "little of the reverence" in which Pringle and Fairbairn held a free press. Later, when they refused to compromise and accept his authority regarding editorial content, he could only conclude that they were "inveterate radicals" and their academy a "seminary of sedition".

Somerset described Pringle as an "errant dissenter who had scribbled" for a publication in Scotland.[77] The governor's irate state of mind can also be attributed to the Commission of Enquiry that meanwhile had been sent to the Cape "to investigate the strained relationship between Somerset and the Settlers".

Some months later, Somerset summoned Pringle to his office, and "[a]fter some admonitory remarks, Lord Charles gave, with obvious reluctance, and with a very ill grace, his sanction for us to proceed with the [magazine] publication".[78]

Somerset must have felt as if there was a conspiracy against him. He also had to deal with the ambitions of Greig as another prospective publisher who was also determined to start a publication.[79] When Greig's original application for the newspaper was rejected by Somerset, he discovered that the law prohibiting publication without prior authority applied only to periodicals – not to newspapers.[80] Thus the first issue of Greig's paper appeared on 7 January 1824. Greig and his associates immediately wanted "their policy ... vigorously to support the liberty of the Press and harmonious race relations".

A new era

All of this culminated in a new era when, in 1824, South Africa's free press was established with the founding of *The South African Commercial Advertiser*, based on "libertarian" and "market" principles.[81]

But for the next number of years, until 1829, the colonial authorities, especially Somerset, would stifle this "libertarian" press. A six-year long fight ensued between the governor and the colonial secretary versus Greig, Pringle and Fairbairn, much of it fought in London. Only in 1829 was the right of a free press recognised in an ordinance, and this led to a proliferation of newspapers. With the outbreak of the SAW in 1899, there was at least one newspaper in virtually "every little town" in the Cape, Natal, Orange Free State and the Zuid-Afrikaansche Republiek (ZAR, or Transvaal), with the key characteristic that the editor was usually also the owner/publisher. It was a press operating in terms of the principles of "free market" capitalism in the true sense of the word.

But all of this could only develop after the first fight for press freedom.

In his application to start a newspaper, Greig stated the publication would "combine the ordinary topics of a magazine, and more particularly such as are interesting to the commercial and agricultural parts of the community". It would "exclude personal controversy and all discussion of matter relating to the policy or administration of the Colonial Government".[82] Still, Somerset refused permission.

Then, as said, Greig discovered there was "*no law* in existence hostile to the publication" of a newspaper, although there was one prohibiting the publishing of a magazine.[83] He therefore immediately compiled a prospectus for *The South African Commercial Advertiser*, dated 30 December 1823, with the address "G Greig, Printer, 1 Longmarket Street".

Greig, 'printer by trade and hawker of news'

After Pringle and Faure had obtained "grudging permission" for their magazine, events developed rapidly.[84] Many "down and out" 1820 settlers had gravitated to Cape Town, among them those who had inspired the petitions leading to the arrival of the Commission of Inquiry. The looming press agitation was part of a general revolt against Somerset, centring around the Society for the Relief of Distressed Settlers, in which LMS missionary John Philip "also had a hand". The "catalyst in the affair, the sputtering fuse which led to a full-scale explosion", was Greig.

Greig was a "volatile character" of whose past not much is known. The printing trade in Britain was "noted for the radical leanings of many of its members". Greig left his London printing office because of "some new arrangements in that department, and other causes", but had "testimonials to his professional talents".

He arrived in the Cape in March 1823. In August, he made the announcement that he was "to set up shop" in Longmarket Street. Later, "he liked to claim the lion's share in achieving the liberty of the press at the Cape". In 1838, fellow journalist Cornelis Moll of *De Meditator* called him a "printer by trade, salesman by coincidence, a hawker of news by habit and a politician out of self-interest". Moll said that, "shortly after arrival", the "smooth-talking" Greig "went from door to door introducing himself to the town's merchants", telling them of his commercial publication "which would hugely benefit the colony".

Greig must have been a person "of vast confidence", as all printing was strictly controlled by government and private presses still were not permitted. And Greig "certainly did not have one", whilst Pringle and Faure had just "tendered" to publish their magazine. Greig apparently knew of Pringle's application and submitted his own "memorial soliciting approval for a literary and commercial magazine". Like Pringle, he undertook to exclude "personal controversy and discussion of colonial policies". He received the "non-committal reply" in August in which Somerset claimed "numerous applications" were awaiting permission. But Greig, as "shrewd spirit", made his "big discovery" that the law did not forbade newspapers, something he discovered through "widespread enquiries". Tired of "living on his capital instead of his profits", he decided to proceed "without official sanction". So, in the last days of December 1823, less than three weeks after Pringle and Faure at last received permission for their magazine, Greig published a prospectus for his *South African Commercial Advertiser*. He did not "tempt fate in the person of Somerset", and emphasised the commercial role of the publication, as the *Advertiser* "will ever most rigidly exclude all personal controversy, however disguised, or the remotest discussion of subjects relating to the policy or administration of the Colonial Government".

Greig was "out to steal Pringle's thunder". As Somerset's "most obedient, very humble servant", he "piously" sent the governor a copy of his prospectus, requesting his patronage. In his note, Greig purposely refrained from asking permission to publish. He never received a reply to the prospectus or the note.

So, on 7 January 1824, while Pringle, Faure and Fairbairn were still "fussing around the layout of their literary magazine", the first issue of South Africa's first independent newspaper, *The South African Commercial Advertiser*, "hit the streets to a rousing welcome from the citizens of Cape Town". The first issue consisted of eight pages, of which more than four were advertising.

A later front page of *The South African Commercial Advertiser.*

The second issue was published on 14 January. Greig said he was "gratefully surprised to see so many of the native [Dutch] inhabitants" among his "supporters". A note arrived from the fiscal's office, informing him of the country postage rate as fixed for his paper. Greig accepted this as official approval of his publication.

When Pringle's *The South African Journal* appeared on 5 March, he and Fairbairn were actually also already editing Greig's newspaper, as the printer realised after the second issue that he needed professional assistance. Unfortunately, the *Journal*, with a print order of a thousand copies and printed on the government's press, was not popular. Three hundred copies were sent to England, 130 were sold in Cape Town, 50 were sent to Grahamstown, and in Paarl it was bought by two people. Still, the two Scotsmen "had fulfilled the dream of a lifetime".

Pringle and Fairbairn and their publishing dreams

But back to how Pringle and Fairbairn's legacy as press pioneers began. When Pringle, within one month after settling in Cape Town, suggested the establishment of a magazine to Fairbairn back in Scotland,[85] Fairbairn reacted: "What should hinder us from becoming the Franklins of the Cape?" He referred to Benjamin Franklin, the American printer-journalist and hero of the American War of Independence, and his brother James, pioneer of independent journalism in the USA.

About the time that Pringle wrote to Fairbairn, he met the "bustling" Faure. Together, they decided to start their journal, agreeing to exclude any "political or controversial discussion". In July 1823, five months after Pringle and Faure had submitted their application to Somerset, the Commission of Inquiry arrived from London. "Emboldened" by the presence of these government representatives, Pringle and Faure approached them but were "politely told that [the matter] fell outside the commission's power to intervene".

When Fairbairn arrived at the end of 1823, he was "confident and fresh" from the intellectual stimulation of Europe, encouraging Pringle to go ahead with the journal. Unexpectedly, on 2 December, Pringle was summoned by Somerset and "abruptly told" that London had permitted publication of the magazine on condition that it should contain nothing "detrimental to the peace and safety of the Colony". Thus, an invigorated "Pringle and friends" promptly "drew up an editorial plan for the journal and made the proper announcements to the public" in the *Gazette*.

But then the *Advertiser* appeared on 7 January 1824 as South Africa's first privately owned and independent weekly newspaper. And Greig got the honour for this.[86] Although it was officially in English, the *Advertiser* soon published news and advertisements in Dutch to also satisfy the needs of Dutch readers and advertisers.

By the second issue, Greig had appointed Pringle and Fairbairn. The motto of the two editors was: "A People without a Press cannot be regarded as civilised."[87] The two, as part of their editorial policy and despite Somerset's anglicising politics since 1822, also tried to improve cooperation between Dutch and English colonists:

> Let us not quibble about words. It does not matter who or what we are – whether we are English, German or Hollander – so long as we live here, have our homes here, and, as the interest of the country in which we live, is our interest, we can call ourselves African.

In the second edition, on 14 January, the Dutch were described as "native inhabitants":

> We were gratefully surprised to see so many of the native inhabitants of this colony among our supporters, and the numerous enquiries which were made as to our

intention in future of translating into the Dutch language the most interesting parts of our miscellaneous intelligences convinces us of the expediency of making arrangements for that purpose.

The paper propagated the notion of a free press from its inception, and nearly every issue contained views on the necessity of a free press, with the slogan "the well-known saying of Johnson": "The mass of every People must be barbarous where there is no Printing."[88]

And in the meantime, the magazine

The first issue of the magazine was eventually published in English in March 1824 under the title, *The South African Journal*, followed in April by its Dutch version, *Het Nederduitsch Zuid-Afrikaansch Tydschrift*.[89] A combined effort by Pringle, Fairbairn and Faure,[90] Pringle and Fairbairn were responsible for the English version.[91] In May, Pringle stopped publication in protest against interference by Somerset. Faure, however, carried on with the Dutch version in cooperation with Pringle and Fairbairn.

Thus, about two months after the *Advertiser*, Pringle and Fairbairn, later "honoured as South Africa's first journalists", started their bilingual periodical.[92] It was immediately "unpopular with the authorities as the content tackled constitutional matters such as the curbing of despotic power and in later issues the freedom of the press". By mid-May 1824, Pringle and Fairbairn were warned that they could only continue publication provided they stopped criticising the authorities. Pringle, refusing to submit to authority, closed the *Journal*.

The first Dutch press pioneer

When Pringle closed the *Journal* in protest against official interference, Faure proceeded with the Dutch version, as it "generally avoided political matters".[93] It lasted until 1843. From this journal came a religious periodical, *De Honigby* (The Honeybee), followed in 1849 by *De Gereformeerde Kerkbode* (The Reformed Church Messenger), forerunner of *Die Kerkbode* – to this day the official publication of the Dutch Reformed Church (DRC).

Although Faure did not play a part in the struggle for press freedom, it is most likely that it "was the whirlwind presence and ferocious enthusiasm of the stubby, dynamic" Faure that kept alive Pringle's interest in the press as "an instrument of public instruction".[94]

Faure was not only the founder of the Dutch-Afrikaans press, but was also "one of South Africa's most amazing pioneer educationists". In 1817, when still a divinity student at the University of Utrecht, he formally requested the secretary of state for the colonies to initiate higher education at the Cape. He became one of the founders of the South African College, precursor to the University of Cape Town, and played a leading role in missionary work and the synod of his church. And, "of course, eventually founded and edited its official publication".

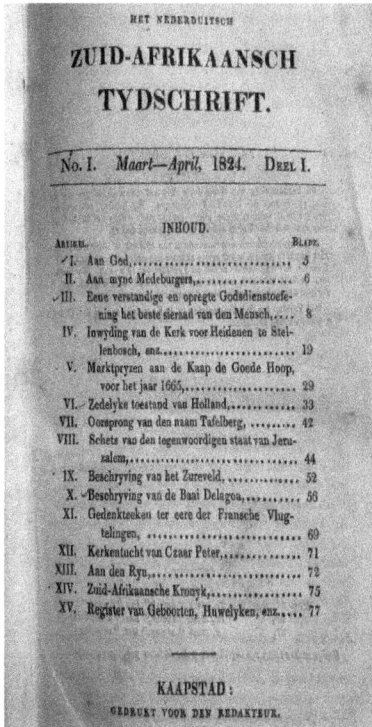

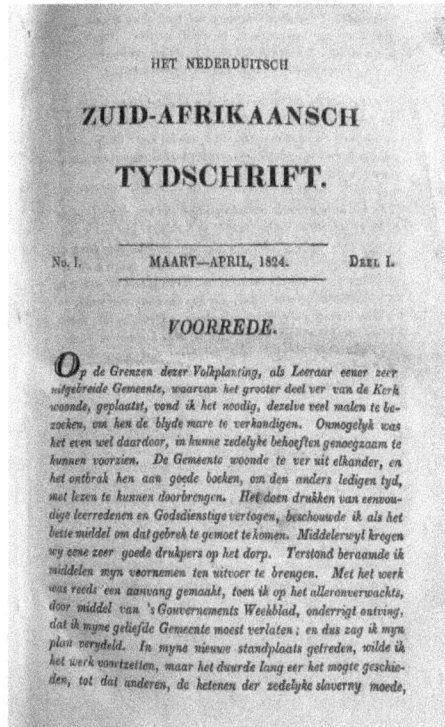

The front page, left, and the editorial, right, of the first *Het Nederduitsch Zuid-Afrikaansche Tydschrift*.
Photos: L. Rabe

Abraham Faure

The struggle starts

The freedom of expression enjoyed by the early press was thus extremely short-lived, followed by a prolonged struggle between the press and the authorities, culminating in Ordinance No. 60 of 8 May in 1829.[95]

The series of clashes between Somerset and Pringle and Fairbairn were about reports in the *Advertiser* with "political implications".[96] Somerset confiscated the *Advertiser*'s eighteenth issue and ordered the publication to be stopped. The government demanded to see the proofs, as Somerset was incensed by the publicity the *Advertiser* gave to court proceedings of libel actions "brought by the Governor against those who had accused him of acting corruptly in the administration of the colony".

When this issue was published, it carried an addendum "that until the position of censorship had been clarified", the *Advertiser* would cease publication. Three days later, Greig was given a month's notice of deportation, with orders that the paper should be closed. Greig decided to go willingly to England, but before his departure he issued a pamphlet entitled "Facts Connected with the Stoppage of the *South African Commercial Advertiser*". He defiantly affirmed his refusal to publish a newspaper under conditions of pre-publication censorship.

All of this happened because the *Advertiser* "grew bolder", with the report on the court case regarding allegations of corruption by Somerset the final straw.[97] The case was on malpractices by the collector of customs, a friend of Somerset. Instead of investigating the official, the complainants were summoned for libel. The reports meant huge increases in circulation. The complainants were eventually acquitted, but Somerset had the final say. His fiscal demanded to scrutinise all proofs of future editions before they could be published.[98]

So this eighteenth issue of South Africa's first independent newspaper, with reports on the governor's "spurious activities",[99] became the feather that tipped the scale in terms of the press freedom struggle at the Cape. Greig, as owner, with Pringle and Fairbairn as editors, comprised the "three tenacious settlers" who broke the 22-year monopoly of the government press.[100] The first reference to the liberty of the press occurred already in the sixth edition of the newspaper, followed by "regular references to press and constitutional liberty" in an "obvious attempt to prod readers into an awareness of these issues".[101]

The harassed fiscal, Daniel Denyssen, who shortly before had been derided in public for refusing a duel with a garrison officer, now sent for Greig. Denyssen told Greig that the "tendency to write about the liberty of the press was dangerous" because "we are not men in this Colony, but merely infants". Besides, in the future, trials could only be reported on on completion and with omission of all "scurrilous" parts.

Greig demanded that the fiscal supply Somerset's wishes and criticisms in writing. A "cat and mouse game" ensued, with the printer demanding that every communication should have the status of an official order. Although Greig "surrendered" the proofs, he later assured readers that not a word was altered because of the fiscal's interference. On Wednesday, 5 May, readers were "astonished" at a notice on page one of the *Advertiser*, stating (italics and capitalisation that of Greig):

> His Majesty's fiscal, having assumed the CENSORSHIP of the *South African Commercial Advertiser*, by an Official Order sent to the printing office by a messenger late in the evening before publication, we find it our duty as BRITISH SUBJECTS, under these circumstances, to discontinue the publication of the said paper *for the present*, in this Colony, until we have applied for redress and directions to His Excellency the Governor and the British Government.[102]

Following this, in May 1824, and after eighteen issues, Somerset ordered the publication to be stopped.[103]

The "defiant announcement" was the "battle ensign" of its editors and publisher in what would become a five-year contest "to wrest control of the press from the authorities".[104] This caused the Cape to be "in a rare state of excitement", with "years after the event people still recall[ing] the audacity of the two young Scotsmen" who had dared "to place themselves in opposition to the all-powerful ruler of the Colony".

Pringle and Fairbairn explained to Greig that they refused to submit to editorial interference, and that he could continue without them. Greig "joined their cause with the fervour of the converted". His "steamroller response" caught the authorities off-guard. Consequently, the month of "May became a red letter month in the history of the press".

Full-out war

On Saturday, 8 May, Denyssen denied in the official *Gazette* that he had threatened Greig with a penalty of 10,000 rix-dollars if anything offensive should appear in future issues of his *Advertiser*. "He simply reminded Greig of the conditions of the prospectus." Greig retorted that he had never received a reply to the prospectus, and that therefore no agreement was in force. The printer seized the opportunity "to make the best of the commercial possibilities of the controversy". The previous day he already tried to place an announcement in the *Gazette* that a paper with advertisements only would be published, instead of the 19th issue of the *Advertiser*. This was rejected, as well as an invitation to the public to order a full report on the controversial trial, to be published in London, so as "to prevent disappointment". A "furious" Greig decided to print these as handbills, including an announcement that on Monday, 10 May, he would produce a detailed "facts sheet" on the stopping of the *Advertiser*. Two men were hired to post these notices all over town – including on a wall facing the fiscal's office. When the fiscal sent an officer to tear them down, also in front of Greig's business, "he was confronted by the pugnacious printer who demanded a badge or mark of identification", and then told the officer to "desist at his peril". In Greig's words, the man "retired accordingly, grumbling to himself'".

On the Sunday afternoon, while Greig was in his house, which doubled as his business premises, "musing" and "sighing" over the "unusual vigor (sic) and rapidity of the movements of the Government against an individual who had not even been charged with a crime", the fiscal's party entered his home. They arrived with instructions to seal Greig's presses and to serve him with an order "banishing him from the colony for sedition and for subverting its peace and tranquillity". Greig set about to "meticulously copy" the warrant himself, "recount[ing] with satisfaction" how, while the "dismal ceremony" of sealing the presses was being performed, one of the officers leaned on a shelf, only to cover his hand with a thick layer of printer's ink.

Thus three days after its "bold" last edition, Greig's press was sealed and the printer himself issued with a deportation order.[105] He had to leave within a month, "in default of so doing he shall be arrested and sent out of it by the first possible opportunity. (Signed) Charles H Somerset."

Although Greig's press was sealed, its type was not and, on Monday, 10 May, he still published his defiant pamphlet.[106] By afternoon, "thousands of copies" had already been distributed.[107]

Black Monday

While Greig was shocked at Somerset's action, he was "gleeful" that the fiscal's ignorance left his type intact.[108] As said, the pamphlet, titled "FACTS Connected With the Stopping of the South African Commercial Advertiser", which detailed his correspondence with Somerset and Denyssen, had already been set up and was ready to be published. That night, the "resourceful" printer and two helpers "worked feverishly by the flickering, dim light, pressing wetted paper on to the inked type".

That Monday morning, Longmarket Street was crowded and people "caught delightedly at the freshly printed copies of the FACTS which fluttered from the upper-storey windows of Greig's establishment". Among those who "lapped up the dramatic events wide-eyed", was 13-year-old Meurant Jnr., who was apprenticed to Greig and would play a major role in newspapers in later years.

Fairbairn would later write of this time: "The Governor's will is law. His disapproval means ruination."[109] He described Somerset's government as a "Reign of Terror".[110] This episode in the history of press freedom in South Africa is regarded as the first official struggle between a newspaper and South African authorities.[111]

While Greig was getting ready to leave what he called "this frightful place", Somerset wrote to London that "the Community here is not deprived of the Convenience of a Public Press, as exclusive of the Government Weekly Paper, The South African Journal under the direction of Messrs. Pringle and Faure, continues to be published every two months".[112]

During this time, however, the next offending publication, on 7 May, was the *South African Journal*. Denyssen confronted Pringle with a "marked copy" of the *Journal* and pointed to the "obnoxious" parts. He warned Pringle, as he had warned Greig, that the tone of the publication was not in accordance with its prospectus. It could continue only on "a pledge that similar outpourings would not appear". This time, the fiscal – "firm but civil and sympathetic" – refused to enter into written correspondence, "having learnt his lesson with Greig". So, on 14 May, Pringle and Fairbairn "curtly" informed the fiscal that, in the light of his communication, they found the continued publication of the *Journal* "inconsistent" with their personal safety.

This is described as "a provocative barb" aimed at Somerset for the arbitrary way he treated Greig. It was reiterated at the "memorial" for a free press, launched in Cape Town the very next day, in which it was stated that "no respectable person will venture to come forward and conduct a Paper without having some security that his person is not liable to violence, and his property to seizure, without his being found guilty of some crime by ... the Court of Justice".

The memorial was signed by 209 persons and led by the principal figures in the Society for the Relief of Distressed Settlers, including prominent British merchants. Somerset regarded them as "a cabal of agitators", but in England, "[p]owerful political forces" had rallied to support the Settlers, with both the British government and British newspapers "snarling at the governor". Somerset, it should be noted, "held more executive power than most in the British colonial system". Described as "[i]mpetuous, intolerant of opposition, vindictive and small-minded", he often "ham-handedly tried to put right errors perpetrated in a fit of temper". For instance, fourteen days after Greig's deportation order, Somerset withdrew it, suggesting that it was meant as a warning. The "impecunious" printer declined the offer to stay, saying he did not need "his Excellency's permission to starve in South Africa". The battle for a free press was not a simple clash between "the pure and the iniquitous", or "St George and the Governor".

Greig left voluntarily for England to put his case before the secretary of state for the colonies, with the struggle for the Cape's press freedom now continuing in London.[113] He was eventually given permission to continue with his publication, provided he adhered to his original prospectus. Within a month of his return, the *Advertiser* appeared again, this time under the editorship of Fairbairn only, as Pringle still had to solve his problems regarding the *Journal*.

Thus the *Advertiser* was revived again on 31 August 1825, after the "drawn-out battle with the colonial office in London".[114] But Greig was victorious: He not only won the right to return to the Cape, but also to continue with his publication.

And then that day in May 1824

It turned out that May 1824 presented a fulcrum period for press freedom at the Cape. As said, soon after the episode between the governor and Greig and his *Advertiser*, it transpired that the English version of the *Journal* also peeved Somerset. In fact, already the second number of the *Journal* carried an "obnoxious" article on the settlers' "lamentable conditions".[115] On 18 May 1824, Pringle was summoned to Somerset's office, where the latter "launched forth into a long tirade of abuse; scolding, upbraiding, and raunting me, – with all the domineering arrogance of mien and sneering insolence of expression of which he was so great a master".[116]

The magazine's offending article was titled "The Present State and Prospects of the English Emigrants in South Africa", outlining the failure of an "ill-planned and ill-conducted enterprise".[117] It also referred to Somerset's "arbitrary system of government and its consequences".[118] And so it happened that the English version of the Cape's first magazine was banned, although the Dutch version continued.[119]

Somerset "was deeply riled by the journalist's role in petitioning the British government for a free press in the colony and his refusal to accept official strictures on the contents of his magazine".[120] He "repeatedly" invited Pringle to continue the magazine, but Pringle replied that he could not do so without "legal protection against official interference". Pringle "walked out of the interview a ruined person", but "unaware that his stand had become a key element in an agitation which changed the future of the colony".

Somerset "spread the word" that he was determined "to oppose and thwart everything, without exception, which emanated from Mr Pringle and Mr Fairbairn, or in which they were concerned". Pringle's stance was to reject "a free press as a privilege in the power of governments to bestow" and "claimed it as the natural right of a free man". Regarding the meeting with Somerset in which Pringle "risked his personal prospects", the principle of an independent press, on which [Pringle] chose to obstinately resist authority that memorable day, was the foundation of a tradition which vitally influenced the character of newspapers, Afrikaans and English, then still unborn. His example remains a signal challenge to this day.

Pringle said "[n]o publisher of principle was safe in the colony and he would rather wait for more liberal times".[121] Besides, "[p]rinters ink had revived Pringle and there was an icy resolve about him", and "[g]one was the solicitous seeker of a secure future in the colony".

Still, "few possibly appreciated the blighted hopes" reflected in the "bland" announcement appearing in the *Gazette* of May 15:

> The SOUTH AFRICAN JOURNAL is DISCONTINUED. All subscriptions that have been PAID IN ADVANCE for the Work beyond the SECOND NUMBER, will be RETURNED.
>
> Thos. Pringle
J. Fairbairn

Pringle could not accept a system "which made the editorial content of his publication subject to the state of Lord Charles Somerset's stomach". He and Fairbairn had "indeed restrained themselves and avoided mere politicking". But: "It was not humanly possible for committed men like Pringle and Fairbairn to forswear public interest or deny a newspaper under their control its relevance to the issues of the day."

Although it was Greig who broke the 22-year monopoly of the government press at the Cape, it was Pringle's enterprise "which tore the shroud which colonial governments had drawn over the intellectual development of its inhabitants". In the second memorial drawn up for a free press, in which the influence of Pringle and Fairbairn is noticeable, the petitioners significantly asked for free expression, not only for South Africa, but also for "other Colonies of the British Empire". It was the principle that was at stake:

> If closing down the *Journal* would add to the demise of Somerset and the system he represented, so be it. But as Pringle gathered himself to face the governor, the deeper reason for his stand on the press was not personal safety or political expediency, but the knowledge that to yield on liberty would be to lose his soul.

Pringle's last stand

Pringle's journalistic endeavours were over, and the "once successful private academy" he ran with friend and fellow-journalist Fairbairn also had to close.[122] He was heavily in debt. Just getting back to England, where his outlook "was equally grim", he had to make up the fare.[123] He had to sell "his precious books" to afford the journey to the Eastern Province, where he still owned property and a few sheep and cattle.

Pringle arrived in London in July 1826. For seven years, from 1827, he "threw himself enthusiastically" into his job as secretary of the Anti-Slavery Society. He also wrote extensively for newspapers, but he "yearned for Africa" and made plans to return, "as usual, in strained circumstances". Pringle, only 46 and ill with tuberculosis, desperately wanted to return to his adopted land. The Society offered help, but it was too late. On 5 December 1834, the "frail-bodied man with the great heart" died – one day before his ship would set sail for Africa. Fairbairn described him as among the "most intrepid and generous defenders of the natural rights of mankind". In 1970, Pringle's remains were brought from London to the Eastern Cape, to "the wild craggy land he first stared at in such wonder from the poop of the settler's vessel". Here they were interred at the Scottish Settlers Memorial Chapel at Eildon, where Pringle had built his first home.

4. The turn of the century and onward

The *Advertiser*'s second close-down

The hard-won permission for the *Advertiser* to be published did not last for long, as the British government suspended publication only nineteen months after permission to continue publication, this time because Fairbairn depicted outgoing governor Somerset as vindictive.[124] This second ban was again as a result of Somerset's direct influence.[125] The paper published extracts from an article in the *London Times* that were critical of a London official, but "leading citizens of the colony" immediately raised funding for Fairbairn to travel to London and "plead the Press's case".

One and a half years later, in October 1828, Fairbairn returned to the Cape. The *Advertiser* resumed publication for the third time. This time, Fairbairn "brought with him the promise from the Colonial Secretary that a Press ordinance, based on the Law of England, would be introduced" at the Cape. This ordinance stated that "printers and publishers who were prepared to deposit £300 as personal surety and a like amount guaranteed by friends, might publish newspapers on 1d stamped sheets paid for in advance at the Capetown [sic] Stamp Office, subject to the law of libel as interpreted by the Judges".

The role of another reverend in the press saga at the Cape

Another "churchman" besides Faure played a major, "if obscure and largely unexamined", role in the Cape's press history.[126] He was John Philip, "controversial head" of the LMS in South Africa. It was Philip who supplied Greig with the mission printing press that launched South Africa's first independent newspaper and kindled a head-on clash with the authorities. As it was described: "Like a rising roll of drums the press controversy marshalled old animosities and summoned hidden ones from the woodwork."[127]

One such incident was described as being the "most acrimonious" between Somerset and the "formidable" Philip. The latter would eventually provide the two printing presses with which Greig had "breached the walls of the Castle". But then Philip "found himself in the embarrassing situation of having to explain to a coolly vengeful governor" how Greig had got hold of mission presses supposed to produce "harmless" educational literature.

Philip is described as the "mystery element in the press affair", but Somerset believed him to be the "guiding hand" behind it, with firm pointers that the "enigmatic" missionary played "a more than passing role" in the press agitation.

The 47-year-old Philip, described as "austere and dedicated", was a successful minister in Scotland before he arrived in the Colony in 1819. He changed the spelling of his name, Philp, to make it "easier on the tongues" of his South African congregation. He "possessed doctorates which the LMS acquired for him in America – to impress the Dutch-Afrikaner population". First he tried to be "on friendly terms" with Somerset, but "gradually became convinced that the fate of blacks in the colony rested on a change in the political order".

It was "natural" for him to "canvass the acquaintance of likeminded men" like Pringle and Fairbairn, encourage intellectual dissent, and involve himself in Settlers' disputes that showed up the "inadequacies of the colonial system". Alert to the cause of his "voiceless flock", he would become "one of the most controversial figures" in early history and "a significant moulder of press attitudes".

Philip dreamt of "an 'empire' of mission stations across the southern part of the continent as a refuge for Blacks against exploitation by white settlers". After the 1832 Reform Act and the freeing of the slaves a year later, "the drive for black emancipation became the litmus test for intellectual integrity". Philip managed to "capture his powerful lobby with often one-sided propaganda", while South Africa became a "hunting ground for philanthropism". He had such influence that at one stage LMS representatives were treated like ministers of state by the British government.

Philip also had a marked influence on Fairbairn, his future son-in-law. The *Advertiser*, to which he contributed under the pseudonym "Colonist", was even labelled the "Philippine press". A son, John Ross Philip, became one of the founders of *The Eastern Province Herald*.

In the wrangle that developed for possession of the *Advertiser*'s sealed presses, Philip "was intent on keeping his political nose clean and on presenting as innocent a picture as possible of his involvement". In England, "his friend" Greig claimed that the minister had offered him the presses, "paying for them when he could", as Philip knew of his plan to start a paper. Writing to the colonial office, "Greig in the nicest way called Philip a liar".

In July 1824, after Greig had left the Colony to pursue the fight against the governor in London, Philip requested the return of the presses, which, "he took care to say", had been "entrusted to the printer ... to arrange and repair". In the end, Philip put the two presses up for public sale, "probably hoping that Greig would buy these and relieve him of all obvious ties with the affair".

In a second letter to Somerset, Philip "reveals a fresh aspect of the troublous, short-lived course" of the *Advertiser*. He wrote:

> From the claim I had upon the Presses I certainly did endeavour to control Mr. Greig in the use of them as soon as I found that his Paper gave offence to Government and I have no hesitation in saying that if matters had been allowed to go a week longer, the measures I had adopted would have led to a satisfactory pledge or security being given on the part of Mr. Greig, or else the Presses would have been taken out of his hands without any necessity for the interference of Government in the business.

Philip's protestations were in response to Somerset's "frigid refusal" to give the presses to the LMS unless security of 10,000 rix-dollars was put up against "the priming and publishing of any matter of political or personal controversy". It was "a cunning lure" to get Philip to accept liability for Greig's "repeated abuse" of his "unrestrained possession" of the presses. It was further pointed out that Greig "has stated positively and unequivocally to His Excellency the Governor, that those Presses and Types were his own property, and that he had sunk a large sum in the purchase of them". Philip was requested to show proof of ownership, also "from what vessel they were landed at the Custom House". Yet, the reverend "washed his hands over and over of the affair", stating that as far as his relationship with Greig was concerned,

> I can scarcely say I had any acquaintance previous to the interview which led to his getting possession of the Presses. He informed me he had come to the Colony as a printer – that he expected to obtain leave from Your Lordship to follow his profession, and he wished to know whether under those circumstances I would lend him the Presses in my possession.

Intrigues, political point-scoring, backstabbing and the role of mission presses

Philip was desperate that the LMS should not be implicated. On 29 July he apologised for previously expressing himself "with unusual warmth and feeling" and lamented that a security levy of 10,000 rix-dollars would prevent mission presses from printing useful "Alphabet and Lessons" for schools. "Quick as a snake", Somerset struck back with an offer to remove the seals from the presses the moment Philip undertook to print only "Alphabet and Lessons". So it was back to square one. In "a closely-scribbled, drawn-out reply the ploy was rejected, finally concluding with [Philip's] revealing assurance" that

> the promise which I now distinctly make [is] that these Presses, while the question of the Liberty of the Press in South Africa is pending, shall never be used in Printing on any political subject whatever, or anything that has a reference to the state of this Government of this Colony.

Somerset simply labelled the clergyman "a villain and a hypocrite", while in London, six months after the Philip-Somerset joust, Greig still disputed Philip's version.

Somerset's "own" paper

The intrigue at the Cape regarding the fight for a free press "was remarkably demonstrated" by the fifth publication to make its appearance on the Cape scene, *The South African Chronicle and Mercantile Advertiser*. It was regarded as Somerset's "front" publication[128] and lasted just more than two years. Its first issue was on 18 August 1824 under two "competent men", William Bridekirk, publisher of Thomas Pringle's ill-fated magazine, and Alexander Johnstone Jardine, journalist and librarian. Jardine's motto as editor "was admirable, if pallid": *No names, but events; no personalities, but principles.* Still, the paper "was well run, with colourful writing, and obviously intended to fill the hole" left by the *Advertiser*.

The paper had probably been "discreetly suggested" by Somerset, who realised that the *Government Gazette*'s "dull fare did not satisfy public taste while fearing the credence an unrestrained press could lend rumour and discontent". The *Chronicle* was instructed to avoid political matters and generally followed "an official line", admitting no criticism or complaints against the authorities. Once it even rejected a letter defending Philip.

Pringle, with his paper closed, was on good terms with Jardine and contributed to the paper's poet's corner. As he was in the process of leaving Cape Town, an advertisement in the *Chronicle* announced the public sale of his furniture (including a bath tub). But the paper could make no headway and Jardine resigned. When the *Advertiser* was published again, the *Chronicle* simply "expired". An "exasperated" colonial government secretary wrote that, despite the government providing it with advertisements, and even copy, the "cause had few friends". With Greig's return to the Cape, the "irrepressible" *Advertiser* "bobbed up again" on 31 August 1825, 16 months after its suspension.

The *Advertiser*'s second life

The *Advertiser*'s second round lasted for 19 months, after which the paper was suspended by the British government, and then "rallied spectacularly 18 months later". Greig was still the publisher, with Fairbairn now the editor. For Fairbairn it was the beginning of an era that would last 34 "tempestuous years", and establish him as "a unique influence and a giant of the South African press".

For this second round, Greig "kicked off by acidly petitioning Somerset for his printing equipment confiscated by the government". They were "the finest materials" that had "at any time reached the Colony". He was livid that they had been sold to the paper that the government started.

Greig's permission from the British government to restart his paper was on condition that he keep to its original prospectus and obtain a licence from Somerset, who "had the right to squash him once more" if he exceeded the prescribed limits in "topics of public disquisition". Greig was exactly where he had been when he left the Colony. Between Greig and Fairbairn, the former was now the cautious one, keen not to tempt the authorities, while Fairbairn was "chillingly uncompromising", "jabbing" at the hapless *Chronicle*, and scathingly commenting on affairs in the Colony. On several occasions, Greig slashed leading articles which he judged to be libellous, while Fairbairn was beginning to show "that dauntless spirit which later drove his press and political opponents to dismay".

On 4 October 1825, Fairbairn said: "An enslaved Press is the most dangerous engine of Tyranny. It not only deprives men of the wholesome nourishment they have a right to expect from the Press, but it administers poison in its stead."[129]

That same October, Fairbairn announced a publication for "educative articles", *The New Organ*.[130] It had only one edition, on 6 January 1826. A week later, Fairbairn was summoned before Somerset's "newly instituted advisory council" and asked why he had neglected to get the stipulated licence. Fairbairn refused to tie himself to "a limiting prospectus" and suspended publication. But only a few months later, Greig was sent for by the same council "for exceeding the restrictions he had agreed to" regarding his newspaper. Somerset was "more pliable than before", but the press battle was moving to a climax. When Somerset left Cape Town for the last time, on 5 March 1826, a scathing report in the *Advertiser* about his farewell accused those who had praised his governorship of "frothing and presumptuous approbation".

New governor, same old control

With a "fresh spirit" in the air, the new governor, General Richard Bourke, favoured a free press controlled only by efficient libel laws. Still, "he cast a heedful eye on local publications" and thought "some efficient control on the Press ... is without doubt necessary".

On 24 May 1826, the final stage in the press battle was sparked in the protracted "paper war" with the authorities. The *Advertiser* published a long article from *The Times* of London of four months earlier. It concerned a 30-month-old incident involving Somerset and a former public servant found guilty of embezzlement that *The Times* "had raked up". No direct evidence could be found for collusion between Fairbairn and the British paper, but ten months later "bureaucracy's ripples" finally reached the Cape. On 10 March 1827, the *Advertiser*'s licence was cancelled on instruction from London. In "an amazing response", the people rose up in Fairbairn's defence. He was made an honorary member of the Commercial Exchange and "within days a powerful statement of support had been drawn up".[131] It showed "how much the hard-hitting newspaper had achieved in the hearts of people in a remarkably short time". It read:

In a Colony ... where a small population is scattered over an immense tract of country, and where the progress of improvement and the diffusion of enlightened ideas are consequently retarded by the difficulty of communication, a newspaper conducted with the ability and integrity which were displayed in the columns of the *Advertiser*, affords instruction to the people, and by inducing them to reflect on their true interests, renders them more useful members of Society. The deprivation, therefore, of this benefit is severely felt by us, as an incalculable loss to the Colonists in general.

It would be superfluous to enumerate the benefits, nay blessings, which would result to this Colony, from the establishment of a free press. These have become apparent from the good effects resulting from the circulation of your independent Journal by which, we take the whole Colony to witness, the principles of loyalty, morality, and good order, have been constantly maintained and enforced. ... [W]e cannot, however, refrain from remarking one circumstance, peculiarly affecting this Colony, namely, that had your valuable Journal existed from the year 1814 the destructive depreciation of the paper currency, with the consequent waste of property and ruin of many respectable inhabitants, would have been foreseen and prevented.

Considering that it is necessarily the lot of the upright conductor of a political publication to point out and expose public abuses wherever they may be found to exist, we beg leave to express our conviction of the impartiality and fairness with which you have performed this painful part of your duty.

The statement was signed by more than a hundred of the most prominent merchants, advocates, doctors, wine dealers, government officials "and others", and the names "were a near equal mixture" of Dutch and English-speaking.

The *Advertiser's* third round

Fairbairn decided to put his case to the British Parliament in person and took with him a report by his advocate, C.J. Brand, who had concluded that the account as published in the *Advertiser* had been a fair reflection of events.

In London, Fairbairn was kept in suspense for more than a year until the mental strain affected his health. He had "numerous interviews with the colonial office" and it "got through to a more liberal-minded British government" that the conflict in the Colony would not cease unless the press was granted freedom from executive control. With Somerset out of the way, the authorities at the Cape supported such a move.

This meant that the *Advertiser* could be restarted again. More importantly, that "an ordinance would follow as soon as feasible". The verbal assurances made Fairbairn "restless", but on 3 October 1828, the *Advertiser* appeared on the streets of Cape Town for the third time.

And on 30 April the following year, the so-called "Magna Carta", Ordinance no. 60, was signed. It was gazetted on 8 May, with effect from 15 May, and it "made the press subject only to the courts and the ordinary laws of the land". Fairbairn had been "jubilantly" welcomed by his supporters and presented with an inscribed silver vase hailing his efforts for a free press. As it was put: "The arduous battle was over. For now."

Fairbairn, the tough Scotsman

It is said that the "iron self-discipline of the man and his dedication to public 'usefulness'" pulled Fairbairn through the hardships in his life.[132] His wife, Elizabeth Philip, daughter of John Philip, died after the "disastrous birth" of their fifth child in 1831, nine years after their wedding. In his sorrow, the *Advertiser* appeared with black rules, "as if for a national disaster". His life "seemed laced with tragedy". Five years after losing his wife and their baby, his oldest son, named after him and who "took mostly after his mother", drowned while visiting his grandfather Philip.

Fairbairn's broad Scottish accent "made him awkward with people", but he moved with authority and eloquence in the printed word, "like a fish in its element". He was a "brilliant leader writer", and "intensely committed to humanitarian principles".

His marriage to Elizabeth Philip "also solemnised his political choices". In the eyes "of a fast-growing number of opponents he became indisputably linked with the philanthropic campaign for black rights" of his father-in-law. He was lampooned as "John Featherbrain", and the *Commercial Advertiser* as the *Hottentot Adviser*.

His career in newspapers and in public life is described as "an attempt to gain South Africa constitutional adulthood". When a "nominated Legislative Council" was granted in 1834, he refused to accept it and pressed for an elected assembly. Fairbairn campaigned for hard roads, the importation of merino sheep and sea-rescue boats as ardently as for the jury system in courts. In 1845 he was a founder of the insurance company which grew into Old Mutual. His opponents "slated" him for "bludgeoning" people in print, of "practising intolerance while worshipping liberty", and of closing his columns to contrary opinion. "This was all true," but his biggest critics would also acknowledge his "unconquerable perseverance". A "valuable penned sketch" of the "dour and dutiful Scot" in the eventual Legislative Assembly, of which he was a member in the latter half of the century, read:

> The immediate neighbour of the Colonial Secretary, is the hon. member for Swellendam (Fairbairn) whom there is never the least difficulty in finding. He is never absent. When in his seat, where he does not keep seated a full half-hour together, he is always seen painfully attentive, his right leg thrown across his left, his right hand tightly squeezed under his left arm, his other hand enclosing his ear ... In his passion to lead his fellow-man to accept, and grant others, those rights which are naturally theirs, Fairbairn developed all the vices of the journalist who assumes the roles of prophet and of teacher, the profession of his youth.

No one doubted the "relentless integrity" which drove him to impose his ideals, regardless of circumstances, on the colony, because as was written much later: "John Fairbairn was building a country." He was "[s]elfless and principled" and disregarded public acclaim. Many of those who hailed him for the free press in 1829 damned him shortly afterwards for his attitude to slavery and other issues. Early in 1832, the Cape wine farmers were experiencing welcome prosperity through a reduction in customs duty – while Fairbairn found it opportune to urge a temperance society. In 1849, after the British government's decision to use the Cape as a penal settlement, Fairbairn became the heart of the anti-convict movement, which drew Dutch and English together against the landing of 282 prisoners.

Fairbairn died on 5 October 1864 at the home of his daughter, with whom he was staying in Wynberg: "The indomitable spirit that had transformed South Africa in such a vital way was of the past."[133]

The one non-negotiable: A free press

It is suggested that it was Fairbairn's uncompromising tenacity that "vitally influenced the kind of press which developed in South Africa".[134] His refusal, with Pringle and Greig, to "horse-trade with the authorities on the issue of the press" was in stark contrast to the attitude of the editor of the ill-fated *Chronicle*, who was willing to accept government restrictions. The fundamental difference lay in the role that Fairbairn and Pringle accorded the press in society, namely that a free press guaranteed the liberty of the individual in relation to the state. As such it was non-negotiable. It enabled the citizen, Fairbairn wrote in 1824, to "bring every part of the system to the test of reason and justice. For no abuse, however sanctioned by time or guided by force, can long resist the action and pressure of enlightened Public Opinion".

To appreciate "the inflexible position these two nineteenth-century intellectuals" held on the press, it should be borne in mind that they were the products of one of the most significant upheavals in Western thought: The birth of individualism. "The community was regarded as a living, rational entity and the press as the instrument of its awareness." It was a case of rather "no press than an enslaved one or a press existing through official patronage". Like Pringle, Fairbairn preferred a suspension of publication to acceptance of compromise.

The Fairbairn-Pringle duo

To achieve this free press, Fairbairn, with advice from Pringle in London, provoked situations with the authorities which would focus attention on the issue.[135] The "Magna Carta" was thanks not only to Somerset's departure "and a change of heart on the part of the colonial authorities", but also to Fairbairn's refusal to allow the British government "to go to sleep on the press issue". He "badgered, argued and petitioned with an obstinacy which not only wore down his health but also those in government". After the 1829 achievement, "he did not rest until all bureaucratic restrictions, like the stamp tax, had been abolished".

When, in 1859, after 36 years in journalism at the Cape, Fairbairn gave up the editorship of the *Advertiser*, the "flagship of an independent press", he was 65, had little money and was in ill-health. In 1860 he visited his constituency, Swellendam (for the first time), and the undemonstrative Fairbairn "was obliged to sit through a procession of horsemen and numerous speeches". The role that his college friend Pringle played in his life was always clear. It was speculated whether he, sitting there on that day in Swellendam, might have thought

> of the bright-eyed university friend with the quick smile who those long years ago tried fruitlessly at first to get him to write for magazines and become a journalist? And when he did not reply, Thomas Pringle wrote back: I know thee, dear John, to be an odd fish, a strange, nervous youth, more sinned against than sinning, more to be pitied than blamed, therefore, I forgive thee.

Pringle was an invaluable influence in Fairbairn's life and, as a professional journalist, tried to teach his "staid" friend the popular touch. From London he criticised the *Advertiser* "as not newsy enough", while also telling Fairbairn to use the anonymous plural pronoun when writing leading articles: "The Editor should always be dignified."

Their relationship was intriguing. After Pringle's death, his wife sent all his papers to Fairbairn, but these never reached their destination – "the mystery of their disappearance has never been solved".

What Fairbairn "missed" in technical competence was compensated for by his deep understanding of the meaning of the press and the "awesome reverence" in which he held "this inestimable privilege". Reflecting on those first, tense steps towards a free press, Fairbairn wrote, "the intention was not to establish a Newspaper or Journal; it was not to encourage or assist in carrying out any particular policy, system or scheme even for the public good". No, it "was simply, solely, exclusively to establish the *Liberty of the Press*".

The 'Magna Carta'

The official gaining of press freedom at the Cape manifested itself in the so-called "Magna Carta". The initial struggle for press freedom on Greig's return from London with permission to publish the *Advertiser* did not mean the fight for press freedom was over. On the second closure of the *Advertiser*, directly under Somerset's influence,[136] Greig, this time supported by 113 "prominent citizens" of Cape Town, drew up a protest letter in March 1827.[137] This time Fairbairn went to London. After the "long struggle", Fairbairn returned to the Cape, restarting the paper in October 1829 for the third time.[138] This led to Somerset's recall[139] and freedom of the press being laid down in Ordinance no. 60 of the Cape of Good Hope.[140] Its "significance is to be seen" in how it was popularly known, namely the "Magna Carta" of press freedom. Sir Lowry Cole ended the "siege of the press" by signing the ordinance on 30 April 1829. Because the ordinance was said to ensure the freedom of the press "to some degree" it was referred to as the "Magna Carta".[141] The government would act against publications only in the case of proven libel, or when irresponsible statements were made. The Preamble to Ordinance no. 60, published on Friday, 8 May 1829, reads:[142]

> For preventing the mischiefs arising from the printing and publishing Newspapers, and Papers of a like Nature, by Persons not known, and for regulating the printing and publication of such Papers in other respects; and also for restraining the Abuses arising from the publication of blasphemous and seditious Libels ...

Five "torrid years" had elapsed from Sunday, 9 May 1824, when Somerset sealed Greig's presses, to that momentous Friday, "which made the publication of newspapers independent of the fickleness of governors". Although the announcement on 8 May 1829 was "couched in peevish terms and smothered in official flourishes", it was "like honey on the parched tongues of those who had fought so long for its achievement".

Altogether, 21 of the 23 sections of the "Charter" spelled out rules and regulations "newsmen" [sic] had to abide by, but "when all the forms had been filled out and stamped, only proven libellous and irresponsible statements could in future give government a reason to interfere". Newspapers had become what Pringle had said they should, namely "a legal right and not a favour". The good news was in the tail of the proclamation: "And be it further enacted, that the Proclamation of 21st July, 1800, shall be repealed, and the same is hereby repealed." The latter was the proclamation by which the corrupt Yonge had banned all public printing by anyone except his nominated cronies. For 29 years it was the "fist which had pinned down the press".

The role of a free press

But this battle for a press independent of "arbitrary decision" had not been a predictable contest. There had been more to it than going to London to claim a free press "as the birth right of an Englishman". Greig's return was with little more than renewed confidence to revive the *Advertiser*, and towards the end of the drawn-out struggle, the "indomitable" Fairbairn's health was also "on the point of breaking down".

In the course of the five years, the government had shifted its ground several times. The "staid old lady of the Castle", the official *Gazette*, on one occasion actually got so carried away "that she lifted her skirts to run with popular sentiment". But its approving quote on "the full influence of free publication on the minds, manners, actions and habits of men in social life" immediately earned it Somerset's censure, and "all light was immediately flung out of the Gazette".[143]

The fight for the freedom of the press was thus not merely for the right to print facts, but to present news critically and to articulate public opinion. What later led to the establishment of the "watch dog" over the "watch dogs", namely the founding of the NPU in 1882, was that

> [e]arly colonial journalism rarely offered news as a faithfully reproduced bleat. This was what set the journalists apart from the peddler of patent medicines and the merchant advertising his wares. The little the newspaper may have had, whether in the form of statement, court case or event, was embellished, examined with a jaundiced eye and, if preferred, ridiculed to the point of insult. Blandness in journalism was a late development in the press. An irreverent tone was a feature of early newspapers and it deteriorated to the point where a storm of libel cases hit the press late in the nineteenth century. The need to protect itself from unwarranted hounding was one of the prime considerations in the founding of the Newspaper Press Union in 1882.

The *Advertiser* as first independent newspaper thus cannot be described as "a good *news*paper". Instead, it was as full of "thunderous homilies" as the official gazette was "of proclamations and regulations". But its success and its stature as an "influential oracle" – for a paper which by 1850 rarely sold more than 300 copies a week – was that the Cape's taste for change and challenge had been awakened by Pringle, Fairbairn and Greig. And the Cape "seemed to find the spicy questioning of an avowedly critical paper, even if they disagreed with it, more credible than an expert marshalling of innocuous facts and events by a commendably neutral one". Thus, only when Somerset was recalled did it become possible to make press freedom a reality, with Ordinance no. 60 described as "a document that provided liberty and political rights to the Press".[144]

Three factors that eventually led to the declaration of press freedom were later identified. They were Somerset's departure from the Cape, the appointment as governor of General Richard Bourke, who favoured a free press, and Fairbairn's "dogged pursuit of matters relating to the press with the British government".[145]

The Press's first 'freedom charter'

Known as the "freedom charter" for South Africa's press, the "Magna Carta" now stimulated the birth of a number of newspapers in both English and Dutch.[146]

In 1885, half a century after this episode, Meurant Jnr. commented on the struggle for press freedom: "How much do editors and the public of the present day owe to the brave men who so manfully and uncompromisingly battled for, and eventually gained, the incalculable victory of the 'Free Press' of South Africa!"[147]

More than one century later, in 1943, this achievement was described as that the struggle for the freedom of the press in South Africa was won.[148] Of course, this was only a relative victory, as the status of press freedom is never absolute. Still, the Cape press after 1829 would be "under the control and protection of *the Law*", and "no arbitrary suppression should take place in future".[149]

This was South Africa's first official victory for press freedom. Since then, the names of Pringle and Fairbairn, together with Greig, have been synonymous with the fight for press freedom.[150] Now the Cape could rely on its "Magna Carta" and enjoy a relatively free period. It also brought with it other freedoms, because "[t]he Star of democracy had risen and that of autocracy was hastening to its setting".[151]

The year 1829 thus heralded a new era for South Africa.[152] In the 1940s it could even be stated that, since 1829, the authorities had been "unable" to curfew the evolution of the press.[153] Such a statement of course also is relative, and depends on whose account it is expressed. In 1844, Fairbairn himself wrote:[154]

> The Liberty of the Press is Freedom to every man in the country to express his thoughts in print, under the same danger and responsibility that surround all other actions in a Free State. If the words printed, injure, the laws punish or give redress. This was the Liberty we contended for; this was the Liberty we obtained for the Cape. And this Liberty the people of this Settlement can never again lose but by their own fault.

The South African press's particular 'blueprint'

It was also argued that, by 1830, a "blueprint" of what was later to be peculiarly significant in the development of South Africa and South Africa's media history "could already be said to have been devised".[155] This referred to the English/Dutch-Afrikaner binary poles in South African society up to democratisation in the 1990s.

The Dutch newspaper DZA was started in opposition to the *Advertiser* and in the interest of the Dutch colonists. Fairbairn, as editor of the *Advertiser*, "had for some time been interested in race relations" and, as said, was "closely associated with the liberal missionary" Philip. Cape advocate Christoffel (C.J.) Brand, "a Dutchman of slave-owning stock" (although a Fairbairn aide in the case against the *Advertiser*), started DZA "with the avowed purpose of opposing" the *Advertiser* on various issues. It also had to help keep "literary Dutch" alive amongst the rural Dutch. By the 1870s, it amalgamated with the *Volksvriend* of J.H. Hofmeyr, known as "Onze Jan", and "was to become more closely drawn into the struggle for 'taal' and 'Volk'". Hofmeyr also started his own newspaper in Cape Town, *Het Volksblad*, in 1849.

The development of the Dutch-Afrikaans press

Het Nederduitsch Zuid-Afrikaansch Tydschrift (HNZAT) lasted longer than its English counterpart, from 1824 to 1843, "partly because Somerset tended to concentrate his actions more against the English press".[156]

Faure's HNZAT published a wide variety of articles and reflected the strong religious background of its editor and the traditionalist Dutch Calvinists at the Cape. The magazine contained articles on the historical roots of the Dutch settlers and was the first South African magazine to concentrate mainly on events reflecting Cape politics and the religious, artistic and social life of South Africa. This focus was intensified when Dutch settlers, mostly in the Eastern Cape, left for the interior in the 1830s as part of the Groot Trek. Faure published a regular feature, "Zuid-Afrikaansche Kronijk" (South African Chronicle), on the fortunes of these "Voortrekkers".[157]

In 1878, Faure's magazine was re-established by Hofmeyr with the new name, *Het Zuid-Afrikaansch Tijdschrift*, but publication was ceased in 1893.[158] An important characteristic of South African publications was the bilingualism of their contents and readers. When DZA – a combination between a newspaper and a magazine (as were many other early Cape publications) – was published in 1830 under the editorship of Frenchman Charles Etienne Boniface, it had a strong Dutch content, but also included articles in English. It subsequently was published as the Dutch/Afrikaans newspaper *Ons Land*. When publication ceased exactly a century later, in 1930, it still carried English versions of its editorials.[159]

Two years after the publication of the HNZAT, in 1826, the first Dutch newspaper, *De Verzamelaar*, was published.[160] Its editor can be described as representative of the medley of nationalities from which the Dutch-Afrikaans population descended. Josephus Suasso de Lima was namely a Jew of Dutch-Portuguese origin. The newspaper was not sustainable, and De Lima went bankrupt in 1830.

Regarded as the first newspaper to speak specifically for Dutch/Afrikaner interests, the already referred to DZA was first published on 9 April 1830.[161] Its owner, advocate Christoffel Brand, was unpopular with the local authorities for his ability to successfully defend cases against the government. The paper was formed "largely as a reaction to the indifference of the English press to the Afrikaner's needs and the attempted anglicisation of the Afrikaner by the government". Fairbairn and his *Advertiser* "clashed bitterly" with DZA.

Early press wars, or the 'East-West cleavage'

Pioneer editor R.W. Murray Snr. wrote that DZA was to the Dutch of the Western Cape precisely what *The Graham's Town Journal* was in Godlonton's time to the Settlers of the Eastern Cape.[162]

This "east-west cleavage", which characterised the press in the post-"Magna Carta" period, ran like a "geological fault right through the centre of Cape Town".[163] The 1830s found Fairbairn "firing broadsides" not only at the distant *Graham's Town Journal*, but grappling at close quarters with his "equally tough" opponent, DZA, as first newspaper to speak for Afrikaner interests. Like the Settlers, "sick" of the *Advertiser*'s philanthropism and Fairbairn's "lashing tongue", the Dutch-Afrikaners "had stirred from their media slumber". This split into factions, still largely on the basis of issues, was inevitable. The granting of a free press in 1829 shattered the alliance of intellectuals and enlightened burghers who had tended to stick together – like a resistance in wartime – under the autocratic shadow of Lord Charles Somerset. The liberty of the press freed opinions previously expressed only round a dining room table or at the literary society.

Fairbairn heard "rumours" of an opposition newspaper early in 1830, co-incidentally while at Grahamstown on a trip through the "frontier districts" with Philip. The paper was most likely the one announced by Cape Town merchants, who, surprisingly enough, included H.E. Rutherfoord, Philip's old friend and secretary of the Society for the Relief of Distressed Settlers. Nothing came of this paper, but the "sensitive" Fairbairn was livid that they had touted themselves as "independent", saying "the insinuation was thus sent forth to the world, that we had lost, or thrown away, or sold our Independence".

The rival paper which did appear was DZA. Its business address was that of the home of its publisher, C.N. Neethling, in Shortmarket Street, and its first issue appeared on 9 April 1830. As said, Brand was also behind this paper, despite once being a Fairbairn acquaintance who, as "canny advocate", had helped him with his case against Somerset with the *Advertiser*'s second banning. Before that, the "enterprising Brand" had made himself unpopular with the authorities by appearing *pro Deo* for a notorious "lawyer-cum-convict" accused of libelling Somerset. Fairbairn and Brand became lifelong enemies, with the latter lawyer-cum-convict later elected as the first Speaker of the Cape Parliament, defeating Fairbairn by one vote.

Fairbairn "never took kindly to opposition", although Pringle, writing from London, had advised "an indulgent attitude". Fairbairn first tried to ignore his press rival. In its first issue, DZA, despite scathingly referring to Fairbairn, also pledged an "unwarlike deportment".

The "sober declaration" of neutrality did not last. The 1830s became a period when newspapers "were used like cudgels in knock-down and drag-out hostility". Fairbairn and the DZA "clashed bitterly" on the emancipation of the slaves and on the Voortrekkers, whom Fairbairn "snidely bade goodbye with the toast to 'the land we live in, and let those who don't like it, leave it!'" DZA was also slated as "a viperous journal" by Jardine's *Cape of Good Hope Literary Gazette*. Fairbairn ridiculed prominent supporters of the paper as "eminent growers of cabbages".

DZA did not see itself as sectional. In its first issue, translating much of its editorial copy into English, it declared:

> In assuming the title of the "*Zuid-Afrikaan*" we hoist a banner which shall serve as a rallying point to all Colonists, both old and new. In fact, all who inhabit this land, and derive nourishment from her bosom, are Africans, and are bound, both by duty and interest, to further the well-being, and guard the reputation of their Country, and whoever wantonly attacks these, should be visited with indignant vengeance of all Africans, whether Dutch or English.

DZA "certainly stimulated Afrikaner awareness". When, half a century later, the robust *Die Afrikaanse Patriot* heralded a rising Afrikaner Nationalism, "it walked a way prepared by the older newspaper". With a "touch of hyperbole", pioneer editor Murray described the paper:[164]

> It was Dutch – heart, soul and backbone, as it ought to have been, to be honest ... Always true to the traditions of its race, it has never affected to hold the people

of the Nation who took the Colony out of the hands of the Dutch with any warm affection ... The columns of the *Zuid-Afrikaan* were as much believed in by the African Dutch as the Bible, and taken to be as unquestionable as the Gospels of Matthew, Mark, Luke or John.

DZA was clear in its first issue's leading article, in Dutch, that the paper was "very much" a reaction to the insistent philanthropism of Fairbairn and Philip.[165] It promised to expose various kinds of "humbugs" to which the colonists had been exposed since the British take-over in 1806. The first "humbugs" were "the FREE-PRESS humbug, INDEPENDENT NEWSPAPER humbug, MISSIONARY humbug, and especially (because this is the paramount or non plus ultra of all humbugs) the PHILIPPINE humbug" (the latter referring to Philip).

The Afrikaners were becoming sensitive to what Pringle called "the insolent and flippant tone assumed by the common herd of English Travellers". Although vigorous in its editorial policy, Brand's paper struggled to survive. Only two months after its first issue, it was sued for libel, with the result that its editor and eccentric Frenchman, Charles Etienne Boniface, left. He was followed by R.J. Stapleton, "who tended overly much to John Fairbairn's philanthropism" and departed after six months. In 1831, eighty sponsors had to keep the paper going. After this, the paper was run by Brand and his brother, P.A. Brand. The paper grew, and after merging with *Ons Land* in 1894, lasted until 1930. During the SAW, the editor, F.S. Malan, was jailed and the paper suspended.

DZA was one of the first moves by Afrikaners to resist anglicisation. Previously, they accepted changes "almost in silence because they believed that complaint would be useless". The British attitude towards "the old colonists", or "natives" as they were regarded, was one of "benevolent superiority". When Fairbairn called "for a fit country for free men, he meant under the British flag". Dutch-Afrikaners were acceptable only as long as they did not insist on asserting their "liberty in choice of language, customs and politics".

The same Fairbairn who in 1827 praised the Cape Dutch for their "love of freedom" and for bearing "the law of liberty in their hearts", pointed out to them in 1832 that the Cape, after all, was a British colony, "captured by British bayonets and purchased with British gold".[166] Also Godlonton, friend of the Voortrekkers but fiercely loyal, changed allegiance when it seemed that the Cape Dutch might challenge British sovereignty.

In January 1828, with Fairbairn and his supporters preoccupied with the press battle, the British "forcibly asserted their presence by scrapping the Dutch local government system of Heemraden and outlawing the Dutch language in the newly constituted supreme court". Once, when Brand spoke in Dutch at a meeting, Fairbairn "had to fall around to find out what he had said". For the Dutch burghers, DZA was their answer to fight against "the radicalism of the negrophilist philanthropists".[167]

More colourful characters

It is said that, as it developed "from its earliest years," the Cape, and thus the rest of the country, "had attracted eccentric characters" who played their part in the growth of the press.[168] Among them was the already mentioned Josephus Suasso de Lima, the "hunchback of Portuguese-Jewish descent" who worked as author, bookseller, publisher, translator and polemicist, and was the first to produce a Dutch newspaper. His weekly *De*

Verzamelaar "bobbed up" in the wake of Fairbairn and Greig's "battle-scarred" *Advertiser* in 1826. It was the seventh publication in Cape Town.

The "highly talented" De Lima was sacked from the VOC's service for "misuse" of documents. *De Verzamelaar* "limped on" with interruptions for 22 years, although De Lima went bankrupt in 1830. Adding insult to injury was that his printing press was then "snapped up" by DZA, under the editorship of his great enemy, Charles Etienne Boniface.

Boniface, a "quarrelsome Paris-born Frenchman", but also music expert and playwright, reached Cape Town in 1807. He and De Lima at first collaborated, but their relationship "erupted in an antagonism which kept Cape Town bemused for many years". Boniface made a wordplay out of *De Verzamelaar*, calling it *Very Similar*. De Lima hit back by publishing his former friend's "legal embarrassments".

Another character was the "mercurial" Cornelis Moll. Together with Boniface, they formed "the odd couple of early newspapering". Between them they started newspapers, mostly short-lived, in three provinces, "more than once staying just one step ahead of the law", and both were described as "disorganised and disdainful of regulations regarding the press". Moll was the 24th child of a Swellendam minister ("which may have had something to do with it"). He was an "outstanding journalist", fluent in both English and Dutch, and "an acerbic and entertaining commentator". Moll cynically compared Fairbairn's lofty claims for the press to gun-powder: "Men begint den oorlog met de eerste, en men eindigt denzelven met de tweede" (One starts a war with the first and ends it with the second).

Moll published his first journal, *The Moderator*, in January 1837. He tried for two years to stave off collapse by changing the name to *De Meditator*, was bankrupt in 1840 and worked as compositor for other papers, but also "as a jack of all trades, including butcher". In the meantime, he had been accused of stealing sheep and, in 1844, when Boniface faced a charge of perjury, he suggested they leave for Natal – "not much persuasion was needed". In Pietermaritzburg they moved into a house doubling as printing works, and Natal's first newspaper appeared on 19 April 1844: *De Natalier en Pietermaritzburgsche Trouwe Aantekenaar.* This "mouthful" soon went bilingual as *De Natalier and Pietermaritzburg True Recorder* (a direct translation of the Dutch). Boniface was editor, reporter and bookkeeper and Moll the foreman and printer. Their paper had a circulation of 40.

The Natal authorities were so unenthusiastic about the newspaper that the two once were fined a hundred pounds for appearing a day late and not on the date stipulated in their prospectus. The commandant of Natal, Major J.S. Smith, protested against Boniface's republicanism and "seditious spirit", and complained to Cape Town about the "mischief caused among this ignorant people ... by an unprincipled Frenchman".

Boniface was described as "a tortured individual" who led a bohemian existence "and drove Moll to distraction". The partnership broke up when Boniface sued Moll for libel after they had quarrelled over some of Boniface's unrestrained leading articles. Boniface was successful, but the *Natalier* closed down in September 1846. Boniface tried "his hand at a few other journals" and eventually died by his own hand in 1853.

Moll's entrepreneurship was from necessity – he now published "other papers sprouting out" to the ZAR (formally founded after the Sandrivier Convention in 1852[169]). He had mortgaged his small hand press in Pietermaritzburg but, when pressed by his creditor, loaded it on a cart "and raced for the border".[170] He published the ZAR's first paper, the *Staats Courant*, in Potchefstroom on 25 September 1857. He then went on to "hold the august post of landdrost in the republic" and left most of his possessions to his printer son, Cornelis Petrus.

The Natal newspaper founded by David Dale Buchanan – "Double D Blow-cannon" to his enemies – on 27 February 1846[171] is today known as *The Witness*, the oldest in continuous existence in South Africa.[172]

The Natal Witness started as a bilingual weekly and later carried a Dutch-Afrikaans supplement, *De Natalsche Getuige*, a direct translation of its title. Buchanan, who was editor for 25 years, "epitomises the passionate self-sacrifice with which many of the early pioneers dedicated themselves to the business of producing newspapers and establishing the presence of a free press".[173]

Buchanan became a South African by chance. In 1829, at age 11, he and his elder brother William, sons of a "well-known educationist", were on their way from Scotland to New Zealand but were persuaded to stay in Cape Town. William later opened a school next to Philip's LMS establishment on Church Square. In 1841 he started a newspaper, *The Cape Town Mail and Mirror of Court and Council*. The paper was unique in that it gave verbatim reports of Supreme Court cases and official debates – William was an "outstanding shorthand reporter". After he and Fairbairn agreed on an amalgamation of their papers, they published the speeches of the Legislative Council as a public service for years. Hansard was established in 1854 "and a record of these speeches would certainly have been lost" if not for Buchanan. A similar service was provided by the *Cape Times* between 1885 and 1910 with the publication, at the paper's expense, of speeches in the Cape parliament.

When Buchanan arrived in Natal he had some type and a small hand press, a parting gift from Greig.[174] In Natal he was soon sued for libel and arraigned for sedition, but refused to pay fines. While in prison, he continued writing editorials denouncing the authorities. As lawyer, Buchanan regarded the freedom of the press as "tenfold more important" than that of the Bar.[175] His paper's motto was "The Truth, the Whole Truth and Nothing But the Truth". Its editor lived by it, "often at hardship to himself". The paper was "a sword in the service of the community" and "an agent of modern civilisation". Buchanan wrote some of "the most vitriolic leading articles" to appear in print, regarded as a sign of the "tremendous strides in public and official acceptance" the press has made in "the short 22 years since Pringle and Fairbairn started their lone battle against Lord Charles Somerset". Although Buchanan directly attacked Natal's governor in his editorials, "his paper remained virtually untouched by officials".

Buchanan's opponents once drew up a petition for the *Witness* to be closed, but among his "fervent" admirers was Theophilus Shepstone. His paper was hard-hitting on Natal's "backwater position" and a "firm friend of the Boers", with Buchanan regularly criticising the "vacillating frontier policies of the British government". Natal had no official gazette until 1849 and Buchanan had the contract to publish government notices – on condition that he did not comment on them until a week after publication. Buchanan was described as "tireless in his role as public watchdog".

And onward

Once freedom of expression through the "Magna Carta" was a given, expansion was rapid. More newspapers started in Cape Town and in Grahamstown – as the main centre for the inland Settlers, and then "spread north and east as the Settlers penetrated the interior".[176]

The so-called "Settler press", confiscated from Godlonton and Stringfellow in 1820, was auctioned off in Graaff-Reinet. The buyer was what can be described as a first publishing tycoon, the already mentioned Louis Henry Meurant Snr. He took it to Grahamstown to start a publication in the fast-growing Eastern Cape centre. The first *Graham's Town Journal* was published in December 1831 with the motto: "Open to all parties, influenced by none."

Thanks to the 1820 Settlers and the printing presses they brought with them, the Europeans in this region soon had a voice with which to express themselves. Godlonton edited the *Graham's Town Journal* and "spearheaded the cause of British and Dutch farmers alike".[177]

Godlonton was described as "the father of the indigenous press [meaning the community press] of South Africa". To him and his fellow editors, "it was the reality of everyday life on the outposts which came first, not the philanthropic views of John Fairbairn and his colleagues in Cape Town". These "[f]rontier editors" furthered the cause of British settlers, Dutch farmers, as well as the Voortrekkers. Godlonton's paper, for instance, published Voortrekker leader Piet Retief's *Manifesto* in 1837.

Godlonton, 'frontier' journalist entrepreneur

When, at Christmas 1834, the "border was aflame" and the Sixth Frontier War had begun, Grahamstown was barricaded. Seven thousand Settlers crowded St. George's Church "to the doors".[178] In "ten violent days the settlers, dumped on bare veld fifteen years earlier, had lost all". But in the "long dark night of distress faced by the maligned and bereft settler community, a commanding voice spoke for them:" Godlonton, "the great frontier journalist". "Allaying fears and passions, he stood rock-like in their defence and would do so for 44 years. His is one of the most impressive figures in the annals of the press in South Africa."

As master printer, Godlonton was also editor of the *Graham's Town Journal* – the first newspaper outside Cape Town. He was over 1,8 m tall, had a prominent nose and a "defiant set to the jaw", and was reputedly a boxer in his youth. "The mere sight of him down High Street on his way to the newspaper office put heart into the townspeople."

At the historic founding meeting of the NPU in Grahamstown in 1882, Godlonton was honoured as pioneer by the "most outstanding newsmen of the time". He was hailed as the "father" of "a colonial or South African" press, with Grahamstown "the cradle of an indigenous English-language press". Also: From "that little town in the eastern province the presses, types and men went on to establish newspapers not only in Queenstown, King William's Town, Graaff-Reinet, Cradock and East London but in Bloemfontein, the diamond fields, Natal and eventually in Johannesburg".

Unlike Fairbairn, Godlonton was a newspaper entrepreneur. In 1850 he founded *The Friend of the Sovereignty and Bloemfontein Gazette*, later *The Friend*, and in September 1853 launched a Dutch paper for the Eastern Cape, *De Grahamstad Register en Boeren-vriend*. Before and after the Great Trek, Godlonton's *Journal* was an "unofficial organ" of the Voortrekkers. In the issue of 2 February 1837, on page 3, Piet Retief's "impressive" "Manifesto of the Emigrant Farmers" appeared. The *Journal* had altogether 27 selling points in the Colony and was also available in London.

Before 1865, when telegraph technology reached Grahamstown and one could get there in four days by sea, the town had been the "remote interior, eight days in a swaying coach over wild tracks from Cape Town". In this "crucible of the eastern frontier the realities of Africa hit white settlers like a blast from a furnace and here the issues of race and territory emerged which would dog a future South Africa". Godlonton wrote for people who knew "death and destruction, insecurity, stock theft and sudden fright and still, in these circumstances, had to try and maintain those values of integrity and decency with which they had arrived in their new country".

In 1882, Josiah Slater, then editor of the *Graham's Town Journal*, toasted the absent Godlonton at the NPU banquet and said that reading the turbulent events reflected in the newspaper files under its pioneer editor "was like looking into a dark pit while involuntarily holding on to the parapet".

Away from "the protective shadow of Table Mountain, a different kind of press had developed". In Cape Town, the "men of the mother settlement faced the sea and the ships" and "remained largely British-orientated". Fairbairn's *Advertiser* carried "lengthy readings from continental philosophers and its editor engaged in polemics not only for his readers but for overseas consumption". He was "widely quoted in British and even Australian papers" and "his views accepted as representative". Those views were coloured "by his growing commitment to philanthropic thought which perceived people as homogeneous and by his aversion to travel". Much of his information came from a single source – his father-in-law, Philip.

Godlonton and Fairbairn were the two great newspaper foes of the post-"Magna Carta" period and symbols of two distinct streams in the English press. Fairbairn referred scathingly to the Settlers as "Brummagem pin makers" who became "frightened at the sight of a natural man". Godlonton "coolly" thought of Fairbairn as "a clever, crafty theorist, nothing more". The Settlers were not "well-fed usurpers advancing Tatar-like, supported by a sympathetic government". Rather, their relative prosperity by 1834 had been "wrenched from nature in a primitive fight for survival in which some were reduced to abject poverty".

In 1820, the Zuurveld was "hopefully renamed Albany" by the newcomers, but it was said that "never was a country so different from what it was represented". When crops failed, the Settlers turned to pastoral farming. This "attracted black raiding parties and bloodshed". Also: "[T]he frontier had two sides and those who faced it with the rising sun on their left saw the whites as invaders grabbing land and grazing rights theirs by tradition." It would be another fifty years before John Tengo Jabavu, pioneering South African editor, "would rise in King William's Town to speak for his people as Godlonton did for the settlers".

Godlonton and Fairbairn, representing opposing views, were both "indignant" at the other's non-understanding of their views and circumstances. Fairbairn, writing from "the sylvan lap of Cape Town", admonished the "harassed border inhabitants for exaggerating their calamity", suffering from "conscious guilt". When he later expressed sympathy, already "more than 700 outraged frontiersfolk" had signed two declarations calling for a boycott of his paper, accusing the Cape Town editor of "a cruel and malignant feeling towards the inhabitants". Meanwhile, Godlonton got in "a dirty kick" at Pringle and reprinted one of his poems to show the "advice" the "savages" had been getting. When Pringle died on 5 December, it was two weeks before "the black onslaught" and, because news from London was slow, Godlonton might have been unaware of his death. Godlonton also "hit out at Fairbairn's slur on the settlers":

We pity the writer of them with our whole soul. We had no idea that the Editor of that Paper could have forfeited his own self-respect and the good opinions of those who would fain have befriended him, by any act so superlatively wicked and foolish, as the composition of that article … Like the branded Traitor who carried the mark of infamy on his own forehead, it only has to be perused to be at once reprobated.

More papers

Godlonton was an "indefatigable" writer who often worked from dawn to ten at night, spending a lifetime "penning his leaden prose in defence of the settlers and refuting philanthropists' charges". His critics called him "Moral Bob". Ambrose George Campbell, an eccentric frontier doctor, attempted an opposition paper in 1840. The pro-Fairbairn "negrophilist" weekly, *The Colonial Times*, was first published on 1 January, but closed four months later, although it was taken over by John Franklin with a policy more in keeping with the inhabitants of Grahamstown and now titled *The Cape Frontier Times*. Described as "irascible", Campbell had an advertisement in the first number of the new *Times*, announcing a literary magazine, *The Echo*, produced by members of the "Fudge Society". The publication saw twelve issues and was denounced as "scurrilous" for ridiculing local dignitaries, with jokes about the sheriff who supervised hangings, such as: "Why is Frederick Carlisle like a canteen keeper? Because he makes a living by giving his customers a drop."

Godlonton himself became a partner in Meurant's firm and bought the business from Meurant five years later.[179] He positioned the *Journal* as the "spokesman for the settlers on the frontier, defending their interests against the sometimes sneering attacks of philanthropists in Cape Town and London". For the Settlers, Fairbairn's *Advertiser* was far too liberal, espousing "the enlightened opinion in London and to some extent in Cape Town", including on the abolition of slavery.

A tale of a man and his press

Godlonton "got into newspapers through a twist of fate he treasured his life-long".[180] When he died in May 1884, aged 89, he "lovingly bequeathed" to his son Benjamin D'Urban Godlonton a mahogany stand – "a portion of the printing press brought by me to the Colony in 1820" when he arrived as one of the Settlers.

This old wooden press had a remarkable tale. Godlonton worked at the King's Printing Office, and when he decided to seek a future in South Africa with his wife and daughter, he and fellow-printer Thomas Stringfellow were presented with a press. The idea was that they should produce a newspaper to act "as a link not only among the settlers themselves but with their home country". The press was a gift – "unless they could make it pay".

When the Settler vessel "Chapman" anchored in Table Bay, the 26-year-old Godlonton did not suspect that he would not see, or hear of, the press for more than ten years, as

> [i]t soon became known that a printing press was among the emigrants luggage and the Government Printer, Mr Van der Sandt, was sent on board to make the inquiry. The result was a prohibition against it going any further, the Acting Governor (Lieutenant-General Donkin) remarking, as we were told, that to allow it to go further would be equal to scattering firebrands along the Eastern Frontier.

It was confiscated without further ado. In the Eastern Cape, at the mouth of the Fish River where Godlonton, as a "city-reared orphan" and now "a printer without a press", was settled, he struggled for nearly 18 months to make a success of farming. In October 1821 he took a job as constable in Bathurst and, in mid-1823, was appointed as clerk in the office of the landdrost of Albany. Here he worked for ten years. While Pringle and Fairbairn were battling Somerset, Godlonton "was pushing a pen and, later, collecting taxes in the district". It turned out these trips around the settlements "provided the lively material for the articles which introduced his newspaper career".

Meurant Snr.'s son, also Louis Henry, experienced his share of the press battle as a young apprentice to Greig during the stopping of the *Advertiser*. In admiration for his (volatile) boss, Meurant Jnr. baptised his fourth child George Greig Meurant.

Meurant Jnr.'s father was a French-Swiss bandmaster in a British regiment who ended up at the Cape and had the £300 to buy printing type off a ship bound for India, where the client's periodical had folded. This he made available to Greig on condition his son was taught "the art of printing".

The younger Meurant was one of the "most dashing characters" in journalism, also a singer, dancer, soldier, magistrate and later member of the Legislative Assembly. In 1861, the dialogues he wrote as "Klaas Waarzegger" (Klaas Truth Teller) became the first book to be printed in proto-Afrikaans.

With Godlonton's press confiscated in 1820 and sent to Graaff-Reinet to print handbills, the government reduced its printing operations and put the press up for sale in 1829, the year of the press ordinance. Meurant Jnr., visiting Graaff-Reinet on a hunting expedition, "jumped at the chance". Though "still in his teens", the following year he set up shop as printer in Grahamstown's High Street.

Meurant Jnr. was "shrewdly aware of the passions which ruled the people of the eastern province". He also "appreciated" the possibilities of a newspaper supporting separatism for the east and providing a voice to combat that of Fairbairn. Still, the first issue of the *Journal*, on 30 December 1831, made it clear that "[t]he Editor does not propose to inflict invariably on his readers what is usually called a Leading Article. Perhaps he has not yet chosen a political hobby-horse; and is not prepared to witch the world with didactic essays". This "impartiality statement" was written by Meurant's associate, Lieutenant T.C. White, who was later killed in the 1834 war. Godlonton, whose articles in the *Journal* had attracted Meurant's attention, was appointed editor at the beginning of 1834 and became a full partner six months later. In 1839 he bought out Meurant, and the press confiscated 19 years earlier was his again.

Apathy of the Dutch

As can be seen from the individuals active in fighting for press freedom, the Dutch colonists did not participate. Besides Faure as founder of the Dutch press, there were none who stood up for press freedom. The Dutch-speaking community's apathy regarding politics was attributed to Somerset's autocratic rule, resulting in the fact that "almost no interest in public affairs existed" among the Dutch, "except for the handful of Anglo men at the Cape".[181]

Few leading Dutch-Afrikaners interested themselves in the press battle that developed.[182] Faure himself refused to sign a memorial to the British king requesting the Cape's press freedom. Still, this did not "help to keep his nose clean with Somerset, who cuttingly remarked that Faure seemed very anxious to focus attention on himself".

The Dutch-Afrikaners were described as "a conquered group without the confidence of the *civis britannicus sum* of colonists of British stock claiming rights from a British government". Outnumbering the British at the Cape, they "were closely watched for rebellious traits" and were "constantly exhorted to fuse with their English-speaking neighbours in a single loyalty to the British flag". To "assist" them, they were subjected to a rigorous anglicisation policy that eventually removed Dutch as legal and official language.

Isolation also bred "an insular outlook which excluded the habit of newspapers". The most significant difference between the two sections of the white population was their concept of liberty. For Dutch-Afrikaners, liberty signified the freedom of the "volk" (nation) or group. The English emphasised the rights of the individual, as symbolised in freedom of expression and a free press. It was much later formulated as that

> [t]o the Afrikaner the press simply never meant that much as a measure of personal freedom. It is a distinction which has influenced the approach of the two groups to the matter of the press to the present day. The Afrikaner sought his freedom within a political structure, that is, the republican ideal; the English-speaker had his rights guaranteed by one.

The Dutch-Afrikaners stood back and "somewhat bemusedly" watched the "English" quarrel. Also, the 1822 proclamation of English as only official language, following the arrival of the 1820 British Settlers, was coupled with the strategic "importation" of Scottish ministers for the DRC; together with English civil servants, all had to contribute to accelerate anglicising the Cape.[183] Cape Town developed an increasingly English character, also thanks to "thousands of British soldiers". In the districts and in rural areas, however, Dutch was still the *lingua franca*.[184]

Dutch burghers at this stage were still mostly apathetic and did not participate in politics, although they "took note" of matters at the district's "drosdy", later the anglicised magistrate's office.[185] One can speculate that, because the Cape was governed for 150 years by a company with an autocratic board of directors in the form of the Here XVII, Dutch colonists were not allowed any opportunity to participate in local government, and when they tried to speak up it was immediately suppressed.

But it was the policy of anglicisation that tipped the scale, turning indifferent Dutch colonists into activists. These cultural-political circumstances were also the reason for the birth of the Dutch-Afrikaans press – particularly as partisan press.[186] The first Dutch publication, the already mentioned *Het Nederduitsch Zuid-Afrikaansch Tijdschrift*, was established in 1824, and the first newspaper, DZA, in 1830, both serving as important mouthpieces for Dutch burghers.

It was said that the Dutch had by then been "indoctrinated" to get by without a paper of their own. Jan Hendrik (Onze Jan) Hofmeyr, Dutch-Afrikaans press pioneer who edited a paper while still in his teens, later wrote:

For the average burgher of 1823, smoking a pipe with his neighbour on the veranda of his residence on the Heerengracht [later Adderley Street], the idea of establishing a private press would have been ludicrous; publishing a newspaper something bordering on lunacy. After all, any printing that was required, had to be done through the government offices. As far as a newspaper was concerned, they had lived without one for so long that the thought of replacing the old order with something new would be something close to blasphemy.[187]

But the "Magna Carta" was an example of an event with unintended consequences. Whereas English now was the only official language, the "Magna Carta" also meant that Dutch papers could be established, heralding a new era for the beginning of Dutch papers. The "Magna Carta" was of as much significance, if not more, for the Dutch colonists as for the English. Dutch as a written language, as well as a church language, and Afrikaans as spoken language, were officially suppressed by the colonial government – yet now a free press supported the development of the Dutch press, morphing into Cape-Dutch, and eventually the Afrikaans press.

Press freedom thus provided for a paradox: While the colonial government suppressed Dutch by declaring English the only official language, press freedom served as impetus for the Dutch press to develop as mouthpiece for the rights of the Cape-Dutch Colonists.[188]

Developments elsewhere

Regarding further developments of the press in Southern Africa up to the 1850s, *De Natalier*, the first newspaper in the then Natal, was a four-page weekly, mostly in Dutch, "with some smatterings of English". Its first edition was published in Pietermaritzburg on 15 March 1844.[189] The Republic of Natalia (today's KwaZulu-Natal [KZN]) was founded in Pietermaritzburg by the Voortrekkers in 1839 and annexed by Britain in 1844.[190]

This first paper's full title was *De Natalier en Pietermaritzburgsche Trouwe Aantekenaar*,[191] and it was edited by Boniface after he "left the Cape hastily" when faced with a libel charge at DZA. It closed in 1846, also after a libel case. *The Natal Witness*, established in 1846, replaced it as bilingual weekly. As *The Witness*, it today is South Africa's oldest newspaper[192] and now is part of Media24. The dichotomy that newspapers took sides either for the English or the Dutch was in the majority of cases not reflected in the language in which they published; irrespective of the "side" they represented, they published copy in both languages. In Durban, the *Natal Mercury* was founded in 1852.[193] Across the border, in the then Orange Free State, *The Friend of the Sovereignty* was founded in 1850 and published until 1986 as *The Friend*. The Orange Free State was founded as a Boer Republic after the Bloemfontein Convention in 1854.[194]

Although the "Magna Carta" paved the way for press freedom in the two British colonies, the Cape and Port Natal, for the rest of the century, it was not the case for the two newly established Boer Republics. This aspect will be covered in the next chapter as part of the discussion on developments in the second half of the nineteenth century.

The development of the 'black' press

Researchers such as Hachten and Giffard,[195] Johnson,[196] Diederichs and De Beer[197] and Switzer and Switzer[198] concur that the "black press" developed in stages. The first phase, from 1830 to 1880, started at mission stations, where publications aimed at an indigenous readership were first printed. LMS missionary Philip, amongst others, reported of the oppression and cruelty suffered by black people resulting from colonial legislation. In the 1850s and 1860s, the Lovedale Press contributed much to the development of the black press.[199] The second phase, from 1880 to 1930, was also called the elitist or independent phase because of its independence from white funding. However, the third phase, from 1931 to 1976, was a white-owned phase, characterised by white funders providing news for black readers. The fourth, from the 1970s, was the multiracial period. From the 1990s onwards, after South Africa's liberation, the next period can be called the integration period, as the deep divides between journalists in the newsrooms had been broken down: Between English and Afrikaans as well as between black and white. Especially since the formation of SANEF in 1996, journalists have united around issues. This phase, the fifth, can also be called the black empowerment phase. It was initiated by cultural-political changes, with black empowerment encouraged since the main media groups were still largely owned and controlled by white people. Mainstream, traditionally white newspaper groups started a process of restructuring to ensure black empowerment.[200] After the elections in 1994, the distinct groupings, described as South Africa's specific "three theories of the press", namely the English, Afrikaans and black press, amalgamated into a truly South African media sector. These developments will be discussed in the following chapters of this publication.

But back to the beginnings of the black press in the first half of the 1800s. In the first period, the so-called missionary period starting in 1830, the origin of the "black press" was "closely linked to the establishment of mission stations in the Eastern Cape and the work between missionaries and black residents".[201]

The first paper for black people was *Umshumayeli Wendaba* (Publisher of the News), printed at the Wesleyan Mission Society in Grahamstown from 1837 to 1841.[202] It was followed by the Presbyterian Glasgow Missionary Society at Lovedale becoming the first centre "of black learning and publishing" in South Africa. The Lovedale Missionary Institute produced *Ikwezi* (Morning Star) between 1844 and 1845, with *Indaba* (The News), a bilingual Xhosa/English paper, following in 1862.[203]

The *Kafir Express*, also a bilingual paper, appeared in 1870.[204] Its Xhosa section, *Isigidimi Sama Xosa* (The Xhosa Messenger), became a separate newspaper in 1876, also considered important as it was the first newspaper to be edited by black journalists, thus also the first newspaper edited by black people for black people. However, the first paper for black people owned by black people was *Imvo Zabantsundu* (Native Opinion), published in King William's Town in 1884.[205] It was owned and edited by John Tengo Jabavu, whose political views were considered to be influential. Jabavu can be regarded as the first black journalist in South Africa. A century later, by the 1980s, this newspaper was part of the now defunct Perskor – but more about this phase of black journalism in the next chapter, spanning the era 1850 to 1900.

The trichotomy of the South African press

Towards the end of the first half of the 19th century, "life was made easier for pressmen".[206] The "Magna Carta" was amended in 1839 to allow affidavits for new publications to be entered into in front of a magistrate, anywhere in the colony, instead of a judge, and stamp tax on newsprint was abolished in 1848. By 1840, Cape Town had seven newspapers and nine printing establishments, and by 1843 its first printers' trade union. The 1840s also saw the arrival of the Cape's first satirical paper, *Sam Sly's African Journal*, founded by the "versatile British journalist" William Layton Sammons, who claimed to be "the first Englishman to edit an independent publication in the colony". Up till then, "the Scots had dominated the field". The "peculiar" Sammons was a friend of Charles Dickens and described as "a middle-aged gentleman, having somewhat of a military air about him, with dark moustachios, and white hair, which sticks out at the sides rather wildly". He had "an excitable temperament" and used "the most expressive action with every sentence". Sammons also helped W.H. Rabone and Alfred Essex to launch the *Graaff-Reinet Herald* in 1852, with a press once used to print the *Advertiser*, fondly called "Old Fairbairn". Letters from readers were taken seriously and given great prominence, and Sammons's *Sam Sly* invited lively response with his motto, "To assist the enquiring, animate the struggling, and sympathize with us all".[207]

South Africa's media inevitably developed along racial lines and as "sectional press" after the first years, when newspapers were established and served both the English and Dutch market. However, for the most part, the English press served the interest of British colonial-imperial ideals, the Dutch press that of the emerging "white tribe of Africa", and the black press the interests of the black communities, leading to South Africa's peculiar "three theories of the press".[208] Race was a distinguishing factor, as race, not language, religion or culture, proved to be the dominant characteristic, and "[w]hite newspapers quite simply ignored the non-European majority".[209] During its early years, the black press did not have political standing, but it emphasised "an indication of the growing westernisation and articulateness of its readers, and an important means of developing a sense of cohesion that surmounted tribal distinction". One of the main functions of black newspapers was to create a reading public.[210]

Allister Sparks, at the time editor of the *Rand Daily Mail* (RDM), said in 1979 that the early newspapers reflected the norm of South African society: "It was a white man's country. Blacks didn't exist."[211] But, between 1837, when the first black publication was established, and 1977, at the height of apartheid, there were more than eight hundred publications "written by or aimed at blacks". Although some were small, others were fully-fledged magazines and newspapers, with circulations up to 170,000. And although "it was a white man's land", "[n]owhere else in Africa was the indigenous, non-European press as diverse, widespread, and sophisticated as in South Africa".

These "trichotomous" characteristics, defining South African media for almost two centuries, were thus laid down in the period between 1800 and 1850, together with the foundation of a free press thanks to the "Magna Carta".

Mijn pen en mijn ink verkoop ik niet!

(My pen and my ink I'll never sell!)

– J.E. DE JONG, Dutch master printer and owner-editor of the predecessor
of the *Worcester Standard,* established in 1880, to prime minister Cecil John
Rhodes when he made an unrealistically high offer to buy the paper in an
attempt to mute criticism

5. THE SECOND HALF OF THE 19TH CENTURY

The two Colonies, the two Republics, the beginning of media empires, and the Newspaper Press Union

Introduction

This chapter revisits the years from 1850 to just after the turn of the century, when the two British colonies, the Cape and Natal, and the two previous Boer Republics, the Transvaal or Zuid-Afrikaansche Republiek (ZAR) and the Republic of the Orange Free State or the Orange River Colony, were united from being four geo-political entities to forming the Union of South Africa after the defeat of the two Boer Republics.

In the Cape, the press flourished. Across the Orange River, or the Gariep, the press developed as these regions developed, especially after the discovery of their mineral riches.

One authority on press freedom, Wessel de Kock, averred that the evolution of the South African press was determined by two powerful factors: The "philanthropic" press, personified by John Fairbairn, and the discovery of gold in 1886.[1] De Kock's analysis was that both "came to represent an imperialism which, in turn, provoked an intense local response". Fairbairn's political ideals for the colony from 1830, even if "deeply sincere", assumed "an intolerant ideological imperialism". His "caustic attacks on the colonists" united Dutch and English speakers and stimulated an indigenous press in both groups. While DZA was established to counter Fairbairn in Cape Town, Godlonton's *Graham's Town Journal* in Grahamstown became the voice for the Settlers. DZA eventually expressed a growing Nationalistic awareness among the Dutch-Afrikaners, which would culminate in the 1875 Taalbeweging (Language Movement).

Fairbairn is regarded as "the rock on which English press sentiment split in two". He was committed to "philanthropic-libertarian ideas" and saw the Colony "as a less privileged extension of Britain". It had "to earn the institutions of the mother country through the education and guidance provided by a free press". Godlonton, on the other hand, was "a frontier journalist who wrote with the smell in his nostrils of settlers' cottages burning and the sight of refugees outside his office window". "Moral Bob" gathered "under his wing a maligned community and spent himself in the defence of their cause". His efforts to get a more sympathetic hearing seemed to be in vain. Like his "Voortrekker friends", he tried to "trek" in his way by "vigorously propagating separatism for the eastern province".

The second factor that influenced the development of the press after 1850 was the discovery of gold. It "changed the face of South Africa and that of its newspapers". In the "frenzied, cosmopolitan atmosphere" of the Reef, a "new thrusting journalism mushroomed". This meant the end of the Cape's dominance in newspapers, "as gold stimulated the ambitions of men like Rhodes and caused the Jameson Raid [on New Year's eve in 1895/1896], a watershed in relations between English-speaker and Afrikaner".

The capitalistic imperialism spawned by gold also split the press on the basis of the two white language groups. The press, originating as "an intermingling of diverse languages and issues", became "two deep furrows in which white emotion and tribal allegiance flowed in contrary directions". This would be the case right up to democratisation in the 1990s.

After 1850, the "Godlonton tradition" of the mutual interests of English speaker and Afrikaner died out. DZA would later "swallow hard" on its "enthusiastic motto" of its early years: "Each African has equal place with me. Whether he be Cape born, or nurs'd beyond the sea ... all who inhabit this land, and derive nourishment from her bosom, are Africans." And, as was emphasised: With "Africans" the paper "meant whites, of course".

Yet, at the turn of the century, when Nationalistic fever rose with the SAW from 1899 to 1902, and "the faces of men hardened against each other", one journalist stood out for his "profound pleas" for peace between the two white races. He was John Tengo Jabavu, editor of *Imvo Zabantsundu* (Native Opinion) of King William's Town – "one of South Africa's great newspapermen". In propagating peace, he seemed "to know instinctively that continuing strife between whites meant the crushed political hopes of his own people, who found themselves buffered from both sides".

The SAW did not stop him from carrying reports condemning attacks on the two republics and from publishing "pacifist sermons". In fact, he became a victim of British censorship when, in August 1901, British military authorities closed his paper for his pro-Boer sympathies. *Imvo* resumed publication in October 1902, after the end of the war.

Among white people, the "swirling passions of republicanism and imperialism as early as the 1880s had begun to harden into the granite attitudes of the future". This was also because Rhodes was "taking an active hand in newspapers". The press was still mostly "scattered" and "at the mercy of vested interests and of government". Often sued, the threat of new, tighter libel laws hung over its head. There was "no cohesion and each did its own thing according to its own lights in its own corner of the country".

Relative freedom

The guarantee for the freedom of the press after the so-called "Magna Carta" was, of course, only relative and would only last until a next government could put measures in place to curtail press freedom. Regarding the political development of South Africa, this second half of the 1800s was a time of war and upheaval that ended with a major conflict between the British Empire and two small Boer republics.

The 1838 Great Trek by disgruntled Dutch led to the founding of the ZAR in 1852 and the Republic of the Orange Free State in 1854. Around 1860, there were in total about

200,000 people of Dutch descent, or Afrikaners, spread over the geographical area that later became South Africa.[2] About 136,000 lived in the Cape Colony, constituting three quarters of the white population. Approximately 30,000 Afrikaners lived in each of the two republics, and about 3,000 in Natal. The Cape had a system of "qualified voting rights". Every male over 21 who earned more than £50 a year, or had property of at least £25, could register as voter. It goes "without saying" that it was mostly white people who qualified to vote.[3]

A 'bristling' bush

The British government's guarantee in 1829 of press freedom "for all times" could only be relative, for obvious reasons. Depending on who irritated whom, euphemistically speaking, there would always be smaller and bigger differences between the press and governments.

In an "amazing proliferation" of newspapers, the Eastern Province saw more than 180 periodicals after *The Graham's Town Journal* first appeared in 1831.[4] In 1858, Grahamstown supported five newspapers, Port Elizabeth three and Graaff-Reinet two, and King William's Town and Cradock each had their own local title. From 1845, when *The Eastern Province Herald* was founded, to the end of the century, at least sixteen newspapers or magazines were published in Port Elizabeth alone. The quality of printing was also "generally better" than that of Cape Town. And, as it was described: "The bush positively bristled with the guardians of the rights, liberties and morals of the citizens."[5]

By 1850, Cape Town was the biggest urban area in South Africa, with more than 10,000 inhabitants of European descent, while the majority of colonists were living on farms or in small towns "across a vast region".[6] As was the norm, no indication of the size of the indigenous population is given – they seemingly did not "count". By around 1858, the Cape's population as a whole was 140,000 people, although the racial percentages were not reflected.[7]

The role of the press at the time is illustrated by what *The Times* in London wrote in 1852, namely that

> [t]he first duty of the Press is to obtain the earliest and most correct intelligence of events of the time, and instantly, by disclosing them, to make them the common property of the nation. The statesman [sic] collects his information secretly and by secret means ... the Press lives by disclosure. Whatever passes into its keeping becomes a part of the knowledge of history of our times ... The duty of the journalist is the same as that of the historian: to seek out the truth above all things, and to present to his readers not such things as statecraft would wish them to know but the truth as near as he can attain it.[8]

This role of the press has been the same ever since, and the "lively succession" of newspaper titles from the 1850s illustrates it, if not the individual commercial success of these papers. By far the most important papers of this period were those in Cape Town, "from whence South Africa's greatest modern newspaper empire [the powerful Argus company, at the time of writing in 1975] has originated".[9] The *Cape Argus* was founded in 1857, after which, thanks to mining capital interests, the company flourished. Almost all of the *Argus's* staff were from England. It would also be the first newspaper to use the new telegraph technology. By 1858, Cape Town had eight newspapers, among them the revived *South African Commercial Advertiser*. At the time, the *Argus* was a triweekly.[10]

After a "short hiatus" following the granting of press freedom in 1829, "as if everyone were catching their breath", "literally hundreds of newspapers and journals sprung up and flowered – or withered". From around 1850 to 1892, seventeen Cape papers existed for less than a year.[11] Still, the number of publications supported by such a small population "is nothing short of astonishing". In hindsight, one can say it was "as if to make up" for the first almost two hundred years of being without newspapers. Following Cape Town's four publications until 1826, their number increased to ten by 1846 – among them the *Companion to the Cape of Good Hope Almanac*, proclaiming that "the Press, that mighty engine of power, is in lively exercise in our midst". The first paper outside of Cape Town, the already mentioned influential *Graham's Town Journal*, was established in 1831 by Meurant Jnr., Greig's erstwhile printing apprentice. Meurant, a ballet dancer in his youth and later to write under the pseudonym Klaas Waarzegger, would become a colourful press pioneer, part of an era of colourful "travelling newspapermen". Among them was Moll, a press pioneer in the Colony, Natal and the ZAR. When yet another of his "numerous journalistic undertakings" collapsed, he tried his hand at everything from wagon maker to butcher and, as said earlier, when accused of stealing sheep, he "slipped" out of Cape Town and set up Natal's first newspaper.

These early papers had "a striking diversity". The press had also "not yet" assumed its "rigidly tribal nature" that characterised the industry later. Also, language was not an indication of "political persuasion", as "men were divided by issue, not tongue". Bilingual papers were common, mostly for circulation reasons. Several Dutch papers were run by English speakers. Etienne Boniface, editor of DZA – the first newspaper to represent "an embryonic Afrikaner nationalism" – was a Frenchman. All these "spirited itinerant newspapermen" with their small presses "wove South Africa into a country", spinning "a net of mutual awareness over the thinly populated expanse of the land and welded loose collections of individuals into communities". One such early printer-editor was T.B. Glanville. When he departed with his printing press on an ox wagon to start a paper on the newly discovered diamond fields, it was "not how to fleece the gullible diggers for revenue". Instead, fearing they might resent criticism "and restrain the liberty of the press", he one day just "upped and left".

Despite this burst of newspapers across the country, a new financial stumbling block made its appearance in 1858. After the "Magna Carta", newspapers were free of charge through the post, but from January 1858 postage was to be prepaid.[12]

The first magnificent media men

The Cape's first parliamentary sessions were held in the 1850s in a Freemasons' hall in today's Parliament Street.[13] There was no press gallery and only "scant provision for reporters – just two small round tables". But there was plenty to report on. The "new" journalism of Victorian-era South Africa was "magnificently personified" in the "restless figure of the newspaper entrepreneur" Richard William Murray Snr.

As a 35-year-old London journalist, he was one of the most experienced when he, unintentionally, arrived at the Cape in 1854 with his family on their way to the Australian goldfields – their ship was wrecked off Simon's Town. His career started as editor of the

Cape Monitor, founded by a "syndicate of merchants" who withdrew their advertisements from Fairbairn's *Advertiser* because of his uncompromising stand on the convict issue (the Cape would also receive a "convict ship" from England).

In January 1857, Murray started the *Cape Argus* with Bryan Henry Darnell. His son, R.W. Murray Jnr., while business manager of Frederick York St. Leger's *Cape Times*, would later play a major role in the establishment of the Newspaper Press Union (NPU), founded in 1882.[14] Of Murray Snr. it was said:

> It is fitting that Murray should have been the one to force Fairbairn's paper from the scene, as he represented the new wave of press pioneers and an emerging sophistication and professionalism in newspapers. The stormy beginnings of the press were over and, in the Cape, at least, the romantic period of intrepid editor-printers was on the way out.

> The future press was not to be an occupation for part-timers and Murray's *Argus* was the first to establish a staff of what he called "first-class" reporters.

Murray wanted the *Argus* to be "complete and impartial", with no party bias, and was himself "a sharp and remorselessly frank" parliamentary reporter. Meanwhile, the Diamond Fields, to which he and other "newsmen gravitated", foreshadowed the proliferation of papers when gold was discovered sixteen years later. These journalists "survived primitive conditions, dysentery, fever, drunken orgies and violent men". Within eighteen years, sixteen papers were founded.

Another Cape press character, described as one of the "most amazing personalities", was Saul Solomon, who printed the *Argus* for Murray. By 1858, he ran "the foremost establishment of the period" and employed 110 printers and compositors. Solomon, also a member of parliament (as many newspapermen of the time), "was a metre-high dwarf who had to stand on a stool when he addressed the Cape parliament". As a converted Jew he was a "man of huge spirit and influence". He learnt "his printing from George Greig and his political beliefs from Dr. Philip". When Murray Snr. left Cape Town in 1863 to start the *Great Eastern* in Grahamstown, Solomon became the owner of the *Argus*, also as "an important voice for black emancipation". He is credited with the success of South Africa's first black editor, John Tengo Jabavu, whose work will be discussed in more detail later in this chapter.

A new era

Fairbairn "lived to see his ideal of an unfettered press fulfilled in his lifetime".[15] On 8 July 1859, the government published an act to repeal Ordinance no 60 of 1829 – it had become superfluous. Where its preamble had spoken sternly of "the Mischiefs arising from printing and publishing Newspapers", the introduction to the new act had a different tone, emphasising the "great benefits" deriving "from the art of printing, and from the printing and publishing of newspapers and papers of a like nature in this colony".

The new act did away with the administrative requirements regarding the registration of newspapers and the identity of editors. Only the name and address of the printer should appear "somewhere in every publication". It "put the seal on a press which had come of age".

However, "fresh assaults" would develop, "more severe in many respects than before", and "it would need a man with the fierce commitment of a Fairbairn to weather these and consolidate that which the press pioneers had achieved".

This person would be Francis Joseph Dormer. He co-incidentally travelled on the same ship on which Cecil John Rhodes returned to South Africa in 1874. Dormer was to take up a teaching appointment in Cape Town. As "an alert, entertaining companion", and "ironic in the light of future developments", Rhodes and he became friends. On arrival in Cape Town, Rhodes greeted him with: "Get in touch with me if ever you come to Kimberley."

First trade unions

With the first printed matter in the Southern Hemisphere having appeared at the Cape, it is not surprising that the first trade unions were that of the Cape's printing industry. The Cape of Good Hope Printers' Protection Society was founded in 1841, and the Cape of Good Hope Printers' and Bookbinders' Society in 1857.[16] By the early 1880s, more printers' unions were established in other cities. In 1898, they merged to form the South African Typographical Union. At one stage it was the most effective and best organised trade union in South Africa. Although not a trade union, the NPU, to be established in 1882, would also become a significant role player.

And an article by Marx in DZA

The diversity of opinion in the papers of this period becomes clear when one considers that, in 1854, a Dutch title carried an article written by Karl Marx.

In London's Soho in 1853, Jan Carel Juta, a Dutch publishing entrepreneur who would become a South African pioneer publisher, and his wife Louisa walked "carefully down the long and narrow Dean Street".[17] Louisa's journalist brother and her sister-in-law Jenny lived in this London slum. Her brother was an "intense, bearded man … a brilliant thinker, [and] a journalist of ability". He was also the London representative of the influential *New York Daily Tribune*. Debt-ridden, he was committed to his ideals, which meant "he and his family seemed condemned to barren neediness". This man was Karl Marx.

Why, asked a concerned Juta, did "Moor", the family's nickname for his wife's dark-complexioned brother, not supplement his income by contributing to DZA, the bilingual pro-Dutch newspaper in Cape Town? The Jutas intended to settle there and the "paper was sure to make good use of copy".

It seems Marx "gratefully accepted" the suggestion. And so "the father of Communism" became one of the first foreign correspondents of the fledgling South African press. In a letter to his friend Friedrich Engels in December 1853, Marx confirmed the invitation to write for DZA. That year he made about eighty pounds from his *Tribune* contributions, his only regular income, although he saw this work as "newspaper muck", interfering with serious writing, and even asked Engels to do articles in his name. At the time, DZA was jointly owned by editor J.J. Smuts and printer I.W. Lotz. Juta's connection to them was not clear, although they "obviously agreed" to the arrangement with Marx.

The only article in DZA to be identified as by Marx (or maybe Engels) appeared on 6 March 1854, without a byline, as was the case, although datelined London, 14 January. Marx's article was a "stimulating and provocative analysis" of the looming Crimean War, "exhibiting an anti-Russian undertone" – not surprising for someone known for his hatred of Russia's "asiatic barbarism". Marx sent the same article to the *Tribune*, an indication that he shared "the attitude of many stringers": "bang through the same story to a number of newspapers and see who uses it". Marx might have sent more articles, "but an interruption of the mail service to the Cape ... may have caused these to arrive late". And, unfortunately, "just in time for the spike".

Juta later pioneered book publishing in South Africa, and he and his wife became "respected members" of the DRC. His son Henricus Hubertus, later Sir Henry Juta, went to London in 1877, where Marx helped him with arrangements for his law studies. Henry later became attorney general and, in 1896, Speaker of the Cape parliament.

The "Marx episode" introduced "a growing sophistication in news content and analysis" in the South African press in this half of the 19th century, even before the advent of the telegraph. News was

> a rare, irregular and hard-won commodity gleaned from passing ships, from the rider with sweat-locks still standing on his horse or from the occasional official dispatch. Papers were restricted to local news and the art of journalism often lay in embellishment, not in substance.

Newspapers quoted "extensively" from overseas publications and "lifting" from rivals was accepted practice, yet not acknowledging it was unforgiveable. Cape papers freely used articles from *Punch*, the *Gardener's Almanac* and other overseas magazines; "Charles Dickens was a favourite". Some of his writings were even translated into Dutch for Faure's *Nederduitsch Zuid-Afrikaansche Tijdschrift*. Dickens eventually had to obtain a *rule nisi* in the Cape Supreme Court to restrain the *Graaff-Reinet Herald* from publishing *Great Expectations*.

A new era

The formation of the Argus Printing and Publishing Company in 1866 was a "landmark" in press history, signalling the end of independent editor-owners and the beginning of "managerial" newspapers.[18] Amongst the later funders was a "young Cecil John Rhodes", albeit through a nominee. He made his fortune in the Kimberley diamond mines and was searching for "outlets" for his political ambitions. Other funders "broadly represented" the Cape's professional and commercial life.

South Africa's first daily was the *Cape Times* in 1876.[19] Started as a "penny paper", by 1880 it forced the *Argus* to switch from thrice-weekly to daily, and also to sell for a penny instead of three pennies.[20]

Politically, the papers made their mark. When self-government was conferred on the Colony in 1872, the *Argus*, under Solomon, "was perhaps in some measure responsible" for the milestone.[21] In 1877, Solomon appointed Dormer as editor, after which Dormer "modified the pro-Native and particularly the anti-British Government policy of the paper". Dormer's influence increased, and eventually Solomon, in financial difficulties, sold out to him. Dormer did not have the capital, but he knew someone who did: Rhodes. His "influence set the paper on a new course". It also meant the "only paper prepared to speak for the Africans was effectively gone".

This happened in 1881, when Solomon sold his paper to Dormer for £6,000.[22] The latter, after gaining experience on the *Queenstown Representative*, had meanwhile moved to the *Argus* as subeditor. In Rhodes, Dormer found an eager sponsor "who desired support of a newspaper to further his political ambitions". The Argus Printing and Publishing Company had Rhodes as major shareholder – and thus "began the powerful Argus group with its close association with mining and commercial interests". The partnership, "skewed as it was towards the provider of the capital", ushered in the era of the involvement of mining magnates and the mining complex as a whole in South Africa to become the "major force and influence" behind the English press.

In 1881, a list of newspapers filed with the Colonial Office in Cape Town included the titles of more than 125 "assorted journals" – a time when the "bush" was "positively bristl[ing] with the guardians of the rights, liberties and morals of the citizens".[23] Among them was *The Eastern Province Herald*, first published on 7 May 1845[24] and one of the oldest papers still to exist, although now just as *The Herald*.[25] John Ross Philip, one of John Philip's sons, acted as "frontman", while the real editor was a schoolmaster, John Paterson, who later became full-time editor after resigning his school position.

Newspapers "proliferated in the most unlikely corners". In 1870, even two schoolboys of 14 and 15, Somerset Bell and his brother Charles, "launched a creditable two-page weekly" on a farm near Grahamstown. It was called the *Ka-riega News* and was described as a "tremendous achievement of improvisation", as the boys constructed their press out of a piece of flat iron and other scrap. The paper "sold well" and lasted a "lively six months".[26]

Meanwhile, in what would become the Empire's other colony, Natal, many smaller papers sprung up between 1850 and 1859, but most were defunct by 1860.[27] Few of the Natal "country newspapers" showed the characteristic bilingualism evident in the Cape and Transvaal.

Halfway through to the turn of the century, most of the oldest, and some still-existing, South African papers were founded. They were the *Eastern Province Herald* (1845), the *Natal Witness* (1846), *The Friend* (1850), the *Natal Mercury* (1852), the *Daily News* (in 1854 as *Natal Commercial Advertiser*), *The Argus* (in 1857 as *Cape Argus*), the *Daily Dispatch* (1872), the *Cape Times* (1876) and the *Diamond Fields Advertiser* (1878).[28]

The right to "publish freely" was carried north by the Great Trek, with the principle embodied in the Constitutions of both Boer Republics. In the ZAR, newspapers were established comparatively late, with the earliest the *Staats Courant*, published in Potchefstroom in 1857. But after the 1886 discovery of gold, "frenetic newspaper activity erupted". The Sheffield brothers of Grahamstown moved their paper, *The Eastern Star*, with their entire printing works to the Reef by ox wagon, to become *The Star* in 1889.

It is said that Britons often viewed "their colonial possessions" as "hot-beds of corruption", where graft and patronage teemed "like deadly nightshade on a dung-hill". In India, a much older colony, most of its press remained "sterile and a means of communication for central government". Right up to India's independence, "it showed little public-spiritedness or identification with that country". In another young country, the USA, newspapers were actively partisan and openly tied to political parties. One president, Andrew Jackson, reportedly had sixty journalists full-time on his payroll. South Africa's newspaper pioneers "showed a robust joy in the adventure of journalism and a gutsy ingenuity in overcoming daunting distances, perilous roads, lack of communications and proper materials". Belief in a free press required more than idealism. It "took muscle", and the "primitive" presses "caused blistered hands and involved sheer physical labour with an editor writing his leading article and then taking off his coat to print the paper himself"; a considerable number of the first journalists were trained printers.

Diamonds and development

The period after the discovery of diamonds in 1869 can be regarded as the beginning of the next phase in the history of the media in South Africa. After the first almost half century of attempting to become established, newspapers "soon followed the news of the riches lying below the African soil".[29]

The first paper established in reaction to the diamond rush was Kimberley's *Diamond Fields*, in October 1870. Soon six papers were serving the "diggings". The *Diamond Fields Advertiser*, founded in March 1878, later acquired by the Argus Group, was the only one to survive. A year after the diamond rush began, Kimberley was the most populous centre outside of Cape Town. Press activities were still concentrated in the western and eastern Cape, but the change in the country's prospects from an agricultural to an industry-based economy also meant a growth spurt for the press, including as carriers of advertising.

And some fascinating characters

South Africa's press history "bursts" with fascinating characters.[30] One, the already referred-to David Dale Buchanan, who was the editor of the *Natal Witness*, had his third trip from prison in 1850 organised by a "cheering party" consisting of the Pietermaritzburg townsfolk. They carried the "genially smiling man" shoulder high through the streets in a wreathed armchair with a copy of the local paper, the *Natal Witness*, tied to it by a red ribbon. On this release from prison, he was not only "escorted by admiring readers", but they also paid his fine. The

> rollicking, pugnacious editor, who refused to bridle his tongue in serving what he regarded as the public interest, exemplified the colourful and irrepressible characters who emerged in the pioneering years of the South African press. No fleeting mention does them justice. They throng the pages of history and of their newspapers, unsparing of authority, their colleagues or themselves.

While the press took some time to gather steam after the "Magna Carta", about two decades later the foundation was laid for "unfettered publishing" and newspapers were found "rooted in every province except the Transvaal". But this changed after "the convulsive events of the period between 1850 and 1900". This period was described as, "if flipped over by its coastal edges, the country tilted north". People were scrambling to the "Diggings" at Hopetown and Kimberley and, in 1886, to the Reef. And where "the dust streaks of the wagons hung limp on the hot veld, the newspapers followed".

Across the Gariep

A number of the English papers established in Natal and the Boer Republics in the second half of the 19th century survived to become major titles in the next century.[31] The Orange River Colony "never developed a multiplicity of newspapers", unlike the Cape and Natal.

After the establishment of its first paper in 1850, nearly twenty years passed before a second appeared, ascribed to the fact that the Cape and Natal were British colonies, whereas the Orange River Colony was an independent Boer Republic and sparsely populated. The Orange River Colony's first paper, *The Friend of the Sovereignty and Bloemfontein Gazette*, changed its name to *The Friend of the Free State* with the acquisition of independence for the region as Boer Republic in 1854. The original paper was founded in June 1850 by Robert Godlonton, owner of the *Graham's Town Journal*, after uploading a press and "a few cases of type" onto an ox wagon and "proceed[ing] to Bloemfontein".[32]

The paper was published in Dutch and English until 1894, when it was published in English only.[33] In 1899, with the outbreak of the SAW, *The Friend* was run by Lord Roberts, who led the British troops into Bloemfontein. As military governor he sent for the editor, Arthur Barlow, requesting "him to continue to edit the paper under instruction from the British rulers". Barlow, a Boer supporter, refused. The Argus Group printed *The Friend* for the British, but Barlow protested against the use of the paper's title for pro-British views. The Argus Group renamed it the *Bloemfontein Post*, published with the help of British war correspondents. Amongst them was Rudyard Kipling, who edited the paper until the troops were evacuated from Bloemfontein. After the war, Barlow restarted *The Friend* under a new company with Abraham Fischer, later prime minister of the Free State, General J.B.M. Hertzog, later founder of the National Party (NP), and other leading Free State political figures. *The Friend* supported the Oranje Unie Party, the Free State equivalent of the Transvaal Het Volk Party.

And across the Vaal

The first newspaper in the Transvaal, *De Staats Courant* (Government Gazette), was started in Potchefstroom, the capital of the ZAR, by Cornelis Moll on 25 September 1857.[34] Two years later, the name was changed to the *Gouvernements Courant der ZAR,* and from 1863, now as the *Staats Courant*, it was published from a building on Church Square, Pretoria.

The first real newspaper in the ZAR was *De Oude Emigrant*, established on 15 October 1859, also in Potchefstroom.[35] Three years later, it was followed by *De Emigrant*, after the collapse of its forerunner nine months earlier after being blamed for bringing journalism into disrepute with insulting articles. The next paper only appeared in August 1873.[36] This was *Die Volkstem* (The People's Voice, also spelled *Die Volksstem*), founded in Pretoria as a Dutch-language newspaper. Under the editorship of J.F.E. Celliers, it supported the Boers and strongly opposed the annexation of the Transvaal. However, the view expressed by *Die Volkstem* "was more the Cape than the Transvaal Boer view", as Celliers "was one of an influential group of Transvaal Afrikaners with Cape affiliations, who were opposed to the Transvaal Boers as epitomized by Kruger and Krugerism".[37] This difference between Northern and Southern Afrikaners would become more pronounced in later Afrikaner Nationalist developments.

Meanwhile, gold was discovered in 1886 and, with Johannesburg beginning to grow, Dormer "was looking northwards" for his company's expansion.[38] The *Eastern Star*, founded in Grahamstown, moved to Johannesburg in October 1887. There were already seven other journals in town. Instead of continuing with his plans to start a new Argus Group paper, Dormer bought the *Eastern Star*, renaming it *The Star*. In 1889, he expanded it from a tri-weekly to a daily evening paper. By 1895, "gold and other mining interests were conspicuously over-represented in the Argus Group's shareholding". Major shareholders in the growing mining companies were also major shareholders in the Argus Group, including Rhodes, Barney Barnato and Solly Joel. The mining and commercial impetus of the company's origins "were to leave a lasting stamp on the company's future policies".

Initially, the sympathetic coverage given to the Kruger government was thanks entirely to Dormer. But, under a new editor, *The Star* switched its support from "progressive Republicanism" to the newly formed Transvaal National Union (TNU), demanding government reforms, "particularly in the existing limited franchise which excluded the 'uitlanders'". These "outlanders" were prospectors who flocked to the Witwatersrand.

The government, however, started to pass laws to muzzle the press. By 1896, the Transvaal Volksraad (Legislature) passed a press law requiring the names of printers and publishers to be disclosed. This gave the president "the power to prevent publication of material which might be dangerous to the order and peace of the Republic, or to good morals". It led to the banning of *The Star* on 24 March 1897. Publications were banned for up to three months because contents could be "dangerous to the peace and quiet" of the Republic. The Argus Group promptly published *The Comet*, "remarkably" similar to *The Star*, including its astral name. The company took its case to court and won, and *The Star* was published again the following afternoon. After the Jameson raid, in which *The Star* "was held to be deeply implicated", TNU members, including Frederick Hamilton, editor of the *Star*, were tried. He left the country after the trial, but was replaced by an editor whose criticism of the Kruger government was even more forceful. *The Star* "ensured the permanent hostility of the Republicans", although the confrontation between "the English-language Press and the Afrikaner Republicans was not to take place for another fifty years".

When the SAW broke out in 1899, *The Star* ceased publication for over two years. After the war, the colonial secretary appointed the Argus Group as sole "printing advisers" to the Government Printing Works. So close was the association between Milner and the Argus Group that Milner "virtually" selected *The Star*'s ninth editor, thereby "earn[ing] a staunch supporter lodged securely in South Africa's most powerful newspaper".

But, already by 1895, Dormer took the "painful step" to leave the company of his making, "bitterly convinced" that Rhodes' influence in newspapers was driving the country to disaster.[39] His offer to buy all Rhodes' shares was declined. As it was formulated: "Too late Dormer realised that the threat against the press that Pringle perceived in Lord Charles Somerset could assume many shapes and need not necessarily wear the uniform of officialdom."

In the Cape, the *Argus* was now under the editorship of Edmund Powell, also a member of the Cape parliament and supporter of the so-called Progressives in the North.[40] *The Star*, under the influence of the Milner government, led the company's editorial policy. At the beginning of the 1900s, the Argus Group stated that its policy on important political issues would

> be as indicated from time to time in the leading columns of the *Star*, and all publications of the company, unless specially authorized to the contrary by the Managing Director, are to follow the lead therein given in all matters of a political nature which are of more than local importance.

The so-called Progressive Movement was not a unified movement, although "its own appellation as the 'Progressive' innovative sector of ZAR society is often taken at face value".[41] At the time, the term "progressive" had been adopted by various South African movements. The Cape Progressive Party, formed in the late 1890s, became the Union Party in 1908. Prior to Unification in 1910, the Progressive Association of the Transvaal represented wealthier English speakers. What was known as the "Progressive Movement" in 1891 in the ZAR was an association of individuals who shared a common antipathy towards Kruger's government, "rather than a cohesive policy to oppose him or an organised party structure". This "shifting alliance of men" needed a mouthpiece, preferably a Dutch-language one to counter the pro-Kruger *De Pers* and the *Weekly Press*, both published from 1889. *De Volkstem*, now under the Dutchman Frans Vredenrijk Engelenburg, was also pro-government, "although ostensibly unaligned". The only independent Dutch-language paper was the "insignificant" Pretoria-based *Land en Volk*. The latter's owners, both having survived a lawsuit (and a challenge to a duel by rival editor Engelenburg), "tended to favour toothless editorials". But, by 1889, Eugène Marais, who had already shown his anti-Kruger credentials, was approached by a Progressive consortium for the editorship of *Land en Volk*. Marais introduced a new kind of journalism, "a break from the staid Anglo-Dutch journalistic tradition" and a shift towards the muckraking of the American yellow press and the radical English penny press. The paper became a vehicle "for the polemics and diatribes of the young Turks".

Both the pro-government press and the opposition press "purported to be independent".[42] Dutchman Engelenburg, appointed as editor of *De Volkstem* by the Krugerites, bought the paper in 1889 and insisted on press freedom – "at least in principle". "Certain papers" won the bulk of "state subsidies and preferential placement of government advertisements", in total for £6,000 annually, with Kruger stating "that it would be simply suicidal to support the opposition press".

Kruger was either portrayed as the heroic "Oom Paul" figure of the "popular imagination", or "a dour intransigent old man, against progress qua progress and intent on dragging his fiefdom back into the eighteenth century, as he feathered the nests of his friends and relations".[43] Marais "vigorously" portrayed Kruger's ZAR as "a kleptocratic, backward government" resisting modernisation and unable to provide the economic infrastructure for the gold mines.

Dutch-Afrikaans titles

But first back to the Cape and the development of Dutch-Afrikaans publications. When the Cape was granted "responsible government" in 1854, English became the sole parliamentary language. Locals could now participate in government, but Dutch-speaking colonists, as the overwhelming majority of the Cape's European population, were "markedly under-represented".[44] This led the Dutch to stand together, but it was not until the 1870s, when DZA and Hofmeyr's *Volksvriend* merged, "that the claims of the Dutch" began to be heard. In 1876, *Die Afrikaanse Patriot* was the first "truly" Cape-Dutch Afrikaans-language newspaper. Both *Volksvriend* and the *Patriot* recognised the importance of language for "group survival and the creation of a nation". One can surmise that the partisan language and ethnic origins of the Dutch-Afrikaans media laid the foundation for the later Afrikaans media to act as mouthpiece for the Afrikaner cause.

DIE

Afrikaanse Patriot.

" Eert uwen vader en uwe moeder, opdat uwen dagen verlengd
worden in het land dat u de Heere uw God geeft."—*Het vijfde Gebod.*

DEEL I.]   SATERDAG, 15 JANUARY, 1876.   [No. 1.

" DIE AFRIKAANSE PATRIOT."

Een Afrikaanse koerant ! Wie het dit ooit gedroom !
Ja, Afrikaanders ! een koerant in ons ei'e taal ! Dit
het baiang moeite gekos om so vêr te kom ; dit kan ek
julle verseker, want die meeste Afrikaanders is nes
steeks pêrde, hulle wil mos nie glo dat ons een ei'e
taal het 'nie. Die ou'e Patriotte hou vas, en klou vas,
an die *Hollanse* taal ; die jong mense vind die *Engelse*
taal weer so danig mooi, en o'ertui'e gaat net so
moeilik, as om steeks pêrde te leer pronk in die voor-
tuig. Ons wil 'nou met ons " Patriot" an die wereld
wys, dat ons wel de'entlik een ta ' het waarin ons kan
sê net wat ons wil.

" AFRIKAANSE PATRIOT,"

Ja, dit is die naam van ons blad ! Een beter naam
kan ons nooit kry nie, want een " *Patriot* " is een
flukse vent, en so wil ons ons koerant ook maak :—
klein , maar fluks.

Op die 15 van ider maand kan julle een besoek van
die " Patriot" verwag, en ek is seker, hoe meer julle
hom lees, hoe liewer julle hom sal kry. En hoe meer
intekenaars julle ver hom sal besorge, hoe meer jul
julle dankbaarheid sal betoon ! Ek sê : *teken in ! dis
mar 5 sielings in die jaar! Sê an al julle vrinde,
teken in ver die* " Patriot," *dis mar 5 sielings in die
jaar !* Myn skepsels ! wat is 5 sielings ver een " Afri-

The first *Die Afrikaanse Patriot.*
Source: researchgate.net

The *Patriot* was the mouthpiece of the Genootskap van Regte Afrikaners (GRA, Association of Real Afrikaners),[45] a group that promoted a proto-Afrikaans as independent language to Dutch. The first issue of the *Patriot* was published on 15 January 1876.[46]

These Afrikaans publications came about not as a result "of professional journalist practice", but to serve the cause of Dutch-Afrikaners.[47] The first editors, "in most cases", were ministers of religion "committed to Calvinistic ethics" rather than "professional journalists". Among them were Abraham Faure and S.J. du Toit. The publications were also not commercial ventures. The Afrikaner cause "weighed more heavily than profits", resulting in many of the Dutch-Afrikaans papers folding. They were seen as "cultural and political crusaders", their "enduring themes" the promotion of the Afrikaans language and political independence. Another characteristic was that they were "committed to Africa and the role of the Afrikaner in South Africa". This in contrast to the English press, which "reported diligently on British affairs", while the Dutch-Afrikaans press focused on affairs of Afrikaners and South Africa, and developed into the foundation for the later Afrikaans press, aligning itself with the Afrikaans language, culture and causes.

When the colonial government turned into a representative government in 1854, English was the only parliamentary language.[48] Dutch was also excluded from schools from 1865. Even the DRC was to be anglicised. This was the situation that the DZA faced, which also led to the founding of the *Patriot*. The "infant Afrikaans press was not one to busy itself with intangibles", but was "a fighting press, trying to stem a tide which it feared was robbing the Afrikaner of all distinctiveness".

If the message of the *Patriot* seemed simple and direct, the motivation was not. It rested on the "utter conviction" that Afrikaners "were doomed" if they failed "to accept and develop their own language". Also, Afrikaners had to be anglicised in a "foreign-ruled" country where their lack of English meant no advancement in public life.

Hofmeyr's DZA was actively campaigning for the recognition of Dutch, not Afrikaans, whereas the *Patriot* led a crusade for the emancipation, culturally and politically, of the Afrikaner. Through pride in their own language, the paper wanted to teach its readers pride in themselves. It had influence up to the Transvaal, "where it encouraged the Boer resistance against annexation which led to Majuba in 1881". Transvaal papers, like the influential *Volkstem*, advised acceptance of British occupation; the *Patriot* suggested that the time for acquiescence was past.

Grahamstown and Paarl, where the *Patriot* originated, were "two towns of marked significance in the history of the press". Each represented a distinctive indigenous response to what was regarded as outside domination, whether ideological or cultural. While DZA fought for Afrikaner rights in a colony where Dutch as a language (let alone Afrikaans) was scorned in courts and in official assemblies, it was the *Patriot* which "uncompromisingly propagated the despised and fledgling Afrikaans language". DZA served the interests of Dutch-Afrikaners within a British-ruled community, whereas the *Patriot* was symbol of "an awakening need among Afrikaners to assert their independence".

But on another level the *Patriot* also represents an "amazing newspaper success story". It had "enormous" influence among subscribers and "rocketed" from 50 to 3,000 in a short time, the latter regarded as a considerable circulation. As an outlet for Afrikaners who found a new voice, it was as "if a wand had touched the lips of a dumbstruck Afrikanerdom, the *Patriot*'s readers poured forth in words: attempts at prose, letters, verse". This response was "brutally attacked and ridiculed" by Dutch-speaking Afrikaner leaders, including the DRC, for promoting the humble "kitchen" language. But it hit back "just as robustly, in the style of a cheerleader edging on a long-maligned team".

The *Patriot* was not a "tossed-off propaganda sheet", but a complete newspaper that took care to supply news, market prices "and everything an Afrikaner needs to know". Because of the "virulent opposition" to written Afrikaans, the beginnings of the paper had "a touch of the clandestine" about it. The two brothers behind the paper were Reverend Stephanus Jacobus (S.J.) du Toit (an "intense genius"), and his elder brother and later editor of the paper, Daniël Francois (D.F.) du Toit. Under the influence of Pannevis, a teacher at the Paarl Gymnasium and one of several foreigners who have played a major role in the development of Afrikaans, S.J. du Toit became a zealous promoter of the language. In 1875 he also founded the GRA, with the *Patriot* as its mouthpiece.

But it was the quiet, industrious D.F. du Toit who kept the paper running after he and his brother had a fall-out. He also attended the founding congress of the NPU in Grahamstown in 1882. D.F. du Toit regarded himself as a professional journalist. He first ran a handwritten newsletter in the Strand for some time before joining his brother's *Patriot*. After the "split in acrimony" with his brother, he joined *De Express* in Bloemfontein in 1894, was captured during the SAW, and afterwards worked on *The Friend*.

While editor of the "besieged *Patriot*", it took "sheer guts to resist the flood of invective from English and Afrikaners alike". In his speech at the NPU's 1882 press banquet, D.F. du Toit "appropriately toasted" the qualities of farmers "and the courage displayed by the neighbouring states", and trusted that "if the Cape Colony were placed in a similar position of danger it would show the same qualities". This was regarded as a patriotic reference to the ZAR and the Free State.

Meanwhile, in Paarl, the "enigmatic" S.J. du Toit became a fervent supporter of Rhodes, whom he saw as a fellow-Afrikaner. After the two brothers parted because of the *Patriot*'s support of Rhodes, the paper "dropped like a lead weight and went out of business in 1904".

The development of the black press

If the development of the Dutch-Afrikaans press was so turbulent, what happened to that of the black press? What scholars identify as the "independent" period developed from about the 1880s to about the 1920s.[49] The missionary stations continued to play a formative role. In 1860, a French missionary, A. Mabille, arrived in what was then Basutoland with a hand press.[50] "Single-handedly and without having had training as a printer," he started publishing literature and translations of large portions of the Bible. In 1864, he also published a small newspaper in Sotho. On his deathbed his last words reputedly were, "Write books for the Basuto".

This "independent" period was initiated by John Tengo Jabavu, who, at age 25, established the first independent black newspaper, *Imvo Zabantsundu* (Black Opinion), in King William's Town on 3 November 1884[51]. At the time he was editor of the *Isigidimi Zamaxhosa* (The Kaffir Express; spellings for these titles as per this source), established during the so-called mission period. It quickly became the most influential African voice and opinion in the Cape, with Jabavu the "most widely known mission-educated African until 1910".

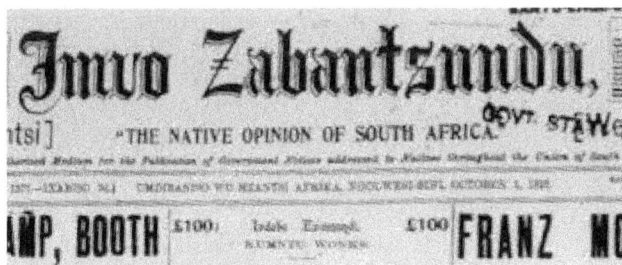

A later front page of *Imvo Zabantsundu*.
Source: http://nhmsa.co.za/news/imvo-zabantsundu-a-brief-history/

Jabavu lacked the funds to start his own paper, but was funded by two King William's Town investors, Richard Rose-Innes and James Weir.[52] *Imvo* published in both Xhosa and English. During the next period, from the 1930s onward – the so-called White-owned phase – it was bought by the then (now defunct) Afrikaans group Perskor, who published it until the mid-1980s.[53] It finally closed in the 1990s due to a falling readership.[54]

Known as the first black-owned newspaper when it was established, it was also popular because "it helped Africans to express themselves without any fear of prejudice and discrimination". Africans were able to share their political views and *Imvo* also became a source of literature.[55]

In this "independent elitist" period between 1880 and 1930, "a widening gap" emerged between those who had a missionary education and the rural-based majority. It led to the formation of a minority black elite "infused with Western values who felt a need for newspapers independent of missionary control".

Jabavu resigned as editor of *Isigidimi* in 1884 to establish *Imvo* in King William's Town as the first newspaper written, owned and controlled by black people in South Africa.[56] It rapidly developed into an influential expression of black opinion and promoted principles of non-violence and cooperation with liberal whites in an effort to bring about reform. However, it soon ran into problems, including financial difficulties and internal tensions, and experienced "intense competition" from *Isigidimi*.[57]

While *Imvo* was in decline, a new paper emerged in November 1897. *Izwi la Bantu* (The Voice of the People) opposed Jabavu on the issue of an organisation representing black rights.[58] With A.K. Soga as editor, *Izwi*, considered far more radical than *Imvo*, had a socialist approach and urged black readers "to improve their lot".

Ilanga Lase Natal (The Natal Sun) was the first important newspaper to emerge for Zulu readers and was started by John Dube in 1903. In 1912, Dube was elected the first chair of the South African Native National Congress (SANCC), which in 1923 became the African National Congress (ANC). Pioneering black journalists were involved in the founding of the SANCC, with the exception of *Imvo*'s Jabavu. He was considered too radical, focusing in his writing on the growing threat of Afrikaner Nationalism and the need for equal rights and public education.

One of the first activities of the newly formed African Nationalist organisation was the establishment of a newspaper to serve as a mouthpiece. It was called *Abantu-Batho* (The People).[59] Other publications from this period also were associated with the establishment of political movements.[60] Mahatma Gandhi, a lawyer in South Africa before he led India's fight for independence, launched *Indian Opinion* in 1903, an "immensely popular weekly in Durban".

'Black' journalism, 'ibali', African Nationalism and a voice of protest

The earliest protest literature can be found in African mission journals in the mid- to late-19th century.[61] South Africa's independent African protest press can be traced to the 1880s, while "designated Coloured and Indian communities" were represented by their own protest publications only from the early 1900s.

According to one source, "African journalism assumes added significance in the context of the paucity of early ANC written records and of formal history writing by Africans".[62] With few publication outlets, many African writers turned to newspapers. This "often accorded with cultural preferences", such as that Xhosa historians favoured "the form of the newspaper article" because it was closer than books "to the form and spirit of the traditional Xhosa *ibali* [tale]". Because of their exclusion from higher education, as well as the rigours of exile later on, "genres such as journalism continued to predominate in African writing".

Nationalism "rarely emerges" without the involvement of "both elites and masses", and the ANC drew support from a wide range of black social strata. In the late 19th century, an elite of educated, Christianised Africans expressed "early forms of national consciousness" through newspapers and organisations. Thus, the "loosely structured" South African Native Congress (SANC) was started in the Cape in 1898, followed by the Natal Native Congress in 1900 and the Transvaal Native Vigilance Association in 1902. As regional pressure groups, they gave way "in the face of the Union of South Africa's white-settler colonies in 1910" to the SANNC, formed in 1912 and later to become the ANC. Many early African newspapers helped nurture African Nationalism, even though the circulation of the early publications was low, as were literacy rates. Besides *Izwi la Bantu*, which existed from 1897 to 1909 and was published in East London, the Natal newspaper *Ipepa lo Hlanga* (Paper of the Nation) was published from 1884 to 1904. It reported on strikes and predicted efforts following the SAW to push down wages.

Gold, the ZAR, British Imperialism and press freedom

But back to the development of the "white" press. Thanks to the Rand's mineral riches, the major development in SA's media followed the discovery of gold in the then ZAR.[63]

After the ZAR's first weekly was published in Potchefstroom in 1857 and taken over as official ZAR gazette by 1859, there were a couple of other newspapers published by different political factions, although most short-lived. After gold was first discovered in the Eastern Transvaal (today Mpumalanga), and then on the Witwatersrand, "hundreds of fortune seekers" flocked to the area. The Transvaal Dutch-Afrikaners, or Boers, were not sympathetic to these "Uitlanders". It was not long before the "Uitlanders" had their own paper to publish their views. The first was the *Gold Fields Mercury*, founded in Pilgrim's Rest in the Eastern Transvaal in 1873. Two similar papers were published in close-by Barberton. All were critical of the ZAR government.

It was also not long before the British Empire viewed the region as desirable, for obvious reasons. Their annexation ideals were described, even up to the mid-1980s, as for "philanthropic reasons". One such formulation read: "Britain, for economic and philan-thropic reasons, now wished to incorporate the independent Boer countries into a federation with the Cape Colony and Natal." Since the "Uitlander newspapers" also pressed for British rule, the ZAR president at the time, T.F. Burgers, established the pro-Boer *De Volkstem* in 1873.

Britain annexed the ZAR in 1876 and censorship of pro-Boer publications followed. During this period, the British administrator declared: "I am afraid I shall have to prosecute *De Volkstem* for sedition; it has been, and still is, most persevering in its efforts to stir up the Boers to do mischief." Indeed, it is thought that due to the "urgings of *De Volkstem*" the Boers revolted in 1880, regaining the ZAR's independence.

Politics, partisanship and the press

After 1882, Kruger made the franchise laws so strict that newcomers "had virtually no chance of getting the vote".[64] The Boers believed the British were after the wealth below the ground. The "Uitlanders" formed the TNU in 1892, with *The Star* "strongly" supporting them. The ZAR was supported by the English *Standard and Diggers' News* – which Kruger subsidised. Through Rhodes, another "Uitlander uprising" was organised by his friend and lieutenant governor of the Cape, Leander Starr Jameson. However, dissent, personality conflicts and poor timing "doomed the exercise" over the New Year's weekend of 1895/1896.

Not surprisingly, in "all this the press played a vital role", leading Kruger to pass new press laws in 1896 to protect himself from criticism by the press. His first victim was the *Critic*, which was suspended for six months. Its editor and proprietor was permitted to carry on publishing under a different title, though, namely the *Transvaal Critic*. At the time, Kruger "had the power to prohibit the circulation of any newspaper, with no right of trial accorded to the parties responsible for its publication and no possibility of appeal". Despite this, the hostility was such that the "English journalists in the Transvaal were outrageous in their language of insult and annoyance".

There is little doubt that these newspapers "served to exacerbate the conflict between the Dutch and the English". In March 1897, after a "particularly insulting cartoon" in *The Star*, as stated earlier, Kruger served a warrant on the editor, banning the paper for three months and judging it to be "dangerous to the peace and quiet of the said Republic". That evening, *The Star*, as stated earlier, simply reported its own suppression at length and the next day the newspaper carried on publishing under a similar stellar title, the *Comet*. *The Star* meanwhile appealed the banning, arguing "that the law under which the paper was suppressed was contrary to the Transvaal Constitution, which assured the liberty of the press". It referred to Article 19 of the Constitution: "The Liberty of the Press is conceded, provided the printer and publisher remain responsible for all publications of a libellous character." Nevertheless, by October 1899, all of the "Uitlander press" was shut down by order of Kruger.

In the other Boer republic, the Orange Free State, its only paper had to do an "abrupt about-face". Although the *Friend of the Sovereignty and Bloemfontein Gazette* had served the English-speaking population since 1850, it supported the Boers when war broke out. When the English captured Bloemfontein, as said, the paper was "entrusted" to a group of war correspondents, among them the already mentioned Kipling. The paper now stood for "the maintenance of British supremacy in South Africa".

Regarding the principle of press freedom, Article 62 of the Constitution of the Orange Free State Republic entrenched the "right to receive information, the right to know".[65] It stated that "De vrijheid der drukpers wordt gewaarborgd mits blijvende binnen de Wet" (The freedom of the press is guaranteed if remaining inside the Law). Similarly, Article 19 of the 1858 Constitution of the ZAR stated that "Vrijheid van drukpers is toegestaan, mits de drukker en uitgever verantwoordelijk blijven voor al de stukken die eerschending, beleediging of aanranding van iemands karakter bevatten" (Freedom of the press is granted on the condition that the printer and publisher remain responsible for all the pieces that contain violation of character, insult, or assault of someone's character).

The Colonial Afrikaners

Back in the Cape Colony, the colonial Afrikaners began to shake off their political apathy by the early 1870s.[66] In 1872, less than a third of the members of Parliament were Afrikaners, despite Afrikaners constituting three quarters of the Colony's total white population. Thus in 1875, the GRA was founded with the slogan, "Our language, our nation and our country". By the mid-1870s, Afrikaner Nationalism, as resistance to anglicisation, began in earnest. The first newspaper in Afrikaans, the already mentioned *Patriot,* was published in Paarl in 1876 and lasted until 1904.[67] It was the mouthpiece of the GRA, and later of the Afrikaner Bond[68] (not to be confused with the Broederbond). The *Patriot* lost many of its readers after 1892 because of S.J. du Toit's support of Rhodes against Kruger. Nevertheless, it was an important vehicle in establishing Afrikaans as a language.[69]

This was followed by the Afrikaner Bond in 1879, the next milestone in what would develop into Afrikaner Nationalism[70] as an idealism aiming to promote Afrikaner culture and interests. Its leader in the 1880s, Onze Jan Hofmeyr, championed the interests of the wine farmers and opposed the replacement of Dutch by Afrikaans. Hofmeyr, identifying "strongly with the Afrikaner community", wanted to build a new nation from the two white language communities by attracting "enlightened English speakers".[71]

In the Cape, the first of the *Volks* newspapers – as expression of a yearning for an own nation or "volk" – came into existence in 1848 with *Het Volksblad.*[72] This was followed in 1862 by *De Volksvriend*, and twenty-five years later by *De Volksbode*. In the Transvaal, *De Volkstem* "became the Boer republic's most influential newspaper". When the ZAR Volksraad approved a tax on newspapers in 1876, the paper's first editor, J.F.E. Celliers, as "professional journalist committed to an independent press", threatened to close his newspaper. The government backed down and the tax never became law. His "passionate" successor, Frans Vredenrijk Engelenburg, even delivered newspapers on horseback "when necessary". The born Dutchman has the legacy that he twice tried to settle political arguments – one with a fellow editor – by publicly challenging his opponents to a duel. These never came off. Still, because duelling was an offence in the Transvaal, "the dashing editor had to answer in court".

The first Afrikaans magazine

In its early stages, the Dutch press protested against "the derogatory way in which Dutch and the growing new language of Afrikaans" were treated by those who regarded English as the only language for the Cape.[73] As stated in the previous chapter, DZA was one of the first publications to protest against the anglicisation of the Cape. When the GRA was founded, it established its own press to serve as its mouthpiece. This included its magazine, *Ons Klyntji*, published from 1896 to 1906. The magazine played an important role in propagating Afrikaans as the language of the future, a task that was eventually accomplished when Afrikaans was added as one of the official languages of the Union of South Africa in 1925.

The industrial revolution, thanks to South Africa's mineral riches, led to the awakening of both Afrikaner Nationalism and Black Nationalism. The former also flared up in response to the annexation of the ZAR in 1877, the First Anglo-Boer War and the Jameson Raid. After the Raid in 1896, most of the Cape Afrikaners were opposed to Rhodes, leading to his resignation as prime minister of the Colony.[74] Colonial Afrikaners who migrated to the

ZAR also experienced the difference between the "Colony" and the "Republic", and it was in resistance to colonial English arrogance that many Cape Afrikaners became increasingly Nationalist.[75]

At the turn of the 19th century there were well-established Dutch newspapers, namely *Ons Land* in Cape Town, *De Express* in Bloemfontein and *De Volkstem* and *Land en Volk* in Pretoria, as well as the Afrikaans *Patriot*, published from Paarl but distributed countrywide.[76]

The NPU

Following the struggle for press freedom in the first half of the 1800s, control by the Cape colonial government no longer posed a threat to the press by the 1880s.[77] Now there were new, indirect forms of pressure, such as a new libel law and the withholding of government advertising. Other issues came to the fore, such as government charging high tariffs for telegraphic services. This essentially cut off the supply that provided publications with news. The government also exploited the constant squabbles between press owners to its advantage in order to keep the press fragmented.

It seems "[a]ll that was fought for by Pringle and Fairbairn was in danger of disappearing".[78] The only way the press "could protect their hard-won liberty and not be done out of their earnings was to unite in a common front".[79] So, organised by Dormer of the *Argus* and R.W. Murray Jnr. of the *Cape Times*, 26 newspapermen met in Grahamstown on 27 November 1882 to form the Newspaper Press Union (NPU) "with the purpose of promoting and protecting the common interests of the South African press". The NPU undertook to fight to amend libel legislation and to establish a fund to help newspapers that ran into financial difficulties.

Dormer, the key personality behind the NPU, was described as "a remarkable man, possibly the most important newspaperman, in overall terms, in South Africa's press history".[80] Francis Joseph Dormer was 28 years old when he founded the Argus Group. His name would spell the advent of a "Modern South African press" based on professional principles, and its beginnings as a competitive industry.

With government control in the 1880s no longer a threat,[81] the "subtler pressures" such as libel laws drove smaller papers out of business. The withholding of government advertising and the already mentioned costly telegraphic services "choked the life's blood of the press". Added to this was "petty squabbling", which kept the press "fragmented in the face of powerful interests". More than anyone, "it was Dormer who set the press on a course to secure its freedom and establish its viability in a vastly more complex South Africa than earlier pathfinders had known".

Dormer argued that the press had to contend with problems peculiar to the country. They included immense distances, inadequate communications and a "sparse reading population" who had to be served in two languages (clearly, the indigenous languages were not a consideration). Plus: "New technology was in the air." The steam press was brand new and the promise of electricity as a source of power "fascinated printers". And, said Dormer:

> [T]he ideals which Pringle and Fairbairn had established were withering in the harsh light of everyday practicalities. No common policy on advertising or the sharing of news existed – individual newspapers made their own arrangements to cut cable

costs. Professional standards hung like a badly cut suit on some newsmen whose unbridled editorial language had outlasted its initial effect.

It was also in the aftermath of Majuba, with "a slow fuse of eventual confrontation between nationalist and Jingoist sentiment" smouldering, that Dormer persuaded his colleagues that whatever might divide them, the press needed unity and rationalisation to survive. He argued that the voice of an individual newspaper, "or an individual newspaper proprietor, strong though it may be, is as nothing compared to the strength of a representation made in the name and on behalf of a numerous and united body".

To guard the legacy of a free press and to ensure that the press as industry "should not be done out of its rightful earnings", newspapers had to unite in a common front.[82] Thus, due "mostly to [Dormer's] untiring efforts", as well as that of his *Cape Times* colleague, Murray Jnr., the 26 men from the most prominent newspapers met in the council chamber of the Grahamstown Town Hall on that morning of 27 November 1882.

A historic picture of the delegates at the founding congress of the Newspaper Press Union in Grahamstown (now Makhanda) on 27 November 1882. Those who could be identified are (back row): – , H.D. Blewitt, *Kaffrarian Watchman*, W. Dewey, *Alice Times*, – , J. Kemsley, *Port Elizabeth Telegraph*, W.S.J. Sellick, *Humansdorp Echo*, – , F.J. Dormer, *Cape Argus*, W. Hay, *Cape Mercury*, T.H. Grocott, *Penny Mail*, J.H. Pocock, *Oudtshoorn Courant*; middle row: R. Vause, *Natal Mercury*, E. Morris, *Port Elizabeth Advertiser*, H. Guest, *Port Alfred Budget*, T. Sheffield, *Eastern Star*, G. Impey, *Eastern Province Herald*, R.W. Murray Jnr., *Cape Times*, H.H. Solomon, *Observer of South African Affairs*, – ; front row: – , – , J.E. Radford, *Diamond Fields Advertiser*, D.F. du Toit, *Die Afrikaanse Patriot*.
Source: De Kock, A Manner of Speaking

With this initiative, Dormer founded "a sound base" for the South African press.[83] As a "quick-witted journalist" he had earlier "sized up the situation" and called on Murray Jnr. to discuss this umbrella body to protect their interests.

There was an air of urgency about him. The Government had rammed through a new libel law with heavy fines for publishers which made it incumbent on newspapers to prove that publication of a "libellous" statement about public figures, even if true, was in the public interest. To make matters worse, the attorney-general had an option to appoint any magistrate, not judge, to hear a case.

In parliament, the "gutsy" Saul Solomon – as many other press men, now a member – "had protested strongly" against this legislation. He even joked that "his useful days were obviously over as he was no longer libeled with regularity". But, he said, he perceived a serious threat to free critical expression, and pointed out that the profits from newspapers in South Africa were not so great as to justify risks. "Public opinion did not rise naturally in defence of newspapermen who were hauled up in court." He also knew "of no respectable paper" that had singled out private people for unwarranted attacks.

Libel had been a "grating point of contention" between the authorities and the press since the days of Somerset. In 1880, the "politically-ambitious" hotelier and railway engineer, George Pauling, and William Houghton, an "itinerant" compositor, published a "scandal sheet" in Grahamstown called *The Comet – A Journal for Men of the World*. They hired a "nominal editor", W.K. Wright, for £20 a month. Between them, they referred to him as the "Prison Editor", as his sole function was to serve any jail sentences incurred by the paper. It is not known whether he ever did – or discovered his real role.

Dormer himself had a libel action against the *Argus* shortly after becoming editor under Solomon. The newspaper acted "on good authority" that there were political motives in the then attorney-general's decision not to "press for the conviction of Koegas farmers who were accused of shooting Bushmen [San]". The *Argus* lost the libel case and its legal costs were severe.

Many of the "representative number of newspapermen" who turned up at Grahamstown were political enemies – the bigger an achievement for convenors Dormer and Murray. The delegates, hosted by Josiah Slater of the *Journal*, met in the city hall's council chamber: "The men who looked one another in the eye or courteously shook hands, some for the first time, exhibited a deep delight in the novel feeling that they no longer stood alone."

Grahamstown was Godlonton's home town. The "Father of the Colonial Press" had been asked to deliver an opening address, but Godlonton, aged 88, could not attend. The "birth" of the NPU, however, continued without him, as it was formed for the purpose of "promoting all objects of common interest to the South African Press, and for the protection of its members in the proper discharge of their public duty".

The fact that Dormer could bring together the people he did around one table "was amazing for the time in which it occurred and a tribute to his tolerance and vision". It was one year after Majuba, where Transvaal Afrikaners rebelled against the British Empire and defeated the British, gaining partial self-government after the Shepstone annexation of 1877,[84] "and Empire loyalists were rampant". Those present represented "radically different political persuasion[s]", including the editor of the *Patriot*, the paper recognised "as having fired the Transvaal sentiment which led to Majuba".[85]

Dormer addressed his colleagues as "my brother pressmen" and said that the press of the country had a need to stand together and share their problems. They faced crucial choices and needed "mutual comfort", seeing that their hard-fought press freedom was in peril of being lost. The only way in which press owners could both protect that freedom and ensure the economic survival of their papers was to unite.[86] Besides fighting libel legislation, they also had to establish the fund for newspapers with financial problems. Although they represented different independent newspapers,[87] Dormer advocated their joining of forces:

> He foresaw that problems such as the vast distances between communities, inefficient means of communication and small readership could slow down any meaningful effect which the press could have on the development of the country

and a fully-fledged newspaper industry. Combining forces would help the press to surmount the obstacles in bringing the news to society.

With the NPU's founding conference, the highly regarded Meurant Jnr. sent a letter of good wishes and "volunteered this graphic description":[88]

> Editors, or Pressmen, as they are now called, have no idea now-a-days of what the labour of conducting and printing a newspaper was fifty years ago. Not only had my dear old friend [Godlonton] to write leading articles, but we had to take off our coats and to print the papers ourselves, he "inking" the "forms", first with "balls" and afterwards with improved "rollers", until our hands were blistered, once a week for a very considerable time.

Unfortunately, less than twenty years later, the bitterness of the SAW would cause a "split down the middle", with some editors in custody for "seditious" reports, others whose papers were suspended, and the NPU barely surviving the turbulence of the war.[89]

Besides resolving to fight for a modification of the libel law and starting the defence fund to assist "harassed newspapers", Dormer also attempted to establish an own press corporation in opposition to Reuters, which he accused of "monopolistic arrogance and intent only on enriching" its shareholders "six thousand miles away, who care no more about South Africa than they care about Siberia or Japan".

This attempt failed, and up to the end of the century, NPU members were involved in several "acrimonious run-ins" with Reuters, who, in turn, accused the newspapers of "lifting, in true pioneering tradition", material to which they were not entitled.

In his inaugural address, George Impey of the *Eastern Province Herald*

> gratefully recalled the legacy of John Fairbairn and spoke of the future: ... within the last thirty years steam has lent its magic power to Press development. Electricity will probably be the next element to serve the Press as motive power; and we shall not only have telegrams and cablegrams transmitted by electric force but we shall have the wondrous power stored up for us and made capable of being supplied to machinery.

The NPU's second congress was held in Cape Town in 1884, and the third in Kimberley in 1885, where Dormer, 31 at the time, was elected president. Membership had risen to 43.

It is ironic that the same page of the *Graham's Town Journal* of 27 November 1882 that carried the report on the congress of the NPU also carried a paragraph about a convicted editor.[90] The "firebrand" editor, Thomas McCombie of the *Lantern*, "surrendered to his bail" that Saturday. He demanded not to be treated as an ordinary criminal and not to have his hair cut, but the Magistrate refused, although he could have a cab to prison if his friends would pay the fare. "He went in a cab with a bag of books." The matter developed into "a celebrated libel test case". McCombie later wrote a book about his "degradation" and how he was "despatched to the Tronk (jail)". He was not popular with his colleagues, though, and Thomas Sheffield in Johannesburg referred to him as "this proven libeller of other people's good names, this cad of the Cape Press".

The beginning of Egoli, City of Gold

The discovery of diamonds and gold changed the nature of South Africa from an agrarian one to an industrial lifestyle. The "horde of alien fortune seekers"[91] not only brought their own ideas of how the Boer republics should be run, but also "their own newspapers to back up their demands".

Johannesburg's first newspaper was *Diggers' News*, founded in 1886.[92] On 6 February 1887, only four months after the Johannesburg diggings – called "the Camp" – was officially proclaimed, "ox wagons loaded with printing equipment rolled into the camp from Aliwal North in the Eastern Cape".[93] The first issue of the "Camp's" second paper, *Diggers' News and Witwatersrand Advertiser*, was printed on 24 February 1887 from a tent put up in Market Square. One day later, the first issue of the *Transvaal Mercury Argus* was printed, followed in March by the *Standard and Transvaal Mercury Chronicle*, all of them produced "under canvas". The *Standard* and *Diggers' News* amalgamated in 1889 as the *Standard and Diggers' News* and was sympathetic to Kruger, rather than to English mining interests.

In his memoire, veteran journalist Joel Mervis wrote that, in its first sixteen years, Johannesburg had proven itself not only a city of gold, but also "a newspaper town".[94] When, in September 1886, Johannesburg was proclaimed, *Diggers News* was published that same month. New titles appeared almost day after day, such as the *Witwatersrand Advertiser* on 24 February 1887 and, on the next day, the *Transvaal Mining Argus*. Three weeks later, on 12 March 1887, the *Standard and Transvaal Mining Chronicle* "burst upon the scene" according to Mervis. By October 1887, two more papers appeared: the *Daily News* and the *Eastern Star*, shortly after *The Star*.

The latter was of course Grahamstown's *Eastern Star*, moved to the Rand in 1887. It grew to become South Africa's biggest daily by the early 1990s.[95] None of the other papers survived.[96] In Grahamstown, the *Eastern Star* was in tough competition with the *Graham's Town Journal* as well as *Grocott's Penny Mail*, the latter founded in 1870. The *Eastern Star* first appeared in Johannesburg as a triweekly evening paper.

In the Cape, Dormer also became interested in the lucrative northern market. With already six or seven established papers, he decided it would be better to rather buy one: the *Eastern Star*. His company also had outlets for stationery in Cape Town and Kimberley and at the time published a weekly edition of the *Argus* in London. Mining financiers, including Rhodes, were "strongly represented" among the shareholders.

Other papers were the *Gold Field News*, moving from Barberton to Johannesburg, and the *Transvaal Truth*, lasting for one year.[97] *Judge* was the unusual name of a paper edited by Douglas Blackburn, whose one claim to fame "was that his bedroom in the Grand National Hotel was also the editorial office where the paper was written and edited". As Mervis wrote: "This was a rare instance of an editor putting himself to bed, and his newspaper to bed, in one and the same room."

By 1895, eight more newspapers had appeared: *Tatler*, *Golden Age*, *Nugget*, *Critic*, *Burlesque*, *Moon*, *Sentinel*, *Transvaal Leader* and the *Johannesburg Times*. While some did not last long, others merged. By 1897, as the SAW loomed closer, the *Standard and Diggers' News* supported the Kruger government, while *The Star* was an "Uitlander" mouthpiece. As Mervis wrote, the two newspapers "could not know that their choice of sides in 1897 was to have a vital bearing on their survival".

The Boer Republics and the thorny issue of press freedom

The two Boer Republics – the ZAR, later the Transvaal and today encompassing the four Northern provinces, Gauteng, Mpumalanga, Limpopo and Northwest, and the Orange Free State – today the Free State, were established in 1852 and 1854 respectively.

The ZAR, although a "republic", was governed as a dictatorship under Paul Kruger.[98] Politics in the ZAR "remained organised along traditionally individual lines, with no formally organised political parties", and although "republican ideology was much alluded to in the political realm, it is hard to know to what extent burghers insisted on or were even cognisant of their republican prerogatives". It was anyway only "literate men" who "kept abreast of Volksraad action through the press". Although "there was an emphasis on participatory volkswil (the people's will) and regular elections", the practical workings of the Republican democracy were "circumscribed by inherent contradictions, like the devotion to strong leaders and a tendency towards nepotism and familial connections".

One such example: In 1886, Kruger issued a law that gave him the power to ban newspapers if they "countered the good values or were a danger to the safety and security of the Republic".[99] One year later, Kruger banned *The Star* for three months.[100] When the SAW began in October 1899, Kruger shut down the "foreign" (English) press.

Land en Volk attacked Kruger for his "autocracy", his tolerance of corruption, "his servitude to Dr Leyds" (his Dutch secretary), his "love of Catholics, Jews and Hollanders" and, at the time, his "loyal help and support for Rhodes".[101] Up to the 1893 election, "the rhetoric of populism allowed Kruger to maintain that he held the volkswil to be sovereign, which meant petitions and armed demonstrations received his Volksraad's attention, but his government was not prepared to accept personalised attacks by a free press".[102]

In 1893, Marais, now as sole editor of *Land en Volk*, found himself arrested by the ZAR's state police on the grounds of criminal libel.[103] A *Land en Volk* article claimed that Kruger, in spite of his £7,000 annual salary, submitted two different accounts for travelling expenses for a visit to Colesberg while he was in fact a guest of the Cape government. Rumours circulated that the ZAR wanted to close down *Land en Volk*.

Kruger summarily denied access to the press banks to Marais, who also worked for the "Progressive" groups' *Transvaal Advertiser*. Marais, during a Volksraad recess, had overheard two members conspiring to silence Jan Celliers, not only a journalist but also a Volksraad member who had been vocal in his opposition to a particular concession granted by Kruger. The next day, Kruger himself disallowed Marais's entry to the press table. Marais wrote in his column: "I had never thought the Chairman [Kruger], that religious man … whose every word is oiled with the grace of God … that this man could utter anything he would blush to see published."[104] Relegated to the public benches, Marais continued to report on the Volksraad, but changed the title of his column from "Glimpses from the Hoekie" (the press corner) to "Glimpses from the benches".

The fight between Kruger and the press

The Volksraad then imposed a draconian censorship law, Law 11 of 1893, which meant that "faultfinding newspapers" faced the loss of a government subsidy.[105] For Marais, one way to circumvent both the libel law and the government's wrath was to couch criticism in the form of letters, rather than editorials. One "letter writer", who called himself "Afrikanus

Junior", was "particularly vituperative". He purported to be a "landzoon" (son of the land, meaning a patriotic ZAR citizen) and a war veteran of the older generation who were increasingly alienated by Kruger's administration. His "Open Letter to the Honourable President Paul Kruger" protested the preponderance of "Hollanders" (born Dutchmen) in government.[106] The Concessions Policy also came under attack. A particularly vitriolic letter was aimed at Dr Leyds, "with the use of the offensively personal 'gij' (you) instead of 'u' (the formal you)". Afrikanus Junior's last "letter" was even advertised in *Land en Volk* the week before it appeared. The editors claimed they had received the letter too late and would have to publish it the following week, but could announce that it dealt with the latest government scandal. The letter duly appeared, and was heavily critical.[107]

There was much speculation over the true identity of "Afrikanus Junior", particularly by those who had been his focus. Some demanded to know the writer's identity, but "Afrikanus Junior" became something of a household name; one advertiser even used him to draw attention to his tobacco and maize.[108] There was speculation that Jan Celliers, or even Piet Joubert, was the perpetrator, but the former died before the letters stopped and the second's usual rhetoric "was entirely removed from the style of the writer". It was also not Carl Jeppe, as Marais himself "tantalisingly conceded", saying that he had known the letter-writer long before and that his name was linked to "great services to his country".

WELVERDIEND!

The "hiding" Eugène Marais's *Land en Volk* got in a ZAR High Court case where the judges were pro-Kruger. This is W.A. Schröder's cartoon of Chief Justice J.G. Kotzé giving *Land en Volk* a thrashing. The twig is labelled "£10 with costs" and the caption "Welverdiend!" (Well-deserved!); it was published on 25 June 1892. Source: National Archives of South Africa, SAB: A. 787 184, Preller Collection, p 79, incorrectly dated 1895.

When the SAW began in October 1899, Kruger had the "foreign" (English) press shut down.[109] As mouthpiece for immigrant grievances and leading English paper, *The Star* was implicated in a conspiracy to invade the Boer Republic and overthrow the Boer government.[110] After the failure of the Jameson Raid in 1895/1896, Kruger passed a law which gave him as president the right to ban newspapers that were "contrary to the good morals or dangerous to peace and order in the republic".

Censorship and war

When the SAW broke out, the ZAR press was severely restricted, first by the Kruger government, then by British colonial rule. With war declared on 10 October 1899, the Kruger government closed *The Star* and the *Transvaal Leader*, both critical of his government, the very next day.[111] The paper that remained open was the loyal *Standard and Diggers' News*. As Mervis wrote: "Things usually moved fast in hectic Johannesburg", so when the British occupied the town in May 1900, it in turn "promptly closed" the *Standard and Diggers' News* and allowed *The Star* and the *Transvaal Leader* to appear again. "Fate, or destiny, now took a hand," as the closing of the *Standard and Diggers' News* in May 1900 became a factor in the founding of the *Rand Daily Mail* (RDM) in September 1902. The owner of the "moribund" *Standard and Diggers' News* sold his press to Freeman Cohen who, at the time, had not even thought of starting a newspaper. But he took a chance and answered the seller that, indeed, he also had an editor, and announced the name of the editor to be before he had even discussed it with him. This would be Edgar Wallace, the "celebrated" London *Daily Mail* correspondent who would write the scoop about the Peace of Vereeniging. Despite the British implementing strict press laws, Wallace managed to outmanoeuvre these. And so he laid the foundation as editor of a newspaper that would eventually play a significant role in South Africa's liberation struggle. The name of the new paper presented no problem at all: it would be the *Rand Daily Mail* (RDM), after the paper Wallace represented in London. He first went back to London, not only to resign from the *Daily Mail*, but also to attend a ceremonial banquet at the Savoy Hotel where he was to be honoured for his great scoop.

This scoop was all thanks to "clever reporting tricks" with which he out-manoeuvred British censorship laws and wrote the scoop about the declared peace before it was officially announced by Kitchener. Wallace was jubilant, but an "embittered Kitchener" could not forget how Wallace had "brazenly stolen his thunder". A "dusty letter" from the British censor, "inspired by Kitchener", followed:

> I am instructed to write and inform you that in consequence of your having evaded the rules of censorship subsequent to the warning you received, you will not in future be allowed to act as a war correspondent; and further, that you will not be recommended for the [war] medal.

Despite this, Wallace "was the man of the hour" in London. The *Daily Mail* owner, Alfred Hamsworth, later Lord Northcliffe, personally congratulated him and expressed his regret that Wallace was leaving the *Mail*. The banquet, "held fortuitously on the night of the coronation of King Edward VII, brought him compliments and cheers".

Thus, the RDM, named after the London paper, was launched in Johannesburg on 22 September 1902 by Cohen, who had formed African Mails Ltd as its "sheltering company". The paper occupied the offices used by the *Standard and Diggers' News* on an upper floor in Corporation Buildings at the corner of Rissik and Commissioner Streets. The contrast between the glitter of London's Savoy and Wallace's new editorial home "could hardly have been more marked". He had to reach his office not by a staircase but by climbing a ladder, and "[d]raughts, noises and smells pierced or pervaded the editorial sanctuary with varying degrees of intensity". The steam-driven printing press was housed in a basement "that matched the tawdriness of the editorial offices". The first serious setback came with the first edition: the printers realised that the supply of fuel for the furnace was grossly inadequate and that the print order would be affected seriously. Fortunately, a large number of wooden crates left in the press room by the previous owner could be used as fuel, saving the first edition.

Wallace did not complain about the inconvenience and discomfort. He was sought after as a man of stature, "one of the leaders in society, either as a guest or a host". Whether dinner parties, the theatre or the race track, "all were frequent and agreeable diversions". Regrettably, his "large salary" was not enough to pay his debts. He had to be "saved frequently" from his creditors by Cohen. As for his paper, Wallace was satisfied only with the best "by way of news reports and features" and paid "exorbitant prices to get them". This raised the paper's status and increased its circulation, "but the money spent went far beyond what the paper could afford". And, clearly: "There could be no point in producing a good paper if the price meant ruin." Six months after the launch, in March 1903, Wallace's "wonderful world began to crumble". Writing years later of his nine months at the helm of a paper that would later become synonymous with media freedom, Wallace referred to it as "one of the two greatest newspapers in South Africa" [the other would probably be the RDM's stable mate, the *Sunday Times*]. He described the RDM as "a bright paper, extravagantly run, but popular from the first". Its competition was the *Transvaal Leader*, "a loyalist which had established itself under the Krugerian regime", adding "but this we eventually killed (not in my time, it is true)".

In the service of Empire and mining interests

In the first edition of the RDM, Wallace published "a declaration of intent" as editorial policy.[112] The context in which it was made must be borne in mind, "as the country [was] recovering from a bloody war in which the Transvaal had changed its character from an independent Boer republic to a British colony". The declaration read:

> The *Rand Daily Mail* will support the Imperial ideal, it will be for progress in Transvaal and South African affairs; and in its general policy it will be for the people, in the same sense that what is best for the State is best for the majority. The *Rand Daily Mail* shares the belief that South Africa, now almost entirely under one flag and a dominant Imperialism which, in the issue, is practically Democratic, has a very great future before it; and that in the cumulative incidence of this future the Transvaal colony, with its incomparable mineral wealth, is destined to enact a prominent part.

It was to be expected that the RDM backed imperialistic capitalism and the mining houses. This was also the interests of mining magnate Abe Bailey, whose path would now cross with that of the RDM. Meanwhile, George Adamson, who emigrated from Scotland in 1880 to take up a post with the *Natal Witness* in Pietermaritzburg,[113] bought the RDM from Wallace. Adamson was aware that "a hostile political group" was poised to buy the RDM, but he "knew just the man to thwart them": Bailey. Thus the paper was bought for £34,500 "first thing in the morning", when Bailey "sen[t] along his cheque".

Having the mining complex's interests as key, and with the *Transvaal Leader* also "well backed by Corner House, headquarters of the Central Mining Investment Corporation",[114] this now led to a new social phenomenon on the Rand: The importation of Chinese labour,[115] which also had an impact on the development of the press in the region.

Many gold mines were closed during the SAW. More than 100,000 black workers did not return when the war ended, meaning a huge labour shortage and that about half the mines would remain closed. Consequently, the "serious post-war slump was likely to grow worse". The mining companies demanded "cheap Chinese labour" to be imported. The choice "was either that or ruin". By 1905 there were 50,000 Chinese labourers, "[t]heir presence ... a recurring source of conflict and disturbance". Still, "[i]t can hardly be denied that the Chinese saved Johannesburg, the Rand and South Africa, and that, as the salvation of the country had been from the first the prime consideration, the less admirable features of the experiment must be regarded as of secondary importance". Thus, "[i]n the best traditions of Chinese puzzles, the Chinese experiment exerted a crazy interplay of contradictory influences on the political fortunes of *Het Volk* and the British Liberal Party".

Racism and racialism - "for whites only"

Interestingly, this also brought about a dichotomy about race on the Rand. Racism was not regarded as what was "standard", namely the "sneering, sweeping references to Chinese and Indians" [and naturally, black people] that were acceptable to white people .[116] These simply reflected a "normal, natural" and "possibly justifiable antipathy towards people of colour", but certainly not "racialism". The latter was "something quite different" and, "[i]n a manner of speaking, it was for whites only". If the English insulted or hated the Boers (the Afrikaners), or if the Boers felt the same about the English: that was racialism. But when headlines reflected the mood of the times as "Yellow Threat", "Asiatic Menace" and "Black Peril", it was not regarded as "racialism". The concept "that colour prejudice was not to be equated with racialism persisted for years, as was to be demonstrated by none other than Sir Abe Bailey himself". Indeed, already in the House of Assembly in 1922, a motion by an English-speaking Natal member asked that the government should consider providing separate areas, urban and rural, for "the Asiatic community".

And racism within the ranks of journalists themselves

With regard to racism within the ranks of journalists themselves at the time, "no amount of argument can excuse a deplorable act" committed by George Herbert Kingswell, the founding editor of the *Sunday Times* in 1906, at an NPU congress in 1912.[117]

The history went back to 1892, when Jabavu, editor of the first independent black newspaper, *Imvo Zabantsundu*, was unanimously elected as NPU member. During the SAW, Jabavu's paper was suspended by military authorities because he condemned the British attacks on the Boer republics. His last attendance at an NPU congress appears to have been in 1905. At the congress in 1912, Kingswell moved that "no coloured or native newspaper proprietor should be admitted as a member" of the NPU. The seconder was D.M. Ollemans of Bloemfontein's *The Friend*. The motion was carried, and the word "European" was added as a qualification for membership. Only in 1975 – 63 years later – did the NPU scrap the condition. Mervis suggests that, while Kingswell had much to his credit as "the brilliant pioneer of a great newspaper empire", his action at the NPU congress "is a regrettable blot on a splendid career".

Kingswell, the Kiwi press pioneer

Who was Kingswell? The born New Zealander migrated to Cape Town,[118] where he bought *The Owl*, a weekly founded by Charles Penstone and taken over by the *Cape Times*. Under his leadership, the circulation increased from 1,000 to 15,000. Contributors included the cartoonist D.C. Boonzaier, later the creator of the cartoon character Hoggenheimer – a bloated mining magnate, symbolising imperial mining capitalism – for the *De/Die Burger*, as well as the pioneering woman journalist "Dadge" (Mrs Julia Hyde Stansfield), who was later to write for the *Sunday Times*.

For Kingswell, South Africa was "the culminating point of his long, restless, rambling, roving career". Johannesburg was his last stop and where he began the *Sunday Times* in 1906. The paper's first print order, for Sunday, 4 February, was 10,000 copies, but 11,600 copies were printed at a rate of just under 1,000 an hour. When this first print run was sold out, the presses started rolling again, printing 5,000 more, even though sixty churches on the Witwatersrand pinned notices to their doors condemning the *Sunday Times* and urging congregants not to buy the paper.[119]

This meant that, for the next Sunday, the print order was "stepped up" to 16,200. By November 1906, sales had risen to 22,450. A year later it was 25,250, and by November 1909 35,000. As a matter of interest, under the editorship of editor Tertius Myburgh (now accused of being an NP government spy),[120] the circulation in 1989 was approximately 530,000.[121] For January to March 2018 it was 260,132.[122]

But back to 1906: Although proclaiming editorial independence, literally in the same sentence it said the paper would be loyal to Britain – up to its "Imperialistic" backbone:[123]

> Tied to the heels of no political party, and as free from Boer bondage as it is from Progressive patronage, the *Sunday Times* will steer an independent course during the coming political storm in the Transvaal ... Though loyal to the finger-tips and Imperialistic to the backbone, the *Sunday Times* will always resent and fight against undue interference by any British Government in the internal affairs of this country.

This statement cannot but remind one of the first editorial of *De Burger*, founded in the name of Afrikaner Nationalism in 1915, almost ten years later, which also proclaimed editorial independence, free from any party political interference, but which also served sectional interests, in this case that of Afrikaner Nationalism.[124]

As to who would be in control of the *Sunday Times*'s editorial policy, it would be mining magnate Abe Bailey: "as long as [he] lives, or retains his interest in the Sunday Times Syndicate Limited, he is at liberty to control the political policy of that paper". This meant that Bailey now controlled the editorial policy of both the RDM and the *Sunday Times*.[125] It seems that being loyal to the British Empire and its mining interests could be equated to the English press being "neutral" and "independent", but that the Afrikaans press's commitment to Afrikaner Nationalist ideals would be the ultimate sin of being partial and partisan.

And the mining complex as a "fifth province"

With the RDM in the hands of "wealthy capitalist" Bailey, the *Transvaal Leader*, shut down in 1899 by the Kruger government, resumed publication after the war. It was owned by the "most powerful financial group" in the Transvaal, namely "Corner House".[126] The Central Mining Investment Company was the largest landowner in the country, controlled by De Beers, the National Bank, the Argus Group, and "many coal mines", and had the nickname of being "the fifth province". Through its investment in the *Transvaal Leader*, Corner House also gained a stake in the *Cape Times,* later to become a partner of the RDM. In 1914, after twelve years of "lively competition" between the RDM and the *Transvaal Leader*, the RDM enjoyed the bigger circulation, and the *Transvaal Leader*, second in the circulation race, was losing money.

But this was only the tip of the iceberg in terms of the rivalry between the then mining magnates and their shares in the South African English press.

When Bailey acquired the RDM in 1905, he was an established mining magnate and was elected to parliament three years later, in 1908. He formed a private company, the Rand Daily Mails Ltd, in which he was the largest shareholder.[127] The RDM and the *Sunday Times* worked in close association with each other, although a single company was only to be formed in 1955, namely South African Associated Newspapers (SAAN). For some time to come, it would be the second largest newspaper group after the Argus Group. From 1915 onward, the Rand Daily Mails Ltd and Sunday Times Syndicate Ltd, either singularly or jointly, "took a number of steps to eliminate their competitors". Today it would be seen as collusion, but together with the Argus Group they also were to assert their dominance by absorbing rival newspapers, sometimes jointly, sometimes in conjunction with other existing newspapers, thus ensuring the elimination of serious rivals, the contraction in the numbers of newspapers and the concentration of ownership in fewer and fewer hands.

The Dormer-Rhodes duo and a new era

But by the turn of the century, with war in the two Boer republics looming and 22 years since "shipboard companions" Dormer and Rhodes first made their acquaintance, this long association was coming to an end over irreconcilable differences.[128] At the "dusty railway junction" of De Aar, in the year 1897, these two men met, the "one a journalist pleading the cause of a newspaper's integrity, the other an imperialist[,] hungrier than ever to conquer a continent".

This meeting at the De Aar junction was Dormer's "last-ditch attempt" to stop the polarising forces that Rhodes had unleashed among the South African press and people. He failed. And, as was written in 1982: It had such severe consequences for the press itself that they "are yet to be fully calculated".

Dormer is described as one of the most formidable journalists to have made his mark on this country. In fact, "his concern for the honour of newsmen and for the newspaper industry as a whole, set him apart from all who had gone before". Starting from a single newspaper, his drive and energy laid the foundations for the first of the four large press groups, which by 1982 published most of the newspapers in the country.

And the story of how it all began

After Dormer arrived at the Cape as a 21-year-old teacher, he went to work for the *Queenstown Representative*, fought in the Ninth Frontier War of 1877 – and reported on it.[129] Two years later he was a correspondent during the Zulu War for Saul Solomon's *Cape Argus*. There he was appointed a subeditor and became editor in 1878. Three years on, on 1 July 1881, Dormer purchased the *Argus* for £6,000 – half in cash and the rest "in monthly notes".

But he had little money, and the investment did not come from him. Indeed, the cash came from his powerful friend, Rhodes, handed to him by "an agent in the strictest secrecy" in the middle of the Grand Parade in Cape Town.

By 1886, he had "co-opted" Solomon's printing works and formed the Argus Printing and Publishing Company. Dormer was one of two directors of the new company in which a number of prominent businessmen had shares. Rhodes was represented by a nominee. This new formation represented "the end of the editor-owner in the South African press and the beginning of newspaper concerns founded on sound management rather than personalities".

In 1889, Dormer bought the Sheffield brothers' *Eastern Star* in Johannesburg. He also "reconstituted" the company and expanded rapidly, including starting newspapers as far away as what was called the "Rhodes' territories". Indeed, the name Rhodesia was coined by Dormer when he began *The Rhodesia Herald*.

But Dormer's direct connection with the NPU came to an end when he departed for "the cauldron of the goldfields in 1889". There he became editor of *The Star* and his "dynamic energy took his company to new heights".

But it was also the situation in the North that "set the scene for his final confrontation" with Rhodes at De Aar on that day eight years later.

Dormer called himself an "Anglo-Afrikaner", and although "intensely loyal to England, his homeland", in "Kruger's country" he kept up "a good relationship with the republican government". He appointed an Afrikaans journalist to report "matters appearing in the Dutch language". Dormer "had no intention to propagate a subversion of the government of his host country". Still, his professional integrity and commitment to independent newspapers were demonstrated by the way he hit equally at Kruger's interference in the press and sponsorship of certain papers, and at Rhodes' influence.

The Witwatersrand appeared to be the Wild West for newspapers as, inter alia, an effigy of Dormer was burnt in the streets of Johannesburg in 1892 "by a wild mob seeking his blood". He was also attacked in a bar and had to get police protection.

But, in 1895, after fourteen years of first leading the *Argus* and then *The Star*, Dormer "suddenly severed all formal links with the company of his making". The reason was Rhodes' pressure on his fellow directors to influence the founder of the company against the latter's "friendly attitude towards Kruger's government". As a "damning indictment of those journalists who sold out to Rhodes", Dormer wrote that he had parted with the Argus Group as the "most emphatic means" that were open to him, and "of marking my dissent from the policy of intervening in the affairs of the Transvaal on which Mr Rhodes had already made up his mind to embark".

By then, Rhodes "had wrapped himself firmly around sections of the press". Amongst those that were "bought" was the first daily newspaper to appear in Afrikaans, S.J. du Toit's *Het Dagblad*, "one of many to come from his pocket, just as years before he had financed Francis Dormer".

With its pro-Rhodes sentiments, Dormer feared that the Transvaal government would be forced to suppress *The Star*. That, Rhodes told him, "is exactly what I want: it will be another nail in their coffin". But

> Francis Dormer could only stare at the man who was willing to sacrifice a newspaper built on the sweat of others, not for the sake of principle but to prove a point. He now thought Rhodes guilty of a "vulgar passion for personal revenge" and capable "of working untold evil in the land".

He "lost" the encounter with Rhodes that day in De Aar, and "[f]earing what the future would hold for South Africa, he moved to Britain". Dormer died in 1928, retaining "a fervent interest in every facet of South African affairs".

Peacemaker journalist, educator and editor

It is an "irony of history" that one of those who withstood Rhodes' "siren song" was a humble man from King William's Town who, in his "dogged dedication" to his paper, became one of the outstanding newspeople of his day.[130] He was John Tengo Jabavu, introduced in the previous chapter, but someone who deserves a closer look.

John Tengo Jabavu
Source: http://www.thepresidency.gov.za/national-orders/recipient/john-tengo-jabavu-1859-1921

He is described as "peacemaker journalist, educator and editor" of SA's first independent black newspaper, *Imvo Zabantsundu*. He started his career during the 1880s, "when the twelve thousand blacks on the common voters' role in the colony had political clout" – later they would make up 47% of the electorate in five Eastern Cape constituencies.

Jabavu was described as a "determined black liberal" who played an influential role in politics and, "if rejected by a more sceptical generation of blacks, the love and integrity with which he set out to serve the cause of his people is a stirring story of South African journalism". In 1892 he was "unanimously" welcomed to the NPU and became for a period "a stalwart member".

His paper was his life's work. On his deathbed in 1921, he implored his son, Davidson Don Jabavu: "Write, and keep it going, Dave." According to his son, his last word, "Yomelelani" (Be of good cheer), was "an expression of faith which characterised his entire life and possibly made him trust men and not principles" – also because men would fail him, "culminating in the bitter blow" after Union when black people were excluded from the vote.

Jabavu was born near Fort Beaufort in 1859 and went to school at Lovedale. Because there was neither a table nor lamp in his parents' hut, he could not do homework and had to memorise his lessons. In Somerset East he became a "printer's devil" – an apprentice – in the office of the local newspaper and started contributing to Solomon's *Cape Argus*. The latter encouraged Jabavu and, in 1881, he edited the Lovedale missionary publication, *Isigidimi Samaxhosa*. He left after the mission would not allow political matter in the paper.

In 1884, at the age of 25, he was assisted by Rose-Innes's brother to establish *Imvo*. "A born editor, his white rivals could sometimes not credit *Imvo*'s leading articles as his own work." The *Port Elizabeth Telegraph* ridiculed it as containing "sesquipedalian words that no Kafir this side of the Tropic of Capricorn could understand or would use".

Jabavu "consistently showed Rhodes the door" because he knew it meant eventual control. This led to the establishment of a rival black paper by the magnate,[131] a time of "strange alliances in politics".[132] Jabavu broke with Rose-Innes in 1898, saying that men like Merriman and J.W. Sauer, whom he supported, "think that the honest, simple Dutch farmer is more to be depended upon for the ends all of us hold in common".

His paper was banned during the SAW. Jabavu, "darkly, and correctly", anticipated that "the new order of things which the present war is said to inaugurate" may mean the introduction of "artifices such as the Native Disfranchisement and the Franchise Act". He, as Dormer, realised the danger of polarisation in a volatile country like South Africa.[133] On 8 October 1902, in the first leading article after the ban on his paper was lifted, Jabavu made a "moving plea for racial peace and accommodation". The suspension of his paper by the British was a financial setback to him, but he fruitlessly petitioned for compensation. The only money he ever received "was twelve pounds from a visiting Quaker".

And then there was the matter with the NPU. His last attendance at a congress of the NPU seemed to have been in East London in 1905, when he was one of only eleven delegates.[134] In 1912, the NPU, responding to demands from "newcomers" – referring to the "aggressive New Zealander" Kingswell – barred all black people from membership. The NPU constitution was redrafted and Kingswell, also newly-elected vice-president, moved that "no coloured or native newspaper proprietor should be admitted as a member of this Union", adding that the word "European" should be added as a qualification for membership. "This conformed to practice in the all-white Transvaal printing industry of the time."

Technological advancement

The first telegraph cable in South Africa came into operation between Cape Town and Simonstown in 1905.[135] The *Argus* published the first exchange under the headline, "By Magnetic and Electric Telegraph". This technology "changed the known world, South Africa and newspapers".

In July 1866, after the laying of the Atlantic cable between Europe and America, *The Times* of London "foreshadowed" the sociologist McLuhan's "global village" by a hundred years:

> Thus is at length accomplished what deserves to be regarded as in many respects the most wonderful achievement of this victorious century ... It would suggest strange thoughts if we could view that slight rope lying insignificant and perhaps almost invisible in the vast depths of the Atlantic, motionless and apparently inanimate, and then reflect that by a still more tiny wire inside the life of the New and the Old World was pulsating to and fro ... For the purposes of mutual intercourse the whole world is fast becoming one vast city.

South Africa shared this "miracle" on Christmas Day in 1879, when a direct link was established between London and Cape Town. Although the technology was "[e]xpensive and erratic", it began the era of "hot news" and made newspaper offices "the centre of excitement in times of crisis". The availability of "facts as news" increased the rivalry between papers "previously content to be custodians of comment".[136] The telegraph service "became the core of the newspaper" and, with it, news agencies and the professional reporter. Although New York's *Transcript* had already singled itself out "as one of the few journals to employ reporters" in 1834, even the "best" South Africa's newspapers employed only "occasional reporters" and correspondents before 1860. Another "novelty" towards the end of the century was something called the interview. It became "a vogue", with a "prominent journalist" writing:

> The innovations which are distasteful to me include the system which has crept in, and is now largely adopted, of "interviewing" all sorts of people on every possible occasion ... This interviewing and perpetual presentation of private men as public characters by block portraiture are innovations imported from American journalism, which to my mind is no improvement in style to the early English.

The end of a tumultuous century

After the discovery of mineral resources, with the whole of South Africa "tilting" North, the press played an important role in this "tumult and ferment of an emerging South Africa, and in the crush of adventurers, idealists and oddballs".[137] It "mushroomed under a new crop of pioneers". By the time the century "slid to its end in a glitter of diamonds and gold edged by the grey of looming war, the press was established as a vigorous, if divided, presence".

The degree of technological sophistication was remarkable as, by the nineties e.g., the *Cape Times* printed more papers in a month "than the issues of all Cape newspapers put together amounted to in a year forty years ago". The old wooden flatbeds, "easy to transport by wagon, had held their own till about 1858", while gradually being replaced with iron hand presses. In 1854, Saul Solomon introduced the first steam press, 40 years after *The Times* of London. The *Cape Argus* had been printed by steam from its inception in 1857, and the following year four Cape newspapers made use of similar presses.[138] *The Advertiser* in Port Elizabeth installed a gas-driven press in 1875, and in Grahamstown Grocott and Sherry installed the first linotype press in 1899.

Printing material, especially paper, remained a problem, particularly outside Cape Town.[139] Moll and Boniface produced their *De Natalier* on paper that varied from red to yellow or green-tinted, and once even used wrapping paper and "stray" grocery paper bags. In 1887, the *Barberton Herald and Transvaal Mining Mail* occasionally "resorted to blotting paper when bad roads or weather delayed consignments". Its editor explained that they had tried "brown sugar paper", but "dry, it would not take ink, and wet, it broke". But print they did.

All in all, the second half of the century saw the establishment of most of South Africa's major newspapers and a rapid rise in the number of rural publications, so much so that "by 1900 scarcely a town of any size or importance in South Africa was without its press".

In 1885, Meurant Jnr. looked back on this achievement: "How much do editors and the public of the present day owe to the brave men who so manfully and uncompromisingly battled for, and eventually gained, the incalculable victory of the 'Free Press' of South Africa!"[140]

He referred, of course, to the "Magna Carta", Ordinance No 60 of the Cape of Good Hope in 1829.[141] It brought with it other freedoms, because "[t]he Star of democracy had risen and that of autocracy was hastening to its setting",[142] heralding a new era for the media in South Africa.[143] As was stated much later, the authorities were unable to curfew the evolution of the press from 1829 on.[144] Of course this "guarantee" for press freedom was only relative and would only last until a next government could put measures in place to curtail press freedom.

For about 50 years after the turn of the century and the forming of the Union, media freedom needs to be understood in the light of this colonial past and of being "influenced by the social mores of colonialism".[145] And it needs to be added that the only opinion that mattered, and the only interests catered for, were those of the white section of the population.

In the latter half of the new century, extremely restrictive press regulations were enforced under the NP government from 1948 to 1994. Malan, the first apartheid prime minister (and, from 1915 to 1924, first editor of the then Nationalist publication *De/Die Burger*), described the English press as the "most undisciplined in the world". He also suggested that journalists had to register like doctors.[146] His successor, Strijdom, would describe the English press as "South Africa's greatest enemy". Verwoerd, Strijdom's successor, in turn blamed the economic depression on the "irresponsible and unpatriotic behaviour of the English press".[147] The prohibitive press laws after 1948 were described as an "avalanche of security legislation" that created "a massive structure of censorship and self-censorship".[148]

But, by the turn of the century, the 19th century's hard-won press freedom could be celebrated with "hardly a town of any size without its own newspaper, the proprietor and editor often being one and the same person".[149] According to one scholar between 1800 and 1910, in total, approximately 639 newspapers were established in South Africa, with 79 "settlements" in the region that had "at one time or another" their own newspapers with 50% to 60% in the Cape Colony.[150] A "strong provincial and very independent press" developed, all of this largely due to the printing presses brought with them by the 1820 British Settlers, and the ensuing struggle for press freedom culminating in the "Magna Carta".[151] The foundation was laid for the development of the 20th century's press.

PART III

The unfreedoms of White Unionism and White Nationalism

The stronger, the freer and more independent the press,
the stronger and freer the country, but I wish the newspapers would
sometimes leave politics alone.

— General Jan Smuts (1870–1950), South African statesman

6. The period 1900 to 1948

The War, Union, Afrikaner Nationalism and partisan journalism on both sides of the language divide

Introduction

This chapter focuses on the developments after 1900, specifically the era spanning the formation of the Union of South Africa on 31 May 1910 up to the unexpected victory of the NP in May 1948.

The era after the turn of the century was marked by the development of two powerful political and societal forces, namely African Nationalism and Afrikaner Nationalism. As political parties, both were founded in the Free State. In hindsight, one can say the fact that they were established in a province with the name "Free State" symbolises both groups' yearning for freedom and the ideal of living, someday, in a "free state".

The ANC was founded as the South African Native National Congress (SANNC) in Bloemfontein on 8 January 1912, later to become the African National Congress. For the next fifty years they could organise themselves freely, until the party was banned and forced underground in 1961.[1] The NP was founded on 1 July 1914 as the National Party of the Orange Free State[2] by General J.B.M. (Barry) Hertzog, first as a provincial party, and later in the other three provinces. The Cape NP was founded last, in September 1915.[3] The NP's four federal parties had different views on Afrikaner Nationalism. This would later lead to internal strife and deep political rifts. It is not surprising that the NP's forerunners as the original two Afrikaner Nationalist movements were founded by the defeated Northern Afrikaners in the Transvaal and the Orange Free State. The first was Het Volk (The People), founded in Pretoria in 1904, followed by Orangia, in the Free State in 1905.[4]

The forming of the Union in 1910 heralded the next stage in South Africa's geopolitical development. The turn of the century, including the SAW from 1899 to 1902, was also key to the development of the media industry for the following period. The outbreak of the First World War shortly afterwards, in 1914, also had a formative impact.

For roughly the first half of the 20th century, media freedom needs to be understood in the light of the British colonial past of the previous century, with the following era also "influenced by the social mores of colonialism".[5] It needs to be stressed that the only opinion that mattered, and thus the only interests catered for, were those of the white population. From a British perspective, South African journalism had a "proud history", illustrated in the example of Edgar Wallace's "scoop of the century" when he broke news of the armistice in 1902 before the British parliament had been informed.[6]

The 1882 founding of the Newspaper Press Union (NPU) was also the first stage in the professionalisation that led to the formation of newspaper groups in the period following the founding of the Union.[7] In fact, as "in many societies around the world", politics and economic factors played key roles in shaping the history of the press during this time. While South Africa's natural riches were exploited, the struggle for control "over the pockets and the minds of people" manifested themselves in newspapers such as *The Star* and the RDM. Mining conglomerates and business enterprises funded and supported English newspapers, whereas Afrikaans newspapers, such as *De/Die Burger* in the South and *Ons Vaderland* in the North, both founded in 1915, were funded by the Afrikaner community for the community. During the first decades of the 20th century, it would not take long before "the cultural differences in the economically active white population group surfaced in the form of a strong English language press and a fledgling Afrikaans language press". "Nation building" among Afrikaners not only led to their empowerment, but also to apartheid, while, simultaneously, the Afrikaans press "reach[ed] economic maturity".

The riches of the Witwatersrand saw "millions of people" flocking there, developing it into an "economic powerhouse", while the black population "was completely negated as a press market". Jim Bailey, son of Rand Lord and newspaper owner Sir Abe, was one of the few publishers who later ventured into the black market. Another white entrepreneur, B.C. Paver, started the Bantu Press in 1932, but the company and its publications, *Ilanga* and *Ikwezi*, were soon "swallowed up" by the Argus Group.

Context

Before the formation of the Union, South Africa consisted of two British-controlled colonies plus two independent Boer Republics, the latter both defeated in the SAW. After the discovery of diamonds and gold, the region developed from an agricultural subsistence economy into an industrial one.

The mineral wealth of Southern Africa was not only irresistible to the British Empire, but it also needed the subterranean riches to sustain itself, leading to the SAW in which a "substantial percentage"[8] of the Boer Republics' Afrikaner population perished.

The "mineral revolution" is considered a turning point because of its economic, social and political consequences,[9] shifting the economic centre of gravity to the north. The majority of white inhabitants initially lived on farms or in hamlets across a vast area. By 1900, about 15% of the total South African white population was urbanised and Johannesburg already had a population of more than 100,000.[10]

The SAW was described as a "devastating instance of white-on-white violence" that stimulated and deepened racial divisions between Afrikaans- and English-speaking South Africans.[11] Imperialistic superiority towards Afrikaners, "deemed as inferior", unified them as a group. Their suppression resulted in a nationalist ideology "around the idea of ethnic supremacy", which ultimately developed into apartheid. The division between Afrikaners and English speakers in itself was a "racial problem".

When, by May 1902, the SAW had officially ended and mines could start producing again, the so-called "Uitlanders" could return to the Transvaal, although it was no longer a Republic but now was under British control, as was the Orange Free State, now known as the Orange River Colony. The British government supported the English-speaking community to re-establish itself as the "dominant white group", also through British officials administering the two new colonies. Simultaneously, British immigration was encouraged and the mining industry was rebuilt.[12]

The Transvaal Colony was granted "responsible government" from 1906 and the Orange River Colony a year later. In Transvaal, the Het Volk party was dominant, and in the Orange River Colony it was the Orangia Unie. This resulted in both colonies having Afrikaner governments under the leadership of Afrikaner prime ministers who were former SAW generals. They were Generals Louis Botha in the Transvaal and Barry Hertzog in the Orange River Colony. In the Cape Colony's 1908 elections, the South African Party (SAP) won the majority, and although John X. Merriman became prime minister, the real power resided with his ally, the Afrikaner Bond (as said, not to be confused with the Broederbond, which was formed later). Afrikaners therefore now formed the majority in three of the four colonial governments.

The SAW and the defeat of the Boer republics probably "did more to unite Afrikanerdom and to foster an Afrikaner nationalism than any other event in South African history".[13] After the Union, two main themes dominated the policies of all parties, namely the Union's position in relation to Great Britain and the Empire, and race relations. The power struggle between Afrikaners and the English was "[a]t the root of the constitutional question" and would overshadow the "Native issue" until 1948. The main concern of both groups was that one or the other "would enforce its own cultural and political pattern on the whole society". In 1910, Botha, "an Afrikaner and a moderate" and first Union prime minister, tried "conciliation between English and Afrikaner". A large number of Afrikaners, in the Free State and Transvaal particularly, did not support him. This led to Hertzog's NP, with its "South Africa first!" policy, putting the interests of South Africa before those of the Empire in 1914. The SAP represented "urban industrial interests and wealthier farmers"; the NP the rural and urban Afrikaner proletariat and the "new Afrikaner intelligentsia". Thanks to the NP's Pact with the Labour Party, described as the "English-speaking party of White labour", it would govern between 1924 and 1933. In 1933, an internal NP breach between Hertzog and the "Malanites" under D.F. Malan widened, especially after Smuts and Hertzog reunited as coalition government that year. This led to Malan's "Purified" NP, while Hertzog and Smuts formed the United South African National Party or United Party (UP) in 1934. But, with the Second World War, Hertzog in 1948 again joined Malan's NP in the now newly constituted Herenigde Nasionale or Volksparty (HNP), which went on to win the 1948 election.

'Vote British!' vs. 'South Africa First!'

Because of internal divisions after the SAW, English-speakers now were the apathetic group regarding politics and did not participate as a unified group in the National Convention of 1908/1909 to form a new constitutional dispensation.[14] Consequently, the Union was politically dominated by Afrikaners. The new South African Party (SAP) that was founded in 1910 united the old SAP, the Afrikaner Bond and Het Volk, with Afrikaners constituting the majority. Under Botha and Smuts, the new SAP had a "South African-oriented policy", based on principles of equality and cooperation between the two white groups. English Natalians, on the other hand, supported independent candidates under the slogan "We are British". In the rest of South Africa, most English-speakers voted for Leander Starr Jameson's Unionist Party, representing British capitalism. Their slogan, "Vote British!", was supported by the mining magnates and the English press; the aim was to strengthen British influence. To complicate matters, the politics of the new Union was soon, in 1914, dominated by Britain declaring war on Germany. Union prime minister Botha had the support of the Unionists and the Labour Party in his support of Britain. But his support led directly to the founding of the first provincial NP under Hertzog in the Free State in 1914. The English were "alarmed", particularly because of Hertzog's "South Africa First!" slogan.

These events led to the formation of the first Afrikaner Nationalist press house, founded in 1915 as De Nationale Pers, Beperkt (The National Press, Limited), soon to become Nasionale Pers, and later Naspers. Today it is a global technology giant,[15] with a spin-off listed as Prosus on the Euronext bourse in Amsterdam in 2019.[16]

In summary, the events after the turn of the century concluded a "bloody century" in South Africa's colonial history, with not "a decade without armed conflict in the bloody 100 years of the pacification and then unification of the region, from Britain's second and lasting occupation of 1806 to Union in 1910, which formalised the single multi-province state of South Africa".[17]

The press post-1900

The press in South Africa in the first decade of the 1900s has been described as the "post-Boer War Press".[18] It consisted of a strong English sector, thanks to its imperial colonial and mining capital support, a fledgling and parochial Afrikaans sector, and a similarly struggling African sector. The "muted" English papers in the north found their voice "anew" after the SAW. Cities were the domain of English capital and their papers reflected these interests. Besides, the two Cape Town dailies, the *Argus* and the *Cape Times,* as well as the Durban-based *Natal Mercury* and Johannesburg's RDM, "support[ed] the imperial ideal".

Rand Lord and mining magnate Sir Abe Bailey financed the RDM in 1902, and in 1906 launched the *Sunday Times*. Like its sister publication, the *Sunday Times* professed to be "loyal [to Britain] to the fingertips" and "Imperialistic to the backbone". These two papers would later become the foundation of the South African Associated Newspapers (SAAN). But it was the Argus Group that expanded rapidly, establishing several papers across the country. In terms of workforce, by 1921 60% of SA's skilled printing craftsmen were British nationals "who had emigrated to warmer climes".[19]

The so-called "British journalistic tradition" was followed at the English papers, with editors and journalists described as "well educated and highly literate".[20] And: "No matter how hard they tried to hide it", they tended to look down on "colonials", considering them to be "lesser breeds". This meant they were "usually quite out of touch with the outlook of Afrikaners and also smugly oblivious of the inequities inflicted on non-whites". While the typical British-born English editor was "well equipped with Greek and Latin quotations",

> his accomplishments did not include the faintest smattering of Afrikaans. Nor had he the slightest inkling of what the Afrikaners thought and felt about matters,

although he was aware of their existence as a group which could be a nuisance as harriers on the flanks of the advancement of the British cause.

Such attitudes "obviously rankled among Afrikaners". Not only did the pro-British slant of the English papers "distress" them, but the papers also portrayed a South Africa focused mainly on powerful financial interests, including the mining industry. This was "evident in both the management of the papers and their editorial policy". Indeed, it was the policy of the daily press "that *ipso facto* whatever is best for the gold mines is best for South Africa as a whole, and that is kept ever foremost in mind".

It is thus no wonder that language and ethnicity have played an important role in the formation of South Africa's press.[21] In the first two decades of the 20th century,

> a political and cultural power struggle took place between the British conquerors, their business interests and their press on the one hand; and the impoverished Afrikaner community which struggled to survive as a group and to assert its own identity and language on the other hand. This formed the basis for the historical division between the Afrikaans and English press.

This situation would last for almost a century, and the division could be bridged only by professional journalism and the democratisation process in the 1990s. But the events at the beginning of the 20th century laid the foundation for the "remarkable dichotomy in politics, with almost all the English daily newspapers supporting white liberal, capitalist-inclined political policies and almost all Afrikaans newspapers being National Party-orientated" – in other words, both English and Afrikaans press were biased towards their own partisan interests. And not to forget: The ailing black press was left to its own devices.

1910 - an un-united Union and a divided country

The establishment of the Union ushered in a new era and was meant to achieve reconciliation between "Boer and Brit in a unitary state".[22] Botha led the first cabinet, with an even split between the two language groups. The new constitution also called for equal status for English and Dutch in official business, as well as a bilingual civil service. Under Hertzog's influence, the Afrikaners campaigned for Dutch as language of education in public schools. Up to that point, English was the only language of education. Hertzog's speeches, with the message "South Africa First!", prioritised South African interests. When the war between Germany and England broke out in 1914, the conflict increased, as the Boers saw their allegiance with Germany rather than with an Empire that robbed them of their Republics. This led to a Rebellion by some Afrikaners in the North.

Still, there was some common front for the press in the form of the NPU. In "numerous skirmishes" with officialdom, the NPU was "the shield behind which the independence of the press, at least, remained intact".[23] The position of a fragmented press without this protection "can be left to the imagination". But it was not a safe haven for all. With its centenary in 1982, the NPU was assessed as having gone through various phases in its hundred years – "not all of which spelt progress". One was when, in 1912, a key NPU congress "brushed aside" the contribution of John Tengo Jabavu and barred black editors and proprietors from membership, a ruling only reversed in the 1970s.

The NPU and a new era

Although the NPU almost did not survive the SAW, the groundwork for a "new future" was also laid at the 1912 congress, its thirteenth, in Bloemfontein.[24] There were now 247 publications, and the printing and newspaper industry employed a total of 4,650 people. The 1912 congress was the watershed, spelling "a decided break with the past". It

> marked the end of the "Colonial" press and of the influence and dominance of the eastern province and the emergence of the north, with larger, professionally-managed companies in a leading role. The era of the editor-owner, of the men who wrote their leading articles with printer's ink on their fingers, was finally over.

During the "disjointed times" of the SAW and immediately after, the NPU kept going, thanks to rural papers, while the bigger publications "stood aside". When the NPU met at Grahamstown in 1902, its first gathering since 1898, only six of the 34 members attended. By 1905, membership dropped to 23, with eleven delegates attending the congress at East London. At the 1910 congress, membership stood at sixteen, but only seven delegates attended, "star[ing] despondently at one another past the empty seats". But in Bloemfontein in 1912, there was a "bustle of forty-four delegates from all over the country and even from Moçambique, at the largest congress ever". Membership now numbered 52, with the enthusiasm "generated by the excitement of a new political dispensation as symbolised by the Union of South Africa".

It was the "old stalwarts" of the Eastern Province, from where six of the first eight NPU presidents came, who initiated the move to turn the union into a national body. They pointed out to the "Transvalers, maybe thinking that was where their hearts lay, that the commercial and administrative aspects of newspapers have become as important as the journalistic side". Before, only 27 out of 87 major papers had NPU membership. The Northerners joined and, for the first time, the Cape was outnumbered. The congress signalled "a telling shift in priorities of a surging press" and "a more complex world". Membership was now corporate and limited to the proprietors of papers and their representatives – editors were excluded. The objectives of the new NPU constitution did not mention the protection of members "in the proper discharge of their public duty", but rather reflected "an emphasis on the hard-headed promotion of newspaper business interest". Fortnightly and monthly publications were regarded as "detrimental to these" and were excluded.

From this new beginning in 1912, "a welter of newspapers" and "four press groups, each with its distinctive history and character", sprang up. With the NPU's 1982 centenary, they were still intact, namely the Argus Group and SAAN on the English side, with Nasionale Pers and Perskor on the Afrikaans side. These four groups would play significant roles in the political development of South Africa in the first half of the 20th century.

A complex situation

The South African press, caught between two World Wars in the first half of the century, found itself in a complex situation. South Africa entered each war on a "split vote".[25] There was at least one editor who was in the chair during both wars: Langley Levy of the *Sunday Times*. As ex-*Sunday Times* editor Joel Mervis wrote:

Although no statistics are available, one can safely assume that few newspaper editors in office during August 1914, at the outbreak of the Great War, would be holding the same post twenty-five years later when World War II began. Langley Levy of the *Sunday Times* was one of the few. This would enable him to add to his curriculum vitae: "Highly experienced in Global War journalism."

Besides South Africa entering the war on a "split vote", other "piquant similarities" were that the two political leaders common to both wars, Generals Jan Smuts and Barry Hertzog, were also SAW heroes. In 1914, Smuts favoured South Africa's entry on the side of Britain, while Hertzog "vigorously" opposed it. This would happen again in 1939: Smuts for, Hertzog against, and on "each occasion Parliament rejected Hertzog". This meant that, in both World Wars, the government had to deal with a "hostile, disloyal and at times violent" group opposing South Africa's participation – the Afrikaners. This led to further polarisation of the South African media and how they reported on the wars. In both wars, the *Sunday Times* and RDM, e.g., were among the papers that supported the government, playing an important part "in the propaganda war on the Home Front".

For the greater part of World War I, newspapers in Britain and her dominions reported news as it was received in its censored form, "with all the distortions that flowed from official army communiques".[26] This censorship on the side of Britain meant "an uncritical attitude in the press, with the result that the enormous loss of life, the prolonged, pointless battles, and the type of strategy employed were simply accepted as the inevitable consequence of war". The press in South Africa "faced one complication that the others were spared, namely, a rebellious, hostile opposition". The SA English papers found "at least some cause for rejoicing" in 1914, as, after the suppression of the rebels, Botha invaded German South West Africa and scored "a brilliant victory".

It was precisely these circumstances in 1914/1915 that led to the creation of the Afrikaans press, not only to express Afrikaner Nationalism, but also literally as opposition to the loyal English South African press. This ensconced the binary positions of the opposing press groups for most of the 20th century.

The development of the Afrikaans press - an overview

The Afrikaans press really came into being after the devastation of the SAW and the wave of Afrikaner Nationalism experienced with the outbreak of the First World War.[27] The impetus for the development of Afrikaner Nationalism was closely linked to being "economically subservient" to the English financial and mining houses.[28] The close links between the English press and the mining houses – the original "agent of the destruction" of the two Boer republics – meant the English press were "enemies and not to be trusted", especially with the Northern Afrikaners "a defeated and impoverished nation". The Milner policy of anglicising the country, including using English as sole language of instruction in schools, added to their resentment. Milner implemented an immigration policy to ensure English dominance, also seen as British political and cultural domination. All of this was "a major spur to Afrikaner Nationalism" and the development of Afrikaner Nationalist papers.

Not surprisingly, the first Afrikaner Nationalist paper was founded in the North, in Pretoria in 1912. Harm Oost's *Die Week* (*The Week*) was dedicated to supporting "political, cultural, and economic agencies" to "rehabilitate" the Afrikaner people. It went bankrupt after two years, but Oost became involved in the Het Volk (The People) political party and backed

Hertzog's NP, established in 1914. When the Rebellion broke out after the declaration of support for Britain in the First World War, Afrikaner Nationalism was born, exacerbated by the execution of Jopie Fourie. In fact, two days before his execution in December 1914, influential Capetonians got together to discuss the forming of a "mouthpiece" for Afrikaner Nationalism[29] – the beginning of what would become Naspers.

While the English press "was beginning its period of contraction", including its monopolistic tendencies, the Afrikaans press was only really beginning to grow[30] and was "inextricably" linked from its start to the cause of Afrikaner Nationalism. In the late 1800s, *Die Patriot* was associated with Afrikaner Nationalism in the broadest sense, including language, the development of group consciousness and Afrikaner culture, but the Afrikaans press in the first part of the 1900s became associated "with a very much narrower and more emotional idea of nationalism, centred on the creation of a political party".

Hertzog broke with the SAP already in 1912, but it was with the establishment of *De Burger* in 1915 that "the Nationalists founded a true party organ". Its first editor was Malan, a DRC minister who "left the pulpit" to edit *De Burger*. Besides "great difficulty" in raising the necessary capital, the company could not even find a willing printer for its paper, let alone advertisements among the hostile Cape English businesses.[31] Coincidentally, the *Transvaal Leader* closed down in 1915 and the newly founded company could buy the equipment from the *Cape Times* company through a third party to whom the *Leader* belonged – and who was blissfully ignorant of the fact that it was intended for the new Afrikaner paper.

Also in 1915, *Die Vaderland* was started in Pretoria as a bi-weekly with the same Nationalist purpose under the editorship of SAW hero General J.C.G. Kemp. Kemp was followed by Harm Oost, who, like Malan at *Die Burger*, remained editor until 1924, when he was also elected to Parliament.[32] In 1931, *Die Vaderland* was taken over by the new Afrikaanse Pers Beperk. With the turmoil in Afrikaner politics, the paper moved to Johannesburg in 1936, now to support the UP. A year later, *Die Transvaler* was founded as mouthpiece of the NP through a Naspers-led Cape initiative, and as a result of the conflict within Afrikanerdom. In its first issue, on 1 October 1937, H.F. Verwoerd, its editor, declared in an editorial that the newspaper had a mission to serve the "Volk" and to ensure that the voice of "sublime nationalism" be heard. Race and republicanism were emphasised. Verwoerd proved "to be more militant and extreme than the Cape Nationalists, including Malan, had intended".

These events in the development of the Afrikaans press came about as a result of political realignments, with, eventually, the split in the UP government about South Africa's participation in the Second World War in 1939. When Hertzog and Havenga formed the Afrikaner Party, only *Die Vaderland*, of all the Afrikaans-language newspapers, gave the former Boer general its support. *Die Transvaler* and the Naspers papers supported Malan and rising star Strijdom. By 1948, "[s]ome measure of unity was achieved" when the Afrikaans press joined together again to support the election of an all-Afrikaner government. In 1951, the Afrikaner Party had merged again with the NP, but it was not until 1962 that *Die Vaderland* was "to be drawn wholly back into the fold". This was also when Afrikaanse Pers Beperk (1962) was formed to incorporate both *Die Vaderland* and the major Afrikaans Sunday newspaper, *Dagbreek*.

In 1947, Marius Jooste, then advertising manager of *Die Vaderland*, resigned to create *Dagbreek*, financed by English business capital and mining interests. *Dagbreek* was meant as "a politically independent" Sunday paper. By the end of its first year, *Dagbreek* acquired the Afrikaanse Pers Beperk's unsuccessful *Sondagnuus*, but by 1951 many of its shares were in the hands of Transvaal Nationalists, with *Dagbreek* becoming an openly Nationalist paper. Amidst speculation that the Argus Group or Naspers might attempt a takeover of Afrikaanse Pers when it suffered financial difficulties in 1962, it was *Dagbreek* that succeeded in amalgamating the "old Afrikaner wing" and the Transvaal wing of the NP. But, by 1965, Naspers indeed decided to do something that "could no longer be stalled": the Cape Nationalists crossed the Vaal and launched the national Sunday paper, *Die Beeld*, headquartered in Johannesburg.

A renowned Afrikaans editor, Willem Wepener, later averred that the Afrikaans press was not founded as a commercial venture.[33] Yet the commercial imperative was clearly always there, even though it was concealed as "volkskapitalisme" (people's capitalism) in the beginning. The main purpose of its press was to be in service of Afrikaner Nationalism, illustrated by its appointment of editors who, in the beginning, were not chosen for their journalistic ability, but because of their party political stature.[34] Several leading figures were directors of the Afrikaans press companies – as, similarly, mining elite were found on the boards of the English companies. In fact, some boards were dominated by the secretive Broederbond, said to be the power behind the throne regarding Afrikaner politics in every respect.

A case study in crowd funding

Die Burger's founding in 1915 was considered to be "the Cape voice of Afrikaner nationalism", as the paper was established "by wealthy professional men who needed a means to air their political views as well as a potential business enterprise for their capital".[35] Because the paper promoted Afrikaner nationalism, it did "not receive a warm welcome from the powerful anglicised minority within Cape Town", with a call in 1917 for an advertising boycott of the paper. At one stage, shares were peddled on the Cape Parade on a Saturday morning – what can be described as an earlier version of today's digital crowd funding.[36]

Up until the mid-1980s, the company served as "perhaps the best example of the history and function of the Afrikaans press".[37] A group of sixteen influential Cape and Boland Afrikaners gathered in Stellenbosch on 18 December 1914, unbeknownst to them two days before the execution of Jopie Fourie, who would become a martyr in the lore of Afrikanerdom.[38] Besides well-to-do Cape Afrikaners among the founders who initially secured some start-up funding, the company relied on "crowd-funding": Members of the Afrikaner community were called upon to buy shares. But the impoverished Afrikaners could barely afford the £1 shares. Still, "tactically it was considered essential to involve large numbers of individual Afrikaners" in the undertaking.[39] The principle of "crowd-funding" was already proven through the highly successful Helpmekaar (Help One Another) Fund, founded to pay damages and fines after the 1914 Rebellion. This fund is still so strong that, one century later, it provides students (of all races) who study in Afrikaans with bursaries.[40] From 2008 to 2010, it paid out bursaries worth an average of R10,5 million per year, and in 2010 about 766 students benefitted from it. In 2011, it was R124,8 million strong.

The "less than promising circumstances"[41] under which the company and paper were founded were due to martial law and the fact that the Cape business community was anti-Afrikaans. Together with the well-established *Argus* and *Cape Times*, businesses did everything they could to ensure the new company would fail. At the time, the *Argus* printed about 15,000 copies compared to *Die Burger*'s 3,000. Also, the latter paper's potential readers were not used to reading a daily paper. Many of them lived in rural areas and out of reach of the paper.[42] A culture of reading, together with the culture of reading a daily, had to be built, and this was done through establishing a magazine in 1916. Other publications soon followed, along with a book club and the cultivation of literature, initially in Dutch/ Afrikaans, and later in Afrikaans only. *Burger* editor Malan was never involved in the day-to-day running of the newspaper; indeed, he confessed that he did not know how to do this.[43] Still, his role as "editor", though only in name, and as party leader was seamless. Naspers's first newspaper – from 1922 in Afrikaans as *Die Burger* – soon had sister publications, also in other parts of the country, such as the company's first acquisition, *Die Volksblad* (today just *Volksblad* and since August 2020 only digitally available) in 1917, together with its printing and publishing works in Bloemfontein. A Pietermaritzburg-based paper and publishing works followed in 1918.[44]

The reason for acquiring the Natal paper and printing company in 1918 was because the NP failed to win a single seat in Natal in the 1915 elections.[45] In the midst of the flu epidemic in September 1918, Nationalist fervour was high, and the biweekly Dutch-Afrikaans *De Afrikaner*, established in Pietermaritzburg in 1904, was bought. Naspers managed the company from its *Volksblad* Bloemfontein offices[46] and also started a branch of its bookshop in Pietermaritzburg.

This sequence of events all started when Hertzog was forced out of Botha's cabinet in 1912, with the subsequent 1914 founding of the NP as the first event "in a series which characterised South African politics for the rest of the century".[47] In 1924, barely ten years after the establishment of Naspers, the NP won the general elections, albeit with a pact with another party, and repeated this success in 1929. In 1933, Hertzog again joined Smuts, to form the UP – the "Smelters" – while Malan led the "purified" NP "into the political wilderness". The "purified" Nationalists were "convincingly defeated in 1938 and even more overwhelmingly in 1943".

This period in the history of South Africa is described as "a study in power" – "hardly less important to newspapermen than it is to politicians", proving "how a so-called powerful Press becomes powerless when faced by a running tide of political opinion which it seeks to oppose". When Hertzog formed the NP in 1914, he could claim the support of only one paper, namely *Die Burger*, although only to be established one year later. The paper had an extremely small circulation, while the English papers in every province had an overwhelming majority of readers, making Hertzog for a decade "the target of constant attack and condemnation", with English readers being saturated with anti-Nationalist propaganda. Yet, in 1924, the NP, together with its Labour Party pact, "handsomely" defeated the Smuts government. Although the English papers "did their best", the "will of the people (assisted by a loaded vote in rural constituencies)" gave the Nationalist-Labour Pact a majority of 27 in Parliament.[48]

These "binaries and paradoxes of power and politics" had a clear impact on news flow and press freedom, to the effect that, in 1933, the two arch-enemies of politics, Hertzog and Smuts, fused the NP and the SAP into a single UP, which achieved "what was thought unattainable", namely a two-thirds majority in parliament.[49]

At the same time, the so-called Native Vote Bill, the Representation of Natives Act No 12 of 1936, "illustrated once again a piquant characteristic of politics, namely that promises, pledges and principles are seldom worth the paper they are written on". After twenty years of bitter animosity "that sprang from apparently irreconcilable principles", Hertzog and Smuts "suddenly discover[ed] they held the same views".

The Broederbond, the Malanazis, and Afrikaner politics

Another role player in the flow of news and press freedom in South Africa came from the formation of a secretive Afrikaner organisation in 1918, founded among Northern, more conservative, Afrikaners.[50]

Called the Broederbond (Band of Brothers), the founders were mostly young Afrikaners and, in a patriarchal Calvinist society, it was only open to men. It was at the height of the forming years of organised Afrikaner Nationalism, with the memories still fresh of the devastating SAW, the outbreak of the First World War in 1914, and the Rebellion.[51] The Broederbond's main purpose was to maintain and secure a separate, "pure-white" Afrikaner nation. It wanted to establish Afrikaner domination and rule South Africa, to "Afrikanerise" English South Africans, and ensure a white South African nation "to be built on [the] rock of the Afrikaner *volk* with the Broederbond as the hard core of that rock".[52]

As South Africa developed during the following years, Afrikaner Nationalism became more pronounced and developed into different strands. In the 1930s, the split between Hertzog (the Northern Nationalists) and Malan (the Southern Nationalists) almost led to a hostile takeover of Naspers, which in the meantime re-registered from De Nationale Pers to become Nasionale Pers in 1922.

In this period, the Hertzog faction's mouthpiece in the North was *Ons Vaderland*, renamed *Die Vaderland*. Naspers now had to establish a mouthpiece for the Malan faction in the North. This was done through the cleverly chosen name Voortrekkerpers, with *Die Transvaler* launched as a daily in 1937. Its editor was Verwoerd, a sociology professor from Stellenbosch.[53] That same year, Naspers also launched a mouthpiece for the party in the Eastern Cape, namely *Die Oosterlig*.

The *Sunday Times* called the "purified" NP the "Malanazis", which infuriated the NP, but the paper persisted in using the term until the outbreak of the Second World War in 1939.[54] The use of such an emotive word was "an indication of the vigour" with which the *Sunday Times* "entered the fray".

The development of the black press

As with Afrikaner Nationalist publications, African Nationalist publications also were organs of their political affiliation and the beginning of the 1900s saw new developments regarding the black press voicing African Nationalism. Following Jabavu's *Imvo*, John Dube founded the *Ilanga Lase Natal* in 1904. Both Jabavu and Dube "established traditions of forthright discussion".[55] Others followed, significantly *Abantu-Batho*, published as mouthpiece by the SANNC.

Abantu-Batho (The People, 1912–1931) was "closely associated" with the ANC and became the official organ of the Transvaal Native Congress (TNC) in 1918, and in 1928 the official mouthpiece of the national ANC.[56] It condemned the 1913 Natives' Land Act, which reduced Africans to "penury and want". Unfortunately, by the mid-1930s, most of the "independent ANC-aligned" publications had either collapsed or been taken over by the white-owned media conglomerate Bantu Press. The estimated circulation of commercial newspapers such as *Bantu World* at this time was only 2,500,[57] and by 1951 the number of African newspapers had declined to seven, all white-owned. Advertising profits, tapping rising urbanisation, fuelled press monopolies and moderated political journalism, while the state's efforts "to assert political hegemony by encouraging a compliant African middle class" increased. Still, "white media domination was challenged by the resilience of an ANC-aligned, non-racial press that sought to represent a national constituency" with a growing portion of workers.

The first African labour union, the Industrial and Commercial Workers' Union (ICU), was formed in 1919. It had two publications, the *Black Man*, in 1920, and the *Workers' Herald*, from 1923 to 1928. *Black Man*'s editor, S.M. Bennett Ncwana, was "sporadically active in the ANC and ICU" and also wrote for *Abantu-Batho*. *Black Man* promoted what was called "Pan-African unionism". *African World*, published in Cape Town from 1925 to 1926, was founded by Western Cape ANC president James Thaele "with the Garveyist slogan 'Africa for Africans'".

Abantu-Batho still served as official mouthpiece of the ANC during the 1920s.[58] The "militant ANC president", Josiah Gumede, purchased a controlling share in the paper in 1929 to provide the party "with a viable organ". In 1930 and 1931, he and fellow editor Daniel Letanka, jailed after a strike in 1918, maintained "an often radical editorial approach". *Abantu-Batho* closed in July 1931, but many of its staff joined *Bantu World*, ensuring "the survival of radical African nationalism". Gilbert Coka, a "radical journalist", referred to a "tide of nationalism" led by *Abantu-Batho* as "truly national newspaper". Still, the ANC during this time "relied almost entirely on the spoken word to get its message across". *Abantu-Batho*'s press was also used to print the *African Leader* (1932–1933), launched as an "unofficial ANC organ". In turn, it incorporated *Ikwezi Le Afrika* (Africa Morning Star, 1928–1932), another pro-ANC paper. *Izwi Lama Afrika* (Voice of Africa, 1931–1932) was published in East London, devoting its space to local issues and declaring "to do away with ... [the] radicalism which is the bane of this country". *Umlindi We Nyanga* (Monthly Watchman, 1936–1941) was also published in East London and expressed "a similar ambivalence toward workers". It was controlled by white business interests and edited by Eastern Cape political leader Richard Godlo. While *Imvo Zabantsundu* earlier on "had little sympathy for the ANC and even less for workers", this changed in 1921, when Alexander Jabavu became editor. He, "unlike his father", expressed loyalty to "the famous ANC".

'Monopolistic tendencies'

Another phenomenon developed in South Africa during the early part of the century, namely "monopoly capitalism".[59] A century later, the term "white monopoly capital" would resonate in democratic South Africa, but the origins can already be found in the gold mining industry of a century ago, which came to dominate the South African economy as a whole.

The media sector did not escape this trend. After the Union in 1910, small, independent newspapers were "swallowed up" by groups, growing larger and larger. This led to press monopolies that only increased their footprint in the second half of the century. The result: The news flow to the South African public was dominated for decades by five media institutions. On the print side they were the Big Four: the Argus Group, SAAN (later Times Media Ltd., [TML]) Naspers and Perskor. In the electronic field, the SABC developed into a state broadcaster, rather than a public broadcaster. Up to the 1980s, the Argus Group was "arguably the most important", as it controlled more major newspapers and other media assets than any of the others.

The already mentioned Saul Solomon, "liberal" Cape Parliamentarian, was behind the initial formation of the Group, which started as the *Argus* paper in Cape Town in 1857. The influence of mining capital started with the transfer of ownership to Francis Dormer in 1881, with Rhodes backing Dormer, as discussed in the previous chapter. The newspaper now promoted "Rhodes' imperialistic dreams, his mining-financial interests and his political career". From the Dormer era onward, the *Argus* furthered capitalist interest – more specifically, that of mining capital. When Rhodes' interest shifted to the Witwatersrand's gold fields, the *Argus* followed. It is said that the "real birth" of the Argus Group started with *The Star* in Johannesburg in 1889. *The Star* not only served as "the voice of mining-capital but also of British imperialism". This led to the shutting down of the paper during the SAW, only for it to reopen after "British imperialism had successfully conquered the Transvaal". In 1910, when the Union was formed, the Argus Group was "solidly entrenched" in South Africa's two main cities, Cape Town and Johannesburg. Over the next forty years, the company acquired papers in Durban (1918), Kimberley (1922), Pretoria (1929) and Bloemfontein (1947), as well as in many towns in both Southern Rhodesia (Zimbabwe) and Northern Rhodesia (Zambia). In 1910, shareholding within the Argus Group "clearly revealed that this was the voice of mining-capital in the new unified South Africa". Rhodes' legacy was perpetuated in the form of shares held by companies formed by him. The gold mining industry, represented by companies as well as mining magnates, dominated. In 1910, these key shareholders were Johannesburg Consolidated Investments (JCI), the Joel Brothers (closely associated with JCI), J.B. Robinson, the Barnato Brothers, the Corner House Group, and Otto Beit (brother of Alfred Beit, a close Rhodes associate). In terms of the Argus Group's gold-mining control, this was "still a pattern" until 1991, shortly before democratisation, despite "changes in the actual number of shares held by different companies and individuals connected to mining-capital". The Argus Group newspapers "therefore supported those governments and political parties who served (and continue to serve) 'English' mining capitalist interests". These were the governments of Louis Botha, Jan Smuts, the Smuts-Hertzog Pact, and parties like the UP, and later the PFP and DP. In 1931, the Argus Group "clearly revealed" its "continued adherence" to Rhodes' "imperialist aims" in Africa through the creation of the Argus Voting Trust (AVT). The AVT's "stated goal" was to keep die company "in the hands of those sympathetic to British control".

The other English language group, which started out with two papers, became SAAN and changed its name to Times Media Limited (TML) in 1987 as part of a restructuring process.[60] The group was founded in 1906 with Sir Abe Bailey gaining control of both the RDM and the *Sunday Times*. Both were described as "products of the new South Africa in which Britain had succeeded, through the war of 1899–1902, in placing all of Southern Africa under a Pax Britannica". Johannesburg's gold fields represented "the heart of this new British order".

Bailey, besides making his fortune in mining, was also a Member of the Transvaal Parliament from 1908 to 1910. From 1910 to 1924 he was an MP for the Unionist Party, the latter "strongly advocat[ing] pro-British imperialist interests".

In 1920 the "Bailey group" and Argus "agreed to split the market" and to "consult" on advertising. It was also agreed that the Argus Group would not compete in the morning market, while the "Bailey group" would leave the afternoon market to Argus – an agreement "that held for six decades". The so-called "Morning Newspapers" was a pooled news-gathering service for the RDM, *Cape Times*, *Natal Mercury* and *Sunday Times*. From the 1920s throughout the 1940s, the "Bailey group" could "generically be seen to have supported the idea of building a South Africa closely tied to London, dominated by English-speakers, and in which whites ruled over blacks".

SAAN was officially formed in 1955 when the Rand Daily Mail Ltd. and the Sunday Times Syndicate Ltd. were amalgamated – "finally consummating a marriage that had existed since 1906". The main SAAN shareholder in 1955 was the Bailey-owned Union & Rhodesian Mining and Finance Co Ltd., with just under 50% of shares.[61]

Whereas the English press looked after its mining/imperialist/capitalist interests, the Afrikaans press developed along "an organised petite bourgeoisie-line". But, like its English counterpart, it was "fiercely focused" on its constituents' interests. In that respect, there was no difference between the two opposing groups, including intra-party and intra-partisan politics to suit the needed outcomes.

On the Afrikaans side, the two main players were Cape-based Nasionale Pers (commonly referred to as Naspers and since 1998 officially registered as Naspers) and the Transvaal-based Perskor. They respectively supported the Southern and Northern versions of Afrikaner Nationalism. The Cape-based company was founded as a direct result of Afrikaner Nationalism, flourishing after the outbreak of the First World War in 1914.[62] In fact, this was the beginning of the "ideological machinery of southern nationalism":[63]

> This new Afrikaner nationalism soon discovered it had no media voice. As a result [the Afrikaans press] was launched as an attempt to break the monopoly over news held by newspapers which were pro-British imperialism and pro-Milner's economic order (an economic order which disadvantaged Hertzog's supporters).

Naspers's financial structure was "in stark contrast" to that of the English papers.[64] "Thousands of pamphlets" were distributed in 1915 in an attempt to raise the necessary capital, yet "great difficulty was encountered in finding subscribers for the new company". But, just after the halfway mark of the century, by 1953, the issued capital of Naspers was £400,000, divided into £1 shares, with the shares registered in the names of 3,239 shareholders. The largest were the Santam-Sanlam Group, the "consortium of all-Afrikaner enterprises in the insurance field", established to support Afrikaner financial empowerment. Santam-Sanlam held 21,67% of the shares, while 10,93% were held by 2,690 shareholders, each with fewer than 100 shares. This spread of shares "most clearly reflected the economic position of the Afrikaners", who were without any capital, unlike the "financier backing" of the English press. Also, conditions regulating the transfer of shares, even in very small numbers, reflected the political rather than profit commitment of the directors of the company, as the "company director" was accorded the right to refuse to transfer or register any share. This term in the company's Articles of Association ensured the continuation of company policy. Shareholders were allowed a maximum of 50 votes at a meeting, no matter how many shares they held. To ensure that "no one unsympathetic" to the company's policy could vote, share sales and transfers were investigated, with the background of the buyer "thoroughly examined". Prospective shareholders would be asked for which party they voted, "and there were indeed instances when share transfers were refused". Still, even despite Naspers' "indisputable political associations and affiliations", its board of directors included the smallest number of party politicians of any newspaper group, including the English groups. By June 1956, only one cabinet minister, C.R. Swart – leader of the Free State NP, served on its board, with only one other political "representative", the president of the Senate, C.A. van Niekerk. The other members were from the Santam-Sanlam Group and Naspers itself. Regarding Naspers, there

> is evidence in the style particularly of *Die Burger* and in the attitudes of the newspaper to the National Party, that the low count of party-political men on [its] board ... had some effect on the running of [its] newspapers. [Naspers] created the most successful financial formula for its newspapers of any of the Afrikaans newspaper companies.

The company was described as "a pioneering example" of the "volkskapitalisme" phenomenon developing between the two World Wars.[65] "Volkskapitalisme" mobilised the savings of middle- and working-class Afrikaners to develop "Afrikaner economic institutions". It did not challenge capitalism *per se*, but challenged "English" (imperial) control of South African capital, with the objective to develop "parallel institutions alongside 'English' institutions". This manifested in the Reddingsdaadbond (Rescue Union), Volkskas (a bank), Santam, Sanlam, the Afrikaanse Handelsinstituut (AHI; Afrikaans Trade Institute), Federale Volksbeleggings (FVB; Federal People's Investments), the Afrikaner Verbond Begrafnis Ondernemings Beperk (AVBOB; Mutual Funerals' Enterprises Limited), Saambou Building Society and, last but not least, also the Afrikaanse Pers Beperk. Later called Perskor, the latter was the Northern voice for Afrikaner Nationalism and was formed after Naspers.

The founder of Naspers, Willie Hofmeyr, and the first Afrikaner actuary, M.S. Louw, were the "key movers" behind many of these initiatives. Both were Cape Town based and "centrally involved" in the creation of "southern nationalism". It is also said that it was no surprise that, through Hofmeyr and Louw, the Sanlam "giant" "financially came to underpin the Cape NP", with the links between Naspers and Sanlam "long and firm". Sanlam also diversified into the related paper-manufacturing field and, through Gencor, it at one stage controlled "the giant paper manufacturers, SAPPI". Through its "Hofmeyr legacy", Naspers has always "been more closely tied to the 'capitalist impulses' within the NP" (i.e., "southern nationalism"), while Perskor "was always closer to the petit bourgeois and working class impulses found amongst the NP's 'northern' constituents".

Thanks to the success of "volkskapitalisme", "southern" Afrikaners, or the "Southern nationalist Cape Establishment", have benefited from this shift and "increasingly did not need the State and the NP to provide them with economic security". Naspers papers were "in the forefront of articulating the voice of the 'liberalising' changes with-in the NP". Although this was articulated more and more during the second half of the twentieth century, the seeds were already sown in the tenets of "Southern Nationalism", with Naspers progressively liberalising itself from the NP.

Piet Cillié, who started his journalism career at *Die Burger* in the 1930s and who would later become editor of the paper as well as chair of Naspers, said contact between the owners, as represented by the board, and the editors "were multiple".[66] Still, according to Cillié, "the board held to the tradition of imposing no directives and of not approaching him individually". Cillié described this relationship as follows:

> I live with many of these people. Every day the managing director comes in for a few hours. The chairman and vice-chairman of the board are both ex-editors of the newspaper and there is a great deal of consultation: they are very useful as sounding

boards. Also I go to them as seniors, particularly if I ever have any doubts – though admittedly that is very rare.

The other dailies in the group – *Die Volksblad* (today the digital-only *Volksblad)* and *Die Oosterlig* (today also digital-only) – took their cues from *Die Burger*. The latter, and Naspers, were "almost as aware of commercial constraints as [they were] of expressing [their] political views", and as such "for a long time unique amongst Afrikaans newspapers in combining the two successfully". It was this "economic necessity" that eventually forced the company to enter the Transvaal in the 1960s and start *Die Beeld*, as a Sunday paper, "since there was an expanding market in the Transvaal which could not be left untouched". Naspers wanted to start a Sunday paper on the Rand much earlier, but "had desisted because of political pressure" via the NP's Transvaal press interests. Although the political opposition still existed when it launched its Sunday paper in 1965, the company felt "it was economically essential to pursue the project to its conclusion". The "need for the Cape to get its political views expressed in the Transvaal was the prime motivation", but clearly "economic necessity" was also valid. Regarding editorial freedom, "[f]or a while it was probably true that the editors of *Die Burger* [Piet Cillié] and *Die Beeld* [Schalk Pienaar] had greater freedom in determining the policies of their newspapers than any English language newspaper editors". However, the editors of the minor newspapers in the group "were strictly supervised from Keeromstraat", Naspers' then headquarters in Cape Town. This "dominance of the editor, rather than the board or management, was consistent with the function that the Cape Press was expected to fulfil within the political machine", and it reflected "the political rather than profit motivations of its promoters".

The Northern Nationalists, however, set the conservative tone for a long time, especially in the first half of the next era, namely the post-1948 period. Perskor, ironically developing indirectly from the Naspers initiative in the 1930s, gave voice to this "northern nationalism" as the key caucus within government from the 1950s to the 1970s.[67] But, after the ascendance of P.W. Botha and the Cape NP in 1978, "the fortunes of Perskor waned", as Naspers had closer links to the "Cape power base of 'southern nationalism'". The "aligning and re-aligning forces" of Afrikaners in the next decades, right to the undoing of the NP regime in the late 1980s, was a key characteristic within Afrikanerdom's press.

The force behind Perskor was the already mentioned Jooste, together with Piet Meyer, "a key NP boss of the SABC". Jooste started *Dagbreek* in 1947, with its holding company the Onafhanklike Pers van Suid-Afrika Beperk (OPSA, Independent Press of South Africa). In 1953, it was "financially advantageous" for *Dagbreek* to support Malan's NP during the first parliamentary elections after the NP's 1948 victory, with "the Hertzog-nationalists (like Jooste) decid[ing] to throw in their lot with the Malanites". In 1962, Jooste merged *Dagbreek* with Afrikaanse Pers Beperk (APB), consolidating the NP's northern faction. APB originally was founded in 1932 as a mouthpiece for the Hertzogite NP, also having been built from the "volkskapitalisme" movement thanks to multitudes of "small Afrikaans shareholders" in the Afrikaanse Persfonds (Afrikaans Press Fund). In the second half of the century, these power formations would play a major role in the development – and demise – of Afrikaner Nationalism, as will be discussed in the next chapter.

The Northern Nationalist press groups started as an organic outgrowth of Naspers when, in September 1935, leaders and supporters of the Cape NP met, again at Stellenbosch, to form a committee to collect funds to establish an Afrikaans daily in the Transvaal to support the NP.[68] Through *Die Burger* and *Die Volksblad*, Malan and the founding committee appealed to supporters to invest in shares in the proposed newspaper company. The first board of directors of the new holding company, Voortrekkerpers Bpk., the name cleverly chosen to not reveal Cape connections, consisted of nine members. Six of them, including the chair, were from the Cape. Four of the Cape directors were MPs and one a Provincial councillor. The first chair was Willie Hofmeyr, also founder chair of Naspers and Sanlam, and by then a Senator.

Through new formations, the already existing Afrikaanse Pers, founded in 1931, morphed into Afrikaanse Pers (1962) Beperk after an amalgamation of Afrikaanse Pers and Dagbreekpers Beperk, which controlled the afternoon daily *Die Vaderland* and the Sunday paper *Dagbreek en Sondagnuus*. But the original Afrikaanse Pers, founded in 1931, "laid down the control", with two of the three board members being Hertzog and Senator W.J.C. Brebner. They were also majority shareholders in the company. In 1935, Hertzog and Brebner created the Afrikaanse Persfonds, with a substantial percentage of shares in *Die Vaderland*, enabling them to appoint two thirds of the directors of the company. Its objects were to "establish and maintain an independent National newspaper in the Afrikaans language ... in the interests and service of the Afrikaans-speaking National Afrikanerdom".

When Dagbreekpers Beperk was formed in 1947, it bought out Afrikaanse Pers's six-month-old Sunday paper *Sondagnuus*.[69] What was not known was that they were backed by an English financier, the Strathmore Group. But when further financial assistance was required in 1953, Strathmore was not prepared to increase its investment. It seems that, apart from finances, Strathmore became "embarrassed by the political views the newspaper had expressed during the 1953 election". The group then offered Jooste the option of purchasing their entire shareholding in Dagbreekpers Bpk. and Dagbreek Trust (Pty) Ltd.

Jooste approached Strijdom, then cabinet minister and leader of the Transvaal NP, who raised the capital. By June 1955, the Transvaal NP held a substantial number of shares in Dagbreek Trust Ltd. By then, the board included Strijdom, who was the new prime minister, and four members of his government. They were Verwoerd, Ben Schoeman and Jan de Klerk (father of F.W. de Klerk), together with Jooste. In 1962, Jooste, as managing director of Dagbreekpers and one of those who broke from Afrikaanse Pers in 1946, acted amidst rumours of takeover bids by the Argus Group as well as by Naspers, and formed Afrikaanse Pers (1962) Beperk.

These power plays within the press groups and the NP in the middle decades of the previous century had an immense influence on the free flow of information, and therefore on press freedom. *Die Burger*, both "because of its tradition and because of the decline in the influence of the Cape in national politics" (after the ascendance of the Transvaal NP leaders), "was forced to assert the voice of Cape nationalism and in so doing to assert itself as a force in national politics".[70] *Die Transvaler*, as voice of "the ascendant and most powerful group in the party", was forced into the role of maintaining the existing power balance in inter-provincial Nationalist politics. With the next prime ministers after Malan coming from the Transvaal and as *ex officio* company chairs, the *Transvaler* "had little opportunity to establish itself as a separate institution within the Government and the party".

And even bigger monopolies

On the English side of the press, monopolies and collusion were still part of everyday business. On acquiring the *Natal Advertiser* in 1918, the Argus Group "extracted" a promise from the sellers that they would not start a newspaper for fifteen years.[71] They also reached an agreement with the *Natal Mercury* about publishing times and advertising rates. Yet there were new "signs of rivalry" by 1934, when, for the first time, the established press "was faced with serious competition from interests outside mining".

L.W. Schlesinger, a "theatre and cinema magnate" who also owned the commercial African Broadcasting Company, started the *Sunday Express* in Johannesburg and the *Sunday Tribune* in Durban. By 1937, he also had dailies in the two cities, namely the *Daily Express* and the *Daily Tribune*. In 1939, the RDM, the *Sunday Times* and the Argus Group together bought out Schlesinger's entire newspaper interests. The strongest pressure on Schlesinger came from the Jewish community, who felt that the English-language press was sympathetic to Jews at a time when the rest of the world was not, while Schlesinger, "the most powerful member of the Jewish community", continued "to oppose and antagonize that Press".

Besides the concentration of newspaper ownership and collusion between existing owners to keep independent papers out, two other factors contributed to maintaining the *status quo* among the English press.[72] One was a news service, while the other concerned distribution. They were the South African Press Association (SAPA), which distributed news to its members, and the Central News Agency (CNA), which monopolised distribution.

SAPA was created in 1938 by the owners of existing papers to provide the South African and then Rhodesian press with a news-gathering service. After 1939, SAPA was the only news agency in the country, with CNA the only concern that distributed papers. The CNA monopoly not only "militated" against the emergence of new papers, but discriminated against existing ones. They gave preferential distribution to English papers by negotiating separate and discriminatory contracts with individual papers, charging higher prices, and insisting that Afrikaans papers be loaded on the distribution vans before their competitors, allowing English newspapers to print later than the Afrikaans ones.

CNA, founded in 1903, initially only distributed the papers of the Cape Times Ltd. and the Argus Group. The owners of both companies became major shareholders, each always with a director on its board. SAAN, after its formation in 1955, also appointed a director to CNA's board. The founders of CNA were also shareholders in the RDM and *Sunday Times*. It was said that there

> can be little doubt that the CNA's virtual monopoly of newspaper distribution and its vested interests in the financial success of a substantial percentage of the country's newspapers contributed to the demise of independent newspapers and operated to the disadvantage of the Afrikaans Press.

Such concentration of ownership was of course by no means unique to South Africa, nor to the newspaper industry. Although with serious implications for press freedom, it has been a feature of business enterprises in many countries, with "the tendency in the newspaper industry ... for fewer and fewer groups to control an often declining number of newspapers".

In South Africa, concern over the monopolising tendency of newspaper ownership was expressed by diverse interests. In 1946, the South African Society of Journalists (SASJ), "representing working newspapermen", conducted an inquiry into the financial control of newspapers. In 1948, the SASJ briefed Bernard Friedman, an MP and member of the then UP government, who consequently asked for the appointment of a Select Committee to inquire into "Press monopolies". After coming to power in 1948, the NP government in 1950 debated a similar motion to the one proposed by Friedman, this time asking for a commission to inquire, inter alia, about the monopolistic tendencies of the Press. The SASJ, Friedman and the NP government "expressed very similar concerns about the financial control of the Press, although from quite different viewpoints". All three agreed "that the freedom of the Press to express a variety of diverse views was seriously hampered by the concentration of newspaper ownership in so few hands". They also agreed that the "close association of the English-language Press with mining interests worked to their disadvantage". Journalists felt "that support for mining interests was imposed on them at the expense of a genuine public service journalism". In 1947, it was claimed that

> before the publication of any items bearing upon the mining industry, it has been the general policy of one group of newspapers to submit the items in question to the mining industry and should they clash with the mining policy they are either scrapped or altered in such a way as to be inoffensive.

The NP government saw this association with mining interests as giving

> the English-language Press a substantial economic advantage over the Afrikaans-language Press as well as an association with interests which historically had been hostile to Afrikaner nationalism and which continued to express their hostility through an extensive network of newspapers opposed to the Nationalist Government.

Indeed, mining interests dominated the English press as much as political interests dominated the Afrikaans press.

The matter of the editor

One of the most important areas of ownership influence on editorial policy was the owners' choice of an editor.[73] Firstly, by "careful selection" of senior editorial staff, they could ensure the perpetuation of general principles. Secondly, owners exerted influence on editorial policy by controlling the financial policy of a paper through determining to what extent they were run "primarily for profit or politics", and making decisions about the allocation of resources. Lastly, owners exerted influence by direct editorial intervention, "whether for commercial or political motives". The British press baron, Lord Thomson, in giving evidence to the British Royal Commission on the Press in the 1940s, said he ran his newspapers as businesses and looked to them to produce profits. Therefore, he would not interfere with the editorial functioning of his newspapers. Another British press baron, Lord Beaverbrook, said his papers "were run for propaganda purposes". But: To ensure that he could continue to make propaganda, his newspapers had to sell.

In South Africa, the English and Afrikaans press "roughly paralleled the Thomson-Beaverbrook distinctions, but with one significant difference": The Afrikaans press "was never prepared to sacrifice political commitment for the cause of circulation". Still, in the 1960s, the Naspers "experiment" with *Die Beeld* "suggested that profit and propaganda were not necessarily incompatible".

It was also claimed that the mining interests of the Argus Group's owners prevented its papers from attacking mining administration – "particularly from campaigning against low mining wages and the conditions of non-White mine labour".[74] Still, in other respects, Argus papers "had been vigorously critical and demanded social reforms for the non-Whites". But the more important point was that no "establishment English-language newspaper" had exposed South African mining interests to severe scrutiny. The financial strength of the mining interests could be seen in the running of the papers, with all editors of Argus papers appointed from within the group itself. They were "tried and tested Argus Group men, conscious of management and of circulation and of the advertising problems of newspapers", although expressing their "firm adherence to the principle of editorial independence".

SAAN, when formed in 1955 and enlarged in 1959 – when the group acquired another two dailies in the Eastern Province – had to answer "the important question" as to what extent its owners were in a position "to influence the policies of their newspapers and what their attitudes to the exercise of that influence were".[75] It was argued that, "undoubtedly", SAAN papers were much less management-ownership controlled than the Argus papers. Editorial independence from proprietorial interference was "extensive", "but it is also true that editors were selected from within a reasonably limited political spectrum".

Collusion on the English side, fierce intergroup fighting on the Afrikaans side

The now established operating lines of the English and the Afrikaans press were firmly in place. Because the English papers were generally financed by "big business" English capital, they co-operated closely with each other to protect their financial interests and to ensure no competitors survived.[76] Prior to 1948, a UP government, representing broadly English mining interests, was in power, and it was those interests that the English press supported without any questioning.

On the Afrikaans side, newspaper groups were owned by many small individual share-holders, all members of the (white) Afrikaans sector of the population, and "relatively much poorer than their English-language competitors". Still, all newspapers were in white hands, including the growing black press. By far the largest sector of the press, the English press was "powerfully profit motivated", while the Afrikaans sector focused primarily on "disseminat[ing] a political view and therefore were prepared to make few concessions to profit". All of this meant that, after 1948, restraints on the content of the press deriving from ownership were of far lesser importance than pressures from government on press freedom.

White-owned "black" press

When *Bantu World*, launched in 1932, was taken over by the Argus Group later that same year, it initiated "the slow death of an independent black press as the ideas of official segregation and later apartheid took hold of the country".[77] The takeover was the result of the interest of "white business and financial interests" in the black press – "an indicator of things to come". The Chamber of Mines launched *Umteteli Wa Bantu* in May 1920, and "soon employed some of the more talented black journalists of the day".[78] This set the stage for the "white takeover" of the black press. The key publisher in terms of the "white-owned black press" was Bertram Paver, an ex-farmer and businessman who founded the

Bantu Press and started his first paper, *Bantu World*, in 1932. Although the black press was in the hands of white interests, it was "staffed and edited by Africans".[79]

Paver, besides being an "ex-farmer", was also an "itinerant salesman" who saw potential profits to be made from the aspiring black market.[80] The establishment of *Bantu World* is regarded as important, as it represents a move from a "local to a national black press in addition to redefining the role and strategy of the press". The paper was modelled on the British *Daily Mirror* as a tabloid. Paver tried to avoid the image of "white control over a black staff", but a new controlling factor began to emerge: economics.

The Argus Group took over Bantu Press in 1932, controlling it until 1952, but by 1945 Bantu Press had already became a media monopoly with publications throughout southern Africa, including ten weekly newspapers, in addition to handling advertising for twelve different publications in eleven languages.[81] Although Paver was a "liberal", he was also motivated by commercial gain. During the Argus period, Bantu Press acquired seven subsidiary companies with their own newspapers. It became the first monopoly in the black press. It also published newspapers and magazines beyond South Africa's borders, including in the former Southern and Northern Rhodesia (now Zimbabwe and Zambia), as well as in the then High Commission Territories (today Botswana and Lesotho) and Nyasaland (now Malawi). *Bantu World* was its leading publication, with a circulation of 24,000. It was widely read – each copy by at least five "adult wage earners", who in turn read it aloud to illiterate friends and family members.[82] It was also a "significant training ground for young blacks in the Western norms of journalism with its stress on objectivity, separation of news and comment, and an event-related concept of news".[83] And, importantly, although it was white-owned, with white corporate control, it transformed the black press into a "contemporary medium of mass communication".

It was impossible for any independent African newspaper to survive the competitive power of this white-controlled Bantu Press – "and indeed this was the intention".[84] The Afrikaanse Pers published *Bona* as an "educational magazine" for Africans, with circulation particularly in schools. Afrikaanse Pers also purchased *Imvo* and *Zonk* from Bantu Press, and Voortrekker Pers published *Our Own Mirror*, formerly published independently in Natal under the name of *Eletha*. Another magazine, *Drum*, was founded by J.R. Bailey in the 1950s, aimed at the urbanised African. J.R. Bailey was the son of mining magnate Bailey. By 1965, *Drum* had "dwindled" into a supplement of another Bailey publication, *Post*, a weekly aimed at the "non-White market".

Newspapers which in the past had an influential African readership, such as the Communist-inspired *New Age* and its "phoenix-like" followers, differed only in name from their predecessors and struggled to continue. An African "underground" press had been virtually non-existent, as the legal penalties and the difficulty of distribution made this inoperable.

This white-owned period in the development of the black press has been reviewed from the years 1930 to 1980.[85] Despite their important contribution to political awareness, most black newspapers lacked capital, equipment, skilled workers and a reliable distribution network.

The yearning for an own voice

Nevertheless, African Nationalism yearned for its own voice. Bantu Press's *Bantu World* had Selope Thema, an ANC member, as editor, but as white-owned African press it only "monitored" African workers' conditions.[86] Several other ANC-linked papers supported African worker rights outright in the early 1940s.[87] *Inkokeli Ya Bantu* (People's Leader, 1940–1942) sought to "champion the cause of the African people". *Izwe Lase Afrika* (Voice of the People, 1941–1942) was the "official organ" of the Cape African Congress, edited by its secretary, Bennett Ncwana. *Inkundla Ya Bantu* (People's Forum, 1938–1951) was more forthright in its support of African workers. This type of "reporting reflected not only the solidarity of an oppressed people but also *Inkundla*'s support for ANC policies". The "alignment" was directly influenced by its editors, namely the first "prominent political activist", Govan Mbeki, and, from 1944, Jordan Ngubane, the Natal leader of the Congress Youth League (CYL). *Inkundla* "articulated a broad, inclusive variety of African nationalism". The solidarity was clear, with Ngubane, writing as columnist "Kanyisa", declaring: "[W]e have never concealed our dislike for Communism ... But we shall never raise our arm against the Leftists just because Malan says we must."

By the late 1940s, the ANC became more militant and, in 1949, declared African Nationalism "as a basis for the fight for national liberation". The ANC's "1949 Programme" also identified the need for a national press. *Inkundla* was the last remaining African newspaper linked to the ANC, but it folded in 1951. The Cape ANC newsletter, *Inyaniso*, said in 1954 that the party "had for years acknowledged the need for its own organ", but it was "well-nigh impossible to establish a newspaper from scratch today", mainly due to "the great monopoly" of the white press. It was also in the 1950s that Bantu Press newspapers "abandoned their nationalist pretences" and uniformly criticised the ANC and "[labour] union militancy". *Bantu World* continued to report on socio-economic issues of interest to workers, "but its coverage of African politics became muted". Still, the ANC found "diverse ways" to communicate through leaflets and short-lived newsletters, like *Inyaniso*, *Izwi La Lentsoe La*, and *Lodestar*, through public meetings, and through a few pro-ANC newspapers, especially the *Guardian*, "which itself became a symbol of anti-apartheid resistance". The *Guardian* championed labour struggles until it was forced to close in March 1963.

When the ANC was banned in 1960, the African Nationalist press was forced underground.[88] With the resurgence of the black trade union movement, the revival of political resistance, and the renaissance of the alternative press in the 1970s and 1980s, workers' interests and needs "became much more visible in mediating the news of South Africa". After the ANC was banned, it could not be mentioned in mainstream media, although "exile publications" continued, among them *Sechaba*, *Workers' Unity*, *Mayibuye* and *Dawn*. In general, the African Nationalist press, throughout its history, "represented African workers as exploited victims of an oppressive system".

One such paper that had an impact was *Ilanga Lasa Natal* (Natal Sun), founded by John Dube and others in 1904.[89] In 1912, Dube was elected the first chair of what would become the ANC. Another influential political journalist of the time was Sol Plaatje of *Koranta*, who "fought for the rights of blacks and condemned racism"[90]. Plaatje's contribution would later, from the 1980s, be put into perspective with a new appreciation for his work, e.g., on land dispossession. Also, Rhodes University established the Sol Plaatje Institute for Media Leadership, stating that he was[91]

> one of the most remarkable South Africans of his generation [as] an outstanding political leader, prolific writer, newspaper proprietor and journalist. He was one of the founders of the African National Congress and became the party's first [secretary-general]. His political book *Native life in South Africa* is an indictment of

pre-grand apartheid discriminatory legislation while his historical novel *Mhudi* was the first novel in English to have been written by a black South African. Sol Plaatje was publisher editor of *Koranta Ea Becoana* (*Bechuana Gazette*) in Mafikeng and later *Tsala Ea Becoana* (*Bechuana Friend*), as well as *Tsala Ea Batho* (*The Friend of the People*). These newspapers were published in Setswana and English.

The first newspaper by Plaatje, the *Koranta Ea Becoana*, lasted from 1901 until 1918 and was published in Mafeking[92] (now Mafikeng). It was owned by SANNC figure Silas Molema. Plaatje gained "added insight into the tribulations" of migrant labourers when, in 1909, he was forced by the financial demise of *Koranta* to work as a labour recruiter.[93] The following year he returned to journalism as editor of the "self-styled" "independent race newspaper" *Tsala Ea Becoana*, later retitled *Tsala Ea Batho*, which existed from 1910 to 1915 and was published in Kimberley. When Plaatje became SANNC secretary-general in 1913, *Tsala* "increasingly was viewed by its readers as an organ of Congress".

Non-White-owned black newspapers

One of the few "non-White owned newspapers" was run by the "more affluent Indian community" in Natal. This was *Indian Opinion*, founded by Mahatma Gandhi in 1906.[94] Although financially independent, it pursued a "closely conservative political line". The Natal Indian Organisation also published *Indian Views*.[95] When Gandhi left the country, his *Indian Opinion* was continued by his son Manilal, until his death in 1956. Gandhi also founded the Indian National Congress in 1894.[96]

In the Cape, Abdullah Abdurahman founded the African Political Organisation, which existed from 1902 until 1919.[97] In 1911 he also founded the newspaper *African Political Organisation*. Although the title and political party refer to "African", the paper and party were aimed at what was known at the time as Cape Coloureds, mainly Muslims.

'The Home Front Propaganda War'

The combined circulation of the English papers in the 1930s was about five times that of the Afrikaner Nationalist opposition, "a preponderance which in ordinary circumstances ought to be decisive".[98] However, circumstances "were not ordinary". Chance "had been made more difficult by a significant event in 1937". When the *Transvaal Leader* folded in 1915, the RDM did not have a rival morning daily. It would come, although much later, in October 1937, two years before the outbreak of the Second World War, and in the form of the already mentioned *Die Transvaler,* a "radical Afrikaner Nationalist publication".

Verwoerd, its editor, was described as a "remarkable man, born in Holland in 1901, went to school in Rhodesia and South Africa, graduated with honours at Stellenbosch University and was appointed to its chair of applied psychology at the age of twenty-six". Whilst *Die Transvaler* was founded to propagate the NP, Verwoerd "carried out his assignment with devotion and skill", running the paper "as a politician's paper for politicians". Its "austere, astringent, doctrinaire approach seemed deliberately to court unpopularity". It was successful "not in terms of profits or circulation, but almost entirely by its effectiveness in disseminating nationalist ideology".

When the Second World War broke out, *Die Transvaler* was "fortuitously on hand" and supported "with zeal and enthusiasm" the NP's anti-war campaign. Without *Die Transvaler*,

English papers "would still have had to cope with the anti-war politicians", but the newcomer "sharpened the tone and temper of the dispute".

And into the tumultuous 1940s

By 1948, English South African-born editors became more influential, and the English newspapers were beginning to question some aspects of mining company policy.[99] In this period, English/Afrikaner relations were again severely tested, with the Union supporting Britain in the Second World War, while most Afrikaners sided, again, with Germany. The partisanship of the press at the time is clear from how the editor of the *Cape Argus* was fired. The policy of the group was that editors "should take care not to undermine" Britain's position "as she strove for peace in Europe".[100] But editor D. McCauseland became more and more critical of Neville Chamberlain's policy – and was promptly fired. It was "a clear demonstration of the close links between the English press and the mining houses and, through them, with Britain". The "amazing point" was that he was fired for criticising Britain, not South Africa, but his criticism "was not at variance" with what was called the "mining press". This was also part of the inherent power struggle between English imperial interests and Afrikaner Nationalist interests:

> The [English] newspapers do not in many instances criticise the British government. To do so would immediately give that section of the Afrikaans press which is bitterly opposed to anything British an added incentive to make the most of it. Criticism of the British government is therefore taboo in the general interests of the mining industry, which is anxious to attract capital into South Africa, and to do nothing that might repel it.

With the war looming, and Afrikaans papers mainly supporting neutrality, it meant the five-year-old coalition between Hertzog and Smuts also split. Smuts formed a new government, his allies now the Labour and Dominion Parties, and led South Africa into war. Nonetheless, there was not much difference between Smuts's UP and the NP. As it was described: "The difference between its attitude to the country's traditional segregationist policies and that of the Nationalists was one of degree, not of kind."

Before 1948 there were confrontations between press and government, but the former had managed to retain a large degree of independence, "not unlike that enjoyed in the other British dominions".[101] Now, during the Second World War, the newspapers were given a choice: government censorship or self-censorship. They chose the latter. The system worked "pretty well", with the responsible minister able to write to editors a note of appreciation after the war:

> The Information Bureau has informed you that all military and navy censorship restrictions have, in view of the cessation of hostilities, been suspended. I assume that the editors who signed the voluntary press censorship agreement will now agree that there is no further reason to continue with the agreement. On behalf of the Prime Minister and the government, I should like to express to you personally and to your colleagues the sincere thanks of the government for your co-operation in the implementation of this agreement. The government expresses its sincere appreciation for the manner in which that voluntary censorship has been applied, thus denying the enemy vital information during the war.

The development of radio

When the first radio service was established in 1927, it followed the same path as that of print media up to that point: it served white interests and, in this case, only that of English speakers.[102] As through much of the development of the South African media, so-called "non-Europeans" were diminished to "eavesdroppers", literally the case when radio was introduced.

The historical development of broadcasting is also the history of the South African Broadcasting Corporation (SABC), as the SABC monopolised the airwaves from its inception.[103]

The early developments followed a similar pattern to that in the UK: first a few enthusiastic radio amateurs, followed by several experimental broadcasts, and only later with more organised programming. It is "easy" to infer that, from its beginnings, the SABC "was shaped not only by the geography of the country and the limitations of technology, but also the ideology of the time which saw the Union government under domination of the UP led by General Jan Smuts".[104] Tight government control was always regarded as "the doing of the apartheid-era and far more hard-line Nationalist Government following World War II". However, "history tells us that it was, in fact, the UP-led Government which united white English and Afrikaans-speakers and was in power from 1933 to 1948, which initiated this policy".

South Africa's broadcasting history can be traced to 1923, when the government called for licence applications for "carrying out official broadcasting by wireless in South Africa".[105] Three licences were granted, each covering a major urban area. In Johannesburg, a private club of amateur radio broadcasters, the Association of Scientific and Technical Services, received the licence. In Cape Town the Cape Peninsular Publicity Association was granted a licence, and in Natal the Durban Corporation received theirs. All three stations began broadcasting in 1924, but soon all were in "significant debt". The Johannesburg operation ceased in 1926. While the postmaster-general unsuccessfully tried to persuade the government to take responsibility for broadcasting, the station was acquired by the already mentioned Schlesinger, "a successful insurance entrepreneur better known for his interests in the burgeoning theatre and film industry in South Africa". In 1927, Schlesinger acquired the other two stations and then connected the three into a single network, naming it the African Broadcasting Corporation (ABC).

Because of poor landline connections, the high cost of programme production and the difficulty of enforcing licence payments, the ABC fell into a deficit by 1929. Schlesinger approached the government with several proposals, none of which were successful. He then turned to the retailing industry and the ABC "reversed its financial position, and within a few years was able to carry out capital improvements, including a much needed transmitter expansion". It still catered to the interests of the English-speaking elite in the urban centres, and reflecting the news agenda of the English press.

With English capital dominating mining, business, government and the leisure industry, the Afrikaans stronghold was in the rural areas. Afrikaner pressure groups lobbied for the development of Afrikaans culture and economic and political empowerment, resulting in the ABC introducing 30 minutes of Afrikaans programming in 1931. By 1936 it increased to 90 minutes. Nothing was broadcast in any of the African languages.

Although a commercial success, the ABC, with "its reliance on entertainment and the complete lack of Afrikaans programming [in 1934, was] much resented" by Afrikaners.[106] The then prime minister, Hertzog, invited John Reith, BBC director-general, to tour South Africa in 1934 to recommend a broadcasting model for the country.[107] His visit was followed by the Draft Broadcasting Bill, introduced in March 1936, and the South African Broadcasting Corporation (SABC) began in August. The ABC was "bought out through a Sanlam debenture issue", with all its assets and staff taken over. The SABC Board had to consist of persons who had "to be unaligned to any specific interest group within the country's political landscape".

After the passing of the 1936 Broadcast Act, Afrikaans programming was prioritised, but it developed slowly due to the fact that the Afrikaans audience lived in rural areas beyond the reach of city-based medium-wave transmitters, which meant that it was still largely an English-language service until 1948.[108]

Regarding programming for black listeners, the 1936 Reith Report made special mention of the provision of programming other than English and Afrikaans.[109] This, however, "at no point" was ever given consideration by the government. It was only during World War II that an initial but unsuccessful attempt was made at providing night-time programming for black listeners through telephone lines to "compounds" in the gold mines, hostels and major townships. Starting in 1949, a daily half-hour programme was transmitted on the English and Afrikaans medium-wave services in Zulu, Xhosa and Sotho.

After 1948, the SABC developed into "His Master's Voice" and, although it was described as providing "the most pervasive and technologically advanced radio and television services in all of Africa"[110] in the mid-1980s, it was an instrument in the hands of the governing NP.

The first half of the 20th century

The development of media during the first half of the 20th century was clearly along the schisms of certain "-isms", from capitalism to nationalism. In this regard, the media were all parochial and partisan, whether they served an elite urban audience, such as the English press, or a semi-urban and rural constituency, such as the Afrikaner Nationalist and African Nationalist press. The English press clearly served English (mining) capitalism, the Afrikaans press the interests of Afrikaner Nationalism, and the Black press African Nationalism. They were all organs of their political-partisan affiliations, and they characterised the development of South Africa for the rest of the century. These "binaries and paradoxes of power and politics" had a clear impact on news flow and press freedom, with messages packaged according to the prevailing sentiments and tropes of the different media concerns. All of this would set the scene for at least the next four decades, up until when, in 1948, the surprise NP victory catapulted South Africa onto its apartheid trajectory. Thus, although there were no clear press freedom violations in the first half of the 20th century, the "unfreedoms" of the dominating English and Afrikaner approaches formed the paradigms for the development of the press in the three sectors serving the English, Afrikaner Nationalist and African Nationalist audiences.

As far as criticism is concerned,
we don't resent it unless it is absolutely biased,
as it is in most cases.
– JOHN VORSTER, SA prime minister from 1966 to 1978

7. THE PERIOD 1948 TO 1990
MEDIA (UN)FREEDOM UNDER APARTHEID

Gagging laws, censorship, Total Onslaught, and a first glimpse of democracy

Introduction

During the apartheid government's rule between 1948 and the early 1990s, the South African media had to find ways to overcome legislation enforced by an increasingly autocratic and oligarchic NP. When the last apartheid state president, F.W. de Klerk, revoked various laws impacting on media freedom in his historical speech on 2 February 1990, in which he announced the release of Nelson Mandela from jail, he also announced that the emergency regulations – also those affecting the media – were being "abolished in their entirety".[1]

The media as mirror to society. This photograph of then South African president F.W. de Klerk surrounded by the press at the international press conference when he announced the release from prison of Nelson Mandela in Cape Town, South Africa on 2 February 1990, also reflects the media situation at the time: mostly male, and all pale. Photo: Media24/Gallo Images

During the four decades of the inhumane apartheid era, the media became more and more paralysed by legislation. This applied to the English "liberal", the Nationalist Afrikaner, as well as what was categorised as the "black" press. Whereas English and black papers challenged the tyranny of the governing party, Afrikaans papers that dared to practise reform journalism were continuously threatened by an authoritarian government.

A society's media system is "intimately connected" to providing the basis – or otherwise – for democratic government, wrote media scholar Eric Louw in the early 1990s, following four decades of NP rule.[2] A democracy implies the possibilities people have to influence society – hence the possibility to live out their own life chances. "Life chances", or opportunities, under the apartheid government turned out to be possible for a small minority, but impossible for the majority.

This resulted in a "low-level civil war of majority blacks against entrenched whites".[3] South Africa was the "polecat of the world",[4] in the words of *Die Burger* editor Piet Cillié after the March 1960 Sharpeville tragedy, with "Sharpeville" becoming a metaphor for the inhumanity perpetrated by the NP government. At the time, *Die Burger* called for a study of "black grievances", cautiously phrased as "even if it means that some fixed concepts may have to be changed". To put this in the context of the totalitarian timeframe of the time: Cillié's formulation was described as "brave words" for an Afrikaner editor and, in hindsight, that timid phrase became "part of South African history".[5]

The NP, after its unexpected election victory in May 1948, started to implement the "strongest segregationist laws possible",[6] part of Afrikaner Nationalism's attempt to implement white supremacy. It soon developed into an oligarchic government, yearning to control every aspect of South African life. Muzzling the media was part of this project in power. The media were subject to two kinds of control – coercive and manipulative. Coercion included legislation in terms of "who may publish and what may be published", as well as intimidation to the point of self-censorship. Manipulative control meant that the "extensive state machinery" used methods to suppress unfavourable information to promote "a positive image of official policies at home and abroad".

All of this implied that media freedom, together with civil liberties, not only deteriorated, but simply did not exist for the majority of the population.

Old game, new players

The NP government, of course, was not the inventor of human rights abuse, nor of muzzling the media. When the NP took control in 1948, "the rules of the game already were well established" in terms of the suppression of press freedom right through South Africa's history.[7] These "censorious and repressive measures" were not something new, but "a continuation of a historical process".

In 1948, the new government "immediately" began implementing racial segregation or apartheid through "a series of laws that stirred a storm of protest at home, and remitting hostility in the media abroad".[8] Amongst them were the Prohibition of Mixed Marriages Act of 1949 and the Population Registration Act of 1950. The Immorality Act of 1927 already prohibited "illicit carnal intercourse between Europeans and natives", but the Immorality Amendment Act of 1950 now included so-called Coloureds and Indians.[9] The Group Areas Act and the Suppression of Communism Act followed that same year. It was clear that the new government steamrolled its policy into practice.

Protest marches against the Group Areas Act of 1950.
Photo: http://www.sahistory.org.za/article/group-areas-act-1950

From 1948 until 1967, every prime minister had direct links with the major Afrikaans press companies, with their boards "under firm control of Nationalist cabinet members".[10] It was only in 1978, after the Information Scandal, that prime minister P.W. Botha "felt obliged" to forbid cabinet members from holding newspaper directorships. But, by the mid-1960s, there was already a growing rift between the "verligte" (enlightened) and "verkrampte" (conservative) Nationalists, the latter mostly associated with the then Transvaal (today the four northern provinces).

While "race" was one of its defining characteristics since the first beginnings of the press in South Africa, "race and racism reached its zenith in the period 1948 to 1990".[11] The NP government's legislation was to strengthen the position of the Afrikaner, most of whom by 1948 lived in urban areas and were "desperately poor".[12] The "rising aspirations" of black South Africans, perceived as a serious threat, were neutralised through "a form of social engineering that became known worldwide as apartheid". After 1948, "a broader and fundamentally political classification of the South African press became established". Newspapers were now clearly either pro- or anti-government. Any efforts at editorial independence were "bound to fail", with government labelling newspapers as "supportive or oppositional". The close bond between the Afrikaans press and Afrikaner politics meant that, under apartheid, the Afrikaans press "found itself in a unique and privileged position". Besides Afrikaans papers receiving special treatment at NP congresses, they were even described as "civil servants responsible for the distribution of information". This proved to be self-defeating. Their close links worked "against good journalism in that they did not expose or investigate graft or corruption, even when they knew something about it", while becoming victims of self-censorship "in exchange for favours from prominent people in government".[13]

Press regulations, otherwise known as censorship, 1948 to 1990

The first prime minister, D.F. Malan, had personal experience of the power of the press: He himself was an editor; in fact, the first, from 1915 to 1924, of *De/Die Burger*.

The post-1948 laws were described as an "avalanche of security legislation", creating "a massive structure of censorship and self-censorship".[14] Malan described the English press as the "most undisciplined in the world" and suggested journalists should be registered like doctors.[15] His successor, Strijdom, labelled the English press as "South Africa's greatest enemy". The next prime minister, Verwoerd, blamed the economic depression on the "irresponsible and unpatriotic behaviour of the English press",[16] while his successor, Vorster, accused the press of "stabbing South Africa in the back".[17] If not for the 1978 Information Scandal, the next prime minister would most probably have been Transvaal NP leader Connie Mulder, who warned in 1972 that "if the press acted irresponsibly, it did not deserve the freedom it enjoyed and the government would act, even if the price was the freedom of the press". In 1973, Vorster repeated previous warnings in his typical "Iron Man style", saying he had "warned newspaper directors and editors and was not going to warn them again"; either "they must come to heel now, or he would step in and bring them to heel". And: "As far as criticism is concerned, we don't resent it unless it is absolutely biased, as it is in most cases."[18] From 1978, under P.W. Botha, the most inhibitive media regulations followed under the state of emergency regulations. One of Botha's cabinet ministers, Stoffel Botha, said "press freedom must be earned by an honest press", implying they were everything but honest.[19]

From 1948 to 1968, the English press was identified as the "external" opposition, while the Afrikaans press, "an institution within the ranks of Government", constituted an "internal" opposition.[20] Threats against the press were part of a "consistent pattern", with "legislation and threats of legislation" used to persuade the press to exercise self-censorship. Two types of mass communication structures developed after 1948. One was a press as "a co-ordinated agency of a centralized party and Government", part of the government's "extensive communication network", and the other independent of government, "which as a matter of general principle believed its independence prerequisite for its functioning".[21] Over time, the Afrikaans press began to function as an opposition, but as an "internal" one and with "very different intentions and consequences from those of the English-language Press in its role of 'external' opposition".

As some context, the racial demography in this period was that, in 1968, the population totalled 19,167,000, comprising 13,042,000 blacks, 3,639,000 whites (with the ruling Afrikaners as 59% of them), so-called Coloureds numbering 1,912,000, and Indians 574,000.[22]

Afrikaner Nationalist manipulation

After 1948, the NP manipulated politics to maintain power. It "steadily became more powerful" by loading rural constituencies, abolishing the Native Representatives Act, eliminating Coloureds from the Cape voters' roll, and continuing the disproportionate representation of South-West Africa (now Namibia) and the "intensive indoctrination" of supporters.[23]

This led to the Afrikaners' "total triumph of political victory and power" in the formation of the Republic in 1961 after increasing their majorities in the elections of 1953, 1958 and

1961. After the 1966 elections, the Nationalists' majority in parliament was more than two-thirds, although "at most 55% of the electorate voted for them". The electoral system was such that even if 60% of the electorate supported the opposition party, the ruling party could still win. It was in this manner that, in 1948, an NP coalition received 40% of the votes and 79 seats, whereas the UP received 50% of the votes but only 65 seats. This was because of an urban concentration of supporters, the loading of rural constituencies and the "constant activity" of the "Delimitation Committee", all working against the UP. Still, there was "not much to choose" between the NP and the UP. It is even suggested that, up to 1968, it was a matter of a "victory of the extremists [NP] over the less extreme [UP]". As NP leadership passed into the hands of "successively more extreme" Nationalists – from Malan to Strijdom, to Verwoerd, to Vorster – it also marked "a shift in the balance of political power from the Cape to the Transvaal".

The NP's "powerful provincial parties" had their own constitutions and held their own annual congresses.[24] The traditional schisms in Afrikanerdom could be seen within this federalism. There were "two persistent and conflicting trends in Afrikaner political thinking": an authoritarian and libertarian tradition, reflecting the conflict within the "Volk" (the people) between a "patriarchal or leadership principle", and a "desire for liberty and equality". This was expressed along provincial lines, with the authoritarian tradition expressed by the "Transvalers" (Northerners), and the libertarian one by the Cape. The "increasing dominance of the authoritarian wing … made its impact on the workings of the political system". Within this system, the Afrikaans press functioned increasingly as the internal "opposition", while the English press assumed the function of an external opposition. And, ironically and paradoxically, almost all "White constitutional politics after 1948 were concerned with the voteless Black opposition".[25]

A cartoon as indication of what was to come

One of the first controversies regarding freedom of expression was a cartoon in the *Sunday Express* in 1949. Following the NP victory, most English-language papers became "more politically aggressive".[26] Toward the end of 1949, a cartoon drawn by the *Express*'s Wilfred Cross depicted a house, representing South Africa, with its front wall "conveniently missing" for readers to see what was happening inside: "a black man lying prone, and a white man sitting astride him and beating him with a stick." Along the side of the house were three black men, representing the three protectorates, who could not see what was happening inside. A "cordial" Malan, standing at the side entrance, is inviting them in. "The reader is left to decide for himself what would happen to the three men if they did enter the house."

In February the next year, summonses were served on the paper's company and the editor and cartoonist under a clause in the Native Administration Act of 1928, which made it an offence to publish matter "with intent to create hostility between white and black". Joel Mervis, at the time with the *Rand Daily Mail* (RDM) and with a legal background, acted as ancillary legal adviser for his company, also in this case. At the trial, Verwoerd was called as one of his company's witnesses, the main purpose to put on record a number of provocative cartoons in the *Transvaler* while he was editor. Their argument was that cartoons are often symbolical and that "things one sees in a cartoon should not be taken too literally". The company, paper, editor and cartoonist were found guilty and fined £50, but the conviction was set aside upon appeal.

The life blood of democracy: a free press

The middle of the 20th century "coincided neatly" with the start of NP rule,[27] leading to a "head-on clash" within the "Three Estates of Democracy" – the Executive and Parliament, and the Courts. The so-called "Fourth Estate", the press, could not "fail to take notice of issues which might undermine the rule of law, political rights, civil liberties and free speech". The nomenclature of a free press as the "Fourth Estate" originated in 1774, when Edmund Burke, speaking in the House of Commons in London, said: "There are three estates in Parliament; but in the Reporters' Gallery yonder there sits a Fourth Estate more important far than they all."

It is accepted that freedom of speech is considered the life blood of democracy. In South Africa it was claimed that the country had the "freest press in Africa",[28] but the country had at best "only a partial democracy" achieved through "various self-defence policies". One was the creation of "homelands", where disenfranchised blacks could vote in their "places of origin", but not for the SA parliament. Still, the demise of white rule started from the mid-1970s, although government "deliberately manipulated and censored" the media "to prevent a breakdown in the morale" and "to appear indestructible". Any dissidence, balanced reporting and criticism were perceived as threats. Nevertheless, South Africa was "culturally, economically and politically isolated", causing the regime to weaken. Despite its "grim determination" to hold on to power, the last white president, De Klerk, started liberalisation with his 2 February speech in 1990. In 1993, an interim Constitution replaced the 1983 Constitution, guaranteeing a free press and the right to information in its Bill of Rights.

Until this era, the media were increasingly under pressure to portray events the way government viewed politics. Restrictive legislation imposed to ensure state security and to project a "more favourable image" globally also had to withstand "revolutionary anti-South African reportage and propaganda". The army and police, plus government bodies such as the Bureau of Information and the National Security Management System, served this purpose. Government's ultimate control mechanism to muzzle the media, "especially the probing foreign press", was to declare successive states of emergency.

Despite these, news was still disseminated to the outside world. It was impossible to suppress press freedom, because it was impossible "to silence those who investigated, probed, ferreted and dared to tell the truth" – all at a time when "the demise of the white government was taking place while a more liberated order was taking shape".

The first commission of inquiry into the press

Malan, as first NP prime minister, "planted the seeds" of the "long running dispute" on whether it was apartheid laws or newspaper reports "that harmed the country".[29] Exposing "guilty" newspapers became a matter of urgency, and Malan "decided to act at once". The first commission of inquiry into the press was appointed on 1 November 1950. But "newspaper failings", so obvious to Malan, clearly "made no instant impact" on the commission. It took thirteen years to complete the inquiry, and when the last reports were tabled in 1964, they were ignored.

South Africa has seen a number of commissions of inquiry into the media since then.[30] The next was in 1979, followed by the "comprehensive" Steyn Commissions of 1980 and 1982. The Erasmus Commission in 1978, although not an inquiry into the press *per se*, "came at a time of high tension" between the press and government in the wake of the Information Scandal. Also known as Muldergate or Infogate, this was the exposure of an R85 million secret five-year propaganda programme consisting of 180 projects aimed at "buying South Africa's way into the international corridors of power".[31]

Fears that politicians would meddle in the press existed even before the NP took power. In 1945, when newsprint was extremely scarce due to the Second World War, Piet Cillié, then assistant editor of *Die Burger*,[32] wrote to his editor, Phil Weber, about his fears that NP politicians could "mobilise" and take over the paper. It was a "minor nightmare", he wrote, that *Die Burger* would become "a slave to the politicians instead of remaining a newspaper". Cillié, expressing his concerns about independence and interference, wrote that there were "politicians who fail to grasp that we owe our power ... which is also in their interest, to the degree of independence we maintain". Their stance "irritates them", and they need "to watch out that the irritation does not turn into a plan and a movement".

The 1950 commission was called for by a former Afrikaans editor.[33] Now, as NP member of Parliament, A.J.R. van Rhyn tabled his motion requesting an inquiry into the "monopolistic tendencies of the press", "internal and external reporting", and the advisability of "control over such reporting". Monopolistic tendencies referred to the then powerful Argus Group, owners of nine of seventeen dailies.

Van Rhyn said freedom of the press was "limited by those who control it". There was a call to deport foreign journalists "who abused South Africa's hospitality", while Malan "insisted that even in peacetime comment ought to be restrained by patriotism", adding that SA's press "was the most undisciplined in the world". Also: Whereas other countries had "proper" organisations for journalists and editors, with "suitable codes of professional conduct", SA had none.

The "very formulation" of the commission's goals "suggested that the findings most likely would be negative". It rather was a case of the press being "served notice" that its activities were under scrutiny and "that it had better watch its step".

The commission, just two years after coming to power, revealed the NP's concern with the press, particularly the English press.[34] The motion read

> That whereas this House is of the opinion that a free Press is essential to a free democratic society, and whereas it is convinced that a self-disciplined freedom ultimately constitutes the best safeguard for the maintenance of the freedom of the Press, and that of all activities and tendencies to undermine and abuse such freedom which exist or are taking root in this country should therefore be combatted, it accordingly requests the government to consider the advisability of appointing a Commission[.]"

Although a free press was acclaimed as desirable, the assumption was that this freedom was abused, "despite the self-disciplinary rider". The commission had to investigate details of media ownership, news agencies, publishers and distributors, and "monopolistic tendencies". It also had to investigate stringers and correspondents for overseas newspapers and news agencies. The third goal, investigating newspapers' responsibility and accuracy, included their "sense of patriotism". The commission met in camera from 1955, taking oral evidence from prominent South African journalists over "many months". For years, their work was "obscured" from both press and public, but numerous "disconcerting reports" from English-language journalists about the methods used led to the International Press Institute's (IPI) Board, consisting of editors from fifteen countries, appointing a "special investigator" to investigate the commission in 1956. Because most of the IPI information came from the English press, the organisation, also with English-only newspapers as members, sent a questionnaire to Afrikaans editors in August 1957 to "gauge their views on the Commission". *Die Transvaler* "immediately" published it, meant as "exposure" of the survey, and issued a "patriotic appeal" to Afrikaner editors not to co-operate.

The commission's first report, dealing with the press's organisational, technical and financial aspects, was published in April 1962. It achieved "very little" and stated the "obvious": The press was dominated by three groups (Argus, SAAN and Naspers), and monopolistic practices were found. Its second report, in May 1964, concentrated on the activities of stringers, resident and visiting full-time journalists of foreign newspapers, and news sent to foreign news agencies from South Africa. The 1964 conclusions were "not much more revealing" than those in 1962: News sent abroad condemned government policies, it was sent by "anti-Nationalist" journalists and "rarely quoted Government justifications for its actions".

The commission's main recommendation was the setting up of a statutory Press Council, as the Board of Reference that the NPU meanwhile had established did not satisfy the requirements "of a body designed to discipline or encourage" self-control. The proposed council could impose "unlimited fines", would be given "powers of reprimand", and could order publication of its judgements. There was no appeal, and contempt was triable by court. Also serious was the recommendation that all journalists should register every year on payment of a fee. Only registered journalists would have authority to send press cables. Also, the Post Office was required to file all cables and make them available to the council. Copies of all reports filed to the foreign press other than by cable had to be filed with the council's registrar. The RDM wrote on 12 May 1964 that it was difficult for "any sensible person to treat it seriously, but unfortunately it will have to be taken in deadly earnest because it can – and almost certainly will – be used as the excuse for legislation", which meant government control of the press. The importance of the commission was not "in any way diminished by the fact that no legislation emerged from it".[35] For fourteen years, the possibility of a statutory body "hung over the press", with the "ever-present threat" already a kind of censorship. Apart from existing laws and regulations governing the day-to-day activities of journalists, they felt "exposed to the ill-will of Government, which accuses them of maliciously distorting the facts and running down the country in the eyes of foreigners". Also, ministers constantly threatened sanctions once the commission's findings were finalised.

For this reason, D.H. Ollemans, Argus Group chair, had earlier proposed an NPU voluntary Press Board.[36] In 1955, two informal meetings were attended by "virtually every daily and Sunday paper" and a number of editors. No decision was taken; it was felt the commission's report should be awaited. Still, Ollemans drafted a code of conduct as discussed by the NPU.

Also in 1954, government set up a "Commission of Inquiry in Regard to Undesirable Publications", which provided its report in 1957.[37] The commission had to deal with pornographic and obscene material only, but recommendations were made for drastic censorship regarding political publications, with books and magazines falling under the jurisdiction of the Publications Board. If uncertainty arose "whether newspapers are undesirable, any authority charged with the enforcement of the relevant legislation" could consult the Publications Board. There was "no doubt" that, had all the recommendations of this commission been accepted, a "blanket pre-publication censorship of the political content of newspapers" would have been introduced. Instead, government used this commission's "extensive and intimidating recommendations" as weapon to persuade the NPU to continue setting up its proposed Press Board. In 1960, then deputy minister of the Interior, P.W. Botha, introduced an Undesirable Publications Bill, providing for pre-publication censorship. After its first reading, it was referred to a select committee, but an "enormous public outcry" from both English and Afrikaans journalists followed. Together with the need to give the NPU more time for its own "measurements", the Bill was dropped. Nevertheless, the Bill was re-introduced in 1961, now without the "pernicious" pre-publication clause, which again was referred to a select committee. It served before Parliament in 1962 and was enacted in 1963 as the Publications and Entertainments Act – importantly, with the South African press excluded from its provisions. But government achieved what it set out to do: Forcing the press to introduce its self-disciplinary Press Board, in exchange for which NPU members were excluded from the Act's provisions.

The parliamentary commission's long-awaited report, which appeared in February 1962 after twelve years, comprised two volumes, 700 pages in total, with seventeen appendices totalling another 1,566 pages.[38] This report did not refer to a press council at all, but was an analysis of South African news coverage overseas. Outdated, it was "tabled without any action being taken".

In the meantime, the NPU's Press Board was established in 1962, in time for the second report presented in May 1964. This report stated that the latter did "not satisfy the fundamental requirements of a body designed to discipline or encourage self-control of the press". The commission was also not satisfied that no journalists or members of the public were represented in the Board. It also did not have any "real powers" and was not "comprehensive enough". The proposed statutory press council was therefore recommended to maintain press freedom; to encourage accurate reporting; to encourage informed and responsible comment; to encourage the press to "maintain the dignity of the state and its officials", and to receive complaints and "try such matters and give judgement thereon".

All of this, finally, would be financed by a levy on the press. The commission's proposed council was something completely different to the already established NPU Board. Fortunately, nothing came of it and the NPU body continued to function.

The first paper banned under apartheid

One of the "defining characteristics" of the NP's policy was its "anti-communist stance and mission" to repress all dissenting voices.[39] After the banning of the Communist Party, the first proclamation to ban a newspaper under apartheid was published in the *Government Gazette*"[40] on 23 May 1952, banning the *Guardian*.[41] The act used in 1952 was later grouped with others as the Internal Security Act of 1982,[42] curtailing press freedom by "imposing draconian restrictions on publications".

Brian Bunting, founder-editor of the *Guardian*, and about 40 colleagues, would be unemployed.[43] Bunting and his team simply went ahead and published under an unbanned title, the *Clarion*, while the banning drew international coverage from the *Times* of London to the *New York Times*. In Parliament, UP members argued that, although they did not support the *Guardian*, it should not be banned, as a lack of media freedom was a characteristic of a dictatorship, "which South Africa should not strive to be".

The *Clarion* was published from 29 May 1952, just six days after the *Guardian*'s ban, and mirrored its content. Its readers regarded it as the same paper, exactly what the staff tried to achieve by "circumnavigat[ing] banning laws". In August 1952, government found that another paper was registered under the same title, leading the *Clarion* to change its name to *People's World*.[44] In November that year, the paper again had to change its name, this time to *Advance*. It could publish for two years, until it became the *New Age* in 1954 when *Advance* was banned. Jack Cope became the editor of the *New Age*. To avoid another banning, he changed both the layout and content.[45] But there was already a certain "resignation": Unlike with previous bans, no publication, save for two newspapers, reported the ban, showing "how normalised banning had become".

The vice tightens

Strijdom succeeded Malan in 1954. Represented as "Lion of the North", a Northern version of Afrikaner Nationalism, he disregarded any politesse in the most blunt and brutal manner, stating in 1955 that apartheid could be called "paramountcy, baasskap [boss-ship] or what you will", but that it, indisputably, was "domination":[46]

> I am being as blunt as I can. I am making no excuses. Either the White man dominates or the Black takes over ... The only way the Europeans can maintain supremacy is by domination ... And the only way they can maintain domination is by withholding the vote from non-Europeans ... The government of the country is in the hands of the White man and for that reason the White man is baas in South Africa.

Strijdom had "little regard for constitutional restraint if it delayed [the] implementation of apartheid".[47] Under him, segregation was enforced in almost all public places. The 1959 Extension of University Education Act,[48] ironically – taking its name into account – severely restricted students of colour from existing ("white") universities and set up four "ethnic colleges". The law compelling African women to carry reference books, or "passes", led to widespread uprisings, including the march on the Union Buildings on 9 August 1956, which today is celebrated as Women's Day. This was followed by the multiracial Congress of the People's Charter, demanding a democratic, non-racial government. The NP government responded by arresting 156 people, and charging them with high treason.[49] Their trial lasted more than two years, leading to "incalculable damage to race relations at home and the country's image abroad". Strijdom's response was in "classic 'kill the messenger' syndrome": attacking the English press as "South Africa's greatest enemy".

Internal Afrikaner feuds - or the political economy of the media

Exactly what was at stake with regard to power and Afrikaner hegemony in the first decade of apartheid rule is also reflected in the internal press feuds among Afrikaners. The *Sunday Express* "nibbl[ed]" for some time at the "anomaly" of cabinet ministers being directors of Afrikaans press companies. The same situation of course also existed in the English press, with mining interests not only serving on the boards of English press groups, but also owning them, and mining companies owning majority shares in the English press. But, on 15 September 1957, the *Express* published an article starting a "series of audacious news reports of a kind seldom seen".[50] It concerned Strijdom's "wrecking" of a cabinet colleague's plan to launch a paper, whilst protecting *Dagbreek* and its similarly named company of which Strijdom was a director. Strijdom also said that internal Afrikaner feuds should not "sabotage Nationalism". The colleague was minister of education, J.H. Viljoen, also chair of Afrikaanse Pers Beperk, who now had to abandon his company's plans to publish its Afrikaans Sunday paper in Johannesburg. As *Sondagstem*, it would be direct competition to Strijdom's *Dagbreek*. Preparations for *Sondagstem* were well advanced. Dummies were prepared and a news franchise from SAPA and staff arrangements were almost completed, while CNA would distribute the paper. But Strijdom "bluntly" told Viljoen *Sondagstem* must be abandoned, otherwise "he would be a saboteur of nationalism".

Thus Strijdom killed *Sondagstem* before it was even published. If Viljoen and Afrikaanse Pers continued, Dagbreek would publish a new daily as rival to their *Die Vaderland*. Viljoen was "in an awkward and embarrassing position". As chair of Afrikaanse Pers he could override Strijdom as chair of Dagbreek. But Strijdom was prime minister and Viljoen "merely" a cabinet minister.

The *Express*'s reporting on this "politico-economic clash" between the two powerful Northern Afrikaner companies was "embarrassing", but "deadly accurate". Strijdom not only prevented Afrikaanse Pers from publishing their Sunday newspaper, he also ended Naspers's intentions to publish a "weekend paper" in Johannesburg by simply telling them to "keep out". The proposed Naspers paper would also provide opposition to *Dagbreek,* but Strijdom's stance was that, if Naspers did so, they would "sabotage nationalism in South Africa". During this time, the English press reported that two of Strijdom's companies were printing "four well-known publications" for government departments. In fact, altogether six government publications were printed. The exposé's ramifications spread, showing that the Cape and Free State administrators had private business activities, as did other prominent NP politicians. Strijdom, in "many such instances", used his position to "boost" private business. One was the youth magazine *Patrys*, printed by Voortrekkerpers, which also was chaired by Strijdom.[51] At the end of 1956, "using his official notepaper", he "strongly urged parents and children to buy *Patrys*". Then, at the end of 1957, he could disclose the magazine's "tremendous growth" – and a record profit of £53,878 for his company.

During this period it was also inferred that "it could fairly be said that not all judicial appointments were based on merit", with a "running fight" with the minister of Justice (later state president), "Blackie" Swart.[52] During the NP's "accession to power"

> [o]ne dared not state openly that a new incumbent was incompetent or unfit for office. Instead, the appointment might be said to evoke "surprise", the new judge appearing to lack the experience of eminent senior colleagues who were overlooked. This certainly became the height of understatement when, as did happen, an appointee rose from the ranks of junior to senior to acting judge to judge within a month.

The three 'South African press theories'

The continuing debate on media freedom from 1950 on illuminated "three distinct concepts" of the press that coexisted "uneasily" in South Africa up to the 1980s.[53] These were the "Afrikaans concept", the "English concept", and the "African concept".

Ironically, the Afrikaans concept closely resembled that of the countries against which government so desperately warned, namely authoritarian states. This "Afrikaner view of the press" developed out of the "cohesive, close-knit Afrikaner tribe". Like the "party press" in Western Europe at the time, it was also similar to the Soviet Communist theory of the press. These concepts refer to the original "Four Theories of the Press" formulated in the 1950s. The Authoritarian theory was based on the idea that "truth" was the product of a few wise men; the Soviet Communist theory expanded on the Authoritarian theory.[54]

The South African English concept of the press was deemed "Libertarian". According to the "Four Theories", the Libertarian theory evolved from the work of Milton, Locke and Mill, based on the "long, three-way struggle between king, Parliament, and the courts"[55] brought to South Africa by British immigrants. Their allegiance to the public instead of government put the English press "at odds" with the former, whereas the Afrikaner view was to be "responsible" to government.

The African concept of the press – historically to publish newspapers to serve their own community – developed into publications serving the "cause".[56] But, while the English press was still tolerated by government, the African press was "too threatening".

Taking these South African "press theories" into account, it was no wonder successive NP governments restricted basically all means of public communication and most of the restrictive laws directed at print media; the SABC, "anyway", was under the control of the government.[57]

Apartheid enacted, press freedom the victim

A "massive complex of overlapping laws" grew between 1948 and 1968 "to preclude an ever widening area of subjects from being available for public scrutiny".[58] In the International Peace Institute's Report, South Africa was named as one of the countries in which the balance between state security and press freedom "had not been maintained". The press suffered "a serious loss in its freedom" because "a body of laws" was "an instrument for maintaining a political party in power rather than an impartial arbiter between competing interests". Three methods of balancing the claims of a free press against government predominated. The first was direct state "interposition", in other words, censorship; the second, internal self-control by the press; and the third the reliance upon courts to impose sanctions. But "[p]erhaps the most unnerving" was that much of post-1948 legislation was so "loosely drafted" that it was "increasingly difficult" to know when an offence was being committed.

The Suppression of Communism Act (1950) was enacted during the first press commission debate in parliament. It "greatly" extended government's existing powers for controlling the press. The governor-general (after 1961 the state president) was enabled

> to ban any publication aimed at furthering the principles or enabled to ban
> any publication aimed at furthering the principles or promoting the spread

of communism[,] and inter alia it became an offence under the Act to convey information, the publication of which was calculated to further the achievement of any of the objects of communism.

It was described as the "first and broadest" of legislation to appear after 1948.[59] Any organisation deemed "unlawful" could be banned, including the publication of such an organisation's views.[60] There was no recourse to law, a matter of "particular concern" to newspapers, as it marked the beginning of direct state censorship as opposed to relying on courts to impose "sanctions". With a law so "loosely drafted", it was "quite impossible" for editors to know whether they were breaking the law.

Another amendment prevented a newspaper from registering under more than one name, as the registration would lapse unless it was published once a month. A "stringent" registration fee of £10,000, forfeited if banned, made the continued re-emergence of papers impossible. Further amendments prohibited papers from publishing any statements by a banned person, "whether alive or dead", without the "express permission" of the justice minister. By 1968 there were approximately 600 banned people in South Africa. This meant editors had to be constantly updated with lists of banned persons. These enactments probably produced the "most serious inroads" into the "free functioning of the press". As it was phrased: "The intention and effect of this Act and its amendments was to eliminate an entire segment of political opinion from the public arena."

After the 1952 Defiance Campaign, there was a "new and more concerted" attack on the English press. The 1953 Public Safety and Criminal Law Amendment Act, with its serious infringements on press freedom, was also enacted. During the Defiance Campaign, nearly 10,000 "non-Whites" and a few "Whites" were jailed for defying specifically six laws. The 1953 amendment made it "extremely difficult" for editors to criticise existing laws, as there was "no way of knowing whether criticism might . . . result in the law being broken".

The Riotous Assembly Act of 1956 defined more "sets of situations" in which publication could be prohibited.[61] The Prisons Act of 1959 was a direct result of *Drum* articles critical of prison conditions, and the Official Secrets and Defence Act of 1965 added "massively restrictive" press legislation. Earlier, the 1955 Criminal Procedure Act provided the "machinery" to subpoena witnesses to answer questions in court, causing "most concern" to journalists.[62] It meant that, if the police believed an individual possessed any information that might help in an investigation, they could force the person to disclose that information.[63] In 1967, in attempting to clarify the relationship between press and police, the NPU reached an agreement with the police commissioner.[64] Government did not use its "extensive powers" to ban newspapers outright or enforce legislation "more stringently and more frequently", because the press was forced to censor itself by exercising "internal self-control".

The later Police Amendment Act in 1978[65] was added in the wake of the Information Scandal, with the Advocate-General Bill introduced in 1979. It included a controversial section prohibiting the publication of articles concerned with public corruption and maladministration before it had been vetted by the advocate-general. This Act followed the exposé of the Information Scandal, which included, *inter alia*, the State's attempted purchase of SAAN through Louis Luyt and the subsequent clandestine setting up of *The Citizen*.

The first state of emergency

In 1959, Strijdom's successor, Verwoerd, blamed the economic depression on the "irresponsible and unpatriotic" actions of the English press. In 1960, in a South Africa that was "closer to a revolution than ever before",[66] a referendum to change the country's government into that of a republic was announced – "a cherished Afrikaner goal" since the defeat of the Boer Republics.

Meanwhile, the ANC offshoot, the PAC, launched a passive resistance campaign against the pass laws, the "hated symbol" of subjugation. In March 1960, blacks were mobilised to go peacefully to police stations, report that they did not have their passes and ask to be arrested. At the Sharpeville police station, policemen – remembering the Cato Manor tragedy just two months earlier when a police raid was set upon, leaving nine policemen dead – panicked and opened fire. Altogether 69 protesters were killed and 180 injured – shot in the back as they tried to flee. Violence engulfed South Africa and government declared its first state of emergency, calling up civilian reserve units, arresting hundreds of people and banning the ANC and PAC.

The march on Cape Town's Caledon Square Police Station, 30 March, 1960.
Photo: Heard, *The Cape of Storms*

The state of emergency also tore the Congress Alliance apart. This alliance consisted of the ANC, the South African Indian Congress, the South African Coloured People's Organisation (later renamed the Coloured People's Congress), the white South African Congress of Democrats (many also members of the Communist Party, already banned in 1950), the South African Congress of Trade Unions, and the Federation of South African Women.[67]

Almost 2,000 activists were detained from March until August 1960. The "dissidents who escaped this dragnet" went underground or fled into exile. The banned groups regrouped and formed underground guerrilla units, both inside and outside South Africa. The Struggle now also "moved into the first stage of armed struggle", with Umkhonto we Sizwe ("Spear of the Nation"), or MK, formed in June 1961.

But the NP was at the height of its power during the 1960s and early 1970s. The "key" was control over African labour. Government tried "to reclassify, redistribute, and ultimately relocate" the entire black labour force in South Africa to "African reserves – referred to as Bantustans, then home-lands, and ultimately national states".

What the first state of emergency meant

When in March 1960 South Africa entered its first state of emergency,[68] it meant the country was governed by martial law. It included a curfew for all people of colour, denied townships basic resources such as water and electricity, and prohibited political meetings.[69] The police also raided homes and offices, including those of *New Age* staff, leading to the arrest of Bunting and his staff members. In the paper's "historically tenacious" spirit, it continued to publish despite being short-staffed. The police also confiscated copies from street vendors, but subscribers still received theirs. Most of the remaining staff worked from hiding to avoid arrest, save for Albie Sachs, the only journalist to work from the Cape Town office. But, by 5 April 1960, the *Government Gazette* published a proclamation that the paper had to cease publication – the first deadline the paper missed since its first *Guardian* edition. The police shut down all *New Age* offices. There was no certainty for how long the state of emergency would last and when the paper could resume publication, but government began to release detainees by August 1960, indicating the state of emergency was over.[70] *New Age* resumed publication one week later – a "significant" edition with the journalists' versions of their detention – stories other papers were not willing to publish.

In 1962, the paper turned 25, celebrating throughout the year.[71] Its silver jubilee edition was published on 22 March 1962, containing several articles by guest contributors, including ANC President Albert Luthuli.

But this was its last celebration – two months later the justice minister banned the paper. He also added a provision to the Sabotage Bill of 1962, which referred to the £10,000 fee a paper would lose if banned. This closed the loophole for the *New Age* to re-emerge after a banning. In its next edition, the paper carried an "open letter" to the minister stating why they had the right to publish and for the ban not to be imposed. But the paper was finally banned in November 1962 and unsuccessfully tried to sue government.[72] Just before the Sabotage Bill came into effect, Bunting went on to print another paper, *Spark*, with the idea that there would be a legal alternative if the *New Age* was banned. So *Spark's* first edition appeared in December 1962.[73] Content-wise it was the same as *New Age*, but focused more on the activities of the ANC and its affiliates. The minister reacted by banning most of the staff, including the editor, in February 1963. Without experienced staffers, the paper struggled to maintain the standards it had set over 25 years, and *Spark* closed in March 1963.

A journalist's account

The clampdown on the post-Sharpeville *New Age* was recalled by journalist James Zug.[74] After government "secretly declared martial law" at three in the morning on 30 March 1960, police "swept into homes across the nation to arrest hundreds of activists". That evening, government "went on the radio and publicly announced what many already knew: South Africa was in a state of emergency". Martial law meant detention without trial was legalised. For the *New Age*, the state of emergency was a "disaster". On Thursday, 31 March, the Security Branch arrested most of its 55 editorial, administrative and sales staff country-wide. Sachs, "a young lawyer who wrote the international news feature", was the only one who remained free. After phoning Caledon Square that Thursday to enquire whether *New Age* was allowed to publish, the police said yes, and Sachs laid out the next edition to be taken to the Pioneer Press plant on Tuesday, 5 April, as scheduled. But on the same day the justice minister issued the *Government Gazette*'s "special proclamation", ordering *New Age* to cease publication for the duration of the emergency. The minister gave as reason a "systematic publishing of matter which is, in my opinion, of a subversive character". For the first time since February 1937, "the weekly was not going to meet its Thursday appointment". Late that afternoon the police turned up at Pioneer, just as the 7 April edition was printed. About 135,000 copies had been printed by then, "with the ink still wet on the newsprint". The police stopped the press, seized all copies and dismantled the type. Pioneer's owner, Len Lee-Warden – also an MP – "snuck one copy away". This 7 April 1960 edition carried a full page on the Treason Trial, and being "[f]orcibly removed from the reading public", the edition "symbolized what the state of emergency meant to South Africa".

By mid-August 1960, with government starting to release detainees, some staffers returned but, like Ruth First, "remained underground".[75] They wanted the weekly to reappear as a sign of defiance, so the paper appeared on Thursday, 8 September, eight days after the state of emergency was lifted on 31 August – "[f]ive months of proscription, fifty-five staffers in jail, and the banning of the ANC were not enough deterrence for the weekly".

Though "[b]lurry and indistinct, the lines between the banned ANC, Umkhonto we Sizwe (MK) and the *New Age* crossed and recrossed".[76] The ANC, now based in London, needed the paper "more than ever to keep its name in the limelight", and "[s]ymbolically, it was vital for Albert Luthuli, the nominal head of the ANC, a well-respected elder statesman and an inspiration for millions of Africans, to be featured in *New Age*". So, "[s]hamelessly fibbing", *New Age* functioned as an essential part of MK, with the paper's four offices providing a cover for clandestine work. Mandela's association with the paper was "further proof of the weekly's direct connection to the armed struggle", and "defending the ANC" through the pages of *New Age* "was easy for Mandela".

But, as mentioned, disaster loomed. The February 1962 silver jubilee was still fêted with a "Grand Celebration Dance" at Cape Town's Banqueting Hall, a dance at the Four Aces Club in Fordsburg, and a special twelve-page commemorative issue on 22 March, but the new Sabotage Bill was being prepared.[77] On 21 May 1962, new justice minister John Vorster waved a copy of the anniversary issue in Parliament, saying it should be banned as it was "the mouthpiece and propaganda organ of the communists". The "House roar[ed] with approval". The Sabotage Bill gave Vorster "the power to outlaw strikes and to ban, place under house arrest, and forbid any person from any specific activity" – a "blanket ban".

The provision that no publication could be published without the "security deposit" of up to £10,000, forfeitable if banned, was aimed at *New Age*. Vorster "slammed shut the loophole" that allowed the *Guardian* to continue to reappear under new titles. Undefiant, the paper came out with a "four-inch-high" banner headline proclaiming "THIS IS A POLICE STATE". The paper "rose to protest its imminent demise" with a number of pages detailing each provision of the bill and its effect on the liberation movement. Vorster just "tightened the noose" as he banned the Congress of Democrats in September and began to "house-arrest" activists in October. Those house-arrested were forbidden to communicate with anyone banned, and since nearly everyone on the *New Age* staff was banned, "inter-office communication" became impossible. On Friday, 30 November 1962, the paper was banned for the third time in a decade. Six days later, however, on Thursday, 6 December 1962, the four-page *Spark* sprung up.

This was thanks to the fact that, shortly before the Sabotage Act, Real Printing and Publishing bought two titles, *Morning Star* and *Spark*.[78] An edition of each appeared in July 1962 already, each with four pages, followed by the same once monthly to maintain their registration status. Both had a "haphazard" look, but readers did not care – it had none. Only five copies of each were published and sent to the required libraries and institutions that by law had to receive a registered periodical. So, on 6 December, the "hitherto sleepy" *Spark*'s four pages quadrupled to sixteen, its newsstand price shot up from one penny to sixpence, and the monthly became a weekly. *Spark* "soldiered on", but 26 years and 1,328 issues after the first issue of the *Guardian* in Cape Town in 1937, the final edition of *Spark* appeared on Thursday, 28 March 1963.

... leading to self-censorship

In the 1960s, South Africa was in the world's spotlight "as never before", leading to boycotts against the country.[79] Readers abroad were better informed about events than South Africans themselves, and editors, unsure about what they could print, "had to exercise a large measure of self-censorship". In England, the *Times* of London reported that the press "has not been bludgeoned by censorship into silence", but had to work daily "under the shadow of the axe".

After the 1961 declaration as Republic and the withdrawal from the Commonwealth, Verwoerd said the "position in which we have landed, both in the Commonwealth and at the UN, is to a large extent the result of inaccurate reports and a wrong interpretation of the policy of the Government". Warning the press to discipline themselves, he said they "should exercise care" and "keep an eye on each other". On 15 April 1961, the RDM wrote that any action by Verwoerd to curb the freedom of the press "will everywhere be interpreted as only the first step towards a general muzzling of speech and opinion in South Africa".

The development of the black press under apartheid

Despite the prohibitive measures by government on the media, some strides – also commercially successful ones – were made with regard to the development of the black press. South Africa's "expanding urban black working-class population" was represented by various socialist publications from the 1920s, but "a non-racial resistance press" emerged from the 1950s.[80]

In May 1951, three years after the NP's victory, Jim Bailey, son of mining and media magnate Sir Abe, launched the *African Drum* and, in March 1955, his *Golden City Post.*[81] These were so successful that Bailey was called the William Randolph Hearst of Southern Africa. By October 1951, Bailey's magazine was titled *Drum* only, and moved from Cape Town to Johannesburg. Its "gee whizz" journalism with its "sex-crime-sports" formula focused on entertainment news. Still, sensationalism was paired with good writing and investigative reporting. As "mouthpiece for the township masses" it was published "with great stylistic verve" in a new "Africanised English" that was "both punchy and colourful". It also had an East and West Africa edition, leading to a weekly circulation of an astonishing 470,000 by 1969.

Magazines directed at the black market became "quite important" after 1945, when "numerous successful black publications" were established.[82] *Drum* was regarded as foremost, with its West and East African editions even more popular than the local one, where it "rode the wave of black protest and social turbulence" in the early years of "Verwoerdian grand apartheid".[83] The magazine broke entirely new ground in African publishing by being at one and the same time a publicist for the ANC's Defiance Campaign, a vehicle for independent investigative journalism, a model of township lifestyles, and a commercially successful picture periodical.

It was through *Drum* that the "pathos and tragedy" of the removal of blacks from Sophiatown was brought to the world's attention, becoming an important mouthpiece to express social and political grievances.[84] When political movements such as the ANC and the PAC were banned in 1960, black publications were severely affected.[85] *Drum* was first withdrawn and then appeared "in a much milder form, devoid of political issues". *Bona*, launched in 1956, together with *Drum*, enjoyed "a virtual monopoly" in the black magazine market, until the mid-1970s and 1980s, when other black magazines "suddenly broke into the market". This was attributed to the rapid rate of urbanisation and literacy.

Bailey's *Golden City Post,* with the same formula of "sex, sin and soccer – plus relevant reporting" – had a weekly circulation of 224,000 in 1968, with about 1,15 million African, Coloured and Indian readers.[86]

But it was *Drum* that had a "lasting impact" on black journalism and creative writing. Several of its journalists became mainstream names, such as Ezekiel Mphahlele, later Wits professor of literature. Others are Peter Magubane, Nat Nakasa, Can Themba, Bloke Modisane, Lewis Nkosi, James Mathews, Alex la Guma and Alfred Hutchinson – all of whom fled the country around Sharpeville. Nakasa left South Africa on what was called an "exit permit" after he could not get a passport when he was awarded the 1964 Nieman Fellowship to study at Harvard. There he tragically died the next year. He wrote:

> I may shut up for some time because of fear. Yet even this will not make me feel ashamed. For I know that as long as the ideas remain unchanged within me, there will always be the possibility that, one day, I shall burst out and say everything that I wish to say – in a loud and thunderous voice.[87]

From his pen also flowed these words: "There must be humans on the other side of the fence; it's only that we haven't learned how to talk." On his death in 1965, Nobel laureate Nadine Gordimer wrote:

He did not calculate the population as sixteen million or four million, but as twenty. He belonged not between two worlds, but to both. And in him one could see the hope of one world. He has left that hope behind; there will be others to take it up … His death must be laid at the door of the people who made him take an exit permit – this government.[88]

Not only did *Drum*'s staff became casualties of the banning orders, but these measures also "killed off most significant black journalism".[89] One of the influential journalists of the time, Don Mattera, referred to censorship as "a dastardly, cowardly deed".[90]

When *Drum* reappeared in its "far milder guise", it steered clear of the aggressive reporting of political issues that had earlier produced "news and photos of meaning to the urban blacks".[91] And then, in 1984, it would be saved by, of all companies, Naspers, which had been established as Afrikaner Nationalist publishing house, although by the 1980s it was a company that had re-invented itself from within;[92] but more on that later.

Bantu Press, established in 1932, was taken over in full by the Argus Group in 1962.[93] Its daily *World* was modelled on the London *Daily Mirror*.[94] A few months after the Soweto uprising in 1976, Percy Qoboza was appointed editor of both *World* and *Weekend World* – "the first African in almost a generation who was free of white editorial supervision" – only for him and his papers to be silenced on 19 October 1977. Until the paper's banning on what would become known as Black Wednesday, it was the "most significant voice in black journalism". Of this banning law, academic Harold G. Rudolph said[95]

Actions taken against black publications, resulting in the black population of the Transvaal being denied its own major newspaper, will affect the whole of South African society. It is therefore vitally important that such actions be both justifiable and justified in the open, otherwise South Africa will have taken another step towards the Orwellian nightmare of 1984.

Meanwhile, government also tried its utmost to work as "mind manager" of the black population with its own publications. Verwoerd, in 1954 minister of "native affairs", established *Bantu* in that year. Later that year, his department also published the *Bantu Education Journal* for black schools. By the late 1970s, the information department published thirteen serial publications in nine black languages.[96] Commercial publications by the white press, the so-called "look-read" magazines, were highly popular. One was *Bona*, founded in 1956, with a circulation of 290,000 in 1983. The white press became increasingly dependent on building black markets and readerships, meaning blacks counted for an increasing share of readership, preparing the way for the next phase in the history of the black press, the so-called multiracial period.

As mentioned earlier, the black publishing scene would change "dramatically" in 1984, when Naspers bought Bailey's "ailing" magazines *Drum* and *True Love* and Sunday paper *City Press*.[97] There was an "uproar" after "probably the strangest marriage conceivable". Yet, by then, Naspers was re-inventing itself as a "new" company, positioned for a "new" South Africa, with reform journalism from within its own ranks at the forefront. This initiative was largely attributed to reform journalist and media leader Ton Vosloo. In 1984, he succeeded liberal David de Villiers as managing director of Naspers, leading the transformation of Naspers from "a decent print media company with a few successful business units" in 1983 to the subsequent "transcontinental multimedia conglomerate", all largely attributed to Vosloo.[98] According to former editor Tim du Plessis, Vosloo was "the one who in the 1980s – our political Middle Ages – persuaded a sceptical board" to persist with the haemorrhaging *City Press*:

> Ton must have had a vista of the kind of media landscape we have today, because he often had to move heaven and earth to explain and to defend *City Press*'s then role as a UDF-leaning Struggle newspaper. At the same time, he had to reassure the edgy Percy Qoboza and his sceptical editorial team about their paper that had landed up unexpectedly in '*Boere* hands'. He did an excellent job in this regard – and this I heard personally from Percy and subsequent *City Press* editors.

But more about this next phase in the development of South Africa's media later in this chapter.

The development of radio

After the 1948 NP takeover, the up-to-then mostly English-language SABC was quickly transformed when the new government gained control of its board.[99] By mid-1980, more than 9,5 million South Africans listened daily to radio programmes and almost 70% of the country's whites watched TV.[100] There were sixteen radio services and three television channels, totalling 2,269 broadcast hours per week in seventeen languages.

At this stage, it was one of the most controversial institutions in South Africa, regarded as "His Master's Voice" because of its close ties to government and being a state broadcaster, not a public broadcaster. It was controlled by Afrikaner elites with "strict Calvinistic morality and cultural values" imposed on all "without reflecting the least bit of the cultural diversity of South Africa".

The NP used the SABC as its propaganda machine, dominating opposition parties and presenting "a world view that conforms to Afrikaner aspirations and fears".[101] White opposition voices were "scarcely heard"; those of African, Coloured and Asian communities "simply not". Through SABC2 and SABC3, aimed at the black population, it had "effectively narcotised and propagandised" large segments of the black majority.

Broadcasting mirrored apartheid: different stations for different language groups. Radio Bantu was an umbrella for a number of different African languages. Yet, despite the SABC being a "useful idiot", its technical developments and expansion were impressive. Another key tenet was how it was used by the Broederbond and, lastly, how long it took to introduce television.

In 1950, the SABC established its own news-gathering service, ending the relaying of BBC news by the SABC. By the mid-1950s, an English and Afrikaans service were "well established", along with a commercial station, Springbok Radio, all receiving an equal share of 70 hours a day broadcast over 52 transmitters.

The "Bantu" services developed from a "re-diffusion system" in Orlando, Johannesburg as a single channel and as a "wired loudspeaker", operated by a British firm. By 1957, when the SABC started to provide sixteen hours of daily programming, it reached 11,910 subscribers.

Because of technical reasons and costs, the SABC could not expand what it called the "Bantu" service to other regions via medium and short wave. By 1959, SABC engineers realised the feasibility of a nation-wide FM system, which also would make programming for Radio Bantu possible. In 1964 it consisted of seven separate services: Xhosa in the Cape, South Sotho in the Free State, Tswana in the Northern Cape and Western Transvaal (North West), Zulu in Natal (KwaZulu-Natal) and south-eastern Transvaal (Mpumalanga), and Venda in the north-eastern Transvaal (Limpopo). This low-cost transmitter distributed "government-controlled programming" – the Afrikaner elite "not underestimating its potential" for political influence.

Meanwhile, the 1960s were "boom years" for the economy:[102]

> While the rest of Africa was in the process of decolonisation, on the southern end of the continent economic expansion saw the rise of Afrikaner capital, increased urbanisation of the black population, and dominance of the AB through the National Party in the political and cultural spheres of the country. Perhaps nowhere were these tendencies more evident than in the SABC which, as a broadcasting institution, was at the confluence of all these sites of struggle.

While the SABC still managed "to maintain a critical distance from the hegemony of the NP and Afrikaner cultural organisations such as the AB" during the 1950s, the "ascendancy" of Piet Meyer as chair of the SABC as well as chair of the AB in 1959 meant it was no longer possible. The result was "a proliferation of top-level managerial posts", most filled with AB and/or NP members. "[N]ational interest" meant a consensus based on government's interests and an attempt "at bridging the gap" between the English- and Afrikaans-speaking white constituencies. The interests of the black middle class were separated from those of the white, with "distinct ethnic identities" for the various black language groups. Four radio categories developed, lasting into the 1980s and early 1990s: the "public service tradition" of the English and Afrikaans services, the African language services, a series of regional music-format stations, and commercial radio.

The Broadcasting Amendment Act No 49 of 1960 brought significant changes in the running of the SABC, including a separate structure for black programmes. These were "isolated" from the rest under 35 white "supervisors" who controlled black announcers and programmes on six channels, collectively called Radio Bantu. Ideologically, it served "to reinforce the separation" between black and white audiences, as well as the divisions among black listeners. In designing the world's first FM transmitter grid, SABC engineers "ensured that black audiences could only access broadcasts and information which the state had specifically directed to them". Although most people owned FM receivers, they could not receive medium- and short-wave broadcasts from beyond South Africa's borders.

The technological development of radio up to the mid-1980s is described as "impressive". Several white-owned commercial stations were also established by now, such as Radio Highveld (1964), Radio Good Hope (1965) and Radio Port Natal (1967).[103] All were "successful and pervasive" thanks to the fact that radio did not have to compete with television until 1976.

The role that the AB played in the development of "His Master's Voice" is significant, as it infiltrated the "higher echelons" of the SABC, thereby accelerating the influence of the NP.[104] The AB, generally regarded as the power behind the throne and influencing all of South African public life, in 1970 counted 12,000 members organised into about 800 "cells" or divisions. As clandestine organisation it was the "real and secret power in South

Africa", "in considerable measure responsible for the political breakthrough of Afrikaner nationalism", its "[p]ower and secrecy ... fused in the crucible of Afrikaner politics".[105]

Up to P.W. Botha, all prime ministers were members.[106] The SABC, among the "strongest opinion-forming and cultural institutions" in South Africa, was so totally under the influence of the AB that Meyer, AB chair from 1960 to 1972, was for the most part also chair of the SABC. At least 49 Broeders were in influential SABC positions,[107] as were seven of a twelve-member commission of inquiry into television in 1970.

The first "Press Board of Reference"

In 1952, the "same political drama" that had been played out "over and over again", namely "first harsh official criticism directed at newspapers, followed by threats of news statutory controls if the press did not 'discipline' itself", led to the establishment of the NPU's first Press Board of Reference in 1962.[108]

It was clear that, if the press did not take action, government would. Thus the NPU held a special meeting in Johannesburg in March 1962. Members of the South African Society of Journalists (SASJ) objected to the proposed Board and its code of conduct, calling it a "first and disastrous step towards censorship over political reporting and comment".[109]

However, the NPU adopted the constitution for the Press Board of Reference, as it was now formally called, but not unanimously. The Argus Group and the Afrikaans papers supported it, while most of the SAAN papers did not. The Board's objectives were to maintain the character of the South African press "in accordance with the highest professional and technical standards", to consider "alleged infringements" and to publish periodical reports. It comprised a chair and an alternate chair, both retired judges, and two members, also with alternates – all appointed by the NPU. The code was "essentially similar" to those in other countries with such bodies and "contained nothing that a conscientious journalist would not normally observe". But there were two significant differences: Journalists were "not required to observe professional secrecy to protect sources", as well as a specific ruling that "comment should take cognisance of the complex racial problems of South Africa and the general good and safety of the country and its peoples".

The Board met quarterly and a "rather cumbersome machinery for adjudication of complaints" was implemented. In its first report, from June 1962 to February 1964, six complaints were heard, five from politicians, the sixth from a political organisation. Rulings were in favour of the press in two and against it in four.

This first Board was gradually modified, with more severe restrictions by the NPU itself to "appease the government and fit its requirements". It was regarded by some as "abject self-censorship" – also to protect financial interests.[110] In the process, the press had "placated the government on each occasion, but [had] also given away more and more of its freedom and independence". It was also acknowledged that the Board was a desperate attempt to "forestall direct government control of the press", with self-discipline "preferable to government censorship".[111]

The Board was "essentially harmless", as it could impose no sanctions and its code comprised "little more than a series of platitudinous statements no self-respecting journalist could object to". Still, there were fears that even a voluntary disciplinary body would be the first step toward more restrictive measures. Government was "determined" to impose some form of discipline. The fears of those who saw the Board as "a first and dangerous step along a slippery path" were justified. Internal and external pressures grew with the implementation of apartheid laws, resulting in the NP imposing more and more restrictive measures on the press. It forced the NPU, through intimidation, to amend the Board's constitution and code "until it largely resembled the kind of disciplinary body the Nationalists had in mind all along". But it was administered through the media by the media, and government could "point with pride to the fact that South Africa had the freest press on the continent".

Although this publication does not focus on how the erosion of freedom of expression played itself out in terms of book publications, movies and university publications, all of these were also subject to censorship even before the NP came into power in 1948, based primarily "on the religious and moral precepts of the Afrikaners as taught by the Calvinistic Dutch Reformed Church and several fundamentalist offshoots".[112] The censoring of literature, film and other creative expression led Nadine Gordimer to write:

> We shall not be rid of censorship until we are rid of apartheid. Censorship is the arm of mind control and as necessary to maintain a racist regime as that other arm of internal repression, the secret police.[113]

In the 1980s, at the height of apartheid, the situation was also described as that "[c]ensorship ... is part of apartheid; it is an authoritarian strategy that imposes on the public an ideology that is Calvinist, capitalist, racist and increasingly militaristic".[114] From the ruling elite's viewpoint, it was necessary to keep out "corrupting" and "obscene" influences.[115]

The press could only fight off "full-scale press control"[116] by disciplining itself, and it was done "masochistically and in public", with "[r]itual public self-flagellation" to keep government at bay – "to a degree". When the first 1962 Press Board of Reference – later the Press Council and then the Media Council – was set up, the NPU denied "any suggestion of outside interference" or pressure. It was a voluntary body, chosen by the newspaper industry, and "in time established high standards and independence under the direction of ex-judges". It had no formal government or statutory recognition, "but a Sword of Damocles hung over its head for years", as government could use existing legislation to step in to "recognise" – meaning to control – the Board. Mainstream papers, through their NPU membership, were exempted from "formal censorship" under the Publications and Entertainments Act of 1963, which "severely controlled" magazines and films, *inter alia*. Still, government was never satisfied with the Board, wanting more disciplining of "erring" and "hostile" journalists.

The single most important factor influencing the political content of newspapers in South Africa was that of governmental restraints.[117] Government's attitude to the press, particularly the "opposition" press, resulted in a "complex variety" of direct and indirect pressures intended to regulate the political content of these papers. It also applied pressure through a "highly discriminatory information policy", which denied one section of the press – the English – access to political or official information. In its "campaign" against the press it had two objectives: to safeguard its political principles and to ensure control of the country. In securing itself in office and eliminating all opposition, government "abrogated to itself very extensive powers" and provided itself with "the machinery to limit the freedom of its institutional or individual opponents".

In the Board's second report, from March 1964 to January 1968, only eight complaints were received, of which four were dismissed, three upheld, and one partially upheld.[118] In its third report, from July 1968 to June 1972, thirteen complaints were listed. Eight were upheld, four dismissed, and one partially upheld – the latter concerning a paper that did print a correction, but without apology or "express[ing] regrets".

In the first ten years of the NPU's Board, it adjudicated a total of 28 complaints, an average of three a year. This also led to a change in SASJ, which, at its 1972 congress, decided to recognise the Board, as it did "a first-class job".

The Code of Conduct

Under the threat of censorship, the NPU finalised its code of conduct in January 1962.[119] SASJ, initially against it, represented only English journalists, as Afrikaans journalists were forced to resign some years earlier by their managements. When the code was adopted at an NPU meeting in March 1962, 25 managements voted in favour, including the entire Afrikaans press, the Argus Group and the *Cape Times*. Seven newspaper managements voted against it, including SAAN and Bailey's *Drum* and *Post*.

In the fifteen cases brought before the Board by 1968, seven were from MPs or Members of Provincial Councils, five from government departments or Afrikaner organisations, and two from "opposition" organisations. The Afrikaans press, having been acquiesced in the setting up of the code, "were surprised to find that they too were subject to the sanctions". Of the fifteen cases, five were against the Afrikaans press.

Still, government's dissatisfaction with the Board was confirmed when, in 1964, the second report of the press commission recommended a statutory press council with extensive powers to replace the Board. This happened against the backdrop of the *Sunday Times*'s "remarkable exposé" of the secretive AB in 1963.[120] Fifteen years later, the *Sunday Times* did it again, "but bigger and better". The 1963 revelations, after police had raided the *Times*'s editor's office in search of AB documents, "changed the Broederbond from being the nation's most secret society into its most exposed".

The 'basic censorship law'

The Publications and Entertainment Act, passed in 1963 and amended in 1974 as the Publications Act, was described as South Africa's "basic censorship law".[121] Under the new post-1994 democratic dispensation, the amendment of this law, through the Films and Publications Amendment Bill, would create even more controversy.[122]

This first all-out censorship law of 1963, however, was predated by other laws that were in existence before the NP's 1948 victory. Although the 1963 law "pulled it all together",[123] imported publications could already be banned under the existing Customs Act, while movies had to be approved by the Entertainments (Censorship) Act of 1931. About 5,000 items had been banned by 1956, and this number had risen to 9,000 by 1963, including works by John Steinbeck and Vladimir Nabokov, as well as D.H. Lawrence's *Lady Chatterley's Lover*. The second of the two-volume *Oxford History of South Africa* (1877–1966) was available in South Africa with 53 blank pages instead of the chapter "African Nationalism in South Africa, 1910–1965". Then chair of the Censorship Board, Jannie Kruger, said there was no truth to the "legend" that the children's book *Black Beauty* was banned because of its title. Of a movie made in the 1960s, the *Sunday Times* wrote: "South Africa's dysfunctional, repressive society just got weirder. Hundreds of Zulu actors in a film about the battle of Rorke's Drift were prohibited by the Publications Control Board from viewing it."[124]

The 1963 law now systemised "haphazard arrangements"[125] and provided "an elaborate mechanism for censorship of virtually all expression".[126] About 30 dailies and weeklies, as well as 88 periodicals that were members of the NPU, were not answerable to this law, but it did not mean they were "off the radar". Indeed not. The threat of censorship led to self-censorship. The divisions between the different press groups – also within the two language groups – made the press vulnerable. Besides the split between the two rivals in the English sector, there also existed the "usual" split between management and labour, with most white English journalists belonging to SASJ, and most black journalists to MWASA. In the Afrikaans sector, the "huge rivalry" between North and South continued.

Government also interfered with ownership.[127] One example was the sale of the newspaper *Landstem*. Founded in the fifties, it was a "lively" Afrikaans weekly edited by the "legendary Piet Beukes", published on Thursdays. SAAN had a substantial share and printed its Transvaal edition. It also shared the "Miss South Africa" competition with the *Sunday Times*. In September 1967, the paper had a loss of R10,067 and was up for sale. Director Jim Bailey asked *Sunday Times* editor Joel Mervis whether he could do something to stop the board selling *Landstem* to Afrikaanse Pers. The Bailey Trust, as major shareholders, and without consulting SAAN, "secretly offered" shares to the Argus Group, thereby "enabling Argus to control SAAN". These "wheelings and dealings" prompted prime minister Vorster to threaten that newspaper takeovers "of this extent, and which so obviously conflict with the public interest, are not in the interest of the country". Legislation was therefore needed to prevent such take-overs, even "if need be with retrospective effect".

Threats and more threats

In October 1971, Vorster accused the press of "stabbing South Africa in the back".[128] At the NP's 1972 Transvaal congress, its new leader, Connie Mulder, gave his warning of "if the press acted irresponsibly, it did not deserve the freedom it enjoyed and the government would act, even if the price was the freedom of the press". The next year Vorster reiterated previous warnings, this time adding an ultimatum: The press had until January 1974 "to clean up its house".

Then still editor of *Die Transvaler*, Willem de Klerk reacted by writing that it was the politicians who were irresponsible. At the very congress where the press was warned, the delegates themselves said "reckless things", including "a plea for dictatorship". De Klerk said the press is "the mirror that reflects what goes on in society ... but where the mirror correctly reflects what has been said or done you cannot blame the mirror, if when you look into it, the face you see there is an ugly face". De Klerk's defiance was described as "staggering"; his paper had "seldom deviated" from the NP.

Following Vorster's warnings, publishers were "far more conciliatory" than editors. The NPU invited Vorster to its October 1973 meeting. He declined, responding, "I have no option but to finalise the contemplated legislation and to proceed with my plans".

Nothing happened, and in 1974 SASJ organised a symposium on press freedom to commemorate Pringle and Fairbairn's stand against Somerset 150 years earlier, coinciding, for maximum publicity, with the opening of parliament. Almost all English titles attended, but no Afrikaans ones. Then RDM editor Raymond Louw said he was saddened by this, "because if representatives of one section of the public cannot congregate with representatives of another to affirm common loyalty to the ideals of a profession serving the public interest, there seems little hope for all of us in the future".

The NPU pledged it would fight any form of government control, yet still revised the (now-called) Press Council's constitution with more restrictive wording, delivered to Vorster two days before the symposium. The powers of the Council were widened, giving it "teeth" by imposing fines up to R10,000. Yet it divided the country's journalists. For the Argus Group and Afrikaans papers it was an effort to keep the contents of newspapers "out of the hands of bureaucrats and politicians"; SAAN papers "vehemently" opposed it.

After Vorster's "show of force" to bring the Council in line with government, he "continued to play cat and mouse" with the press, refusing to say whether he accepted the new proposals. Furthermore, he sowed division by setting one group up against another, exacting a self-disciplinary code and "continue to boast of a free press". By December 1975, Vorster returned the NPU's code with "suggested" changes, scheduled for discussion in 1976.

But then 1976 happened: Simmering unrest exploded in Soweto in June and quickly spread throughout South Africa.

Government responded with draconian measures, "rushing through" the Internal Security Act that widened the scope of the 1950 Suppression of Communism Act under which organisations and publications could be banned. People could be imprisoned or "restricted" for merely "expressing views or conveying information the publication of which is calculated to endanger the security of the state or the maintenance of public order".

During this time, Vorster said he regarded the press as a "necessary evil".[129] Besides "powerful likes and dislikes", he "cherished" an "institutional hostility" toward the English press. At a "private meeting" of English-language editors, he said: "Let us be candid about it. You hate me and I hate you. You have tried to bring me down at every turn."

Vorster's "favourite cat-and-mouse game" with newspaper owners was to tell them to "put your house in order", meaning "to control critical editors and journalists". He knew owners and managers "scared easily" and therefore kept "notes on press lapses". Vorster also prepared "elaborate newspaper legislation, but did not pass it". He furthermore pressed for the Press Council, later the Media Council, to "be given more teeth" to "punish newspapers more to his satisfaction". When, in 1972, he tried to secure the "compliance of the press" in calling an "informal" state of emergency, it involved self-censorship "which the public never knew about". Opposed by editors, the attempt failed. Although Vorster never tried anything as "all-embracing" as Botha's media regulations under the state of emergency, neither of them "was a democrat"; however, as party leader, "Botha went marginally further along the road to repression".

Thus, to "sidestep threats of direct state control", the Media Council was founded on 1 September 1983 as the next version of a voluntary press control body and as the NPU's solution to the growing conflict between press and government over press freedom.[130] In 1995, the name was changed back to Press Council and in 1997 an ombud was appointed.

The SABC morphing more into His Master's Voice

The SABC, functioning as propaganda tool for government since the NP takeover, was mandated as public broadcaster according to the tenets of the BBC. But "the dominant Afrikaner elites", "operating through the secret Broederbond", gained control, turning it into a broadcast monopoly to "further the goals and interests" of government and the NP.[131] At the height of apartheid in 1984 (and just before the introduction of subscription TV), the SABC had sixteen radio services and three TV services, now broadcasting 2,269 hours per week in seventeen languages – "a powerful force for moulding public opinion". Still, constant government interference reached the public domain, such as President Botha's infamous late-night phone calls to the SABC with instructions to "recast" the news in a more favourable light.[132] A single comprehensive study of South African broadcasting during the states of emergency is that of Teer Tomaselli, describing the SABC as state broadcaster instead of fulfilling its mandate as public broadcaster.[133]

The North/South split

The eventual democratisation process and undoing of the NP had already started in the North/South press wars. In the North it was soon clear that Marius Jooste, as Northern media "empire builder", planned to consolidate a voice for Northern nationalists – a conservative one.[134] Jooste had formed Dagbreek Trust Beperk as a controlling subsidiary within Dagbreekpers as early as 1951. Through all the subsequent mergers and name changes, Dagbreek Trust remained the controlling body within what later became Perskor. On its board sat Strijdom and Verwoerd, as well as government ministers. Press unity was "fostered" by the 1940s Reddingsdaadbond, which created "the conditions for the nationalist class alliance" bringing the NP to power in 1948. But the "emerging dominant fraction of Afrikaner capital" soon polarised "capitalist and petty-bourgeois interests", a polarisation that would "once again manifest itself as a North-South conflict". The second Ekonomiese Volkskongres (Economic People's Congress) in 1950 marked "the ascendance of Afrikaner finance capital", which flourished under NP rule. Volkskas investments doubled between 1948 and 1952, with State intervention strengthening Afrikaner finance houses. It was not long before Afrikaner and English capital began to co-operate in joint ventures, such as the 1963 Anglo-American and Federale Mynbou project to control the General Mining and Finance Corporation, or Gencor.

Afrikaner politics in the 1950s and 1960s saw a renewed outcry from the North against the "geldmag" (money power) of the South (primarily Sanlam and Rembrandt), with *Die Burger*/Naspers supporting Cape interests against Northern "provincialism". With Verwoerd's assassination in 1966, the conflict between Southern "capitalists" and Northern "verkramptes" "burst into the open".

Jooste acted against these dynamics within Afrikanerdom. Identifying the "rise of Southern capital", a strong "Northern voice" was needed to articulate "Afrikaner worker – and especially petty-bourgeois – interests". In July 1962, he merged Afrikaanse Pers with Dagbreekpers, forming Afrikaanse Pers Beperk (1962) (APB1962). *Die Vaderland* and *Dagbreek en Sondagnuus* were now in the same stable. Naspers was "not slow to perceive the need for a 'verligte' voice in the Transvaal" and launched its 1965 Sunday *Die Beeld* amid "bitter controversy". The paper was printed simultaneously in Johannesburg, Cape Town and Bloemfontein. The ensuing circulation battle between the two groups' Sunday papers was one neither could win. Jooste meanwhile "consolidated his empire" in 1967 by buying the Cape weekly *Die Landstem* and incorporating it into *Dagbreek en Sondagnuus* as *Dagbreek en Landstem* in 1969. In 1968, Jooste's APB1962 collaborated with Voortrekkerpers and launched the Pretoria daily *Hoofstad*. Andries Treurnicht, editor of the DRC publication, *Die Kerkbode*, and later CP leader, was its first editor. By the end of the 1960s, the circulation battle between *Die Beeld* and *Dagbreek en Landstem* was so great that it led their two companies to merge the two under editor Willem Wepener into a new Sunday paper, *Rapport*, in November 1970. The next year, Jooste consolidated the Northern "voice" even further by merging his APB1962 with Voortrekkerpers to form Perskor. Dagbreek Trust was now the controlling body of *Die Transvaler*, *Die Vaderland* and *Hoofstad* and, by 1972, also *Oggendblad*. By early 1970, Jooste had consolidated Northern control over every major Afrikaans Transvaal paper except *Rapport*, thereby "effectively establishing an unchallenged voice for petty-bourgeois conservatism" under the "banner of the 'authentic' Afrikaner voice".

In 1974, Naspers made its second major effort to establish a "verligte" Northern voice by launching *Beeld* as Johannesburg daily, again under the influential editor, Schalk Pienaar. Perceived as a direct challenge, Perskor's board (and cabinet ministers Schoeman and Mulder) were outraged and "actively" undermined *Beeld*. Indeed, Afrikaner politicians have "always taken strong views on their partisan press", with Verwoerd already calling for an outright boycott of the Sunday paper *Die Beeld* in 1965. In the 1970s, politics "were more clandestine and dirtier". In 1977, for instance, Mulder allocated 98% of his information department's publishing budget to Perskor. That same year, Perskor began submitting inflated sales figures to the ABC, attempting "at all costs" to hold together "the Afrikaner conservative consensus based upon images of 'Volk' and 'Vaderland' that had proved so successful in … 1948". But it could not succeed. History and "a very real Afrikaner class split" were against it. At the beginning of the 1980s, both Perskor and Naspers claimed support for the NP, but promoted different notions of Afrikanerdom while locked in a struggle for a fast disintegrating readership.

The "Fight for the Heartland": 1982-1983

In 1973, "astute" theologian Willem de Klerk, brother of later state president F.W., was appointed editor of *Die Transvaler*. De Klerk was a "Dopper", belonging to one of the three Afrikaner "sister denominations", a version of "Christian Nationalism" that can "be crudely characterised as theologically and socially conservative but relatively liberal in political terms". It was De Klerk who coined "verlig/verkramp" in 1966. For him, as for other Afrikaner editors, "some form" of Afrikaner unity behind the NP was essential. When the first wave of "verkramptes" led by Albert Hertzog left the NP in 1969 to form the HNP, the press and later the AB "closed ranks and effectively expelled" them from mainstream Afrikanerdom. With the second split in 1982, neither the press nor the AB "were so sure any more". This was particularly since, under Botha's premiership, "Afrikaner business was the dominant grouping, dictating issues of policy and reform". The crisis "called for strong leadership", with the press "not slow to accept this responsibility". This led to "a highly contradictory press situation" and a widening class division, after the "identity and community" that previously had unified Afrikanerdom.

When, in February 1982, Treurnicht, leader of the Transvaal NP, led 21 MPs out of Parliament and established the Conservative Party (CP), the traditionally conservative Northern cultural organisations felt a "very strong pull" towards it. *Beeld*'s Vosloo attacked *Oggendblad* and

Hoofstad for supporting Treurnicht. Accusing Perskor of "shifting its political allegiances", it drew Jooste's "angry riposte".

This was not the "only bone of contention" between Naspers and Perskor. In April, Perskor's circulation fraud was exposed. It inflated its figures from January 1977 to September 1980, but the real issue was Perskor's readership in conservative Afrikanerdom's "heartland".

Perskor was found guilty of fraud in September 1983, but a further threat to the company's dwindling support arrived in the form of the ultra-right fortnightly *Die Patriot* as voice for the CP, named after the first Afrikaans paper.

Beeld meanwhile conquered the market with a combination of "hard-nosed pragmatism and uncompromising support" for reform. The Afrikaner press scene was one of Naspers advocating reforms, as "it had always done", and was "essential for the continued prosperity of the big capitalists, still largely based in the South", while Perskor "was increasingly speaking with a forked tongue". When Jooste sacked De Klerk for his "verligte" views, six senior *Transvaler* staffers resigned in protest and seven more took leave to consider their futures. But, "[a]s always, regional differences became a convenient way for expressing what was essentially a class conflict".

The Afrikaner "press wars" ended when Perskor left the morning market in 1983 to Naspers's *Beeld* and tailored "two different constituencies" for its afternoon papers. *Die Vaderland* was "verlig", while *Die Transvaler* faced "firmly North and in the general direction of the CP". For the first time since 1948, the Transvaal had "a sizeable non-NP class alliance of Afrikaner farmers, workers and petty bourgeoisie" opposing an NP government, and a major Afrikaner publisher now confronted the NP. "Christian nationalism" could hold only so much "diversity of interest", and hence fragmented. Politically, it split the NP, and in the media it translated into a vicious conflict between Naspers and Perskor as they struggled for the soul of the "real" Afrikaner.

The state of the nation at the height of apartheid

In 1984, South Africa was described as a country with deep divisions and racial tensions, but as "a dynamic and changing society".[135] On their side, the black majority had "powerful influences" of demographic change, increasing urbanisation, continued industrialisation, rising personal income and spreading education and literacy. This affected all facets of society, including mass communication. The press and other media, "quite independently of the pressures" from government, underwent "far-reaching modifications" in content, nature and size of audiences, and also in their relationships with each other. The political system also was clearly unstable. Almost every political faction, from the ruling NP to the moderate PFP and the then still outlawed ANC, advocated sweeping, albeit different, changes. Traditionally, the media were produced "by and for" the white elite, with other population groups "essentially eavesdroppers", but this also changed. In 1984, the bulk of newspaper readers and radio listeners were African, Coloured and Indian. It was exactly this growing diversity of audiences that provided a major reason for government to control content. Black publications venturing "into active politics" were "likely" to be suppressed. Media usage was divided by demography, also among the four main African groups with about sixteen different languages. The population now consisted of 3,5 million Zulu speakers, 2,8 million Xhosa, 2,5 million Afrikaans, 1,5 million Tswana and 1,5 million English speakers. In 1980, about 70% of the population was black, 17% white, 9% Coloured and 3% Asian. About 90% of whites and Asians lived in towns and cities, as did about 77% of Coloureds and about 38% of blacks. Johannesburg was the media hub.[136] The combined circulation of all dailies in 1982 amounted to about 1,4 million copies, or 50 papers per 1,000 population, putting South Africa well below industrial, but above most developing, countries. Fifteen dailies were published in English and six in Afrikaans.[137] In 1936, less than half of Afrikaners lived in urban areas; in 1984 it was about 90%.

Attempting to address a multiracial audience during 1957 was perilous.[138] Even the "first and most dramatic thing" new RDM editor Laurence Gandar did, namely to drop the word "Native" in favour of "African", caused an "outcry" – followed by the "biggest wave of cancellations" in the paper's history. Gandar also appointed Benjamin Pogrund as the first "African affairs reporter" – although he was white.

As in the past, the "form and substance – and comparative freedom" – of the media were influenced by politics.[139] It was during 1980 that Botha's statement, "We must make adaptations, otherwise we will die", was abbreviated to the popular "Adapt or die". For Botha, white survival depended on "making changes that would satisfy the political aspirations of the majority Africans, as well as the Indians and Coloureds". In 1979, minister Piet Koornhof even told a US audience that South Africa had reached a "turning point": "Apartheid … is dying and dead." But besides "a few cosmetic alterations" there were "no fundamental changes". Instead, Afrikaner leadership seemed to become more conservative, also with the 1982 formation of the CP under Treurnicht. By "its own count", the new right-wing party had 1,100 branches. Commentators predicted it could win enough seats to become an important opposition party. Fortunately, the "resounding support" in the national referendum for constitutional reform in November 1983 indicated that right-wing opposition was less widespread than feared. But it illustrated the Afrikaner's dilemma: Although verligte Nationalists controlled government, verkramptes retained a veto power over reform.

More enlightened thinking can be ascribed to the reform journalism now practised by Naspers papers. They were "in the forefront of articulating the voice of the 'liberalising' changes".[140] Already in the 1966–1969 "Broedertwis" when the HNP broke away, then the CP in the 1980s, as well as with the Tricameral "reform", Naspers papers supported "verligte" thinking. When De Klerk took over, Naspers papers "ha[d] been central components in the ideological task of re-orienting" Afrikaner thinking. They advocated reform, negotiations, one-person-one-vote, the recognition of the mistakes of apartheid, and even "some redistribution of wealth into black hands" – although "within a capitalist framework". It is even said that, in the early 1990s, some Afrikaans Naspers papers "moved further to the 'left'" than certain Argus Group papers.

All of this followed gradual reforms since the 1970s, accelerated in the 1980s, especially with Botha from September 1978 and De Klerk from August 1989.[141] It seems "they had no choice", as South Africa's economy was in a downward spiral. The rand plummeted from $1,29 in 1980 to $0,35 in 1985, with economic sanctions imposed by the US, the British Commonwealth except Britain, and several other countries.

All of this was regarded as the "total onslaught", to be answered with a "total strategy". The former "was conditioned by the belief" that South Africa was a major target of the communists, the ANC being a "puppet" of Russia.[142] Meanwhile, Angola "became a nightmare for South Africa akin to Vietnam" for the US, draining the country financially and morally.

Another trend in 1984 was the "militarisation" of South African politics.[143] Botha sought military, rather than political, solutions to the "total onslaught". Instead of political reform, he "embarked on military adventures". In 1981 and 1982, the defence force, "by far the most effective military force" in sub-Sahara Africa, undertook raids into neighbouring Mozambique, Angola and Lesotho. This was in response to the rising level of "terrorism" within South Africa, leading to an "Ulster-like pattern of low intensity civil war".

By 1983, either a slow, evolutionary change, marked by a growing level of sporadic violence, or a slow descent into civil war was foreseen.[144] This meant that government aimed its "Total Onslaught" against the press, with greater restraints on journalists and more restrictive legislation. English papers "probably exercise[d] even more self-restraint through self-censorship", while the black majority turned "to greater violence and the Government to ever more repression". It was anticipated that press freedom would decline even further and that "black" journalism, or publications seen to carry a political message to blacks, would be suppressed. All of this boiled down to an authoritarian regime, with all freedoms jeopardised. South Africans learnt the truism that "freedom is indivisible". Press freedom was subject to arbitrary government actions, but even more so to "a slow whittling away through legislation duly enacted by an elected parliament".

Government as 'arbiter' of what could be read, seen and heard

Although South Africans "ha[d] long lived with official controls of what they read, view[ed] or hear[d]", by the mid-1980s censorship laws meant government was "the final arbiter of what could be consumed by the public".[145] The 1963 Publications and Entertainment Act and the revised 1974 Publications Act were applied by an "elaborate bureaucracy". Established novelists like Gordimer were getting published, but unknown black authors and those writing in Afrikaans were prime targets.

Censorship expert John Dugard said the reason for these "elaborate censorship measures" was that any political expression was "limited to the cause of white supremacy" to protect the "ruling Afrikaner oligarchy".[146] There was especially concern that "permissiveness" would lead to communism – although, ironically, "communism is not known for its permissiveness". The "real objection to the social and cultural freedom" was that, if exported to South Africa, "it might release the average" Afrikaner from the tenacious grasp of those institutions that controlled "both his mind and his voting habits". These were the Afrikaans churches, Afrikaner cultural organisations, the Afrikaans press and the NP. Dugard emphasised that[147]

> [o]ne of the most skilfully nurtured South African myths is that there is a genuinely free press. This myth was perpetuated by the apparent freedom with which the English-language press criticises governmental policies and practices in certain legally and conventionally defined areas; by the praise of foreign critics who are continually surprised to find any criticism tolerated; and, particularly, by the shower of abuse poured upon the English-language press by Government spokesmen who regularly accuse it of disloyalty and subversion and threaten to deprive it of its "freedom".

The object of censorship was to "retard social change and to maintain the status quo".[148] But the gradual "secularisation" and "detribalisation" of the Afrikaner led to some controls being eased.

In 1973, André P. Brink's *Kennis van die Aand* (*Looking on Darkness*) was banned because of "interracial sex and police brutality". Published by Naspers, it practised a strange dichotomy of "independence under the NP Government and the vice of the Broederbond". Koot Vorster, DRC moderator and brother of the prime minister, said "sex perverts started to write poems". Also: If Brink's book was art, "then a whore house is a Sunday school". He added that "dirt spouts [vuilspuite] put their creations on paper", all of which resulted in what he termed "septic art".[149] Brink said during one of the trials to get the ban lifted that "censorship is a boil on society's bottom".[150]

The revised act - or how to improve the image of censors

The public outcry and support for the Brink publication, as well as the attack on the Censorship Board even from inside government, led the NP to revise the 1963 Act into the 1974 Publications Act.[151] The law became "an obvious embarrassment". A commission of inquiry suggested amendments to revise the structure and procedure of the "censorship machinery". It wanted to improve the "image of the censors" by removing the right of appeal to spare the censors "the embarrassment of having their decisions reversed". Secondly, the most outspoken critics were "wooed" by efforts to include them in the review committees (it did not succeed), and thirdly, insulting and belittling the Appeal Board was made an offense. This, in effect, muted criticism.

The key criterion for the new act was whether something was "desirable". In 1978, it led to a severe test after the public outcry when Etienne Leroux's *Magersfontein, O Magersfontein* (also a Naspers publication) was banned. After a huge court battle, it was eventually unbanned.[152]

Of the 2,138 items reviewed by 1979, 1,207 were found to be "undesirable".[153] In 1981, more than half of the publications submitted were still deemed "undesirable". Each week the *Government Gazette* would publish a list of "undesirables", from books to T-shirts. According to the UN's Unit on Apartheid, more than 20,000 items were banned by the mid-1980s, including a T-shirt with the slogan, "A woman needs a man like a fish needs a bicycle". Even those with a peace symbol and the motto "Black is beautiful" were banned. This also had an impact on academic work. Stellenbosch University's André du Toit warned that academic study in his discipline, political philosophy, "could become virtually impossible". This, while black writers, whether journalists or creative writers, had "long been harassed and frustrated in their efforts to communicate their views and feelings through the written word",[154] as was the case for Afrikaans writers,[155] while many works in English ironically slipped through below the censors' radar.

'Independence'

Good contacts and sources are an essential requirement for effective journalism, "but so then is some measure of independence from those sources".[156] In South Africa, the English press had a great deal of independence from government in that it opposed them on almost all issues and "consequently had very few inside sources". The Afrikaans press had all the sources, but little independence. For both, the extensive deprivation of the primary asset of good journalism resulted in the English press being "largely ill-informed" and the Afrikaans press unable to publish "much of the information they had". The English press adapted by relying – "very extensively" – on the Afrikaans press as source of information by "learning to read between the lines". They also championed social campaigns, forcing issues into the "political realm". In doing so, the English press acquired additional information by eliciting statements on relevant issues. The Afrikaans press mitigated its lack of independence by sometimes manipulating government to its advantage. Before 1961, the Afrikaans press rarely reported on NP conflicts. But after the founding of the Republic in 1961, disagreements "seep[ed] into the news more frequently". By 1966, *Die Beeld*'s campaign against the "verkramptes" during the "verlig-verkramp" split forced a breach within government and party – also in the Afrikaans press – which "shocked and surprised" most Nationalists, "particularly NP politicians themselves".

How journalists had to watch their step is illustrated in the permanent "banishment" in 1964 of the *Cape Times*'s political correspondent Anthony Delius. As "staunch and consistent" critic, Delius was parliamentary correspondent from 1958 until 1964 and was first suspended in 1962. The reason was an article criticising Parliament regarding the removal of historical portraits. His article infringed on the ruling against reporting anything heard or seen in the House other than formal speeches. A one-year suspension, "clearly out of all proportion to his offence", followed. In 1964 a similar offense led to the permanent withdrawal of Delius' admission. He had reported that Koot Vorster, brother of minister of justice (and later prime minister) John, sat in the visitors' gallery – a breach of parliamentary rules. Delius was informed he had "now filled up [his] book". Before the "final message", Delius was warned his paper would lose its contract for printing the House's papers. The company responded by forming a separate company to handle printing contracts. But the consequences for Delius were severe, ending his career as political journalist. He left the country following his expulsion. Importantly: The actions against him was a message to other political journalists. SASJ wrote to the Speaker to clarify what "constituted a punishable offence against Parliament's dignity". The Speaker declined to answer – so ensuring that he alone could define an offence and decide when to implement rules to exclude "unacceptable" journalists.

The advantages of the Afrikaans press lobby, on the other hand, extended beyond "simple confidences" between journalists and MPs. At each session's beginning, prime ministers met with Afrikaans editors, discussing policy for the forthcoming year. Under Malan, Strijdom and Verwoerd it meant joint meetings with all Afrikaans editors. Vorster "varied" the system, holding joint and private meetings with individual editors. Verwoerd, "in spite of his approach, or perhaps because of", was on several occasions opposed, particularly by *Die Burger*'s editor. In the conflict on direct representation of Coloureds, the paper openly refused to accept a "Prime Ministerial directive" at a pre-parliamentary meeting.

Under Malan's editorship, "*Die Burger* was Dr Malan".[157] After him, Naspers established, at an early stage, the principle that the paper should have "an independent existence within the party" by appointing journalists, and not politicians. *Die Burger*'s relationship with Strijdom, as a "Transvaal man, whose closest associates were fellow-Transvalers", was strained. In fact, *Die Burger*'s role now was described as that of "pioneers, scouts and protagonists", the paper increasingly coming into conflict with NP leadership. *Die Burger* "enjoyed its pioneering role and its influence in the party", but under Verwoerd the "party line as laid down by himself" had to be adhered to strictly. After Verwoerd was shot – and survived – *Die Burger* "lost the battle". A "fierce loyalty" to the Verwoerdian persona developed at the paper's expense. The rift had already begun in 1960 with the "Cape Nationalist intellectual viewpoint" that Coloureds should represent themselves in Parliament. Verwoerd tried to stop the paper from discussing the issue in its news and letter columns. Eventually, Verwoerd assembled the NP Federal Council to force *Die Burger* to stop. This, in conjunction with a door-to-door campaign by Verwoerd loyalists instructing subscribers to stop buying *Die Burger*, forced the paper to halt its campaign. In the process, editor Cillié offered his resignation, which was not accepted.[158] Verwoerd's successor, Vorster, surprisingly "chose to be guided" by *Die Burger* rather than by Perskor papers.[159] "To a large extent *Die Burger*, together with *Die Beeld*, saw itself and was seen by many Nationalist politicians and newsmen as the creator of 'verligte' thinking."

Die Burger's stand against Verwoerd and NP policy meant the paper ceased to be the Cape NP's official mouthpiece. Although the significance was "mainly symbolic",[160] it was certain that the dropping of *Die Burger* as official "organ" was on instructions from the PM himself.

Die Beeld's establishment in 1965 in competition with Verwoerd's *Dagbreek* was evidence that the rift had taken place, as it was founded "against the wishes" of Verwoerd. Following Verwoerd's assassination in 1966, *Die Burger* "quite deliberately" ventured to win Vorster to their way of thinking, described as "Cape verligte" thinking.[161] Cape Nationalists saw themselves as

> less brash, more tolerant, democratic and "civilized" than the Transvaal Nationalists … [T]he Cape Nationalists, through a more constant contact with the British in the Cape, were more deeply imbued with British concepts of democratic processes as well as the idea of compromise.

Yet Nationalists feared that Vorster had become *Die Burger*'s "puppet". There were frequent accusations that the paper was trying to rule the party. Unlike *Die Burger*, *Die Transvaler*, as official organ of the Transvaal NP, was unable to free itself from "the party's shackles and create an original role" for itself.[162] It was so close to the NP because, as early as 1953, when Naspers wanted to start a Sunday paper in the Transvaal, the Transvaal NP and Strijdom blocked them and arranged Northern papers to be funded by the Transvaal NP.[163] In 1965, Naspers's *Die Beeld* met with "ferocious opposition" from the Transvaal NP, the PM and even the Church. But the "spirit" of the Naspers Sunday paper embodied a belief in its "mission" to propagate Cape Nationalism and undermine "the ever-growing dominance of Transvaal Nationalists in Government". While *Die Beeld*'s editor, liberal Schalk Pienaar, was vilified by Transvaal Afrikaners, other editors experienced more subtle forms of pressure,[164] such as an out-of-the-blue raid on an editor's office by Special Branch detectives. Giving no reasons, in one incident they arrived three-quarters of an hour after the post, when the latter included a communist weekly that was illegal to possess. But the editor found its unexpected arrival suspicious, suspecting it was "planted" in an attempt to convict him of an offence. There was no trace of it when the police arrived. These measures added to "an atmosphere of fear", resulting in less and less politically contentious news. Editors found it increasingly difficult to get reporters to take on risky assignments, which led to certain stories "simply eliminated" from the news list.

Until the 1950s, the English press had concerned itself primarily with the rights of English-speaking South Africans, while the Afrikaans press "never sought to win a wide, general audience, or to provide a comprehensive 'news' service".[165] It served Afrikaner Nationalism, although in later years was "an extremely powerful pressure group for change". Indeed, "[t]here can be little doubt" that the Afrikaans press brought about, "or arguably, speeded up", the first split in the NP after 1948.[166] In 1968, the battle in the NP "raged furiously", with the Afrikaans press "at the very centre".[167]

Until the split in the NP, a single party, representing a single sector of a minority group, governed South Africa and supressed any opposition.[168] To the "Afrikaans press's credit" it must be said that, during the 1960s, after Sharpeville and the creation of a republic, it "forced the discussion of serious differences" in the party and government to be debated in public, demanding "a new role for itself".[169] The Afrikaans press progressed to "[become] the most powerfully organized force of opposition".

The Afrikaans press and its complex relationship to the NP

All of the above was built on an intriguing relationship that developed between the governing party and the supposedly subservient Afrikaans press. In the words of liberal editor Schalk Pienaar, it was a relationship steeped in "onafhanklikheid in gebondenheid", meaning "independence with bonds", or "freedom with commitment".[170] He phrased this in 1973, adding that it can stand as the only formula for all Afrikaner institutions. Also: "[T]he Afrikaans newspaper has the other important function: not to use today to accept yesterday, but to help others to prepare to get ready to meet tomorrow."

In 1965, with South Africa in the firm grip of Verwoerdian apartheid, "Southern" Nationalism crossed the Vaal with *Die Beeld* and thereby also crossed its own Rubicon. It rung in a new era for reform journalism and thus reform politics. Pienaar would eventually receive a posthumous honour in 2007 with the order of Ikhamanga Silver[171] for "fearlessly" playing the role of catalyst for a South Africa "where the rights that the Afrikaners claimed for themselves would be for all". He "rais[ed] consciousness in the Afrikaner community … about the immorality of apartheid and making them open to change through his daring questioning [of] the status quo". In 1974, Pienaar also laid the foundation for reform journalism as founder-editor of the new daily, *Beeld*.

Earlier, with the attainment of the Republic in 1961, Pienaar prophetically said that Afrikaner Nationalism was exhausted after achieving the ideal of having an own republic, and that it would lose momentum.[172] Inherent divisions between the more conservative North and the more liberal South again became clear in terms of this "Republican ideal".[173] It also played itself out in the 1970s Information Scandal with yet another power struggle between North and South, supported by Perskor and Naspers respectively.[174]

Die Beeld's 1965 launch was already a "significant step in the emancipation of the Afrikaans press from slavish obedience" to the NP.[175] The paper exacerbated the conflict between the "verkramptes" and "verligtes" and, by "forcing" the issues into the open, *Die Beeld* and other Naspers papers not only stimulated public debate, but also created "considerable uncertainty and anxiety among the Nationalist rank and file". The "ritual attack" at NP congresses against English papers now included the dissident Afrikaans papers, accused of "spreading heresies" and undermining party leadership.

Pienaar's understanding of press freedom was not a "watertight concept, but part of the various liberties enjoyed by every free and independent state", with the power of political, or constitutional, freedom guaranteeing press freedom – not the other way round.[176] Newspapers were to be recognised as equal partners, not "ventriloquist's dummies".[177]

In 1970, although *Rapport* was a 50/50 merger between Naspers and Perskor, Naspers had control over editorial content.[178] It continued with its independent political editorial policy with a "remarkably liberal line" under editor Willem Wepener, known for his phrase that journalists are "a nation's scurvy inspectors".[179] It was Wepener's contention that were it not for papers such as *Rapport* that "cleared the way" for new ideas and made them acceptable, the government's "liberalising changes would not have been possible".[180]

The change in the Afrikaans press after the formation of the Republic was "significant".[181] The more liberal Cape Naspers approach was "anathema" to the more "doctrinaire" Transvaal Nationalists. This approach was also illustrated in the earlier historic fall-out between Cillié and Verwoerd in 1960 on the representation of Coloureds in Parliament.[182]

Still, English observers described them as "occasional" disagreements. For news South Africans "really wanted to know", they had to turn to the English press for "a far more complete picture of developments" – including the "super-secret Broederbond".[183]

For Afrikaans journalists, their independence from party politics but loyalty towards Afrikaner Nationalism was more complex than seen from a simplistic outsider view. In 1988, Cillié wrote that an "opposition journalist" once said, "You people are not journalists – you are crusaders".[184] Cillié responded: "That remark is more incisive and closer to the truth than the usual envious but futile mocking of the bigger Afrikaans papers as yes-men, party pamphlets and government apologists." Cillié added: "The relationship between 'the Afrikaner' (who is he?) and 'his newspaper' (which one?) is in any case more intricate than what can be encapsulated in a sentence."

Cillié thought the influence of Afrikaner journalists was "envied (and sometimes rather overestimated)" by opponents. They saw themselves "at the forefront and the growth points of the rejuvenation and renewal of South Africa". They saw "visions of Nasionale Pers as a powerful cohesive factor in the new South Africa that is now being born with such difficulty". For Cillié, the "fruitful continued existence" of Naspers was "totally interwoven with the evolution" of, as he put it, "an orderly and creative co-existence of free nations and cultures in southern Africa". This was "the core of our idealism, the binding principle in our diversity and our growth".

But the "class rifts" at every level of Afrikaner institutional life in the late 1970s and early 1980s left their mark on the Afrikaner media, the result of "[o]pposing interests that had been cobbled together by Christian nationalism in a remarkable feat of consensual organising".[185] What had begun in the early 1900s was, by the 1980s, a "generalised crisis" "separate[d] out again with a vengeance". In the "Afrikaans press wars", publishers took one another to court, leading to two dailies that closed, another moving from Johannesburg to Pretoria and a major editor sacked – all of which happened "roughly between February 1982 and February 1983".

These events as "indicators of rupture" were not only due to ideological differences, but also the result of "political allegiance, economic mobilisation and class struggle", specifically regarding the North/South split. From 1915 up to 1981 there had "always been a simmering animosity between the smooth, cultured and affluent southern nationalists in the Cape and the rougher, poorer, less culture-conscious northerners in the Transvaal". Many hypotheses exist for this difference, including "a difference in political or ideological style". The century of colonisation had "left its patina of gentility on the southerners as well as giving them practice in the ways of civilised resistance". But there was an additional difference in "the relative class composition of Afrikaners in the Cape and in the Transvaal". Cape Afrikaners had greater numbers of "wealthy farmers, urbanised and prosperous professional people and emergent capitalists". The Transvalers, starting from a predominantly rural base, were "proletarianised and urbanised by social forces", resulting in "a large, destitute white working class eking out an existence in the cities". In 1900, 10% of Afrikaners were living in towns; by 1926, the number had grown to 41%. "Economic mobilisation", channelled through an "ethnic nationalism", was needed. Newspapers had to give voice to this strategy, with "every important Afrikaner newspaper" founded for this purpose. But because of divergent provincial class interests, there was continuous tension, "mirrored in the relations between the press" in the two provinces up to the 1980s, all based on "the messy, confusing history of Afrikanerdom from 1915 until the Nationalists came to power in 1948".

Control, propaganda, news flow and self-censorship

A crucial aspect in the control of South African society lay in the use of propaganda, with criticism of government considered unpatriotic or even treasonable.[186] World-wide condemnation of apartheid grew and South Africa remained high on news agendas. This led to government trying even harder to control the flow of information to sustain apartheid. By mid-1970, the NP had to deal with negative news coverage internationally, while domestically they had to "do something" about "the unpatriotic and rebellious" English press. A strategy developed to control the press "based on propaganda and political action". This included

- declaring a commitment to press freedom in parliamentary debates;
- accusing the press of being disloyal towards South Africa and in collusion with her enemies ("usually the communists");
- threatening the press with legal action unless it "sorted itself out";
- appointing commissions of inquiry, usually pro-government, to investigate the press;
- discussing regulatory legislation with press owners, and
- encouraging the press to draw up codes of conduct and setting up control bodies.[187]

Through this, government "could lay claim to be placing a high premium on press freedom" while simultaneously getting the press to regulate itself through self-censorship.[188]

'That evil box' - introducing television

The fact that, by the end of the 1960s, South Africa was probably "the only developed country in the world" not to have television, "greatly increased" the significance of other media.[189] The refusal to introduce TV was because of "Nationalist fears" about its effects on the "non-White population". Most importantly, "fears of producing a cultural imbalance weighted in favour of English-speaking South Africans and against the Afrikaans culture", as the service would had to rely on programming from English-speaking countries.

During the 1960s, the NP, with then minister of posts and telegraphs Albert Hertzog, regarded TV as "a negative influence on society throughout the world", calling it the "evil box".[190] No other industrialised nation waited longer, or debated at greater length, the "perils" of the "evil black box".[191] The NP and SABC were "frankly afraid" that TV would release "unsettling forces of change" on the "euphemistically" called "South African way of life". Calvinistic Afrikanerdom perceived a threat to the Afrikaans language and culture because of the heavy dependence on UK and US programming, but also realised the "potential psychological and political impact" on urban blacks. And they were concerned about the undermining of the "traditional moral values of Afrikanerdom" and the DRC.

Fact is, the British-based J. Arthur Rank Organisation had already wanted to introduce TV in South Africa in 1953, but the government blocked it as "the time was not ripe". The demand for TV started to build again by 1956,[192] but besides the influence on Afrikaners' "cultural independence", it would "disrupt" family life.[193] The next year, Verwoerd added economic arguments: Other countries could first carry the "full costs of experiment and development" before South Africa introduced a "non-essential service". By 1962, Hertzog confirmed that South Africa would not introduce TV in the near future.

But opinion polls showed South Africans wanted TV, and "South African businessmen kept the pressure on". In 1964, another group, now under Anglo-America's Harry Oppenheimer, planned to establish a TV service and to market sets. Hertzog blocked this. But then "one major obstacle" was removed when Vorster removed Hertzog from his portfolio in 1968. And the first moon walk in July 1969 made "white South Africans also realise that they were virtually the only people in the developed world unable to observe the historic moment". A film showing the event drew 6,000 people to a 500-seat theatre in Johannesburg. The UP even called for a referendum. In December 1969, the NP named its "twelve-man" commission, headed by the SABC's Meyer. By now it was clear that government had considered the introduction of TV for some time already, as plans existed for studios at the SABC's Auckland Park complex.

After the commission's 56-page report was tabled in March 1971, it was announced in April that TV would be introduced within four years. It was clear government was "convinced that they would control the news medium for their own purposes", as the service would be statutorily controlled and integrated with radio. TV should also "advance the self-development of all" and foster "pride in ... own identity and culture".[194] This "set the stage" for NP control for almost 20 years.[195] Test transmissions began on 5 May 1975 and the service officially opened on 5 January 1976. The "political and social impact of apartheid" dictated its "form, structure and content" until around 1990. Globally, public service broadcasting has been characterised by centralised state control – "no less so in South Africa during apartheid". Government thought "it had a right and a duty to make strategic interventions on behalf of the public".

The introduction of TV meant "a profound change in South African leisure time activity".[196] One channel broadcast for five hours an evening, divided equally between English and Afrikaans. A second was introduced in 1982, carrying TV2 and TV3 as "split signals", beamed to different geographical areas of the country "along a supposed ethnic logic". TV2 broadcasted in the Nguni languages of Zulu and Xhosa, and TV3 in North and South Sotho and Pedi.

A boycott by the British actors' union Equity "severely restricted" programming.[197] This meant the English service was dominated by American programmes such as *Dallas* and *Santa Barbara*, with the Afrikaans service "sustained" by dubbed American and German programmes.

Technically, by 1984 the SABC's facilities and services were described as "impressive".[198] For the first five years, about R150 million was spent to launch the service – an expenditure that mainly benefited five million whites. By 1979, exactly 2,099,596 radio licences had been sold, "although obviously many listened without acquiring a licence"; by 1983, radio licences were no longer required. For services in African languages, more than 4,8 million adults listened from Monday to Friday. By the end of 1979, almost 1,25 million TV licences had been issued and, by the end of 1982, 1,6 million. In 1983, altogether 78% of the white population watched TV from Monday to Friday. Despite the "white" content, 48% of Coloureds and 71% of Asians also watched. In 1984, TV1, TV2 and TV3 offered content described as "bland, innocuous, and 'safe', clearly designed to be unoffensive to the moral and religious values of Calvinistic Afrikaners".

In 1982, the SABC claimed to have 71,3% local content on the English channel and 88,7% on the Afrikaans service. Earlier, in 1978, an SABC spokesman said that, because South Africa was a "Christian nation", only Christian denominations were invited to participate in religious programmes. Several religious leaders took exception, saying the "policies pursued in this country ... were anything but Christian". Besides, the SABC "ha[d] long taken positions much closer to those of the most conservative elements of Afrikanerdom", rather than those of the increasingly urbanised, sophisticated and *verligte* Afrikaner mainstream.

Yet, by mid-1980, the SABC was still "safely in *verkrampte* hands", meaning the AB was in charge, its influence heard every weekday in 269 news bulletins over sixteen radio services in seventeen languages. The news was characterised by "selection, omission, and placement". Combined, they gave a "weird" picture of the world besides a "self-centred view" of South Africa as "a badly misunderstood and wrongly persecuted little nation that is a bastion of Christian democracy". An SABC director-general said they were "objective after being subjective in favour of South Africa". What was clear was that news and current affairs programmes became "increasingly subject to propaganda".[199]

1976 – the beginning of the end

The year 1976 was the tipping point regarding South Africa's media-technological development of introducing television. But, by far, it was a political watershed, following the Soweto uprising on 16 June, today Youth Day, blasting the lid off the political Pandora's Box.

The first official TV broadcast on 5 January, after TV had been withheld from the public for political-social reasons, was a quantum leap for South Africa's media development. Despite being state-controlled, this powerful visual medium now brought the images and sounds of the "riots" into homes during the state of emergency, albeit from the perspective of a state broadcaster.

The message that a white Afrikaner minority could never control a black majority could not be clearer. While 16 June began as a peaceful protest by black learners in Soweto, it soon moved as an unstoppable wave across South Africa.

In the eighteen months following the uprising, more than 600 people, mainly young and black, were killed and 3,000 were wounded.[200] By 1978, more than 2,000 had been detained. A number would be killed in detention, including Steve Biko. It is estimated that "perhaps" 5,000 left South Africa to join the ANC and other exile organisations. In October 1977, eighteen organisations were banned, including the *World* and *Weekend World*.

With the uprising having started in Soweto, it was especially the RDM and the *World* that covered the events thanks to their black journalists,[201] along with black journalists who stringed for the Afrikaans daily, *Beeld*.[202]

As early as on 11 June, Andries Treurnicht, then deputy minister of "Bantu administration and development", rejected applications from Soweto schools to deviate from the 50-50 mix of English and Afrikaans as languages of instruction.[203] But even before this, liberal daily *Beeld*, established just two years earlier, warned of the danger of compulsory Afrikaans in black schools.[204] The resistance already began in May, with a "mostly underrated" school strike. On 26 May, *Beeld* wrote: "Lord Milner has started stalking the Rand again in recent days." Readers were reminded of how Milner tried to force English "down the throats of small Afrikaners" – and that the Afrikaner government should not do the same. On 7 June, it was followed by an opinion piece, "Don't force Afrikaans on black schools", by Reverend Sam Buti, secretary of the Synod of the DRC in Africa. He repeated the Milner argument: "Shortly after the Anglo-Boer War, the Afrikaners rose up and fought when English was forced on them in their schools. The same arguments that they advanced, apply to the black people!" The time "for dictating and unilateral decisions" was past.

After the uprising, *Rapport* "lashed" out at Treurnicht: "Stop! We don't want blood on our language!"[205] For *Die Burger* it was a "painful thought" to realise Afrikaans was rejected as "the language of the conqueror, the oppressor, the tyrant".[206] Referring to Afrikaner history under British oppression, it said "[c]oercion can be counterproductive". And: Afrikaners "should understand that better than anyone else". The paper warned, "more than once", that an "antipathy" against Afrikaans is induced when white Afrikaans speakers "behave offensively". Afrikaners responsible for causing damage to the language are the real "enemies of Afrikaans".

Government "cracked down on those reporting the event".[207] Months later, black journalists were still in detention, held under the Terrorism Act. Most were released without trial later.

An increasingly toxic government became internally unstable from the mid-1970s, dehumanising itself through *kragdadigheid* (forcefulness). Boycotts began taking their toll on the economy. To the credit of Afrikanerdom, serious moral-ethical questions were asked in the public domain. One example is that of Stellenbosch philosophy professor, Willie Esterhuyse. His contribution to the "talks about talks" towards the end of the 1980s gave rise to a film, *Endgame*. His *Farewell to Apartheid* was published by Naspers in 1979, again illustrating the binary, paradoxical position of the company, with its newspapers still supporting (a more liberal) NP government, yet not interfering with its own publishers' right to print "controversial" titles.

Although government blamed the press for "fomenting the riots", the Cillié (not the newspaper editor) Commission of investigation not only exonerated the press, but "expressed appreciation for the balanced reportage".[208] The investigation also gave the official toll of the tragedy: 575 dead, of whom 494 Africans, 75 Coloureds, two whites and one Indian. Altogether 451 deaths were the result of police action, and 124 from causes other than police. Of all the victims, 134 were under eighteen, 113 of them killed by police. Among them was Hector Pieterson, with Sam Nzima's picture becoming a symbol of the uprising.[209]

The iconic photograph of Hector Pieterson that became synonymous with the 1976 uprising, taken by Sam Nzima.
Photo: https://www.sahistory.org.za/people/hector-pieterson

Reporting the riots and its consequences

Khulu Sibiya, later *City Press* editor from 1988 to 2001, referred to *Beeld*'s reporting during the Soweto uprising: "I bumped into a fellow journalist, Jon Qwelane, at one of the trouble spots … He was petrified and had just escaped being shot by the police."[210] Qwelane was commissioned by *Beeld* to cover the unrest. According to Sibiya, Qwelane was the first black reporter to work for an Afrikaans newspaper. No white reporter dared venture into Soweto; even black reporters "survived only because they could easily mingle with the rest of the crowd". Sibiya, contributing stories to the RDM, was asked by Qwelane to also write for *Beeld*.

Between June 1976 and June 1981, about fifty black journalists were detained without trial for periods of up to 500 days.[211] In 1976, black reporters were arrested just "because they had reported the events". Fifteen or more "disappeared into custody", including Peter Magubane, Nat Serache, Jan Tugwana and Willie Nkosi of the RDM, Joe Thloloe of *Drum*, and Duma Ndlovu of the *World*. Many were arrested under the Terrorism Act. Photojournalist Peter Magubane, who worked for *Drum* and the RDM, was banned for five years, imprisoned several times for a total of two years, with 586 days in solitary confinement – yet he has never been convicted of any crime. Even NP supporters "felt that the actions were self-wounding and unnecessary", particularly in the light of the promise that "many aspects of apartheid, especially certain 'petty apartheid' laws, would be rescinded".[212] There was also a "well-circulated jibe", also among "loyal Afrikaners", that in Pretoria there were "two secret agencies, the Department of Bad Timing and the Department of Dumb Mistakes". Although "super-secret", they worked "very closely together".

But it was no joke when, in the October 1977 press crackdown, the 150-member Union of Black Journalists (UBJ) was among the numerous organisations banned. Government "obviously perceived the UBJ as a Black Consciousness [BC] movement and therefore subversive". The Writers' Association of South Africa (WASA) was formed a year later. Whites were initially "officially and explicitly" excluded, but WASA later decided to open its membership to all in the media and changed its name to the Media Workers Association of South Africa (MWASA). Barely two years later, government acted against MWASA's leadership. On 28 December 1980, MWASA president Zwelakhe Sisulu, then news editor of *Sunday Post*, and Marimuthu Subramoney, BBC correspondent and MWASA's national vice-president, were banned for three years and placed under house arrest under the 1950 Internal Security Act. This was followed by the closing of the *Post* papers, which "merely led to greater alienation between white and black journalists working on the same newspapers". Black reporters resented the way their stories were handled and often rewritten by white sub-editors, who "frequently" toned down or "sharply" edited black-written or black-reported items – "often to conform to the harsh and complex laws restricting what the press can report".[213] It was said that what really disturbed the authorities were the "glimpses of themselves".[214] Apartheid was based on division, exploitation and an authoritarianism "that involved the law, administrative process, and brute force". It was a "philosophy so compelled by its own nightmares that it presides over every activity from bowel movements to burials" – all of which were regulated by "a massive structure of censorship, both legislated and informal, legal and illegal".

Black Consciousness, Black Wednesday, and the continuing madness

The origins of BC "lay in the political vacuum" of the mid-1960s, after the main opposition groups had been banned and the state crushed armed resistance.[215] The first stage, between 1969 and 1972, was generated by an attempt to establish "an alternative to the dominant, non-racial, liberal discourse that had engaged generations of African nationalists". The second, between 1973 and 1977, resulted from issues that made the apartheid regime "more vulnerable and hence more likely to resort to repressive measures to contain internal dissent". In 1975 and 1976, the economy slipped into recession, paralleled by an increase in the rate of inflation. And then Soweto happened, followed by severe government clampdowns. The climax came on 19 October 1977, later called Black Wednesday, when government did what it had threatened to do all along: It cracked down under the Internal Security Act on eighteen organisations and a number of "dissidents".

Government "swooped" upon various organisations with all its "dictatorial and autocratic might" – a "cataclysmic event" for the black press.[216] The crackdown was especially aimed at those associated with BC leader Steve Biko, who died in police custody on 12 September. The *World* and *Weekend World*, as the largest and most influential papers, were closed because they were "contributing to a subversive situation"; their editors Percy Qoboza and Aggrey Klaaste were arrested.

Beyers Naudé, one of those banned, afterwards said his banning orders made him "monddood" ("mouth dead"), "a very appropriate expression",[217] as nothing written by a banned person could be published, nor could their "words, opinion or thoughts" be quoted. As an outspoken cleric, anti-apartheid activist and leader of the Christian Institute, Naudé wrote after Biko's funeral that Biko was the young leader who might have become prime minister or president one day.[218]

Suppression of press freedom thus also entered a new chapter on 19 October, the reason why it is commemorated as Press Freedom Day today. Besides the *World* and *Weekend World* (both Argus Group), the *Daily Dispatch* was also banned, as well as 47 prominent leaders. The *Dispatch*'s Woods was literally pulled off a plane bound for the US and banned from practising journalism for the next five years.[219]

The Argus Group bought the *Natal Post* to fill the void left by the *World* and began publishing it as the daily *Post*, with Qoboza as editor after his release months later.[220] Even "supporters of Botha and the NP felt that the actions were self-wounding and unnecessary". But it did not prohibit government from drawing up new laws, such as Section 205 of the Criminal Procedure Act of 1977, according to which government could subpoena journalists to reveal the identities of confidential sources.[221]

Organised black journalism

It was said that perhaps the "most police repression of black journalists result[ed] not from suspected political activity but from resentment of reporters' *reporting* the news".[222] In hindsight, the target was not even the papers, but black journalists who organised themselves into MWASA as successor to two previous unions, UBJ and WASA.

In the October swoop, the 150-member-strong UBJ was among the many banned organisations.[223] Altogether 26 black journalists were fined after taking part in a protest march against this action. The UBJ was founded in 1973 after meetings convened by Harry Mashabela to discuss discrimination against black journalists. Under SA law, the white-controlled SASJ could not bargain for salary increases if black journalists were members. Still, they invited black journalists to join. Mashabela, then at *The Star*, and his black colleagues rejected the invitation and established the blacks-only UBJ, with Mashabela as president. WASA was formed a year after the UBJ's banning. Whites were "officially and explicitly excluded". In 1980, it opened membership to all workers in communications, changing its name to Media Workers' Association of South Africa (MWASA).

But a generation gap existed within black journalism in the 1980s. Younger journalists were "more angry" and identified with MWASA. Peter Magubane, who stood up to repression, was even "ridiculed by some younger colleagues for belonging to SASJ".

Government action against MWASA increased. A MWASA officer, Joe Thloloe, for instance, was given a two-and-a-half-year sentence for possessing a single banned book.[224] Despite the "decimation" of its leadership, MWASA survived. In early 1981, its membership counted 288, of whom 210 were journalists.

Alienation between white and black journalists "working on the white man's newspaper" increased. At the time, one white journalist remarked that polarisation meant that, "even in journalism, whites are getting whiter and the blacks are getting banned". There was such "mutual hostility" that white and black journalists did not talk to each other. Their companies' "extra" editions, aimed at blacks, were almost unanimously resented by black journalists, who also resented the way their stories were handled and rewritten by white sub-editors. Besides, many were not full-time employees but worked as stringers on "modest retainers". Salaries for those employed full-time lagged behind those of whites, and they were also usually in lower positions. As was said: "Such a subordinate role for the black journalist is particularly galling in light of the impressive history of black journalism in South Africa."

At the time, *Beeld* drew a correlation between Afrikaner Nationalism and African Nationalism. Commenting on the banning of two black journalists, both MWASA members, *Beeld* wrote that MWASA was not so much a journalistic organisation but an arm of radical black power. Plus: "We don't blame MWASA for it. Indeed we are painfully aware that Afrikaners in similar circumstances did the same to achieve power."[225] It referred to how Afrikaans newspapers "[were] an instrument for mobilizing forces so that victory could be gained at the polls". *Beeld* called on government "to put things right", proposing lifting the ban on *World* and *Weekend World*. Also: "We are eager to make this suggestion."[226] The ban was not lifted. In fact, just more than a year later, government also banned the papers' successors, *Post* and *Sunday Post*.[227]

'Extra' news - 'black' news in 'white' papers

A number of daily and weekly papers developed what they called "Extra" editions for the "non-white" market. These included RDM, *The Star*, *Sunday Times*, *Daily Dispatch*, *Sunday Tribune*, *Sunday Star* and *Rapport*, as well as *Die Burger*.[228] These "extra" pages were carried as supplement inside the paper. The first to do this was the RDM, with its *Mail Extra*, developed during Benjamin Pogrund's time as African Affairs Reporter prior to 1963, when blacks were employed on a "tip-off" basis only. In 1963, the RDM appointed its first black journalists, Laurence Mayekiso and Sidney Hope. Gradually, the RDM developed *Township Mail*, beginning on page 3 "as ordinary news and later bec[oming] a separate edition". For this separate edition, the shares page was replaced with a full page of "black" news, the rest of the paper contained the Late Final edition. By 1970, this edition was selling approximately 20,000 copies a day "and a small corps of black journalists had begun to form".

The *Township Mail* was renamed *Rand Daily Mail Extra* in 1973. More important was the "limited degree of autonomy" assigned to the *Extra*, with greater use of black reporters and photographers and the appointment of a black sub-editor. Still, it was "a makeshift and disjointed publication". *The Star Africa Edition* also replaced two or three pages of news with "township, black show business and sports news". The reaction to *Extra* editions by black readers was "equivocal". Qoboza called the *Mail Extra* and, by implication, other such editions, a "monumental insult" to blacks.

Technological quantum leap, political watershed

Ironically, the 1976 quantum leap for South Africa's media, with the first official TV broadcast on 5 January, would become, despite state control, a powerful visual medium to bring the "riots" into people's homes.

Another irony is that the Theron Commission's report that had investigated matters relating to the Coloured population was submitted to parliament two days after "Soweto", on 18 June. Its recommendation of direct political representation for Coloureds on all levels of government was rejected, despite the revolt that was already raging countrywide.[229] *Die Burger*'s political commentator "Dawie" (the editor, Cillié) wrote that the report, released "in the shadow (or flame-light)" of the unrest, could be considered an "ironic blessing", giving the report "the perspective of a warning and a call".[230] Still, government did not heed this advice from the ranks of its most loyal support.

On 6 July, government scrapped the compulsory use of Afrikaans in black schools.[231] But, as was the case with other matters, it was too little too late. On 25 August, Vorster, on his tenth anniversary as PM, acknowledged that the country had "problems", but denied it was a "crisis".

So many papers, so many readers, so many markets

To provide some context in terms of who provided what news to the South African public, there were ten newspapers "vying for two million white readers" in the Johannesburg-Pretoria region alone in 1976, when Soweto was the tipping point.[232] With the establishing of TV that year and increasing publication costs, profits were under pressure. In the black market, the *World* still seemed to be growing. The "extra" edition of the *Sunday Times* had a combined readership across South Africa of 100,000. The *Rapport* "extra", serving the Coloured market, had a circulation also exceeding 100,000 in the early 1980s.[233] In this period, black journalists, originally hired for the "township editions", moved to mainstream editions, "albeit in lower positions".[234] The *Cape Herald*, founded by the Argus Group in 1965, served the Coloured community. The Indian community, based mainly in Durban, was independent of white financial control and had the most viable titles of all "non-white" publications, with the *Leader*, founded in 1941, and *Graphic*, in 1950, as the main titles.

Black journalists were handicapped because of bad education, resulting in low competence in English as well as lacking the broad background needed in journalism. Editors thought their "standard of work leaves much to be desired". The need to train black journalists resulted in short courses by the Thomson Foundation and the South African Catholic Bishops' Conference. The Argus Group and SAAN offered cadet courses, but of the 40 to 45 journalists per year, only a handful were black. At the time, Rhodes University had established its journalism department, today the School for Journalism and Media Studies.[235] Due to apartheid restrictions, it was not open to as many black journalists as they could accommodate. At the Potchefstroom University for Christian Higher Education, a historic Afrikaans university and now North-West University, an Afrikaans communication course was established a couple of years later. The first university-based postgraduate honours course specialising in journalism training and education was established at Stellenbosch University (SU) in 1978.[236] Although SU at the time still was an "Afrikaans" university, the programme was offered in both Afrikaans and English. It accepted its first black student, Mohamed Shaikh, in 1979.

'Underplaying' the news

The reporting of racial unrest "tells much" about SABC policies.[237] One such incident of "American Indians" demonstrating in Washington was broadcast by both radio and TV on

16 July 1978 and "repeated all day long", along with actor Marlon Brando's quote that "America is the world's last colonial power", and that in South Africa "they have even given blacks their land back again in the homelands". At the time of the 1980 Cape Town school boycotts, it did not show any footage of student rioting, only "talking heads", and then switched to visuals of rioting in Miami. The message in both cases was obvious: things are not so bad in South Africa, just look at the rest of the world.

With the Soweto riots in June 1976, barely five months after television began, both radio and television "deliberately underplayed the events". The SABC's 1976 annual report read: "Every effort was made to place disturbances in the black townships in the proper perspective, and to control passions." The next year, the report stated:

> Television news, in reflecting the sporadic unrest in various parts of the country, accepted from the start that its information function demanded precise reporting, but that coverage had to be sober and unemotional, in order to avoid the internationally recognized risk of television only inciting excitement and unrest.

The consequence was that "anxious South Africans" were assured by the SABC during the evening that all was quiet – and then read the morning newspapers "to find out that more rioting had occurred the night before".

Proof of this bias was the biggest political scandal in this period. Secret funds of the department of information were found to be misused, culminating in the Information Scandal.

The 'Total Onslaught'

In 1977, a White Paper spelled out that South Africa was threatened by a "Total Onslaught" which could only be countered by a "Total Strategy".[238] Apparently the phrase was first used in a White Paper on Defence in 1973. "It was only a passing reference to the concept, which was, however, articulated in detail in the White Paper of 1975 and especially that of 1977."[239]

To retain the grip on the "hearts and minds" of Afrikaners, Afrikaner politics went into overdrive. Whereas Verwoerd had openly declared a boycott of *Die Beeld* in 1965, the politics of the 1970s were "more clandestine and dirtier".[240] In 1977, for example, Connie Mulder allocated 98% of his department's publication budget to Perskor, as the alliance between the Northern NP and its Northern Nationalist press was aimed at maintaining the "conservative consensus" among Afrikaners "based upon images of 'Volk' and 'Vaderland'" at all costs.

But, while receiving almost 100% of the information department's publication budget, Perskor simultaneously started providing inflated circulation figures to the ABC. While both Perskor and Naspers supported the NP, they promoted "different notions of Afrikanerdom" and were "locked in a struggle for a fast disintegrating Afrikaner readership". All of this created the ideal press-political landscape for the ideology of the "Total Onslaught" to flourish.

The Newspaper Press Bill of 1977

After the Soweto uprising, the worldwide attention led the government to focus – again – on regulating the South African press.[241] And to blame the messenger.

In February 1977, government gave the NPU a copy of proposed legislation that would impose direct state control on newspapers. This was rejected "out of hand". Still, the government introduced the Newspaper Press Bill in March. It "embodied" the Nationalist ideal of how the press should be controlled, with a statutory Press Council backed by state authority. It also authorised the Council to impose "reprimands" or fines of up to R1,000 on individuals and R10,000 on newspaper owners. Most of all: It could suspend publication.

For the first time, English and Afrikaans journalists were united in an "unprecedented show of opposition". The RDM wrote: "We are all in peril. In proposing to destroy press freedom as it has been known in South Africa, the Government's reason has finally snapped."

Before retiring as *Burger* editor, Cillié, in 1977, would still wage this last battle together with his English and Afrikaans colleagues against the "fiercest assault" yet on media freedom, also against his "own tribe", the "white tribe of Africa", as he referred to Afrikaners in a *New York Times* article in the 1960s. To take a stand inside an increasingly authoritarian NP regime was regarded as brave. Behind the scenes, part of the bigger media freedom battle was another political scramble for positions within the Naspers Board. Seen as a "development that could undermine Naspers's independence", it was a tussle about the position of chair. Again Cillié played a "substantial" role in averting the threat.[242] It was "fairly certain" that Cillié, at the time still *Burger* editor, would become a director – "probably" chair. However, politicians on the Board – P.W. Botha, Fanie Botha, Piet Koornhof and Nak van der Merwe (they would all resign one year later as a result of Cillié)[243] – started mobilising to elect Flip la Grange, a Senate member, as chair. As "party man", La Grange would be under Botha's direct authority. Naspers's independence was at risk and Cillié "gave notice" that he would not serve as director under La Grange.

While this internal power struggle went on there was the bigger threat of state legislation against the press. When government announced the new legislation, *Die Burger* carried a front page banner – an exception – on 11 March: "Government shocks Press: big storm ahead" (translated). This was seen as a direct challenge to government.

The Newspaper Bill represented the most draconian censorship to date, with the intention of introducing a statutory council, the immediate closure of newspapers and huge fines for newspaper owners and journalists.[244]

On the day of the "daring" headline, NP leader Botha "summoned" Naspers's leadership to his office regarding "Cillié and *Die Burger*'s headline". Naspers stood its ground, emphasising that it had been resisting state control "all these years and it would create a serious crisis if the same Pers now suddenly had to advocate it". It was also stated that Naspers journalists were "not paid advocates or hirelings, and that has always been the Pers's strength". This dichotomy was present all along: There was a fierce loyalty to Afrikaner Nationalism, but not to what was regarded as party political fallacies.

The above was a manifestation of a serious clash – seen "as the first major confrontation" between the Afrikaans press and the government,[245] although there were many others before. In this particular case, the statutory council, with a tough new code of conduct and the power to impose fines and with no appeal to the courts, led to a "tone and outrage" in Afrikaans papers "now rivalling that of the English press". The Afrikaans papers "pulled out all stops" to block the legislation, with the "spectacle" of both English and Afrikaans papers "ganging up" to berate government unique in the country's history. But, whereas government was never "deflected" by English papers, it was now "faced with revolt by its own party press".

A week after the introduction of the Bill, Vorster met with an NPU deputation, including the chairs of all four major press groups. Discussions continued for three days. On 23 March 1977, Vorster announced that the Bill would be withdrawn, but the NPU had one year to "test" its new self-disciplinary measures.[246] The Bill had been tabled in Parliament, but its eventual withdrawal meant "statutory control of the South African press" was prevented – once again.[247]

So the press had a year to regulate itself.[248] The NPU's South African Press Council (PCSA), as it was now called, founded in 1962 as the Press Board of Reference, was reconstituted with an amended constitution, code of conduct and rules of procedure.[249]

As to Naspers and its independence, once the bigger battle for press freedom was won, the internal issue could be attended to again. The upshot was that Cillié was appointed chair, again defeating party political interests inside the company.[250]

Still, not a press victory

The NPU victory was by "no means a victory for the press", as it had to agree to accept a code of conduct almost identical to that in the Newspaper Bill.[251] Eventually, the "essentially toothless council" set up fifteen years previously had evolved into "something far more to the liking" of government.

In its first two years, the PCSA received almost 400 complaints, of which 95 were settled between parties, seventeen were adjudicated, and the rest dismissed or allowed to lapse. Of the seventeen heard, eleven were upheld, five settled and judgement was reserved on one. The figures for the next year, 1978/1979, showed the same trend. Between May 1981 and September 1982, the council received 145 complaints, 34 from government. About 35% were dismissed, the other 65% lapsed or were settled, leaving only 10% to be dealt with.

Laurence Gandar, then RDM editor, said of the 1977 PCSA that it "was a reluctant response to raw political pressure applied over a long period – an act of appeasement, in fact". For him, the PCSA had nothing to do with the need to codify the ethics of journalism, but everything "with the political clash in South Africa of two fundamentally different outlooks as to the nature of society and how the public good can best be served".

Still, government was not to be appeased. In the 1980s, the Steyn Commission of Inquiry into the Mass Media would follow, calling for new measures.

Muldergate, or Infogate - yet another beginning of the end

But first the shock of a state scandal with epic dimensions had to be absorbed. The 1978 Information Scandal shocked Afrikanerdom and was popularly known as Muldergate or Infogate, after the US's Watergate scandal. Muldergate was derived from the name of the responsible minister, Connie Mulder.

The scandal "rocked"[252] government when it was revealed that the information department engaged in clandestine propaganda exercises to "sell apartheid to the world".[253] The political career of Mulder, tipped to be next PM,[254] ended, but the scandal led to more repressive measures, including legislation requiring newspapers to get permission from the advocate-general before exposing corruption in state administration – another way government tried to muzzle the press. But this move also drew such sharp reaction that the legislation was amended. All in all, however, "it marked a turning point in the cosy relationship between the Afrikaans press and the apartheid government". The event also split the Afrikaans press, with the Cape-based Nasionale Pers condemning the government openly, while Perskor attempted to protect the National Party leadership. Following the scandal, the Afrikaans press began to express misgivings about the government and apartheid with an increasing frequency, producing cracks in the apartheid system that ultimately led to self-destruction.[255]

If "political warfare" involves two basic strategies, censorship and propaganda,[256] apartheid South Africa applied these by making "use of various forms of censorship". Its "major propaganda offensive" had its origin in November 1961, after South Africa's withdrawal from the Commonwealth when it found itself "in a state of increasing international isolation". Government decided to create a fully-fledged information department to replace "the underfunded and ineffectual" state information service, set up in 1937. The media now had to focus on the positive, "on process-oriented and developmental news, rather than on negative, event-oriented reports" – an approach containing "the seeds of Muldergate". Also, the first 1950 press commission, with its first report in 1962, found that the news was "unfair, unobjective, angled and partisan". The second report, in 1964, found that foreign correspondents, apart from printing "untrue statements", "failed to give an account of the problems the government faced in restoring law and order; gave undue prominence to statements by opponents of the government and played down government statements". The new information department would rectify this imbalance with a straightforward message, as "it was essential to portray the country as a stable, profitable environment for investment and a desirable place for Europeans with useful skills to immigrate to".

The 1960s was a period of "high economic activity", but politically "the position was less satisfactory". Despite huge funding increases, the information department was unable to influence policies. The situation became "particularly acute" in the early 1970s, when the Portuguese dictatorship collapsed, leaving Angola and Mozambique independent, which meant that the *cordon sanitaire* on South Africa's borders comprising a "comfortable buffer of friendly states" was gone. The country was "in effect at war". And, in a time of war, "the rules of war" must apply.

That is how South Africa's secret propaganda project began in 1972, when Mulder appointed Eschel Rhoodie to the department's top position, as secretary for information. Rhoodie earlier served as information attaché in Australia, the USA and the Netherlands before returning to South Africa in 1971 as deputy editor of a new news weekly, *To the Point*, one of the department's first secret projects. More than R17 million was funnelled into it, although this was "strenuously denied". Another early, but unsuccessful, venture was to covertly buy an existing English paper, the *Natal Mercury* – a Durban morning daily and one of the few English papers not owned by either Argus or SAAN. Also, it had "to sell apartheid through some of the world's most respected newspapers". Rhoodie told Vorster he wanted "his approval for a propaganda war where no rules or regulations would count". Vorster agreed; an amount of R64 million could be spent over the next five years.

The "propaganda war" even included an offer for an English press house from "an unlikely source".[257] In October 1975, millionaire Louis Luyt announced a bid for the entire issued share capital of SAAN at R4,50 a share. At about R9 million in total it was more than double the trading price at the time. This infuriated the English establishment, with English papers denouncing the bid as an NP attempt to take over the English press. The RDM, the "real target" of Luyt's offer, said in a front-page editorial that if he were to succeed, "a devastating blow will have been dealt to the cause of press and public freedom in South Africa and a wide range of public opinion stifled". Nothing came of it. Thus "spurned", Luyt started a new English morning daily in Johannesburg in direct competition with the RDM. Translated directly, *The Citizen* means *Die Burger*, and it was launched in September 1976. Indeed, for the most part, *The Citizen* read "like an English translation of the pro-government Afrikaans newspapers".

Despite denials by Luyt, it was implied that *The Citizen* was getting secret support from government. Already in 1974, *Rapport* had run a story of "hidden links" between the information department and *To the Point*. *Beeld* and the *Sunday Express* also carried the story, but Rhoodie "reacted violently", "haul[ing]" the papers before the PCSA, where he swore under oath that he and his department had no connection with the magazine.

The Afrikaans press also played a "significant role in investigating and exposing" Infogate.[258] And, once the scandal was documented by Judge Anton Mostert and the Erasmus Commission, "they became as fierce in their criticism as the English papers", partly because of "a sense of betrayal":

> Afrikaners have a strong respect for authority, especially when it is associated with political power. And however misguided and narrow Afrikaner leaders may appear to outsiders, they have always been respected for their sincerity and honesty. Corruption and graft in high places were considered typical of the rulers of developing countries to the north, not of a government of God-fearing Calvinists.

A second reason for the aggressive probing by the Afrikaans papers had to do with "political and commercial factors". The scandal became a major issue in the power struggle between the Transvaal and the Cape NP fractions, supported by Perskor and Naspers respectively. Mulder was the Transvaal NP leader and Perskor director. Botha, minister of defence and Mulder's chief rival as premier, was Cape NP leader and had the support of Naspers, of which he was a director. The Erasmus Commission eventually found that R85 million was spent in the secret five-year propaganda programme on 180 projects aimed at "buying South Africa's way into the international corridors of power".[259] *The Citizen* was funded by about R32 million of taxpayers' money channelled to a front organisation headed by Luyt.[260] "Infogate" even included an attempt to gain control of the *Washington Star* at a cost of R10 million.

The scandal was yet another nail in the coffin of the NP government. The disillusionment of Afrikaners, who, despite the immoral policy of apartheid, thought themselves to be upright and righteous in the best Calvinistic tradition, was clear in how liberal, pioneering Afrikaner journalist Rykie van Reenen described the disbelief that took hold of the "volk" in her typical satirical way.[261] It was, she wrote, such a "strange relief" – after having overcome the "worst shock" – that Afrikaners are not "examples of greater diligence or piety" they thought themselves to be, part of Afrikaners' superiority complex and the result of a "divine call" – as Mulder indeed himself concluded in his doctoral dissertation in 1956.

Different numbers are given by different sources regarding the cost of Infogate. According to one, it started with $74 million in a secret fund.[262] At the time, R1 was equal to $1,15. In total, an estimated R32 million was used as backing for the *Citizen*. But this was only the tip of the iceberg. Besides funds to subsidise the internationally distributed *To the Point*, the *Washington Star* attempt was also part of "extensive secret efforts to buy media influence around the world".

All of this was part of the "Total Strategy" against the "Total Onslaught" government led itself (and Afrikaners) to believe in.[263] It included the 1975 invasion of Angola, of which the South African public were uninformed because of a "total black-out" media policy. Some papers, desperately trying to inform the public, could only hint at the real situation and rumours of an invasion, as in fact, were published in overseas media. It was the beginning of the militarisation in every aspect of society in the country.

The sophisticated Rhoodie, the brain behind the Information Scandal, was described by *Cape Times* editor Tony Heard as "stylish" and "slick".[264] The department's "elaborate secret plan to use funds irregularly to try to sell the unsaleable apartheid to the world" was funded by money "voted by an unsuspecting Parliament in the belief that it was for the Defence Special Account". But the Mulder/Rhoodie objective, to carry out "an ambitious propaganda war at home and abroad" "with Vorster's knowledge and connivance", backfired. Mulder, though, "made it clear that virtually any actions were justified" in the cause of South Africa – "by which he meant the National Party". On 3 November 1978, Mulder still said "no rules applied when the existence of South Africa was at stake". It turned out that journalists also were bought. General Hendrik van den Bergh, head of Vorster's security apparatus called BOSS, said that it had 37 South African journalists on its payroll. Three were parliamentary correspondents, one an editor-in-chief, and eight "worked on news desks in one capacity or another". Infogate also led to the demise of Perskor because, when Mulder resigned as director, the company lost multimillion-rand contracts from the State.[265]

According to editor Joel Mervis, the RDM and *Sunday Express*, although working independently, probably did most to expose the scandal.[266] It was only thanks to timeous intervention that the Luyt attempt to take over SAAN was stopped,[267] but it was all part of the information department's "long, lingering, festering trail of lies and deception".[268] Even when the "information bubble" burst, Mulder proclaimed in parliament on 10 May 1978 that the department "owns no newspaper in South Africa and runs no newspaper in South Africa". Specifically: "The Department of Information and the Government do not give funds to *The Citizen*."[269]

But it was all over by September 1978. Vorster announced he was stepping down as PM after twelve years – but that he was available for election as President.[270] Mulder, still regarded as front-runner for premiership, lost the internal power struggle to Botha.

The political effect of all these disclosures "was profound".[271] Mulder's defeat to militarist Botha meant that, for the next decade, press freedom would become "emasculated" in the NP's desperate attempt to stem the tide.

Ironically, as part of the strategy to support the Total Onslaught narrative, government designed, as per a 1974 memorandum, a blueprint for a "Bantu film industry".[272] As Rhoodie later bluntly explained to RDM reporters, the idea was "to combine censorship and indoctrination".

Infogate: Continued

The real extent of the Information Scandal was revealed when Supreme Court judge Anton Mostert was appointed as a one-man commission in 1978 to investigate violations of foreign exchange control regulations.[273] He "stumbled" upon funds laundered through European banks to pay for the information department's schemes. Among them were "large sums of money from secret funds" to finance *The Citizen* – revelations that "hit the country like a bombshell".

When Mostert released his report, corroborating numerous newspaper stories over months, the SABC "chose to downplay the biggest political story in years" because "it was not sure the law permitted it to report the story".[274] It did refer to Mostert's report, but then quoted the Commissions Act, which prohibited the publication of Mostert's findings. But by then the afternoon papers were "on the streets with the full story".

The SABC kowtowed even more by giving disgraced Mulder an *audi alteram partem* opportunity the next day to reply to the report that the SABC had chosen not to cover. The RDM quoted an opposition leader saying that the fact that the SABC chose not to report the scandal was a scandal in itself. The liberal, yet still pro-government Naspers *Beeld*, wrote:

> The events underlined the differences between the role of newspapers and the strange role of radio and television. The SABC did not broadcast the substance of evidence under oath of Judge Mostert but was prepared to give Connie Mulder the chance to air his side after the other side had been censored by the SABC.

The SABC had access to the prime minister and other ministers "not enjoyed by the opposition English press or even the Afrikaans press". This meant direct censorship from government itself. One example was when the first 25 minutes of a 30-minute bulletin on a Sunday evening was used for an "obsequious interview" with foreign minister Pik Botha, explaining government's "views on the continuing unresolved issue of Namibia". No other views were provided in this bulletin. Botha, as a matter of fact, appeared so often on a public affairs programme that it was called the "Pik Botha Show", and the SABC "nothing more than an agency" for the NP. This meant that, during the 1977 and 1982 whites-only elections, TV was, for the first time, a "powerful new instrument to help the Nationalists win once again".[275] It was found that 80% of the SABC's political coverage was devoted to government views.

Censorship under Botha - an editor's tale

Although the press "won" against Vorster after the Info Scandal, it lost to his successor Botha, writes editor Tony Heard.[276] Botha "was determined that the secret business of government should not be at the mercy of press disclosure again". Although he had been "the political beneficiary" of the scandal – denying involvement or knowledge and "wangling himself into the leadership … over the battered corpses of Vorster and 'crown prince' Mulder" – he turned "savagely" on the press.

By then, the media had "got[ten] used to coping with a regular flow of unsolicited notices from defence which stopped or inhibited the flow of information". They were issued according to an agreement between the Defence Force and the NPU, and "monitored by a special liaison committee made up of a hotchpotch of editors, newspaper managers, and bureaucratic brass". It "was supposed to ease the news flow, and lots of tea was cordially consumed". In practice, it was a one-way mechanism facilitating "the flow of defence propaganda and whitewash to the unsuspecting public". The "supposed communist onslaught" was used as justification "to browbeat the press" and stop it "from delving into dark corners of government". There was the "draconian" Official Secrets Act, later called the Protection of Information Act, "not unlike the British one in wording but far more severe in application". It could be used on the "purported ground" that newspapers "were giving away state secrets". "Almost nothing" could be said about defence and arms supply, nor the reason why the public "was left in the dark about a matter as important" as the 1975 invasion of Angola.

Also, those banned or listed by the government under the Internal Security Act could not be quoted. Promoting "communism" – meaning "espousing anything marginally to the left of Attila the Hun" – was a serious offence. The Inquests Act was applied in cases of controversial deaths, such as Biko's, as well as "scores of other political detainees". The Commissions Act also "shrouded matters being investigated by any state-appointed commission". The list of restrictions "went on endlessly", and "tomes were written by lawyers to guide editors, tomes that had to be updated frequently". One was *The Newspaperman's Guide to the Law* – the "editor's bible". Just a "slip-up" could lead to a lengthy court case and the possibility of a heavy fine or even jail. The English papers' boards of directors, "not roaringly liberal and concerned about newspaper assets and profits, were not keen on over-adventurous editing", as was "made clear" in private discussions with editors, "though they openly gave lip service to their editors' independence". It was frequently, but not always, a case of "external" independence but "internal" subservience to managerial or proprietorial pressure, with strong editors resisting; however, "the weaker buckled". An example was the National Key Points (NKP) Act of 1980 that gave government power to declare certain "national key points" for the "safeguarding thereof" [still not repealed, meaning that journalists are still prohibited from reporting, e.g., on Nkandla, as "key point"]. "Key points" included "oil refineries, storage depots, explosives, or armaments manufacturing plants" to make them safe from sabotage and spying. The problem was knowing what and where the key points were, as government "refused to supply any information". Newspapers could stumble into a contravention of the law by identifying a key point "without knowing it was a key point". The fine at the time was up to R10,000, or three years in prison, or both, with the Act "rushed through" Parliament in the last days of the 1980 session. The NPU complained ("behind the scenes") that it was not given an opportunity to "make representations". Government consulted the NPU and editors only "when it suited its book"; the rest of the time they were treated "in cavalier fashion".

When, in 1985, "the country was aflame with black unrest", Botha introduced a "limited" state of emergency, including curbing the right of the press to report what was going on. This was lifted early in 1986, simply to be replaced on 12 June with a far more extensive, nationwide emergency, re-imposed annually "in ever-repressive form" until 1990. Editors "ingeniously managed to get round" the legislation. Heard's *Cape Times* regularly published the "famous three monkeys", depicting "see no evil, hear no evil, speak no evil", to alert the public. Indeed, "[m]ost newspapers published daily front-page warnings to readers that they were not getting the full picture of what was happening". Also, "editing under the emergency meant editing by *Government Gazette*". "A myriad of taboos and rules locked the press" out of reporting reality. But the "supreme insult to journalism" was a provision that required that journalists immediately leave an area if unrest broke out. They could not even be "within sight":

> The iron clamp fastened itself round the necks of journalists, and when the Supreme Court intervened and found loopholes and weaknesses in the drafting of the emergency, the government cynically re-imposed the curbs in revised, more watertight wording which was often more repressive. The prime objective of the state of emergency was to shroud the security forces' actions in secrecy.

"[R]egular bulletins" were issued by police or government's "propaganda clearing-house", the Bureau for Information. Meanwhile, from September 1984 to September 1986, nearly 2,000 people died in unrest, with deaths continuing at varying degrees of intensity thereafter.

Throughout the "largely clandestine involvement in Angola", lasting well into the 1980s, government "kept up a barrage of confidential messages to editors, giving advice and guidance – or containing outright prohibitions on publication".[277] In February 1978, for instance, it requested editors "in the national interest" to refrain from speculation regarding the length of the "call-up", warning that "any speculation or repetition of previous statements in this regard" might cause reaction "which will definitely not be in the national interest".

And a young man's death: the first victim of P.W.'s War

The press, however, can only "be suppressed up to a point and a nation held as fools up to a point", as editor Harvey Tyson wrote:[278]

> It was only when the army began to be deployed in internal operations against South Africans; when President P.W. Botha's concept of Total Onslaught became a political device embracing even the armed forces; when they attacked neighbouring states; and when Military Intelligence was used as a weapon against some of its own citizens, that relationships between the press and the SADF fused into mutual hostility.

On 9 August 1975, the SA military invaded Angola near the Ruacana Falls on the then South-West Africa border. The RDM protested against censorship measures by carrying blank spaces on its front page. It also protested because foreign media could obtain news and photographs national media were denied. The first blank space appeared in the RDM on Saturday, 15 November, its main story about Russia backing the MPLA in Angola. But there was also a small white box below the main story, reading that an item "which would have occupied this space has not been published because permission which is required in terms of the law for such publication has not been granted". This concerned a report on British TV showing South African troops and army vehicles in Angola.

One of the most shameful acts by government, however, was when the first soldier was killed. Chris Robin's parents were ordered to put a notice in the paper to "the effect that he had died in an accident". Raymond Louw, then editor of the RDM, "lifted the advertisement out of the classified columns and placed it on Page One, immediately below the SADF denial that South African soldiers were at war in Angola". The charade lasted until Botha acknowledged the SADF's official involvement in Angola. According to one source, just one operation, Operation Savannah, cost the South African taxpayer R89,915 million, not including costs such as soldiers' wages, running and replacement costs.[279]

The Steyn Commission

With criticism against apartheid policies on the increase following the Info Scandal, government felt "some response" was needed, particularly given the importance of the media, and especially the press, in "supporting apartheid".[280] With press-government relations at a low, the Steyn Commission was appointed in June 1980 "as a further attempt to control the flow of news and information". This was seen by government "as a legitimate way of dealing with a troublesome and disloyal press". The commission's brief was to "inquire into and report on the question of whether the conduct of, and the handling of, matters by the mass media met the interests of the South African community and the demands of the times, and, if not, how they can be improved". It was "without surprise" when the commission found many shortcomings.[281] Some of the recommendations were:[282]

- professionalisation of the media by registering journalists. Any journalist convicted of subversive activity would automatically be disqualified – "a move which would have silenced most black journalists"

- establishing a press council to set norms and standards for objectivity and fairness, particularly matters relating to the peace, order and safety of the country, thus effectively prohibiting any reporting on the rising Black Consciousness

- breaking up the major press groups, particularly that of Argus and SAAN, under the guise that these monopolies were a threat to press freedom.

The commission was controversial from its inception. Afrikaner journalists also refused to be associated with it.[283] It was not a surprise that the final report "was met with indignation by both pro- and anti-government newspapers". "Oddly," government did little to implement the draconian recommendations despite the fact that the proposals supported its view. It is speculated that the conservative US Reagan administration persuaded the government to rethink.[284] Another factor, as with Infogate earlier, was that the English and Afrikaans press stood together in condemning the report.[285] Still, legislation was introduced in June 1982 to establish a new media council and forcing all newspapers to join the NPU.

Where there were 247 publications in 1912, with the printing and newspaper industry employing 4,650 people, it provided a livelihood for more than 36,000 with the NPU's 1982 centenary.[286] South Africans consumed more than nine million copies of newspapers and magazines, not including monthly and fortnightly publications.

The Steyn Commissions' second report in 1982 proposed three pieces of legislation which, "together, provide[d] a matrix of coercion under the guise of 'voluntary' censure".[287] The first was the Internal Security Act, No 74 of 1982, which prohibited the circulation and debate of ideas relating "to alternative social, political and economic policies". The second was the Protection of Information Act, No 84 of 1982, which repealed the old Official Secrets Act, with numerous additional clauses. The third was an amendment to the Registration of Newspapers Act, No 92 of 1982. This offered newspapers the choice of falling under the Publications Act of 1974, and thus under direct control of the Directorate of Publications – the State's censorship machinery, or subjecting themselves to the code of conduct and disciplinary powers of a new Media Council, "a body complementing the NPU", as the

Press's own attempt to stave off government interference through its own "self-policing body". The NPU had previously enforced "a comprehensive degree of self-discipline" on the press. The provision that none of the members of the new Council would be appointed by government lent credence to it being an independent and voluntarily constituted organisation. Nonetheless, it derived its power from statutory recognition. Coercion, however, was not the only tactic used by government to harness the press. There was "a discernible pattern" in government's strategy towards the English-language press. When co-option failed, it introduced legislation to coerce it. The introduction of each successive stage of legislation raised "the threshold of co-option", followed by further coercion "as the perceived crisis escalate[d]". The long-term ability of the press "to articulate alternative viewpoints [was] increasingly curtailed". The legislation prior to 1976, for example, was inadequate to cope with the "Soweto crisis". Thus "[e]xtreme coercion" – the banning of newspapers and editors and detaining of editors and journalists – was followed by a period of "co-option", as government first tried to purchase a section of the English press, then to set up its own paper. After the "limited success" of this strategy, further coercive measures followed with the Advocate-General Bill. Thus, the Steyn Commissions set the climate for further co-option in the form of the Media Council and "voluntary" self-censorship. Simultaneously, the already mentioned three Bills, rushed through Parliament in 1982, provided "the most comprehensive arsenal" against the press. Even before the first Steyn Commission Report in 1980, Allister Sparks, then RDM editor, said that the "Total Strategy" would include pressures on the press to secure its co-operation in the "national interest" by drawing it "into the system".

Successive governments had to "discipline" the press to become "responsible" without showing "overt censorship", while the press regarded its claim to be the "freest press in Africa" as "one of its few assets in world public opinion".[288] South African journalist Patrick Laurence, arrested twice under apartheid (the second time the slogan "Free Laurence of Azania" was spray-painted on a wall[289]) said: "The Old Nats always prefaced their attacks on press freedom with affirmations of their belief in a free and responsible press."[290]

Botha's "major effort" was to find a "lever" through the Steyn Commission. Named after its chair, retired Judge M.T. Steyn,[291] hearings were held from November 1980 to April 1981. The first 1,367-page report, along with draft legislation, was tabled in parliament on 1 February 1982. The proposed "Journalism Bill",[292] a system of licensing similar to that of the medical profession, was regarded by the media as yet another "Botha proposal" to control the press without actually having a "government censor in every newspaper office". Both the English and Afrikaans press opposed this.

The commission's mandate, to "inquire into and report on the question of whether the conduct of, and the handling of matters by the mass media meet the needs and the interests of the South African community and the demands of the times, and, if not, how they can be improved",[293] was controversial from its inception. No press representative, English or Afrikaans, agreed to serve on the five-person commission. In the end, it was highly criticised "for pandering to government ideology".[294]

Also, no black journalist was willing to appear before the commission, and spokespeople from both English and Afrikaans press groups showed "a rare unity" in agreeing that the "press was already bound by too many restrictive laws", with no need for any further legislation, "especially a register of journalists".[295] Ex-editor Joel Mervis said the register was "sinister and dangerous".

The NPU's presentation represented both English and Afrikaans papers. South Africa was "a country under stress", but it "did not mean that the nation should dispense with freedoms painstakingly acquired over three centuries". The principle "should be a free flow of information". Ton Vosloo, then editor of the influential *Beeld*, said the commission should rather recommend to government a revision of press restraints.

The most far-reaching recommendation was a "vague code of conduct to be enforced by a central general council of journalists". The proposed "Journalists Bill" implied not only the registration of journalists, but also that they should have certain qualifications and pass certain examinations before being allowed to practise.

Still, the commission, although finding that the media were "not effectively meeting the demands of the time" and that "the interests of the community were not being sufficiently served", rejected state control and censorship, but paradoxically also "unbridled press freedom".[296] Its second report again proposed the compulsory register and "the splitting of ownership" to prevent monopolies. Only the latter was incorporated in the new law on the registration of newspapers. Religious organisations, specifically the World Council of Churches and the SA Council of Churches, were "strangely" singled out in a "scathing attack" in the report's "242 page digression on black theology".[297]

The recommendation on ownership stipulated that major shareholders would be forced to sell off large parts of their companies to get as wide a spread of shareholders as possible.[298] No one was allowed to hold more than 1% in a public company, and no more than 10% if privately held.

The eventual compromise – "as was now the rule in these matters between the press and Government" – was that the NPU had to set up a new media council to replace the old PCSA.[299] Still, government had the last say. When, in the last hours of the 1982 parliamentary session, the Registration of Newspapers Amendment Act was accepted, it meant that the minister of internal affairs could cancel the registration of a newspaper if it did not subject itself to certain disciplinary measures. And all of this happened amid the apathy of South Africans, who "could not care less" about media freedom:

> As a group, white South Africans show little understanding of or concern for freedom of the press and do not feel that their own freedoms are jeopardized when black newspapers are closed down or journalists arrested. The white public, with the exception of a comparatively few liberals, are far more concerned about the vague "total onslaught" than what has happened to civil liberties of fellow South Africans.

The Steyn Commission was indeed part of government's strategy of "divide and rule".[300] If there would be a conflict between state and media, national security would weigh most and the media would apply self-censorship on the activities of the "internal and external enemies of the state (enemies as defined by the state)". The media had to propagate and maintain a positive view of the state's security and defence forces, and was expected to mobilise public opinion regarding the "Total Onslaught" against South Africa. In the end, most of the commission's findings were not implemented, and press and government "continued their uneasy relationship until the next crisis when the [next] state of emergency was implemented".[301]

'A massive, perhaps fatal attack' on your right to know

The response to the initial recommendations of the commission was "immediately and blunt".[302] The RDM wrote that it would be "a massive, perhaps fatal, assault on your right to be kept informed of what is happening in your own country", and "a hammer blow to standards and to freedom of information". Influential Afrikaans editors, including Vosloo and Willem de Klerk, expressed strong opposition to government.

Thus, government hesitated to push through the "Journalists' Act". Again, the NPU mobilised and held a series of meetings. After "five months of bargaining", government once again backed off. Instead, the NPU's agreement to set up a new media council worried editors that it may lead to an indirect system of government control. Still, editors "felt they had won a victory of sorts and that this compromise was far less ominous than the register of journalists".

With regard to the Newspaper Registration Amendment Bill, the newspapers again presented a united front against its proposal.[303] Government wanted to "rectify" a "fatal flaw" in the PCSA, namely that newspapers that did not belong to the NPU were exempt from its code. This was aimed at the far-right Afrikaner fringe papers, *Die Patriot* and *Die Afrikaner*, to reduce their influence. Again, English and Afrikaans papers were unanimous in denouncing the bill, their opposition voiced through the NPU as well as the Conference of Editors, a grouping of white editors.[304] Government "obviously feared" the influence among *verkrampte* Afrikaners through the two far-right Afrikaans papers, supported by right-wing Afrikaners who broke away from the NP.[305]

Under the compromise law, the Registration of Newspapers Amendment Act No 84 of 1982, the registration of newspapers could be cancelled if publishers did not subject themselves to the new Media Council, implying the two far-right Afrikaans publications would also have to adhere.

In the end, the inquiry just "added an important new chapter to the continuing struggle for control of the printed word in South Africa," although the report, with its "somewhat paranoid and extremist perception of the 'total onslaught' was ridiculed by many South Africans". In time it became "something of an embarrassment" to government.

In sum, the major result of the commission was the creation of the Media Council, which replaced the PCSA in 1983.[306] For the first time, the Council included working journalists and members of the public – intended to "include members of all race groups". Besides the NPU, the white Conference of Editors, representing editors of both English and Afrikaans papers, were part of negotiations ensuring the commission's recommendations were not implemented.

The new Media Council consisted of a chair and alternate chair, plus 14 media and 14 public representatives. Six of the media representatives were nominated by the Conference of Editors, six by the NPU, and SASJ and MWASA could nominate one each. The 14 public representatives were selected by former judges from a panel of candidates submitted by the NPU – all in all, a Council meant "to promote freedom of expression and higher professional standards".

The 'alternatives' and others

But, while Vorster had secretly already tried, and failed, to get the press to observe an "informal state of emergency" on security matters in late 1971,[307] a "much more serious effort" came in 1986. The main target now was the "alternative" papers which "mushroomed" as unrest grew after 1984 and "operated outside the clubby atmosphere of the NPU", with which government would hold "regular, confidential discussions". Botha wanted the established papers to destroy the alternatives. Once again, the press had to accept "guidelines", meaning the papers had to work under the same conditions as in a state of emergency, such as that a journalist on the scene of unrest would have to leave immediately. But this time it would be worse – "the public would not even know about the arrangement". Through these secret, voluntary guidelines, and not being openly coerced by the state, participating newspapers would escape fines, or jail, for their staff. "The price was treachery against others." The "alternative" publications could then be dealt with under the state of emergency by government – and government would get what it wanted: A "'responsible' and 'patriotic' (which means compliant) established press, with the rest bludgeoned into submission". After much discussion, the English-language newspaper groups refused to go along with the Afrikaans groups in their acceptance of these guidelines.

In terms of the Internal Security Act of 1982, as amended, all publications, and not only newspapers, were already subject to severe censorship.[308] For instance, the already referred to *Oxford History of South Africa Vol 2: South Africa, 1870–1966*, appeared with a missing chapter on African Nationalism. At least one international newsmagazine appeared with a blank page, explaining that the state of emergency "made this necessary". This "all happened against the background of a growing clamour" for government to talk with the ANC. Circles "close to government" took up the refrain, such as in 1980, when Vosloo, verligte editor of *Beeld*, predicted this by saying the day would arrive when a South African government would sit at the negotiating table together with the ANC. "[B]ig business", on the other hand, led by Anglo-American head Gavin Relly, met with Tambo and other ANC leaders in Lusaka.

The coercion of the media continued, however, such as when, in the mid-1980s, "dropping or modifying the law on quoting banned or listed persons" was considered. A paper would be "secretly offered" a list of names of people who could be quoted on a six-month trial basis, but the paper would still have to get formal approval from the "powerful State Security Council", chaired by the state president and "bristling with security chiefs", before anyone on the list could be quoted. The editors, though, "did not want to get involved in deciding, with the minister or anyone", who could be quoted and who not – the "professionally correct position", as a "list of quotables was as bad as a list of unquotables".

'Social control' over the 'urban African'

The "black" radio service, Radio Bantu, was described by sociologist Heribert Adam as "one of the most powerful tools of social control over the urban African".[309] It was one of the most obvious "and most expensive features" of apartheid, as it "undoubtedly reinforced Nationalist policies on apartheid". Besides its paternalism and propaganda, it nevertheless "accumulated and preserved a large and valuable archive of cultural materials relating to major ethnic groups".[310] While critics of Western broadcasting derided its destructive influence on traditional culture, the SABC, paradoxically, preserved and encouraged traditional music, drama, legends and folklore.

With the establishment of "black" TV in January 1982, "only the architects of apartheid" could "produce such an innovation in broadcasting". About 1,000 blacks were recruited as staff – at a time when blacks owned 235,000 TV sets, although most black homes did not have electricity. The answer to why the SABC proceeded with "black" TV was simple: It was part of the initial 1971 Meyer Commission "Master Plan". And it was executed because the SABC was convinced it could "control the black channel" and use it for its own purposes.

By mid-1980, the SABC enjoyed a state-run monopoly.[311] But, with new technology, the video cassette player flourished, as did video-hiring companies. Also, Swazi TV could be received in certain areas. Regarding radio, Johannesburg could receive Radio 702 broadcast from Bophuthatswana in competition to the SABC's Radio 5.

Although SAAN editorially condemned the existence of homelands, they were eager to go into a business partnership with the Bophuthatswana "government" as part of the 1981 consortium of newspaper companies – Argus, SAAN, Naspers and Perskor – for a TV service from Bophuthatswana. Government was reluctant to issue a TV frequency – an "interesting dilemma" – as the homelands had to appear to be independent, including being given radio frequencies for Radio 702 and Capital Radio, but government did not welcome any "incoming radio nor TV signals" which could take away "both audiences and advertising revenue".

And Afrikaner press wars

The already referred to Afrikaner press wars started in 1965, when Naspers decided to launch a publication in the North – traditional territory of the Northern Afrikaner Nationalist press groups. There was "bitter opposition"[312] from Perskor, the by-then amalgamated group between Dagbreek Pers and Afrikaanse Pers Beperk, which earlier amalgamated with Voortrekkerpers. There were even open calls to boycott the new paper and the "liberalism" that dared to transgress on their territory. The "newspaper war" lasted for almost two decades, estimated conservatively to have cost each R20 million,[313] and which ended in a fraudulent Perskor lying to the ABC about its circulation.[314] The final court ruling in 1983 was a settlement giving the morning market to the more liberal Naspers and the afternoon Afrikaans market to Perskor, together with a significant fine. Perskor also had to pay advertisers the sum of R1,3 million as refund, or give them advertising space to the value.

The scandal became known as Syferfontein, a wordplay on Watergate.[315] Meaning more or less "Numbersgate" or "Circulationgate", the manipulation of figures had in fact started as far back as in 1976, when *Beeld*'s circulation topped 50,000 for the first time. The "bombshell" came in September 1980, when the ABC announced that circulation for *Die Transvaler*, *Die Vaderland* and *The Citizen* had been "inflated" by several thousands.[316] Perskor CEO Jooste described it "somewhat demurely" as "an incorrect version of loyalty and enthusiasm". But the extent of the fraud went far beyond just circulations. The concomitant financial loss for Naspers was one aspect, the political agenda another. At issue was "the perceived readership for Perskor in conservative Afrikanerdom's heartland".[317]

The South-North dynamic, while no longer definable in geographic terms but rather as *verlig* and *verkramp*, was emphasised.[318] *Beeld* was "increasingly cornering the market" with "uncompromising support" for the proposed reforms,[319] but it also got its commercial reward: sole control of the Afrikaans morning market.[320]

Reform journalism the Afrikaans press way

The Afrikaans press wars indicated the "war lines" between the traditionally conservative North and more liberal South. By the mid-1980s, the Afrikaans press, once subservient to Afrikaner Nationalism, developed to become "dynamic political institutions in their own right"[321] with what can be called "reform journalism".[322]

Afrikaans papers at first did "little more than toe the party line".[323] But, as the party became more and more dictatorial, they "increasingly ventured to step over the line". In the mid-1980s, "they ha[d] begun to suggest where the line should be drawn". Afrikaans papers often were "far ahead" of government, "calling for sweeping changes in traditional Nationalist policies" and becoming an important "internal opposition", with Afrikaans editors "increasingly" setting the pace and determining the goal of the party while adopting a "more Western concept of the role of the press". They saw themselves not "merely as propagandists for the government, but watchdogs over the implementation of government policy", as "a forum for exploring alternatives to apartheid, and as a teacher whose task it was to wean Afrikaners away from the idea that the country's problems could be solved entirely within the context of white politics". The Afrikaans press's growing independence was not welcomed by party superiors. Trying to suppress Afrikaans editors' "newfound freedom", some "powerful Nationalists", preferring a tame "mouthpiece for their views", came down on the press with more legislative and other restraints. These new threats meant that Afrikaans editors, in order to preserve their "newfound independence", had to work together with their English peers – traditionally their rivals and "opposition" – as they found that freedom of expression "was not divisible".

With ever more constraints on the press, the Afrikaans press developed a "growing independence" in their attitude toward government restraints.[324] Afrikaans editors backed the NPU in setting up the PCSA and, especially after Vorster's threats, "some alarm appeared in the Nationalist press". The Afrikaans papers welcomed the new code of conduct "if it would head off direct government control". Afrikaans editors found themselves "on the firing line" as conservative Nationalists "took aim" at them for trying to "re-educate" readers to accept political changes they had long been taught to resist. Simultaneously, "an increasing sense of professionalism" developed among Afrikaans journalists, "several of whom by now [had been] exposed" to Harvard's Nieman Fellowship.

By the mid-1980s, the Afrikaans press might have become more objective, more critical, and more aligned with Western concepts of journalism, "but the very substantial changes" since 1965 did not mean that they had "ceased their primary function of serving" the NP.[325] As "purveyors of a political message" it was an "uncomfortable dilemma" for them. This was problematic on two levels: As newspapers they had to be independent of direct party control, but as Nationalist newspapers they had to maintain their influence on the Afrikaner elite. It was an uneasy path, as "neither side could afford a split". They had to "keep a foot in the door of the establishment", otherwise it became powerless, and simultaneously the Afrikaans establishment could not afford a war against their papers, "as it [was] too vulnerable, especially within itself".

Although the Afrikaans press was founded as a "servile press", it started to change from being a "lapdog" to a "watchdog" as early as in the 1960s.[326] The Afrikaans press's support for the NP was the primary reason for its existence, but it had become more and more critical since 1970. Clashes between political figures and Afrikaans editors were "the rule rather than the exception". Contrary to popular belief, the Afrikaans press was not the NP's "monolithic undifferentiated publicity arm".[327] Before South Africa became a Republic, the Afrikaans press was "loath to criticise the policies and direction of the party to which it owed its allegiance". Unlike the English press, financed with corporate capital, Afrikaans papers were funded through a large number of small investors. By 1953, for example, Naspers was registered in the names of 3,239 shareholders. The largest then was still Santam/Sanlam, then a consortium of Cape-based Afrikaner enterprises created with the intention of consolidating small capital. Afrikaanse Pers was not only financed through Transvaal NP supporters, but also directly by the Party itself.

By 1948, the Afrikaans press had achieved its "greatest ambition", and the next ten years were spent consolidating the Afrikaner power base.[328] But by late 1950 it was clear that "there were differences between an unequivocal support for an entrenched Government and the building up of a cultural entity under perceived attack". For the first time, "elements of the Afrikaans press" were prepared to challenge NP leadership. After some reforms, and consequently conservatives breaking away, the Afrikaans press succeeded "in projecting verligtheid as the image of the responsible Afrikaner and verkramptheid as the deviant, the dubious and the self-deceptive, even the stupid".[329] Verligtheid obtained an "image of decency, respect and credibility, particularly via the Afrikaans press".

The 1982 CP breakaway also reflected the traditional Cape/Transvaal division. Afrikaans papers have long been the "site of struggle" between the two. Their animosity also dated back to the premiership of Verwoerd, who was "adamantly opposed" to the establishment of a Naspers paper in the Transvaal – the stronghold of the conservative Perskor. Indirectly, the introduction of Naspers's *Die Beeld* led to more "verligte" Perskor editors in the persons of Willem de Klerk at the *Transvaler* and P.G. du Plessis at *Hoofstad*, indicating that the Naspers paper opened up opportunities for enlightened thinking in the North. However, after De Klerk's dismissal, Perskor "returned to its old strategy" of backing the more conservative elements of Afrikanerdom.

A country at war with herself

Meanwhile, South Africa was getting more and more unstable. Biko's arrest and death while in police custody in 1977, after "several days of brutal treatment", led to September of that year becoming known as "Black September".[330] Justice minister Jimmy Kruger's remark that Biko's death "left him cold" became a statement that would reverberate long after. Willie Esterhuyse, Stellenbosch University philosophy professor and, towards the end of the 1980s, peace broker, said Kruger's words were "like a cannon shot to the hearts of many NP-supporting Afrikaners whose consciences were increasingly troubled by the megalomania of their leaders".[331]

That same year, another censorship battle was being fought over the publication of a book.[332] As Naspers chair Ton Vosloo would later state: The protracted battle around the novel *Magersfontein, o Magersfontein!* was the best example of his company's defence of freedom of expression. To Vosloo, "there is no doubt that the significant changes that were subsequently made to the Publications Act" had been influenced "to a considerable extent" by the *Magersfontein* rulings. The battle lines regarding book publications were already drawn in 1963, when 117 writers and 41 artists presented their view against the Publications and Entertainments Act, stating the Act was contrary to the "most basic principles of art".[333]

The Publications Amendment Act followed in April 1979. In the same month, the Suid-Afrikaanse Akademie vir Wetenskap en Kuns (the Afrikaans South African Academy for Science and the Arts) announced that the Hertzog Prize – Afrikaans literature's highest recognition – was awarded to Leroux's *Magersfontein*, although still banned. The court case continued, but the ban was lifted by April 1980, with bans on most of the other prohibited books also lifted in the 1980s.

On being a foreign correspondent

From the earliest years of NP government, "spokesmen have fulminated against foreign correspondents" who sent "irresponsible and slanderous reports" abroad, also against "unpatriotic" or even "treasonous" local newspapers and journalists.[334]

As early as in 1952, the annual report of the State Information Office complained that there had been "a resurgence of an organised press campaign" against South Africa.[335] The Foreign Correspondents' Association had only six members in 1974, thirty in 1977, and by 1984 had "burgeoned" to 85 journalists, with about 20 of them American. It represented 53 organisations from ten Western countries, Japan, and Taiwan. "Such a concentration of journalists has assured that South Africa ... was the most thoroughly reported area of Africa". During the same period, Western news coverage of other sub-Saharan countries generally declined.

In the 1980s, authorities kept track of foreign journalists' reportage.[336] Some journalists' telephones had been tapped and some had been denied renewal of work permits. In 1980, eight West German journalists were denied visas, while in 1982 a Dutch radio and TV correspondent was expelled. On occasion, "harassment became prosecution". Government in the 1980s was "less tolerant" of foreign correspondents "and clearly any newsman who tries to investigate and report on the political activities among blacks is particularly vulnerable to expulsion". These abrasive relationships between government and foreign journalists may have resulted in "some self-censorship by the journalists", but the flow of news was "indisputably negative because that is the kind of news South Africans" were making.

Another step towards the Orwellian nightmare of 1984

In 1981, Harold G. Rudolph, senior law lecturer at Wits, wrote that the January 1981 "gagging" of two of the most important black newspapers, *Post* and *Sunday Post*, "and the comparatively small public outcry which resulted, show that little press freedom survives in South Africa" and that the "public has been forced to accept, without demur, invasions of this freedom".[337] He emphasised that the term "press freedom" was misleading, "because it conveys the impression that the freedom to tell, that is, the right to publish, is of paramount importance", but "ignores the equally, if not more, valuable freedom – the right to be told or the right to know".

The rationale behind the concept of press freedom "must surely be that every member of society should be able to acquire information from all sources, not only from those that are officially approved". Quoting PCSA chair Judge Galgut, he said "[freedom of the Press is not something which belongs to the journalist. It belongs to the public."

In the 1980s, while "struggling to find an equitable solution to its complex racial problems", government faced increasing pressure from both internal and external sources. It was crucial that all South Africans "be exposed to the greatest possible divergence of opinions and policies" to enable them to "exercise judiciously those rights that they do have". Rudolph quoted Professor J.D. van der Vyver, who wrote in 1976 that the press

> is free to publish whatever it pleases in whatever form or terms it pleases, except in so far as its right and competency to do so have been curtailed by law. Press reports and comments are not subject to government approval, and as such the South African press has not fallen victim to governmental censorship in the narrow sense, that is in the sense of the press having to obtain *a priori* permission from the government to publish whatever it may wish to publish.

One therefore could conclude that the press in South Africa enjoyed "a fair measure of freedom". The opposite was the case, Dugard wrote in 1978, namely that "one of the most skilfully nurtured South African myths is that there is a genuinely free press". This myth was perpetuated

> by the apparent freedom with which the English-language press criticizes govern-mental policies and practices in certain legally and conventionally defined areas; by the praise of foreign critics who are continually surprised to find *any* criticism tolerated; and, particularly, by the shower of abuse poured upon the English language press by government spokesmen who regularly accuse it of disloyalty and subversion and threaten to deprive it of its "freedom".

Dugard referred to Professor L.M. Thompson, who in 1966 wrote that the "liberal Press has been reduced to insecurity and near impotence", while the "great English dailies are impeded from discovering and reporting the worst evils of apartheid and are under great pressure to refrain from fundamental criticisms of the government".

The right of unrestricted discussion of public affairs, or the "right to know", was "of peculiar importance" to both SA's white and the disfranchised black population. Newspapers, especially those serving the black community, were "vital to the quasi-democratic process that exists in South Africa", as they articulated their readers' hopes and aspirations "and acted as a forum or as an outlet for the expression of their views". Black opinion could be expressed on current matters and "Government and non-black people of South Africa [could] gain an understanding of black opinion".

Still, "interference with the freedom of the Press is an interference with the public's right to know", depriving the public "of the information it requires to form a proper judgment". Ironically, government "has repeatedly avowed its adherence to the concept of freedom of the press", often boasting that South Africa is one of the few countries in Africa that possesses a "free press", justifying its actions "to protect our 'Western' way of life".

Legislation against the press was preceded by government's standpoint that, "while it is committed to freedom of the press, such freedom is not unlimited and may not be abused", meaning "newspapers are free to publish whatever they wish as long as they do not publish whatever they are told not to publish". Despite government's "avowed commitment" to press freedom, its actions belied its words. Whatever press freedom survived was "despite the actions" of government, "not because of them". The "right to information" has never been absolute in South Africa and was not provided for in the Constitution, although government "boasted of the right South Africans have to dissent". Dugard quoted a 1968 publication, *South Africa and the Rule of Law*, stating it was no offence in South Africa to oppose its "separate development" policy. Indeed, "it is opposed by the opposition party in the South African Parliament itself". Also, "a large section" of the press vigorously criticised government as well as government actions on a daily basis, with no action taken against critics "as long as their opposition is conducted in a constitutional manner". This statement would be "unexceptionable in a society in which the majority of the citizens participate[d] in the electoral process", but in South Africa it was misleading, as "the limits of constitutionality are dictated by a small white oligarchy representing one-fifth of the total population".

It was not only misleading, but untrue, as action "can be, and often has been, taken against both individuals and organizations, and any recourse to the judiciary denied them". According to the South African Institute of Race Relations, some 1,240 persons were banned between 1950 and 1974. At the end of 1978, 149 banning orders were in force. In January 1981, the minister of justice was quoted as saying that there were 195 "restricted" persons, of whom 38 had left the country.

Also, since the NP took power in 1948, a number of newspapers were silenced, despite the "commitment" to a free press. It was "extremely difficult to obtain an accurate assessment" of the number of "silenced" papers, as there was "no comprehensive, official index". A case in point was when, under the 1952 Suppression of Communism Act, *The Guardian* was banned but reappeared after each banning under the names of *Clarion*, *Advance*, *New Age* and *Spark* until 1962, when new legislation prevented a newspaper "considered to be furthering the objects of communism" from appearing under a new name. Also, the significant deposit to register a newspaper was a factor, unless there was "no reason to believe that it will ever be necessary to ban it". If a ban was imposed, the deposit was forfeited, which was intended to discourage new publications and empower the justice minister to silence a newspaper – thereby relieving the president of the "unpleasant task of banning it". Other newspapers that were banned were *Fighting Talk* in 1962 and *African Communist* the following year. The October 1977 crackdown closed *Pro Veritate* of the Christian Institute, plus *The World* and *Weekend World*. This caused a public outcry both in and outside South Africa. Justice minister Kruger explained "he had to do this as the administrative procedure" by the PCSA "was too slow and cumbersome" and because "the security of the country was at stake".

When *Post* and *Sunday Post* were closed in January 1981, a similar explanation was given: The papers "aimed at creating a revolutionary climate in South Africa". No evidence was given, although the papers were accused of propagating the aims of the banned ANC. Besides, it was said Section 6 of the Internal Security Act does not oblige the minister "to give reasons for his actions", "nor is the public's right to receive information or their right to know provided for in the Act".

But, argued Rudolph, the public's right to know, inherent in a democratic society, was ignored. With the "security situation being what it is", South Africans would "accept some form" of media control, provided it "is both limited and reasonable", also that it "is exercised and is seen to be exercised independently" of government "by a body of persons divorced" from government. It should have no power to close papers, should represent all sections of society, and should ideally be chaired by a judge of the Supreme Court. And:

> It should be empowered to act as a type of watchdog to guard the interests of both the public at large and the press in particular; its decisions should be made subject in the ordinary course to both review by and appeal to the Supreme Court; the hearings should be in public, so that whenever action is taken against a newspaper, for any reason at all, the public will be assured that such action has been taken only after all the evidence against the newspaper has been tried and tested in public and found to be correct.

Only in such a way could the public's right to know be protected and enhanced, because "[f]reedom is indivisible", and "actions taken against one section of society inevitably affect other sections of that society". Actions taken against black publications "resulting in the black population of the Transvaal being denied its own major newspaper" would therefore affect all of South Africa. Also: They should be "both justifiable and justified in the open" – otherwise South Africa "will have taken another step towards the Orwellian nightmare of 1984".

Treading a fine line

In 1981 it was said that "[n]ewspapers serve as the lone megaphone of dissent"[338] and, without the still moderately free press to spread news and "unpopular" ideas, the country's "political lopsidedness would be near complete". In fact, "[m]ore than any powerful force in the country", newspapers stood between government and "totalitarian darkness". But some critics said they should do more, as they represented the "forces of the status quo",[339] with none of the media publishing or broadcasting "material undermining the principles of their owners or the elements upon which they depend financially".[340] Indeed, the South African press "essentially serve the narrow class interests of the dominant whites".[341] Other critics said "all sectors of the established media support one or more factions of the hegemonic alliance".[342] In hindsight, though, the "media played a more pivotal and complicated role" in South Africa's democratic transition "than the democratisation literature would lead us to expect".[343] No consensus exists on this, as the "far too simplistic" narrative of casting the English so-called liberal press as the angels and the Afrikaner Nationalist press as the demons is by far not nuanced enough "to assist in understanding all the idiosyncrasies" of a complex period.

In 1987, the English press was dominated by Argus and SAAN, with the former owning 40% of the latter.[344] The shareholders of both were concerns "traditionally associated with the mining industry; most notably Anglo American and JCI". Considering the composition of the holding companies and their directors, it was not surprising that the English press was "closely associated with the aims, objectives and interests of the hegemonic bloc as a whole". This "convergence of interests should not be viewed in the mechanistic fashion" in which the English-language press was seen to be "controlled" by individuals such as Harry Oppenheimer and Gordon Waddell. Before 1948, and the years immediately after, the NP and the UP "vied with each other" to be the "real custodians of white interests". The

NP strategy of Afrikaner cultural and political exclusivity "meant the exclusion of English-speaking elements", and more particularly "a legitimisation of the notion of racial purity".

Critics viewed apartheid not as "an illogical and irrational ideology hinged on racial and cultural differences", but as "an externalisation of the class struggle in a capitalist society historically divided by race".[345] There were many tenets common to both Nationalism's apartheid and its liberal English counterpart. The most important was the need to develop a black middle class as "a skilled stratum of the workforce". Still, the English press's "limited resistance" to government met with "fairly severe repression". One example was the RDM's "Take Care Mr Vorster" story.[346] Laurence Gandar and reporter Benjamin Pogrund were accused of "[r]unning a campaign to vilify the Prisons Department, of publishing one-sided reports, and of rejecting information favourable to the prisons". Both were charged under the Prisons Act and found guilty three years later. Minimal penalties followed, but the case was important in "clarifying the contradictions of a 'free' press in a repressive state". Crippling legal fees were a bigger deterrent to further contentious stories. Another example is the investigation by East London's *Daily Dispatch* into the death and detention of Biko and the banning and exile of editor Woods. The action against Woods was far harsher than that against Gandar. One reason was the *Dispatch*'s growing influence as a black-orientated news medium.

Despite the *Dispatch*'s attempts to comply with the requirements of Transkei bureaucracy, the paper was also banned for three weeks in April 1980 after a report on the arrest of 200 people after an alleged assassination attempt on Kaiser Matanzima.[347] The *Dispatch* was the only regional paper, meaning its banning created a vacuum, with government tenders that could not be published as well as no platform for the Transkei cabinet. For the paper it meant a drop of approximately 20% in circulation, as well as advertising losses, particularly from Transkei government offices.

The states of emergency

During the apartheid era up to De Klerk's speech on 2 February 1990, a number of states of emergency were declared. These severely infringed on the media's right to report on events – one of the purposes of the declarations. Ken Owen, described as South Africa's "Last Great White Editor"[348] who retired as editor of the *Sunday Times*, said "the consequences of censorship are always perverse".[349] He did not spare criticising his own profession: "If our newspapers are liberal, they are, by and large, the wettest liberals on earth."

Altogether seven states of emergency were declared between 1960 and 1990, "plus the subsequent proclamation of unrest areas" – implying severe censorship, even though "without them, South Africa existed in a state that amounted to permanent emergency".[350] Besides the "no-go areas" as deterrent to gathering news and the power to suspend newspapers, detention was a "constant underlying threat". "Emergency powers" were as much a psychological tool for government "as a necessary source of power". This included the security forces' right to act in "an arbitrary and often blatant fashion", "unchallenged by courts or parliament". Journalists could not even use phrases or words such as "white minority regime", "draconian", or "riot-torn". Not only was the concept "Right to Know" "foreign" to South Africa, but to believe in it "was tantamount to treason". At its most blatant, censorship involved the "straightforward banning of the printed word", often "rendering individuals and corporate bodies invisible in a literary sense". The 1974 Publications Act and the Internal Security Act were part of "an integral police state culture".

Between 1975 and 1990, 23,435 titles were submitted to the Publications Control Board, 88% by the police, customs officials or employees of the Directorate itself, and only 5% by the public and publishers.

When reformist editor Ton Vosloo headed Naspers as executive leader from 1984, he fought against government's threats and said of yet another plan to form a media regulatory body in 1988 that the formation of such a body would be

> to cross the Rubicon of press freedom in this country. Either you have some degree of press freedom, or you have an Iron Curtain situation. The government already has the necessary law and is just waiting for an opportunity to implement it. If it were to do so, it would be a day to mourn and I strongly advise against it.[351]

But fellow Afrikaners in government did all they could to annoy, muzzle and blindfold the media. As one minister, Adriaan Vlok, said: "We give all the basic information, but, of course, we don't give the story behind the story." Another minister, Louis Nel, declared: "We do not have censorship in South Africa. What we have is a limit on what newspapers can report on." He emphasised:

> I want to put it clearly today: it does not matter whether limitations are imposed on the freedom of the Press; nor does it matter whether there is a degree of control over the Press; nor does it matter whether action is sometimes taken against the Press. The Press is free, of principle.

Cape Times editor Tony Heard commented that the "caricature of a bloodthirsty ANC was carefully nurtured by the South African government and its faithful media, the pro-Nationalist press and the SABC".[352] In 1985, Heard conducted an interview with Oliver Tambo in London,[353] leading to a court case, heard in November 1985.

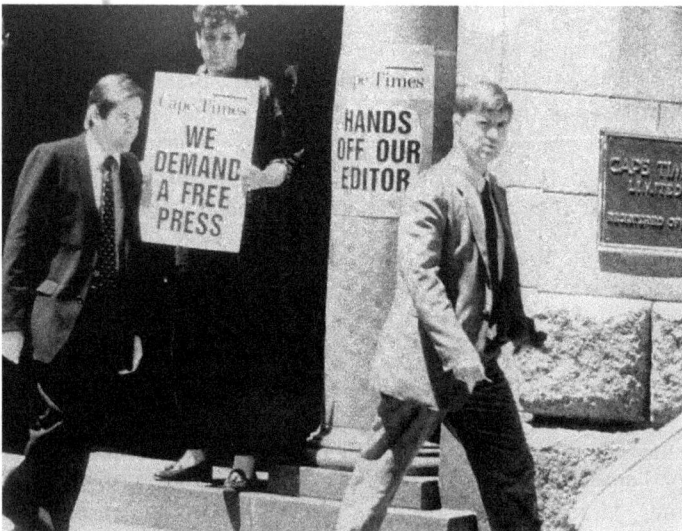

Tony Heard (left) being taken to court by a police lieutenant in November 1985 after publishing the Tambo interview, with Marianne Thamm (behind) holding a placard.
Photo: Heard, *The Cape of Storms*

Heard's "offence" was quoting a "banned or listed person". Legislature did not provide for a fine and the charge carried a maximum prison penalty of three years. Heard thought the authorities would "duck a trial".[354] If not, it could be "a celebrated case, involving the fundamental right to know", with a defence that could "draw on Milton, Voltaire, the United States First Amendment Act and other powerful free-expression sources and statements to make the point". Charged with violating the Internal Security Act by publishing a full-page interview with Tambo on 4 November 1985,[355] the charges were withdrawn in July 1986, although SAAN paid "a small admission-of-guilt fine". Heard was awarded the International Federation of Newspaper Publishers' Golden Pen of Freedom in May 1986, as well as SASJ's Pringle Medal for the Defence of Freedom of the Press.

But it cost him dearly. In August 1987 he was dismissed as editor. Tony Weaver, then assistant news editor and Western Cape SASJ vice-president, "was highly critical of the decision" to replace Heard. Whatever "weak excuses" were given, there could only be one: "buckling to government, police and right-wing pressure". There was such an outcry that Stephen Mulholland, managing director, sent a note to attorney Richard Rosenthal on 12 August 1987 to give a "categorical assurance" that the decision "had nothing whatsoever" to do with Heard's "integrity or moral probity". And: "If Tony so wishes we are prepared to issue a public statement to this effect." The decision was based on "practical, commercial" reasons, "and our view that we need a new Editor to apply a fresh mind to the problem of increasing circulation, and tackle various managerial and related problems".

The 1980s 'Big Four'

By the mid-1980s, newspaper publishing was dominated by the "Big Four": two English and two Afrikaans groups. Of the four, the Argus Group, officially the Argus Printing and Publishing Company, was a "mammoth" – not only the largest, but the "most powerful".[356] Among its seven dailies were the *Cape Argus* and the Johannesburg *The Star*. SAAN included among its four dailies the RDM and the *Cape Times*. The Argus Group held 40% of SAAN stock, while SAAN held a somewhat smaller Argus stake, both tied to mining and industrial interests.

When, in 1978, Argus made an attempt to buy a 65% share in SAAN it was prevented by the Monopolies Act, but Argus nevertheless made slow "but effective incursions" into SAAN and, by 1981, owned 39,9% of the company.[357] Despite strong "interlinks", the two struggled for dominance in the market from the early 1980s. The "gentlemen's agreement" was that the morning and Sunday papers would be SAAN's, while Argus would serve the afternoon market.

In the mid-1980s, the two Afrikaans groups were parochial compared to the English groups. They were financially unallied, highly competitive and represented the two NP factions, the more liberal Cape and more conservative North. Naspers owned four dailies, including *Die Burger* and *Beeld*, and Perskor also four, including *Die Transvaler*.[358] The Cape group, innovative from its start,[359] was on the brink of establishing itself as a major force with the introduction of the subscription TV service M-Net in 1986. This transformed the company from a strong local media company into an electronic media entity, giving it the financial muscle to ride every new technological wave, and morphing the company into the tech giant it is today, with its global businesses listed under Prosus on Amsterdam's technology stock exchange.[360]

Naspers as company had already proven to be entrepreneurial from its start, always finding new markets.[361] One was the much longed-for urban Afrikaans market across the Vaal, where political conniving first stopped it until it decided to take control and established the Sunday newspaper *Die Beeld* in 1965.[362] Naspers's eventual "victory" over Perskor "mirrored the success" of the Southern caucus within the NP itself, following power shifts within the party after the fall of Transvaal's Vorster and Mulder and the rise of the Cape's Botha.[363] The "power shift" from Johannesburg-Pretoria to the Cape implied serious problems for Perskor. *Beeld* was now also a new daily voice of "Southern Nationalism". Perskor eventually closed *Hoofstad* and *Oggendblad*, and *Die Transvaler* moved from Johannesburg to Pretoria, although closing shortly afterwards. Politically, Northern Nationalism was fractured by Cape "reformism". All of these events first led to the neo-fascist HNP, and then to the far-right CP. Those who remained in the Transvaal NP "became *de facto* extensions of Southern nationalism".

By the 1980s, the black press was effectively banned, with "not even a handful titles" serving the "black market", with the *Cape Herald* serving the Coloured, and in Durban the *Post/Natal* the Indian, market.[364]

As an indication of demographics, the South African population in 1984 consisted of about 21 million Africans, with Zulus the majority.[365] There were about five million whites: 2,5 million Afrikaans speakers, 1,5 million English speakers and one million "others", mainly Portuguese, Italians and Greeks. The Coloured population counted 2,7 million and the Asians 840,000, mostly Indians. In 1984 there were 21 dailies, eight Sunday or weekly papers, about a hundred biweekly "country papers", and about five hundred "periodicals", ranging from family magazines to specialist journals.[366]

Winds of change blowing harder

In the mid-1980s, the apartheid bastion started to crumble, also as a result of a new global liberalism. By 1989 the Berlin Wall had fallen and the Cold War had come to an end. South Africa, on the brink of a civil war, could not be isolated from such global liberating forces. The NP increasingly lost its vice-like grip on the minds of Afrikaners, who progressively realised how an inhumane policy humiliated the majority of fellow South Africans. This change was also ascribed to the role of the Afrikaans media: After being "mind managers" for most of their existence, they realised they had to "re-programme" Afrikaner readership by starting to practise what can be termed reform journalism.

Technology also played its part. Bophuthatswana, then a "homeland", on 31 December 1983 launched the first TV service that offered competition to the SABC.[367] It used the SABC's signal network, subject to restrictions, and broadcast to Bophuthatswana as well as to areas outside the "homeland". "Bop-TV" carried less biased news and drew a "considerable" number of viewers away from SABC TV1. This led the SABC to block signals reaching "affluent white viewers in the advertising-rich Johannesburg", beaming it to Soweto only. More signal blocking followed when Bop-TV proved more popular in Soweto than TV2 or TV3.

And then a new era dawned with more sophisticated technology: TV that could only be received via a decoding system.

Subscription television

The first subscription TV was established in the US in the mid-1970s.[368] M-Net was South Africa's first, and till the mid-1990s, only, subscription channel, officially beginning on 1 October 1986. It grew rapidly, with local subscribers reaching one million by 1996, when it launched four digital services as part of a "bouquet of channels" via satellite. They were M-Net, Movie Magic, SuperSport and K-TV, which also reached one million subscribers in 36 countries across the continent.

This development did not come from the broadcast sector, but from print. The move by newspapers into broadcasting was not a uniquely South African phenomenon, but a worldwide one.[369] Locally, the Argus Group led the way with investments in film production, strengthening its holdings in CNA-Gallo and purchasing half of INFO, a computer-based data service. INFO's goals, together with the now defunct SAPA, was to make news available via telephone, and eventually through TV screens. In 1982, the newspaper groups also had shares in Bop-TV. The same happened with the new satellite initiative: The consortium consisted of Naspers, as initiator and major shareholder, with SAAN, Argus and Perskor, and the *Natal Witness* and *Daily Dispatch* with smaller shares.

The idea was already born in 1984 when Naspers approached government with a request for pay TV, owned and operated by a newspaper consortium.[370] The press's revenue base was "rapidly eroded" by the growth of advertising on SABC. By 1986, the SABC received almost a quarter of the total adspend. Just ten years earlier, in 1977, newspapers and magazines received 86% of the adspend. By 1990 this had dropped to 51%, with TV and radio climbing from 17% to 44% over the same period. A licence was consequently awarded to the Electronic Media Network, or M-Net. Management resided in Naspers. When it listed on the JSE in 1990, Naspers's share was 26%, that of Times Media (previously SAAN) and Argus both respectively 18%, Perskor 12%, the Natal Witness 2%, Dispatch Media 2% and the public 22%. In 1991, government gave M-Net permission to broadcast news, excluded from its licence, provided there was no direct competition with the SABC as information provider. These plans were never executed.

M-Net used terrestrial encryption technology as opposed to cable, which was used in the US.[371] This required a decoder plus a subscription to "unscramble" the scrambled signal. The development signalled "[o]ne of the biggest and most surprising changes to the broadcasting scene".[372] It also was the first "over-the-air subscription" TV service in the Southern Hemisphere. Thanks to the fact that government could be convinced that the Afrikaans press's future – and thus their support base – was in danger, it was a "quid pro quo" approval, with the proviso that it limit itself to entertainment as it was not allowed to compete with the SABC, over which the government "exerted a strong influence".

The freest media in Africa …

Despite all the media legislation, government still prided itself that South Africa had the freest media in Africa.[373] This was regarded as testimony to its practitioners, as the South African press was "fettered by over a hundred laws". By the mid-1980s, press freedom was in severe decline. Government succeeded in closing off important information "from press and public", especially concerning police, prisons, military and security matters. Furthermore,[374]

[p]olitical critics have been harassed, banned, detained or imprisoned under a policy that equates normal (by Western democratic standards) criticism, dissent, or even repeated expressions of black political aspirations with disloyalty, subversion, or treason. Black journalists and black newspapers have been singled out for particularly harsh treatment.

This led to a "virtual obliteration" of black political expression through either print or electronic media "by, and for the 24 million plus Africans, Coloureds and Asians".

Botha would often "give lip service" to press freedom and stressed that "the press should *always* support government aims and policies".[375] With Botha's heavy-handedness, "black militancy rose in equal measure", leading to yet more press restrictions. As one government official said: "We can't see ourselves governing this country as long as some newspapers go on as they do." Botha declared he would curb all newspapers if they continued to report on "activities of subversive or revolutionary elements". In 1980, journalists were barred from entering townships – declared "operational areas" – for the commemoration of the Soweto uprising. Photographs were also prohibited, with journalists' passports confiscated, while the controversial Advocate-General Act, as government's response to Muldergate, led to more outrage from the press. It was called the "gagging act", intended to eliminate the media's watchdog function regarding corruption and misconduct. As soon as the "advocate-general" started an inquiry, the matter would become *sub judice*, meaning the press could not report on it. This led to "a new position" among Afrikaans papers, as they opposed the legislation as vigorously as did the English press. Another restrictive action was the Second Police Amendment Act, prohibiting reportage of police actions or, in one editor's words: "The first step toward the Gestapo."

The intention of the 1979 Advocate-General Bill after government was "[s]haken to its foundations" after Infogate was "to prevent any further publication of allegations of state corruption and maladministration".[376] The post of "advocate-general" was created to investigate allegations of bribery or corruption, with no newspaper to report on them without permission. When this "Press Gag Bill" set off a storm of protest in both the Afrikaans and English press, government (again) backed down and dropped the most contentious sections, including restrictions on reporting. In virtually every instance of government trying to restrain publication that led to court action, the courts sided with the newspapers. Stephen Mulholland of the *Sunday Times* said it was fair to say that, "if South Africa can let it all hang out this way, it can rightly claim that it is not, racial matters aside, a totalitarian state, even if it is an authoritarian one".

When the Argus-owned *Post* newspapers were suspended in 1981 and several black journalists were banned, it had a circulation of 112,000 and readership of 907,000, and the *Sunday Post* a circulation of 118,000 and readership of more than a million. They were the only two black papers in the country with significant circulations. Argus CEO Hal Miller said, "another bar has been added to the cage which is beginning to circumscribe our freedom", while the PFP described it as a "fascist step that is bringing the revolution nearer".

Another act to control the flow of information was passed in June 1982: the Protection of Information Act, with jail sentences of up to ten years.[377] Zwelakhe Sisulu, president of MWASA, and Marimuthu Subramoney, MWASA's Natal vice-president, were banned – both restricted to their hometowns and forbidden from participating in journalistic or political activities. Just weeks later, banning orders were served on *Post* journalists Mathatha Tsedu,

Phil Mtimkulu and Joe Thloeloe. Later the same year, Tsedu and Thloloe were also detained, with Sisulu held in detention for over eight months.

The first South African Ombud was appointed in 1979 in terms of the Advocate-General Act 118 of 1979, amended as the Advocate-General Amendment Act 55 of 1983. The office of the advocate-general could be compared to that of the special prosecutor in the US, instituted after Watergate. But the office was replaced by that of the Ombud in 1983 after amending the Advocate-General Act to the Ombudsman Act of 1983. Later, the Constitution Act 108 of 1996 repealed the Interim Constitution Act 200 of 1993, paving the way for the promulgation of the Public Protector Act 23 of 1994, which provided for the establishment of the office and the governing principles of the Public Protector.[378]

Besides legislation, editorial teams also had to contend with managerial intervention. Mervis recalls how, as early as in 1973, a managing director, "without mincing his words", "clearly and unequivocally" stated the company's position: "It is well understood by the editors that the board is finally responsible for policy. There is no question of editors being given free rein to say what they like."[379] This situation should "be seen in its proper perspective", but even a fellow (English) journalist once said to RDM journalists: "If I were the chairman of the company, I'd fire the lot of you. You aren't journalists. You're a bunch of political activists."[380]

The same could be said for both sides of the "language divide". The *Sunday Times*, especially from 1959 until 1975, provided a "perfect example". Its political reporters as well as its editor were unquestionably "political activists". Few will dispute that a large part of the paper's success flowed from its undisguised political activism. But this also applied to some, "or possibly most of the Afrikaans papers", as *Die Burger* and *Beeld* "[were] loaded" with "political activists" – indeed, "from birth, and [they] make no secret of the fact".

An authoritarian state of affairs

Although for many years government proclaimed the "freest press in Africa",[381] the opposite was true – especially during the state of emergency declared in 1985/1986, when many critics "were vehement in their condemnation of what they regarded as draconian measures against the media".

The state of emergency banned film and video coverage of "political violence", and curtailed "coverage of violence by the print media". The next state of emergency, declared on 12 June 1986, restricted both local and international media. These measures were the strictest since World War II and "there was a general outcry against their severity". Publications could be seized, with fines of R20,000, and journalists jailed for up to ten years. Copies of *Sowetan* and *The Weekly Mail* (later the *Mail & Guardian*) were seized, and overseas magazines like *Time*, *Newsweek* and *The Economist* appeared with reports and photos censored with black ink. These measures were "unanimously rejected or strongly criticised" and described as the strictest measures any South African government had ever taken against the media. Ex-editor Tyson commented that press freedom did not die in 1986, but already in 1977, when authorities closed the *World* and arrested Percy Qoboza without charging him – one of the many examples of "detention without trial". The states of emergency muzzled the media from 1986 until February 1990, when most of the restrictive measures were lifted. In 1996, through the Bill of Rights, freedom of expression and access to information was guaranteed. But during the apartheid years, more than a hundred laws and regulations had a direct or indirect influence on what could be published. Legal advisers described press legislation as a "minefield". Assessing the "white" media during the height of apartheid, Archbishop Desmond Tutu said:[382]

> My basic thesis was that the South African press, controlled exclusively by powerful white bosses, had by and large been pandering to white interests at a time when they should have been opening the eyes of the white public to the dangers to which our country was exposed by the iniquitous system of apartheid and its draconian state of emergency measures. They were lulling whites into a false security, usually telling them those things which they wanted to hear. The South African press was on the whole at that time giving the impression that our country was passing through a time of calm and stability when in fact it was facing traumatic times.

When *Cape Times* editor Tony Heard was dismissed because of an interview with Oliver Tambo, it was because of "a serious contravention of the security and the emergency laws". And: It was not government that "got him", but "the white business interest which controlled the press which had it in for him". He was "sacked for daring to want to tell the truth".

Heard himself wrote that the right of the media "to publish and to comment freely was restricted", with "vast areas such as defence, police, prisons, oil supply, nuclear fuels, the statements of banned or listed persons placed out of bounds".[383] It was also in this time, "[a]s things turned full circle and political expectations burgeoned in the 1980s", that Cape Town's walls "became alive with protest".[384] One graffito, referring to jailed Nelson Mandela, read: "NELSON IS NOT A SEAGULL, HE'S A JAILBIRD." Someone added: "HE'S AN ALBATROSS AROUND P.W. BOTHA'S NECK." Although the city council attempted "to paint over the daubings", they would "sprout anew overnight".

By the mid-1980s, government had "unlimited" power to close papers.[385] Described as a "more insidious" power, the requirement was now that a new paper must register with a deposit of R40,000 as a "guarantee of good behaviour", to be forfeited if the publication errs, as was the case with *Vrye Weekblad*.[386] Journalists themselves could also be banned, as happened with "great frequency" in the 1980s.[387] "Banning" implied house arrest, with severe restrictions regarding visitors. Besides being banned, a journalist could also be detained, especially under the Terrorism Act, and they could also be prosecuted under the Official Secrets Act, the Terrorism Act, and the Prisons, Defence and Police Acts.

Besides, the freedoms that existed were enjoyed only by whites, and only "as long as they do not directly challenge by word or deed the prevailing political ideology". The English press "enjoyed freedom" because it operated within an entirely white framework, with "many journalists" who felt they could "oppose apartheid more effectively by staying on their jobs rather than emigrating as many liberal whites ha[d] done".

The liberal press in the mid-1980s was described as having been reduced "to insecurity and near impotence", with the English dailies "impeded from discovering and reporting the worst evils of apartheid" and under great pressure to refrain from fundamental criticisms of the government.[388]

It was said that if press freedom in South Africa would finally be extinguished it would not be through the passage of one law. Rather, "it will merely be the end of a long process in which this freedom was eroded by many laws". Piecemeal legislation was introduced, "in the guise of measures needed for public safety or state security". By 1985, the major laws affecting the free flow of information were the:[389]

1. Internal Security Act, 1950

2. Sabotage Act, 1962

3. Terrorism Act

4. Unlawful Organisations Act, 1960

5. Riotous Assembly Act, 1956

6. Official Secrets Act, 1957

7. Prisons Act of 1959 and 1965

8. Police Amendment Act, 1979

9. Advocate-General Act, 1979

10. Protection of Information Act, 1982

11. National Key Points Act, 1980

12. Petroleum Products Amendment Act, 1978

13. Atomic Energy Act, 1967

14. Hazardous Substances Act, 1973 and the

15. Radio Act, 1952.

In 1986, professor of law Anthony Mathews stated the power to ban publications in the interests of internal security or public safety was secured by the 1974 Publications Act and the 1982 Internal Security Act.[390] The 1957 Defence Act authorised "the imposition of general censorship", including banning publications. Under the 1982 Internal Security Act, government could "prohibit the printing, publication or dissemination of any periodical publication or the dissemination of any other publication". These included newspapers, magazines, pamphlets, books, hand-bills and posters. Under the Act's predecessor, five publications were already banned from 1962 to 1964, followed by a further three in 1977.

The "chief engine of censorship" was the 1974 Publications Act, dealing with indecent, obscene or blasphemous material. Grounds for banning were that something should be "prejudicial to the safety of the state, to general welfare or to peace and good order". Another was that it could cause harm "to the relations between any sections of the inhabitants of the Republic". But the definition was so wide that even "writing or a drawing on underpants" could be offensive. As soon as the declaration of "unlawfulness" was gazetted it was a criminal offence to distribute it, meaning the "mere possession" of a banned publication was also a crime. In addition, the 1957 Defence Act, which until 1977 authorised general censorship only in times of war, was amended in 1977 to authorise the president "to impose a general censorship" over all postal, telegraphic, telephonic or radio services, as well as certain written or printed matter "in defence of the Republic or for the prevention or suppression of terrorism or internal disorder".[391]

All these laws affected freedom of expression and information, meaning the "notion of a free press had strong mythical elements about it".[392] Newspapers had to avoid publishing speeches and writings by "listed persons", as just two examples of press restraints. It was illegal to publish an unregistered newspaper. The registration fee meant that "[i]t goes without saying that the poorer black publishers" were the chief victims. While the established press, mainly white, catered for interests that were "predominantly, though not exclusively, white oriented", it was the press freedom of the disenfranchised that was gravely restricted. The 1980 National Key Points Act meant any place could be declared a key point[393] and reporting on almost anything, "from bare ground to buildings (of any kind)", was subject to drastic penalties – while journalists were in no position to establish whether or not it was a "key point".

The cumulative effect of the "entire corpus of permanent security legislation" was to give government "many of the powers normally associated with martial-law or crisis rule".[394] By 1986, a "growing and virtually unbroken law-and-order crisis" was in place, more than three decades since the first emergency in April 1960.

With democracy only meaning "democracy for some",[395] the Westminster governing system used in the Cape and Natal in 1910 was also accepted for the Union, providing "some justification" for it being called a "democracy". Black participation before 1910 "was at best nominal" and "finally eliminated after Union". The 1983 "tricameral" system, providing separate Indian and Coloured parliaments, "set the seal on the constitutional exclusion of blacks". Before this, the Westminster system "was steadily drained of its contextual lifeblood" and became, even within the limits of white politics, one of "unrestrained majoritarian-ism". Assaults on the rule of law and "the associated liberties of person, speech, movement, assembly and association" reduced freedom "to a state of extreme debilitation even for white voters". Extra-parliamentary organisation, association and dissent were prohibited by the detention and banning of individuals, organisations, assemblies and publications – all imposed by "arbitrary executive decrees". This destruction of the rule of law became catastrophic for blacks, who, already deprived of political power, lost all remaining freedoms associated with democracy.

(Not) a new political order

As part of government's desperate measures to remain in power, it "reformed" itself through the so-called Tricameral Parliament. Up until then, legislative power was vested in a central parliament consisting of a Lower House, the House of Assembly, the President's Council (until 1981 the Senate), and a state president.[396] Political power centred in the House of Assembly, with 165 white members. Under Botha, this Westminster system was adapted in 1983 with segregated chambers for Coloureds and Asians, but no provision for South Africa's then 22 million blacks. It was called "power sharing", although the president could still rule by decree. Frederik van Zyl Slabbert, leading Afrikaner thinker and Opposition leader, said the Constitution made "racial discrimination a cornerstone of its operation".

This Constitution was implemented after the November 1983 referendum (white voters only), which was won by 66%. Dugard commented that South Africa was not a democracy, but "a pigmentocracy in which all political power is vested in a white oligarchy, which in turn is controlled by an Afrikaner elite". In the absence of a real opposition, the fifteen to twenty English newspapers became the *de facto* opposition, with government also directing its "counterattacks at the English press, not the opposition party". The latter was the PFP, which replaced the UP in 1977. By 1981, the NP celebrated its ninth consecutive victory, now with the highest margin ever, winning 131 seats of the Assembly's 165. The PFP had 26 and the NRP eight. Parliament was described as a "legislative tyranny", with "Parliamentary sovereignty taken to its logical and brutal conclusion at the expense of human rights".

But inside the NP the split was growing between reform-oriented Nationalists and the hard-core Afrikaner right, leading first to the formation of the HNP and then the CP. More than three decades of NP rule had led to "a certain arrogance and deceit" among prime ministers and their cabinets, including deceiving the South African public in 1975 when Angola was invaded, and Infogate in 1978.

The "racial oligarchy" – also called "a limited democracy for whites with political tutelage for blacks" – had a security system "irreconcilable with democratic values and civilised behaviour",[397] leading to authoritarianism "and hence ... denying its constitutionalism, ... dropping all humane restraints and checks on power". Ultimately, it became a paramilitary police state and mirror image of the terrorism it was supposed to be defeating. An as example of the inhumanity of the system: The per capita education expenditure in the 1983/1984 financial year on a black child was R234; on a white child it was Rl,654.59.[398]

The suppression of the press

Between 1 July 1986 and 31 December 1987, a total of 1,177 publications were submitted to the Directorate of Publications.[399] Of these, 729 were found to be "possibly prejudicial" to state security. The "undesirables" numbered 355, with 675 "not undesirable". In September 1987, *New Nation* was banned, alleged to be "prejudicial to the safety of the state and to the maintenance of good order and public safety". Its December issue also was banned, followed the next year by a number of alternative publications being "prohibited" or warned. Author André P. Brink said the "so-called liberalisation of censorship" was a ploy:

> South Africans are living with a "Third Reich Syndrome" in which the real target is the journalist ... What is feared is the dissemination of factual information by the media. If the Press is curtailed, it is easier to relax in the belief that unpleasant events happen only when they are reported to have happened.

Publications Appeal Board chair Kobus van Rooyen said in September 1989 that "South Africa had the strictest form of censorship in the western world", although he acknowledged "that freedom of speech and choice" were principles to be guarded.

This followed after the Information Bureau played a cat and mouse game with the media in 1986. It was the only official government news source to get information from, and held "news conferences" and issued daily "unrest reports". These could not be verified, with press queries "delayed until the news had turned stale". The Bureau refused admitting "that it was playing the role of censor", although it allowed "only one version of South African affairs" to be published. Spokesperson Dave Steward appeared regularly on TV, warning journalists "to tone down their language". From June 1986, questions were only answered if they had been submitted four hours before "briefings", and from September the Pretoria "Media Centre" closed and only responded to telexes. Daily "unrest reports" were in "a carefully sanitised and truncated form", telexed to Sapa for dissemination. And then daily briefings stopped altogether. The Bureau said unrest-related news "was no longer worthwhile". Editors protested to the deputy minister of information, Louis Nel. Briefings resumed, only to be terminated again in September "in the interests of accuracy".

Telephone responses to queries were minimal. After an enquiry, Steward responded: "We are still perfecting the flow of information."

Under Nel, the Bureau recorded a "peace song" titled "Together we build a brighter future", costing taxpayers more than R1,5 million. He was promptly dubbed "Louis Liedjie", but was soon replaced by Stoffel van der Merwe, leading to editor Harald Pakendorf's comment that government had moved "from Louis Liedjie to Soft-Shoe Stoffel". Van der Merwe later apologised to parliament for reporting incorrect costs regarding the Bureau's projects, including the song, which was also translated into Afrikaans and seven African languages. By 1988, the Bureau had 697 employees, 14 offices and a budget of R33 million.

This was the debilitating bureaucracy to which the news media were subjected. Of the 201 inquiries received between 17 and 22 December 1986, only 19 were "authorised". The bureaucratisation of course was a gatekeeping mechanism. *The Star* concluded that, "as it had feared", news that readers should know came back from the censors, saying "[p]ermission to publish refused".

Within a progressively paranoid government, another body had already been formed in 1983: the National Security Management System (NSMS) based within the State Security Council Secretariat.[400] It devised strategies to counteract "the battle of words or, to call it by its name, the propaganda campaign against the RSA". The NSMS believed "that the vanguard of modern warfare is psychological". The responsibility of the Strategic Communications Branch (the infamous "StratCom") was "advice and co-ordination" regarding efforts "in combating the war of words".

This bureaucracy had one objective: to ensure the NP disseminates news. In November 1989, after the fall of Botha, the NSMS was dismantled and the Joint Management Centres were replaced by Joint Co-ordination Committees, with the State Security Council "downgraded" to cabinet committee status.

The black press at the height of apartheid

The crisis on all levels of society by mid-1980 – the political (also inside the NP), the ideological (through media legislation), and the economic (through recession, unemployment and deteriorating labour relations characterising the economy in the 1980s) – led the State "as guardian of the welfare of capital in general" to establish "a coalition of interests between the politically dominant groups and the white and black middle classes".[401]

The South African press has historically appealed to "political and social elites", starting as early as the "missionary press" in the 1880s, with titles such as *Izwi la Bantu* produced by and aimed at missionary-educated black South Africans.[402] *Bantu World* in 1932 "spearheaded the shift from a local to a mass black press".[403] Like other attempts to develop the black market, this failed due to three factors: finances, a fear of political militancy (by State and advertisers) and the intervention of white entrepreneurs.[404] These, combined with the monopolies of the four white groups and close state vigilance and intervention, ensured no mass tabloid press developed until 2002.[405] After 2000, the mass press did spring up in a few short years, from nothing to a "powerful dominance" of the newspaper market under now media behemoth Naspers.

The black middle class could only "articulate their feelings and grievances" through the commercial mass media in an indirect way.[406] With the exception of a few trade union and community-based papers, there were no radio or TV stations nor commercial press owned or controlled by blacks, leading to grievances in the form of school and consumer boycotts, industrial action and subversion. These, because of their "dramatic nature", drew attention from the mainstream press.

Some brief context: This era followed on the turn of the century's African-owned publications that could voice black aspirations, such as the Xhosa *Imvo Zabantsundu* (1884), the Zulu *Ilanga lase Natal* (1903), and the Tswana and English *Koranta ea Becoana* (1901). They were described as "highly individualised, non-corporate, elite press for literate blacks" in rural, usually Christian, peasant communities and for the emerging urban areas. A number of "non-white" political organisations were responsible for the "spate" of African-language newspapers before 1930, but all fell prey to economic restraints and political suppression. The second generation of black publications, like the ANC's *Inkundla ya Bantu* (1946), *Torch* (1946) and *Spark* (1952), were banned after Sharpeville. Bantu Press, established in 1931, would later be bought by the Argus Group. The first paper, *Bantu World*, was the forerunner of the daily *World*. Bantu Press "gradually" assimilated the major surviving newspapers, including *Imvo*, *Ilanga* and *Evening Post*. The Argus Group, realising the commercial potential of Bantu Press and funded by Anglo American, acquired a first major interest by 1950 and total ownership by 1963. Their investment found "substantial reward". *World*'s circulation rose from 11,000 in 1959 to 90,000 in 1968. By 1976, its penetration equalled that of the RDM, at 145,000 copies, despite the fact that the early 1960s saw a "low point" in black journalism because of political militancy in South Africa. No independent African paper could survive the dominance of the white-controlled Bantu Press – as "was the intention". *World*'s slogan, "Our Own, Our Only Newspaper", was described as a "curious reflection" of the interests attributed to black readers, as it mainly covered "sensational crime, violence and sex". It avoided politics; its general manager said this elicited "apparently very little interest among the Bantu". *Post*, a bi-weekly with similar content, replaced *World* after its banning in 1976.

Drum "flourished" in the 1950s and 1960s. As discussed, it was owned by Jim Bailey, son of mining and media magnate Sir Abe, and carried exposés of issues such as prison labour on farms, brutal prison conditions for blacks and apartheid repression from a black viewpoint. Afrikaanse Pers established *Bona* as an "educational" magazine, publishing in Zulu, Xhosa and Sotho, to "counteract" *Drum*. *Bona* was distributed free to black schools. Afrikaanse Pers also bought Bantu Press's *Imvo* and *Zonk* in 1964. The information department tried to buy *Drum* in 1977 but, failing, started *Hit* under Johnny Johnson, later editor of State-funded *Citizen*. A second magazine, *Pace*, regarded in the 1980s as the "most highly capitalised publication", was established by a front company, Hortors, as direct competition to *Drum*. *Pace* was taken over by the Argus Group through the acquisition of shares in Caxton's *Golden City Post*, established in 1955 and also by Bailey. Argus finally bought the paper in 1964. After the banning of *World* and *Weekend World*, the Argus "elevated" its smaller *Post* and *Weekend Post* to "exploit the readership previously served" by *World*. *Post* journalists went on strike in October 1980, calling for improved salaries. The two-month strike resulted in the paper's registration lapsing, and when Argus applied for a condonation of the lapse, it was informed that resumption would result in banning – a threat "designed to intimidate" Argus into reducing its operations amongst black readers. *Post* and *Weekend Post* were then replaced with yet another small weekly, the *Sowetan*, published from Monday to Friday in 1987. Many of the *World* and *Post* journalists continued with the *Sowetan*, but Argus thought its company's activities in the black market would "be considerably" reduced because of the *Post* papers' closure.

In early 1982, Bailey and SAAN launched *Golden City Press* to fill the gap left by the banning of *Weekend World* and *Sunday Post*. Published from Bailey's *Drum* offices, it was printed by Perskor. With its 1950s' formula of "sex, violence and gang war", it experienced financial difficulties, but when SAAN changed the paper into a "Kaizer Chiefs propaganda sheet" it attracted "attention in the townships". A Friday edition, "to capitalise" on black interest in horse racing, was also introduced. By November 1982, its circulation of 100,000 surpassed that of its chief rival, *The Sowetan*. But Bailey and SAAN could not see eye to eye, and SAAN gave Bailey an ultimatum of either resigning as executive manager or SAAN withdrawing from *Golden City Press*. Bailey refused, SAAN withdrew, and the paper closed on 31 January 1983. On 2 February, after an "acrimonious wrangle" over copyright, Bailey brought out a new title under the masthead *City Press*. A year later, Raymond Louw, formerly of SAAN, took over as general manager and Percy Qoboza as editor. And, in April 1984, Bailey sold *City Press*, *Drum* and *True Love* to Naspers. The English press, along with Perskor as printer, had been given first option but could not raise the funding. Naspers was still seen as the "faithful voice" of the Cape NP. But Naspers had already bought into black media in 1982 by acquiring Chain Publications, with its five freesheets delivered to 125,000 homes in the PWV area. *City Press* immediately grew "enormously" under Naspers, with its circulation increasing by 34% from July to December 1984, and with a further 21% from January to June 1985; editor Qoboza was "no doubt spurred by the paper's vociferous anti-apartheid stance".

In the "homelands", a number of black-owned or black-managed newspapers stressed "ethnic consciousness, which ideologically is compatible with apartheid". Some were soon banned. One was the Transkei weekly, *Isasizo*, banned in 1977. It reappeared as *Isizwe* in January 1978, but was banned six months later. The publisher moved to Lesotho, where he set up that country's first commercial news service. The only rural-based paper attempting to penetrate urban areas was *Nation*, the mouthpiece of the Zulu Inkatha movement. It ceased publication in March 1979 after nine consecutive bannings.

It was clear: It was impossible for an independent black press with a "critical, if not radical" stance to survive in the 1980s. *Nation* was replaced by *Clarion*, a much more "sober" monthly and, in January 1986, *The New Nation*, a fortnightly published by the South African Bishops Conference and edited by Zwelakhe Sisulu, was launched.

The black press under the "protection" of white publishing companies was "virulently anti-apartheid, but not necessarily anti-capitalist". Still, they did not only face State intervention but were subject, "in varying degrees", to white editorial policies. In the case of *World* there was "editorial control from white overseers". In the early 1970s, black journalists on *World*, as well as those on other white-owned papers, "became increasingly disillusioned with the conciliatory policies adopted by the editorial staff", and founded the UBJ in 1973. Described as "a black consciousness union", it sought "to mobilise black journalists and synchronise their aspirations". Qoboza's appointment as editor of the *World* in 1974 "brought no immediate change", but after his 1976 Nieman Fellowship he "returned with a greater determination to fight for the black cause". His return coincided with the Soweto uprising in 1976, changing the editorial content of *World*. With better marketing and a morning edition, it led to a "dramatic" increase in circulation. When it was banned on 19

October 1977, the paper was "more widely-read and ... more influential than almost all other newspapers black or white" in South Africa.

Before this, conflict between Qoboza and his white editorial director, culminating in the latter being transferred to another newspaper, meant editorial policy now vested in Qoboza. This "ushered in the beginning of black editorial control on white-owned newspapers". Qoboza described black journalists' contribution during the Soweto uprising:

> When the Soweto riots raged in earnest, the black journalists were there right in the middle of the crossfire. Because his white colleague was refused entry into the black areas, and because of the dangers that faced whites in general, it fell on the shoulders of the black journalists to keep South Africa and the outside world informed about what was going on there.

This led to black journalists being harassed by police, culminating in the detention of 30 black journalists without trial, including Qoboza, who was held for eight months. The police's intimidation included taking down names, confiscating press cards and car keys and ordering journalists to report to police stations, as well as questioning sessions, arrests, detentions and assault. Five reporters of *World* were detained, the editor interrogated for eight hours, and "the highest number of telephone calls" from the minister of justice, "containing a mixture of threats, demands and requests".

The 1976 unrest "seemed to mark a turning point" in the editorial control of *World*, but "in retrospect it did not put forward a radical point of view", with the "consensus theme" still present. The *World* and *Weekend World* have been described as a "crisis sheet, doing little more than recording day-to-day happenings with a modicum of comments". They were also not exempt "from the editorial process whereby the final presentation of the story coincided more closely with the views of the white media managers than of the reporters themselves". Even Qoboza's position was not without contradictions. Comparing him to the previous white editorial director, who "wanted to play it safe", a *World* reporter said: "Mr Qoboza talks my sort of language ... but when it comes to the crunch I sometimes feel a guilty stab against my editor. He is also one of the big money boys and walks to the tune."

General dissatisfaction, increasing harassment, the banning of *World* and *Weekend World* and Qoboza's detention, however, led to increasing radicalisation. Salary scales were still an issue, with black journalists arguing they were discriminated against, including the few permanently employed black journalists working on white-oriented papers – "even during Allister Sparks' editorship" of the RDM.

MWASA pledged to uphold what they called "commitment journalism", which included rejecting "ideological controls" such as the principle of objectivity. By 1987, this, together with "their grassroots support amongst unskilled media workers and deliverymen, placed them in a powerful position vis-à-vis management", "set[ting] them against the white-owned English liberal press and the State". Government deemed MWASA "sufficiently dangerous" to ban successive leaders, leading to "a vicious, but confused, attack" from the second Steyn Commission. Its "heavy-handed recommendations" regarding the "captive black press" seemed "entirely inappropriate and superfluous at a time when this press had been weakened by successive closures and financial bankruptcies". Newspapers serving black readers were all "firmly under the control" of white-owned parent companies, and were "unlikely to espouse a radical discourse".

Still, in the mid-1980s, black journalists and the "black press" were at the "cutting edge" of the confrontation between Afrikaner Nationalism and African Nationalism.[407] Government's primary motivation for repressing political expression was "to prevent blacks from speaking (or writing) to other blacks about political alternatives or using the printed word to report in any depth their serious affairs and describe their common problems".[408] Many thought a civil war had already begun, one in which the black journalist "plays a curious and perhaps pivotal role", also one, "like much else in that troubled land", that was "contradictory, precarious, and enmeshed in politics".[409] Africans, Coloureds and Asians lived in what amounted to a police state, "virtually without protection against its excesses and abuses". In 1985, journalism was "one of the most dangerous occupations for blacks in South Africa", with about 200 black journalists working at publications owned and controlled by whites.

In this period there were no newspapers owned and controlled by Africans, Coloureds or Asians, and none to "express the real political concerns of the non-white majority". The black readership of some of the English papers, such as the RDM and the *Daily Dispatch*, was greater than their white readership. Overall, 33% of daily newspaper readers in 1962 were African, Coloured or Asian.[410] By 1977, it was 45%. Between 1962 and 1978, readership of dailies had risen by 30% for whites, by 125% for Coloureds, by 80% for Asians and by almost 250% for Africans. Papers served readerships in two contrasting ways: generalisation and specialisation. The Argus Group "specialised" with their weeklies *Ilanga* (in Zulu), *Cape Herald* (for Coloureds) and the daily *Sowetan* (for Africans). Critics saw this as an extension of apartheid.[411] The RDM and *Daily Dispatch* "generalised", aiming their publications at a "mixed" readership, with the RDM having twice as many black readers as whites and the *Dispatch* four times as many. The growing importance of urban blacks as consumers of mass media was a major reason to establish a black TV service. As said, the "extra" editions had also been a way of serving the black market since the 1970s. *Die Burger* established its *Extra* in 1970, appointing its first journalist of colour, Conrad Sidego, a teacher who acted as correspondent for Tulbagh[412] and who would later become head of Naspers's Corporate Communications as well as ambassador to Denmark and mayor of Stellenbosch.

But no true independent black press existed during this period. In 1985 it could be summarised[413]

- that the English press served as "surrogate", with reporting by blacks and being edited for blacks;

- that weekly "black-oriented" papers were *Imvo Zabantsundu* in Xhosa, *Ilanga* in Zulu, *Cape Herald* for Coloureds and *Bona* as a "look-read";

- that *Sowetan*, although owned by the Argus Group, was produced by blacks;

- that *Golden City Press*, established by SAAN and Bailey in 1982 after the *Sunday Post*'s banning (followed by their split in December 1982 and the paper continuing as *City Press*) was "in a shaky financial condition", but was then bought by Naspers, together with *Drum* and *True Love*;

- that several marginal publications existed, such as *Graphic* and the *Leader*, two Asian publications in Durban, *Muslim News* in the Cape, with two black weeklies, the *Voice*, sponsored by church groups, and *Nation*, Inkatha's mouthpiece, the latter two folding in 1985.

In this period, black journalists increasingly rejected any sort of moderation after government's "silencing black voices of moderation", thereby radicalising "non-whites" into supporting violent measures. Between June 1976 and June 1981, about 50 black journalists were detained without trial for up to five hundred days. At least ten were detained more than once, and ten were banned.

A 1977 survey counted 3,761 white journalists and only 220 black journalists. Months after the 1976 uprising, some black reporters were still in detention. Fifteen reporters "disappeared" covering Soweto, among them Peter Magubane, Nat Serache, Jan Tugwana and Willie Nkosi of the RDM, Joe Thloloe of *Drum*, and Duma Ndlovu of the *World* – mostly arrested under the Terrorism Act, with many released without trial or ever being charged. *Sowetan* editor Klaaste said that, under apartheid, "Black journalists were guerrillas with a pen".[414]

The story of a photojournalist

Peter Magubane's career is a good example of the hazards a black journalist had to endure.[415] He was born in Vrededorp (today Pageview), a Johannesburg suburb,[416] in 1932 and grew up and completed high school in Sophiatown. His interest in photography began as a schoolboy after being given a Kodak Brownie. In 1954 he got a position at *Drum* as driver and messenger, but the "highly motivated and resourceful" Magubane managed to get a position as darkroom assistant to Jürgen Schadeberg, chief photographer and picture editor. One year later he got his first photographic assignment, covering the 1955 ANC conference in Bloemfontein, which launched his career as one of the legendary "*Drum* generation". He covered most of the major political events and befriended liberation leaders. In 1957, Magubane applied to join the all-white Photographic Society of South Africa, but was turned down. Tom Hosking, *Drum* editor, led the magazine's photographers to form the Progressive Photographic Society, which organised the first non-racial "Salon" where Magubane won the first prize. This was the first of a large number of local and international awards, including honorary doctorates. In 1961 he held a one-person exhibition, the first photographer ever to exhibit in South Africa. He worked for the RDM from 1966 to 1980, but was banned for five years as RDM staff photographer. Confined to his home, he was not allowed to practise journalism.[417] He was imprisoned several times and spent six months in ordinary and 586 days in solitary confinement – "a record for a journalist" – yet was never convicted of any crime. Of this, Magubane said his experience was not unique: "I am no martyr. I am no hero. I am a photojournalist."

Mervis recalled that, when his company first recruited black staff, they worked as freelancers.[418] Later, as permanent employees, the Group Areas Act obliged them to work in a separate office in the RDM building. But Magubane needed to share the photographic department and darkroom with whites. This was thought to be against the law, and Magubane was given a room in another building a few blocks away which served as his studio and darkroom – and solved the Group Areas problem. But then editor Raymond Louw was visited by the police, indicating "they were calling in connection with Magubane's studio". The colonel asked whether they knew that they were breaking the law. Louw responded that they "had done all this to comply with the law". But: "You are breaking the law. You can't have a black man working in a white office building in the centre of town without being under the supervision of whites." Louw responded that Magubane was supervised from his office. No, said the police, "it must be direct supervision". Louw:

"Are you saying that we must place Magubane in our photographic studio? They said 'Yes.' I said, 'I am delighted'."

Peter Magubane
Photo: http://www.sahistory.org.za/people/peter-sexford-magubane

An iconic Magubane image: the mass funeral of Sharpeville victims.
Photo: http://www.hopecohnprojects.com/peter-magubane/

And ... enter Naspers as saviour of the remains of the black (white-owned) press

Of historical significance for the media was the boundary-shifting development when Naspers entered the "black" market. Naspers itself was catapulted into a new era. In the words of chair Cillié: serving a national market rather than a Nationalist market.[419] As company it was innovative from its founding. It published its first English book in 1919, and its first black publication in 1922.[420] In 1965 it captured the highly profitable English women's magazine market with *fairlady*.[421] But, when the acquisition of *City Press*, *Drum* and *True Love* became known,[422] it evoked "shock rather than surprise".[423] People were "baffled" and "perhaps there were also suspicions that Naspers had ulterior motives". The deal was struck on 1 April, but it apparently was so sensitive that the news was only "made public" on 4 April. In particular, the media world "was abuzz". The SABC devoted an entire news programme to the transaction, while reports in a "negative and mistrustful tone" appeared in newspapers.

Cillié said in a TV interview that "the Pers" was "rooted in the Afrikaner struggle of the past, and therefore well-equipped to take the lead in reconciling people from different backgrounds and language communities ... to promote mutual understanding". CEO Vosloo stated that, with their knowledge "of Afrikaner nationalism, the Pers is equipped to understand Black Nationalism".[424]

Bailey, as son of mining and media magnate Sir Abe and for many years SAAN director, was an important publisher in his own right.[425] He lost "a good deal of money" with *Drum* and *Golden City Post*. At the time it seemed it did not concern Bailey, as it "was his purpose to educate, enlighten, amuse and entertain black people" – and "he succeeded magnificently". His contribution to literacy among blacks is regarded "as probably greater than that of any other individual South African".

But, with his publications in trouble, there was no support "from other quarters".[426] The fact that his titles' "saviour" was the very company that had been founded to advance Afrikaner interests raised eyebrows. Naspers regarded the growing purchasing power of South Africa's "developing black population" as "a market factor that increasingly" had to be "reckoned with". In addition:

> For a publisher that seeks access to people's thinking with a view to promoting peaceful co-existence in the country, this section of the population is much more than merely a destination for consumer goods; they are also co-creators of wealth and have to be the co-exponents of peace and goodwill to create a future for the country.[427]

Naspers, in fact, had previously negotiated unsuccessfully with Bailey – in 1979, 1980 and 1981. According to a Bailey employee, his comments were that, if he should sell his publications to Naspers, he would be "acting like someone who packs off his mistress to an old age home".[428]

City Press editor Qoboza thought the takeover was "an act of faith" on the part of Naspers, yet

> [f]aith it had to be for the staffers too. But the consensus was that it would be a matter of months before things other than the towels in the loo were changed. Suspicion runs too deep – certainly amongst black journalists whose history had been one of constant siege – for Afrikaner and African to find a way to be partners, despite the hopes of Mr Bailey.[429]

Regarding editorial independence, suspicion indeed ran deep. SASJ's chair declared that "society is opposed to any move which will further restrict the already limited diversity of viewpoint by the Press". In front-page commentary by Qoboza, he referred to a meeting between seniors of the publications and Naspers where they insisted, and Naspers agreed, "that we will maintain our highest journalistic integrity and interpret our people's aspirations the way they expect us to do". This agreement to protect their independence was cynically referred to as "a document they called 'The Charter' in a sly perception of linguistic loyalties", because it had the ring of the ANC's Freedom Charter to it.

Bailey was "bitterly unhappy". The *Sunday Express* reported that, in a "bitter moment over gin and tonic", he said that "the great liberal establishment was not prepared to put up a cent". Also, Bailey later indicated how difficult it was to "swallow" the takeover: "Suddenly he had to discover that the Nationalist Afrikaners, who had always maintained close ties with the Government, had become his bosses."

Of all three publications it was the newspaper that stood to lose most regarding its integrity and credibility, but also the two magazines could lose their entire readerships. Qoboza said he was more acerbic in his commentary, and the newspaper more militant than before, as a way of publicly showing off their independence. Naspers lived up to its undertakings, soon engendering trust. Also, Naspers's conditions of service were introduced immediately, "and they were much better from the outset".

A later editor, Khulu Sibiya, wrote about Vosloo's non-interference: "True to his promise, in my more than 20 years as a senior editorial member of *City Press* there was never any interference from the board. The same cannot be said about the so-called English liberal newspapers that I worked for in the past."[430]

An impotent press?

In 1989, Mervis recalled a conversation between him and NP "strongman" BJ Vorster, who "once chaffed me about the impotence of the Press".[431] "Your paper", he said, "is powerless. You have attacked the National Party year after year and election after election; and yet with each succeeding election our majority gets bigger and bigger. Why don't you give up the struggle?" Mervis conceded "there was some merit" in what Vorster said. He replied:

> You are correct, Prime Minister. The only weapons available to us are words. On the other hand, when you restrict your power to words only, how much better have you done? Year after year, election after election, you have attacked the *Sunday Times* and what is the result. Year after year, election after election, our circulation grows bigger and bigger and bigger. In fact, Prime Minister, we probably have more readers than you have voters.

Certainly, the forty-year-long confrontation between the NP and the *Sunday Times*, from 1948 to 1988, "has shed an interesting light on Press power and political power". In 1948, the Nationalists gained power with a small parliamentary majority. By 1988, their majority was one of the biggest in history. Compared to this, the *Sunday Times,* in 1948, had a circulation of 240,000; by 1988 it had grown to 530,000 – by far the biggest paper in the country. "A piquant paradox," Mervis concluded. "People vote for the party which the paper dislikes, and they read the paper which the party dislikes."

The role of an alternative media

An alternative press "usually becomes active when the political, economic, social or cultural views of certain social groups" are excluded from the popular media market.[432] Although the alternative press came to the fore particularly after the Argus's *World* and

Post were closed, the alternative press in South Africa "has a much longer history", with its emergence and development paralleling the Struggle.

The South African press "probably underwent greater challenges and changes" than during any other period in the history of its media during the last quarter of the twentieth century.[433] Its most specific challenge was the states of emergency from July 1985 and their press restrictions. Major newspapers could not cover events, and readers viewed them with suspicion – "as being too close to Government and too concerned about making profits and maintaining white readership to be concerned with labour and life in the townships". This led to the alternative press.

Louw[434] and Johnson[435] identify three phases in the development of the alternative press, namely from the 1930s to the 1960s, the 1960s to the late 1970s, and the 1980s to the mid-1990s. The first "was a complex period in the development of resistance", with alternative publications reporting the development of political movements "against a background of ongoing internal conflict and political apathy".[436] The dwindling of black-owned papers meant no independent liberal voice existed. One, *Inkundla*, openly supported the ANC and played a key role in Albert Luthuli's election as president. It closed in 1951 and is today considered a "transition journal" because it was independent, relatively liberal, and with a wide and sympathetic coverage of the ANC. The *Guardian*, also promoting the ANC, was founded in 1937, became the *New Age* in 1954, and closed as *Spark* in 1962. It has been described as "a good example of a radical newspaper".[437] The next era, the 1960s to the late 1970s, saw the rising of BC, with the alternative press emerging again "as part of an expression of rising black consciousness, taking the form of massive labour strikes", such as the one in 1973.[438] BC's rise prompted the "re-emergence of independent non-commercial alternative publications" such as the *SASO Newsletter* of the South African Students' Organisation. The 1980s to the mid-1990s saw the climax of the alternative press, linked to the MDM and UDF while the ANC was still in exile. This era was marked by a "bottom-up style of resistance" and the alternative press played an important part. Government viewed this press as part of the "Total Onslaught", blaming outside influences "for corrupting the people".[439]

Three categories of the alternative press have been described:[440]

- The progressive-alternatives, known as the "people's media", expressing the Struggle at community level as part of the national Struggle. Examples were *Grassroots*, *Saamstaan* (Stand together) and *Al Qalaam*.

- The left-commercial, which developed as resistance grew, although this was "generally ignored by the conventional press". The "left-commercial" press evolved after 1983 as a "hybrid development" of the capitalist and progressive-alternative presses. Covering national news, it was financed by selling ad space, "but with a heavy reliance on assistance from sympathetic donors", plus journalists "prepared to work for very little". Titles included *New Nation* in Johannesburg in 1986, *South* in Cape Town and *New Africa* in Durban, both in 1988.

- The independent social-democrat press, aiming for financial independence and supporting broad democratic ideals while maintaining independence from any specific movement. Examples were the *Weekly Mail* after the closure of the RDM in 1985, and the Afrikaans *Vrye Weekblad*. By 1992, the latter had 37 criminal charges, eight libel suits and five court interdicts against it.[441]

The resistance press

The vacuum created by the demise of the *Post* in 1977 was filled on 2 February 1981 by the Argus Group's "substantially transformed" former freesheet for the African market, *Sowetan*.[442] This was the start of the 1980s' resistance press. Repositioned into a daily, it employed 32 former *Post* and *Sunday Post* journalists. *Sowetan*'s first editor in its new format was Joe Latekgomo, who said the fact "that we will be serving the same market makes it imperative that we reflect the same concerns and aspirations as were reflected by *The World*, *Post* and *Sunday Post* … and that we continue to fight for a just society for all".

Examples of smaller alternative voices were *Grassroots*, *Staffrider*, *Graphic*, *Muslim News* and *SASPU National*, the latter a student publication circulating on both black and white campuses. Meanwhile, as sign of sure, although far too slow, reform, the hated "Pass laws" were abolished in 1986.[443]

Paradoxically, the majority of the alternative media that worked against all odds and impossible laws towards freedom, forming "an integral part of the social movement that transformed South African society", were unable to survive the transition.[444]

Some could not survive the "dire pressures" of a police state in the late 1980s, while others "withered" because of a lack of capital and management skills, while "still more failed to adapt to the new times and changing audiences".

The "freeing of South Africa lost some heroic voices", but also led to mainstream media changing "beyond recognition". Although the "erstwhile 'people's' publications" did not survive to see these changes, their role in realising them was fundamental. Many of the "resistance journalists" moved into the "commanding heights" of post-apartheid mainstream media, thereby shaping the early 21st-century South African mediascape. But "the former white establishment media", both English liberal opposition and Afrikaner reformist", also "deserve credit" alongside the resistance media.

Newspapers, newsletters and magazines that confronted the state after 1960 and contributed to reviving a mass movement inside South Africa as a marginalised press "had an impact" on their audience. Although this impact cannot be measured in small circulations, limited advertising revenue, or the absence of marketing and distribution strategies, this press "provided a voice to alienated communities that were too often voiceless" and contributed "immeasurably to broadening the concept of a free press".[445] In no small way, "the guardians of the new South Africa owe these publications a debt of gratitude that cannot be repaid".

This resistance press evolved in three phases. Phase one represented "the end of a period of protest that began more than eighty years earlier", when almost all African nationalist newspapers, "the dominant voices of alternative news and opinion before the 1940s", were bought, closed or depoliticised after the Great Depression and merged "with a new captive black commercial press controlled by white entrepreneurs". The only independent African Nationalist publications in the 1950s and early 1960s were "a few pamphlets and short-lived newsletters like *Inyaniso* (subtitled *Voice of African Youth*), *Isizwe* (Nation), *Africanist* and *African Lodestar* – all aimed at limited activist township audiences. The 1940s to early 1960s was represented mainly by socialist newspapers, part of, or independent of, the Communist Party, which was banned in 1950. ANC-aligned publications were *Liberation* (1953–1959) and *Fighting Talk* (1942–1963), positioned as non-racial, non-sectarian and "perhaps more representative" of left-wing working- and middle-class interests.

Phase two was associated with the BC movement during the 1970s, and phase three consisted of alternative papers during the 1980s and early 1990s, when the Struggle was mediated through UDF affiliations. Although the commercial press covered the escalating protest, it did not provide the kind of "political conscientising" favoured by the UDF. Controlled by the Big Four, the commercial mainstream 1980s press accounted for 95% of daily readers and 92% of Sunday and weekly readers. Of the two English and the two Afrikaans groups, it was Argus and Naspers that "towered" above their rivals. The fourteen English and five Afrikaans dailies had an estimated 1,3 million readers in 1991, the year in which *Sowetan* became the largest daily. In the 1980s, there were a number of left-wing academic and student journals, newsletters, newspapers and 45 pamphlets produced at "white" universities. The community press also played "a central role in chronicling" the Struggle and helping to build a level of defiance "that sustained and broadened the resistance movement". Another actor was an Eastern Cape alternative source of news and opinion provided by a network of local news agencies known as the East Cape News Agencies (Ecna).[446] Consisting of four agencies launched between 1982 and 1987, they were Veritas in King William's Town, elnews in East London, Albany News Agency in Grahamstown and Port Elizabeth News. By 1990, Ecna had become a single organisation.[447] It was "no accident" that "a successful regional news service" developed in the Eastern Cape. Ecna's 1991/1992 annual report describes the region's significance: Some of the oldest institutions of black education were to be found there. Regarding media, "it has also played a pioneering role", with "probably the oldest black newspaper", *Imvo zabaNtsundu*, founded by John Tengo Jabavu in King William's Town in 1884.

People's power

In 1985, the UDF decided that "political education required a more specialist vehicle"[448] and launched *Isizwe* in Cape Town in November. Its second issue only appeared in March 1986, when the UDF had a new strategy of "people's power". But government responded to the "people's power" threat with its June 1986 state of emergency. In February 1988, it banned the UDF, making the production and distribution of *Isizwe* impossible. Still, "political education" was continued through a new journal, *Phambili*. The first appeared in April 1988, a second in October, but while government renewed the state of emergency year after year, "more and more white South Africans adopted dissenting political positions".

Cape Town also was home to two of the most important community papers, *Grassroots* and *South*, aimed at Coloured and African readers.[449] *Grassroots* journalists did not see themselves as journalists, but as "community activists with an unashamedly propaganda mission". While the commercial press "presumably anesthetized" its readership with 'sex, sin, and soccer'," they meant to conscientise their readers "to promote change through collective action". It was launched in early 1980 and closed in August 1990 after being unable to survive without foreign subsidies and unwilling to transform from "struggle paper" into a "professional, general-interest commercial" one.

South as a southern voice

South was launched in Cape Town in March 1987.[450] Less dependent on foreign donors, it reported "more widely" on regional and national issues, promoting UDF policies and activities. As "media activists" they "jealously guarded" their editorial autonomy.

Unfortunately, it also could not adapt to political changes. Even after a "facelift" with a more commercial layout, it closed in December 1994, "unable to compete with the establishment commercial press and unable to sustain a readership within the Coloured community to support the newspaper".

As an independent weekly, *South* had to fight successive states of emergency and the measures to muzzle the media in the latter half of the 1980s, "the bleakest years in the annals of press freedom in South Africa".[451] *South*'s founders realised it was an extremely difficult time to launch a paper, "let alone one with a radical anti-apartheid agenda", and also in a newspaper market monopolised by "big business". The English press was criticised for its conservatism, "shirking its social responsibility", accused of shutting its eyes to the crisis in South Africa and "anesthetising" readers with a diet of "sunshine journalism". Although critical of apartheid, the English press was still "essentially supportive of the status quo of white privilege", its reporting "generally" ignoring "news of interest to blacks". They also employed few black journalists, and none in senior positions. The English press also was often hostile toward the resistance movement. *South* was the first "left-wing commercial" paper in the Cape since the *Guardian*'s *Torch* had been "snuffed out". After the UDF was founded in August 1983, and with the upsurge in popular protest, the possibility of establishing a mass-circulation weekly to articulate the "grievances and aspirations" of the black Cape working class became possible.

South was published by a public company, South Press Services Limited, with capital donated by ICCO[452] and managed by the Ukwaziswa Trust, consisting of political and community leaders. The first edition, on 19 March 1987, was "an important milestone" in the history of protest journalism in the Western Cape. The paper "lifted media activism to a higher plane". Struggle news was covered "more widely and more efficiently" than in other contemporary, left-wing community publications. It wanted "to articulate the needs and aspirations of the oppressed and exploited" and serve the interests of the working class. The paper served as a voice for extra-parliamentary protest movements, especially the UDF. It also kept South Africans "abreast of news the apartheid government wanted to suppress" – and it challenged the monopolistic control of the media of both government and large corporations.

South's greatest threat was state harassment, with government "coercing alternative newspapers into compliance" rather than shutting them down, as it wanted to create "an illusion for the outside world that press freedom existed".[453] Also, government's "hard line" against the alternatives "had the added advantage of intimidating mainstream newspapers into toeing the line".

The paper was banned for three issues, from 23 July to 6 August 1987, because "they were helping to create a revolutionary climate and cultivat[ed] a positive image of the ANC and its guerrilla fighters". But *South* won "an important political and moral victory" when it succeeded in having the Publications Appeal Board lift the banning orders. In November 1987, *South* received an official warning that it was publishing "subversive propaganda and promoting the public images" of the ANC and PAC; in March 1988, it received a second warning and a third in May, which led to the three-month banning order. It became the second paper, after *New Nation*, to be banned. But anticipating the banning, *South* planned a special edition for 9 May 1988, although it had to withdraw most of its 20,000 copies already printed when the banning order came through on the same day. Still, the paper resumed publication after only five weeks because the emergency regulations expired on 10 June. It seemed government used the banning order as intimidation tactic, rather than to close *South*. But the harassment "was extremely damaging", taking up much of management's time, involving costly litigation and adding to the staff's insecurity. According to editor Moegsien Williams, as many as twenty-four court actions were brought against them in the 1980s. The paper faced seven charges simultaneously under the emergency regulations in early 1989, which ensnared the paper in a "web of legal regulation". To "wear it down in a courtroom war of attrition" seemed to be a deliberate strategy. The paper was also subjected to "a range of informal harassment tactics". This involved *ad hoc* victimisation by security police and "shadowy operators" within the State's security apparatus. Security police regularly visited the paper's offices and, on occasion, the homes of staff when they were not there, harassing their families. Threatening phone calls were received and journalists "were regularly followed and sometimes detained". In some instances, journalists "found their [car] locks jammed with glue, their tires cut along the inside rim, or their wheel nuts loosened". There was also at least one informer on the staff. No one suffered serious injury, but journalists at other alternative papers paid dearly. Several papers, including *Grassroots*, suffered arson attacks on their offices.

But it was *South*'s inability to sustain a commercially viable circulation that led to its closure. Its relationship with the Argus Group was also "uneasy" – critical of the *Argus*, but dependent on the company for printing and distribution.

And then 2 February 1990 happened, launching South Africa "on a four-year course of transition to democratic rule".[454] *South* realised it had "to shift with the times and reposition itself". It attempted repositioning in March 1989, and again in late 1990, with "a more commercial look". But in August 1991, Moegsien Williams accepted a post at *Sowetan* and Guy Berger was appointed editor. With the emergency regulations lifted, establishment media "started encroaching on the terrain of the alternative press". *South*'s role "as the voice of the democratic movement" was "greatly diminished". Its highest circulation, 23,000, was the issue of Nelson Mandela's release, but by mid-1991 it slumped to between 6,000 and 7,000.[455] A new *South*, relaunched on 27 February 1992, increased its pages from 24 to 40, with a "trendy commercial format", but even this could not save it. In March 1993, it entered into a contract with Naspers for its printing and distribution.[456] It also launched the free sheet *Southeaster* in February 1994. By October 1994, it had a circulation of 150,000 and was also delivered to Cape Town's black townships. But *South* suffered severe losses, shrinking from sixteen pages to eight by the end of 1994. It had a monthly deficit of R80,000, owing its printers R400,000. In November 1994, its board tried to sell South Press Services to New Africa Publications (NAP), the publishing arm of NAIL (New Africa Investment Limited). The latter intended using *South*'s infrastructure to produce a Cape edition of *Sowetan*, but talks collapsed on 22 December 1994 and the company was liquidated. The last issue of *South* was published that same day, managing to survive for nearly eight years during the "last, decisive phase of the apartheid era".

Real *Grassroots*

Grassroots formed part of the "new" alternative media of the 1980s "to contest the prevailing world view of the mainstream white-controlled commercial" papers".[457] While commercial media was seen as upholding the status quo, non-profit community media saw themselves as part of the movement for political and social change. The new paper was a tabloid with a five-week publication cycle, articulating the views and aspirations of communities and workers. The five-week frequency, rather than monthly, "was a tactic used to avoid falling within the legal definition of a newspaper" and thus not facing the requirement to register and pay a "security deposit" of R40,000.

The paper built a network of activists in the Western Cape, "thus laying the foundations for the UDF".[458] Also: "People's Power had to manifest itself in all spheres of life, including the media." This "People's Press" had to challenge the power of the "ruling class media" to minimise their influence "and eventually take over state media and commercial newspapers, and use their institutions to serve the interests of the people".

Grassroots became a target of the police, with their offices raided twice in 1985.[459] Staff members were repeatedly detained. In October 1985, the building that housed *Grassroots* and other progressive organisations was gutted by fire. The following year, Veliswa Mhlawuli, *Grassroots* organiser for black townships, was shot, leading to the loss of her right eye. Still, the usual number of eleven issues was produced in 1985, the print run doubling from 20,000 to 40,000. After the 1986 state of emergency, *Grassroots* could no longer continue as an above-ground operation as staff members went into hiding. But, by August 1986, *Grassroots* was on the streets again. Government now instituted new restrictions, including temporary closure and the threat of cutting off foreign funding. *Grassroots* and its sister magazine, *New Era*, were indeed closed for three months in 1989. But, after 1990, *Grassroots* shared the fate of most of the alternative newspapers: It could not survive.

Grassroots "certainly" contributed to popularising the ANC in the coloured areas.[460] While the ANC had been "unmentionable" at the beginning of the decade, "ANC symbols and slogans had become commonplace" toward the end of the 1980s. But *Grassroots* was not effective as "an organizing tool across the racial divide, and probably it could not have been". A large part of the African population, "notably" those in informal areas, were illiterate and "beyond the reach of newspapers". Still, the paper was part of the "arsenal of alternative newspapers", challenging "dominant ideologies". Especially in its early years, its "attempts to give a voice to the voiceless was an important innovation in the alternative press". But, by remaining an "orthodox struggle paper" and preserving "its ideological purity", it missed the opportunity "to develop a more popular appeal".

Other alternative papers

New Nation was launched in January 1986 and was aimed at the Roman Catholic (RC) community, with regional and national coverage of the Struggle, subsidised mainly by the RC Church.[461] *Sowetan*, launched in February 1981, started out as an alternative voice, but would later become a mainstream paper under its NAIL ownership. It was seen as "really the successor" to the Argus-owned *World/Weekend World*, banned in 1977, as well as the Argus-owned *Post/Weekend Post*, which ceased publication in 1980 after reregistration was refused. The Argus Group adhered to government's "racial classifications" in all categories of life, with the black staff of *Sowetan* "tend[ing] to absorb this mind-set". In the 1980s, the paper analysed Struggle issues in "racial terms", providing coverage to BC groups as well as to the UDF/MDM, but producing "editorials sympathetic to the BC position". The paper catered to the top two income groups (at the time, incomes of more than R500 a month) and "provided extensive coverage to African business groups". When, in 1993, *Sowetan* was bought by NAIL, the new owners, "apparently under pressure from the ANC", ensured that *Sowetan* would support them. *New Nation* was also sold to NAIL in 1995, but was forced "to tone down its socialist content". It folded in May 1997. *Sowetan* "managed its affairs by submitting to the demands of whatever market player obtained the greatest return for its investment". In 1993, NAIL was headed by Nthato Motlana.[462] While many of *Sowetan*'s editorial staff remained "within the orbit of the evolving" BC movement, it "became in effect an organ of the ANC". Editor Klaaste said because the paper

> was considered to be anti-ANC, our new owners were under pressure from the ANC to ensure that they reformed the paper. We were also dragooned into buying *New Nation* because of its obvious connections with the people it supported during the liberation struggle.

Alternative Afrikaans voices

Regarding the Afrikaans alternative media, *Vrye Weekblad* (VWB), *Saamstaan*, *Die Suid-Afrikaan* and *Namaqua Nuus* are of significance.[463]

The main Afrikaans alternative paper was VWB, first appearing on 4 November 1988 – "during the worst decade of government repression of media in South Africa since the era of Lord Charles Somerset as governor of British colonial Cape Province in the 1820s".[464] The significance of this publication was that, for the Afrikaans press, it was "like taking a deep breath after loosening a restrictive corset". This "debilitating corset" was fastened by successive NP governments with their institutionalised apartheid after 1948. The "corset" was also fastened by mainstream, establishment press and the SABC, "which toed the line". The party ruled "with intrepid bravado against world opinion", "blunting" resistance from the 1960s onwards and banning political opponents, with their leaders either in prison or in exile. Apartheid ideology "underwent a few cosmetic changes", such as sporting contact between race groups and "acquiescing to governments from Africa appointing black ambassadors to South Africa", but instability increased and came to a head after the institution of the tricameral parliament in 1983, leading to the partial state of emergency in July 1985. For the first time, dissident Afrikaans voices made themselves heard in the Afrikaans media.

It was "widely accepted" that the liberal Johannesburg-based Afrikaans papers *Die Beeld* and *Beeld*, in particular, and later also other Naspers papers, played a more important role in changing apartheid than the Afrikaans establishment press "have generally been credited" for. James McClurg, "highly regarded" ombud for the Argus Group – at the time the largest media conglomerate in Southern Africa – asked rhetorically, shortly after the ANC were unbanned, that when "historians turn their eye on this era, will they reserve a chapter for the contribution of the verligte (enlightened) Afrikaans press towards change in South Africa?" If not, "an injustice will have been done".

In the "symbiotic relationship between Afrikaans publishing houses and the NP", the Afrikaans press's struggle was against Afrikaner right-wing factions and publications, as well as government's "ultrasensitive reaction to criticism of its policies from main-stream English-language newspapers". This led government to impose stricter controls on the media. The outcry of the press, through the NPU and including its Afrikaans members, led to compromises under which NPU papers had already established a voluntary Press Council "to forestall direct government control of the press".

When, in June 1982, the minister of home affairs, Chris Heunis, tried to introduce a new press law to ensure the voluntary council became a statutory body, it was actually aimed at the right-wing Afrikaans papers outside the NPU to force them to join the NPU and adhere to its rules. But this was also abandoned after strong opposition because of the new press law's potential impact on NPU members. In September 1985, the NPU agreed to replace its existing council with the South African Media Council. This included broadcast as well as print media, and the body could "reprimand and fine". Although the original legislation was directed primarily at the two right-wing papers, they never submitted to the Media Council's authority, remaining "a thorn in the side" of government. But, with the countrywide state of emergency in June 1986, government sidestepped the NPU. Trying to "crush" the alternative press, the "Directorate of Media Relations" was created in September 1987. This was linked to the Directorate of Publications, the Department of Law and Order, the Department of Defence, and the Bureau of Information – all under the authority of the Department of Home Affairs. Thus, by the late 1980s, there were five separate government bodies responsible for policing South Africa's press.

The Directorate of Media Relations had to monitor the "progressive press" and hold them accountable.[465] In 1988 the decree became retroactive, creating a situation in which a publication could be reprehended for subversive statements that were published even before government announced the restrictions in 1986. Besides the work of the Directorate, the "progressive press" could voluntarily send their work for clearance to the Interdepartmental Press Liaison Centre (IPLC) from December 1986. In its first week, the IPLC received 201 inquiries. A mere nineteen were considered fit for publication. The Afrikaans press responded by being "as cautious as possible in their interpretation of the definitions of a subversive statement" to avoid action. An exception was *Beeld*, which openly expressed its view that it reported only on what was happening and "that it is not their fault if Government is not pleased with reality". Initially, the English "liberal" media expressed disdain for the IPLC, but in October 1987 they were "strong-armed" into coming to terms with government's interpretation of all content regarding opposition parties amounting to "a subversive statement". Needless to say, the IPLC soon became defunct and was disbanded by 1988.

But it was in this climate that VWB was founded by Max du Preez, who wanted it to be the first Afrikaans newspaper committed to a "non-racial, democratic, united South Africa".[466] He described himself as someone not "detribalised, and don't see any reason to be". But, at the same time, he saw no conflict "between being an ethnic Afrikaner, writing Afrikaans, loving Afrikaans, being Afrikaans in my environment". He also wanted his paper to "have the side-effect of changing the image of Afrikaans as the language of the oppressor". Indeed, VWB broke new ground when it "deviated from the path of traditional Afrikaans newspapers in its use of language, often using a colloquial mix heard more in informal discussions than in standard and written Afrikaans".

Yet it was not "an ideal climate for a new, rebellious Afrikaans newspaper". Other alternatives were shut down in the preceding months – *New Nation* from March to June 1988, *South* from May to June, and the *Weekly Mail* in November 1988 – the same month in which VWB launched. At least seven other publications had been under government scrutiny since October 1987 and warned they might be closed. These were *Al-Qalam*, *Grassroots*, *New Era*, *Out of Step* (the End Conscription Campaign's publication), *Saamstaan*, *South*, the *Weekly Mail* and *Work in Progress*.

VWB was published by Wending (meaning change) Publikasies and had a provocative style "that was absent from the mainstream Afrikaans press". Beneath its masthead it declared it to be "Die nuwe stem vir 'n nuwe Suid-Afrika" ("The new voice for a new South Africa"). This phrase would become the NP's slogan during its reform initiatives a year later. The paper launched itself with a front-page headlined "Mandela: 'n Nuwe era" ("Mandela: A new era"). It was the first time that readers could read in Afrikaans about Mandela without him branded as "violent, a terrorist, and a godless communist".

Two weeks after VWB's launch, government began a campaign against it. In a front-page story on 25 November 1989, the paper reported about a faxed letter received on 11 November from justice minister Kobie Coetsee warning that the paper could "be used as a means to express the views of illegal organizations as stipulated by the Internal Security Act of 1982". The Act empowered the minister to require a R40,000 deposit. Normally, a nominal deposit of R10 was required. This act was used to intimidate newspapers that, if banned, they could forfeit the deposit. This was the first warning of a newspaper under the Security Act since the June 1985 partial state of emergency, the same act under which the *Guardian* was closed in 1952 and the *World* and *Weekend World* in 1977. Media regulations announced in June and August 1988 also gave the justice minister permission to ban a paper "if he believed they endangered the state and the maintenance of law and order". Several reasons were cited why VWB should be warned. It responded to each point, concluding that "no grounds exist that we should be treated differently from commercial newspapers like *The Citizen* and *Beeld*". Still, they had to pay a registration fee of R30,000 – the highest ever for a South African newspaper. After three editions, the paper had an overdraft of R10,000 and could not pay salaries. Readers "rallied to the support" and sent in more than R60,000.

But intimidation went on. At the end of 1988, government sued the paper for R100,000 for libel for a report headlined "Pik, PW en die Mafia-baas" (Pik, PW and the Mafia boss). It alleged that P.W. Botha and his foreign minister, Pik Botha, had dinner with a notorious mafia leader, Vito Palazzolo. The editor refused to apologise or pay, stating the report was based on a sworn statement to the police by a Pretoria accountant in January 1988. With P.W. Botha's retirement in 1989, the libel case was withdrawn.

Du Preez called it a government-sponsored "low-intensity war" against the alternative press. When VWB quoted Joe Slovo, banned SACP secretary-general, Du Preez was charged and found guilty of contravening the Internal Security Act, which prohibited the media from quoting a banned person. Meanwhile, fifteen stories quoting Slovo had already been printed in mainstream and alternative newspapers, none of which were charged. Du Preez was found guilty. VWB printed a front-page story headlined "Vendetta!" Du Preez was sentenced to six months suspended for five years, and Wending Publikasies was fined R1,000, also suspended for five years. Hours after the sentence, the security police notified VWB that it was under investigation for contravening various provisions of the Internal Security Act.

VWB helped "set the news agenda" of the alternative press, questioning and criticising the NP, exposing the existence of politically motivated death squads in the security police, documenting planned terrorism by right-wing groups and reporting the existence of a secret "Third Force" creating havoc in the peace process. Final vindication for Du Preez came from the Truth and Reconciliation Commission in June 1998 – but it was too late.

However pioneering the publication was, money, as with other alternative media, was always a problem and a lack of advertising was a major factor in VWB's demise.[467] It received assistance from the Independent Media Diversity Trust when the latter was established in 1991, but by 1993 the paper had serious financial problems. Still, its impact "cannot be calculated", as Professor Sampie Terreblanche, one of its directors, emphasised: "*Vrye Weekblad* gave Afrikaners hope. It gave them an intellectual debate outside the borders of the mainstream Afrikaans press." As recognition for his contribution to the Struggle, Du Preez was honoured with South African journalism's Pringle Award. The last edition of VWB as newspaper appeared in May 1993. A new, 86-page fortnightly news magazine, *Vrye Weekblad die Nuustydskrif*, was launched on 24 June 1993. It lasted less than eight months, ceasing publication on 2 February 1994, exactly four years after De Klerk's 1990 speech. Of VWB, veteran Afrikaans journalist Martie Retief Meiring said it "truly, good and solidly, cracked the oppressive corset of guilt, apartheid and painful, formal rectitude we as Afrikaners had worn".[468] VWB was resurrected as an online weekly in April 2019.[469]

Die Suid-Afrikaan appeared in the spring of 1984, published by Voorbrand Publikasies in Stellenbosch under the editorship of historian Hermann Giliomee.[470] Leading "verligtes", such as André P. Brink, Jakes Gerwel and André du Toit, were part of the editorial board. The last edition appeared in December 1995/January 1996.

The other Afrikaans resistance press was *Saamstaan* ("Stand together") and *Namaqua Nuus*. *Saamstaan* was published in the Southern Cape after the introduction of the tricameral parliament in 1983, when communities decided to "stand together" in their protest against the exclusion of Africans from the new dispensation.[471] It was initiated by *Grassroots* and, by the end of 1984, had a circulation of between 60,000 and 80,000. From December 1984, the newspaper appeared monthly, mostly in Afrikaans, with a few articles in English and Xhosa. *Saamstaan*'s office in Oudtshoorn was partially gutted in a paraffin bomb attack in May 1985. In subsequent attacks, Reggie Oliphant, director of *Saamstaan*'s board, was nearly killed by someone driving at night without headlights, and journalist Patrick Nyuka was shot by a municipal constable while covering a story. There were three arson attacks on the newsroom, one with reporter Mbulelo Grootboom present, who doused the flames. When the partial state of emergency was declared in 1985, *Saamstaan* was formally warned that it could be closed. Its editor-organisers were Mansoor Jaffer and Humphrey Josephs. The latter, and his successor, Derick Jackson, were both arrested under the Internal Security Act. Josephs was jailed under the Act and Jackson spent three months in jail. "Every time we were released, we again started the newspaper," Jackson said. "Even the cashier was arrested." The newspaper finally closed at the end of 1994. Established with foreign donor funds, it also could not survive democracy.

The *Namaqua Nuus*, in turn, was launched in September 1988 by *Die Suid-Afrikaan* under its DSA Trust. It was a monthly community paper, primarily in Afrikaans, aimed at readers in rural communities in the north-western Cape-Namaqualand region. It was a free newspaper with a monthly print run of 30,000 copies. The paper never attracted the attention of the authorities like *Saamstaan* because it was not as militant.

The flagship: the *Weekly Mail*

Between 1985 and 1994, the *Weekly Mail* was the "flagship" alternative paper.[472] It was launched in June 1985 by a group of journalists left jobless after two liberal mainstream papers, the *Sunday Express* and RDM, folded. With its "social-democratic" political perspective, the paper attracted what were called "slumpies": "slightly left, upwardly mobile professionals" – plus "an influence out of all proportion to its circulation".[473]

The editors were regarded as pioneers in the use of desktop technology for editing, lay-out and design. The paper never received overseas funding and was largely dependent on advertising to survive as a commercial newspaper. The *Mail* began an "association" with the British *Guardian*, with the latter's weekly international edition integrated with the *Mail* in 1992. Renamed the *Weekly Mail & Guardian* in July 1993, it was later shortened to the *Mail & Guardian*, and continued to be "jealously protective of its editorial and financial independence".

The *Mail* first appeared on 14 June 1985. The jobless journalists used their severance pay to found their paper and to "carry forward the ideals of the RDM".[474] To sidestep a high registration fee, co-editors Anton Harber and Irwin Manoim decided to apply for registration. To their surprise, and "probably because the authorities did not anticipate the *Weekly Mail* would become such a thorn in their flesh", the application was approved at the relatively modest fee of R5,000.

Thanks to new digital technology, there was a huge saving on production costs. An initial problem to find a press ended in irony. Printers were not prepared to get involved with what might be "subversive content", but the *Springs Advertiser* was willing to print the *Mail* – they also printed the right-wing Afrikaans *Die Patriot*.

Within days after its first issue appearing on Johannesburg streets, government announced the first state of emergency since 1960. The July 1985 emergency covered only parts of the country, mainly the Cape and Transvaal. A countrywide state of emergency was imposed the following year; its major aim was to control the flow of information. The authorities hoped "to write the ANC and the SACP out of current news coverage and out of the experience of ordinary South Africans". On average, one new emergency regulation "was introduced each week during 1986 and 1987". Among forbidden topics regarded as subversive were reports that normalised or legitimised the liberation movement, speeches of restricted persons or officials of restricted organisations, photographs of and reports on "unrest", activities of the security forces, reporting on "restricted" gatherings or strikes and boycotts, and on detainees. Qoboza said these regulations were to reduce the credibility of the press, especially in the eyes of township residents. Yet the *Mail* was defiant. Firstly, they portrayed "them for what they were". Harber called it a "sjambokracy – where the rule of law has been replaced by the rule of the whip". Secondly, the paper "succeeded to some extent" in getting around even the most severe emergency regulations, although, of 28 pages in the issue of 20 June 1986, fourteen contained blacked-out text or empty space where articles, even a cartoon, had been removed. It also adopted "an attitude of mocking humor".[475] With new censorship regulations, readers were advised: "For further information, telephone your Minister", with the minister's work and home numbers provided. The newspaper drew attention to censorship "while keeping sufficiently within the law to survive". At the end of 1986, censorship was tightened and, in January 1987, reports and ads about unlawful organisations were banned. Even blank pages were now proscribed. By Christmas 1987, the Directorate of Media Relations sent the *Mail* a series of notices and warnings of "possible closure" under emergency regulations. After three warnings, the paper was proscribed for one month, from 1 to 28 November 1988 – the month in which VWB was launched. The paper pointed out that minister Stoffel Botha once objected to a mere 1% of an issue. Harber by then had already created a new verb: to "stoffel", meaning to snuff out. He urged colleagues "to stop worrying about the law and adopt the attitude of journalistic street fighters".

The *Daily Mail* was launched in June 1990, but it folded in September.[476] This left the *Mail* with a large debt to Caxtons, then a subsidiary of Argus, which printed both papers. The solution was that Argus was allowed access to *Mail* reports until the debt was paid back – eventually in April 1991. The paper later developed South Africa's first internet news site.[477]

'Press Freedom' in quotation marks

In 1987, newsrooms experienced "contradictions" of, as they themselves wrote in quotation marks, "Press Freedom".[478] Various "external constraints as well as the internal consensual pressures" to which South African media were subject, limited their degree of independence, but could not "nullify it". The English press, to some extent the Afrikaans press, "and even the SABC at times", expressed views that were offensive to various "establishments", whether in "politics, culture, crime, religion or morals". While this resulted in the banning of a number of publications, "the harassment of even more", and the censuring of the SABC from party political platforms, "there nevertheless remain[ed] a substantial degree of tolerance and latitude within the media". Despite direct state control, the SABC "has or has had islands of critical expression". But even such "allowable dissent" operated "within the larger structure of exploitation".

Black journalists continued to experience "suppression of their reportage on politically sensitive issues".[479] The situation at the *Argus*, e.g., was said to be that "[r]eporters were never directly told that they had to follow a certain line or could not report on certain things". Still, stories would be cut, "buried downpage or simply spiked". A "more sinister example of news suppression" was how, "when police announced a clamp-down on the coverage of unrest", the editor ordered two major feature articles to be removed. One was on the views of black political organisations on Afrikaans-speaking students' attempt to speak with the ANC, the other on clashes between white vigilante groups and black youths in a Cape Town working class suburb. They were replaced with a picture of Table Mountain and "an article on penguins".

The 'worst onslaught in modern times'

In 1990, Thami Mazwai, then editor of the *Sowetan*'s business section, wrote that South Africa's media experienced its "worst onslaught in modern times" from 1986 until early 1989.[480] Black journalists especially had

> cause to be worried. They know what harassment is, having suffered it all of their professional lives. The harassment of the *New Nation*, *Saamstaan* and *South* is testimony to this. Thirteen years ago *World* was banned and its successor, *Post*, suffered a similar fate. The *Sowetan* has also found that life is not that easy and, like the *Weekly Mail*, has consistently enjoyed unwanted and unwarranted attention from the authorities.

Mazwai recalled the "resilience of the press in the days of granite apartheid", their leadership roles and how black journalists dealt with censorship from all sides, also problems "they had to expect in future". Pressures were from government, "elements in the liberation movements", as well as newspaper owners, the latter generating "a fourth evil, self-censorship".

With the 12 June 1986 state of emergency, two of the biggest issues concerned the prohibition on the taking or publishing of photos or sound recordings of "unrest situations" or of security forces, and on the publication of a "subversive" statement. Publishing or distributing "subversive" statements would be an offence punishable with a maximum penalty of R20,000 or imprisonment of 10 years, or imprisonment without the option of a fine. Copies of a publication "detrimental to public safety" may also be seized.

Government enforced self-censorship by "ruthlessly dealing" with first offenders. Only one day after the promulgation of such regulations, copies of the *Weekly Mail* and *Sowetan* were seized. "The message was clear." The regulations were also formulated "as vaguely as possible, a ploy used by politicians" to enable interpretations "as suited the occasion". Government acted on mainstream media "as viciously as it did with the alternative media". Among the first organisations to challenge these measures was NUMSA. Trade unions could not be classified as political organisations, but while government "was not prepared to precipitate industrial disruptions", NUMSA "virtually took over" the functions of political organisations. Various court cases succeeded, allowing for clauses to be scrapped – "although these would later reappear free of loopholes".

On 28 August 1986, government published another major set of regulations aimed specifically at the alternative media, but also at the black press. A minister could shut down a paper for up to three months. The *New Nation* was its first casualty. The *Weekly Mail* and *Sowetan* received notices that they were being "investigated", while *South* was closed, as well as other small publications.

As a way of "beating the system", a "taskforce" was formed of MWASA officials, the Association of Democratic Journalists, SASJ and the Anti-Censorship Group, also including other organisations, to launch a press freedom campaign. The new regulations turned journalists into "the most demotivated workers" in the country – but ways of beating the system were found. Although the press was barred from reporting police action, newspapers used terms such as "so-and-so was taken away by white men travelling in cars and in uniform". When Zwelakhe Sisulu was detained, these "couched" phrases were also used, and only then people realised "that the police were armed with the most awesome powers for any law enforcement agency to have".

Another way of "beating the system" was to place "illegal" stories next to the classified pages, or in the middle of church and community news sections, on the reasoning that the police would be interested in the front and the following couple of pages. One such story was "mistakenly" placed in a paper's sports section. But the police censors "were very thorough", as warnings about reports appearing in innocuous parts of newspapers kept coming. As another strategy, *Sowetan* used one or two government propaganda stories on page one, and somewhere in the middle "a hot story", assuming readers would spot the hidden stories, while government officials, "obviously grinning from ear to ear after reading the front page story, [were] likely to gloss over the remaining pages".

There were "three-dimensional" demands from community organisations. Black journalists were expected to ignore news concerning certain organisations, while highlighting those of others. They were also "expected to publish atrocities of the one and ignore those of the other" in a period of "boycotts and necklacing". It was taboo to criticise these, even "as reprehensible as they were". However, *Sowetan*, later joined by *The Star*, "was not prepared to abdicate its responsibilities". *Sowetan* refused to accede, leading to a strong anti-*Sowetan* feeling in "certain circles", with accusations of it being anti-ANC. After a boycott threat, it published its side of the story after meetings with unions and community organisations, but "[b]y then the damage had been done". Anti-*Sowetan* feelings "were being whipped up at meetings, and trucks carrying our newspapers were barred from entering one or two townships". *City Press* suffered similar pressures. The irony: "[T]his was quite laughable: we had played right into the hands of the government." Interior minister Stoffel Botha wanted these newspapers closed down; now his job was being done by blacks themselves.

Worse was to come, leading to some serious "accidents". At a funeral in Soweto, "a group of youngsters, all armed to the teeth and carrying the 'trusted tyre', came looking for any reporter from the *Sowetan*". By now the newspaper did not send reporters to certain areas, including Soweto. In the Northern Transvaal, a *Sowetan* reporter and photographer were cornered by activists wanting to necklace them. "Fortunately some of the comrades intervened and stopped what would have been an ugly situation." As a result, "quite a few black journalists wanted to leave the media. A few did."

Another type of pressure experienced by black journalists came from newspaper owners. Taking the "easy way out", they avoided "political news like the plague". The owners "of those liberal English language newspapers serving the black community were supportive of the campaign against press censorship", but there "was a sting in the tail". "Everybody knows what the managing director means when he says: *I am behind you but please note that they can close us any time. It might be advisable for you to check everything out with the lawyers.*" Every "stitch of copy" had to go through lawyers "who were kept busy making changes here and there". *Sowetan* journalists told lawyers that, instead of telling them a story could not be published, "they should tell us how it should be worded for publication". Lawyers were "pushed so hard that one actually said: *Look, my job is to tell you what the law says and the risk is yours thereafter*. This suited us fine, but obviously the bosses were unhappy."

All of this led to self-censorship, "the most vicious form of censorship, for newspapers and journalists tended to become more severe on themselves than the government would". This, coupled with community pressures, "made coming to work a nightmare". Papers were torn between giving the facts and protecting themselves and their journalists by "being extra careful". There was nothing "wrong with being extra careful (we are like this every day)", but the reasons "were no longer normal, and our reactions tended to be abnormal". Self-censorship, both as a result of actions by government and community organisations, was severe. Pressures also came from different political groupings, including the ANC, PAC and BC supporters.

When reporting on township violence, papers stopped quoting the names of organisations for the safety of reporters – "but readers were the sufferers with incomplete information". It became so severe that political leaders were approached by *Sowetan*, *Star* and *City Press* reporters, which helped, but sentiments flared up "time and again".

The black press, over the years "at the forefront of the struggle for human dignity" and civil liberties, was central to the struggle for press freedom. The majority of senior black journalists had been detained, imprisoned, or both; besides Qoboza, Klaaste and Sisulu, also Moegsien Williams, Vincent Mfundisi, Willie Bokala, Rashid Seria, Gabu Tugwana, Quoraish Patel and Vuyiswa Mhlawuli. Also imprisoned were Moffat Zungu and Thami Mkhwanazi. Thami Mazwai served two prison terms, the second for refusing to give evidence in a political trial. Other black journalists in exile were Nat Serache, Charles Nqukula, Tenjiwe Mtintso and Enoch Duma, and before them "the Lewis Nkosis, Bloke Modisanes and Can Thembas left the country". These journalists "wielded the power of the written word and what they said carried more credibility with the black community". Government therefore "never hesitated" to close the *World* and *Weekend World* and detain Qoboza. When the *New Nation* represented a new threat, they again did not hesitate to shut it down, as with the *Weekly Mail* and *South*. After "the initial shock of the regulations and the challenges in court, newspapers did become adventurous and published unrest material", but "the timing had to be perfect". During "relative calm" periods they "could get away" with these stories, but when "things were hot the censors were more vigilant".

When the *World* was closed in 1977, condemnation came from all corners of the globe. Still, the cost for anti-government newspapers to be shut down, "even in this blaze of glory", was too high. It also had a debilitating effect on the morale of the remaining papers, "[which] would no longer be that brave and continue the fight" – and then the field would "be open for our friends in Auckland Park [the SABC] and Height Street [Perskor]". Defiance could only work if all newspapers participated. The question was, "would *Beeld*, *Business Day*, *Star*, *Sunday Times*, *Pretoria News*, *Financial Mail* or *Argus* agree to face closure?"

In 1990, the battle for control of the media continued. While government got sectors of the press to act as its apologists, it became "commonplace for all organisations to try and do the same". This "type of thinking" was "given credibility" in the rest of Africa, "where governments control the media". The reasons were "noble, but the practice itself is ignominious", as governments "manage to get the atrocities they perpetrate ignored, as was the case during the regimes of Idi Amin and Adolf Hitler", where they took control of the media and then unleashed "unheard of brutality on their people".

Although this might not be the case after an "ANC or PAC take-over", an independent press was important. During the transition period in the 1990s, Mazwai appealed to organisations "to allow us to carry out our duties" – "the very essence of the press freedom [these organisations] preach about".

This was also the reason why *Sowetan* launched a *Freedom of the Press* campaign, as this freedom "is indivisible" and cannot change from situation to situation; "neither is suppression of the media by a black government less severe than that [by] a white government". Both are human rights abuses. And: "We cannot have our cake and eat it too."

Mazwai quoted Justice Frans Rumpff, former Chief Justice:

> The freedom of speech – which includes the freedom to print – is a facet of civilisation which always presents two well-known inherent traits. The one consists of the constant desire by some to abuse it. The other is the inclination of those who want to protect it, to repress it more than necessary. The latter is also fraught with danger. It is based on intolerance and is a symptom of the primitive urge in mankind to prohibit that with which one does not agree.

The newsroom's guide to the law

In the mid-1980s, the more than hundred laws restricting the press were described in *The Newspaperman's Guide to the Law*, written by SAAN board member and practicing attorney Stuart Kelsey.[481] An RDM editor estimated that lawyers were consulted ten or twelve times a day, while police would often harass reporters and seize their cameras and film.[482] Tyson said of the myriad laws censoring the press under apartheid that[483]

[w]e have reached a point where I cannot believe any individual within government or without, knows how to handle the mare's nest of rules on a rational efficient basis. I don't believe anyone but God and Peter Reynolds & Associates (the latters are our legal advisers), know how many regulations actually exist. And I think God must have forsaken the subject. The only certainty for newspapers is that, if they do nothing to upset the government, they will be safe.

Tyson added: "If we don't have a public sympathetic to a free press, not only will we not have a free press, we won't have a democracy either."

Bun Booyens, later to become editor of *Die Burger*, wrote that, with Botha's announcement of the state of emergency on 12 June 1986, South African media, "for all practical reasons, were muzzled and blindfolded", and journalism as profession "abolished" – so severe were the restrictions.[484] As for the situation in the newsroom, he referred to lawyers in *Die Burger*'s newsroom as a constant presence, "circling low" to ensure they remained inside the law.[485]

At "any given time" in South Africa in the mid-1980s, there were "numerous journalists who ha[d] possible jail sentences hanging over their heads", with "a good number of reporters and editors, black and white", demonstrating on almost a daily basis "a good deal of courage, defiance, and professional skill in telling their readers (and the world) the continuing story of racial conflict and crisis in South Africa".[486]

The partial state of emergency in July 1985 was the first since Sharpeville in 1960 and covered mainly the Eastern Cape and Transvaal.[487] It was followed by a nationwide one in June 1986, imposed yearly until De Klerk's speech in February 1990. In 1981, under the Public Safety Act, numerous BC organisations, including AZAPO and 32 UDF-aligned organisations, "were prohibited from engaging in any activity whatsoever, and thus effectively banned". Trade unions now played a major role in maintaining the Struggle's momentum.[488] By 1986, it was estimated that 75% of workdays lost to strikes were because workers supported community-inspired protests; only 25% were disputes over wages, benefits or working conditions.

Meanwhile, support for apartheid diminished dramatically.[489] Young white males refused conscription and the emigration rate of whites rose. English "and even Afrikaans-speaking politicians", students, journalists, businessmen, and other members of the white elite ignored government and met the ANC in London, Lusaka and Dakar. At the same time, the NP was under pressure from the right-wing CP, formed in 1982. In the 1989 elections, the CP became the official opposition with 23% of parliamentary seats – 31% of the white vote. Afrikaner politicians to the left of the NP joined the PFP, forming the Democratic Party (DP), a new multi-racial party, in April 1989. The DP won 20% of parliamentary seats in the 1989 elections. The NP's majority "had gradually [been] whittled away", from a high of 81% in the 1977 elections (66% of the white vote) to just under 57% in the 1989 elections (48% of the white vote). By the end of the 1980s, only 23% of MPs and less than one-third of the white electorate "remained committed to the Verwoerdian vision of grand apartheid". This pushed NP leaders toward negotiation.

And then fate stepped in. P.W. Botha suffered a stroke in January 1989 and was replaced as party leader by De Klerk in February. Botha was forced to resign in August, with De Klerk elected as president in September – "a decisive turning point in the long quest for majority rule". De Klerk acted "decisively". In his first few months he dismantled the National

Security Management System, "which had virtually governed South Africa in the mid-late 1980s". ANC secretary-general Walter Sisulu and seven other "lifers" were released from prison. The "stage was also set" for the historic announcement on 2 February 1990 that Mandela would be freed and the ANC, the Communist Party and the PAC unbanned, as well as all restrictions lifted on the UDF, Cosatu and 31 other organisations. Many political prisoners were released and the death penalty suspended.

Mandela's release on 11 February 1990, after 27 years in prison, "sent an unmistakable signal" that the NP was ready to negotiate. Formal talks began in May. In June, the state of emergency was lifted in all provinces except Natal, where fighting between the ANC/UDF and Inkatha continued. This was recalled in October, but the Inkatha Freedom Party (IFP), as it was now called, and the ANC and its allies would battle one another "for years to come". The ANC announced an end to the armed Struggle in August 1990, with all political prisoners released by this stage. By the end of 1990, ANC president Oliver Tambo and other exiles had returned to South Africa, while the NP announced in October that its membership was open to all races, as did the IFP. The UDF, after eight years "of turbulent history" as ANC surrogate, disbanded in March 1991. Mandela succeeded Tambo as ANC president in July 1991, at the party's first legal national conference in South Africa since its 1960 banning, while the NP government repealed "virtually all" remaining apartheid laws in 1991, including the Native Trust and Land Act of 1936 and the Group Areas Act of 1950.

The last years of apartheid

This ended a period up to 1990 when journalists had been imprisoned, and newspapers closed or confiscated and prosecuted for publishing "restricted matter". Perhaps, "worst of all", a total blackout was enforced on "news of detentions, police action in quelling unrest, and on boycotts, strikes, stay-aways, gatherings and other protest action" for short periods during the states of emergency between 1986 and 1990.[490] In 1989, the IPI "once again" singled out the South African government as "one of the main villains" in its annual *World Press Freedom Review*.[491] Apart from banning alternative papers for a month or more, government in 1989 concentrated on harassing foreign correspondents and local journalists from both the alternative and liberal press "in an attempt to stop them from getting to the 'coal face', and so preventing them from 'seeing the action'". Arrests, detention, harassment and censorship "on an unprecedented scale" were used during 1989 as part of government's attempt to allow only "acceptable" information to be published.

But then 1990 dawned. De Klerk's announcement was a "giant step towards a society where individual rights were protected against excess of government" and where freedom of association and of speech were "again real and tangible concepts". The prohibition to quote banned persons fell away, and the press was "now free to report and publish the views of even the most outspoken and vehement" of government's critics. Despite the new leniency, "at least a hundred different laws affecting the Press were still being enforced more than a year later". In 1991, newspapers could, *inter alia*, still be closed, journalists could be sent to jail if they failed to disclose confidential sources, and the Internal Security Act still held negative ramifications for the media – although De Klerk has expressed himself "positively in favour of the freedom of the press and individual freedoms". Government also requested the Media Council to undertake a comprehensive survey of the remaining restrictions, with the Council committing itself to the "eradication of all forms of censorship based on ideology and arbitrary actions by the state".

Afrikaans papers had already joined their English counterparts during the 1980s in protesting against Botha's states of emergency, which seriously affected freedom of speech and other measures affecting the free flow of information.[492] After February 1990, both the NP and the ANC made statements supporting a free press.[493] Despite this, various groups still wanted to "control, direct, censor and manipulate the media with an authoritative hand to suit their purposes". After February 1990, a number of official positions regarding the future of the media were announced, such as the ANC's Media Charter. Interestingly, the NP did not have "specific ideas" regarding the relationship between a new government and the media.

The transformation of the SABC

On 25 August 1990 2,000 South Africans marched on the SABC carrying banners reading: "The People Shall Broadcast! Democratise Radio and Television!"[494] This was the democratic movement's response to government's plans to unilaterally restructure broadcasting ahead of constitutional negotiations.

Government appointed a "Task Group" to propose new policies and a new controlling structure.[495] This secret inquiry by the SABC Board's chair and a group of male Afrikaner civil servants, known as the Viljoen Task group after chair Christo Viljoen, backfired. Widespread opposition to its secrecy followed, including the march on the SABC. Demands later formed part of the Convention for a Democratic South Africa (Codesa) discussions and resulted in a "spirited" crusade by the Campaign for Independent Broadcasting, a coalition of the Campaign for Open Media, Cosatu, the Council of Churches and other organisations.

By 1990, South Africa was "highly politicized".[496] De Klerk's 2 February speech meant South Africa was to be radically transformed. The civil war and military conflicts of the 1980s now were in the form of a "struggle for power via negotiations and political manoeuvring".

The nature, organisation and content of broadcasting were described as critical in the change from a pre-democratic society to the "new South Africa".[497] Thus the late 1980s and early 1990s saw "a plethora of proposals for the re-regulation of broadcasting". When the Viljoen Report was published in August 1990, despite criticisms, many of the recommendations were similar to those of radical media groups. The Report called for an independent regulatory body, the Independent Broadcasting Authority (IBA), and for the democratic and transparent appointment of a new Board. This happened in May 1993. The 1993 IBA Act No 153 also required an enquiry into the protection and viability of public broadcasting services.

Two models of radio broadcasting existed: the commercial, based on "libertarian theories of free trade", "giving the audience only what they want and thereby making a profit"; and the public service model, based on social responsibility.[498] A third model developed in the early 1990s, namely community radio.[499] In August 1991, the Jabulani! Freedom of the Airwaves Conference proposed public, commercial and community broadcasting. In January 1992, the Media in Transition conference outlined "an operating space for community radio within a broader system of broadcasting regulation". Community stations developed from the Struggle's 1980s "street committees" that gave individuals and groups the opportunity "to ask direct questions, express opinions and be informed of decisions taken and pick up useful information".[500]

By 1996 there were 22 regional and national radio services.[501] Eleven, one in each of the official languages, were "full spectrum" stations with a full range of programming genres and with the mandate to "build national identity". Many were given new names according to the IBA's 1995 Triple Enquiry Report, which stipulated that "the identification of stations' reference to language or ethnic group will not be permitted".

Freedom is … indivisible

Existing in a capitalist society, South Africa's media were driven by commercial principles, failing "dismally" to service South Africans with the full range of information they needed to make rational decisions about their world.[502] Mainstream press had traditionally blamed government censorship for failures, but while there were enormous restrictions on the media, "a significant part of the problem [lay] in the market mechanism". The claim that a libertarian ("free enterprise") media guaranteed a "free market place of ideas" was not true. Rather, a commercially-oriented media meant "market-censorship", and a media controlled by advertisers plus middle-class interests "to which they pander". Advertisers are interested in the middle class's disposable incomes, which "editors of the commercially-driven media must attract if they are to survive".

Tyson quotes John Stuart Mill, who said in 1859 that truth "is not a single element", but "a gem of many facets, each capable of different, even contradictory – appearance".[503] Mill's words "[encapsulate] the entire argument for a free press", as it is "impossible to grasp the whole truth from a single point of view". Conversely, every "honest point of view achieves an aspect of truth". In the "turbulent" period between 1990 and 1994, rather than nationalising the press, "we need[ed] to ensure that the press deserve[d] to be free".[504] Tyson emphasised that, in a time of instability and transition, the media must be constructive, not destructive, hard-hitting without being intolerant, and critical without being emotionally or misleadingly destructive.[505]

Talk of "nationalisation"[506] came mainly from the SACP and socialist academics, not from the ANC and PAC. The "so-called monopolistic press" was "more than happy to share, willingly, a century and a half of effort, talent, sweat, investment and experience in order to ensure fairness and balance, equal opportunity and diversity of opinion and news analysis". And: "Only by working hard to provide these can press freedom be achieved."

At the beginning of 1990, the Media Council examined "all the regulations and statutes which appear to conflict with the principles of any proposed Bill of Rights". More than "50 or so laws that inhibit the media" were compared with those in the US and Germany. It became clear that "not a single restrictive press law [wa]s necessary to guarantee orderly government or a responsible press", as "[b]oth freedom and responsibility can be properly tested in the courts in terms of a Bill of Rights". Instead, the focus should be "on the fundamental value of freedom", emphasising "simplicity in protecting freedom of expression", as in Article 19 of the UN Charter.

It was argued that every qualification placed on freedom of expression created a flaw. While "almost all politicians support the principle of 'freedom of the press', each wants to insert provisos in the name of responsibility, or democracy, or justice or some other word which will protect that politician's own interests". But freedom is "indivisible" – also the reason why government, "even in its worst days", was unable to suppress a hostile press.

But to whom then should the media be answerable? As Tyson said: "Certainly not to itself." Nor to any government, or to "the people's representatives".[507] It must only be answerable to the law:

> It is the Courts who will decide where the right to free expression infringes on the right to individual privacy; on communal moral values; on the interests of the State. And it is the independent judiciary who must protect the independence of the press – just as the press must protect the independence of the Courts. This symbiosis is part of democracy, while a State press, or a press subservient to the party and/or "the people" is not helpful to democracy or to freedom.

A free press must demonstrate fairness, play a part in building a fair and just society, be undivided and vigilant in its support of free expression, help to protect the independence of the judiciary, respect the authority of the courts and ensure that opposing views are given a voice.

The notion that, once power changes in nations with politically controlled media systems, dramatic changes soon follow in the media,[508] was also the case post-1990, having started gradually since 1985, also with the development of subscription TV. Up until then, South Africa's population was subject to "semi-totalitarian" control by the SABC/NP power bloc – assuring a "sterile status quo force".

The transition to a new era of political pluralism, free-market economics and media liberalisation also followed the fall of Communism sweeping the African continent in the 1990s.[509] To provide some context of the power of the apartheid economy and how it diminished as a result of boycotts: In January 1980, R1 could buy one \$1,30; in May 1990, R1 equalled 38 US cents.[510]

Up to the new dispensation, the media were censored by legislation, but after 1994 they were governed and protected by legislation. Mandela, the first democratically elected president, said of the role of newspapers, while still in jail, that they were more valuable to political prisoners than gold or diamonds, more hungered for than food or tobacco, and that "they were the most precious contraband on Robben Island". They were "not allowed any news at all, and we craved it".

After a long and tragic Struggle, South Africa and her people were free at last – both the oppressed and the oppressors, as the "Total Onslaught" had equally manipulated the minds of Afrikaner Nationalists. The words of Steve Biko, namely that "the most potent weapon in the hands of the oppressor is the mind of the oppressed", was also applicable to the oppressors.

South Africans were free at last. Or were they?

PART IV

The new democracy dawns

The theory of the free press is not that the truth will be presented
completely or perfectly in any one instance,
but that the truth will emerge from free discussion.
– attributed to both E.E. Cummings and Walter Lippmann

8. The period 1990 to 2009

Democracy and its pillar, media freedom

Introduction

At the beginning of the 1990s, South Africa suddenly found herself on the cusp of democracy after 250 years of colonialism and fifty years of apartheid – the last years of this period in a state of civil war. This new era also brought far greater, never-before-experienced and constitutionally protected media freedom. Yet, after years of clashes between the media and government, the initial honeymoon between the media and the ANC government was soon over.

This "dawn of democracy" had a significant impact on the South African media landscape, which up to then could still be described according to the three South African press theories, namely a traditionally English, Afrikaans and black press. In terms of media policy, regulation and ownership, South African media now faced major new challenges in a completely new political, cultural and societal ecosystem. What normative and professional practices were now needed? Media owners, media bodies and journalism practitioners had to reimagine themselves while emerging from a suppressed, restricted and distorted past and while still serving the South African public.

This meant that, from the beginning of the end of apartheid in the 1990s, South Africa's media also experienced a democratisation.[1] The "old" disappeared quickly and the media underwent swift shifts, transforming the industry in terms of race, politics and economics.[2] The ownership of major titles, such as the *Sunday Times*, was transferred to black empowerment consortia. Also, foreign investors, like Tony O'Reilly's Independent Group and Pearson Plc, became major players, while the Media Development and Diversity Agency (MDDA) was founded. The first independent licensing body, the Independent Broadcasting Authority (IBA), was later incorporated into the Independent Communications Authority (ICASA), which issued licences to community radio stations. This led to a diversity of voices and "far greater pluralisation" as well as normalisation than South African media had ever experienced. But these developments were coupled with "growing commercialisation and tabloidisation", the latter appearing almost literally as a "new dawn", as the *Sun*, aimed at the Gauteng black working class, started to rise. But alternative media such as the *Weekly Mail* and *Vrye Weekblad* did not make it. With their *raison d'être* disappearing, so did their funding. The former could reposition itself thanks to the British *Guardian* as the *Mail &*

Guardian, but the latter went under (to survive again as an e-paper in 2019). Simultaneously, the ANC's ideal of establishing an own paper did not materialise.[3]

When, in 1992, the ANC introduced its Media Charter,[4] it was regarded as the foundation for the recognition of freedom of expression as well as media freedom. The document is ascribed to the work of civic organisations and NGOs during apartheid, among them the Campaign for Open Media (COM), the Campaign for Independent Broadcasting, Jabulani, the Media Institute of Southern Africa, the Freedom of Expression Institute (FXI), and the Open Society Initiative of Southern Africa (Osisa).[5] The Charter provided for

- the protection of freedom of speech,
- freedom of the press, or media,
- the freedom to collect, use and disseminate information,
- the development and implementation of processes to guarantee the legal and economic democratisation of the media,
- the protection, growth and independence of private as well as public media,
- improved access to media for all,
- the rights of media workers, including their right to education and training and, in general,
- the promotion of a free and democratic media culture.

In the first years after the demise of apartheid, "it went well for media developments". Policies, policy development and implementation "were in sync" with the Charter and its principles of freedom of speech. Local developments reflected global developments, such as the liberalisation, privatisation and internationalisation of media ownership. Global developments in information and communications technology (ICT) could be assimilated by South African media companies, including multimedia convergence. New developments were the restructuring and transformation of the SABC as public broadcaster, establishing community radio, the empowerment of black media ownership and management, and the "partial" liberalisation of the telecommunications market. New regulatory bodies in line with international standards and practices were established, and new media groups with new products, TV channels, radio stations, newspapers, magazines and the internet were established. And despite all of these developments, some ANC officials had already started shortly after 1994 to threaten the media, "mimick[ing] the attitude and actions of the apartheid government".

Still, there is consensus that South Africa had witnessed "the most remarkable changes in the media", as well as in society in general.[6] In broadcasting there was "an efflorescence of new stations" and, besides changes in the ownership of existing stations, the completely "new layer" of community media begun in an extremely short space of time.

The socio-political imperatives of the "new South Africa" were compounded by an on-going "rampant" globalisation of the international media environment as a result of the digital revolution and the impact of satellites, all "changing the communication landscape completely".[7] From 1994, international capital invested in local media companies on "an unprecedented scale", with local black empowerment consortia purchasing shares in previously "white" media companies.

The media industry itself also shifted to greater independence and a system of self-regulation after the extremely legalised apartheid media environment. A non-racial body was founded for the first time: the South African National Editors' Forum (SANEF), from the amalgamation of the (white) Conference of Editors and the Black Editors' Forum.[8] Within the bigger picture of news events in South Africa, this "specific element of reconciliation almost went unnoticed".[9] In 1996, editors "joined hands" and formed, for the first time in the country's history, a united forum. After its November 1996 founding, bold headlines proclaimed, "Defence of free press now in black and white", "Breakthrough at historic editors' meeting" and "The big story: a milestone in building a non-racial media". SANEF announced a number of action programmes, including the monitoring of black empowerment and affirmative action, media education and training, and press freedom.

But although formed after a merger of the newspaper-based (white) Conference of Editors and the cross-media Black Editors' Forum, it was regarded as "relatively elitist" and its non-racial character "spurred" the growth of the FBJ.[10] SANEF quickly showed its strength, however: In 2000 it brokered an agreement limiting the use of subpoenas under Section 205 of the Criminal Procedures Act. Under apartheid this was used to force journalists to reveal information.

Although media freedom was protected in Article 16 of the Bill of Rights, which was accepted in 1996, it was clear that the new government also did not really grasp what media freedom really meant. Even within government it was clear there was no consensus. And, as stated by editor Aggrey Klaaste in referring to new black media bosses shortly after democratisation: African Nationalist media owners were also "just capitalists who just want to make money".[11]

The last years under apartheid

At the beginning of the 1990s, the media status quo was very much the same as it had been for almost a century.

In an assessment of the state of newspapers and news dissemination in South Africa during the last years of apartheid, it was said that the "wide cultural variety of the country's peoples and the sheer vastness of the land" had played an important role in presenting and disseminating information through newspapers.[12] The "historical link" to the West, as well as certain "Western values", gave South African newspapers "their form", with British and American influences "most visible". The Western model of the "liberal press" could be seen in anti-apartheid English-language newspapers such as the RDM, *The Star* and the *Sunday Times*, while the Afrikaans press was "generally considered to be pro-segregation or apartheid, especially up to the late 1950s". But from the 1960s, and especially with the founding of the daily *Beeld* in 1974, the Afrikaans press moved away from "strict adherence" to NP policies. *Beeld* and its forerunner, the Sunday *Die Beeld* (from 1965 to 1970), were an independent voice within "the previous political-cultural hegemony" of Afrikaners. Among the "alternative" press, regarded as the "social-democrat independent press", were *The Weekly Mail* and *Vrye Weekblad*. Among the smaller, "progressive-alternative community press" were *Grassroots* and *Saamstaan*. Within this grouping one could distinguish between the "left-commercial anti-apartheid press", such as *South*, *New Nation* and *New African*, and the "small neo-fascist, pro-apartheid and right-alternative press", such as *Die Afrikaner* and *Sweepslag*.

But the ground shifted when the democratisation process started in the 1980s and accelerated in the 1990s. White monopoly was being "broken down" and the press "democratised to accommodate a wider scope of voices and interests in the country". The four major publishing houses were still the English Argus Group and SAAN, and the Afrikaans Naspers and Perskor, although they did not publish exclusively in these languages.

In February 1994, the majority of shares in the erstwhile "behemoth" Argus Group, founded in 1889 with mining capital such as that of Rhodes, were bought by Irish press magnate Tony O'Reilly. The group was renamed after O'Reilly's Independent Newspapers Holdings Limited. Argus Holdings, the former owner of Argus Newspapers, became Omni Media, which in turn was incorporated into Anglo American's Johnnic. It absorbed the stake of Anglo American and JCI in Times Media (91,3%). This was "in line" with the ANC's black empowerment policy, but in real terms it transferred ownership to an international conglomerate that owned 65% of the newspapers in Ireland as well as interests in Australia. The group now controlled more major newspapers than any other and was considered the "largest player" in printing and publishing. One of its papers, the *Sowetan,* was the biggest daily with a circulation of 211,433 in 1996, followed by *The Star,* with a circulation of 163,179; the two papers had a combined readership of more than two million.

Towards the end of the 1980s, in March 1987, SAAN became Times Media Limited (TML), replacing its "ailing mother company", also originally founded as a conglomerate with English mining capital, and which since May 1965 had developed along with Sunday Express Limited, dating from 1931.[13] As in the case of the Argus Group, the historic links with mining interests abounded. RDM and the *Sunday Times,* as daily and weekly, shared staff and facilities. In 1937 the *Sunday Express* was also bought, consolidating the group before the formation of SAAN. Both the RDM and the *Sunday Express* closed in 1985, after financial losses of R23 million. In 1996, the *Sunday Times* was the biggest newspaper in South Africa, with a circulation of 468,084. While Times Media was still controlled by Anglo American through JCI until early 1996, their black empowerment deal that year meant the National Empowerment Consortium (NEC) bought control of Johnnic, an industrial holdings group, which controlled 91,3% of Times Media through Omni Media. Anglo American then sold most of its 47,7% stake in an "historic deal" to put a substantial portion of South Africa's print and electronic media interests under black control, as the NEC represented black businesses and trade unions. The two Afrikaans companies, formed because of "the Afrikaners' wish to rule their own affairs and to have a medium through which to express their hopes, fears and dreams",[14] were "deeply rooted in the struggle of Afrikaner nationalism". By 1978, this close link was broken when Afrikaner politicians were banned from being board members, a suggestion made by Naspers chair Cillié to P.W. Botha, after which "guidelines to effectively remove the politicians from these positions" were formulated.

Naspers, traditionally the biggest Afrikaans press group,[15] and regarded as a proponent of "Southern" Afrikaner Nationalism, in 1965 moved into the then Transvaal because of industrialisation and Afrikaner urbanisation. First to be published there was its Sunday *Die Beeld,* and in 1974 its daily *Beeld. Die Beeld* amalgamated with Perskor's *Dagbreek* to form *Rapport* in 1970, with both companies owning a 50% stake. Naspers bought out the other 50% when Perskor ceased to exist.

In 1990, the year when political transformation was announced, it was clear the Afrikaner intellectuals had also moved on, as the "emphasis on Afrikanerdom and its ideals" had changed. Naspers chair Cillié stated in his 1990/91 annual report: "We want to be more representative of the whole community in our undertakings. We see our destiny as that of a 'national press', a country-wide, nationwide communication industry."[16] The company had already bought three black titles in the mid-1980s, with one of them, *City Press*, doubling its circulation to 266,717 between 1992 and 1996.[17]

Perskor, or Afrikaanse Perskorporasie, also owned magazines through Republican Press and held majority shares in *Imvo Zabantsundu*, based in King William's Town. Perskor's holding company was Perskor Beleggings (Persbel), in turn controlled by Dagbreek Trust, in which Rembrandt had a 32% share. In 1996, a deal was made between this "old money" and Perskor's "conservative heritage" and the Kagiso Trust's "new money". Perskor's contribution to the partnership was 13 consumer magazines and 23 regional newspapers, while Kagiso represented a "huge" educational publishing business with a market value of more than R300 million. A characteristic of the two Afrikaans publishing houses was that both had a solid magazine market in both English and Afrikaans.

'Seismic changes' in a new media ecosystem

With the 1989 fall of the Berlin Wall and the end of the Cold War, South Africa could not escape global trends. This liberalisation and global trend to democratisation was followed by the "triumph of liberal democracy".[18] In this, the media had played a significant role as "site and agent for change",[19] even under apartheid's severest restrictions. Of course, the media's commercial interests also played an important role under the new dispensation – as they did during apartheid. Emerging from a history "of violent conflict and marked by continued severe economic inequalities", criticisms of the media's role and its relationship regarding development and the "marketplace of ideas" and access to media "become even more pertinent".[20] With such competing imperatives in a new, free society, the meaning of media freedom was not self-evident, a situation that could be exacerbated when the media wanted to protect and practise their new-found freedom, also because of deep social divisions inherited from the previous era which problematised notions such as "public interest".[21]

To add to the challenges facing South African media during this period, digital development, with its "internet of things" and online free speech, became more and more of a reality, leading to the fact that the freedom of the internet was later also the focus of media freedom indexes. Legislature regarding the internet, especially regarding the protection of children, became crucial.

It was clear that, post-1994, there would be seismic changes in every sector in South Africa. Despite the relatively peaceful transition to a constitutional democracy, heralded globally as an inspirational moment in history, the road would be "hard and bumpy" after the first "glory days, or couple of years". The "miracle" of racial reconciliation led to Nobel peace prizes for Nelson Mandela and F.W. de Klerk, with South Africa initially on a new, although brief, path of political and economic development. But reforming 350 years of statutory discrimination was not easy. After the first five years of democracy, South Africa's parliament was "unrecognisable" from the pre-1994 one. Everything was different, even the "pictures on the walls", as was the atmosphere ("far less stuffy") and the buildings ("certainly far more lively").[22] Besides, the membership of parliament comprised "a majority of black people who suffered under apartheid, serving political parties, a number of whom were banned until 1990". Most importantly, "its institutional construction has been almost entirely overhauled".

Key to this was the writing of South Africa's new Constitution, with the interim one adopted in 1993 and the final one in 1996. Its Bill of Rights contained, in Article 16, entrenched rights to media freedom and general freedom of expression. South Africa's first democratic government passed 534 Acts in its first five years, in itself a "huge achievement",[23] although not all the laws concerning press freedom were abolished. The scrapping or suspension of most of the repressive media laws after 1994 meant "space for media to contribute to democracy".[24] What was "especially noteworthy" in the transformation of print ownership was how ownership affected editorial control. Under apartheid there was little distinction between the two.

In 1996, at least 20 urban daily and weekly newspapers were registered with the NPU as part of Print Media Association of South Africa (PMASA),[25] with three independent dailies and four independent national weeklies. As in the 1980s, corporate ownership of newspapers remained the norm, with the four major groups "continuing to control" the publications with the highest circulation, although there were some "new dynamics" following Nthato Motlana's New Africa Investment Limited (NAIL).

Besides the NPU, which had already celebrated its centenary in 1982, other industry organisations in 1994 were the Magazine Publishers' Association of South Africa (MPASA), the SA Typographical Union (SATU), the South African Printing and Allied Industrial Federation, the Conference of Editors, the SA Society of Journalists and MWASA. PMASA was established in 1994 and consisted of the NPU, MPASA, the Provincial Press Association and the Specialist Press Association.[26]

An 'interim' period: 1990 to 1994

One can identify two periods of significant policy development in South Africa: from 1990 to 1994, with preparations being made for a new democratic dispensation; and from 1994 to 2007, when the policies were implemented and refined.[27]

In April 1990, two months after the release of Mandela and the unbanning of the ANC, "a small team of ANC strategists arrived in South Africa". Returning from "many years in exile" they had to prepare for the negotiations between the apartheid government and the ANC. Among them were Gill Marcus and Joel Netshitenzhe, who had to engage with the South African media establishment. Their involvement was two-fold: To establish a channel of communication through which the ANC could disseminate its views, and to discuss the transformation of the media. In 1992, Mandela, as ANC president, said the party valued "a free, independent and outspoken press", but made a number of criticisms that "cut deep in South African media circles".[28] One was about the lack of diversity in control and staffing that led "to one-dimensional journalism". Besides criticising white journalists' "pessimism", he also "strongly criticised black reporters", suggesting their allegiances lay with their "white bosses rather than with the imperatives of the liberation struggle". All of this "put pressure" on all editors. White editors felt they were being told it was time to leave, while black journalists felt the attack was added pressure. Even editors "sympathetic to the ANC" found their journalistic independence to be under question.

Regarding broadcast media, the "drive to sever" government's grip on the SABC dominated media policy between 1990 and the 1994 election.[29] However, it was said that it "is highly debatable" whether it secured the SABC's impartiality. After the ANC victory, there were

> repeated incidents of interference by the state in programming selection and content, the appointment of senior staff and management, the choice of commentators and in the restructuring of the SABC itself, strongly suggest[ing] that the public broadcaster remains very much at the whim of government and the majority party.

This also played out massively in 2016, as will be seen in the following chapter. With regard to print, with the "general reluctance" to interfere with the freedom of the press in the early 1990s, mainstream print media was left "largely untouched" by specific regulatory constraints. The ANC was "very keen", though, to establish "a foothold" in the print sector.

One option was a party newspaper; the other to buy a paper and convert it into a party organ. The issue "absorbed considerable energy" within the ANC. An ANC working group was formed under the leadership of Moeletsi Mbeki, brother of the later-to-be second president, to do a feasibility study of a party political paper. Establishing a new paper, or buying an existing one, never materialised. At the time, though, "perhaps" the strongest contender was the *New Nation*. Edited by Zwelakhe Sisulu, son of senior party leader Walter, it was an alternative weekly that already served as an important conduit for ANC information during the late 1980s and early 1990s. The reasons for the ANC's reluctance to enter the newspaper business were given as both financial and political.

Relationships, relationships

The relationship between media companies and the political elite is also a matter of interest – as was the case with the Afrikaner Nationalist ruling elite and Afrikaans media companies. Dominant media companies tended "to support the social and political status quo", with examples of "intimate relations between senior politicians and media barons ... relatively commonplace".[30] One of the best examples of such a "personal arrangement" was between Irish press baron O'Reilly and Mandela. According to an anonymous Independent Newspapers senior executive, when "Mandela was having a hard time, in particular over Winnie" (his wife, Winnie Madikizela-Mandela) in 1993, "O'Reilly called and said: 'You're working too hard, I'm sending my plane to fetch you. You need a holiday.'" O'Reilly's plane took Mandela to the billionaire's "exquisite holiday home in the Bahamas". This was followed "soon after" by a meeting in Switzerland. Mandela, accompanied by Pallo Jordan, met O'Reilly in his hotel where he asked "businessman questions". The most important was: "If I put hundreds of millions of pounds into your country, will my bid meet with your favour? Are you okay with me buying in?" According to the source, no guarantees were given, but there was "a tacit understanding" that Mandela knew about O'Reilly's intention to bid for the Argus Group "and approved of it". This was followed by negotiations with Anglo's Michael Spicer, "who, in 1993, bought a controlling stake (31%) in the company". The "myth about the friendship" was that "O'Reilly woos Mandela", and if the latter "approves the Argus purchase, he will make sure the group is pro-ANC for ever".

According to Moeletsi Mbeki, as media consultant, the arrangement between O'Reilly and Mandela was "endorsed" by the ANC "on the understanding that some black shareholding would be facilitated".[31] This, however, did not occur. In hindsight, the "O'Reilly deal" was criticised,[32] especially the "oft-made charge that the Irish parent company had embarked on an asset-stripping strategy according to which excess profits were repatriated to Ireland".

From 1994 to 1996

When the prospects of an ANC newspaper were exhausted, the focus shifted to the SABC through the South African Communication Service (SACS) as one of the ANC's few potential tools to influence the media.[33] The process began "in earnest" in 1995 with the Conference on Government Communications, which led to the Communications Task Group (Comtask), established in 1996, and the founding of the Government Communication and Information System (GCIS) soon after.[34] Still, the ANC "had a history of supporting a free press that militated against direct intervention". Already in 1943, the ANC annual conference unanimously adopted the "Africans' Claims in South Africa" document. Included was a Bill of Rights that called for the "right of Freedom of the Press", seen as the genesis of ANC media policy. It was based on the 1941 Atlantic Charter, drawn up by US president Franklin D. Roosevelt and British prime minister Winston Churchill, "to see sovereign rights and self-government restored to those who have been forcibly deprived of them". Absorbed by the ANC, it later became enshrined in South Africa's 1996 Constitution, as well as in "Acts of Parliament, government policy directives, regulatory authority directives, licence conditions, self-regulatory structures and in corporate regulations".

The formation of media policy began in earnest in 1990, corresponding with the setting up of the ANC's Department of Information and Publicity by Marcus and Netshitenzhe. A series of conferences, debates and even protest actions followed, giving "significant impetus to policy matters" and focusing attention on the importance of the media and its role in the transition to democracy "and beyond". Many laws and policies concerning the media existed prior to 1990, "not least the 120 laws that the apartheid government put in place over decades to restrict the media and limit freedom of expression and association".[35]

The UN's Universal Declaration of Human Rights was announced on 10 December 1949. Its Article 19 has become a "landmark" of media policy,[36] as discussed earlier. As "lodestone" for media activists, it continued to influence constitutional law and media policy globally, as also seen in the 1955 Freedom Charter at Kliptown. Although the latter did not mention the media specifically, it declared that South Africa would one day be governed by a law that would "guarantee to all their right to speak, to organise, to meet together, to publish, to preach, to worship and to educate their children". It also referred to the "free exchange of books and ideas", the right of all people to use their own languages and to develop their own culture and customs. Paradoxically, in this period from the mid-1950s to the late 1980s, SA media policy "was principally about the imposition of censorship and repression".

But, by the end of the 1980s, things started to change. In 1989, COSATU set up "a national consultative process" regarding media policy that "crystallised a rudimentary network of left-wingers interested in media policy work". This "floundered" because of more pressing national priorities, "but a seed had been planted". Central was the belief that being able to communicate, and to receive and transmit information – rather than just the right to information – was as important to democracy and development as other, "more traditional", human rights.

As referred to earlier, on 25 August 1990, 2,000 people marched on the SABC in Johannesburg. This was a watershed moment in the evolution of media policy, as it "marked the galvanisation of progressive media workers to resist the top-down reform of broadcasting" as enacted by the NP "in its dying days". It was a protest against the Viljoen Task Group, headed by Christo Viljoen, then SABC chair, to investigate the SABC's future. The protest was led by COM, established by the Film and Allied Workers Organisation (FAWO), and COSATU's anti-privatisation committee. But it turned out that even the ANC had to concede that the Task Group made "some useful recommendations", including the establishment of an independent regulatory body, the framing of a new broadcasting act, the devolution of political control, and improving accessibility. The Task Group's nine members were initially unrepresentative and biased towards the NP,[37] as it did not include blacks and women or represent advertising and marketing. In 1993, public hearings on nominees preceded their appointment as members of the first post-apartheid SABC Board. Although still seriously criticised, also in the way it eventually was appointed by then state president De Klerk, "it was by far the most representative and democratically appointed board ever". The new 25-member board immediately started internal restructuring. One recommendation, the IBA, was one of the most significant events in the history of SA broadcasting. The IBA Act was passed in October 1993 and the IBA's first meeting was in March 1994.

By the early 1990s, the SABC was already an affirmative action employer with a full-time staff complement of 4,700, including journalism, administration and technical staff.[38] About 30,000 people were engaged as freelancers.

A series of influential conferences in the early 1990s brought international experience and gave substance to early media policies.[39] Most important were the Jabulani! Freedom of the Airwaves conference in Amsterdam in August 1991. Also important was the Patriotic Front Conference in Durban in October, and the ANC's Department of Information and Publicity seminar in November 1991, at which the draft Media Charter was circulated. The Charter "drew heavily" on earlier debates and highlighted issues like the equitable distribution of media resources, diversity, access, skills, ownership and affirmative action. It was described as a "crucial turning point within the ANC's approach to the media" and was adopted by the ANC's National Executive Committee (NEC) on 13 January 1992. The Charter was a "deliberately Utopian statement of intent". It included a clause stating: "All communities shall have access to the skills required to receive and disseminate information." The draft called for the democratisation of the South African media and stated that "the forms and methods of the media shall take account of the diversity of communities in respect of geography, language and interests". Diversity of ownership would be ensured, while affirmative action would be implemented. The ANC's priority was to minimise the SABC's pro-NP impact in the first democratic elections, but it also focused on print media.

Three resolutions were adopted with specific reference to print. The first was the founding of a national newspaper "for the democratic movement", the second the monitoring and regulation of print, and the third the implementation of a media development programme. The seminar was "an important indicator of the broad democratic movement's attitude" to print. Only the third resolution, the media development plan, would come to fruition – more than a decade later. The idea of regulating and monitoring print "was vehemently rejected by several key figures", including the chair of the Argus Group, Murray Hofmeyr, the editor of The Star, Richard Steyn, and Argus director and former editor of The Star, Harvey Tyson. In 1992, they jointly issued a statement declaring that "the monitoring of the print media during the interim period or after the election of the new government is an unacceptable principle which conflicts fundamentally with freedom of expression".

An "accord of journalistic practice", as called for by the seminar to ensure "a minimum of bias in the print media and to prevent distortions in the information process", was also not established.

New print ownerships, no interference?

With the emergence of NAIL, press ownership was widened to five major groups, with still "an extent of cross-ownership" among them.[40] As an example, Independent Newspapers had a 42,5% share in the *Sowetan* as part of NAIL, while it owned 37% of Times Media. It was acknowledged that the concentration of such media ownership "diminishes the diversity and pluralism of news", while a democracy is best served by a "diversity of competing voices" providing the public with "a multiplicity of information and opinions". Besides NAIL's entrance into the media scene, there was also a rise in black access and empowerment in other sections of the newspaper industry. Black empowerment started on a "significant scale" in 1993, when Independent Newspapers decided to "liberate" the *Sowetan* by selling it to NAIL. The decision to sell the largest-selling daily "revolutionised" the industry. Independent kept 42,5% of the stake, giving NAIL a majority of 52,5%, with 5% for staff. The other four big groups also applied black economic empowerment. In April 1996, Times Media sold 30% of its Eastern Cape operations to a consortium of local black businesspeople and community organisations. Kagiso Trust Investment (KTI), a black consortium with interests in book publishing, bought a 16,3% share in Persbel, the holding company of Perskor. Naspers also repositioned itself. Ton Vosloo, then executive chair, said at the end of the 1995/1996 financial year:

> We are striving to involve fellow-countrymen who were excluded from the business process, more and more in our activities. If current confidential negotiations with black and brown business sectors are successfully concluded, we want to implement these imaginative new partnerships in the current financial year.

In 1996/1997, Naspers broadened its shareholding by inviting members of staff, as well as the community in general, to take up shares, with "[a]ll interest groups ... represented in the body of 7,000 shareholders". As part of its black empowerment programme, the company sold 51% of its shares in *City Press* to the Western Cape black business consortium Ukhozi Investments. South Africa's largest and only "black" Sunday newspaper was now controlled by black owners. It was expected to "revolutionise the Sunday market". Cynics argued that monopolies were only willing to sell assets that were not profitable, or those that would not be competition to their titles, although "the *City Press* sale proved the contrary".

These changes and acquisitions were not without controversies. One of the problems new and prospective owners faced was the issue of editorial independence. It was expected that these problems would only exist when "buying into 'white titles'", but it was "no less intense" at the *Sowetan* when Motlana took over in 1995. At a series of staff meetings there were complaints about Motlana's "interference". It was perceived to be on directives from the ANC, "and from President Nelson Mandela, in particular". Then *Sowetan* editor Aggrey Klaaste said "[g]uys like Motlana who own this newspaper are itching to interfere, because black guys also like interfering in things".[41]

Similarly, when a bid to buy Johnnic was getting stronger, Times Media distributed an "editorial charter" among its staff, demanding guarantees from NAIL (then led by current

South African president Ramaphosa) that it would not interfere in the editorial policy of any Times Media title "during and after the signing" of the Johnnic deal.[42] Nigel Bruce, former editor of the *Financial Mail* and at the time editor of *Finance Weekly* and, according to sources, the author of the charter, said that despite "some protestations to the contrary", the NAIL "syndicate" was intending to interfere with Times Media editors.

Another challenge was the issue of editorship. Although "the bidders and buyers" gave assurances that they would not interfere, "major changes in the editorial boards of most of these newspapers were likely". It was a particularly "delicate balancing act". The new owners had to satisfy the need for affirmative action, but also assure the commercial viability of the papers. One issue was also whether the press "under black control" would be as critical of the ANC government as it should be, with some doubting whether "South Africa would not drift back to the old days when newspaper editors resorted to self-censorship" to not offend the NP.

At the time, deputy president Thabo Mbeki appointed the Comtask to investigate the media, including issues of ownership and affirmative action. The problem was that only "a handful of black businessmen were buying into the industry". When six SABC commercial radio stations came up for sale, the same groups bid, namely NAIL, KTI and NEC, raising concerns that the South African media were moving towards a position of black elite monopoly. This was seen as just a reversal of the 48 years under NP rule, especially as ANC leaders and supporters were appointed in top positions in business groups with media interests. Ramaphosa became chair of Johnnic, while the owner of Times Media, Motlana, was the chair of NAIL, the owner of the *Sowetan* and *New Nation*; Oscar Dhlomo, the founder of Dynamo Investments, had interests in *City Press*; and Eric Molobi, a former Robben Island inmate and head of KTI, bought into Perskor.

Morphing, morphing

Prior to 1993, broadcasting was almost entirely a state monopoly, "tightly controlled not only by the government and the propagandist board it appointed, but by the Broederbond and latterly military 'securocrats' and in a few cases by Bantustan dictators".[43] The only private TV broadcaster was M-Net, licensed to the newspaper industry but forbidden to broadcast news.

Historically, the SABC played "an important role in both constructing and supporting the apartheid structures of pre-1991 South Africa".[44] In the 1980s, the SABC "uncritically supported the NP" in the "Total Onslaught" narrative. When the process of restructuring began in January 1991, the "dominant ethos" was pragmatism, rather than propaganda. FAWO, COM and the Community Radio Working Group and its various affiliates were the "fulcrums around which a series of initiatives" were undertaken. Among them were the march on the SABC in 1990, a media policy workshop at Rhodes University in the same year, and the "highly influential" Jabulani! Freedom of the Airwaves Conference in the Netherlands. Following the ANC's Media Charter in 1991, COM hosted a conference in 1992 titled "Free, Fair and Open Media". This helped to establish the Campaign for Independent Broadcasting, leading to the first democratic and transparent appointment, in May 1993, of a new SABC Board and the setting up of the IBA the following year. The IBA Act No. 153 required an enquiry into the "protection and viability of public broadcasting", cross-media control and South African content, known as the Triple Enquiry, completed in 1995. All of this was the turning point heralding a new broadcast environment. At the beginning of 1996, the SABC had 22 regional and national radio services. Eleven, one in each of the official languages, were full-spectrum stations, meaning they offered a full range of programming genres, from news, actuality, sports and discussions to entertainment and education.

Thus, between 1994 and 2000, the SABC made "great strides" in transforming itself from a state to a public broadcaster, while implementing "one of the most aggressive affirmative action programmes yet seen in a public entity".[45] The SABC was one of the first institutions to be partly privatised under the new government.[46] The sale of six commercial stations increased diversity by adding to the growing number of private radio stations involving black ownership, but "had a disastrous effect on the Corporation's finances". In 2000, the SABC underwent another round of restructuring, aligning it with the then adopted Broadcasting Act, which had to set the SABC "on the road to self-sufficiency".

Most of the decade leading up to 2000 was a period of restructuring and establishing a broadcasting regulatory authority.[47] In 1992, the SABC's partisanship towards the NP government and its credibility in the run-up to the 1994 elections was still of concern. This period also saw the introduction of the three-tier broadcasting system, namely public, commercial and community broadcasting.

Regarding black empowerment, in April 1998 the IBA gave the first free-to-air commercial TV licence to the Midi group, a consortium of previously disadvantaged groups. Known as e.TV, the station was "awash with criticism and controversy", starting with allegations of political interference in the allocation of the licence.[48]

But the SABC also seemed to be "doomed to be abused". From 2000 to 2007, it was ridden with "the ambiguities of post-apartheid broadcasting". Despite efforts to "shake off the stigma" of a crisis-ridden organisation, criticism "ha[d] compounded … since democratisation in 1994".[49] Although the SABC's independence was guaranteed by law and reviewed by an independent regulator, it continued "to stumble from controversy to controversy over its relationship with the government and the ruling party".[50]

The beginning of the new South Africa also saw the demise of the alternative media. After their *raison-d'être* was erased, overseas funding dried up.[51] Although they were spurned by mainstream press and the apartheid government, they survived against all odds, only to become redundant in a new political dispensation.

The media as critical observers?

Until the early 1980s, South African critiques of the press were "few and far between".[52] Five broad categories of studies existed until the 1980s. They were "reminiscences of retired journalists and editors"; uncritical descriptions "which by and large ignore[d] the very existence of a black press"; works within the "orthodox western Liberal framework" that "generally lack[ed] analysis of structural conditions"; more rigorous work such as that by Potter and Hepple, but which also excluded analyses of the black-oriented press; and lastly, in the fifth category, structural analyses, but limited, and only after the late 1970s.

Commentators were split, e.g., over whether the newspaper industry was helpful or harmful regarding the maintenance of apartheid.[53] Most fell into the category of "reminiscences of retired journalists and editors", such as Joel Mervis's *The Fourth Estate*.[54] H.L. Smith's *Behind the Press in South Africa*[55] was also criticised. Although it asserted that the policy of the daily

(English) press was "that *ipso facto* whatever is best for the gold mines is best for South Africa", something "kept ever foremost in mind", it concluded that the mining industry only had a "benign influence on the autonomous press". By not abusing its power, the press remained "a responsible, free agent capable of opposing the state". Potter also identified the structural links between the English press and mining capital. For her, the English press was an "external opposition" and "uniformly opposed the government, its ideology and its supporters". This was supported by *inter alia* Neame (1956),[56] Hepple (1960)[57] and Pollak (1981),[58] who said that newspapers were "the lone megaphone of dissent". Without the "moderately free press to promulgate news and unpopular ideas", South Africa's "political lop-sidedness" would be near complete. They stood "almost alone between the Afrikaans government and totalitarian darkness".

But there was also criticism that newspapers represented "the forces of the status quo", and that none of the media could publish or broadcast "material undermining the principles of their owners or the elements upon which they depend financially".[59] The press "essentially serve[d] the narrow class interests of the dominant whites",[60] with other critics writing that "all sectors of the established (South African) media support one or more factions of the hegemonic alliance".[61]

But now democracy brought with it the first black-owned print media companies, such as NAIL and Johnnic. Although NAIL was widely regarded as "black" and had a major stake in the *Sowetan,* historically disadvantaged groups owned less than 5% of the company.[62] With the important changes taking place in print ownership, it meant also foreign ownership took root.[63] Although the print media have undergone "highly significant changes" regarding ownership, they still faced an "ever-increasing problem of access".[64] Although access to and consumption of radio and TV had grown, reflecting international trends, newspaper circulation shrunk from 19% to 17% between 1990 and 1996. In 2000, South Africa had the second lowest number of titles in the world in relation to population size. The "effects of commercial restructuring" could be seen in newsrooms, namely "more and more centralisation to ensure editorial and economic efficiency gains", such as Independent Newspapers' centralised parliamentary bureau. This led to the critical question of what the implications of such "syndication" meant for editorial diversity: Was it, e.g., healthy for "one political opinion alone to circulate in all Independent titles?"

Attempts to support black empowerment were already showing strain. Naspers, e.g., had repurchased the *City Press* stake sold to empowerment groups.[65] This was the first major black empowerment deal to be unwound after the sharp deterioration in "trading conditions" that began in this period. Businesses relied on borrowed funds, while the cost of these funds increased and profits in the newspaper industry "[were] squeezed".

At the same time, the broad alliance of parties that formed the first Government of National Unity (GNU), consisting of the ANC, the then New National Party (NNP) and the Inkatha Freedom Party (IFP), collapsed when the NNP "realised it had no real say in the determination of policy".[66] This "arrangement" also "soon tested boundaries" and questioned the role of the media in the "new democratic dispensation". The political system was based on a constitutional and legal framework that included media freedom, but "a powerful democratic state [was] also more than capable of stalling, if not reversing, the process of differentiation to ensure its own narrative [was] the one that predominates in the mass media".

Simultaneously, the rules and requirements of journalistic professionalism changed after 1994.[67] Despite the country's "long and proud history of journalistic excellence" in the print media, the relationship between state and media had shifted. The arrival of global investors, tabloids, client magazines and accelerated commercialism threw "traditional practices into question and introduced new forms of journalism". The collapse of the major professional organisation for journalists, SASJ, only "exacerbated the dwindling of journalistic standards". By 2007, however, South African journalists had achieved a "significant degree of autonomy" and had "a largely collegial work process" with a formal and hierarchical structure in most newspaper newsrooms according to which "almost all material [was] subject to review". While it was in this time "extremely rare" for corporate management to dictate the political content, "there exist[ed] an unwritten consensus among senior staff of the print sector that determines attitudes to different political players".

Access to print was hindered due to the "big factor" of illiteracy.[68] Due to the legacy of colonialism, and apartheid towards the end of the 20th century, almost half of South Africans were still illiterate. This high rate of illiteracy, together with the low purchasing power of the black population, were some of the reasons the black press struggled, while the political and social impediments of apartheid further hampered the growth of the black press and black ownership "until as recently as 1993".

1994 – but first, the glory days

At the IPI's conference in Cape Town on 14 February 1994, just before the first democratic election in April 1994, Mandela referred to the role of a free press in a democracy:

> A critical, independent and investigative press is the lifeblood of any democracy. The press must be free from state interference. … It must enjoy the protection of the constitution so that it can protect our rights as citizens. It is only such a free press that can temper the appetite of any government to amass power at the expense of the citizen. … It is only such a free press that can have the capacity to relentlessly expose excesses and corruption on the part of the government, state officials and other institutions that hold power.

Referring to this time as the "halcyon days" of the early 1990s,[69] one critic wrote[70]

> [t]here will be few years in South African history with as much significance as 1994, the year the country became a democratic state, held its first elections with universal franchise and elected its first black president. Though the world had begun to warm up to the idea of a new South Africa in the lead up to the election of April 27th 1994 – sanctions had eased and foreign investment had started to trickle in – the doors to the world were well and truly flung open in the heady days after the poll. The country's shift from global pariah to universal icon of hope and reconciliation was as rapid as it was largely peaceful.

It seemed that newspapers could not have big enough print orders to answer to the need of information. *The Star* held a "big party" in Johannesburg in 1994 and printed special T-shirts with the number "275,000" on them – their highest circulation.[71] Circulation was higher than it had ever been "and people were in a mood to celebrate". Newspaper managements and staff "believed they were riding the crest of a wave that would keep on growing and gathering momentum". Unfortunately, the bubble soon burst. Called "transition fatigue" and "reader exhaustion", people "simply grew tired of politics".

This political "switch" had "massive repercussions" for every aspect of South African society, significantly also the media industry. Up to then, "for more than a century", the print industry had "enjoyed a tightly structured fraternity with barriers to entry as high as the barbed wire fences surrounding the country's military establishments". In 1994, 80% of South Africa's population was black, but a "black" press "had not been allowed to develop". Instead, laws "expressly forbade" publications from reporting on black leaders or parties, or even from covering political and social developments "in zones designated as black living areas". With the late arrival of TV, and its state monopoly, there was "little opportunity for the convergence of technologies" or for the amalgamation of multi-media empires that "was in full force" globally during this period. South Africa's isolation meant no substantial foreign investment until 1993, "leaving largely undisturbed a language- and race-based oligopolistic division of the spoils" between two Afrikaans and two English groups.[72]

This situation might have accounted for the fast changes in the following period, also in unexpected areas, such as the severe drop in newspaper circulation after the 1994 elections. Virtually every title, whether urban or rural, experienced significant declines in circulation. The *Cape Argus* lost almost 20% between mid-1994 and the end of 1995; Durban's *Daily News* dropped from just under 100,000 in the first half of 1993 to 75,960 in the last half of 1995, and in Johannesburg *The Star* fell from 216,684 for the first half of 1993 to 165,171 for the last half of 1995. The circulations of dailies fell by 11%, or an average of 134,564 copies, between June 1994 and December 1995, a "huge loss of revenue and a dramatic shift" within the market. And, with the digital revolution "waiting in the wings", these losses were permanent. In 2006, the *Cape Argus* was selling 74,000 compared to about 105,000 ten years before. And this was only the beginning of the digital disruption of the mediasphere, as will be indicated in the next chapter.

But it was not only the quantity of sales that fell; the quality of print media also suffered. In 2002, SANEF commissioned a skills audit as indicator of the state of South African journalism. The results showed, in the words of then SANEF chair and *City Press* editor Mathatha Tsedu, "not a nice picture".[73] Amongst others, the audit found that 82% of South African journalists surveyed showed poor interviewing skills, while a low level of reporting skills in general was common.

During this time, the major trade union for journalists, the South African Union of Journalists (SAUJ, formerly SASJ), collapsed and was finally liquidated in 2005.[74] MWASA and SATU continued, but accounted for only a small proportion of working journalists, also due to major shifts in technology. Both MWASA and SATU primarily looked after employees working on presses. By 2007, no alternative to the SAUJ seemed likely, and "the support and regularisation of professionalism" was left to editors, "who have traditionally and historically been antagonistic to the rights of journeymen journalists in South Africa". From its inception, SANEF experienced various crises of division and disagreement.[75] Another issue was "[r]epeated and public ethical blunders such as cases of plagiarism, biased reportage in support of political factions ... and wide-scale inaccuracy", all of which "embarrassed the industry in the post-1994 period".[76] The recession from 1999 to 2002, together with the bursting of the global internet bubble, led to a huge reduction in staff and budgets, also for remuneration and training, all leading to the so-called juniorisation of the newsroom with the laying-off of experienced staff and responsible work left to inexperienced juniors.

In this scenario, "probably the most important overriding factor" was the need for transformation – indeed, the government's "urgent challenge to the media [was] to transform". But not only skills, circulations and transformation had an impact on journalism. The structure and dynamics of the media sector itself experienced a shift.

While the alternative press consisted of about a dozen foreign-funded anti-apartheid newspapers before 1994, post-1994 the majority had to close because of funding and positioning problems. Only the *Weekly Mail* survived as the *Mail & Guardian*, supported by the UK *Guardian*. The "Big Four" changed dramatically with black and foreign capital entering the market. Both the Argus Group and TML were bought up, while formerly partisan Naspers expanded into "an imposing, multi-platform, multilingual global presence" that was already active in 50 countries in 2007.

In the same year, South Africa was served by 43 daily, weekly and bi-weekly papers, representing a wide range of audiences and interests.[77] Most were owned by the (new) Big Four of 2007: Naspers, with its media division positioned within its subsidiary Media24 since 2000, Johnnic, Caxton, and Independent Newspapers. There were 50 "knock-and-drops" or free sheets, all owned by the major companies as "commercial carriers". In 2004, there were around 100 community-run newspapers, ranging from regular weeklies to sporadic newsletters distributed by hand.[78]

The rise of the tabloids

From 2000 on there was "rapid growth" in the newspaper industry, thanks to new entrants into the market, which meant rising circulations and readerships.[79] Between 2000 and 2005, the total circulation of dailies increased by 38.4%, from 1,13 million per day to 1,57 million – all thanks to the new tabloids. Established papers remained in a "steady downward curve", reflecting global trends due to digital disruption. Still, South Africa had an "unreading" population: In 2000, the country had the second-lowest number of print titles in the world relative to population, with a circulation per capita that was the world's fifth-lowest.[80]

Two interesting phenomena developed post-democracy. One was the rise of the tabloids, the other the emergence of print media in the vernacular. The Media Monitoring Project (MMP) remained sceptical over the tabloids. Their concern was the tabloids' use of "shocking visuals, inflammatory headlines, blatant sexism and xenophobia", while ethical practices were side-lined, resulting in lower-quality news and "an equally low regard for human rights".[81]

Three regional vernacular papers appeared in Zulu in KwaZulu-Natal. The youngest was the daily *Isolezwe*, starting in 2002, which quickly reached daily sales of 97,370 copies. *Ilanga*, founded in 1876, was not only one of the oldest papers in South Africa, but also one of the biggest, selling over 100,000 copies. Also, with a long history of more than 60 years, the weekly *UmAfrika* became more niche orientated, focusing on issues with in-depth features "for the more sophisticated reader".

Another post-1994 trend was the commercialisation of print,[82] especially with the rapid development of contract publishing. By 2005 there were about 350 ABC-audited monthly magazines, totalling about 20 million, many of them contract or custom magazines. This meant a challenge in media ethics in terms of the "grey area" of advertorial content. According to AMPS, 40,4% of the adult population in 2000 read a newspaper at least once a week – low by developed-world standards. This figure, however, is skewed by the large rural population – almost half of the total population – who were beyond the reach of newspaper distribution or who could not afford or read a publication.

Paradoxically, the urban lower range of the market, consisting of blue-collar labourers, gave newspapers a "never foreseen injection". The arrival of tabloids heralded a new dawn for print, with "few developments [regarded as] more significant" post-1994. In 1994, the biggest-selling daily was *The Star*, with 191,322 copies per day. By 2007, the top-selling daily was the *Daily Sun*, selling 450,000 copies a day. The increase in circulation between 2000 and 2005, by 38,4%, was entirely thanks to the *Daily Sun* and *Isolezwe*, which, in 2006, had a daily circulation of 86,232. Excluding these two, the remaining 17 dailies lost 10,8% in circulation.[83] The 2003 Naspers annual report stated that "most sectors of South Africa's magazine and newspaper markets are overtraded".[84]

The *Daily Sun*, founded in 2003, spawned other tabloids such as the *Sunday Sun* and the Afrikaans *Son*, all Naspers-owned, and Independent's *Daily Voice*. These titles, though criticised for their flippant content, built a new, never-existing reading market.

Another factor was the skewed South African economy, as the "entire South African economy was distorted during the colonial and apartheid eras and this affected every single sector".[85] The "massive" wealth of the mining houses, together with the economic isolation during apartheid, "nurtured a process of economic cannibalisation in South Africa". Mining houses "consumed" all other sectors on the stock exchange, from insurance and paper production to beer brewing and pharmaceuticals. By the end of the 1980s, the economy was concentrated "into half a dozen mine-based corporations". The most powerful was Anglo-American, with a controlling share of more than half the companies in the economy, including diamond mines, retailers, manufacturers – and newspaper houses. The two companies that monopolised the English-language newspaper industry until the early 1990s, the Argus Group and SAAN (later TML), were both owned by Anglo-American. This "lack of competition enabled by the concentration of capital", together with the "deep pockets of the media houses' mining benefactors", allowed for "gross inefficiencies to creep into the South African newspaper market". When O'Reilly acquired the Argus Group in 1993, it had only a 4% operating margin on turnover. The standard global benchmark was 15% to 20%. This was "symptomatic of the structural problems". The poor margin was only one indicator of the "scale of the wastage". Independent Newspapers had 14 parliamentary correspondents, representing each of the company's individual titles. Each correspondent "not only [received] a handsome salary – relative to other journalists at the time – but the company was obliged to pay a government-approved tax-free parliamentary allowance which virtually doubled correspondents' packages". The allowance was a "relic" from the days when government shifted annually from Cape Town to Pretoria and "imitated the grant parliamentarians received for the upkeep of a home in each city".

Another factor was the rise of a strong middle class post-1994. Considered "one of the key engines of the country's rapid economic growth rate", it has fuelled a retail, housing and travel boom post-2000, in turn leading to a strong surge in ad spend. Independent's flagship *The Star*, e.g., quadrupled its profitability between 1999 and 2005. A survey showed that, between 2002 and 2004, almost 300,000 black South Africans "climbed up the socio-economic ladder to join the ranks of the middle class"; another 500,000 achieved lower middle-income earnings in the same period. The tabloids' growth was based precisely on the emergence of these so-called "black diamonds".

At the same time, the growth of subscription TV

MultiChoice, as a "pay television, subscriber management company",[86] had by 1996 grown into its own behemoth group of businesses. Besides broadcasting content, it included encryption and access-control services, management and repair of decoders, sales and marketing, billing and fees collection, and technical customer support. By 1996, MultiChoice offered 23 international satellite TV channels and 48 audio channels on its subscription service, called DStv (Digital Satellite Television). Two years later, in 1998, MultiChoice had 2,7 million subscribers in 43 countries, 31 of which were African countries.

By 2000, M-Net was described as part of the international subscription TV group Nethold, active in 59 countries in Europe, Africa and the Middle East.[87] It did not have a public service mandate and did "little to alter its positioning within the post-apartheid milieu". Originally a "service division" of M-Net, it was from this foundation that MultiChoice started operating as a separate company, although still providing subscription management for M-Net. After consolidating the company's subscription TV business into the Network Holding Group, as holding company for the whole of the "M" family, it included at the time M-Net, M-WEB, MTN (Mobile Telephone Network) and DStv, as well as a number of engineering and electronic manufacturing companies.

Regarding free-to-air services, the first commercial licence was awarded to e-TV in 1998. It was 80% owned by a black empowerment consortium in an equity partnership with Time-Warner, which had 20%. Technologically, it was the most sophisticated channel on the African continent, with 100% digital broadcasting, although "[v]ery little" local programming content. In 2000, local programming was approximately 2%, excluding news, with "most of the programming" in English. e-TV did not require a subscription or decoder, but its footprint "was curtailed" to the "heavily populated urban areas". Unless one had a DStv subscription via MultiChoice, it could not be received in rural areas.

The technology factor

Another factor with an impact in this transition period was computer technology, already beginning in the 1980s. The rapid evolution of printing technology always had "fundamental impacts" on the structure and functioning of societies.[88] For the media industry it meant that desktop-publishing phased out hot-lead typesetting and the "expensive editorial systems". This was also a "key element" in South Africa's alternative press, as it now was possible to publish a newspaper at one third of the normal costs. Indeed, it "brought newspaper publishing within the budgets of communities around the country".[89] Within a few months, an alternative weekly press had mushroomed, all based on the *Weekly Mail*'s production techniques. The digital revolution led to "an industry-wide shift in technology" by 1996/1997, with "massive repercussions" for the newspaper industry. It also meant traditional typographical tasks were phased out.[90] Equally, it transformed an "old-fashioned, patriarchal industry". Or, as an anonymous Independent Newspaper manager said in 2005: "When someone was promoted, the joke was you would ask 'Who died?'" A new era dawned as "[t]he days of the old press lords, where proprietors in the mould of Lord Beaverbrook owned and manipulated newspapers as an amusing pastime, were gone".[91] Newspapers were now "a big, bottom-line, global business":[92]

> For years South African newspapers had been protected. The English-language press had enjoyed a cosy relationship with the major mining group Anglo-American while the Afrikaans press, principally Naspers and Perskor, had been created as an instrument of the volk and had never been intended to be a business. Suddenly, in the early 1990s, as the country itself crawled out of apartheid isolation, the South African mainstream press entered a new realm. Virtually overnight, it became a large, commercial enterprise in which the rapid evolution of technology was a common and powerful force.

Restructuring of print

While the pre-1994 printscape was dominated by the "Big Four", together with some smaller print concerns, Naspers also owned M-Net,[93] and the whole sector was "tightly managed, with closely regulated advertising, printing and distribution arrangements". Between the media conglomerates of the apartheid era and other South African capital interests, "complex relationships existed". When the Argus Group restructured in 1993 via "unbundling" – meaning selling off "constituent parts of the company" – it "was punted as indicating a commitment to black empowerment". First, 52% of the largest daily targeted at black readers, the *Sowetan*, was sold to black-owned Corporate Africa. Sanlam, described as "Afrikaner-owned insurance and financial conglomerate", held 17% of Corporate Africa in September 1996, and Corporate Africa owned 75% of NAIL. Argus retained 25%, as well as the printing, advertising and management contracts. By the second half of 1998, black shareholders and directors owned 10% of the NAIL equity, with public shares making up a further 18%. The rest of the shareholding was divided between "traditionally white insurance and investment companies". This arrangement was

> reminiscent of the centralised action/power and structure/determination processes of the white-owned press under apartheid which has re-emerged in relationships between black-managed newspapers, their holding companies, and emergent black-dominated capital.

In 1994, the *Sowetan*, now owned by NAIL, acquired the last of the alternative papers from the 1980s, namely *New Nation*, a "union-supporting weekly with socialist tendencies". It was donor-funded from its founding in 1986 until 1994. After 1994, the paper was unable to get sufficient advertising and was shut down shortly after its takeover.

When, in 1994, South Africa was "reopened" to foreign investment and Irish-based Independent bought 31% of Argus from Anglo-American in January of that year, increasing it to 58% in 1995, 75% by 1999 and a 100% by the end of that year, it was the largest company in O'Reilly's international stable. O'Reilly listed the company separately on the JSE as Independent Newspapers. This was described as the "first phase" of the restructuring of South Africa's print media.

The second phase began in April 1994, when Independent purchased TML's shareholdings in companies previously owned by Argus, thereby "securing a majority hold over much of the English-language print media". Only the sale of *The Sowetan* and the consequent formation of NAIL were "an unbundling exercise in the strict sense".

The third phase was the NEC deal in late 1996, signalling "a pivotal advance towards the interpenetration of black and white dominated fractions of capital". In early 1994, Anglo-American/JCI decided on unbundling, following ANC demands for blacks to play a greater role. The unbundled JCI had direct and indirect interests in the CNA chain, the recording company Gallo, subscription TV MultiChoice and Times Media. NEC, in 1994 a "loose association" of smaller businesses and unions, was joined by NAIL after January 1996. The NEC takeover of Johnnic was the biggest cash deal in South African history. Within two years after the 1994 elections, black-dominated capital controlled 10% of the JSE, "a rate of accumulation far greater than that of previously disadvantaged Afrikaner capital growth at any time during apartheid".

Phase 4 of the print media transformation was how, against "all predictions", NP-supporting Afrikaans media underwent "a sea-change during the early 1990s". In 1996/1997, Naspers formed new firms and sold shares to companies owned by black business. Its managing director announced the group was "selling the family silver" to black interest groups for moral and practical reasons. As said, of *City Press*, 51% was sold to black investment groups. Also, Perskor's restructuring was described as "instructive". In 1996, Perskor owned a number of profitable magazines, a stake in M-Net, *The Citizen* and half a stake in *Rapport*. KTI, a large ANC-supported NGO, became a joint controlling shareholder of Perskor, but in 1998 the two "parted company". The "new-found libertarianism" amongst Naspers and Perskor resulted in some "unexpected shifts of political allegiance during the four phase transitional period". *Die Burger*, "mother of Afrikaner Nationalism", editorially supported the "small liberal" Democratic Party (DP) while criticising the NP during the 1994 elections, and – "what would have been a heresy and politico-economic suicide prior to 1994, even donated funds to the DP, ANC and NP election campaigns".[94]

The pre-1994 "Big Four" all had "a range of stakes in apartheid, notwithstanding limited contradictions that derived from differing ownership interests, cultural traditions and institutional rationales".[95] While the two English groups "were ultimately sourced to mega-corporation Anglo-American", Naspers and Perskor "were tied to Afrikaner financial capital". They formed "interlocking companies and pyramid structures" and

> there was a form of horizontal integration of the newspaper sector with the oligopolistic and protectionist pulp and paper industry on the one side, and ownership of printing and distribution facilities on the other. Worse, there was very little direct competition between the groups – an oligopoly existed even to the extent of a legal agreement specifying that Caxton (at the time, part-Argus owned) would not enter the sold-newspaper business and, for its part, the Argus group would not compete in the free-sheet or magazine market.

The initial foreign ownership of 35% of the Argus Group, rising to 58% in 1995, included gaining full control of the *Cape Times*, the *Natal Mercury* and the *Pretoria News*, "papers that until then were not wholly owned".[96] In April 1999, O'Reilly bought out the rest and de-listed the company in South Africa. In terms of concentration, this foreign investment was not a positive development. After O'Reilly, other "fresh foreign ownership" was introduced, "again in the higher end of the market", namely the UK-based Pearson PLC, which bought half of *Business Day* and the *Financial Mail* from TML. Together with TML, they created an internet publishing operation called I-Net Bridge. The foreign investment trend was also clear when 62% of the *Mail & Guardian* was bought by the UK *Guardian* in March 1998, "a move that undoubtedly prevented the closure of the loss-making South African paper".

Here comes … the internet

The internet "arrived" as a new medium in the 1999 elections, when old media "were routinely trounced by the interactivity, speed, breadth and depth of online coverage". Still, in terms of transformation of race and/or class ownership, the impact was minimal compared with TML and Pearson's I-Net Bridge. But then Naspers "became a force" with its 24.com, which merged with its internet service provider M-Web in 1999. At the time, Naspers also part-owned the global media company OpenTV, as well as international media technology Mindport. The internet service provider (ISP) business became a "hotly-contested terrain" when Telkom entered the market, claiming monopoly rights for its Intekom offshoot against private contenders.[97] With the issue "simmer[ing]", there was already a phase of rapid mergers and take-overs with Naspers's M-Web "leading the way". Still, the internet "remained largely white-owned", although "worth noting" was that government unbundled the signal provider Sentech from the SABC. By 1999, Sentech announced its intention to launch educational and health TV channels.

The honeymoon over

Despite constitutionally entrenched guarantees of press freedom, the relationship between media and government in South Africa became increasingly conflicted after the initial "honeymoon period", as was recorded by Jacobs as early as in 1999,[98] Fourie in 2002,[99] Hadland in 2007,[100] and Louw[101] and Berger[102] in 2009. Fourie even drew parallels between the apartheid state and the ANC regarding the latter's intolerance of criticism.

A significant trend in the post-1994 era was the "realignment" in the relationship between media and state.[103] It was seen as an "inevitable development", although in retrospect it was clear that both sides "struggled to come to terms with their new roles and responsibilities", leading to "heightened tension" between the ANC and the media. The specific "points of conflict" were that, at best, the ANC's relationship with the press had been "distant and neurotically suspicious", and "at worst, pathologically hostile".[104] There was also the State's "growing willingness" to interfere in various ways, its reluctance to reform legislation affecting the media, its own entry into "mass newsletter publishing" and the establishment of a variety of "clientelist-type bonds" between government and the "nascent community media sector".

The media also faced the challenge, "both to and within" itself, to "revisit its traditional, liberal role of Fourth Estate watchdog in favour of a more conciliatory, less adversarial voice".[105] This "corresponded" with "an increasingly cosy relationship between majority party political leaders and media owners". The changes in the post-1994 period can be summed up as journalistic professionalisation, issues regarding state-media relations, the proximity of the media to the political system, and the structure of the market.

Outright clashes

The antagonism between government and media concerned apartheid-era legislation. This was "high on the agenda" of several "important discussions" between editors and "high state officials", including president Thabo Mbeki.[106] More than one decade later there was still no resolution on these issues, and the State continued to use these laws to limit media access to information and prevent publication of what was deemed sensitive content. A number of meetings between government and editors and managers were held from 1999, with both sides "plagued" by mutual antagonism and "a possible breakdown in communication".[107] This led to the March 2001 SANEF meeting with Mbeki to discuss the "sense of disengagement". Later that year, the so-called "Sun City Summit" was held under the title, "The role of the media in a changing society". SANEF chair Mathatha Tsedu stated that the "present level of mistrust and animosity has gone beyond a tolerable and acceptable point". While acceding that there was "too much shallowness, superficiality and unprofessionalism" in the media, government was also "communicating inadequately, not properly articulating policies and resorting too easily to media bashing when failures were reported".[108] A plan to establish a Presidential Press Corps (PPC) in 2003 to improve communication between the media and the presidency never came to fruition. By mid-2006, SANEF noted "it had probably died".

Other "points of conflict" included the Human Rights Commission's (HRC) subpoenas to editors in its inquest into racism in the media in 2000, "bitter ANC reaction" to "speculation" about the Aids-related death of presidential spokesperson Parks Mankahlana, also in 2000, a court action for defamation brought against the *Mail & Guardian* by minister Jeff Radebe in 2001, and the ANC's defensiveness over criticism of Mbeki's Aids denialism and his Zimbabwe policy.[109] These "flashpoints" were regarded as "systematic hostility". The State's "lack of effort" to deal with it through professionalised communication was "noteworthy". The core of the clash was the dilemma over the media's role in a democracy:[110]

> The ANC prefers the political sphere to remain distinct and privileged, reported on by a media from the sidelines and, at the same time, to claim an authentic, unmediated relationship with what it variously calls the people, the masses, or the majority. The media are seen as unnecessary to this relationship and are unwelcome to it.

It boiled down to government "consistently" expressing its "exasperation and frustration with the mainstream media and its role in the post-apartheid, democratic order".[111] The launch in mid-2005 of *Vuk'uzenzele*, a bi-monthly magazine produced by the GCIS with a circulation of 1,1 million (increasing to 2 million for the SONA), did not come as a surprise. With an annual budget of R20 million,[112] it was "perhaps the eventual realisation of the ANC's hopes in the early 1990s for a newspaper of its own"[113] – although it was funded by government. The publication was available from GCIS offices across the country, also online and as an app, with Twitter and Facebook accounts and in all eleven official languages.[114]

The ANC also had an online mouthpiece, *ANC Today*.[115] In 2001, Smuts Ngonyama, head of the presidency, wrote about the "tricky" relationship between government and the media:[116]

> One aspect of the media's role which has proven difficult to effectively debate, not surprisingly given the country's history, is the relationship between the media and the government and the ruling party. Some people view this as a simple choice for

the media: either be a watchdog keeping a beady eye on the ruling party or a lapdog which happily swallows anything the ANC might dish up. Neither dog is particularly desirable. What South Africa needs is a truly critical media. A truly critical media is not one which opposes the government at every turn ... a 'critical media' is a media which thinks.

The debate in the post-1994 years continued to "circle" around what the role of the media should be in a democracy.[117] The year 1997 "will probably be regarded as the year of revolutionary changes in the country's media" as the debate about how the legacy of apartheid could "urgently be shaken off" was refocused on what the "proper" role of the media within a democracy should be. The frustrations were shared by "dozens of government and ANC statements" in this period.[118] Some stated:

- Mere declarations of media freedoms on their own are not enough, but must be "underpinned by an equitable distribution of media resources, development programmes and a deliberate effort to engender a culture of open debate. ... Ownership of media resources, production facilities and distribution outlets shall be subject to anti-monopoly, anti-trust and merger legislation", as was formulated in the ANC's *Ready to Govern* policy guidelines adopted at its National Conference in 1992;

- That mass media institutions were lagging behind other sectors in transforming themselves to suit the new South African environment ... "it is precisely because we need a diversity of ideas that we need diversity of ownership". The principle extends both to the number of institutions that are able to publish and broadcast, and to the ownership structure of those individual institutions, as formulated by Tokyo Sexwale, Gauteng Premier, in an article entitled "SA needs a diversity of media ownership" in the ANC journal *Mayibuye* 6(6), in October 1995;

- That, to "some extent", the media have transformed. The SABC was "now free of government control"; major changes in ownership have taken place and the media industry was starting to deal "seriously" with shortcomings regarding skills development and black advancement. But "[h]uge strides" were needed regarding equality and in building the diversity and depth that a developing society needed, as formulated in *The Role of the Media Under Apartheid* in the ANC submission on Media to the TRC in September 1997;

- In the words of president Mbeki on World Press Freedom Day in 2001: None "of us [can] remain content while press freedom in its fullest sense remains in practice something enjoyed mainly by an elite – urban rather than rural, rich rather than poor, industrialised rather than developing";

- That ultimately, there is a need to "continually engage" with the media on their "attitude towards the democratic movement and government" – "difficult though this may be". In 2002, the ANC said: "As we challenge the media on its relationship with the progressive movement, care should be exercised that criticism of the media and its particular behaviour should not lead to a situation in which the ANC is perceived as opposed to the freedom of the media in general ... The ANC must put media reform on the political agenda. This should be aimed at dealing with anti-democratic tendencies within the media system," as written in "Media in a Democratic South Africa" in the ANC magazine *Umrabulo*, no. 16, in August 2002.

It was clear that the ANC government "expressed a particular interest" in a range of possible interventions in print media. The state's antagonism was grounded in its demand for a media that is "more efficient at delivering on the state's agenda", whereas the print media believed it must retain an oppositional role. The ANC's "urgency" stemmed from the "gradual concentration of power within the state executive and its consequent anxiety to direct the polity", something "widely noted by academics and authors". One academic, for instance, wrote that "[f]reedom of speech is a meaningless right if group pressure demands conformity".[119]

1996, the Constitution, and media freedom entrenched

For the first time in the existence of the geo-political region that would become South Africa, media freedom was constitutionally protected. After the acceptance of the new Constitution in 1996, media freedom was subject to and protected by the Constitution's Bill of Rights. Article 16, as referred to in Chapter 2, entrenched media freedom, including it being subject to certain responsibilities. Media freedom was now also protected by the South African Press Code (PCSA), the Broadcast Complaints Commission of South Africa (BCCSA), as well as individual media companies' respective ethical codes.

Under this newfound freedom, cognition also had to be taken of the grey area of ethics – namely what might be *legal*, but *unethical* – a reality leading to the perception by the public that "the media" is only after sensation and profit.[120] It should be added that this was and is due to a general population-wide low media literacy, the result of the country's totalitarian past, as the citizens did not understand their media rights, nor that their freedom is closely linked to media freedom.

With the introduction of South Africa's liberal democratic Constitution in 1996, it was "commonly assumed" that a new era lay ahead and that freedom of the press (or the media), freedom of association, freedom of access to information and freedom of speech were all enshrined within the Constitution's Bill of Rights, "fortifying" the media's classic liberal democratic Fourth Estate function.[121] It was accepted that the media would no longer be curtailed and circumscribed by an authoritarian regime, and that draconian laws would no longer "determine what could be printed in the nation's newspapers and what could not". Also, key High Court judgments on press freedom "eased once onerous libel and defamation laws". It seemed as if South Africa "now had a framework in place that would make a cast-iron Liberal model for its media system inevitable". This never-before-experienced media freedom now formed the basis for the about 600 print media titles in South Africa, compared to the 20 that existed in 1910. Still, despite the entrenchment of media freedom in the new Constitution, it seems media leaders expected more. As *Sunday Times* editor Ken Owen recalled: South Africa's constitution-makers "baulked at entrenching free speech or giving it anything like the weight which it enjoys under the First Amendment of the American Constitution".[122] The "constitution makers" seemingly did not trust the newspapers or the idea of free speech,

> so they brushed aside the modest request of the Conference of Editors [the mainly white English and Afrikaans editors] for full entrenchment of free speech, and instead assigned to that right a lesser status and a lesser protection than they gave to other rights. In effect, they put into the hands of legislators and judges the power to decide how much freedom would be 'reasonable' in the new democracy ... This

reluctance to relinquish control of discourse was, given the centrality of free speech to both democracy and to the wider search for truth, revealingly ominous.

Indeed, many loopholes existed and countertendencies emerged. Apartheid-era legislation, such as the 1968 Armaments Development and Production Act and the 1982 Protection of Information Act, containing deeply anti-press restrictions, have been used by the state repeatedly in the new democratic era.[123] Some of these "archaic" laws demand the revelation of sources' identities, or prevent newspapers from publishing articles. These were some of the measures that SANEF has campaigned against since its founding, but it has yet to be successful.

In 1998, for instance, under Section 205 of the apartheid era's Criminal Procedure Act of 1977, photographers were expected to testify as state witnesses in a case about the murder of gang leader Rashaad Staggie.[124] A delegation from SANEF met with then justice minister Dullah Omar and safety and security minister Sydney Mufamadi about the "'old laws' problem". An interim proposal was drawn up. Ironically, just days after the meeting, three Cape Town editors were issued with subpoenas in the Staggie case. They publicly refused to cooperate.

In 1999, a "Record of Understanding" was signed between SANEF, Omar, Mufamadi and the National Director of Public Prosecutions, Bulelani Ngcuka.[125] The need "to continue to negotiate" on Section 205 was included, and the final agreement was signed on World Press Freedom Day on 3 May 2000. Despite this undertaking, various newspapers were raided without warning by the authorities looking for information on the Staggie case. Forty editors protested outside the Cape High Court in June 2001, when Arrie Rossouw, editor of *Die Burger*, appeared with regard to his application for the withdrawal of a search warrant.

The solidarity between previously "opponents" and the deep schisms that existed between English and Afrikaans media during apartheid was illustrated by the fact that one of the "outstanding characteristics" of post-apartheid media was how newspapers from previously opposite sides of the political spectrum were joining voices to protest against government's restriction of press freedom.[126] With regard to Section 205, SANEF "repeatedly argued that journalists should not be put in the role of police informers nor do police work, because this damaged their ability to gather information in the public interest".[127]

The TRC and the media

In 1997, the TRC also led hearings on the media's role during the apartheid years.[128] While "most people probably thought that the Afrikaans press would attract the main attention of the TRC" because of its support of apartheid, a "ruckus broke out" about the role of the English language press.[129] Afrikaans media companies did not support the idea that they should "confess" their role during apartheid to the TRC, "where gross and horrifying testimony" was heard about illegal security operations, especially the Vlakplaas horrors. The "mainly white" English press held two points of view. One was expressed by former editor Rex Gibson, namely that "journalists who fought apartheid have nothing to apologise for at the TRC". The other was that the English press should express "regret for its failures and shortcomings in the sphere of human rights during the apartheid era", in the words of *The Sunday Independent* editor John Battersby. The Independent/Times Media group submitted voluntary submissions. Black journalists "almost unanimously" agreed that the English press should give submissions to the TRC. Although the white English press had opposed apartheid, "not enough" had been done about the "humiliation, pain and suffering of black journalists, and the forgetful minds of white bosses during the apartheid era".

Anti-media statutes still 'on the books'

In April 1999, SANEF contracted the Wits Centre for Applied Legal Studies to compile a list of anti-media statutes that were still "on the books".[130] It was completed by May 2000, after which the justice ministry referred the document to the Law Commission for proposals. Yet, by early 2007, no progress had been reported.[131] Section 205, in fact, had been invoked several times, and other laws, such as the National Key Points Act, had been used to block journalists' access to information.[132] Between 2000 and 2006, SANEF made several representations to parliament, issuing statements expressing criticism of various legislation containing anti-press measures. These included the Broadcast Amendment Bill, the Anti-Terrorism Bill, the Convergence Bill, the Interception of Electronic Communications Bill and the Film and Publications Amendment Bill.

How pliable the law was, was again seen in January 2007, for instance, when the Gauteng government announced that reporters were barred from contacting local police stations directly (a normal daily procedure) and had to work through the police's head office. Raymond Louw, ex-editor, media freedom advocate and, at the time, deputy chair of the South African branch of MISA, said it showed "how fast the government is creating an information-starved state".[133] By 2007, the limitations on press freedom "[weren't] about political party partisanship or banning an opposition point of view", but rather "classical liberal dilemmas about the trade-off, for instance, between national security and access to information".[134]

In 2005, Joel Netshitenzhe, then head of GCIS, said at the conference on "Transformation of the Media in a Society in Transition" that, although "access to information is the lifeblood of democracy",

> you can't have media freedom in a vibrant democracy if there is a situation of conglomeration and homogenisation of news. You can't have media freedom where there is no diversity of ownership. This means the poor are not just consumers but producers of news. You can't have media freedom if commercial pressures limit editors' use of content or where editors are held on a leash to satisfy the dictates of advertisers. ... Freedom is not an amorphous concept without values. ... Is it possible where the media is an opium to dull the senses and connives in the destruction of the very values that make media freedom possible? Media freedom should add value to the national endeavour, not support conspicuous consumption, greed and impel the people to live above their means.

The paradoxes of 'pre-liberation' and 'post-apartheid'

In 2001, the new-found media freedom consisted of "two paradoxes", described as "Pre-Liberation" and "Post-Apartheid".[135] Under apartheid, censorship involved a "massive system of thought control" by a "national minority of whites and their allies" over a "numerically superior and largely hostile population". There were a number of "sub-plots". One was the need to suppress knowledge "of the nature and scale of repression" to sustain apartheid; another the inhibition of ideas and information that "might counter the customary view of the differences between the groups"; and yet another "a desire to minimise understanding of non-racial opposition to apartheid". The need for censorship was identical to that of any authoritarian regime in its desire "for conformity, orthodoxy, mass values and suppression of the enquiring mind". By the mid-1980s, police state legislation accumulated in the Internal Security Act, which "allow[ed] the authorities to control individuals and organisations, proscribe publications and, in effect, declare war on the anti-apartheid movement by regulating peaceful expression". Section 205 of the Criminal Procedure Act of 1977 was also still used to force journalists to disclose sources. But it was particularly the law on defamation that was "a major stumbling block" for media freedom. *Vrye Weekblad* can be regarded as "perhaps the most famous case", where the paper was forced to close after publishing allegations about Lothar Neethling allegedly supplying poison to "police death squads". The TRC found in favour of the paper and its editor, Max du Preez, but this, of course, was too late. The threat of censorship in the latter years of apartheid became "increasingly physical". By the end of the 1980s,

> informal, extra-legal low intensity conflict provoked by the securocrats who ran South Africa during that decade had developed into the most important facet of the censorship system and the one that had the potential to become the most deeply woven into the fabric of society.

Although it was realised that the most important purpose of the states of emergency in this era was to influence the media, and thereby control "perceptions of the struggle", technological advances in the 1980s made the gathering and dissemination of information possible in different ways. Ultimately, the government "lost the battle" and, to a large, "although immeasurable, degree", this was achieved through the documentation efforts of civil rights campaigners. The second half of the 1990s can be regarded as "one of the most tolerant" in history, built on the Bill of Rights, as well as the Promotion of Access to Information Act (PAIA) and the Archives Act. But the paradox lay in the fact that their impact had been "subverted by political forces operating openly within a liberal democracy". By then, it was argued that much would depend upon the PAIA. Bizarrely, it was "subject to secrecy in its drafting as a Bill". This Act would give "effect to both vertical and horizontal rights" through the establishment of the right of access to any information held by the state or by another person, although, for the latter only, "when required for the exercise or protection of other rights". It not only had to foster a culture of transparency and accountability, but also to "guard human rights while protecting privacy, commercial confidentiality and good governance". It was also hoped that media freedom would be improved with the repeal of the Newspaper and Imprint Registration Act of 1971. In the past, this act thwarted the founding of "opposition" papers to both the left and the right through bureaucracy and high registration fees.

However, other publications were still in jeopardy, as the Film and Publications Act of 1996 had as objective to regulate certain publications through a Board and a Review Board – a structure that was "alarmingly reminiscent of censorship bureaucracy of the apartheid years". It was also feared that it could be interpreted in such a way as to restrict the "ability of commentators to reflect the true nature of South African society", including "undesirable elements", or that "unscrupulous authorities could use this provision to clamp down on straightforward robust speech".

Although the poet Breyten Breytenbach wrote in 1993 already that "only a fool will pretend to understand comprehensively what South Africa is really about, or be objective or far-sighted to glimpse its future course", other commentators were "more optimistic". It was stated that "whatever else it may be", South Africa as society had "a very strong dissident tradition", although others thought dissent was still "a thing to be whispered behind cupped hands" using "much the same tones as … in the old South Africa", as dissenters were treated as "counter-revolutionaries".

In 2001, one commentator argued that the future of media freedom and freedom of expression "will depend upon the newly acquired statutes that have yet to be interpreted by the courts". However, under the second presidency "the atmosphere shifted to one of paranoia", with "[t]he idea of shooting the bearer of bad tidings" still "deeply entrenched" in South Africa's culture and psyche. Examples of "explicit and implicit" suppression of information and expression "abounded". One was the "infamous *Sarafina* affair, an expensive and dubious exercise in AIDS education" by the department of health in 1996. It was said that "[d]emocratically based governments that succeed authoritarian regimes often find a residue of repressive legislation useful to them". Another example was the so notorious Section 205 of the Criminal Procedure Act. Increasing crime, including gangsterism, in 2001 resulted in the fact that "[m]any South Africans cannot be described as true citizens, but live in areas dominated by clientelism and patrimony in which sectional loyalty is a prerequisite for material improvement". Under such conditions, "individual freedoms do not flourish" and there can "be little doubt that the circulation of opinion in South Africa is badly affected by political correctness". During Mandela's presidency there was an "understandable tendency to dwell on legislative achievement", but under Mbeki's, there was "a growing realisation that a culture of political intolerance and paranoia and a tendency towards a lack of transparency" also severely threatened "hard won academic rights". Another commentator saw the "first warning signs" in 2002, when the ANC government started to re-enact the apartheid government's attitudes to media freedom.[136]

Media diversity and media freedom

The MDDA was established in 2002, following discussions since 1991, and especially following the appointment of the Comtask in 1996.[137] Among its recommendations was "the very specific call for the establishment of a structure that would support diversity" in the media. It was an independent, statutory body funded by government, the media industry and donors, and had to assist with the development of community media and promote media diversity. The MDDA Act was accepted in 2002, with its slogan "access to diversified media for all".[138] The agency had four objectives and four methods of intervention. The objectives were to encourage

- ownership and control of, and access to, media by historically disadvantaged indigenous language and cultural groups;
- the channelling of resources to community and small commercial media;
- human resource development and capacity building in the media industry, especially among the historically disadvantaged; and
- research regarding media development and diversity.[139]

By the end of 2004, the MDDA had only just commenced its work, and on a limited budget. It had such a small impact that, by 2007, no one could "honestly claim" that it had made a "deep impression" on mainstream media. According to its annual report, it had disbursed close to R20 million by March 2006, but conceded "it is too soon to judge the broader impact" as this could not be measured by the number of grants or the fact that grant funds had been committed.[140] The "real measure" would be whether projects supported by the MDDA continued to thrive "years after support has been concluded".

This government agency, unfortunately, also fell victim to mismanagement and corruption. In 2017 it was reported that the official who "blew the lid off massive mismanagement" at the MDDA, Donald Liphoko, was no longer at the entity.[141] His secondment to the MDDA as acting CEO was rescinded by the then communications minister, Ayanda Dlodlo. Seconded in May 2017, his "relationship with the board was fraught, culminating in a dramatic meeting of the portfolio committee on communications" in August that year, where "much of the blame for the agency's woes" were put on Liphoko. He, in turn, blamed the MDDA board for mismanagement, stating that workers were being intimidated. The portfolio committee rejected the MDDA board's presentation. Three days later, Liphoko reported a "very unusual event" at his house on which he did not expand. In September, at a next portfolio committee meeting, it was said that the relationship between Liphoko and the board was "non-existent". Liphoko had cancelled "irregular contracts" – the reason why the board tried to fire him. He also indicated not only intimidation, but attempts to lock him out of his office and illegally suspending him. It was said that the MDDA was "in a total state of dysfunction" and a parliamentary inquiry was called. At the time, the MDDA had a deficit of almost R13 million, irregular expenditure stood at R6,7 million and the auditor-general found that the accounting office did not have sufficient monitoring and oversight controls, nor had "senior management adequate controls of performance and compliance". The MDDA's initial promise of "diversified media to all" was described as a "rotten agency".[142] The board was also inquorate for some time, with the chairperson having "a track record of terrorising everybody at the MDDA". The portfolio committee was asked to intervene in the same way as was done at the SABC in 2016, which in the meantime had deteriorated into yet another "Master's Voice", and a parliamentary inquiry led to an ad hoc committee investigating the SABC board.

In December 2017, the MDDA was one of the topics at the ANC's Nasrec conference, when William Baloyi was appointed as its new acting CEO while the recruitment of a permanent CEO was under way.[143] After the conference, NEC member and chief whip Jackson Mthembu reported on the ANC's subcommittee on communications and "the battle of ideas", speaking about the concerns regarding the MDDA's capacity to assist community media and saying that the agency had "all sorts of problems, including management".

And another stalwart biting the dust

In 2002, the SAUJ, which had replaced SASJ, folded, but there was "some staff representation" at most media houses in forums like pension fund trustee committees, although journalists seldom participated "at a strategically significant level".[144] At the then Johncom, a staff association took over from the SAUJ, which lost its majority membership at the company some time before it went into liquidation. Journalistic organisation was practically non-existent in all companies in 2007, and "organising journalists was also more difficult in some companies than in others". The SAUJ, e.g., never succeeded in unionising at Naspers, later Media24, where there was "an historic hostility to unions". Membership declined after 1994, and dwindling subscriptions fell "short of the union's day-to-day costs". Moving from an oppressive system to a democratic, constitutional state led to the irony that journalists did not feel the need to belong to a trade union anymore, although journalists joined other unions, such as MWASA, when the SAUJ collapsed. By 2007 it was estimated that 5% or fewer of working journalists were unionised.

Another organisation representing journalists and the media now was PMASA, previously the NPU, which was established in 1882.[145] In 1998, its membership included major urban, daily, weekly and Sunday newspapers under the NPU subsection, all the major consumer magazines under the MPA subsection, a large number of local newspapers under the Community Press Association subsection, and specialist, trade and technical publications under the Specialist Press Association subsection. PMASA played "a significant role" in the establishment of other press bodies, such as the Audit Bureau of Circulations (ABC), the Advertising Standards Authority (ASA) and the PCSA. All major newspapers and magazines were members of the PMASA, which had a membership of 509 in 1996. Besides SANEF, which was also founded in 1996, MWASA, SATU, the Foreign Correspondents' Association, the Black Editors' Forum, the Association of Democratic Journalists, the South African Association of Industrial Editors, the South African Printing and Allied Industries Federation and various press clubs in the larger centres still existed in 1998, before the era of digitalisation disrupted all these bodies and new ones started to form.

'Instrumentalism'

Besides the ever-present serious matter of self-censorship, the matter of "instrumentalism" remained an issue.[146] While there was a "considerable degree of political instrumentalism" post-1994, it was also the case in the apartheid era. The Afrikaans press was unashamedly an "instrument" for pro-Afrikaner nationalism – indeed, "a living monument to instrumentalism in the pre-1994 era".

Senior journalists have "repeatedly got themselves into difficulty" over this issue.[147] Probably the "most glaring example" was one in 2003, when an article was published in *City Press* by journalist Ranjeni Munusamy. Later the subject of a judicial enquiry, known as the Hefer Commission, it was found to have been planted by supporters of then deputy president Zuma. It was aimed at discrediting Bulelani Ngcuka, director-general of prosecutions, who was preparing a probe into allegedly corrupt activities by Zuma. The "abusive allegations" made against Ngcuka, including that he was a spy for the apartheid government – "a permanently damning allegation in the South African context" – brought "broad disgrace on the profession".[148]

SANEF and self-regulation

Since the forming of SANEF in 1996, together with its press code, the self-regulatory system of South African journalism not only became stronger, but was worked at continuously. Although self-regulating, South African journalism was underpinned by an ethical framework, "the principles of which are commonly adhered to in day-to-day practice".[149] Many titles also had their own individual ethics codes, some with an internal ombud. Those that were members all resorted under the PCSA and its ombud, the latter also established in 1996.[150] The system was revised constantly,[151] especially to prevent government from interfering with legislation.

However, after 1994 there was a "marked deterioration in journalists' understanding and implementation of ethical guidelines".[152] Inaccurate reporting grew "from being an irritation" to the ombud in 1999 to "constituting the majority of his work by 2004".[153]

In 2005, the ombud received 200 complaints, up by 26% over the previous year and constituting the highest number of complaints received until then.[154] There were also allegations of plagiarism concerning several senior journalists, including columnist Darrell Bristow-Bovey, editor Cynthia Vongai and authors William Mervin Gumede and Antjie Krog. By 2004 it had reached such "crisis proportions" that SANEF made an appeal to all journalists urging them to address this problem.

Although the ombud system means self-regulation, its authority and scope "have been challenged from a number of quarters and has therefore come under review".[155] At the end of 2006, when the first ombud, Ed Linnington, had to retire, SANEF established a sub-committee to review its functioning and role. The emergence of tabloid journalism "caught the self-regulator short repeatedly", with "several titles disrespect[ing] the office altogether".

Transformation and an HRC consternation

By 2004, several conferences on the transformation of the South African media had been held. A series, the International Seminars on the Political Economy of the Southern African Media, was held in 1996, 2000 and 2002.[156]

At the end of the 2000 seminar, Rhodes journalism Professor Guy Berger suggested that, "in response to the consternation caused by the utterly flawed research on racism in the media" commissioned by the HRC, a new approach to media research should be considered. The research by Claudia Braude and the MMP for the HRC "gave a lot of people an excuse to avoid dealing with the real issue of racism" and discredited the HRC inquiry severely.

The situation translated into "a looming boycott" by many journalists of the hearings, which in turn led to subpoenas being issued to media that had been named in the research. To undo the damage, it was suggested that researchers needed to take "extra special care to produce quality research".

A new PCSA - facing a new onslaught

Despite the consternation regarding the HRC media inquiry, the media themselves started to get their house in order regarding self-regulation – similar to what had been done ever since the first threats of government control after the first inquiries into the press in the 1950s, leading to the first Press Board in 1962.

The new PCSA was established on 1 August 2007, although the history of self-regulation "officially goes back to the early 1960s".[157] The system changed "repeatedly" over the decades, with the new PCSA replacing the Press Ombud's Office in 2007. The new PCSA would be appointed for five years, and the system would be "adjusted in response to social and political change, both in South Africa and elsewhere". Some changes were negative, as when the PCSA "in a previous incarnation" tightened sanctions in response to pressure from the apartheid government. Others, however, were positive, such as when, in 1997, the code and constitution were changed in line with the new SA Constitution.

The PCSA was "a self-regulatory mechanism to provide impartial, expeditious and cost-effective arbitration to settle complaints" about the editorial content of newspapers and magazines.[158] It consisted of six press and six public representatives, chaired by a press representative and with a public representative as deputy chair. The members' five-year terms could be extended at the end of that term,[159] and the body was funded by press organisations represented in the PCSA.

But, at the ANC's Polokwane conference at the end of 2007, there would be another onslaught on media freedom with the proposal of a statutory Media Appeals Tribunal (MAT). While press self-regulation had changed "in form and nature" since the NPU's 1962 Press Board of Reference in response to the NP's threats to impose statutory regulation,[160] the latest amendments were still not good enough for the ANC. The on-going evolution of the first Press Board into the Press Council, followed by the Media Council and then the Press Ombud's Office, before it was transformed yet again in 2007 into the PCSA, did not satisfy the ANC government.

The state of media freedom

Even when Zuma was still a deputy president, the threats to media freedom were loud and clear. There were several statements on the role and the position of the media during this period, with vague threats by the ANC leading to more concrete and clear threats of legal action by Zuma against the media when he attempted to sue editors, journalists, cartoonists and media companies for R63 million in 2006. What follows are some of the statements regarding the importance of media freedom, its basic role in society, and threats from the state:

> "I cannot overemphasise the value we place on a free, independent and outspoken press in the democratic South Africa we hope to build."[161] – *Nelson Mandela*

> "Governments are always in the service of the citizenry. The media must remind them of that, to the point of being sick and tired of them."[162] – *Ton Vosloo*

> "No-one can be satisfied when press freedom is mainly enjoyed by a select group. ... It is the core right of all people to have access to media that expresses their opinions and which adequately reflects their life experiences and aspirations."[163] – *Thabo Mbeki*

> "Censorship has two effects, one obvious and the other obscure. What is obvious is that you know you are being misled, and you have seen through the deception. But the second effect is subtle: the influence on your thinking starts to work because you don't know what you don't know. You haven't heard the other side. The trouble is, neither does the propagandist, who ends up as much victim as his target, the citizenry."[164] – *John Matisonn*

> "South Africa [has] experienced a new dawn – one heralded by the new rainbow nation whose conscience, for the first time, has been unchained to utilise its

intellectual capacities to the full, to think, speak, articulate and write freely. The media in general has been freed to remain the focal point of the nation's conscience."[165] – *Tokyo Sexwale*

"Media freedom and freedom of speech [are] not something that 'just should be there', an object that you keep in a safe, a display cabinet or a constitution, as if to brag with. You should do something with it. It must have value for a country, for a community, or for humankind."[166] – *Tim du Plessis*

"Is suppression the real goal of the national democratic revolution? If so, what about all the freedoms since 1994? Are we on our way back to a police state without freedom of speech and without the supreme authority of the law?"[167] – *Henry Jeffreys*

"When a political party starts a statement with three paragraphs outlining its commitment to media freedom, you know there is trouble coming for journalists."[168] – *Anton Harber*

"The quality of our democracy is measured not only in holding regular, clean elections and socio-economic empowerment (all of which are exceedingly important), but also on how the state respects the media's right to remain critical without worrying about any threats. We hope there will be due regard to the important role the media plays in society more broadly and in enhancing the quality of our democracy."[169] – *Mpumelelo Mkhabela*

By 2007, media freedom was under pressure because of "a high degree of concentration of capital in media markets", which created an "environment in which cosy relationships … developed between senior political and media players".[170] The country's shift from authoritarianism to democracy also "resulted in a blending of the system's paternalistic, authoritarian (and traditional) inclinations together with more pluralist elements". These elements "existed in a state of tension" because of "a concentration of power and a diminishment of accountability". All of this may "exacerbate emerging democracies' vulnerability to heightened state intervention in the media". In South Africa's case, "with a single-party dominance within a majoritarian system with a weak level of accountability", it led to "repeated bids by an active state to roll-back media power and autonomy". This did not mean that democracy itself was jeopardised, but that the "expansion of media freedom is less likely in a democracy that is dominated for long periods by a single political party".

This led to a situation in 2007 in which the media were under "great pressure" to resist a series of anti-press measures in proposed legislation, "as well as a raft of old laws still resiliently inscribed in law and occasionally called upon by the authorities".[171] There were a "number of controversies and debates" between media and government that heightened tensions. The contention included the role the press should play in a developing democracy.

Although by 2007 there were many changes in South Africa's media sector, print media were still dominated by "four or five companies and their products, just as it was a century ago". Still, in key areas, such as ownership, diversity, products, audience and even roles and functions, the South African media were "virtually unrecognisable compared to the early 1990s". The "catch", however, was that the government, "perhaps like other emerging democratic, one-party states", was intent on redefining the role of the media by "picking at the edges of the media's legal, Constitutional and ethical framework".[172] The media even took a "conciliatory and submissive mode", which threatened to "unravel the media's liberal functions and duties". Such a situation could be "exacerbated by various forces", including deteriorating professionalism, undermining editors' roles relative to corporate management, as well as by the "ethics-shredding and controversy-averse impact of commercialisation". It was already argued in 2004 that the "globalisation-shaped transformation process" taking place in South African media had "created and enhanced a competitive media environment, access and diversity". On the other hand, it "[had] shed many non-performers and annihilated small media corporations, creating an environment in which only conglomerates thrive".[173]

Changes since democratisation

There is no doubt that "profound changes" were made in the print media between 1994 and 2006/2007.[174] According to one analyst, these were:

- The emergence of tabloids, reaching mainly a new audience of first-time newspaper buyers;

- The disappearance of two of the four largest media conglomerates, namely Perskor and TML. Perskor "realigned" with the "black" publishing house KTI, but sold off its print interests, and TML was bought partly by Johnnic and Pearsons, owners of the London *Financial Times*;

- There was "significant entrance of black capital", such as through the National Empowerment Consortium, NAIL and also Media24, including trade union investment vehicles such as that belonging to the Paper, Printing, Wood and Allied Workers' Union;

- The purchase of the erstwhile biggest newspaper group, the Argus Group, by the Irish Independent Newspaper group;

- Foreign investment, such as in *Business Day*, the *Financial Mail*, the *Mail & Guardian* and *ThisDay*;

- The growth of Naspers from a (mostly) unilingual print business into a multinational, multilingual, multi-billion rand business, "by far" the biggest company in the South African media market by 2007;

- The rise of local newspapers, in 2007 accounting for 30% of the country's newsprint;

- The racial transformation of newspaper editors and management;

- The deregulation and liberalisation of the country's broadcast system, with implications for cross-ownership and synergies with print media; and

- Growing state support for the diversification and subsidisation of community newspapers by up to R20 million by March 2005.

These changes were described as "substantial and far-reaching". Although another critic argued that there "has been little change", he consented that the post-apartheid restructuring of the Argus Group, as well as the acquisition by "black-dominated capital" of TML and the share offerings to black investors by M-Net and Naspers in 1996, "emerge[d] as a significant departure from the pattern of concentration of ownership that historically characterised the South African print media".[175]

Media audiences

At the beginning of the 1990s, altogether 88% of the South African population could access radio, and about 70% TV, primarily the SABC.[176] The SABC had nineteen radio stations with 20 million listeners daily, producing 2,000 programmes a week. SABC TV consisted of three channels with a daily audience of about 12 million. Thanks to the introduction of community radio as part of the democratisation process, there were about 100 community radio stations. But, simultaneously, the circulation of dailies and weeklies decreased. Also, compared to global figures, the consumption of print media was not high, with readership of dailies of just over eight million, or 31% of the population over 20, or 26% of the population over 15. Only 36% of South Africans used print as a source of information.

In 1996, a statistic showed that more South Africans owned radio receivers than mattresses.[177] This "simple fact" illustrated that radio is "the most appropriate means of communication in South Africa".[178] AMPS 1995 indicated that 90% of the population, then consisting of 41 million people, had access to radio. This medium had "far greater reach and accessibility" than print, also because of the country's high illiteracy rate, estimated at 45% of the population. Radio was also more affordable than TV, "and since it is also battery powered, it is not dependent on electricity", an important factor in a country where at the time an estimated 60% of rural areas were not part of the power grid. Also, TV signals were limited to certain areas. About 12 million people, 50% of the then adult population, watched TV on a daily basis, compared to nearly 16 million, or 65%, of adults who listened to radio daily. Radio could draw on "South Africa's rich oral tradition" and was "ideally suited" to a country where the majority were illiterate and lived in poor rural or peri-urban areas.

Transformational stumbling blocks

By 2007, the arrival of global investors, tabloids, client magazines and "accelerated commercialism" threw "traditional practices into question, introducing new forms of journalism".[179] The formal organisation of South African journalists collapsed, while self-regulating codes and structures were found wanting. Maybe importantly: Racial transformation at newspaper companies was handled poorly. The juniorisation of newsrooms was already an issue, as well as the downgrading of in-house training and the "undermining of editors' authority". Wide-scale poaching by government and the corporate world of key black staff also contributed to "dwindling journalistic standards".

In 2003, South African journalism was experiencing what the MMP's William Bird called its "worst year".[180] Incidents involved an editor's fall from grace and cases of plagiarism, but one of the most "worrying trends in media reporting" was "the violation of people's right to privacy and dignity, which often occurs in time of trauma and grief". Also: "Given the media's public service roles and their responsibilities and their importance to the functioning of a democratic society, they can be expected to hold themselves to the same standards that they measure others against."

The 'Declaration of Table Mountain'

The state of global media freedom led to the "Declaration of Table Mountain", adopted at the World Association of Newspapers (WAN) and the World Editors' Forum (WEF), held during the 60th World Newspaper Congress and 14th World Editors' Forum Conference in Cape Town in June 2007.[181] Especially in Africa, the press was "crippled by a panoply of repressive measures". They included the jailing and persecution of journalists and the "widespread scourge" of "insult laws" and criminal defamation, all of them used "ruthlessly" by governments to prevent criticism and to "deprive the public from information about their misdemeanours". It was stated that Africa urgently needed a "strong, free and independent press to act as a watchdog over public institutions". The declaration also recognised that a free press was needed to sustain peace in Africa and to fight corruption, famine, poverty, violent conflict, disease and lack of education.

The Declaration of Table Mountain reaffirmed the responsibility of the owners, publishers and editors of global media organisations to conduct "aggressive and persistent campaigning against press freedom violations and restrictions". Media freedom, as basic human right, was an indispensable constituent of democracy in every country. The declaration also referred to Article 19 of the Universal Declaration of Human Rights, and said that freedom of expression is essential to the realisation of other rights. Exactly these principles were stressed five years before, in the 2002 Declaration on Principles of Freedom of Expression in Africa adopted by the African Commission on Human and Peoples' Rights and the AU, which required member states to uphold and maintain media freedom – as was also emphasised in the 1991 Windhoek Declaration, which led to UNESCO declaring World Press Freedom Day in 1992.

In terms of a wider media freedom focus, African states had to recognise "the indivisibility of press freedom", as well as their responsibility to respect their commitments to African and international protocols upholding the freedom, independence and safety of the media. As a matter of urgency, they also had to abolish "insult laws", in use in 48 of the 53 African countries, as well as defamation laws. Since the beginning of 2007, the aforementioned laws had already caused the harassment, arrest and/or imprisonment of 103 editors, reporters, broadcasters and online journalists in 26 countries. The declaration also called on the AU to include in their criteria for "good governance" in the African Peer Review Mechanism the "vital requirement" for a country to promote free and independent media. WAN and WEF made

> this declaration from Table Mountain at the southern tip of Africa as an earnest appeal to all Africans to recognise that the political and economic progress they seek flourishes in a climate of freedom and where the press is free and independent of governmental, political or economic control.

The declaration was the idea of media freedom stalwart Raymond Louw, then chair of SANEF's Media Freedom Committee and Africa representative of the World Press Freedom Committee.

Self-censorship

Although journalists achieved a "significant degree" of autonomy within their news organisations in the first decade after democratisation, the issue of self-censorship remained.[182] Although it was "less usual, but by no means unheard of", senior non-editorial management did put pressure on newsrooms "to cover particular events or stories". According to Hadland, "many" South African newsrooms had "anecdotes about this kind of intervention". He himself referred to his time as senior reporter at *Business Day* from 1987 to 1988 and 1991 to 1994, where "it was implicitly understood that no article could be written about the newspaper's parent company, associated companies or board without the explicit approval of the editor". Quoting Bagdikian, he said, "when their most sensitive economic interests are at stake, the parent corporations seldom refrain from using their power over public information". Hadland also quoted an Independent Newspapers managing director who referred to "frequent interventions" at his company. One senior executive "interfered in editorial from the day he arrived", thinking "nothing of calling the editor to have some story or other changed or redone". And: "Some of the other managers also never knew where the line was." One example was the

> order from above to the newsroom staff in 2003 to ensure the opening of a new pottery shop was given prominent placement in Independent Newspapers Cape's group newspapers, the *Cape Argus* and the *Cape Times*. The pottery shop, Wedgewood, was owned by the wife of Independent Newspaper proprietor Tony O'Reilly. The opening of the establishment had no apparent news value but still gained prominent placement.

There were "many, many other examples of such interventions, and not only at Independent Newspapers or at *Business Day*".

Still, the media as political pawns were "more indicative of the trend", rather than "commercial interference". It was "extremely rare for corporate management to dictate the political content of South African newspapers on a day-to-day basis", as there was "more often than not an unwritten consensus among senior staff that determine[d] a title's attitude to different political players". Usually, this consensus consisted "of a broad sympathy with the ruling party and a disregard bordering on subtle ridicule of the opposition parties".

And then the Polokwane bombshell – besides the Mbeki-cide

The ANC's 2007 conference in Polokwane produced two bombshells. The one was Mbeki-cide, when the Zuma faction within the ANC successfully elected him as president of the party, leading to the recall of Mbeki as state president by 2009. But the other was the announcement that the ANC was considering the introduction of a "media tribunal", followed soon afterwards with the threat of the Information Bill.

With growing criticism from government that the media industry failed to regulate itself, the government issued the threat of this statutory body – as had the apartheid government over and over for years – to ensure the media act "responsibly" and uphold human rights.[183]

By 2009, it was feared that there may be a return to the repressive "techniques and strategies" of the apartheid government, despite the fact that the ANC had a far more liberal approach to the role of the media in society and, of course, the fact that media freedom was entrenched in the Constitution.[184]

Despite the ANC's Media Charter, a "foundational document" regarding the principles of freedom of expression, as well as certain "progressive transformations" in the media since

1994, there was a steady decline in media freedom under the ANC. The party threatened the media with tighter regulation, more control, and with legal action. It also interfered with the independence of the public broadcaster and discredited the media, including questioning the professionalism of the media and inciting tension amongst journalists.

Specific apartheid laws could still be used, such as the "dreaded" Publications Act of 1974, the Law on Internal Security of 1976, and certain measures controlling the media under the various states of emergencies. The ANC also drafted a new version of the Films and Publications Amendment (FPA) Bill (2003), and of the Bill on the Protection of Information (2008). Regarding the interference with the public broadcaster, the controversial Broadcasting Amendment Bill (2002), as well as efforts to interfere with the appointment of the SABC board, "raised eyebrows".

There were "numerous examples" reminiscent of the apartheid government concerning discrediting the media, as well as attacks on the media. The NP government blamed the English and foreign press for "misinterpreting" its policies; the ANC's constant criticism was that the media were still mainly in white hands, and therefore anti-government.

Also, both regimes attempted to acquire their own media. The apartheid era had its Information Scandal, while the ANC government tried to purchase Johnnic Communications in 2007, and in 2008 the *Sowetan*. Under apartheid there were a number of commissions of inquiry into the media, sometimes lasting for several years and resulting in threats of statutory regulation, despite existing regulatory measures. In 2007, the ANC started to threaten the media with the MAT, despite the existence of ICASA, the BCCSA and the PCSA.

During apartheid, the government, "intentionally or unintentionally", created tension between Afrikaans and English journalists, whereas in the "new" South Africa there was tension between black and white journalists – regarded as something that could cause harm to the "solidarity between journalists, as such solidarity is necessary for the well-being of freedom of expression". All of these could contribute to increased self-censorship, which would have "a devastating effect on the media's task to inform and enlighten the public". Despite Constitutional protection, it seemed the struggle for freedom of expression was a case of "a luta continua".

Threats now included stricter regulation, interference with the SABC's independence and autonomy, objections to and discrediting the media, questioning journalists' professionalism, and "encourag[ing] strife" amongst journalists.[185] These were all based on an "ongoing questioning of the role of the media in society". It not only led to uncertainty among the media, but to distrust in the media by the public – both having consequences for how the media execute their role of informing the public. Questioning the role and value of the media is of course not a uniquely South African problem; governments across the world "are often uncomfortable with their media". However, it seems "a bigger problem in Africa". Democratic values such as freedom of speech do not have "a long and built-in history". The media are still expected to serve the interests of the government, and "too often the role of the press as government watchdog [is] overshadowed" by its role as "public cheerleaders for development efforts". Also, the media's developmental role in South Africa was often called for, as in the rest of Africa.

The apartheid government's actions against the media could already be compared with those by the ANC in the field of the law, in interference with the SABC, accusations, complaints, discreditations and attacks on the media, attempts to acquire its own media, commissions of investigation and threats of further regulation, and inciting divisions among journalists to interfere with journalistic solidarity. Under apartheid, the government had "unrestricted power" to withhold information from the public in terms of the law, which made it difficult for journalists "to know when they acted in or outside of the law". The "infamous" Publications Act of 1974 was so vague that it was difficult to establish, e.g., how "a movie, a book, a newspaper, a pamphlet, a magazine, or whatever else" could be judged as obscene, offensive or harmful to the morality of the public, and defamatory or offensive to the religious beliefs or feelings of any part of the population. This law led to the banning of international works, including award-winning books. The laws implementing the state of emergency after the 1976 Soweto uprising introduced even more stringent restrictions, and censorship worsened in the 1980s, with newspapers that were banned or closed down. There were even calls for journalists to be registered.

Although most of the restrictive legislation was abolished under the ANC government, there were "a number of recent laws, bills, and amendments reminiscent of the apartheid years" that caused concern. One such amendment was the proposed FPA, originally tabled in 2003. In July 2008, this law had not yet been accepted (as was also the case more than a decade later). There were many objections, and although the proposed law's primary objective was to extend legislation about child pornography and e-commerce, the bill was formulated in such a way that all the content of all print, broadcast and new media had to obtain approval pre-publication. In September 2008, SANEF sent an urgent request to then state president Mbeki not to sign the amendment law.[186]

Yet another example of legislation that could endanger media freedom was the 2008 Protection of Information Bill. Like the FPA Bill, this one also raised concerns about "unclear definitions and their interpretations".[187] In 2007, there were also threats to arrest the editor and a journalist of the *Sunday Times* in terms of the National Health Law after the minister of health's file was allegedly stolen from a hospital. The paper denied this allegation, but also said it was in the public interest to publish concerns about the minister's alleged alcoholism and her alcohol-related illness.

Under the apartheid government, the SABC was a state broadcaster rather than public broadcaster and a pawn of government, thus the NP's criticism was directed mainly at print. Labelled "His Master's Voice", the SABC boards ensured that the ideology and principles of "Christian nationalism broadcasting" were followed. Under the ANC, the Green and White Papers on Broadcasting, leading to the acceptance of the 1996 Broadcasting Act, were regarded as an example for African countries of how to democratise broadcasting. But it was not long before the ANC began, "if not to influence, … to take control of contents". In 2002, a controversial amendment to the Broadcasting Act was seen as a blatant attempt to gain political control over broadcasting. The words of minister of communication, Ivy Matsepe-Casaburri, were compared to those uttered by Strijdom, Verwoerd and Botha, namely that "foreign rulers are given carte blanche access to our living rooms to propagate their propaganda when our own leaders cannot enjoy the privilege to air their views on important matters about our country". After several debates, the Amendment Act was revised to refer issues to ICASA – "as it should be". But still it was not the end of the ANC's efforts to interfere with the SABC's independence. In 2006/2007 there were "regular reports" not only about interference, but also about the SABC's "growing willingness" to adhere to these "demands". Included were reports about the SABC's decision not to broadcast a documentary about Mbeki, as well as the existence of a "blacklist" of commentators who should not be used as they were too critical of the ANC. Other incidents indicated that there was "growing consensus" that the SABC was deteriorating. One commentator concluded that the "growth of greater executive control over broadcasting could well constitute some of the 'shreds of evidence' that media freedom has declined" under Mbeki's administration.[188] RSF, MISA, Freedom House and the African Media Barometer came to the same conclusion. The apartheid government discredited the media as far as was possible to validate the government, and the same started to happen under the ANC, the latter "seemingly just taking over from the NP".[189] Under apartheid it was complaints and accusations about "a lack of patriotism"; now it was complaints and accusations that the media "do not contribute to development".[190] White media ownership was also a negative and provided a reason for the launch of the ANC's weekly e-newsletter, *ANC Today*. Mainstream media, according to Mbeki, were anti-government because they were owned and controlled mainly by whites. Mbeki wrote in the first newsletter:[191]

> We therefore have to contend with the situation that what masquerades as "public opinion", as reflected in the bulk of our media, is in fact minority opinion informed by the historic social and political position occupied by this minority. By projecting itself as "public opinion" communicated by an "objective press", this minority opinion seeks to get itself accepted by the majority as the latter's own opinion.

There were more similarities. The ANC started to hold meetings with the media, as had the apartheid government.[192] In 2001, SANEF and the Mbeki cabinet met to discuss their deteriorating relations. This was when the so-called presidential press corps was supposed to be established. Zuma, then deputy president, argued that reports were often full of errors, had a lack of focus and purpose, were poorly researched, and that depth of analysis and balance were lacking. Western news values and how these should be adapted were also discussed. The media's role was again on the agenda at a meeting in February 2008. This time, SANEF protested against ANC security staff actions against the media and the poor handling of the media during the Polokwane congress. SANEF accused the ANC of "boorish behaviour towards the media" and attempting to refuse media access to public sessions.[193]

In January 2008, shortly after the Polokwane congress, Zuma, as newly elected ANC president, attacked the media, upon which SANEF publicly expressed concern about his hostile remarks.[194] Zuma argued, amongst others, that the political majority, thus the ANC, had no representation in South African mass media, that the media represented the opinion of a minority that was sold as public opinion, and that journalists' prejudices were responsible for their inaccurate political forecasts. He also referred to his election, which the media had not foreseen. Zuma argued that if a country's media system was compiled from its different political, social, economic and cultural sectors, it should be diverse, which was not the case. On the contrary, it presented itself as an opposition. In addition, Zuma said, there were "ideological motives" to bring the government to a fall, driven mainly by economic considerations. Zuma proposed that a mouthpiece like *ANC Today* should be available to more people and that the ANC would be working towards the transformation of all of South Africa's media system.

Regarding government ownership of media, the apartheid government's Infogate after spreading propaganda was well known. But the ANC also "had a plan for its own newspaper" as early as in 2000 and 2001. Again, as under apartheid, the motivation was that the media were "too critical". In late 2007, memories of the Info Scandal were "rekindled" when it became clear that a multibillion rand offer by Koni Media Holdings, consisting of top government employees, had been made for Johnnic Communications (Johncom). As it was structured at the time, the company owned, amongst others, the *Sunday Times*, *Sowetan*, *Daily Dispatch* and 50% of *Financial Mail* and *Business Day*. Koni Media Holdings was co-owned by Groovin Nchabeleng, a prominent figure in the advertising industry, Titus Mafolo, presidential advisor, Ronnie Mamoepa, foreign spokesperson, and Billy Modise, previous head of state protocol. The transaction did not succeed, but by July the next year there were again rumours of government planning to buy a newspaper.

Regarding commissions on the media, the apartheid and ANC governments' threats could also be regarded as similar. Under apartheid there were "regular commissions of inquiry" into the content, behaviour, ethics, ownership and regulation of the media; the ANC government's threats against the media are comparable. Especially the MAT "strongly" recalled the history of "apartheid-style commissions". Before the MAT threat, the closest was the HRC's controversial investigation in 1999/2000 on racism in the media. The ANC's policy discussion document was called "Communication and the Battle of Ideas". It contained, as in previous such discussion documents, 26 points on the media, including freedom of speech, diversity, public broadcasting, media and social cohesion, and media and gender. One of the main concerns was the effectiveness of the existing self-regulation by the PCSA, its ombud, the press code, the appeals panel and the BCCSA, among others. Therefore, at the 2007 Polokwane conference, the MAT was suggested with the aim "to strengthen, complement and support the current self-regulatory institutions in the public interest". Related to this was the need to balance the right to freedom of expression and freedom of the media with the right to equality, to privacy and human dignity for all.[195]

The media and various related organisations expressed serious concerns. The MAT was not only seen as a way for government to interfere, but as a serious threat to media freedom.[196] In 2008 it was said that, similar to the apartheid government, the ANC also created distrust among the public in the media, often leaving the perception that "the media is part of the enemy".[197] Underlying this was a totalitarian and authoritarian view of the role of the media in society, and therefore the media as instrument to be used to promote its own political ideology and power. The ANC's actions could be described as a repeat of those of the NP government. These actions had to be regarded as serious threats to media freedom "under the guise of the ANC's apparent libertarian views on freedom of speech and media freedom".

Indeed, the message could not be clearer: The struggle for freedom of speech and media freedom continued, even under the party of liberation, and despite it having entrenched these freedoms in a Constitution regarded as an example to the rest of the world.

Or, in other words: *A luta continua*.

– Mpumelelo Mkhabela, ex-editor, SANEF chair and media commentator[1]

9. The period from 2009 onward

The Tribunal, the Secrecy Bill, Zumacracy, Ramaphoria … and a pandemic

Introduction

Nothing new out of Africa? Well, the political beasts wanting to hoard media freedom as the sole property of a political party – admittedly, elected to govern – continued to do so. History repeated itself. The disillusionment with the ANC government after South Africa's liberation was therefore perhaps even bigger. Together with the threats against media freedom, the role of an independent media became even more important as words such as "state capture" and "rogue state" became part of South Africa's vocabulary during almost a decade of rule under a leader who knew how to maintain the "President's Keepers".[2] The latter refers to an investigative project by journalist Jacques Pauw that led to a bestseller that mostly reads like a thriller. Except it was reality, not fiction. At the beginning of the era under Jacob Zuma, it was especially the threat of the MAT that dictated the relationship between the media and government. This threat against democracy, with media freedom as the only guarantee of an individual's freedom, was as real as in any other political era in the history of South Africa. Any naivety left after the euphoria of the Rainbow Nation evaporated in the new reality of South Africa's harsh daylight.

The Battle of Ideas - or a luta continua

The ANC's 2009 Discussion Document on communication – ironically, besides being extremely badly edited and still called "The Battle of Ideas" – restated its concern about the slow pace of transformation in the print media.[3] The "noble principles of editorial independence" were recognised, but the "question of the degree of impact of ownership and control to editorial content" remained debatable.

The document gave insight into valuable media statistics. Radio was still the most accessible medium, with 94% of SA's adult population having access. TV reached almost 84%. The major media companies in 2010 were Avusa, Caxton/CTP, Media24 (a division of Naspers), the Independent Newspapers Group, Kagiso, Primedia and the SABC. Newspapers and magazines had a respective reach of 48% and 40%, and more than five million newspapers were sold daily in South Africa. With 18 public radio stations covering all official languages, divided into 15 public broadcasting service (PBS) stations and three public commercial service (PCS) stations, the SABC had 41,6% of the total radio audience. Altogether 13 private commercial radio stations operated as regional or provincial stations, reaching 16,5% of the total adult radio audience. In 2007, ICASA licensed MultiChoice, On Digital Media (TopTV), Telkom Media (called Super5Media in 2010), and Walking on Waters to provide satellite TV subscription services. ICASA also licensed three other commercial radio stations in so-called "secondary markets". At the time, more than 126 community radio station licences were issued, of which more than 87 were active. These community stations accounted for 4,6% of the total radio audience. According to AMPS 2008 data, there were 11,1 million TV sets in South Africa that year. The SABC provided three public terrestrial TV channels, SABC1, 2 and 3, with 69,3% of the total TV audience. According to its 2009 report, MultiChoice had 1,6 million DStv subscriptions. The only private free-to-air commercial terrestrial TV station was eTV, with an audience of 18,1 million representing 22,3% of viewers. The four licensed community TV stations were Soweto Community TV in Soweto/Johannesburg, Bay Television Station in Empangeni/Richards Bay, Cape Town Community TV and Trinity Broadcasting Network (TBN) in the Eastern Cape.

In 2010, print media was still "by far" the largest sub-sector of media in terms of the number of titles and ownership, mostly in English and Afrikaans, with very few in black languages. About 940 million newspapers circulated in South Africa per annum, including mainstream commercial, as well as small commercial and community papers. AMPS 2008 gave the national newspaper readership as 15,2 million. Altogether 71,9% was in the economically strong provinces of Gauteng, Western Cape and KwaZulu-Natal (KZN), accounting for 69% of the total readership. Gauteng printed 26,6% of papers, KZN 25,5% and the Western Cape 19,8%. The Northern Cape and North West had the smallest circulations – below 10%. There were at least 504 magazine titles, with a readership of 12,6 million. The highest magazine readership was in Gauteng, with 3,5 million, followed by KZN with 1,9 million.

Regarding media ownership and control, the ANC document reported that the 13 private commercial radio stations had ownership that on average comprised 58% historically disadvantaged individuals (HDI). As for TV, private commercial TV stations' HDI ownership was about 64,4% per station. This was attributed to the IBA, established under the Independent Broadcasting Authority Act of 1993, and ICASA's regulatory and licensing interventions. In print media, ownership was concentrated in Media24, Caxton, Avusa and foreign-owned Independent Newspapers, with Media24 regarded as "dominant". These companies had "some degree" of HDI ownership, with Avusa's 25,5% HDI shareholding and Media24's 15%. Caxton and Independent had no HDI investment.

The ANC document stated that free, independent and pluralistic media could be achieved not only through many media products, but also through diversity of ownership and control. As "sites of transformation, information and communication", the companies were subjected to "contested politico-economic tussles". These included ownership and shareholding, control of management and production of content, and the composition of the workforce. The transformation of this sector implied "a special place in the changing milieu of the socio-political landscape, since it is a key of reform and revolution in the broader society".

Pre-1994 broadcasting, with all its inequalities, had no clearly defined regulatory system, leading to a "disjointed" system. All of this was transformed by the IBA. The ANC document also referred to media control as "one of the most important tools in the apartheid arsenal", with the "battery of censorship legislation" that ensured the survival of apartheid.

The ANC therefore wanted to "vigorously" communicate its outlook and values regarding "a developmental state, collective rights, … a caring and sharing community, solidarity, ubuntu, non-sexism, and working together" versus the current mainstream media's "ideological outlook" of "neo-liberalism, a weak and passive state, and overemphasis on individual rights, market fundamentalism, etc". There was "no question" that the media as institution deserved to flourish as a critical platform for freedom of expression, which was the reason why the ANC "has always fought for media freedom" as cornerstone for a democracy to flourish. Everyone had to defend media freedom and editorial independence from any form of compulsion, whether political, economic or commercial.

The document, however, stated that "independence" does not presume journalists to be "unique human beings with unique journalistic genes and genealogy". Rather, they are the products of the environment within which they operate and "the circumstances that spawn them". For the ANC, media remained "a contested terrain and therefore not neutral", reflecting "ideological battles and power relations based on race, class and gender". The media therefore could not claim that they "merely" "reflect interests". Instead, they shape them. Journalists are not "passive transmitters – "a clean slate" – on whom "events imprint themselves". The media do not "merely" reflect, but "help to shape social preferences". And they can also "facilitate" or "serve as a break on social transformation".

The document stated that the media would be relegated to the status of "social irrelevance" if journalists had absolute freedom – only the "inconsequential in social processes have a semblance of absolute freedom". The media were not a victim "waiting to be abused"; instead, they were "a repository of immense ideological, economic, social and political power". And so the ANC's National Democratic Revolution (NDR) expected the media to contribute to transforming South Africa. In fact, "building social cohesion and promoting values of a caring society are an essential part of the battle of ideas and must underpin and inform" the manner in which the media operate. Accountability and fair reporting were therefore central "to the objective assessment of the gains of the NDR", as the media needed to contribute towards the building of a new society and be accountable. Media transformation had to target "the entire value chain" and investigate anti-competitive behaviour.

According to the document, even a "[c]ursory scan" of the print media revealed an "astonishing degree of dishonesty, lack of professional integrity and lack of independence". In editorials, papers would distance themselves from "these acts", but apologies were "never given due prominence". In fact, they were mostly "forced through" by the press ombud. And none of these were sufficient "in dealing with this ill".

Although the so-called "brown envelope" journalism initially arose in an ANC local provincial government, the document referred to the abuse of positions of power, authority and public trust "to promote narrow, selfish interests and political agendas inimical to our democracy" – "the problem" that is called "brown envelope journalism". It was a much more serious "rot" than the media were willing to admit and ran "even deeper tha[n] meets the eye". Clearly, the internal problems in the tripartite alliance were the cause of these irritations. The document referred to what has now become something "like permanent briefing sessions between faceless leaders within the ranks of our Alliance and some journalists about discussions taking place in confidential meetings". They "possibly" also involved "payment arrangements".

The "flowers of free speech to bloom"

The ANC document stated that it was "inadequate" to posit media freedom in constitutional and legal terms only. Fundamental expressions of media freedom, such as ownership and control, also had to be discussed. With growing conglomeration of ownership and homogenisation of content there could be no realisation of media freedom. The ANC conceded that it

> is quite true that there can be a temptation, especially in political office, to constrain such freedom of expression and media freedom in particular; but in our society we can say without fear of contradiction that most of those who believe in democracy (led by the ANC) know that there can be no real transformation without freedom of expression and media freedom.

Although media freedom had to be defended, it should not be a refuge for "journalist scoundrels" to hide "mediocrity and glorify truly unprofessional conduct". Under the heading "Media freedom put into perspective", the document made a number of points considered crucial for media freedom. It opened with the statement that media "faces the danger of consigning itself to social irrelevance if it ignores the national mission". Media could become a "popular source of amusement – the opium that dulls the senses – and an institution that connives in the destruction of the very values that make its existence in freedom possible". It reaffirmed that media and communication were "highly important strategic sectors in the process of economic development and reconstruction". But given "the history of monopolistic broadcasting and an oligopolistic print media in South Africa", the ANC equated democratisation with the introduction of more competition and the entry of black empowerment capital. Besides having "many media products", free, independent and pluralistic media could only be achieved through diversity of ownership and control. There could be no real media freedom "under conditions of unique manifestations of censorship such as self-censorship", also "peer censorship" or "the tendency among journalists themselves to seek to dictate to others how they should cover issues". An example was that "anyone who dared to acknowledge progress in service delivery and government performance was condemned by peers as a lapdog". It was not that "sunshine journalism" was required, but the media needed to critique government in such a way that it added value "to the national endeavour". The media needed to reflect "on the broader questions" about how "our souls are being poisoned by the spirit of conspicuous consumption in a socio-economic formation that encourages greed".

The document restated self-regulation, although the need for an independent media tribunal "should be brought back onto the agenda". Under the heading, "Recommendations and processing of the Congress resolutions on the Media Appeals Tribunal (MAT)", it stated that "freedom of expression and the right to information also imply the right to speak and even the right to be heard". One should not only be the recipient of the views of others, but have the right to impart own information and ideas – information "should not be the preserve of the rich and the powerful".

The MAT was considered after "concerns raised by a number of citizens and complaints from a number of people" who were "victims of unfairness and unsatisfactory decisions" of the self-regulatory body. After its decision to investigate the establishment of the MAT at its 52nd conference in Polokwane in 2007, the ANC reaffirmed that the media situation was "untenable" and that there was a need "to strengthen, complement and support" self-regulation "in the public interest". The fact that the press ombud was "from the media ranks, a former journalist, and is not an independent person who looks at the media from the layman's perspective" meant an inherent bias towards the media. The document also referred to the media's reaction to the initial Polokwane MAT resolution, namely that they were not "lacking in bravery behind the armour of collective self-defence", with reaction that showed "hypersensitivity" to criticism and missed "the point that people need recourse when media freedom trampled their rights to dignity and privacy". The MAT would "legalise and strengthen" and "complement and support" the work of the ombud. It would not be an ANC body, but a statutory, parliamentary one "in order to guarantee the principles of independence, transparency, accountability and fairness" – as ICASA's BCCSA for broadcasting. As a final point regarding the MAT, parliament had to investigate the ownership and control of print media and "what needs to be done to change the tide".

The document stressed the fact that there was a need for a Competition Act for the media "precisely because of market failure". It also had to ensure that those who do not have access to resources can get that access in order to participate equitably. The media's "uncompetitive" and "monopolistic" behaviour, "price collusion, access to general services and so on" should be the focus of such an act.

Regarding a media charter, the document referred to the decision in the late 1990s to introduce new policies aimed at broad-based black economic empowerment (B-BBEE). In 2003, the government released its B-BBEE strategy, defining it as "an integrated and coherent" socio-economic process. The B-BBEE Act of 2003, promulgated in 2004, had a "generic score card" of seven criteria. In addition to this, the ANC document proposed that "a public hearing process" should probe the necessity of a media charter, similar to the inquiry on advertising that led to the Marketing, Advertising and Communications Charter, "to bring about transformation and to change the tide in the print media". The document concluded that

> Freedom of expression, today, still requires staunch and determined fighters, under new conditions, to confront the real issues facing contemporary South Africa. The ANC government should find mechanisms to speed up the process of improving the media environment by creating conditions for the flowers of free speech to bloom for all of society and every citizen.

It was also reaffirmed that it was the ANC's responsibility to set the agenda for change to "dominate the battle of ideas" and "that our voice is consistently heard and that it is above the rests" [sic].

The MAT, still - or again

Thus, at the ANC's 2010 National General Council in Durban, the MAT threats became more explicit.[4] As spelled out in the discussion paper published before the meeting, the ANC reiterated that:[5]

- The mere fact that the press ombudsman was from the ranks of the media, a former journalist and not an independent person who looked at the media from a "layman's perspective" was an inherent bias towards the media, which the ANC regarded as grossly unfair and unjust.

- For a complaint to be accepted by the ombud, the aggrieved had to waive their constitutional rights to approach the courts if they disagreed with the verdict.

- It took long to clear the names of alleged wrongdoers.

- It was an "expensive exercise for an ordinary citizen".

- Many who found themselves "in the news" were "unhappy about the way their story ha[d] been presented or the way journalists … obtained information". Many laws restrict what can be published, "but not the behaviour of journalists", and there were few legal remedies for inaccurate reporting.

- Legal aid was not available for expensive libel cases, with no statutory press regulation in this regard.

- It was "an entirely voluntary system" which did "not have the force of law".

- Also, in public debates, members of the ANC Alliance argued that the ombud's office was "toothless".

Contested paradigms

Also in 2010, a study was done by foremost media academic Herman Wasserman among journalists and other role players on their perceptions of, *inter alia*, media freedom. It was found that freedom and responsibility were contested in South Africa as a "transitional democracy". Still, there was wide agreement on the formal aspects of media freedom thanks to the democratisation process.[6]

The study found that journalists, politicians and other role players "mostly agreed" that democracy had brought unprecedented freedom of expression linked to a human rights culture.[7] This manifested in constitutional guarantees protected by watchdog organisations, including the FXI, the ombud system and SANEF, and it was also visible in the transformation of the industry. There was an "increased transnational news flow", indicating that South African media "became less parochial" and took a less "provincial" view on world affairs.

Still, the participants disagreed on the nuances or "application" of notions like freedom and responsibility, as they could be used to "disguise political agendas". New threats to freedom of speech were identified that were "more subtle than in the past". Although democracy brought "a freer flow of information locally", it "opened up the local media for global/transnational influences", both structurally and culturally. The former led to an influx of capital, leading to increased commercialisation and profit-seeking with South Africa operating in global markets. Culturally, it led to the "adoption or contestation" of media behaviour that was imported from "elsewhere".

Respondents from both party-political and media spheres indicated that democratisation did not lead to "a complete transformation of political communication", as its "actors" often still belonged to elite classes. Despite claims to independence, media were seen "as aligned with government in privileging an elite discourse associated with neoliberal economic policies".[8] Other concerns were commercialisation and juniorisation, limiting the media's capacity to be "watchdogs" or to do investigative work. Tabloidisation and sensationalism were "lamented". Another concern was the "abuse of notions of 'responsibility' by the state for political ends", such as covering up sensitive information or diverting attention from scandals. Conversely, the media could abuse their freedom to justify "unfettered commercialisation". Media played "an important role in shaping political debate" in a new democracy, but the media themselves also became "the focus of debate and contestation". The vigour of these was "a sign of the vibrancy of the mediated public sphere, even as its boundaries" were continuously renegotiated.

One of the more subtle pressures on media freedom was bullying. Politicians were "heavy-handed", especially towards black journalists who were expected to "toe the line" or contribute to "nation-building".[9] While economic pressures "prevented the media from fulfilling their investigative watchdog function", the SABC was "time and again" singled out as an institution in which press freedom was threatened, either by state intervention or by increased commercialisation.

Interestingly, post-apartheid South Africa created the opportunity for media "to emerge as a political player in their own right". This could be compared to other emerging democracies, where the media also shaped the behaviour and expectations of political participants – even where the media, as in other parts of Africa, emerged as "an alternative power centre to government" thanks to far greater freedom.

This differed from the immediate postcolonial era when media were expected to play a supportive role to the developmental state.[10] Still, in post-apartheid South Africa the media functioned as opposition, countering the ANC's "power bloc" in the absence of a major opposition party.[11] Alas, some participants saw the media's new-found freedom as not making "a real difference in the lives of the poor majority".

In 2010, the main threats to media freedom were

- Political threats, among them the proposed MAT to replace self-regulation. New legislation, e.g., the FPA Bill, could make pre-publication censorship possible. More subtle threats were government influence in the SABC's editorial content, as well as "politicking" on its board.

- Economic threats resulting from increased commercialisation.[12] Because overseas funding stopped, "vibrant alternative media" disappeared. The Irish Independent Group took over large sections of the English press, and the former mostly Afrikaans Naspers began operating as a global entity. Some media houses unbundled, selling off parts to BEE firms, thereby leading to new conglomerates. The juniorisation of newsrooms, already identified in SANEF's 2002 National Journalism Skills Audit, was also a threat.[13] The negative impact of commercialisation and juniorisation meant that a lack of investigative and in-depth political reporting threatened press freedom, as the media could not fulfil its watchdog function. With the absence of grassroots community media and increased conglomeration, the media seemed to be "moving upwards" instead of down.

- Despite examples of "excellent and far-reaching investigative work", the media was accused of favouring "entertainment and diversion in the form of infotainment".[14] This was problematic in a young democracy; the media rather had to strengthen democratic institutions and root out corruption. A lack of investigative journalism in the post-apartheid era was seen "as particularly ironic or unfortunate", seeing that media were freer to do so than under apartheid, leading to a sad conclusion: "[H]ard-won freedom was seen to be squandered for short-term commercial benefit."

A 'dire threat'

In 2010, three former newspaper editors felt so strongly about the "dire threat" looming over media freedom that they issued a statement warning about "anti-freedom" legislation reminiscent of apartheid.[15] Harvey Tyson, Rex Gibson and Richard Steyn, editors who "spent decades opposing press censorship in the apartheid era", issued their joint statement after the Protection of Information Bill and the proposed MAT.

Tyson was former editor of the *Star*, former member of the IPI and board member of the former Argus Group, Gibson was an ex-editor of the RDM and Steyn a former editor of the *Star* and the *Witness* and a member of the IPI. Although the threat was "naïve", it was "dangerous". Also: "It appears to come in an uninformed attack by a few legislators who don't like criticism." And: "Freedom is killed that way in most dictatorial states."

The Protection of Information Bill, "even if shorn of its follies and evil", was a serious threat to freedom of information as it "almost certainly" would be used "at some stage as a blunt instrument by some demagogues proclaiming their love of democracy".

Even worse was the "second blunt instrument being forged by the democratic government". This was the proposed "independent" MAT to discipline the media and stop "unfair" criticism. Successive apartheid governments had tried to enforce "this blatant form of popular censorship no less than eight times in 48 years" – and "failed every time, simply because the device, in every form, was too blatant and utterly crude".

The three said "inferences in the Info Bill" and the MAT's "uncalled-for" legal authority to oversee media "excesses" would "injure democracy and besmirch the name of South Africa". The MAT in itself created "an ominous precedent". And: "For the sake of everyone, and in the name of democracy and freedom, please don't even begin to try to do it."

Leading to the Right2Know

All of these concerns led to the Right2Know campaign, or R2K, launched in August 2010.[16] It has grown into a movement centred on freedom of expression and access to information. It is a democratic, activist-driven campaign that strengthens and unites citizens to raise public awareness, mobilise communities and undertake research and targeted advocacy that aims to ensure the free flow of information necessary to meet people's social, economic, political and ecological needs and live free from want, in equality and in dignity.

This new campaign added to a number of still existing non-profits acting as watchdogs over South Africa's fledgling democracy. R2K mobilised itself on three focuses, namely the right to protest, the right to communication, and the establishment of a participatory democracy. For the latter they also wanted to support other civil society organisations (CSOs), especially in poor communities, to ensure their rights.

The organisation consists of three democratic provincial working groups – in Gauteng, KZN and the Western Cape, as well as a national committee representing CSOs, community groups and social movements.

Fighting what it called the Secrecy Bill (the Protection of Information Bill), it mobilised a network of activists and organisations across the country. In 2013, R2K's founding history was published by the Rosa Luxemburg Foundation[17] and, when celebrating its fifth anniversary in 2015, it published a timeline of milestones.

The Right2Know logo.
Source: https://www.r2k.org.za/about/

The Press Council's new reincarnation

In 2011, the report on a substantial review of the Press Council (PCSA) was tabled after a year of submissions.[18] The first five-year period of PCSA and the ombud system, after being established on 1 August 2007, was coming to an end. In August 2010, a PCSA task team was appointed to review this system, also because of growing criticism against the print media by the ANC as well as members of the public, all calling for stronger press regulations.[19] The PCSA's members were the Newspaper Association of SA, the Magazine Publishers Association, the Association of Independent Publishers, the Forum of Community Journalists, and SANEF, together representing at least 1,227 publications.[20]

This comprehensive review dealt with the PCSA's constitution, press code and protocols for complaints, with hearings held throughout the country. Other systems of press regulation were investigated, while the task team also corresponded with press regulation bodies as well as regulatory bodies in other spheres.

As PCSA chair, veteran journalist and editor Raymond Louw said his approach was that "press self-regulation was a tried and tested method", but "it also opened his mind" to "accommodating any other process that would achieve the objectives".

This review was only "Stage One", as the report was then handed to all bodies that drew up the 2007 policy. "Stage Two" included handing the PCSA's own review to the independent Press Freedom Commission (PFC), set up by SANEF and Print Media South Africa (PMSA). The PFC would conduct its own investigation, with "Stage Three" the end of this "lengthy procedure", after which the PFC produced the "South African Press Freedom Report" with its recommendations. The results would ensure

> a strong and effective Press Council acting as a watchdog over press misdemeanour, while contributing to excellence in the practice of journalism and upholding the freedom and independence of the press, all essential elements in promoting the concepts of democracy.[21]

It was an opportunity for the PCSA "in its current incarnation" to reassess its first five years of existence, but simultaneously respond to what it called "political pressures".[22] Besides regular attacks on the media, the real threat was the ANC's 2007 Polokwane MAT resolution. After it was amended at the ANC's 2010 Durban meeting, by 2011 a parliamentary commission was requested to investigate all press regulations with "the intention of deciding which is best for South Africa". Thus, the PFC was led by three criteria:

- Will the proposals lead to improving the quality of South African journalism?
- Will the proposals make "our system more efficient and effective"?
- Are the suggestions practical?

The PFC also had to survey public submissions and regulatory frameworks of international media councils to determine a suitable local press regulation system.[23] Chaired by former Chief Justice Pius Langa, it comprised nine independent persons and submitted its report in April 2012. It examined four forms of regulation, namely

- self-regulation,
- co-regulation,
- independent regulation and
- state regulation.

The PFC found that independent co-regulation, defined as "a system of press regulation that involves public and press participation with a predominant public membership but without State or government participation", was the best form of regulation for South Africa. Independent co-regulation, which was eventually adopted, was not "widely preferred" by the public submissions,[24] but in almost all cases there were "explicitly" negative comments regarding statutory regulation.[25] In its submission, the ANC referred to

> continuous shabby journalism, declining of journalism standards, inaccurate, unfair and irresponsible reporting, the inadequate powers of the Press Ombudsman to deter and discourage this practice, continuous noncompliance and adherence to the very existing Press Code; and the lack of accountability from the media.[26]

Regarding regulations, the task team concluded that statutory regulation "[wa]s not warranted". The structuring of the new regulatory system included[27]

- a director, to concentrate on public engagement around issues of standards and media freedom,
- a public advocate, to assist the public with their complaints and help negotiate for an early solution with the publication, and who may assist complainants during hearings,
- the ombud, to arbitrate matters not resolved through negotiation; and
- a chair of appeals, to deal with appeals.

This structure facilitated a "more proactive" approach, while creating "a useful distinction" between the PCSA's functions of mediation, arbitration, appeals and public engagement. The public advocate would also "unambiguously [be] on the side of the reading public".

Altogether 100 codes from around the world were assessed, including 25 from Africa.[28] Proposed amendments included the rights of children, guidelines on privacy, dignity and reputation, independence and avoidance of conflicts of interest. Guidelines for the use of confidential and anonymous sources were expanded, and the rules about discrimination and hate speech were strengthened.

There was a steady increase in the number of people using the ombud's office from August 2007 to 2011.[29] By mid-May 2011, the office had received 104 complaints compared to the fact that the 104th complaint in 2010 was only received late in August. In total, 213 complaints were received for 2011.

Still, the Secrecy Bill

In 2012, South Africa ranked 52nd out of 179 countries in RSF's index of press freedom – down from 42nd the year before.[30] The annual Worldwide Press Freedom Index, covering the period December 2011 to November 2012, reflected the degree of freedom journalists and news organisations enjoyed in each country and efforts by states to support this freedom.

Contributing to South Africa's lower ranking was the threat of the Protection of State Information Bill, or the Info Bill, which was also popularly known as the Secrecy Bill. After a year of debate, the contentious, already amended bill was passed by the National Assembly in April 2013. Yet, it has still not been signed into law. Siyabonga Cwele, state security minister at the time, told parliament that the bill was "aimed at protecting sensitive state information and the information of ordinary people, such as marriage certificates and business registrations". The bill gave the minister control over the classification of information, while the government insisted that whistle-blowers would be protected "and no one will be able to use the bill to hide corruption". Yet opponents, including human rights and legal experts, opposition parties and CSOs, said the bill, also in amended form, "preferenced state interests over transparency and freedom of expression".

Apartheid-era laws still on the books

Added to this, by 2013 South Africa seemed stuck with "apartheid-era laws" that remained on the law books. Under the heading, "Scrap apartheid-era laws!", veteran journalist and former editor Raymond Louw wrote that, after eighteen years of democracy, it was "high time" for these laws to be removed from the statute books.[31] At least ten – among many – required urgent review. A campaign for a review was started in the early 1990s, when apartheid was crumbling and it was hoped that these laws would be scrapped or amended, but almost two decades later there still were laws "heavily restricting media freedom". And, worse, they were in direct conflict with the Constitution.

The National Key Points Act (NKPA), for instance, came in "handy" in attempts to prevent the media from obtaining information about the upgrading, using taxpayer's money, of Nkandla, Zuma's private homestead in KZN. In 2008, Louw wrote there was "a surge of hope" when the Law Commission announced it would review 2,800 laws enacted since 1910. Yet, four years on, in 2012, there still was no indication of any progress. And, according to Louw, also not a word about legislation affecting the media.

The MAT making waves

Meanwhile, the MAT continued to dominate headlines in 2013. It "revealed" the ANC's "own insecurities, fears and hysteria in its desire for a media appeals tribunal", wrote academic

Glenda Daniels.[32] But such control could "not sit comfortably in an open democracy". The MAT showed the ANC's need "for more hegemonic control over a media it finds lacking in any loyalty and gratitude to it, the liberation party". It also implied a "desire" for more consensus and unity with the media, but that was "also out of sync with a real democracy".

Still, the ANC was convinced the MAT was needed because "the self-regulation system [did] not work". It deemed the PCSA's decisions as skewed in favour of the media; that there was insufficient protection for those whose rights had been violated; that the PCSA was "toothless" because it could not levy fines and "merely asked for" apologies and, when these were made, they were "insufficient in size and stature" compared to the damaging article; and finally, that the media were unaccountable.

The MAT was passed as a resolution at the ANC's Polokwane conference in 2007, which meant it had to be followed-up. The 2010 discussion paper, "Media Transformation, Ownership and Diversity", at the National General Council meeting in Durban reaffirmed the resolution. Described as the ANC's "ideological social fantasy", it meant there should be "only one outlook in a democracy – its own one". The ANC's conception of democracy was of unity and consensus, the reason why the party found "it difficult to accept the different perspectives in the media, as well as criticisms of its performance and exposés of corruption". These were viewed as "oppositional" and "un-transformational".

While it was a given that the media had to be accountable – "that has never been in dispute" – it was "to the norms and values of professional conduct and to the public that it serves – not to Parliament". Otherwise, it would constitute "political control and an unprogressive hegemony". The ANC's other need for the MAT, namely that apologies were not always printed on front pages, was "a matter for discussion", not one of "imposing a draconian measure such as a tribunal".

It seemed there was "some détente" when the ANC accepted the PFC's recommendations for "independent co-regulation", which implied more public involvement. In 2010, ANC spokesperson Jackson Mthembu accused the media of being "just hysterical" regarding the proposed MAT. Also: "If you have to go to prison, let it be. If you have to pay millions for defamation, let it be. If journalists have to be fired because they don't contribute to the South Africa we want, let it be." According to Daniels, the ANC's "ideological fantasy" of the role of the media was evident in this statement. By November 2012 it seemed as if Mthembu had "softened his stance", as he now asserted the need for "an independent press". Still, the ANC had "a conscious fantasy that South Africa should take the form of its own vision, which it appropriated once it obtained hegemonic power". The ANC's "conscious fantasy" that the "whole of the people" supported the party meant that "the whole of the media should support it as well".

ANC secretary-general Gwede Mantashe also maintained that a MAT was required to deal with the "dearth of media ethics". It would also help "correct" the anti-ANC bias, as the media were driven by a "dark conspiracy to discredit the national democratic revolution". Shortly after Mantashe's statements the SACP's Blade Nzimande suggested the media was simply "a reflection of its owners", a "capitalist media bastard".

While the "meanings of democracy" can be contested, Daniels wrote, they should be understood "as a plurality of public spaces". One of them was "noisy and nosey journalism". Also: Journalism was "not supposed to be in sync with the ANC, or indeed any political party". This referred to then president Zuma, who criticised the media for being "ideologically out of sync with the society in which it exists". Daniels said that what he really was unhappy about was that the media was "out of sync with him and the ANC". And: "The ANC and 'society' is not one and the same. No wonder from time to time there is hysteria, fear and insecurity."

Keeping secrets secret

At the beginning of 2014, futurist Clem Sunter wrote about "breaking futures", whereby he meant issues that would become crucial for the planet's survival.[33] A week later he expressed surprise when three of his "breaking futures" forecasts became breaking news. Besides his climate-change forecast, another was what he called "Snowden's torch". It referred to the role of whistle-blowers concerning global intelligence networks and states' invasion of privacy of other states, as well as that of individuals.

This "breaking future" regarded the "extensive influence" of the "Edward Snowden affair" on the intelligence community. Sunter: "Traitor or hero, he has compelled every country to review the way it keeps its secrets secret." He said the practices of security agencies, particularly in collecting phone records, had to be reformed and regularly reviewed by a panel of private advocates. Ironically, Snowden, "meanwhile, remains holed up in Russia, once hailed as the land of Big Brother".

At the same time, South Africa's "Secrecy Bill", the Protection of State Information Bill, was again under scrutiny.[34] The Public Protector's investigation took approximately two years, exceeding the deadline, as there were "significant delays" while questions around secrecy – "inconveniently for some" – kept "cropping back up". One of the main concerns, also raised by CSOs, was how secrecy can "mask corruption". In fact, the Public Protector raised concerns about secrecy hindering her work in her submission to the parliamentary committee dealing with the Bill. This, for example, played out in how prescient the issue was in delaying the "Nkandla report", as it was "classified information" and "Top Secret", meaning the information was of such a nature that its unauthorised disclosure or exposure could be used by "malicious/opposing/hostile elements" to "neutralise the objectives and functions of institutions or the state".

But this situation was regarded as unconstitutional. According to Wits academic Jon Klaaren, it had its origin in a military information security policy that had been "crudely and inappropriately adapted to attempt to cover the entire public sector". The Public Protector had already said in her 2012 submission that "a public interest override" was not the same as "a public interest defence clause", defined as a defence that allows anybody who discloses classified or protected information to avoid criminality by claiming it was in the public interest to do so.

Although civil society was derided "as somewhat hysterical" in its reception of the Secrecy Bill, the changes to the legislation have not given "much comfort". There were already international examples, such as the US government "making every effort to hide the footage of the Apache helicopter attack on Reuters journalists in Baghdad". It meant that precisely what people were concerned about could happen, namely that the state could use secrecy laws "to try to hide evidence of wrongdoing". The Public Protector identified as main issue delaying the 2013 Nkandla report "access to classified information". Or, rather, the lack of it, as the "essential allegation of civil society, that secrecy would be used to cover up national security wrongdoing, amongst others, has been proved correct".

In the 2008 version of the Bill, it was already pointed out that the issue of the public interest was inadequately covered. A mandate to release information through a general public interest override had to be built into it, plus protection for whistle-blowers. In 2008, when the controversial Bill was withdrawn in the chaos after the Mbeki recall, the reason given was that it was "problematic and needed redrafting". But when it was reintroduced it was "significantly worse". Three years later, the Protection of State Information Act of 1982 and the NKPA still remained in place, despite "their dodgy constitutional status". In spite of these "apartheid tools to hand", it seemed government "proved rather inept in keeping secrets". The solution was one of "weak states everywhere", namely to "try to make more and more secret, and require more and more people to be secret keepers".

The question at the time was why the president hesitated to sign the Secrecy Bill when the chief state law advisor reassured over and over "that it is constitutional, in all its forms". But, by 2014, the minister of police was again directed to review the NKPA, "something he ha[d] been promising to do", while the minister of justice promised to review the protection for whistle-blowers in the Protected Disclosures Act. The conclusion: "Everyone promises to behave well, on the understanding that no one concedes behaving badly. And the case for a public interest defence clause in the Secrecy Bill only grows stronger."

No surprise then that that same year, Freedom House reported that global press freedom for 2014 was at its lowest level in decades.[35] Only 14% of the world's population lived under conditions in which the media could be rated "free", with 44% living in areas where the media was "not free", and 42% where it was "partly free".

The media's ability to fight corruption

To mark Press Freedom Day on 3 May 2014, SANEF's chair, Mpumelelo Mkhabela, said the Protection of State Information Bill must be sent to the Constitutional Court (CC) for ratification before it is signed into law.[36] A "public interest defence clause" in the bill would "truly enhance the ability of media to assist in the fight against corruption". SANEF reiterated its call to the ANC and the president "in particular" to send the bill to the CC for ratification. Mkhabela said it was "arguably the biggest threat to press freedom and freedom of expression since the dawn of democracy. We stand ready to challenge it in court should the president sign it into law."

Although the media landscape had been transformed since 1994, ensuring diversity, Mkhabela said ownership in print was still "a sticking point". The 2013 Print and Digital Media Transformation Task Team had to draw up a blueprint to provide "a way forward". Its report found that print and digital media failed to "sufficiently transform" in terms of ownership, management, skills development, and employment equity, especially with reference to women and the disabled.

Mkhabela also urged African governments to speak out against the persecution of journalists in countries like Swaziland (now eSwatini), where a journalist was arrested and jailed for an article critical of its judiciary. "The silence of African governments and the general African public on all these violations is a cause for grave concern", Mkhabela said. He added that SANEF expected the SA government to raise these issues "at appropriate forums".

Twenty years down the line

Ex-editor Tim du Plessis also said that, after 20 years of democracy, the "concept and the practice of media freedom did not undergo a similar decisive moment on April 27 1994".[37] Under apartheid, South Africa

> experienced a sizeable degree of media freedom ... And I'm using the word experienced instead of enjoyed very deliberately, because what media freedom there was during the previous dispensation, was not bestowed by a generous and wise government, it was seized by brave editors and fearless journalists who were more or less supported by owners who could occasionally force themselves to look at a bigger picture instead of the bottom line only.

Du Plessis said a "vigorous and outspoken opposition press" developed during apartheid. From the early 1970s, papers aimed at black readers "joined the fray" in attacking the apartheid government, including *The World*, and later *Sowetan* and *City Press*, all promoting the banned liberation movements. Under the "late and great" Qoboza in the 1980s, *City Press* was regularly referred to as "nothing but an ANC mouth piece". The banning of *The World* and the arrest of its then editor Klaaste, together with Qoboza, in 1977, "was perhaps the most grotesque infringement of media freedom in South Africa's whole history".

To say there was "no or very little press freedom in South Africa prior to 1994 would be somewhat of an injustice to those editors and journalists who used every inch of manoeuvring room they had in those grim days" to oppose apartheid, Du Plessis said. The "sea change" between 1994 and 1996 was that freedom of speech, including media freedom, was enshrined in Article 16 in the Constitution. The political elite "obeyed the letter of this article ... but less so the spirit thereof". However, upholding media freedom not only involved adherence to the letter of the law, "but also encouraging and enabling the free flow of information, including information the government may not like". The Zuma era heralded "worrying signs" that South Africa's "20 year honeymoon" with media freedom may not be as everlasting as was thought. Du Plessis listed some reminders that media freedom can never be taken for granted:

- The Polokwane MAT resolution;

- The "pernicious Info Bill";

- Verbal attacks on journalists and publications, reaching a peak during "The Spear" debacle, when the ANC called for a boycott of *City Press*, with Media24 having to ensure the physical safety of its editor; and

- The irritation of the political elite with media and journalists "that [was] permeating into the state bureaucracy".

And still, that Bill

Du Plessis said that, although some of the most "invidious measures" in the Secrecy Bill had been watered down, it remained problematic, "if not outright dangerous". Had the Secrecy Bill been law at the time, the papers exposing the Nkandla scandal would have been prevented by law from doing so. Also: "The conduct of the ruling party in Parliament this week when they shut down Parliament's ability to hold the president accountable, is clear evidence that they will stop at nothing to protect their political interests."

R2K also described the bill as carrying "the fingerprints of the securocrats who have remained the 'hidden hand' behind this process from the start".[38] Even the final version criminalised the public for possessing information that had already been leaked, protected apartheid-era secrets, and "still contain[ed] broad definitions of National Security that will in all likelihood be used to suppress legitimate disclosures in the public interest". It was a clear threat to South Africa's "right to know". If pushed through, the Bill will end up before the CC and, should that happen, "it will be the first time the proponents of free speech and the free media will invoke the Constitution to safeguard their rights".

Du Plessis predicted that the "incremental encroachment on media freedom will ease at the demise of the Zuma era".[39] South Africans "ha[d] tasted the fruit of an open society" and would not allow the ruling elite to start "rolling back well-established rights such as media freedom and freedom of expression". In any case, the digital revolution would make it difficult to "enforce the kind of suppression of information envisaged in the Secrecy Bill".

The fear of the 'dead hand'

Also commemorating World Press Freedom Day on 3 May 2014, Aidan White, founder of the international Ethical Journalism Network (EJN), said the media should not confuse self-censorship with "sound editorial judgement":[40] The ethical decisions that journalists take on a daily basis require "choices about content", from headlines to audio clips. They are not acts of self-censorship, but when made by "well-trained, free-thinking professionals they are the bedrock of journalism at best".

When politicians and others complain that these choices do not "portray them in a good light", feeling they are victims of bias rather than the subjects of fair reporting, it boils down to "self-interest or reveals a poor understanding of the craft of journalism". Systems of internal self-regulation are therefore essential "to defend and explain the way media and journalism work". Good journalism is subject to editing, rewriting, or other alteration, in the name of style, taste, precision and clarity – "not internal censorship", but simply the application of sound editorial judgement.

White admitted that the "competitive, breakneck pace of the modern newsroom" and the pressure to deliver "faster and for different platforms" had "squeezed" the "ethical information space". Besides less time for editing, extra research, fact-checking and verification, fewer journalists are employed with the skill set and experience to maintain editorial standards. This leads to mistakes, "particularly as web content and social networks become increasingly important as sources of news and information".

While this undermines quality journalism, "even if it is creaking", self-regulation remains at the heart of producing "credible, trustworthy and timely journalism". Self-censorship – journalism driven "not by editorial concerns but by fear" – is a different matter. If decisions are motivated by "the threat of reprisal", whether from state, police, owners or advertisers, "it has nothing to do with the principles of good journalism". Internal threats "are not unusual" and not new. A survey in the US in 2000 showed that 40% of journalists admitted they shaped stories "to suit company interests". That is why ownership should be known in order for audiences to judge themselves whether to trust a news source. But, as long as "fear of retaliation stalks the newsroom", there can be no press freedom or independent journalism – journalists should always be alert "to the dangers of the dead hand of politics in media". Because: "Independence in the newsroom is not an optional extra; it is the solid foundation of the craft of journalism."

Still a 'battle of ideas'

The ANC policy documents for its 2015 conference still titled its media policy document as "The Battle of Ideas, Media Transformation & Diversity, and Accelerating Digital Future" [sic].[41] Prepared as a discussion document for its October National General Congress, it stated there was "a ganging up on the ANC and the movement's representatives" by media analysts and commentators as well as "the ultra-left and ultra-right".

After more than two decades of being the ruling party, it still referred to the "National Democratic Revolution", saying that media, "including unfortunately the public broadcasting outlets", are persistently attacking the "National Democratic Revolution". Besides, the quality of journalism continued "to deteriorate with increasing signs of gutter journalism". The document alleged that "young graduates in media studies have been exposed to a media studies curriculum and journalism that … promote sensational reporting and lacks [sic] a great deal regarding development communication and with little training in terms of government communication". The ANC's "battle plan" therefore included "engagements with strategic allies and other progressive forces that can influence media and help drive the thrust of the National Democratic Revolution in the media platform spaces". The "battle plan" should also "reignite the national dialogue and focus it on the radical transformation trajectory".

The ANC "has not effectively demanded its rightful share of the media space". In many instances, the "right to reply" to "baseless attacks" was not followed up on. In fact, it is "usual" to hear attacks on the party "without ANC cadres and spokespersons participating". The ANC should "measure its successes" and "package the success stories and disseminate" them through all media platforms. Also, its own network must be strengthened, *inter alia* by identifying journalism schools "of choice" and reviving the ANC News Service "and incorporat[ing] these onto [sic] the ANC Communications Business Plan".

This "war of ideas must be fought like a real war". Community and public media should offer "an additional potentially progressive opportunity for the ANC", depending on "the ability to influence this media and provide it with adequate support" – although it also stated that the ANC remained "committed to a media climate that is free from vested political and commercial interests".

Online has arrived

In 2015, the PCSA officially announced that it would henceforth also oversee online publications.[42] This was seen as yet another argument against the proposed MAT. Besides, 2015 saw the second "makeover" of the PCSA since 2013's PFC review.

The PCSA's independent co-regulatory mechanism provided "impartial, expeditious and cost-effective adjudication to settle disputes" between newspapers and magazines and the public, but did not regulate their online versions. The SACP's Blade Nzimande also questioned papers' positions on racism, arguing that no action was taken to censor racist comments – "[l]eave alone Twitter and Facebook". He said media houses must take responsibility "for people who comment on stories".

Following lengthy negotiations with several bodies, including SANEF, a new constitution, code of ethics and conduct for print and online and complaints procedures were adopted by the PCSA. It was seen as another response to the MAT threat. As said by Joe Thloeloe, PCSA executive director, the body had to be "reimagined", especially after the closure of Print and Digital Media SA following "dramatic changes in technology in the media industry". Previously, only the online sites of member publications could sign up to the PCSA's Code of Conduct. With the new policy, any site could sign up, giving it "the credibility of a Press Council stamp of approval".

'Potential political capture'

Despite the revised PCSA, the MAT remained a threat. In 2015, at the conference of the international Organisation of News Ombuds (ONO) in Stellenbosch, Karabo Rajuili, representing investigative journalism grouping amaBhungane, stressed the MAT's "impeding danger".[43] The threat was diverted through the PCSA's "proactive reform". Another threat was the "much amended, but still deeply problematic Secrecy Bill", at the time still "sitting on Zuma's desk". The minister of state security's suggestion that "it should be finalised" caused "an environment of increased securitisation of state and overreach of intelligence activities".

Ironically, on exactly the same day on which Rajuili spoke at the ONO conference – 23 April – the Films and Publication Board (FPB) had public hearings in Cape Town "on a new fundamentally flawed policy". Rajuili called it "a wolf dressed in sheep's clothing of a Bill". Drawn up "under the pretext of protecting the public", especially children, from harmful online content, the bill imposed "a new set of ill-conceived heavy handed regulations". The FPB's first hearing was in Durban, but notice of the hearings was only posted after the date: the press release was dated 18 April, while the hearings were held on 10 and 11 April. This despite "emphatic statements" by the ministry of communication stating that "no one is being side-lined", with "ample opportunity to discuss and change the policy document".

With the interregnum in the media industry due to the digital revolution, audiences changed dramatically. Between 2010 and 2015, the circulation of the ten largest newspapers in South Africa dropped by 29%, resulting in sharply declining revenues, also due to a decrease in advertising spend. The 2015 PricewaterhouseCoopers media forecast predicted that "mobile internet subscribers" would increase from 15 million in 2013 to over 35 million by 2018. Rajuili said the FPB correctly assessed that the internet would become "one of the most popular media distribution platforms in the country" – the reason why it was investigating "innovative mechanisms" to regulate the internet. Yet, in effect it would entail "a regime of state driven pre-publication censorship", with the "real possibility" of some content being banned and placing publishers and distributors at risk of punishable offences.

The FPB wanted to develop and implement a content-regulation framework and strategy that ensured "100% classification and labelling of classifiable content distributed on online, mobile and related platforms". Another goal was to "form and maintain national and international partnerships with key stakeholders, other regulators and law enforcement agencies for improved regulation of content distributed through online, mobile and related platforms".

Rajuili averred that the "over-concern on the harmful content is out of step with the reality". Moreover, the FPB Act on which the policy was based was already ruled by the CC in 2012 as containing large sections that were unconstitutional. This "landmark ruling" concerned the FPA of 1996 and its subsequent amendments, and dealt with the issue of prior restraint of publication. The "free flow of constitutionally protected expression" should be the rule, with "administrative prior classification" the exception. This principle was in line with the "highest democratic standards in international jurisprudence" and "in accordance with which any limitations on freedom of speech are treated with great circumspection". The new bill "simply ignored this".

The PCSA already regulated both print and online news. It was not clear if the new regulations would duplicate or claim jurisdiction over the PCSA. Implications were also that it meant pre-publishing approval for online content – something that just was not practicable. Even uploading "any video material, such as a family holiday, onto YouTube or Facebook" had to be pre-approved. Online distributors and large international online platforms had to register with the FPB at a fee of up to R750,000 per year, determined "at the discretion" of the FPB.

Rajuili emphasised that studies showed that an independent co-regulatory mechanism, "not including state participation", best serves press freedom. Self-regulation was seen as the best means "to enhance the role, accountability and responsibility" of the media in promoting democratic values and in upholding "the rights, dignity and legitimate interests of the people". A MAT "threatened to whittle away media freedoms", as would the FPB. It was "not the time to be losing ground, or for the media to be in deep slumber about this". Rajuili said the FPB had "overstepped" its mandate, playing "judge, jury and executioner". Should the policy "ever see light of day, it would have a suffocating effect on internet freedom", as it was not "in line with the spirit of the Constitution, or in the interests of free flow of information". The UN had already in 2011 declared the internet a basic human right, stating "every citizen in the world should have the right to meaningful participation in the Information Society".

The dis-ease of slowly declining freedom of expression

Besides the FPB there were also other red lights. Academic Julie Reid, writing about the decline of media freedom, especially since 2010, said there was a "slow but significant decline in South Africa's freedom of expression status, across all sectors of society and not only for the press".[44] In terms of the latter, the year 2015 was especially "a little sickly".

"Symptoms" included the SONA signal jamming, as well as the SABC's "selective camera shots" of the National Assembly, resulting in visuals broadcast to the public that did not include how EFF members were forcibly removed. In a following court case, media houses and R2K challenged, amongst others, a clause in parliament's broadcasting policy that allowed for the broadcast feed to be cut if there was disorder, as it contravened the Constitution. Another "symptom" was a *Sowetan* journalist's conviction of criminal defamation, which was overturned on appeal. Initially it seemed like a victory for freedom of speech, but it turned out the judge ruled it was because the state failed to prove the journalist acted with the intention to defame; the judgment itself still found criminal defamation consistent with the Constitution. This opened a "large door" to criminalising free speech. It was ironic that the Table Mountain Declaration called for the decriminalisation of defamation in Africa, but a South African court moved to criminalise libel. And "while one hopes Africa is moving forward on this issue, South Africa takes a step backwards".

Another symptom was the increase in attacks on journalists. This included police harassment of reporters, including wrongful or illegal arrest, and forcing journalists to delete photographs and barring them from entering particular spaces. Besides several such cases, the death of a freelance photojournalist raised another red flag. In February 2015, the State Security Agency also handed then Mpumalanga premier David Mabuza (who, by 2018, was deputy president) intelligence reports on the lives and movements of journalists in his province.

Besides these incidents, there was also "renewed movements to infringe" on media freedom. As early as in July 2014, SABC acting COO Hlaudi Motsoeneng called for the registration of journalists. After displaying "such an unfathomable dearth of understanding of freedom of expression rights", Motsoeneng was "rewarded" with a permanent appointment as COO "of the largest media outlet in the country", in spite of the Public Protector's report finding him guilty of maladministration and abuse of power.

Still looming was the unsigned FPB bill. If accepted, it would amount to pre-publication censorship of any digital publication, of any kind, on any digital platform, including websites, blogs, Twitter and Facebook. Besides having an impact on free speech beyond the media, it would have a hugely negative effect on the ability of digital news media to publish content timeously – "if at all". Besides being "un-workable" and "impossible to practically administer", the majority of users would "simply ignore the classifications procedure prior to publication", as well as paying a publications fee to the FPB. Besides: It was "all too obvious how this could be used as a post-publication political tool to silence dissenting voices in the digital space".

In April 2015, then president Zuma used xenophobic violence as "a thinly-veiled excuse to take another stab at the press". In the process, the department of communications was split into two new ministries and departments. The one, confusingly also called the department of communications, "was described in a manner more akin to a ministry of propaganda". Its newly appointed minister, Faith Muthambi, "seems to have read this memo". She assisted Motsoeneng in "painting a rosy picture of the SABC's finances" – despite the fiscal's projected loss of R501 million, as well as its loss of R1,1 billion in value a year after Motsoeneng's leadership. Muthambi "danced the propaganda tune further" by telling MPs that parliament should "initiate action on a regulatory system for the print sector" for "meaningful transformation". In other words: "resuscitating" the ANC's 2007 and 2010 calls for the MAT.

One could "only assume" she was ignorant of the various changes to the PCSA since then. Or perhaps "our minister of communications has not heard of the work of the Press Freedom Commission, nor read its final report". The minister was "clearly oblivious" to how members of her own party "frequently" made use of the ombud system – and how often papers were sanctioned in their favour. Besides: One should hope that she knew that the ANC delegation at the PFC's public hearings "called for an independent, as opposed to a statutory, system" of press regulation. Most worrying was that the minister seemed to believe "the regulation of the content of the press, and the transformation of the print media sector, [we]re the same thing". And, although print media needed transformation, it was a weak argument for justifying the MAT. While there were "many problems" within the print media, administration of complaints against "alleged bad" journalism was not one.

The cause of all these "symptoms" was "a general intolerance by the powerful [of] criticism and dissent". Besides a growing culture of state secrecy and unaccountability motivated by the desire "to conceal corruption, self-enrichment [and] maladministration", there was also "simply an arrogant irritation at the thought of investigative probing" into what the public "rightfully ought to know".

According to Reid all of this did not happen in a "vacuum". Rather, the "disease" had to be seen in the broader context of societal symptoms, such as the militarisation of the police, described as "a collective psychology of authoritarianism", and the securitisation of the state by security and intelligence services. There was not only harassment of whistle-blowers, but also assassination.

The "cure" was preserving a critical media's "investigative function". But the media were "frustratingly complacent" in defending their own right to freedom of expression, as much of the responsibility for the preservation of press freedom lies within the media sector itself. Indeed, media freedom does not apply to the media, although it is about the media being able to do their work, but "involves the freedom of the ordinary person to access that work". It not only applies to what is allowed to be said via the media, but involves access to quality media. The media also should not rely on others to defend their freedom, but must become activists for their own rights. And: If the media do not want to be "fixed" via authoritarian measures "enacted by a paranoid state", then they need to "fix" themselves.

The PCSA 'showing teeth'

In a study on the efficacy of the PCSA's press regulation released in November 2015, it was stressed that the media's accountability system had been the "subject of scrutiny" since the 2007 ANC Polokwane conference, which found it to be "ineffective" and "toothless".[45] The MAT was supported by the ANC "with even more vigour" in 2010, but by then the PCSA's own reviews were underway.[46] After the PFC's recommendations in April 2012, it released its new press code, complaints procedure and constitution in October.[47] Its most significant change was that the accountability mechanism moved from being self-regulatory to independent co-regulation involving public and press participation. At the time, it was enough to stave off the MAT.[48] In early 2013, when the ANC published its resolutions from its national conference of December 2012, it acknowledged these revisions, yet still stressed the intended parliamentary MAT investigation. By 2015, the ANC reinforced these resolutions, saying it "remained committed" to the MAT.

Meanwhile, the PCSA's 2015 report showed the number of complaints submitted, the nature of the complaints, the publications being complained against, and the PCSA's rulings over a five-year period.[49] Between 2009 and 2013 1,433 complaints were submitted, of which 1,083 were dismissed before ruling, deemed "superfluous or unacceptable due to anonymity, maliciousness, fraudulent complaints or most commonly, because the nature of the complaint fell outside" the PCSA's mandate.[50] If resolved amicably, complaints were dismissed. Still, 350 complaints were formally ruled upon and the findings published on the PCSA website. The PCSA sanctioned 200 cases for breaching the press code, while 147 were dismissed as it could not find that the publications were at fault, nor did they contravene the press code. Altogether 26 "public figures and celebrities" laid complaints, besides numerous members of the public.[51] National government ministries submitted 25 complaints, provincial government departments also 25, and local municipalities 20. Altogether 29 complaints came from political parties – twelve from the ANC, six from the IFP, three each from COPE and the DA, and one each from the Boerestaat party, the SACP and the ACDP. The Office of the President submitted three complaints, SAPS two, and the SABC six. Schools and universities submitted fourteen complaints and businesses 140. The ombud found that the press code's first article, on truth, accuracy and fairness, was breached in 115 of the 179 of the complaints sanctioned.[52] Regarding the code's second article, in terms of balance, context, distortion, exaggeration, misrepresentation, omission and summarisation, the ombud sanctioned 60 publications. The principle of seeking comment prior to publication – the *audi alteram partem* rule – was breached in 51 of the 179 instances. Regarding accuracy, 35 of the 179 articles were found to be guilty.

More than 640 publications, mainly members of PDMSA, subscribed to the PCSA and thus fell under its jurisdiction.[53] For the five-year period, 83 national and local publications were brought before the ombud, including those sanctioned and not sanctioned.

It was found that infringements were, "in fact, low", despite the criticism that the print media "display a continuing decline in the quality of journalism, especially with regard to ethics".[54] In fact, overall the print media were "performing well". The report said it was "encouraging to note that the largest majority" of publications operated within the ethical framework "for the greatest majority of the time". It was stressed that the PCSA's responsibilities "should not be conflated with the problematics surrounding a perceived lack of content diversity", besides the digital challenges faced by print. The PCSA said it could not be held responsible for these, as it was not its responsibility to address these problems. Regarding the PCSA being accused of "toothlessness", contrary to criticism, the PCSA and ombud had not displayed "significant bias" towards the press over the five-year period, nor were they in favour of the press at the expense of the complainant.[55]

The report also found that the introduction of the public advocate improved the PCSA's functioning and made the complaints process more accessible to the public, regardless of literacy. The turnaround time of complaints also improved significantly, and the prominence of apologies was now stipulated by the ombud, with publications complying 100%. Overall, the PCSA "improved in its functions" thanks to its policies, procedures and office.

The malaise 'a luta continua'

With many apartheid-era media laws lifted in February 1990, it was soon clear that, in the "new" South Africa, not all apartheid media legislation had been abolished.[56] The commitment to media freedom seemingly only applied as long as it suited the governing party, even though media freedom is entrenched in the Bill of Rights. This was also apparent in the days leading to the first election, when it became clear that censorship had not "departed on the coattails of PW Botha".[57]

By 2013, almost two decades after the first democratic elections, there were still so many laws relating directly and indirectly to the media that it urged the headline, "Scrap apartheid-era laws!"[58] At least ten laws had to be revised urgently as they were in direct opposition to the Constitution. One was the already mentioned NKPA of 1980, applied to prevent the disclosure of information regarding Zuma's private Nkandla homestead.

While the 1996 Constitution meant a new era for media freedom, barely a decade later the media were constantly criticised by government for being too critical, leading to a number of private and public clashes between the two. Fortunately, SANEF, formed two years after the first elections, could "speak with one, strong voice", not only to government, but also to owners.[59] Its media freedom subcommittee became more and more important as it became increasingly pertinent to what should be in the public interest, and what in the national interest.[60] After that, the initial "honeymoon" relations deteriorated to the extent that Zuma criticised the media for being "ideologically out of sync with the society in which it exists".[61] The differences could be reduced to what can be described as serving the public interest versus the interests of the specific political party and government. Mathatha Tsedu, influential editor, previous SANEF chair and SANEF executive director, had already described these differences in 2001, namely that the media held the view that national interest was encapsulated in the Constitution, and that those abiding by the Constitution were adhering to national interest. Although it seemed government believed national interest to be "something else", the media "maintain the position of watchdogs of the society and for the society, and we operate in the interest of the greater public".[62]

Altogether about 80 apartheid-era laws of the NP government to prevent the media from publishing anything negative about defence or police activities still remained on the statute books. The NKPA was the "standard bearer" and was invoked regarding reporting on Zuma's Nkandla residence.[63] The 2008 announcement that the SA Law Commission would do a "major review" of the 2,800 laws enacted since 1910 to modernise and simplify the statute book and remove those that are discriminatory or in conflict with the Constitution, led to nothing – and nothing has been done since.

Besides a number of other disillusions, the "wake-up call" was probably the proposed MAT.[64] The latter, along with the Secrecy Bill, the scrambling of technology signals during the 2015 SONA and the amendment of the FPA, led to the media and CSOs realising that the hard-fought-for media freedom – despite being entrenched in the Constitution – was being eroded under their feet.

The MAT still had the status of being "a resolution".[65] There was consensus that, should it be pursued, it would become a "battle" in the CC. Yet it remained on the ANC's agenda[66] and, when it surfaced again in 2015, constitutional law expert Pierre de Vos described it as "wrongheaded, self-serving, deeply reactionary and unnecessary".[67] According to De Vos, Zuma indicated "that such a Tribunal would protect politicians from the publication of facts about their 'private lives'". For Zuma it was more a matter of curbing the "ideological" media.[68] Clearly, he preferred a "more sympathetic and less critical press", and certainly did not like investigations "such as the arms deals and the Oilgate scandals". For the R2K, the MAT would mean "significant closures for freedom of expression, media freedom and therefore democracy" – as has occurred in a number of post-colonial African countries. The MAT remained "on the Government's agenda", with the minister of communications reporting to the communication portfolio committee in April 2015 that "the parliamentary investigation must be re-instigated for a more balanced and satisfying regime in this [print media] industry".[69]

The second clear threat to media freedom still was the Protection of State Information Bill[70] of 2010. Almost immediately dubbed the Secrecy Bill, it kept opposition parties as well as SANEF and other CSOs busy lobbying against it. But, even after revision, it still had, *inter alia*, an "open-ended definition" of national security that provided "scope for abuse of the law, or at least an inconsistent approach to what will be classified".[71] The eventual law could punish researchers, activists, whistle-blowers and journalists with prison sentences of up to 25 years and was directly against the Constitution. If passed, it would be contested in the CC.[72]

The grouping Democratic Left Front (DLF), with academic Jane Duncan among them, concluded that the Bill, together with the MAT, was part of "a bigger malaise in South African society and politics".[73] The "ruling elite [was] enhancing the coercive capacities of the state" and "centralising power in an increasingly unaccountable security cluster". Also, media professor Franz Krüger said the ANC's "animosity" towards the media regarding the Secrecy Bill was "not new". Although the two parties "meet from time to time and declare that they respect each other's role … in truth tolerance seems to be shrinking".[74] The Bill has also been described as the "most substantial infringement of media freedom we have seen". By 2015, it still sat "on Zuma's desk". In the wake "of an environment of increased securitisation of state and overreach of intelligence activities", the minister of state security suggested it should be finalised.[75]

A third clear example of threats to the free flow of information was the scrambling of signals during SONA on 12 February 2015. According to several days' news reports following the chaotic SONA, those responsible for this breech of the Constitution were state security individuals, or the department of state security as a whole.[76] Media24's parliamentary editor at the time, Janet Heard, described the chaos in a "dysfunctional Parliament" as "an hour that shamed South Africa".[77] Ultimately, the State Security Agency was responsible for the signal blockage, described as "undoubtedly a constitutional transgression".[78] Besides the signal blockage, the SONA saw the "heavy-handed eviction" of EFF members by unidentified men "in white shirts and black trousers", as well as a walk-out by the DA.

Following this, on 24 February 2015, journalists were barred from the Gauteng Legislature's press gallery during its opening; the explanation was that important guests had to be accommodated.[79]

Since these incidents it seems that state officials felt they had a licence not only to violate media freedom, but even to attack journalists, as happened at parliament on 11 March 2015 when the police's assault on a journalist was described by SANEF as "thuggish behaviour".[80] Since then, it became the rule, and not the exception.

Another example of how media freedom was eroded in this period is that of the amendments to the FPA, with hearings conducted by the FPB in an almost underhanded way.[81] Despite an "emphatic statement" by the communications ministry that no one would be "side-lined", with "ample opportunity to discuss and change the policy document",[82] this was not the case, as stated earlier. The new FPA was "fundamentally flawed". Under the pretext of protecting especially children, the Bill imposed a new set of "ill-conceived heavy handed regulations". The original Act had already been ruled unconstitutional in a "landmark" CC case in 2012.

Meanwhile, the media were still busy with earnest self-investigation to ensure their regulation system was above distrust. As in the Declaration of Principles on Freedom of Expression by the African Commission on Human and Peoples' Rights, "[e]ffective self-regulation is the best system for promoting high standards in the media".[83] It was "the best means to enhance the role, accountability and responsibility of the press in the promotion of the values of a free and democratic South Africa" while upholding everyone's "rights, dignity and legitimate interests".[84]

Introducing the February 2013 revised PCSA system, press ombud Joe Thloloe[85] said the previous one was

> slow in responsiveness, low in profile, violating the principle of separating player and referee, being exclusive author of their code of conduct, reactive rather than proactive in initiating complaints, structurally empowered to impose only symbolic sanctions, giving insufficient weight to rights like dignity and privacy, and failing to raise standards in the press as a whole.[86]

The revised system could be compared to what French academic Claude-Jean Bertrand termed "Media Accountability Systems", defined as "any non-state means of making media responsible towards the public".[87] Still, while self-regulation systems might be imperfect, government control would be "infinitely" worse. A MAT would ultimately ensure political control of the media, with the fear that journalists would self-censor instead of "offending" the MAT.[88]

The 2013 PCSA, ombud, appeals system and Press Code provided "impartial, expeditious and cost-effective adjudication to settle disputes".[89] It was based on two pillars: a commitment to freedom of expression, including media freedom, and excellence in journalistic practice and ethics. More than 640 publications subscribed to it, the majority PDMSA members.

But it was clear that, despite these measures, the ongoing threat of the MAT, the Secrecy Bill, seemingly *ad hoc* decisions by the State Security Cluster such as the SONA scrambling of cell phone signals, and threats such as still-existing apartheid-era laws, as well as the FPA and its amendments, remained. In fact, journalist Ferial Haffajee described the chaotic SONA as the beginning of a new era in South Africa – "the beginning of a police state".[90]

SANEF's chair at the time, Mpumelelo Mkhabela, stressed the fact that it could not be accepted that "because we have freedom of speech in South Africa there will be no threats. No, we have to fight for it".[91] Legal systems had to safeguard media freedom, but it also was paramount to explain to citizens what media freedom means. In his words: "Media freedom has nothing to do with the media, but with the freedom of citizens."

Besides these threats, there also was direct political influence over editorial decisions in certain media houses. Then Western Cape premier Helen Zille even described it as a matter of "state capture" of the media.[92] The "powerful ruling elite" took over "independent entities one by one" as an "extension of the ruling elite".

Constant vigilance

It was clear that the media had to be in a state of constant vigilance. In 2002, South Africa was ranked 26th on the first World Press Freedom Index.[93] This was exceptional for a country that had experienced official media freedom for the preceding eight years only, as opposed to other countries where freedom of speech had been entrenched as part of their civil liberties. At the time, the US ranked 17th and the UK 21st.

But, in 2015, two decades after 1994, a litany of media freedom impingements led to South Africa's demotion on the index, now ranking 42nd.[94] Another body that measures media freedom, Freedom House, categorised SA as "partly free", despite its constitutionally entrenched media freedom, downgrading the country from 33 to 37 on its 2015 scale.[95] This was the biggest downgrade on its index, together with that of Botswana and South Sudan.[96]

The words of Nelson Mandela, even before the first democratic elections, echo two decades later: "A critical, independent and enquiring press is the lifeblood of any democracy."[97] The SA media might have taken a long walk to get to their constitutionally protected media freedom, but this does not mean the journey has ended. For a democracy not only to survive, but to thrive, the "lifeblood" of "a critical, independent and enquiring press" needs to pulsate through its media's veins. As the R2K campaign stated: "We need continued, unified action to resist a growing culture of secrecy and authoritarianism."[98] While media freedom is always conditional and never guaranteed – nor resolved – and despite a *pro tempore* credence that it might be the case, it must be a constant dispute and a continuous struggle – and as much an issue in a so-called liberal democratic dispensation as it was in a dictatorial colonial era. As before: *A luta continua.*

And the role of the Afrikaans press, looking back

Ex-editor Tim du Plessis said in 2016 that, in the pre-1994 dispensation, opinion-forming newspapers used the media freedom that existed to help bring about change.[99] The Afrikaans papers "played an important role in convincing [their] community of the need for change – a good example of useful media freedom for the greater good". Du Plessis made a number of observations regarding media freedom:

- Media freedom is "in a better place than ever before, without a doubt", with Article 16 of the Bill of Rights entrenching freedom of speech and the media.

- With the courts and institutions of civil society, the free media, "especially the opinion-forming newspapers", have emerged more and more as "important brakes" for a ruling party with a great deal of power.

- Various black editors and journalists have not allowed that "a struggle solidarity" prevent them from robustly criticising the ruling party. "It took much longer for Afrikaans editors in the previous dispensation to discover their own voices."

- Threats of the MAT and certain clauses in the Information Bill have "the potential to be serious threats" to media freedom. Both are worrying indications of the "distorted thinking about the free flow of information of those in power", although it will certainly not stand a test in the CC.

- There is a much greater threat than the MAT and the Information Bill, and that is self-censorship, "an evil thing that appeared like a thief in the night". What makes it so bad is that it happens "unconsciously", and later "just happens by itself". This should cause "bigger concern than any restraints by a mostly incompetent state".

Social media have "overthrown" the rules and conventions of "public debate in the media" that have been established over decades. Besides "horrible defamation", there is little talk of "hearing both sides" and of "granting the right to reply". It is more a case of "ad rem" rather than "ad hominem", "with stereotyping and gross generalisation as weapons of

choice", resulting in inhibiting the free flow of thinking and ideas – "a disadvantage to all".
Du Plessis added:

> It's one thing to say, think – and read again – before sending on Facebook or Twitter.
> But it's altogether different when those voices that need to be heard, are not, out
> of fear of the lynch mobs on social media. This does not only threaten speech and
> media freedom, it also prevents South Africans from reaching a shared consensus,
> about their past, their present and their future – a consensus without which South
> Africa has no chance of upgrading our country from just muddling on.

If people are labelled as racists, apologists for apartheid or, on the other hand, beneficiaries
of corruption and patronage, a "vital dialogue that must lead us to a shared truth" is
extinguished. It is not about "absolute and unrestrained" speech and media freedom. While
it was difficult to predict what the outcome of self-censorship would be, Du Plessis warned
that what appeared on social media was not representative of South Africa's everyday
reality. Self-censorship "works like a slow poison. When you find out, it's usually too late."

A veteran's voice

Another ex-editor and media freedom expert, Raymond Louw, warned about inhibitions to
freedom of expression, particularly regarding another draft bill that was prepared towards
the end of 2016.[100] His "high hopes" that the "common law crime of criminal defamation",
as promised by the ANC to be repealed in April or May 2016, "were dashed when the
draft repeal Bill had not even been submitted to Parliament by the year's end". The justice
ministry postponed the Bill's tabling indefinitely "because the repeal could raise the
possibility of unintended consequences".

A new date has not been set for its submission, although the ANC's legal team that
initiated the repeal process emphasised that "defamatory statements made through the
media should not be considered a criminal offence". Civil litigation should be used to
pursue defamation claims. The delay raised doubts whether the ANC intended to proceed
with the repeal. But journalists' fears were heightened by the publication, in the closing
months of 2016, of the Prevention and Combating of Hate Crimes and Hate Speech Bill.
The media and CSOs were "dumbfounded", as the contents proposed "sweeping inroads"
on freedom of expression and media freedom. Several organisations, among them SANEF,
FXI and PEN South Africa, made "highly critical submissions". Offences included conduct
and speech "normally regarded as irritating or even offensive but not meriting a criminal
charge". It also impinged on what would be regarded "as humorous commentary on the
mores of society". The Bill would "stifle artistic expression, media analysis and critique of
public figures, cartoons and other forms of political satire". It equated certain forms of
expression to offences in terms of "insult laws", an offshoot of criminal defamation laws.
A key component of hate speech, as defined in the Bill, was an expression by any person
who intentionally

> by means of any communication whatsoever … communicates in a manner that
> advocates hatred towards any other person or group of persons or is threatening,
> abusive or insulting towards any other person or group of persons … and which
> demonstrates a clear intention … to incite others to harm any person or group
> of persons[.]

The grounds on which the bill was based related "to 17 human characteristics, including race, gender, sex, which includes intersex, ethnic or social origin, colour, sexual orientation, religion, belief, culture, language, birth, disability, HIV status, nationality, gender identity, albinism or occupation or trade". There were concerns that these characteristics were "defined extremely broadly", encompassing "practically any conduct" and extending to "virtually any characteristic or activity of people". The "temptation" for authorities, including police officers, was to "base charges on almost any human emotion as expressed by facial or bodily expression or innuendo".

The dangers of censorship were that certain clauses in the now-called "Hate Speech Bill" illustrated the major problem when trying to deal with hate speech and that leads to an intrusion into freedom of expression and the application of censorship: Penalties could be severe. For a first offence, a three-year jail term or a fine – according to commentators likely to be heavy – could be imposed. For a second offence, the prison sentence could be ten years or a commensurate fine.

Coupled with this was the "reappearance in discussions" by the ANC's policy-making committees that the MAT should be finalised. Meanwhile, the Protection of State Information Bill, or "Secrecy Bill", with its provisions for censorship and heavy prison sentences, was still awaiting the signature of the president, now already three years after its passage through parliament.

Other laws that were still an issue were the NKPA, preventing the publication of information related to certain institutions and buildings; the Protection from Harassment Act, which, despite "the good causes it serves", restrict journalists from gathering information by "staking out" the office or home of a person who refuses to answer questions over the telephone; anti-terrorism legislation, called the Protection of Constitutional Democracy Against Terrorist and Related Activities Act; and the Promotion of Equality and Prevention of Unfair Discrimination Act.

Simultaneously, the media were confronted by a phenomenon "that has taken on a more ominous character in the past year": increasing hostility by SAPS as well as violence during service delivery protests.

There were many examples of the intimidation and harassment of journalists by police, security staff and protestors during #feesmustfall in 2015. Also, government continued to call the press "the opposition", adopting practices that obstructed the press and prevented the public from being informed. In response to criticism of "the misrule, lack of service delivery, ever-increasing levels of corruption and other deficiencies in government", the latter resorted "to cloak its activities in secrecy". Louw said officials obfuscated or withheld information, including official reports that had to be released. SANEF raised its concerns about police brutality several times, including actions such as deleting images from cameras. It distributed a booklet with guidelines for the behaviour of journalists and police, "but it is uncertain how effective it is". Also, the public attacked journalists during demonstrations, probably fearing that photographs may lead to them being identified and charged.

Meanwhile, the media's 'dire' situation

In his 2016 report, Louw also referred to the media's "dire economic situation".[101] While the resulting retrenchments had "a negative impact on the comprehensiveness of news coverage", the impact on circulation and advertising revenue was "spectacular". The *Sunday Times*, once SA's biggest paper, was selling about half of its more than 500,000 copies of just years previously. It seemed there simply was no formula that could improve profitability, despite huge strides on the electronic side. In the traditionally "English" media houses, distress resulted from a high staff turnover, including of editors. There were also allegations "of improper management interference".

In October 2016, Independent Media, bought in 2013 by Iqbal Survé's Sekunjalo Investment Group,[102] withdrew from the PCSA. Independent appointed its own internal ombud and "so-called Media Press Appeals Tribunal" to adjudicate complaints.[103] Louw stressed SANEF's position, namely that self-regulation "should be executed at arm's length by an independent regulatory mechanism … and not by employees of media companies".

In 2016, the SABC also came "under critical review" by CSOs. Among them were Media Monitoring Africa (MMA), critical staff members and "interested parties". All warned that the SABC was deviating from its role as public broadcaster and had returned to being a state broadcaster "serving the interests of the ruling party", as during apartheid. An editorial instruction that visuals of violence and destruction of property during protest demonstrations were not to be broadcast was widely criticised.

Staff members reported "they were told not to use stories that spoke ill" of the president. Eight staffers who objected to the "departure from independent and public interest journalism" were dismissed. A "reckless reign of impunity" and a "culture of tyranny and fear, interference and censorship" were introduced by COO Motsoeneng. It turned out he lied about his matric certificate when first interviewed for a position at the SABC. Later, he was irregularly appointed in a senior position and his salary "improperly raised". There were also allegations that the SABC paid for the establishment of the TV channel ANN7 (now cancelled), and funded *The New Age*'s events. Acting Group CEO Jimi Matthews "resigned in disgust", referring to a "corrosive atmosphere" inside the SABC. All of this resulted in media freedom organisations and journalists picketing outside the SABC in Auckland Park and Sea Point in protest against censorship and in support of the eight staffers, now called the "SABC 8", which also led to a publication titled *The SABC 8*, written by one of the targeted journalists, Foeta Krige.[104]

The Struggle continues

As was the case in all of 2016, it was clear that media freedom, although constitutionally entrenched, was not guaranteed. As in cartoonist Zapiro's 2017 cartoon to show how "prepared" the security forces were for any disruptions at SONA, it turned out that the media was actually their target, together with the EFF. Ironically, the real threats, symbolised by armed terrorists, were totally missed.

Zapiro's cartoon before the 2017 SONA.

The 2017 Freedom House report indicated that, although South Africa's internet was free, its media was "partly free."[105] South Africa scored 38 out of 100, two points lower than the previous year. Freedom House said global press freedom was at its lowest point in 13 years.[106] One of the key developments in South Africa was that, in July 2016, ICASA ordered the SABC to reverse its ban of covering violent protests during the run-up to local elections, which would have avoided images that could be "unflattering" to the ANC.[107] The eight SABC journalists who were fired for resisting the ban successfully challenged their dismissal, but still endured intimidation and physical attacks after their request to the CC to order a parliamentary investigation. This led to an unforeseen tragedy. One of the journalists, Suna Venter, died as a result of a cardiac condition caused by severe stress,[108] ascribed to the continued intimidation, victimisation and death threats the SABC 8 suffered. Before this, Venter was even shot in her face with a pellet gun.

Despite this, Freedom House stated that, in 2017, South Africa had "a diverse and pluralistic media environment" supported by several press freedom advocacy organisations that regularly challenged media freedom encroachments.[109] Courts and regulatory bodies also consistently reaffirmed media freedom and the right to information, with judgments and rulings supporting an open and accountable government and media independence. Yet concerns grew amid increasing government pressure.

Already in September 2016, the Supreme Court of Appeal invalidated two rules that limited media coverage of parliamentary activity, ensuring the principle of an open parliament and journalists' right to report from within. The court also overturned a rule prohibiting the broadcast of footage depicting "grave disorder", invoked in 2015 to block coverage of protesting EFF members being ejected from parliament. It also ruled that the security service's signal-jamming was unconstitutional. All of this was thanks to a coalition of NGOs, as well as one media company, Media24, who challenged these rulings after the chaotic 2015 SONA.

Zumacracy and Ramaphoria

While South Africa saw the dawn of a new era under Nelson Mandela in 1994 and a moral high ground of a yet untainted ANC government, as ruling party it slid down a slippery slope into a morass of corruption under the country's fourth president, Jacob Zuma. This situation was eventually called "state capture".

When Cyril Ramaphosa was elected as ANC president at its 52nd conference in December 2017 and Zuma recalled as state president in February 2018, one commentator, Max du Preez, wrote that "South Africa's era of being ruled over by an African Strongman, almost a traditional chief, is over and a new era of modern leadership has started".[110] It ushered in a fundamental shift of which "historians will one day write a special chapter on". On the wave of what was called Ramaphoria, Du Preez wrote: "Did we, with our history and demographics, perhaps have to go through a Zuma period before we could cross a kind of Rubicon and become the country we're ready to be?"

Zuma, the "traditionalist", was for nearly a decade "a singing, dancing head of state", not "averse to wearing the traditional dress of leopard skins", and "a patriarch who sat on a throne like a king" while "dishing out and receiving favours and gifts".

The new president was the first "not coming from the ranks of the ANC in exile or the Mandela-era Robben Islanders". But Ramaphosa led a fractured party with "its culture of entitlement, corruption and nepotism that built up over years still largely in place".

When Zuma admitted to his "recall" as president, it was "entirely appropriate" that he did not leave office "in a dignified way, in a way that is in the interest of his party and the country".[111] His presidency was "arrogant, defiant, destructive, giving the democratic process the middle finger, only serving his own interests".

It was hoped that Zuma's demise would "be an end to the darkest chapter in South Africa's history since we became a democracy in 1994". Summed up, the "Zuma years" were a litany of "excesses, corruption, abuse of power and immoral behaviour". In the words of Du Preez:

- Zuma ripped through the fabric of our society and compromised many important state institutions.

- He outsourced the political power we, the people, entrusted him with to an immigrant family in exchange for favours and money. He allowed this family to insult us and subvert our sovereignty and national pride.

- He undermined our judicial system and repeatedly violated his oath of office and our Constitution.

- He blatantly lied to parliament on several occasions.

- He destroyed many of the hard-won gains our society had made between 1994 and 2009.

- He sat on a throne like a feared king, dishing out and receiving favours and gifts.

- He did serious damage to our economy and singlehandedly caused a credit downgrade.

- His personal life is a mess and he embarrassed his country in the eyes of the African continent and the world.

- He ruled by fear and division.

- He discredited the concept of a rapid transformation by using the concepts radical economic transformation and white monopoly capital as a smokescreen for large-scale theft of public money.

- He was driven by greed, lust for power and paranoia about ending up in jail.

- He systematically destroyed political accountability.

- During his nine years in power, money meant for development and alleviating the plight of the poor was brazenly stolen by his inner circle and "business buddies".

- He brought back something the ANC had successfully fought against for a century: tribalism and ethnic chauvinism.

- And, when it was his time to go, he threatened and mobilised and played dangerous games.

Zuma's legacy was a South Africa mired in an immoral morass. The problems plaguing the media were almost a mirror held to society and reflecting the general state of the nation. Thanks to media freedom, a number of items of longform investigative journalism appeared towards the end of the Zuma "reign", among them the highly successful *The President's Keepers*.[112] Written by well-known investigative journalist Jacques Pauw, who had been a member of the small but brave *Vrye Weekblad* during apartheid, it was a thriller-like account of exactly who the "President's keepers" were and how the wheeling and dealing behind the scenes played out to ensure "Number One" remained at the helm in order for all his cronies to benefit from "state capture". Another longform investigative journalism publication was Pieter-Louis Myburgh's *The Republic of Gupta: A Story of State Capture*.[113]

But at last, at the end of 2017, it seemed as if beleaguered South Africa glimpsed a new dawn. In a highly contested election bid for the ANC presidency, Cyril Ramaphosa narrowly won against Nkosazana Dlamini-Zuma, ex-wife of the president and seen as part of the Zuma-ANC faction.

Guptology, Guptacracy … Zuptacracy

It was time for the Zuptacracy can of worms to be opened. The main actors were the Gupta family, born in India and not South African citizens, although they received citizenship astonishingly fast. They benefitted not only from BEE benefits intended for previously disadvantaged South Africans, but also thanks to their corrupt relationship with Zuma. The family also ensured they had media interests. By early 2018 it was clear that the contract of the controversial ANN7, or "Gupta Channel", on MultiChoice would not be renewed. After what was called the "Gupta Leaks", none of civil society's media freedom fighters came to the defence of ANN7, not even to argue for the principle of a diversity of voices.[114] It was even said ANN7 "did not deserve activism" since it was not "legitimate media", but a tool to serve "corrupt interests" with disinformation and propaganda – all of it done with "stolen tax money".

Max du Preez lauded how the media "has shown in dramatic fashion that it is a central part of our freedom and democracy" – especially when Zuma "gave many of the powers the voters had given him to an immigrant family in exchange for gifts and favours". The Gupta family then "created a shadow state where they could even appoint Cabinet members, senior civil servants and members of the boards of state-owned enterprises". Aided by Zuma and by state security services, the family embarked "on a project to get rid of virtually everyone in the state who could investigate or prosecute corruption and state capture".

This project included "a massive propaganda onslaught to camouflage state capture and to discredit and harass its critics", all produced by the "Gupta/Zuma cabal". ANN7 was a central pillar, while Bell Pottinger, a British PR company, "refined" the strategy. Du Preez: "In a manner unforgiveable in any democracy, they started to disrupt, manipulate and undermine the national discourse and the way South Africans relate to each other." Their methods included "[s]implistic, cheap populist concepts" like radical economic empowerment and white monopoly capital that had "to cover up the grand theft of state money that would otherwise have gone to development and to alleviate the plight of the poor". The TV channel never attempted to let "suppressed voices be heard or opinions outside the mainstream". Instead, it was "purely and simply" a tool "to glorify the Guptas and the Zuma faction of the ANC, to cover up these elements' criminal tracks, camouflage state capture and harass those who stood up to corruption".

Bell Pottinger was hired and paid by the Guptas. "Zuma faction structures", like the Youth and Women's Leagues and the MK Veterans' Association, were provided with speeches and statements, while ANN7 gave them maximum publicity. On social media, the "massive Gupta onslaught" involved "fake news websites and hundreds of thousands of bots".

Although "serious questions" needed to be asked about MultiChoice's ethics in giving ANN7 a national platform and paying them "many millions", these do not belong "in the same debate as the merits or demerits of ANN7". The consequent "sale" of ANN7 to Mzwanele (previously Jimmy) Manyi "was nothing but a smokescreen". Nothing changed and it was still "a tool of state capturers and Zuma loyalists". It would have closed down anyway after the Guptas "fled the country for good". Du Preez said while he did not want to see ANN7 banned, he was glad it lost its privileged position on a national platform – and the SA "media landscape will be better off without ANN7".

And still the FPA …

Despite a new president and high hopes for a soon-to-be clean government, implications for online free speech and digital content still hung in the balance in 2018, when the department of communications and the FPB once again attempted to resuscitate the FPA. Richard Firth, "stalwart of SA's IT industry"[115] and CEO of a South African software developer, said that, while the primary mandate of the FPB was to protect children from "adult and other harmful materials" and to provide consumer advice to make informed viewing, reading and gaming choices, it was "overreaching" its mandate.[116]

The policy fell "incredibly short". The "insurmountable obstacles" the FPB would face in implementing the act were the most obvious. Everyone, irrespective of being an individual or a business who "publishes or facilitates" online material, would be held liable by the FPB. This included bloggers, small and medium enterprises, giant corporations, social networks and news agencies. It also included online learning material. The FPB's system to charge "service providers" a flat fee included an allowance "for those who don't want to pay the flat fee". The bottom line was that, unless a company or individual "has all their ducks in a row with the FPB, they cannot publish, and that leaves South Africans the poorer for the lack of content". This while a "digitally enabled and educated generation" was South Africa's best hope of building "a globally competitive and prosperous economy".

While educational organisations were trying to convert course material into "massive open online courses" thanks to new digital possibilities, South Africa is "actively blocking access to many existing educational media because they have not been approved by the FPB". And, while government "is handing out iPads", there is "little point if learners can't access half the materials available". Firth argued the FPB should rather try to preserve the internet "as a vehicle for social and economic development" to create an environment where political, social and economic innovation can flourish. And: It should encourage and facilitate an open and competitive online landscape, one that enforces the right to free speech and expression for both users and platform providers. Firth said the legislation should be rejected as overly restrictive and presenting the internet as a threat, as opposed to the "empowering, democratising entity" it potentially could be.

And yet another Bill: The Electronic Communications Amendment Bill

Also in 2018, Research ICT Africa recommended that the Electronic Communications Amendment Bill should be withdrawn because, among others, the government's plan to create a single "wireless open-access network" or "Woan" is a "high-risk intervention that South Africa cannot afford".[117] The department of telecommunications and postal services solicited inputs ahead of a planned industry debate on the Bill scheduled for early March 2018, already later than planned.

Research ICT Africa conducted independent research on ICT policy and regulation, concluding that the proposed Woan created an "uncertain investment environment". Other ways of entry into the market, more efficient use of spectrum, and preservation and extension of "common needs" could rather be implemented.

Government's plan to create a "wholesale provider of communications services" to which most, "if not all", future mobile spectrum will be assigned, was criticised by mobile operators and the Free Market Foundation. It would "simply result in an infrastructure monopoly" and harm investment. They argued that the Bill was unconstitutional and would be challenged if enacted. The Bill also provided for the "extensive powers" of the minister of telecommunication and postal services, not only in overseeing the sector, developing policies and representing the country at international forums, "but also in the management of scarce resources such as spectrum". The bill also eroded the powers of ICASA, a body that had "the necessary technical expertise and grasp of the dynamics and trends within the broad ICT sector". It also undermined ICASA's independence, making the bill unconstitutional.

South Africa's position on the Press Freedom Index

While the RSF's 2018 World Press Freedom Index reflected growing animosity towards journalists,[118] South Africa moved up on the index. This was not because trends improved in South Africa, but because of negative trends in other countries. In 2015 and 2016, South Africa ranked 39th out of 180 countries, in 2017 31st, and in 2018 28th. In 2019, the report ranked South Africa at position 31, down three from the previous year, with press freedom "guaranteed, but fragile".[119]

The report found that hostility towards the media, openly encouraged by political leaders, and the efforts of authoritarian regimes to export their vision of journalism, posed a threat.[120] A "climate of hatred" was steadily becoming more visible. Hostility towards the media from political leaders was no longer limited to authoritarian countries, where "media-phobia" was so pronounced that journalists were routinely accused of terrorism, and those who did not "offer loyalty arbitrarily imprisoned". More and more, "democratically-elected" leaders saw the media as adversary, openly displaying their aversion. The US, "country of the First Amendment", was again downgraded in the index under Donald Trump. In 2019 it occupied position 48, the report stating that Trump had continued to declare the press as "enemy of the American people" and as "fake news" in an apparent attempt "to discredit critical reporting".[121] The report stated that Joseph Stalin also referred to reporters as "enemies of the people". RSF secretary-general Christophe Deloire said the unleashing of hatred towards journalists "is one of the worst threats to democracies". Political leaders who "fuel loathing for reporters bear heavy responsibility", as they undermine public debate based on facts instead of propaganda. Also: "To dispute the legitimacy of journalism today is to play with extremely dangerous political fire."

Emily Bell, director of the US Tow Center for Digital Journalism and professor of professional practice at Columbia University's Graduate School of Journalism, said the assumption that "there will always be a well-funded commercial press is already shattered".[122] While "voices are drowned out or distorted by those with greater resources, better tactics or worse motives", press freedom is "a sacrosanct article" of a democracy, and "even at its most abusive, it remains better than the alternative". There are principles that identify good practice, just as there are in medicine and law, and "there are consequences for transgression". It is also not about "the rights of the press", but the rights of the citizenry "to have access to and receive reliable information".

Apocalypse now?

As early as in 2000, the World Bank identified "state capture" as a phenomenon in "post-transition countries" and posing a threat to growth more far-reaching than "ordinary" corruption.[123] This included "repurposing the state to serve the president, his family and friends, and certain other rent-seekers who fit into this camp, at the expense of other entrepreneurs, economic reform and, of course jobs". When this happens, policy, legislation and regulation no longer serve the national interest. Countries in post-communist Eastern Europe, including Russia, fell into this category. It was no wonder for journalist John Matisonn that ties between Russia's Vladimir Putin and South Africa's Zuma "played a role in both the biggest deal of the state capture era", namely the proposed purchase of R1 trillion worth of nuclear energy plants, and as a "model" for sustaining Zuma's "ascendancy despite growing challenges". Fortunately, South Africa's constitutional and civil society cultures – including freedom of the media and freedom of expression – proved "decisive" in reversing the tide. But during the period of state capture, the National Development Plan, a "widely supported blueprint for growth", was adhered to in name only.

It was this "state of the nation" that Ramaphosa inherited as state president, and while everyone, unrealistically, expected him to right all the wrongs, he had to play his cards well to ensure the ANC remained a "collective", while addressing the myriad of problems in the wake of the "Zupta" tsunami.

A basic human right

Also in 2018, SANEF "strongly" supported a new initiative to ensure that South Africans have "a daily standard level" of free basic access to the internet "to exercise their constitutionally guaranteed access to information rights".[124] The body was joined by the IAB SA (an independent non-profit focusing on growing the digital industry), MMA, and the Association for Progressive Communications (APC), and it followed the APC's research project titled "Perspectives on Universal Access to Online Information in South Africa: Free Public Wi-Fi and Zero-Rated Content".

The report was launched in 2017 on the International Day for Universal Access to Information at the conference of the Forum for Internet Freedom in Africa (FIFAfrica) in Johannesburg. Following this, the ANC resolved at its December 2017 National Conference to encourage efforts by government and the private sector "to deploy broadband infrastructure and services and also ensure accessibility of free Wi-Fi as part of the development of economic inclusion". The ANC emphasised that free Wi-Fi must be provided "in rural areas as well as metros and in all public schools, clinics, libraries, etc". In 2018, a further initiative was embarked on when an online industry and media delegation, led by the IAB SA and including SANEF, met with the SAHRC to discuss possibilities of free access. Based on existing government policies and the fact that universal internet access is "a pre-requisite and enabler for access to information", the delegation argued it should be included in the SAHRC's mandate. Their seven-point plan consisted of:

1. Free access to the internet at sites such as schools, libraries and health facilities;

2. Zero-rated access to government websites and data, as envisaged in e-government policies;

3. Free Wi-Fi access to be a basic municipal service and run as a public utility (alongside water, electricity and other services);

4. Minimum standards for the provision of free internet access, including for all commercial offerings, with a minimum data allocation per person per day and with standards for privacy, security, access quality and fair access to information in the public interest;

5. The introduction of the concept of "My Internet Rights" (or "My i-Rights"), namely that every citizen should be entitled to a daily minimum of free internet access (the example was 500 MB per day, the "standard" for many free Wi-Fi schemes), to exercise access to information rights;

6. The introduction of digital literacy programmes in education curricula as part of free internet schemes, especially aimed at children "and those unfamiliar with risks and opportunities related to the internet"; and

7. The need for the SAHRC and other oversight bodies to monitor and report on the "progressive realisation of internet access rights", in particular the adoption and implementation of legislation, regulation and policies governing free access to the internet as a basic human right.

In terms of other realities facing South Africa, this seemed like utopian ideals, but the COO of the SAHRC, Chantal Kissoon, indicated that the commission would consider incorporating the monitoring of government's internet access plans for inclusion in national, regional and international reports on human rights issues. They would also investigate convening experts and stakeholders to explore aspects of the action plan and raise the issue of free access in stakeholder engagements.

To emphasise the importance of the issue, SANEF chair Mahlatse Mahlase stated that access to information is "a fundamental human right and access to the internet is fundamental to exercise those rights". At the time, the government already made commitments as part of the global Open Government Partnership to set up open data portals and e-government services. Unfortunately, this ambitious plan has remained just this: ambitious, and a plan.

In 2018, communications regulator ICASA established its Consumer Advisory Panel to advise the regulator on consumer-related issues in broadcasting, telecommunications and postal services.[125] It planned to "reach out to consumers" to understand concerns and recommend what consumer protection research should be undertaken. The panel comprised eleven members, nominated through a public process, also representing those living in areas "poorly served by ICT". For ICASA it was an important milestone because they would receive "first-hand information" to assist them to better execute their "consumer protection mandate", and to ensure that they "indeed live up to our vision of ensuring that we regulate in the public interest".

And the power of a free press

In 2018 the Taco Kuiper Award for Investigative Journalism proved that 2017 was "an extraordinary year", wrote media professor and veteran journalist Anton Harber.[126] After experienceing a number of years of "facing an impervious culture of impunity", accountability at many state institutions faltered while corruption undermined democracy and destroyed the economy. But: "[S]mall groups of investigative journalists beavered away." Eventually, they "pieced together" the elements of what grew into "a remarkable story of a systematic attempt to control the machinery of state for personal gain" – what was to become known as "state capture". The award was won by a joint team of amaBhungane, *Daily Maverick* (DM) and *News24*.

After the "back-and-forth of allegation and counter-allegation, charge and denial", a "trove of leaked emails" appeared, providing evidence of "the depth and breadth" of the attempt to take control of parts of the state. The journalism teams "did meticulous and highly skilled work", mining the material and then weaving together "a full picture". The centrality of professional journalism and a free media in this "sad chapter in the history of South Africa" was undeniable. Harber wrote:

> I know of only a few times in the history of a nation when journalists have played such a clear and crucial role in bringing a country back from the brink. South Africa's journalists were not alone in this. They worked side-by-side with civil society and

the judiciary in particular. But never has it been clearer how important a free press, skilled investigative reporters and the support of brave editors is to a democracy, its economy and the people who live in it.

It was also a tide turner for journalism. Some clear trends surfaced. The major one was working collaboratively, not only as teams, but also across media outlets and types. This reflected an international pattern, with the scale and complexity of large investigative stories "often too much for one journalist or even one newsroom to handle".

Another trend was how journalists from different newsrooms not only cooperated, "but helped, promoted and protected each other". Also: Most of these projects were done thanks to philanthropists and foundations, rather than through commercial newsrooms – "a major signal of where South Africa's journalism is headed". Besides the winning entry there was also "a remarkable array" of other investigative work.

But a worrying trend was the rise in the intimidation and harassment of journalists, including attacks on reporters, threats to those covering contentious issues and the "weaponisation" of social media by using robots and fake news to target journalists. "Thuggish protesters" threatened an editor in his home, while others disrupted a public meeting of journalists. Editors were targeted by fake news outlets, resulting in, as far as Harber knew, journalists for the first time ever needing restraining orders "against organisations and individuals". Jacques Pauw, veteran muckraker, was pursued by authorities threatening him to stop publishing. Another negative trend was the "few" news outlets that promoted or supported state capture, with journalists "availing" themselves "to be used by those who wanted to cover up what they were doing". It drove home the need "for vigilance and the utmost professionalism" to ensure journalists build trust and credibility and serve the public interest, not "narrow, personal or factional interests".

Open season

It seemed the position of journalists became more and more precarious, as neither police nor politicians understood their role in society. In March 2018, SANEF expressed its shock following an attack on a journalist within the parliamentary grounds.[127] The incident was filmed and the "disturbing" video "widely circulated". It showed EFF deputy president Floyd Shivambu physically attacking Media24's Adrian de Kock. According to De Kock, he asked Shivambu for comment on the disciplinary inquiry against then Cape Town mayor Patricia de Lille. Shivambu declined to comment. The video shows how Shivambu, accompanied by two unidentified men, is heard demanding that the images are deleted while he and another man violently grab De Kock, with Shivambu also slapping him. De Kock was "pushed around" whilst the men tried to remove the camera from around his neck. Shivambu later walked away while the other two continued to harass De Kock.

SANEF condemned the incident "in the strongest possible terms", saying it was "extremely disappointed by Shivambu's actions" and that this "type of intolerant behaviour" was unacceptable in a democracy. As MP, Shivambu "is entrusted with protecting our hard earned media freedom and freedom of expression as is enshrined in our constitution" and he should "lead by example and champion journalists' protected right to do their work without fear or favour". It would take up the matter, as it was "unacceptable" for an MP "to intimidate a journalist whatever the circumstances". They also welcomed the fact that De Kock planned to lay a charge of assault against Shivambu. SANEF "have repeatedly called on police to assist" and, despite "numerous and often public attacks on journalists, to date no perpetrator has been brought to book". Failure to prosecute attacks "allows for a culture of impunity to continue".

A cartoon by Zapiro on 23 March 2018, indicating the EFF's attitude towards the media.

And still, SA's 'censorship bill'

The FPB's Amendment Bill still caused ripples, years after it was initially tabled, when ISPA took up the cause and said it raised serious concerns about freedom of speech and should be rewritten.[128] The bill was a "classic example of good intentions gone bad". The draft got lost "in vague definitions and ill-considered attempts" to expand the role of the FPB into an "internet policeman".

As all South African internet users are "online content distributors", it meant that WhatsApp messages and Facebook and Twitter posts and comments on online news articles were all content that the bill wanted to regulate. The bill proposed different definitions of the term "distributor". One was that of a "non-commercial online distributor", defined as "any person who distributes content" on the internet, or enables content to be distributed for personal or private purposes. It went "well beyond the original mandate" of FPB legislation, which was "to regulate the activities of people in the business of distributing films, games and publications". Now the bill sought to regulate all South Africans who distributed electronic content, including private communication between individuals, which would have a "[dangerous impact on] fundamental constitutional rights such as freedom of expression". ISPA said a "quasi-government body" appointed by a minister should not be making "extremely complex legal judgment calls about something as fundamental to our hard-won democracy as freedom of expression". Before the bill could be signed into law there should be "careful consideration" of how it "interacts with South Africans' constitutional rights". And, if all else fails to remedy the bill, the act "should be repealed and rewritten from scratch".

The growing threat of fake news

Meanwhile, the distribution of fake news, or disinformation, became more and more problematic as technology became more and more accessible. In 2017, a joint statement was issued by various global and African bodies on freedom of speech, "expressing alarm" at the spread of disinformation and propaganda, with attacks also on news outlets as "fake news".[129] The ICFJ issued a guide to fake news, stating that "fake news" was nothing new and dated back to ancient times, but the 21st century saw the "weaponisation of information" on an unprecedented scale. Bodies representing freedom of speech were

> [a]larmed at instances in which public authorities denigrate, intimidate and threaten the media, including by stating that the media is "the opposition" or is "lying" and has a hidden political agenda, which increases the risk of threats and violence against journalists, undermines public trust and confidence in journalism as a public watchdog, and may mislead the public by blurring the lines between disinformation and media products containing independently verifiable facts.

In South Africa, the production of fake news by the once prestigious UK PR firm Bell Pottinger became a case in point. Thanks to professional journalism, the firm's disinformation campaign – described as a "large-scale fake news propaganda war in South Africa" – collapsed in 2018.[130] Bell Pottinger and a marketing firm based in India "had been part of a long and secret campaign to foment racial polarisation", a campaign carried out to discredit critics of Zuma and the Guptas, "who paid the (expensive) bills". The disinformation was spread through websites and tweets, amplified by bots, misleading online adverts, covert exploitation of Facebook and Wikipedia, as well as hacks and malicious leaks. Journalists who exposed the state capture by the Guptas were the subject of accusations and being lapdogs of "white monopoly capital".

And another case in point

As if it was not enough that the credibility of professional news media was attacked, the news media themselves also stepped into it. With both feet, in fact. In 2018, SANEF met with the management of Tiso Blackstar, a media group that now owned the *Sunday Times*, in the wake of the "deeply disturbing developments" at the Sunday paper after its reportage on a so-called SARS "rogue unit".[131] It turned out to be false and, while SANEF welcomed the paper's apologies, these "breaches of editorial standards" have undermined public trust beyond the publication itself, "undermining the credibility of journalism for the public good". Besides affecting the media's credibility, it "had a devastating impact" on individuals' lives. SANEF appealed to "media houses to seriously introspect and review editorial systems to ensure" the debacle was not repeated.

Besides an "an independent investigation into issues of editorial integrity", SANEF also undertook "a major training campaign on media ethics for journalists". More ominously, the episode led to new calls for a MAT. SANEF reiterated its opposition to state control because of its inherent dangers to media freedom. The Editors' Forum said the PCSA was an independent co-regulation system, headed by retired judges. Besides already proven to be effective and quick, it was also cheaper. The system was also revised over and over to respond to needs of the time.

The efficacy of the PCSA could be found in the fact that complaints against the *Sunday Times* were laid by the three individuals concerned in the story. The eventual cases were Pravin Gordhan vs *Sunday Times* (15 December 2015), Ivan Pillay vs *Sunday Times* (16 December 2015) and Johann van Loggerenberg vs *Sunday Times* (16 January 2016). The PCSA forced the paper to apologise even before the official revelation of the bogus stories and the paper's later apologies.

Brown envelope journalism

The so-called "brown envelope journalism" from a previous era surfaced again in 2018, forcing SANEF to issue a statement about its concerns that journalists might be "receiving bribes from newsmakers to stop them from publishing certain stories".[132] This was clearly violating the press code that binds journalists "to practice ethical journalism at all times, reporting the truth and being motivated only by the public interest". SANEF requested those with evidence of journalists accepting bribes to contact the PCSA's public advocate, Joe Latakgomo.

The press code clearly states that journalists must avoid conflict of interest, and also that

- The media shall not allow commercial, political, personal or other non-professional considerations to influence or slant reporting. Conflicts of interest must be avoided, as well as arrangements or practices that could lead audiences to doubt the media's independence and professionalism.

- The media shall not accept a bribe, gift or any other benefit where this is intended or likely to influence coverage.

- The media shall indicate clearly when an outside organisation has contributed to the cost of newsgathering.

- Editorial material shall be kept clearly distinct from advertising and sponsored content.

On payment for information, the code states that the media must avoid "shady journalism" in which informants are paid "to induce them to give the information, particularly when they are criminals", except where the material concerned "ought to be published in the public interest and the payment is necessary for this to be done".

SANEF concluded that it expected journalists to abide by the code "at all times"; also that it expected editors to "continuously ensure that training on the press code is done and journalists understand their obligations and responsibilities".

A slow tsunami

But another threat to media freedom was "shrinking newsrooms". Glenda Daniels, an academic and chair of SANEF's media and ethics diversity committee, wrote in 2018, just before the commemoration of Black Wednesday, South Africa's Media Freedom Day, on 19 October that, "[l]ike a slow tsunami, South African newsrooms are shrivelling".[133] If "journalists all but disappear, whose freedoms are we worrying about protecting?" she asked. Journalism is meant to serve through offering the public a voice, diversity and plurality to deepen democracy, but, by 2018, the number of full-time journalists had halved from ten years before, when it was about 10,000 strong. Some researchers said there could well still be about 10,000 "media workers", but some were freelancers and most in PR or part of the "gig economy" – "a day here and a day there of editing or hustling".

Community newspapers shrunk from 575 in 2008 to 275 in 2018, with the CEO of the AIP, Louise Vale, who felt the latter number "could be on the optimistic side" as it may be even less than that.

It became the rule rather than the exception to be retrenched as part of cost-cutting, with companies serving "section 189" notices on employees according to the Labour Relations Act. The SABC, the biggest employer of journalists, at the time had debts of R622 million and said "it may be serving the 189 notice". Between 2008 and 2018, retrenchments, voluntary packages, dismissals, "being laid off" or "asked to take early retirement" took place "in waves". Media companies came up with "rational" and "somewhat scientific" terms, such as "consolidation", "convergence" and "centralisation". But Daniels said all "these Cs sound politer than the S words which are more apposite descriptions of the reality: shrivel, shrink, sink and squeeze".

The majority of the retrenched journalists had no union support, were not trained for the digital age "even though they were keen", and the majority were part of the so-called gig economy – "doing a mix of journalism and other things", such as PR. A small percentage was studying towards MAs or PhDs, "while an even smaller percentage moved completely out of journalism to selling property or Bitcoins". The majority were "mostly disillusioned with the media world". A study also found that "[a]ppallingly low freelance rates" had not kept up with inflation". But, as one said: "We take whatever we can get, really, after being chewed up and spat out by the company, which didn't have the courtesy to even say thank you, never mind a farewell party after 20 years."

And women were still worse off

Daniels also referred to the so-called glass ceiling research on women in the media, launched on Black Wednesday/Media Freedom Day on 19 October 2018. It showed that women were still experiencing a backlash in the newsroom and media companies. Despite men understanding "sexism a lot better … than in the past", women still earned less than men. Sexist jokes were "still the order of the day", and being ignored for promotion and the "old boys' network" continued to exclude them.

Daniels asked rhetorically: What have job losses in journalism got to do with Black Wednesday/Media Freedom Day? In a democratic South Africa it was "highly unlikely that any such gross and obscene mutilation of our human rights" (clamping down on newspapers) could ever take place again. But job losses meant "we are also losing voices, plurality, context, and experience". With media companies consolidating, they are hiring young people "who they can pay R10,000 a month or less, but provide no mentorships and training, so they swim or sink". Also, such a loss of plurality meant "you see the same story with the same quotes, intro, angles, etc." in a variety of "different" websites and papers, sometimes with the same byline, sometimes with different bylines, "discombobulating readers in the process".

Daniels also identified other serious threats:

- Government interference in the SABC board. "Government tends to think it owns the public broadcaster", thereby conflating state, government, ruling party, SABC and the public;
- Police bullying at crime scenes: Police need to know that journalists are allowed to be at crime scenes, to interview people and record events from outside the cordoned-off area;
- Protesters and police guilty of harassing journalists, "particularly photo-journalists and women";
- The Protection of State Information (Secrecy) bill, still remaining "unsigned on the president's desk".[134] It should be scrapped, as information rights and media freedom activists have already sent it to lawyers to check for constitutionality;
- The establishment of the MAT, which had remained an ANC resolution since 2007. Although unimplemented, "some elements" in the ANC would like journalists to be "licensed". Daniels added: "This is a joke in the digital world where everyone can publish and the definition of who is a journalist becomes more fluid every day";
- Surveillance, with a number of investigative journalists reporting that their phones were tapped;
- The increase in the bullying and online trolling of women, with bullies using "sexualised images" to shut women up when they expose investigations on corruption;
- Fake news (or misinformation/disinformation/propaganda and lies) was a huge threat "and will probably increase" moving to the 2019 election, also with politicians being accused of attempting to "brown envelope" (bribe) journalists;
- The huge loss of professional journalists meant a "loss of institutional memory, loss of political memory and context, with more mistakes in print and online"; also subs' desks have been cut back radically;
- As a last threat, Daniels said that, although the police "may not be throwing journalists into jail and the government is not closing papers", media companies "are discombobulated, and have resigned themselves to participating in the tsunami; they have not provided support or training either".

Daniels identified the following media trends:

- Collaboration and sharing, with investigative journalists sharing information and helping each other. "Competition is healthy, but media wars are a bit passé." The trend is rather for collaboration "to hold power to account to fight corruption, disinformation and lies";

- To fight corruption – probably "the biggest threat to poverty alleviation", meaning investigative journalism must be supported;

- Without investigative units, titles "are likely to continue to shrink". Some that once carried 64 pages have been downsized to 32. News companies need "to have a niche area to survive", otherwise they tend to be full of opinion, not based on research;

- The backlash against women; but the good news was that women were more assertive in media companies about salary disparities and were putting "up their hands more for leadership positions";

- Although social media usage is deepening democracy, data in SA is more expensive "than anywhere in the world", with most people in rural areas without smartphones to access social media, leaving "the middle classes who are addicted to their echo chambers";

- Newsrooms will continue to hire younger people, "who have the skills of uploading videos with smartphones" and who can do "content producing" – "which isn't necessarily about telling a story skilfully". In deconstructing the term "content producing", Daniels said, it "can be likened to a vase: pour anything in, including flowers, and it holds 'content'";

- Time stress: journalists having to do multiple stories a day without getting the time to do in-depth, complex stories;

- Newsrooms not only shrinking, but also closing, and not just in print;

- The growth was in online media; in 2018, the country counted 108 online publications, which did not exist a decade earlier, and with most of them registered with the PCSA;

- Yet, until broadband is made available to all, and made cheaper, "as promised by the government ten years ago, the unemployed, the poor, and rural folk will continue to be the losers in accessing information".

And a minister threatening "War!"

Shortly after the commemoration of Black Wednesday in 2018, the media establishment was shocked by finance minister Tito Mboweni's social media posts threatening war against editors.[135] In fact, SANEF stated it was "deeply disturbed". In a statement it said that Mboweni tweeted without context:

> Wars start in different ways. Spears and shields, gun powder, bullets and now through media: printed and electronic (eg trade wars by a super president), and then Social media!! Well, the SA Editors must be Editors!! If needs be, we will be forced into the fight, War!

In a second tweet, Mboweni said he was a "product of the warrior commanders of the mighty Zulu army" and that "there will be collateral damage".

SANEF said the comments were unacceptable. As a cabinet member, Mboweni is a custodian of the Constitution and "has taken an oath of office to protect and uphold the Constitution that guarantees media freedom". Whilst the minister has "every right to engage with the different media houses if he feels aggrieved", or alternatively, approach regulatory bodies like the BCCSA or the PCSA, "threatening editors with war is unacceptable and very dangerous whatever the circumstances". SANEF said it hoped to meet with the minister "to discuss the unfortunate tweets".

Facts matter

Towards the end of 2018, Max du Preez asked whether the media should allow the EFF as "loud-mouthed" group to dominate the national discourse.[136] They "are controversial and make the most noise". But should the media allow "the distortion of public opinion", Du Preez asked rhetorically after a controversial live broadcast of the EFF. He added: "Do editors and journalists have the guts to do what should be done now?" As veteran Struggle journalist, he suggested that there should not be

> another live broadcast of an EFF press conference or rally, not after the one last week outside the Zondo Commission when Julius Malema and Floyd Shivambu's blatant lies, threats against the media, hints at coming violence and crude racism were broadcast on live television.

Du Preez argued that footage and recordings of all future EFF events should be viewed and fact-checked "and stripped of incendiary talk and wild defamation" before being aired via radio or TV. Stating that "[m]any in the South African media appear to be oblivious of the fact that the reality of post-truth and alternative facts has also arrived in our society", he appealed to them that "facts matter". "And it is our primary job as journalists to make sure that they do."

He referred to the US media, which had decided not just to repeat Trump's "disregard for the facts" and not to "simply report them, but to also point out his blatant lies". He referred to "Truth-O-Meters" that were being used "to quickly fact-check politicians' utterances".

Journalists should guard against acting as "publicists" for the EFF's "theatrics and publicity stunts". If journalists "don't fall for their politics of spectacle every time, they will have to come back to earth and practice proper, issue and policy driven politics".

Regarding the EFF's blatantly racist statements, it should be reported as is done with right-wing racism: "as an exposé of racism and with commentary, rather than as run of the mill political statements".

The irony was that the media, as guardian of an open society and in turn the backbone of democracy and characterised by tolerance and free speech, were "aiding and abetting the EFF's all-out assault on our openness and tolerance". The media did so with its "generous, often unquestioning publicity" – and all of this "completely out of proportion" to the EFF's popular support.

It is ironic that those politicians who attacked media freedom in a way "unprecedented since we became a democracy, and victimised, intimidated and threatened them with violence (even acting on these threats on occasion), became the media's darlings". This after the media "were all on our high horses, flaming sword in hand, fighting Bell Pottinger's propaganda onslaught during the Zuma-Gupta era", yet "the EFF is Bell Pottinger on steroids, but now our horses are suddenly lame".

Malema "played the media like an organ", and "too many of us danced to his tune like trained monkeys". When he feels "unloved or under attack", he holds a "rambling" press conference, "mostly spewing nasty gossip, innuendo, insults and threats". Du Preez argued that the media hung on to every word, partly "because some journalists confuse entertainment with substance, but also because of fear".

The fear included being called a racist or "a tame black in the service of whites", but also "a very real fear that they be called out by name and threatened with retribution by the EFF mob, on social media and, as has been happening increasingly recently, in person". Du Preez wrote that, when the EFF did not like what journalists reported, they were labelled "Stratcom agents" – "even journalists with well-established struggle credentials". According to him, "[t]hat label is hung around my neck every week on social media", despite public knowledge that he was one of the journalists who exposed the apartheid government's "strategic communications" project of propaganda and disinformation in the 1980s.

Du Preez said he felt like "a stuck record" because of the media's handling of groups to the left and right "who have little public support, but scream their hatred, lies and intolerance out so loud" that they are allowed to dominate the public discourse. Deciding how to report on such matters is not censorship, but the opposite: "If we allow loud-mouthed groups to dominate the national discourse purely because they're controversial and make the most noise, we oversee the distortion of public opinion."

While the media have to make judgment calls every day regarding what should be on the news agenda, not all events can be covered in the same detail. Decisions should be made regarding balance and fairness, "and the public should keep us honest". Du Preez appealed to the media to "carefully consider" whether an EFF statement or event is really newsworthy, "or an attempt to obfuscate, mislead or manipulate the media". Also: "Journalists who give unnecessary oxygen to politicians who undermine our democracy and our open society, are betraying their real calling as servants of the truth and of freedom of speech."

A war against the media is a war against democracy

At the same time, Ralph Mathekga, senior researcher at the Centre for Humanities Research (CHR) at the University of the Western Cape, wrote about the "war" against journalists and politicians' "willingness" to "openly name" journalists they did not like.[137] Even though "it was generally accepted" that a free press strengthens democracy, there has been "significant regression" regarding the media's role in society. As a global phenomenon, the Trump administration in the US openly threatened the media with contempt, causing "ripple effects … in the most remote corner of the world". "Fake news" became "the standard response to negative media coverage", with some even "manufacturing fake news to counter and neutralise legitimate adverse reporting". Those sceptical about a free press now "openly attack[ed] the media". In South Africa, there has been "a growing hostile attitude" among some influential political leaders, with a "level of intolerance" to the extent that "it has become a political project to express that intolerance towards a free press".

The *Sunday Times*'s "rogue unit" reports "did not help". Also, "[q]uite often", when one media house made a mistake, it was used to create "the impression that the entire media is compromised and cannot be trusted". There should be nothing strange about occasional tension between the media and governments, but the South African situation "is strange" in that it is not only those in government who resent a free press, but also "some elements" in the opposition who show intolerance. While opposition parties usually gain from a free press, "as it helps them to point out the shortcomings" of government, opposition parties in South Africa "seem to be obsessed with power to a point where they believe a free press would bother them once they are in power". Even within the "dominant opposition parties" there was a growing level of intolerance towards a free press.

Mathekga wrote that there are those "who really relish in calling media conferences to berate others", but opposition parties in South Africa have to reflect on "what type of relationship they want to build with the media". The media cannot be seen as important only when those political parties have "juicy gossip" about government. Furthermore, South African politicians have openly named journalists they dislike. The tactic of trying "to isolate journalists simply because they are uncooperative is what we see also in Donald Trump's White House", with some journalists intimidated and threatened with withdrawal of their accreditation. If an organisation or department "decides to bar a media house from covering its events, the most appropriate thing is for other journalists to boycott coverage". The media "should sharpen its reporting and become more vigilant and robust in its coverage". This will ensure that the "only thing that eventually triumphs is the truth", to be delivered "with no agenda other than to unmask the full extent of the story". Otherwise, the "war between the media, the powerful and the politicians will escalate further".

Mathekga said the murder of journalist Jamal Khashoggi was no coincidence. Trump's "openly hostile attitude" towards the media created "favourable conditions for Saudi Arabia's government to stage a broad daylight murder". The message: "One can openly take up battle against a free press and face no consequences." Mathekga said South Africa is getting to a point where one can target the media without facing anger from society. "It's doable, and it's sadly underway."

The media's realities after the 'new dawn'

South Africa as a country on which a free media have to report is far from simplistic. After the swearing in of Ramaphosa as president in May 2019, the 66-year-old Ramaphosa had to overcome many challenges, but few in his "long career as an activist, businessman and politician" were as daunting as those awaiting him as president of a "state captured" country.[138] He had to consolidate his position in a deeply divided nationalist liberation movement and was "politically weaker" than he looked. For some, he was too "pro-business" to take the "radical measures" needed to redistribute wealth "in one of the most unequal countries in the world". But others disliked "and feared" him "for more venal reasons". Although succeeding in having removed Zuma from power, his task was to "move decisively against the extensive networks of patronage and graft" entrenched in both party and state under Zuma. By May 2019, unemployment was officially at 27%, but it was accepted to be much higher. Nation-wide load shedding, with Eskom's debt at the time standing at $30 billion, meant economic growth was impossible. A situation of "very high violent crime" and "troubled" education and health systems added to the country's woes. Despite Ramaphosa's "immense charm, intelligence, energy and charisma", and him not being an ideologue but a pragmatic and careful politician, "who often outfoxes opponents and competitors", analysts said "Ramaphoria" "rapidly ebbed when it became clear that there would be no sudden improvements".

And the media literally under fire

With World Press Freedom Day on 3 May 2019, Zapiro's cartoon of "Still shooting the messenger" emphasised the stress under which also South African journalists worked.

Zapiro's cartoon on World Press Freedom Day, 3 May 2019.
© Cartoon by Zapiro, Daily Maverick © 2017 -2020. All rights reserved.
For more Zapiro cartoons visit www.zapiro.com

Towards the end of May, SANEF issued a statement that it was "pleased to announce" that progress has been made regarding the case in the Equality Court initiated to protect journalists against harassment and abuse.[139] It concerned a case that SANEF lodged against the EFF in 2018 following "a barrage of abusive and dangerous threats". Besides defending media freedom, SANEF also sought for the protection of journalists. It called, in relation to the EFF leadership, for

• Interdicting them from intimidating, harassing, threatening and assaulting journalists;

• Interdicting them from publishing personal information of journalists on public platforms, on social media, or by other means;

• Interdicting them from expressly or tacitly endorsing the intimidation, harassment, threats or assaults by supporters or followers, whether on public platforms, social media or by other means;

• Directing the EFF to publicly denounce the harassment and abuse of journalists; and, finally

- Directing them to publish an apology to the specific journalists listed as complainants in the court papers, directing the EFF to publicly acknowledge the constitutionally protected role played by journalists.

After initial delays, SANEF was informed that a timeline had been agreed on with the EFF to file their answering papers by mid-June. SANEF had to reply by the end of June, with a pre-trial meeting scheduled for mid-July, and the first week of August scheduled for hearing the matter. This was critical to SANEF, particularly in the light of the "ongoing harassment" of journalists. The "most recent chilling case" was the harassment of investigative journalist Pauli van Wyk after her reportage on the EFF and VBS Bank. Malema, while not "naming individuals", urged his followers to "go for the kill" and to "hit hard"; this despite the fact that the timing pointing "to a veiled threat" against Van Wyk. SANEF wanted the court case to "finally hold the EFF leadership to account in its sustained abuse of journalists", as well as its abuse of South Africa's hard-won constitutional principles of freedom of expression.

SANEF also acknowledged its own shortcomings. In June, after its AGM, it noted "a number of disturbing trends" in the media, including "the erosion of public trust, the decline of editorial independence due to a number of issues including the encroachment of media owners and shrinking newsrooms linked to large-scale retrenchments".[140]

Trust in journalism was eroded because of fake news and misinformation, "as well as journalists sometimes backing certain political factions, which ... muddied the waters" and tainted the whole industry. The large-scale retrenchments were noted "with alarm". The annual *State of the Newsroom Report* quantified that approximately half of the professional journalist workforce had been slashed, from about 10,000 journalists to about 5,000 over the past decade, plus on-going closures of news organisations.[141] As in the rest of the world, advertising moved from media companies to media tech companies such as Facebook and Google.

Yet Advocate Hermione Cronjé, Head of the Investigations Directorate at the National Prosecuting Agency (NPA), said as keynote speaker at the Nat Nakasa Award for bravery in journalism that journalism "has never been more important than now".[142] Had it not been for investigative journalism, the various commissions of inquiries, e.g., the PIC, Zondo and Nugent, "would not have taken place at all".

SANEF, in "this highly pressurised and difficult era", again committed itself to fight to strengthen journalism in a three-pronged way. The first was its Inquiry into Media Ethics. The panel of commissioners was headed by retired judge Kathleen Satchwell, and included panellists Nikiwe Bikitsha and Rich Mkhondo. It had to investigate "what went wrong with some of our journalism in recent years and how we can fix these gaps and loopholes so that trust and alliances between us and the public can be built". Secondly, SANEF would be investigating a campaign to tax the large tech companies through cooperation with government and civil society; and thirdly, it planned to embark "upon research into new models of journalism" as "public funding and philanthropy appear to be some of the trends".

But first, the 2019 elections, journalists and media freedom

After the national elections in May 2019, Angela Quintal, the CPJ's Africa Programme Coordinator, wrote that, in the lead-up to the elections, journalists cited online harassment and threats as the biggest challenge to their work.[143] She herself was prevented from covering the pre-election violence of 1994 when her editor stopped her from covering the Shell House Massacre, where ANC security guards opened fired on members of the IFP "in a day of violence around Johannesburg that killed over 50 people". She quit her job because she "refused to witness South Africa's first democratic election from behind a desk". This happened almost a month before the elections, with the country "on a knife-edge". By then, Abdul Shariff, a freelancer for AP, had already been killed, and *The Star*'s chief photographer, Ken Oosterbroek, would also be killed in crossfire days before the election. Quintal's editor "insisted it was too dangerous for a female journalist". Also, they had no "riot cover".

A quarter of a century later, Quintal returned to Johannesburg for the sixth democratic election on 8 May, this time as an international observer for the Electoral Commission (EC). Quintal focused on press freedom and whether politicians were adhering to the electoral code of conduct in their interactions with journalists to ensure free and fair elections.

Whereas there was a clear risk of physical violence in the 1990s, journalists in 2019 had to contend with online harassment, cyber-bullying and "toxic" social media – and fear and uncertainty whether the digital threats could turn into physical attacks. As was so often the case, "it was a court that would ultimately provide journalists with a shot at redress," Quintal wrote.

Ranjeni Munusamy, an associate editor at Tiso Blackstar, publisher of the *Sunday Times, Sowetan* and *Business Day*, and who covered the political violence in KZN in the 1990s, said that those making the threats did not know what it was like "to live in a war zone and did not witness people being killed because some or other politician declared them as an enemy". Yet they were using "inflammatory language to fire up their constituencies, but seem not to realise that words have direct consequences".

Munusamy was one of five journalists who made an affidavit in SANEF's case against the EFF, following "a barrage of threats against journalists from the party's leaders and supporters". SANEF initially sought a meeting with the EFF; when the party responded that its schedule was "very tight and fully booked", SANEF requested the Equality Court to prohibit the party from "using any platform, including social media, to intimidate, harass, threaten or assault journalists". Munusamy's affidavit, as well as those of the other journalists, detailed the threats and how they were affected, personally and professionally.

The EFF "vowed" to oppose SANEF's case, yet did not file the requested replying affidavit, leaving the Equality Court lawsuit "in limbo". Quintal wrote that "[g]iven the heightened rhetoric and vitriol in the election, the legal stalemate left journalists feeling vulnerable, while politicians and party supporters appeared emboldened".

Some journalists tried to downplay the threats, insisting they are not "cry-babies" and that colleagues in Africa "had it far worse". Younger journalists, "in particular", said harassment and intimidation were "normal".

Although there were no formal complaints about misconduct, it did not mean the election was without problems. Some journalists were robbed on assignment or accosted during live broadcasts. Even the communications minister, Stella Ndabeni-Abrahams, tried to block the media from filming disruptions at an ANC election manifesto launch in the Eastern Cape. She later apologised. Four days before the election, the Durban offices of the Zulu-language newspaper, *Iphepha laboHlanga*, were burgled and equipment was stolen, thought to be an attempt to silence it. "Unable to publish, it denied Zulu speakers election coverage in their own language."

But, wrote Quintal, the biggest issue was that social media platforms spreading disinformation were used "to discredit, threaten, and harass the press". While social media were "weaponised", Munusamy and other journalists were also singled out for verbal abuse at rallies or in party statements. The EFF was not alone in harassing journalists, but had the biggest impact. Their main target was "people not on the ballot paper", namely journalists, as "public enemy number one". Munusamy did not cover their rallies and avoided writing about the party, and was considering "getting out of journalism" to "get away from the fire". Quintal contacted the EFF, which did not respond, but later said they would respond to the CPJ.

According to Quintal, the press "battled the threats alone". It did not get support from the EC, nor Chapter 9 state institutions like the Commission for Gender Equality and the SAHRC, whose mandate it was to support constitutional democracy. And the "police weren't much help either".

Cases in point

It is not a coincidence that the following cases all concern women journalists. Foremost among them is Ferial Haffajee, CPJ's 2014 International Press Freedom Award honouree, who said it appeared that the EFF enjoyed "virtual impunity".[144] All seven cases laid against the EFF in 2018 – "its year of violence" – have become "virtually cold cases". Haffajee was also concerned how cyber bullying affected journalists. And if anyone "would know about harassment, trolling, bot armies and cyber hate", it was Haffajee.[145] She was harassed after publishing the infamous Muhammad cartoon, had to take legal action against the now defunct Bell Pottinger for defamation and breach of privacy after being harassed along with two other editors as part of a disinformation campaign, and was "singled out" by the EFF after being publicly labelled, together with other senior journalists, as the "Ramaphosa Defence Force" because of their "supposed bias" towards Ramaphosa and Pravin Gordhan. In an interview with Quintal, Haffajee said she "continues to report critically", but acknowledged there were times that she definitely censored herself.

Haffajee was also concerned about the impact on younger journalists and how cyber-bullying affected journalists' mental health, adding that she did not "trust the system to protect us". This was emphasised by a *Sunday Times* political reporter, Qaanitah Hunter, who tweeted less than a month before the election about the impact of threats: "Being a journalist is terrible for your mental health … simply because no one speaks about the effect of this on our lives." She was sent an image of a gun from a mobile phone number used by an official of the ANC's Women's League. The official later apologised, but denied being the person who sent the image. Hunter experienced "automatic trolling" after every "big story about the internal dynamics of the ruling party", including being discredited – with a picture of her with captions stating, "this is what a liar looks like".

Hunter was also body shamed. After such an incident she tweeted: "And then ANC comrades zoom ó [sic] to my picture and body shame me on their whatsapp groups. I'm done. Taking a mental health break. Sometimes that thick skin gets withered [sic]."[146] Hunter received overwhelming public support, including from Chief Justice Mogoeng Mogoeng.[147] Three weeks later, she won SANEF's Nat Nakasa Award for courageous journalism. Judge Joe

Thloloe said that her courage was "displayed in revealing her own anxieties, in writing and talking and sharing her fears about mental health, in warning us all to find equilibrium in the demanding and volatile jobs we do".

Radio and TV journalist Karima Brown was "doxed" (to publish the private documents of an individual) during the election campaign. After being doxed by Malema, there was "an onslaught of graphic messages on social media", both through voice and WhatsApp messages, "many threatening rape and murder". She laid a charge of harassment with the police and, because the Electoral Code of Conduct was in force, also complained to the EC.

Brown felt the EC "dragged its feet" and made a case in the Johannesburg High Court, arguing that Malema and the EFF had contravened the electoral code. Malema had to apologise on Twitter and pay a penalty of R100,000. Quintal wrote she sat in the public gallery and watched as the EFF lawyer "attacked Brown, her journalism, and her credibility". While judgement was reserved until after the elections, the cyber-hate continued.

During the same time, and following the already referred to exposé by *Daily Maverick* investigative reporter Pauli van Wyk implicating the EFF, Malema "turned to his 2,4 million Twitter followers". While not mentioning Van Wyk or her publication, those commenting took it to be a reference to the specific article. Malema's tweet was viewed as incitement, especially "with its apparent reference to a 1838 massacre of Boers by Zulu King Dingane. It read: "We are still cruising nicely, bana ba baloi (children of wizards) are not happy. Go for kill fighters, hit hard … ."

Almost a month after the election, it was ruled that Malema and the EFF had violated the Electoral Code of Conduct and they were ordered to pay Brown's legal costs. The judge said their conduct had the effect of jeopardising free and fair elections "by fostering a chilling effect on robust media reporting". Malema was not ordered to apologise on Twitter or pay a fine. Instead, the judge noted that Brown's "strident and political tone" had "fuelled the flames of discord". It remained a victory for Brown and journalism, however, setting "an important precedent that could stand to offer South African journalists some protection". SANEF's Equality Court case against the EFF was still expected to be heard in August, and it was speculated that, if the application succeeded, South Africa's journalists "might well have renewed trust in the system to protect them".

But the harassment continues

In July 2019, SANEF had to issue yet another statement condemning the harassment of journalists after attacks on Newzroom Afrika's reporter Mweli Masilela and the harassment of two Independent Newspapers journalists.[148] Masilela was "violently accosted" while investigating the death of a 16-year-old who allegedly fell into an open mine. His attackers "forcefully took his camera and deleted his footage". They also took his car keys. He eventually got his equipment back, but was told to leave the area immediately. Local police also initially refused to assist Masilela, turning him away twice and telling him to get a protection order against his attackers. Because he had no visible injuries he could not report a case, despite witnesses to the incident. Only after Newzroom Afrika management escalated the incident to provincial and national police did Masilela get assistance. It was unacceptable to SANEF that journalists could only get assistance when they "are beaten, with visible injuries". Many community news organisations "suffer this kind of treatment and don't have the luxury of access to provincial and national officials".

SANEF was concerned about the "ongoing attacks, harassment and intimidation" and called on "elected leaders" and law enforcement to take journalists' safety seriously. But just one day later, SANEF had to issue another statement on the harassment and arrest of journalists during a protest in Durban.[149] At previous protests, journalists were verbally threatened and SANEF expected the KZN ANC to "take swift action" against those who disregarded the role of the media and attacked journalists.

SANEF reiterated the media's "important role" and said that there were several channels for recourse for grievances, from contacting the editor to filing a complaint with the PCSA regarding print and online media, and with the BCCSA for broadcast complaints.

Later that same month, SANEF again had to put out a statement condemning the harassment of journalists, this time referring to a "number of incidents" that happened that week, from intimidation to bullying.[150] The first concern was the Hawks' attempt, via the KZN SAPS, to force *Daily Maverick* (DM) journalist Marianne Thamm to reveal her sources following an article.[151] The Hawks were investigating the alleged theft of documents and the disclosure of information meant for SAPS only. The police requested Thamm to reveal her sources, despite the MOU between SANEF and the ministers of justice and safety and security of 19 February 1999, which suspended the application of Section 205 of the Criminal Procedure Act. According to the MOU, the matter must be referred to the National Director of Public Prosecutions instead of resorting to Section 205 – "an apartheid-era law which SANEF wants amended".

In another incident, SANEF was concerned about a visit by a police lieutenant to DM's Johannesburg offices, asking for "the whereabouts" of journalist Aidan Jones. Refusing to say why he was looking for Jones, the officer only said that "he would come back if he didn't come right elsewhere". The police were investigating charges by a Durban businessman against *GroundUp*, Jones and Trevor Stevens after Jones wrote an article for *GroundUp* exposing alleged corruption involving the person in relation to the Passenger Rail Association of South Africa (Prasa).[152] The article was published in both DM and *The Citizen*. According to SANEF, SAPS wanted to take "warning statements" from Jones and Stevens regarding their sources and were not investigating the allegations regarding the content of the story. SANEF said it was unacceptable that a businessman "appears to be using the SAPS to fight his personal battle" instead of approaching the ombud, or the courts, to independently assess his grievances.

SANEF also noted that these incidents happened while they were working on scheduling a meeting with the National Police Commissioner "to discuss crucial aspects of engagement" between the media and law enforcement agencies.

It also noted "with grave concern" the SABC's statement on "death threats" its journalists received after covering various stories, including alleged corruption, as well as "political and corporate bullying" directed at its journalists, some of it on social media.

SANEF emphasised that the SABC was a national asset and that news and current affairs need to be "free of political or any other influence". They requested the SABC board to monitor the situation and ensure security for journalists. With complaints procedures in place, editorial independence had to remain "sacrosanct". Any attempts to muzzle journalists, both inside and outside the SABC, were serious, because when political leaders "impinge" on the rights of journalists, their supporters follow, leading to "disastrous consequences" that impact "negatively on the work of journalists who are there to serve the public good".

Exactly because of these threats, UNESCO noted that journalism "is one of the dangerous professions in the world", with 94 journalists and other media workers who were killed in 2018.[153] According to the RSF's 2019 World Press Index, there was "a growing trend of hatred" against journalists, culminating in increased violence. The number of countries previously regarded as safe for journalists declined every year "as authoritarian regimes tighten their grip on the media". Of the 180 countries surveyed, only 24% were classified as good for journalists. Journalists working in the remaining 76% work in regions where killings, threats and attacks have become part of their "occupational hazards".[154]

According to Freedom House, the media was "under attack", and part of this assault came from elected leaders who should instead have been the "ardent defenders of media freedom". Freedom House also observed that the "slump in media freedom" was closely linked to the general decline in democracy across the world.[155] UNESCO's Director for Freedom of Expression and Media Development, Guy Berger, noted that there were several instances of "mobilisation of mobs" at rallies and online, creating an environment in which journalists "are treated as liars and trouble causers who deserve the ill treatment they receive".[156]

The general decline in media freedom was both a symptom and a cause of the breakdown of democracy, but also partly caused by a decline in media freedom in regions like Europe and America, previously known to uphold media freedom. In Africa, media freedom remained "fragile", with threats, harassment, kidnappings and detention of journalists "common place across several countries". In the first half of 2019, three journalists had already been killed in Africa.[157] According to the African Freedom of Expression Exchange, eleven journalists were killed in African countries in 2018.[158]

Journalists and media freedom as social media's 'roadkill'

Ferial Haffajee, a journalist who experienced the venom of a political party, wrote about her experience in 2019 after having been targeted by political trolls and bots on social media for several years, and how these platforms were a rising threat to media freedom.[159] As a trend targeting women in particular, it is called cyber-misogyny – but "naming it makes it no less painful, as I have found," she wrote. Also:

> Every morning, I pick up my phone and check WhatsApp messages. Then, I open my Twitter feed. "Bitch!" reads a response to something I've posted or written or reported. I block. "Cunt," reads another. Block. "Racist, go back home," says another.

> "I will smack you so hard, you won't know your name," I type. And then block.

Another journalist, Pieter du Toit, referred to the EFF as "violent, anarchic and populist".[160] The party's structure "is modelled on an autocratic and despotic system of command and control", with Malema styled as "commander-in-chief", a position usually "reserved for the head of state as commander of all armed forces". The party's top structure meeting is a "war council", evoking "memories of Asian resistance and revolution"; its supporters are "ground forces" – an "obvious military term". Even its name is "associated with violence: the Economic Freedom Fighters". Members wear red berets, headgear associated with the military, and have adopted "red uniforms as their clothing of choice". It was no surprise, Du Toit wrote, that the way in which they engage with journalists "would wind up in court".

According to Haffajee, online abuse "has become so commonplace that blocking is part of the daily routine now".[161] However, "[j]ust occasionally, you have to fight back". She referred to Donald Trump's message to four US congresswomen "to go back to where they came from", which "ignit[ed] a fusillade of stories from people who had been told so". This made Haffajee think about writing about "the black digital Trumps in South Africa" who instructed her to "Go home" and "Go back to India if you don't like it here".

Haffajee's next trauma was caused by a fellow journalist. It happened in July 2019, when he started "his infamous thread numbering and naming a group of journalists", calling them the "Cabal". They were "part of a narrative of disinformation" – he himself not realising that it was him "deliberately misleading the public". On his list, Haffajee was number 29. She muted him on Twitter because "the deluge of responses was too abusive to cope with". But it had "real-life consequences". She literally felt it shortly after, at the Zondo Commission, where she sat near the back in a crowd accompanying Zuma to give testimony. During tea-time, somebody started "stage-whispering" the word "cabal". Then it was picked up, and "soon it was repeated". And "[t]hen they laughed. It stuck to me like spat venom." Haffajee remembered that she still was not sure whether she did quality journalism that week, as she kept hearing "cabal", "cabal", "cabal". And: "I've worked hard for 29 years as a journalist to not be part of any cabal, so the whispers cut to the heart of me."

The internet and (more) violence against (female) journalists

Haffajee was of the opinion that the internet's powerful social media platforms hosted among the "worst forms of violence against journalists". UNESCO and other advocates saw it as a rising threat to media freedom, as women journalists were particularly targeted in cyber-misogyny. Haffajee experienced it physically:

> I realise that when reporting, I walk with a stoop now, bent from the world as if to protect myself. It's not like me. At news events, like EFF media conferences, I make myself small and will ask questions in a way that sounds to me, as I reflect, almost obsequious. It's definitely not like me.

Haffajee decided not to be part of SANEF's case against the EFF – "not because I don't identify with it or support it with my full heart". It rather was a need that "the spotlight should turn away because the insults sear at me" and that she "imbibe[d] the insults and opprobrium, to cut my cloth to fit the words flung with abandon and to begin to second-guess myself".

She read "with disbelief" Malema's responding affidavit in SANEF's Equality Court case to have journalists declared as requiring protection under Section 10 of the Constitution, which governs hate speech. In it, she got "a high-five" from Malema for not being one of the journalists in the case. The five were Ranjeni Munusamy, Pauli van Wyk, Adriaan Basson, Barry Bateman and Max du Preez. She was "lauded" for "still going to EFF press conferences" – some journalists do not "because it's a risk" – and for "engaging as an equal". Haffajee's reaction: "I am no equal. I am a roadkill."

The SANEF case also followed Malema's speech in November 2018 outside the building in which the Zondo Commission sat, "when he outdid even himself in the rhetoric of hate". His "wide-ranging speech" came "to define how the EFF positions itself in the era of State Capture 2.0". He aimed at the minister of public enterprises, Pravin Gordhan, the "clean-up" at SARS, and the Commission itself, and then he named the "Ramaphosa Defence Force". They were publisher Palesa Morudu, editor Max du Preez, activist academic Nomboniso Gasa, legal scholar Pierre de Vos, journalist Ranjeni Munusamy and Haffajee herself. Haffajee remembered she was the only one at the rally that day "and so got special treatment". Malema addressed her directly: "Ferial with all her skills as a former editor why are you not asking Pravin if he has an account outside South Africa. Ferial never asks [these questions], instead, she attacks [the] EFF." Then Malema "told his supporters to write down all our names" and to "attend to them decisively everywhere you see them". In the "world of trolling armies", it was "an instruction to attack, either online or even 'IRW' (in the real world)".

Haffajee recalled: "But then something happened that made Malema pull back." The crowd around her literally "started growling", despite "at least two lines of police officers" as security for the precinct around the commission. Malema saw what was happening, and "being the brilliant (perhaps Machiavellian) politician he is, he changed the tune". He then said they must "engage with them from a civilised point of view" and "must never be violent with them" – warning against harming those he had named straight after telling them to "attend to them decisively".

The EFF said in its defence "that political speech is often only rhetorical and that Malema cautioned his supporters". But it also argued that journalists cannot be given special protection under the Constitution's Section 10 because "it could open the floodgates for other groups, such as politicians, to claim similar treatment". This again, it was argued, would harm Section 16 of the Constitution, which enshrines free expression. Haffajee said it was a clever argument "and one that resonated with journalists". She said she did not want to curtail free speech, "but neither do I want to feel so permanently nervous".

Haffajee was unsure that "the battle against online violence" would be won in the courts. But the "powerful social media platforms", like Twitter, Facebook, WhatsApp and Google, had to do more "to prevent technology being weaponised in the way it has been".

Another such case was when Malema, on the instruction of Twitter, had to take down a tweet in which he clipped a WhatsApp message from Karima Brown, including her phone number. At a press conference he said he only agreed because "I need that thing [Twitter]".

Haffajee: "Malema is a general and Twitter is his army of 2,4 million followers." He was not unique in using social platforms this way, as "trolling armies are now used around the world by politicians to grow or protect or gain power". There were many examples, mostly targeting female journalists. Social media has made democracies more democratic "by giving people a voice, by making sure the media is more accountable". It is also "not the only platform in town" anymore, because everyone "with a smartphone or a data point is their own media", thereby "smashing media monopolies". But it also spews threats severe enough "to make the life of journalists so dangerous that they quit". Or it could result in the election of authoritarian regimes "or political change so seismic that it turns the clock backwards". Haffajee referred to how disinformation played a part in the Brexit referendum and how the Cambridge Analytica disinformation campaign "scraped and sold Facebook data", possibly a contributing factor in "delivering the era of US President Donald Trump".

Speaking from experience

Haffajee is a veteran of being targeted precisely because of practising courageous journalism. As editor of *City Press*, she published a review of the work of artist Brett Murray. Part of the exhibition was a controversial painting, *The Spear*, depicting then president Zuma painted as Lenin, "but with his penis exposed in a piece that referenced the parable of the *Naked Emperor*, the cautionary tale of what happens to leaders whose followers are too scared to tell them the truth".

Murray is an activist artist, with his first works dating from the Struggle "as part of the cultural resistance". He "hadn't stopped resisting, especially as the governing ANC descended into corruption".

The review caused one of "the first Twitter storms", with Haffajee the target, "as the hive of hate swarmed". Cabinet ministers, party leaders and one of the president's wives marched against the painting. Ten years later, Haffajee said she had forgotten "most of the hate", but some stuck. She said the contents of the tweets made her "feel ill", although she did not "know the words yet to explain why". There was more to come: "There was mayhem. I was scared. People knew where I lived. We didn't have the language to describe digital misinformation or disinformation." Haffajee pulled the digital image from her paper's website "after the First Lady personally burnt copies" of her newspaper.

Haffajee's personal feelings towards Twitter as a platform to "micro-report, to live blog, to carve an opinion in the constraints of 140 characters" is that it is "a liberating tool and a democratising one". Indeed: "I enjoyed Twitter. Until it turned on me."

Another example happened a day "after publishing an essay that took me months to report and which had been done with due care and consideration". Haffajee opened her social media "to find distorted images of myself as a gargoyle and a mad elf staring back at me". Alarmed, she scrolled through images "of myself jumping out at me".

The topic of her reportage was an in-depth study of state capture as "sophisticated corruption where policy and positions across the state are commandeered by powerful patronage networks". In this case, the patrons were the Gupta family who, as Indian immigrants, befriended Zuma "and then proceeded to enrich themselves spectacularly". In the process, Zuma "fired a highly regarded finance minister, ostensibly at their instruction".

Haffajee heard "that a group of journalists who had written about the Guptas were under surveillance and were a target, but I had given it little thought". And then she became one of them. "The images bombarded Twitter for weeks." After the first distortions of her image, "they morphed into images of more destructive hate". Amongst others, her face was photoshopped on to a "barely clothed dancer" and onto a "busty cheerleader wearing a barely-there costume", onto a dog being walked by Johann Rupert, the "face" of so-called white monopoly capital, and onto a cow being milked by him. A dog, a cow, a prostitute – "the nasty purveyors of online hate could not get more stereotypically sexist".

It became clear that Bell Pottinger designed the campaign in the same way it had designed "black ops" in countries such as Iraq, using "click farms and designers in India from where the Guptas ran some operations". Haffajee, plus others, were suing Bell Pottinger "or its insurance company, as the PR giant went bankrupt", although they are not sure that they will succeed.

"I'm roadkill, not an equal of Malema's and other trolling armies, because they have impacted on me," Haffajee wrote. The images of her, the words of a journalist colleague who turned on her, and Malema's trolling army "fill me with shame". She has asked herself "so many times how this digital misogyny impacted as hard as it did, shaming me and causing me to hide the images and to hide from them and to feel like I had to explain them". She still lacks an answer, "except that I have realised that when hate comes to you packaged and delivered on to your phone and into your palm, it gets into you".

The "designers and purveyors of cyber-misogyny" use online attacks to silence journalists, and it is part of Haffajee's routine to spend part of each day blocking hate. SANEF's court case was an attempt "to get the judiciary to declare that this kind of hate is hate speech in terms of our Constitution and that it impacts on the founding statute's freedom of expression provisions".

Haffajee even experienced a man being so incensed by what she tweeted "that he sent me a direct message in which he said I deserved a bullet to my head". He did not even "bother to hide his identity". She reported it to Twitter. Eventually, she got through to the bots who take reports and he was blocked – "but only for a time", as there "is no life sentence for making death threats against women on Twitter". Haffajee said that, while social media executives "flood the free media conference circuit" and "speak the language of ending cyber-hate and online misogyny against journalists", the situation is so severe that UNESCO has recognised the trend as a rising threat to free expression.

Despite social media executives' assurances of fighting online misogyny, Haffajee's experience was the opposite. Trying to report such incidents, she found "Twitter's chatbots, which field first line reporting, to be singularly unhelpful". Reporting such messages and attacks, "most times I get a bot (or a poorly paid and poorly trained casual worker in one of their outsourced customer complaints teams) which or whom, in essence, tells me I have to put up and shut up when called 'bitch', 'cunt', 'witch' or any of the casually flung epithets that come at us day after day". The response would be that they do "not violate Twitter rules", followed by the advice "to block or to mute the hate". It's the "digital equivalent of telling women journalists … to go and cover easier beats than investigative and political journalism that do not generate hate". Something, "I guess, is just what the online merchants of hate want – to get us off the beat".

The case for media freedom (and against the EFF)

SANEF and the five journalists requested the court to interdict Malema and the EFF "from intimidating, harassing, threatening or assaulting any journalist".[162] It also asked the court to interdict Malema and the EFF from publishing the personal information of journalists, as well as preventing Malema and the EFF "from openly or tacitly endorsing such actions by its supporters or followers".

Malema and his party were "known for their threatening and violent language and behaviour towards journalists and others who differ from them", including those "who look different from them". EFF MPs have assaulted a journalist and parliamentary staff, they have been "physically ejected" from the National Assembly on "countless occasions", and their "posture, approach and philosophy are violent". SANEF's advocate argued that Malema and the EFF have created a "toxic environment" for journalists. Malema's statements "need to be accepted at face value" because "words have consequences". Malema's statements amounted to "a call to violence", even starting "long before he declared that journalists should be treated as politicians". In effect, Malema said that if journalists "don't write what he likes they will continue to call them out". This meant "journalists will be fair game and the abuse and harassment will continue, because they are regarded as politicians".

Malema's assertion that neither he nor the EFF could be held responsible for the actions of supporters or followers were rejected by SANEF, as they had to foresee that their words can have consequences. They did not "dissuade their supporters from making threats and harassing journalists".

The EFF argued that not only does SANEF not have *locus standi* to bring any complaint to the court, but the complainants have failed to locate the matter under the Equality Act. Thus the application should fail on those grounds alone. However, they argued that journalists themselves are complicit in the creation of the "toxicity" because of their bias towards Ramaphosa and Gordhan. Journalists were "too deferential" to the "new dawn", implying that they "may be engaged at a political level".

It was clear that the case could become "a seminal issue in the evolving case law on what constitutes hate speech", how "the murky world of social media and politics intersect", and whether political leaders can be held accountable for their supporters' actions.

Social media threats 'undermining media freedom'

The PCSA, at its AGM in August 2019, stressed that violent threats through social media "are intended to undermine media freedom" and that "aggrieved members of the public and politicians should use existing channels to lodge complaints".[163]

Latiefa Mobara, executive director of the PCSA, said that adherence to the press code and the PCSA's mediation and adjudication mechanisms would protect the media "when our media freedom is threatened and when the credibility and trust of our newsrooms are being eroded by the peddlers of misinformation and disinformation". She also referred to the "cabal" tweets shaming senior journalists. Mobara urged the public to use the PCSA to resolve disputes. The code was also translated into Zulu and Afrikaans to "improve access to the Press Council's processes".

In 2018, the PCSA received 533 complaints, up from 499 in the previous year. The new ombud, Pippa Green, had by then issued seven rulings. She found in favour of the complainants in three cases, three in favour of the media, and the seventh partially in favour of the complainant, but with most of the complaints dismissed. One concern of both the public advocate and the ombud was the increase in the number of complaints in which publications failed to give a right of reply to the complainant – the *audi alteram partem* rule – a matter they would address with the media through workshops in their next fiscal.

And setting the record straight

Still on the topic of the Equality Court application against Malema and the EFF, Mahlatse Mahlase, SANEF chair, said they noted and welcomed the public debate in the wake of the court case.[164] She believed the discussion would strengthen and improve "our national discourse on the importance of media freedom and freedom of expression". Unfortunately, some commentary misinterpreted SANEF's case, brought under Section 10 of the Equality

Act, and "falsely accuse[d] SANEF of undermining freedom of expression", as this "could not be further from the truth".[165]

The case followed the "spate of abuse and harassment by people purporting to be EFF supporters against journalists who had been specifically named by Malema". This singling out of journalists and the creation of an "enabling environment" for abuse and harassment was "at the heart" of the case, as SANEF believed it constituted hate speech and harassment. SANEF approached the Equality Court, as it was believed to be "both appropriate and relatively expeditious". Besides infringing on constitutionally protected media freedom, SANEF also believed the EFF's statements and the resulting conduct of their supporters constituted hate speech and harassment under the Equality Act.

Mahlase said Sections 10 and 11 prohibit hate speech and harassment on grounds that "negatively affect human dignity and enjoyment of rights, such as, in this case, the complainants' occupation as journalists".

The EFF's statement was that the basis of this abuse was "the complainants' occupation as journalists and the perceived bias in their reportage on the EFF". Mahlase wrote that, although SANEF welcomed fair criticism of journalists, they "cannot condone individuals being subjected to harassment or hate speech on the basis of their occupation, in contravention of the Equality Act".

The trigger in the case was Malema's speech outside the Zondo Commission, in which he named several journalists as "the enemy" who need to be dealt with "decisively". In the following tweets, the journalists were subjected "to a barrage of abuse and harassment", ranging from name calling and insults to threats of violence and calls for the addresses of journalists to be made public. It "appears to be a direct result, and in support, of the statements made by the EFF". SANEF informed the EFF about the results of their utterances and requested that they condemn the abuse, but they refused and, in doing so, created "an environment which enables the abuse and harassment of journalists whose reportage the EFF and its supporters do not agree with".

Max du Preez, one of the applicants, outlined in his affidavit what he experienced after he attended one of the Zondo Commission sittings:

> I left after lunch. While I was waiting for my Uber driver to collect me ... some of the EFF protestors walked by. One of them recognised me and shouted my name. About a dozen of the protestors then mobbed me, shouting threats and abuse at me. One threat I remember was "You're not safe on these streets, you white bastard". I was distressed by this incident and feared for my safety. Fortunately two policemen were very close by and intervened. The protestors then moved away and I was not harmed. It did make me wonder, though, what could have happened if there were no policemen around.

Three days after Malema's speech, Ranjeni Munusamy was harassed at a shopping mall. Her affidavit stated:

> At approximately 18:00 on that day, I visited a shopping centre near my house. I go there often on my way home from work. I do not wish to disclose the precise location because I do not want a repetition of what happened on the day. While shopping, I noticed three men looking at me. As I walked past them, they repeatedly

called my surname in a mocking tone. I tried to ignore them, walking past them quickly. The men were waiting for me at the entrance of the shop when I left. As I passed them they hissed at me and shouted my name. I was so distressed by the incident that I tweeted what had happened. As a consequence, I am wary of going out to public places.

SANEF felt these physical and "online threats, abuse, harassment and hatred levelled at the applicants" were directly as a result of Malema's speech. Therefore, their complaint was "not to stifle criticism of the media and journalists", but that they believed that the comments "by the EFF, Malema and Malema's purported supporters go beyond fair criticism of the media", and in fact constitute hate speech under the Equality Act.

SANEF tried to resolve their concerns with the EFF "through direct engagement and twice requested a meeting", but the EFF refused to meet and they "had no option but to seek legal recourse".

The crux of the complaint was the "nature and effect" of the statements. Malema made "inflammatory statements which he is aware will incite a violent and abusive response from his purported supporters", but refused to condemn the abuse when it was brought to his attention. As leader of the country's third biggest party, he should be aware that his "words and actions, or lack thereof, have consequences", and that the party is responsible for the consequences. It also has a duty to protect the rights enshrined in the Constitution, including to condemn the violation of media freedom as a result of its statements.

After the attempts to resolve the matter amicably, SANEF again approached the Equality Court, as the alternative was not an option: To do nothing "and wait for a journalist to be assaulted, injured or killed before we approach the courts to determine if the EFF's utterings meet the test for hate speech".

The internet as Trojan horse for tyranny and oppression?

South Africa's rating on the index for internet freedom slipped by three points between 2018 and 2019, although the country still had a "free" internet according to a new report by Freedom House.[166] It included 65 countries, or about 87% of internet users. Globally, Freedom House concluded that internet freedom had declined for the ninth consecutive year. In South Africa, it was as a result of election-related factors, as "neither the state nor other actors block or filter" content, with also no evidence of blocking or content filtering on mobile phones, nor blocking, filtering or other restrictions on the use of online mobilisation.

However, self-censorship, online harassment and online manipulation all increased in the run-up to the May 2019 election. Freedom House said that, although South Africa had "a reputation as a proponent of human rights and [is] a leader on the African continent", the ANC had been accused of "undermining state institutions in order to protect corrupt officials and preserve its power as its support base began to wane". The government did not have direct control over the internet or international connectivity, with no "intentional" disruptions to connectivity. The biggest obstacle was high data costs, despite mobile operators gradually providing more low-cost data packages. Most South Africans without internet access, representing 42% of the population, were earning less than R7,200 a month. Amongst others, Freedom House noted in its report:

- In November 2018, parliament passed a "substantially revised" third version of the "controversial" Cybercrimes Bill. This version dispensed with other provisions that concerned rights activists;

- Encroachments on privacy rights remained a major concern, among them

  - inadequacies in the legal framework surrounding surveillance and the interception of communications; and

  - a 2018 report by Citizen Lab identifying South Africa as one of 45 countries using Pegasus, a "targeted spyware software developed by the Israeli technology firm NSO";

- The withdrawal in February 2019 of the Electronic Communications Amendment Bill, criticised for granting extensive regulatory powers to the department of telecommunications and postal services at the expense of communications regulator ICASA's independence;

- In March 2019, parliament passed the FPA Bill, empowering the FPB to issue "takedown orders" for a wide range of content. The bill was meant to protect children from adult content and to prevent hate speech, but "the vague wording" still made online content vulnerable to censorship;

- Online attacks against journalists intensified before the May 2019 election, and analysts believed it contributed to increased self-censorship;

- South Africa has few restrictions on anonymous communication or encryption. No laws require internet users, website owners or bloggers to register. Users are also not required to use their real names when posting comments online;

- ICASA's independence "has been compromised due to encroachments on its mandate by several government entities". The proliferation of regulatory bodies led to poor coordination and contributed to the perception that there is no comprehensive approach to the regulation of the sector.

- Internet restrictions are "generally transparent and proportional". ISPA, representing many of the country's ISPs, takes "a self-regulatory approach to restricting access" to unlawful internet and digital content. ISPs often err on the side of caution by taking down content upon receipt of a notice to avoid litigation. There is no incentive for providers to defend the rights of the original content creator if they believe the takedown notice was requested in bad faith. "Takedown notifications" lodged with ISPA increased from 464 in 2017 to 608 in 2018. Of those, 233 were accepted (up from 210 in 2017), 366 were rejected, and nine were withdrawn. Of those accepted, 216 requests resulted in content being removed. The main reasons for removal included copyright or trademark infringements, fraud, malware or phishing, defamation, hate speech, harassment, and invasion of privacy.

Freedom House said an area of concern was South Africa's capacity "to undertake bulk and targeted surveillance". It was "particularly concerning because (interception legislation) Rica's oversight applies only to domestic signal interception and not to the interception of foreign signals, which include communications such as emails". The National Communication Centre "is responsible for intercepting foreign signals and does so without oversight". Although SAPS has the international mobile subscriber identity technology

(IMSI) known as "stingray" for bulk interception, "the extent of its use is unknown". Also: "The ministry of state security does not believe that IMSI is governed by Rica, and its use is therefore unregulated." Although government said the technology was used only for national security, "consistent weaknesses in oversight mechanisms within the state security departments leave surveillance open to abuse".

The report stated that journalists "have been frequently targeted for surveillance by the state, usually as a means of identifying confidential sources". One example was in May 2018, when phone conversations of investigative journalist Jacques Pauw were intercepted while he researched state capture during the Zuma administration. So-called "non-state actors" have also targeted journalists for surveillance.

While the internet globally is less free than a decade ago, it is "getting worse as some governments expand efforts to use social media to manipulate elections and monitor citizens". While governments have monitored speech on social media all along, advances in artificial intelligence (AI) "have opened up new possibilities for automated mass surveillance". In fact, it is "driving a booming, unregulated market for social media surveillance". More than half of internet users live in countries where certain political, social or religious content is blocked. Also, 71% of users live in countries where individuals have been imprisoned for posting on political, social or religious issues. China was the worst abuser of internet freedom for the fourth consecutive year, reaching "unprecedented extremes". But even in democratic countries, internet freedom has declined. Freedom House cited disinformation around politics "as an issue in the US".

The future of internet freedom rests on the ability "to fix social media". Since the platforms are mainly American, the US has to be a leader in promoting transparency and accountability in the digital age – the only way to stop the internet "from becoming a Trojan horse for tyranny and oppression".

A luta continua: SANEF, the EFF and media freedom

In December 2019, the skirmish between the media and the EFF was still on-going. The EFF denied access to certain journalists at its elective conference, while SANEF requested them "to include a diversity of journalists".[167] The media denied access included DM, Scorpio, amaBhungane, *Rapport* and Caxton. The EFF decision was regarded as unconstitutional. Besides, the journalists applied for accreditation in time. DM and amaBhungane, instead of accreditation, received emails that included two previous EFF press statements, titled "EFF is not moved by SANEF and its double standards on so-called investigative journalists", and "EFF notes testimony at the Zondo Commission against a journalist paid by State Security".

The first statement was "particularly instructive", arguing that the EFF had the right to freedom of association. It had the right to decide "who we associate with, in our events and platforms", including the right to exclude specific media organisations. This, SANEF stated, infringed on the right of freedom of expression enshrined in the Constitution's Article 16. It also stated that

- the EFF's ban was in effect diminishing citizens' right to receive information to make informed decisions about politics – including on their view of the EFF;

- the ban was imposed to "punish" specific media organisations for reporting on their alleged corruption and theft – meaning journalists were being excluded for doing their job;
- the EFF's actions "signal a warning" to other media houses not to report critically; and
- the ban was "an act of intimidation".

The real victims, SANEF said, were "the voters and citizens". The organisation also referred to an earlier statement in which it said that Malema, as MP, took an oath of office to uphold the Constitution. His calling for a ban of journalists was "at odds" with the oath and with accepted standards of conduct for MPs. SANEF urged the EFF to allow the journalists to attend – otherwise for MPs to sanction Malema. The EFF retorted that its exclusion of the specific media was due to a "lack of space at NASREC". However, SANEF knew of some media houses that received several accreditations – a lack of space could not be a reason.

Zapiro's depiction of "media screening" at the EFF conference, 18 December 2019.
© Cartoon by Zapiro, Daily Maverick © 2017 -2020. All rights reserved.
For more Zapiro cartoons visit www.zapiro.com

The matter of fundamental media freedom rights

Branko Brkic, founder and editor-in-chief of DM, was not to be silenced after the EFF's "ban" on his journalists. He said they believed it was unconstitutional and intended to test it in court.[168] There was "no uncertainty" as to why the EFF made their decision. It was because of DM's reporting, specifically on the VBS scandal. The fact that the EFF refused "to even give us a clear response to our accreditation application" was a "passive-aggressive tactical move", designed to prevent an urgent court action.

But, wrote Brkic, the EFF "is mistaken in its action". Not only was the "ban" against "the spirit of a new, democratic South Africa, it is also not an enforceable sanction". Many of the EFF's "politics and actions may date back to the 1920s and early 1930s", but "technology has since moved on". DM, in collaboration with its media colleagues and specialist journalists and writers, would "still provide the great insight and quality analysis we are known for". The "ban" achieved "nothing but expose[d] their totalitarian bent".

Brkic encouraged colleagues from other media houses to cover the EFF congress "as vigorously as they can". It was the media's role "to shine a light on society, including the parts who openly wish us harm and advocate for our demise". Despite South Africa looking like a country living on a precipice, "defend truth we must".

Political analyst Piet Croucamp also climbed into the ring. According to him, the media added to the damage done to media freedom.[169] While "fascists like the EFF" prohibited its meetings from being covered – "a step in the wrong direction" – it was partly because journalists in the age of social media took on roles that went further than those of the "traditional reporter". As example, he used "brilliant investigative journalist" Pauli van Wyk. She uncovered corruption "to the bone", then also became involved in "fierce Twitter arguments" with Malema and Shivambu. The style of these "Twars" made it possible for the EFF and its supporters to "virtually" attack Van Wyk, "molest her", and stigmatise her work as nothing but a personal vendetta and "fake news". The public tirades made it possible for whoever was sceptical about the media to "buy into" this new perception of the media. It was not only Van Wyk who was exposed to verbal violence, but almost every journalist or opinion writer.

Croucamp wrote there was no doubt that criticism against the media was welcome and healthy, but the "messenger's back" was clearly a target in the age of social media. The biggest danger was that opposing "truths" could lead to an "irrational outcome". The EFF was mostly "a black middle-class party", with about 60% of its members having access to social media, as opposed to the ANC's percentage of about 10%. This meant that "reality does not have to be backed by facts to find traction among EFF supporters". By "literally creating thousands of false accounts" on social media, the EFF created "a totally new narrative", which among others had an effect on elections.

The party's ban on certain media attending its conference was "clearly the result of the conflict on social media between the EFF and the media", with the EFF trying "to manage the risk" by banning or avoiding journalists. The fact that the "plundering" of VBS Bank was again in the news definitely played a role, but there was "no doubt that the Twars on social media ha[d] made the differences a personal issue".

It was also "most probable" that delegates would have confronted Van Wyk personally if she had attended. But, for Croucamp, the "peculiarity" was that the media that could attend "just carried on" reporting "as if media freedom, in their presence, had not been violated in the most banal and public manner". The EFF "trumpeted" from a public stage that it was limiting media freedom by not accrediting "bloody agents". eNCA did the "right thing" by withdrawing from the conference, "creating huge disagreements within their ranks". Some journalists were "clearly not prepared to work under circumstances where media freedom had become a relative term", but the "drama of kneeling Fighters at the feet of a fire-breathing Fascist" was clearly too fascinating for some. Croucamp wrote that "[f]ixation leaves some of us without peripheral vision".

News24's Adriaan Basson announced that all electronic media that were not accredited could use their copy. For Croucamp, this was nothing less than acknowledgement of the damage done to media freedom, but "also an attempt to legitimise Media24's presence", as Basson "must have been aware that media freedom received a lashing". Despite what *News24* wrote, it was "filtered" by the will of Malema and "his gang of political fascists". Democracy suffered "because some of the media danced to the tune of Malema and Co amidst the humiliation of their colleagues". For Croucamp, the fact that "this unbelievable breach of media freedom" gained little attention confirmed his point that "the lobster became used to the temperature of the water". The media should act in solidarity, and in the name of media freedom, "not as a prop in the theatre of the EFF". All media should have boycotted the conference – not because the EFF and their actions were to be boycotted, but to make an important point for media freedom. Besides, the EFF was "totally" dependant on "cheap coverage"; without it they were doomed.

For Croucamp, the "blood" was already "on the water" in 2010 when Malema made defamatory remarks against a BBC journalist as a "bloody agent" and "bastard with white tendencies", and then chased him from its news conference. "Not a single journalist stood up to protest." A similar situation happened in 2017, when Gordhan singled out an ANN7 journalist and accosted him in an "almost personal tirade", although that was not Gordhan's point. "He wanted to spread the lies of the channel on the specific journalist's bread." At the time, some "journalists actually clapped hands and jeered the journalist". In the US, Trump used the same tactic to silence female journalists. By silencing their voices, Trump, as Malema and the EFF, hoped "an important dimension of the political discourse can be smothered". Despite diverse perceptions about the South African media, Croucamp wrote that more or less the majority of the population understood that the country's democracy hung on a "thin thread" thanks to a fearless and independent media. State capture, for instance, would still be "an enigmatic riddle wrapped as mystery", were it not for the country's media. But media freedom was not only in danger when the EFF prevented journalists from attending its meetings. It was also damaged when the media "kick[ed] for the pavilion rather than to attack".

A victory for journalists and journalism

In January 2020, the Stratcom defamation case against the EFF came to a close with a verdict against the party. Anton Harber and Thandeka Gqubule-Mbeki were accused by the EFF of being members of the notorious "Stratcom" in the 1980s. The two journalists made a case against the EFF, and the South Gauteng High Court ordered the EFF to withdraw its statements, apologise within 24 hours, and pay damages, declaring all allegations "as untrue and unlawful".[170]

The judgement was "a victory for truth" and "welcomed by all of those who want to see public figures held accountable for making unsubstantiated and defamatory attacks on journalists and others". Harber and Gqubule-Mbeki said the statements were not just an attack on them as journalists, "but an onslaught on our capacity as journalists to do our work unhindered. The ruling is a victory for journalism and journalists."

Also, SANEF issued a statement congratulating them "for their well-deserved victory in their long battle for justice".[171] The court ordered the EFF "to apologise for calling them spies, and also ordered that they pay them each R400,000 in damages". The statement said the labelling of journalists as Stratcom members – "a notorious propaganda and disinformation unit of the security police unit of the apartheid era" – was "dangerous and demeaning". The EFF had "peddled and perpetuated" the statements on social media almost two years previously following the publication of a *Huffington Post* documentary in which Winnie Madikizela Mandela made the unsubstantiated claims. The *Huffington Post* subsequently apologised. The court also interdicted the EFF "from making such claims about the journalists in future", as they were "defamatory and false". The EFF's statement "was and continues to be unlawful", and had to be removed from all their platforms within 24 hours of the order. They also had to publish within 24 hours a notice on all their platforms in which they "unconditionally retract and apologise for the allegations made". Furthermore, they were also "interdicted from publishing any statement that says or implies that the applicants worked for or collaborated with the apartheid government".

SANEF emphasised that "political formations and interest groups" should use the PCSA's ombud "when feeling aggrieved or unfairly treated". It was better "to have an incorrect report properly investigated and sanctions imposed" than to resort to social media attacks on journalists and to "creat[e] a toxic atmosphere of conspiracy-mongering and hatemongering towards the journalists and media in general".

But, a luta continua …

Barely four days later, SANEF had to issue another statement declaring its "deep concern" regarding the "increased trend of death threats and social media harassment of journalists". The difference now was that it was not the usual suspects, the EFF, but right-wing groups and their supporters.[172] The harassment "by certain right-wing linked elements and groups" was an attempt to silence or stop the media "from investigating their activities". SANEF cautioned "against the threats of any nature and crimes against the media that continue with impunity", as they fuel and perpetuate a cycle of violence. The consequent self-censorship by journalists deprived "society of information and further affects press freedom", besides directly affecting the UN's "human rights-based efforts to promote peace, security, and sustainable development".

The incident concerned the news editor of *The Citizen,* Daniel Friedman, who was forced "to abandon social media platforms" due to "a barrage of threats on his life and a relentless campaign meant to paint him as an unfair and biased journalist". In an apparent fake news attack, a video from 2015 showed him "making fun of the torture and murder of farmers". The video was "debunked" by *The Citizen*, but the campaign against Friedman escalated. He received "hundreds of abusive messages, including death threats and antisemitic hate speech". Some of the claims were that he called for the death of right-wing South Africans – something he denied as "wilful misinterpretation" of an edited version of a joke he made at an event where he performed as stand-up comedian. It was also claimed that he called all Afrikaans people "racist scum". Friedman described this as "baseless and untrue". He was also accused of attacking Afrikaners in general, resulting in calls to "make an example" of him, using "many other expletives" that suggest how he should be attacked and harmed.

Again, SANEF asked political formations and interest groups to use the services of the PCSA or the BCCSA when "aggrieved or unfairly treated", as it was better to have an incorrect report properly investigated and sanctions imposed than to resort to "mob justice through social media and creating a toxic atmosphere of conspiracy-mongering and hatemongering towards the journalists and media in general".

And SAPS (still) not knowing media protocols

From an incident near Paarl in the Western Cape it was clear that SAPS (still) did not know what the protocols were regarding the presence of journalists at crime scenes and resorted to manhandling journalists. SANEF was, once again, "deeply concerned" about the arrest of a journalist, this time covering a shooting incident.[173] Within the prescribed regulations, it is "a journalist's right" to cover a crime scene and it "is essential that the police are properly informed about the role of the media". SANEF arranged a meeting with the commissioner of police to raise these and other issues, including the problem of the centralisation of police communication, in September 2019, but felt that "problems are arising once more". They would now meet with all provincial commissioners to deal with specific issues in the different provinces.

And the media gets a deserved slap in the face …

The former SARS executive who was one of the falsely accused victims of the made-up stories concerning a "rogue unit", Johann van Loggerenberg, called the media to account after the debunked articles.[174] In his submission to SANEF's inquiry into media ethics and credibility, he called on SANEF to recommend changes to the way in which journalists and publications are held accountable for publishing false news. Van Loggerenberg called for widespread changes to media regulations after his career "was tarnished" following reports, which have since been debunked, that he was part of an "illegal spying unit". The articles about SARS's "spying unit" under former commissioner Gordhan were exposed "as false and part of a broad campaign to remove credible employees from SARS and hollow out its investigative units".

Van Loggerenberg said he had "consistently denied every single adverse aspect, theme, allegation or claim" regarding the "rogue unit narrative". He challenged journalists to publish evidence, "not supposition and rumour".

SANEF's inquiry into media ethics and credibility, led by retired judge Kathleen Satchwell, was launched in October 2018 following the *Sunday Times*'s retraction and apologies for the "rogue unit" reports. Van Loggerenberg said the paper with its "leaked false intelligence", was the primary driver of the "rogue unit" narrative, but he also criticised *City Press, Carte Blanche, Sunday Independent, Noseweek, NewzroomAfrika, Radio 702* and *Power FM* for their reporting and commenting on the issue.

He resigned from SARS while it was led by Tom Moyane, "who perpetuated the claims against those allegedly involved in the investigative unit", while facing criminal charges along with Gordhan and former deputy commissioner Ivan Pillay. While one or two media errors "are perhaps acceptable", the "rogue unit" narrative raised questions. Indeed: "The outcomes were disastrous for our nation." He continued:

> There can be no doubt that the period of State Capture, coinciding with the developmental challenges of a young constitutional democracy such as ours, still heavily under constraints attributable to the apartheid regime's legacies, combined

with the modernisation of the media in the information age, and our own unique political dynamics, have caused much harm and damage and trauma to our nation, the state, government departments, capacities and capabilities, officials, their families and our future.

He detailed his "extensive efforts" to rectify the false reports and to hold journalists and publications accountable. They often "came to nought" and at "considerable personal cost". He suggested a merger of the oversight bodies, the BCCSA and the PCSA, in order for them to introduce "harsher punitive punishments for not only publications but individual journalists who breach the industry's ethical codes".

Van Loggerenberg said that punitive consequences only affect the media entity, with no form of culpability for the actual journalists involved. "They move on as if nothing happened." He added:

> As our judiciary has the legal obligation to develop law, so too should a self-regulatory media oversight system. It needs to move with the times. Is it still relevant and applicable in the age of fake news, media manipulation and infiltration, fraudulent leaks and the like?

As registered tax practitioner, he said his industry required him to log points annually that show he has the required training and experience, and questioned whether a similar practice should not be instituted for journalists. He also said complainants should be assisted financially when lodging claims against the media to level the playing field. And, in his words:

> Where mistakes were made, let those be identified, acknowledged, understood, dealt with and prevented in future. There will be no magical fix. Our media has also suffered as a result. As the last vestiges of protection, we have our judicial system and our Fourth Estate. They dare not fall completely.

'Strong-armed bully boys'

Despite media freedom being enshrined in the Constitution, strange things continued to happen, as journalist Marianne Merten reported.[175] A "little like the *sub judice* rule, frequently used by politicians and officials to sidestep questions", it looked as if "an investigation" was also sufficient reason not to answer questions regarding the National Joint Intelligence Structure, or the so-called "Natjoints". It actually boiled down to "strong-armed bully boys". The fact that "a probe was underway" was cited as a reason "to not fully respond" to a series of detailed questions DM had submitted for comment to both parliament and SAPS. Included were an incident of DA interim leader John Steenhuisen being blocked from the parliamentary precinct by a senior SAPS officer, a journalist being prevented from filming the incident, as well as additional security measures for the 2020 SONA. Also, "[i]n contrast to past years", it remained in place for the three-day SONA debate from 18 to 20 February 2020 and "reappeared" for the 26 February budget speech. The spokesperson for parliament, Moloto Mothapo, only responded the Monday, after the questions had been put to them the previous Thursday, that they were "unable to issue commentary on the matter while this investigation is ongoing". For "specifics", DM was referred to the Parliamentary Protection Services (PPS). When contacted, the PPS referred DM back to Mothapo. Also, the SAPS national spokesperson "sidestepped" a question about who the person was who had referred the matter to the Speaker for an investigation. It turned out it was DA Chief Whip Natasha Mazzone who asked for the investigation. Citing the 2004 Powers, Privileges and Immunities of Parliament and Provincial Legislatures Act that prohibits anyone from threatening or obstructing an MP from attending any parliamentary business, Mazzone said several MPs, including Steenhuisen, were blocked by SAPS – although Steenhuisen even had a "parliamentary member's gold access card". SAPS thus broke a rule, "creating an illegal act and bringing your good office into disrepute". The Speaker indicated that she would ask for an investigation, while "also in her in-tray" was correspondence from the Parliamentary Press Gallery Association (PGA) to raise its concerns over one of its "properly accredited members who was prevented from doing his lawful work as a journalist". A SAPS brigadier, the identity known to DM, "slapped away the cell phone, effectively stopping the filming, after demanding to know who had given permission to film an interaction with Steenhuisen". In fact, no such permission is needed, and taking photos of MPs and officials is "a regular practice on the precinct". The journalist also laid a charge of assault, and Steenhuisen at the time was preparing an affidavit against the SAPS officer who tried to prevent his access.

Merten wrote that these were "not the only incidents". At least two guests "correctly invited" by an opposition party "were walked off the parliamentary precinct by police" because they did not have "the gold invite from National Treasury". The police insisted this was the only correct documentation. For about two weeks in February, the "parliamentary grapevine was unsettled" by accounts of "aggressive and rude police at the gates" and elsewhere on the precinct, "both in uniform and in plain clothes".

The so-called Natjoints comprises various departments, including SAPS, "for ensuring the safety and security of all major events throughout the country". Yet Natjoints "is not a structure of law or regulation or one that publicly accounts to anyone on its actions or monies". According to two senior SAPS officers, it was established by "a Cabinet memo" during the Mbeki presidency. Mertens wrote that what happened not only on Budget day, but also during the SONA parliamentary debate, "seems to indicate the SAPS, and Natjoints, believe they can get away with doing as they please". If that is "how they conduct themselves in a space where according to the law, security services operate only under the authority of the presiding officers, hard questions must be asked about how police behave in communities, where the powerful are not at hand to ensure scrutiny". How these complaints would be dealt with "is a fundamental test" to prevent executive encroachment, she wrote.

Multi(ple)choice…? Uhm… actually, none?

Meanwhile, at the Zondo Commission the spotlight also fell on transactions between a "media giant" and the state broadcaster,[176] after other sources had pointed out over a number of years how MultiChoice coerced the SABC into selling its "family jewels". Now "[d]amning testimony" about MultiChoice's role "in blocking government policy over digital migration has continued to be heard" by the Commission.

A former SABC group CEO, Lulama Mokhobo, claimed that ex-COO Motsoeneng acted in support of MultiChoice at the SABC. She said the SABC was "effectively robbed of potential billions in digital revenue thanks to the support pay-TV giant MultiChoice received in protecting its commercial territory". Mokhobo said she had "raised very sharply her discomfort" with the tabling by Motsoeneng and former SABC board chair Ellen Tshabalala of a non-encryption stance as the official position of the SABC. If the SABC acted instead in accordance with government policy on digital migration, it would have been "able to provide subscription-based programming via encrypted set-top boxes". But Motsoeneng, "in particular", "bullied" SABC executives into adopting a position against encryption, thereby ensuring MultiChoice's dominance of the pay-TV market.

Zapiro's cartoon on 4 March 2020 depicting Naspers chair Koos Bekker, his competition bludgeoned by MultiChoice, a previous Naspers filial. Bekker was CEO when the founding company M-Net was erected in 1986, with Naspers as major shareholder. In February 2019 it was spun-off as freestanding company.
For more Zapiro cartoons visit www.zapiro.com

Mokhobo said they were all "taken aback" when a proposal was tabled contrary to the government's policy on the matter. According to her, "one of the ways" in which Motsoeneng exerted pressure on colleagues was "by bragging about his powerful connections", boasting that "he had been at the president's house till 2 am". Given the fact that the SABC had 60% to 70% of total South African viewership, the state broadcaster could be very successful as far as pay TV was concerned. Through MultiChoice's subscriber base of 7,4 million households, the company received a total revenue of R40,4 billion in 2019, with a "base average" of R342 per month per subscriber. Without the "SABC bouquet running on it", MultiChoice "would probably not have those kinds of audiences". If the SABC used its "vast footprint" "to go head to head" with MultiChoice, offering a R40 monthly subscription fee, it could raise an annual revenue of R1,9 billion through only four million subscribers – though the figures were "obviously very, very conservative". It just "did not made sense" when it was said that the SABC cannot move into pay TV. Still, Motsoeneng "ensured that the SABC agreed to adopt a non-encryption stance as part of a 2013 agreement with MultiChoice" – signed during Mokhobo's leave – in exchange "for the supply of two DStv channels for R553 million over five years". Mokhobo thought this was "a nonsensical deal", given the revenues "that could have been generated from the SABC going digital".

Former communications minister, Yunus Carrim, told the inquiry "that he was particularly horrified" to discover the 2013 deal, which gave MultiChoice "exclusive access to the SABC's entire archive". The archive "contained priceless historical footage". In an investigative journalism project in 2017, the #GuptaLeaks emails revealed how MultiChoice paid off the Gupta family and drafted government broadcasting policy for Carrim's successor as communications minister, Faith Muthambi.[177] Following Carrim's testimony, MultiChoice's share price at one point dropped almost 8% from its closing price the previous day.[178] In a letter to staff, MultiChoice's CEO, Calvo Mawela, "noted with disappointment the baseless allegations" made by Carrim and Mokhobo. He not only "emphatically" denied the allegations, but said the company "conducts its business in a lawful and ethical manner". Mawela also urged staff "not to be distracted by the reports". Instead, they should "continue to deliver world-class service in order to delight our customers". Naspers spokesperson Shamiela Letsoalo said "the company had concluded that it did not have a case to answer at the Zondo Commission because it had not been accused of any illegal behaviour". The company also "notified the commission that Naspers did not intend to exercise its rights to give evidence, to call witnesses or to cross-examine witnesses in response to the notice received from the commission". Carrim said in his testimony that "the private sector lobbying government for or against policies" was "perfectly normal in a democracy" and "standard practice" in South Africa. But, added Carrim: "The question is where do the boundaries begin and end?" To him, the fact that MultiChoice "could contribute to drafting a Cabinet memo" on broadcasting policy was "astonishing". He suggested that "the media giant's behaviour" was an example of "regulatory capture".

The planet's tipping point

And then a virus got the world in its grip, leading to a tipping point in modern history. A member of the coronavirus family causing an illness called Covid-19 washed like a tsunami around the globe. Without a shot being fired, the human and economic costs of a Third World War left all countries exposed.

The threats to the media sector were clear: print would be one of the casualties of war. But, paradoxically, information and a free media were more important than ever, as the editor of the DM, Branko Brkic, emphasised in a special newsletter to DM readers.[179] The chair of SANEF, Mahlatse Mahlale, said in her Press Freedom Day message on 3 May that the media was more important than ever, as was also evident in the phenomenal spike in consumers going online for quality information.[180] The threat in the form of Covid-19 "represents a different side of evil, one we have never experienced before".[181] As was also pledged by other news institutions during this time,[182] it will be a case of "defending the truth" and "inform, help, advise, report and truly fulfil our public service role".[183] Covid-19 would "disrupt every area of our lives", but it is also "an opportunity for us to come together, to lead and to help those most vulnerable in our society." Indeed, journalists in South Africa were now the country's eyes and ears, living their job. In the words of Henriëtte Loubser, editor-in-chief of *Netwerk24*: "Journalism is not a job, it's a way of life and a calling." And: "Journalists realise they are in fact the soldiers in the trenches in a war between a virus and humanity."

SANEF issued warnings to journalists to take their own safety seriously, as media workers were included in those professions deemed "necessary services" in the lockdown period, which started on Friday, 27 March.[184] It was essential that journalists were allowed to do their jobs "so that ordinary citizens have a clear understanding of what is happening in their country – so that they can contain and fight the disease". SANEF called on media houses to not only make sure journalists themselves are protected, but also to avoid sensationalism. What was needed was the distribution of "responsible, fact-checked, credible news and information".

The initiative "Quote this woman", or QW+, provided the media with a list of names of women who were experts on various issues around the pandemic, updating it regularly to ensure that expert women's voices were also heard in the reportage on the virus.[185] Language has consequences, and while Covid-19 was the "greatest disruptor many of us will have known in our lives", QW+ saw the pandemic as "starting to rewrite the rules of media engagement: both in terms of what makes news, but also in terms of who gets quoted in news stories". The names included health experts, as well as "analysts of community panic, the economy, South Africa's ability to build more hospitals, and more". One week later, the database had been used over 100 times a day by national and international media.

'In the shadow of a crisis, authoritarianism looms'

At one minute before midnight on Thursday, 26 March, South Africa, was declared to be under lockdown, with strict rules for the next 21 days. The country had already been under a state of disaster since Sunday, 15 March. The initial 21 days would be extended for another two weeks, after which a gradual lessening would be implemented to ensure the economy could start functioning again while the health services prepared for South Africa's peak, expected in August and September. But, with some sectors already in the grip of corruption, award-winning journalist Richard Poplak analysed the country's context for such a crisis in an acidic article, indicating how the much-needed "tough leadership, leadership from above, disciplined leadership" was "already fraying.[186] Though as "Un-Trump-like" as was possible, South Africa's president virtually "imprisoned" South Africa in an attempt to halt the pandemic. But unlike other governments, the ANC was not an "organisation" in the "strictest sense of the term", but rather a framework "through which power is acquired and expended" – also "a syndicate through which patronage is nurtured and maintained". The result was that the government functioned as "disconnected", with "often competing spheres of influence". This was also still a result of the "Zuptacracy" government under Zuma.

Under Ramaphosa, the presidency "ha[d] been transformed into a modern technocracy that operates by consensus and rule of law, linked to formal systems of wealth creation", like "banks, big business [and] Western-style financial/monetary best practices". Yet, the "ghosts of each system howl at each other endlessly, and the argument is never won". It is hard enough to "govern during peacetime", Poplak wrote, indicating that what awaited the country was a potential war. Also, while the ANC "has never done trickle-down well", "nothing [was] trickling down" with the outbreak of the virus. Every minister "ha[d] embarked on his or her own bespoke Covid-19 policy initiative". The "ancient ANC habit" of placing "politically expedient muppets" in cabinet positions "has its downside that become most obvious in times of trouble". For Poplak, the "booze ban" was just "a hint of how creepy puritanical authoritarianism" can become during a crisis. As for the cigarette ban, the "cigarette Mafia will be enjoying a halcyon age", as it was known that cigarette smugglers "enjoy close relationships with powerful politicians". To Poplak, it seemed as if government "[wa]s *trying* to create the perfect conditions for organised crime to flourish".

While finance minister Tito Mboweni was "desperately" trying to stave off a downgrade (he failed), the "non-moves" were designed to "mollify" Moody by insisting that the country was committed to austerity, while "[o]ver the road at the SA Reserve Bank, Governor Lesetja Kganyago is now minting money in order to buy government bonds", a practice known as "quantitative easing".

Poplak then asked: "And who is watching the watchmen through all of the lockdown lunacy?" It was not the DA, which "ha[d] rendered itself meaningless". As for the EFF, "the most influential politician in the ANC is Julius Malema", although everyone in Ramaphosa's "walled-in citadel thinks the man is a fool". But: "[Y]ounger ANC members are minutely responsive to his proclamations, sharing the view that transformation is the single ideological imperative".

The striking front page of the second edition of Daily Maverick168 (DM168) on 3 October 2020 depicting all the horrors of an already captured state being captured beyond all imagination as a result of Covid-19 corruption. DM168 launched a pilot edition on 29 August, stunning the media world with launching a weekly despite the Covid-19 media chaos and when other print operations were either closing down, or published with new frequencies and formats. DM168 was officially launched on 26 September, ringing in a totally new era regarding print media, with a brand-new business model and an impressively innovative approach to lay-out and design.

Most disturbingly, the Covid-19 crisis presented "certain opportunities", because "in the shadow of a crisis, authoritarianism looms". The disease was "a technocrat's nightmare" but "an autocrat's dream". Poplak asked rhetorically: "Has any place been more prepared for the unpreparable?"

In her analysis, Ferial Haffajee referred to the South African economy as "fundamentally incapacitated".[187] The opinion of Business Unity South Africa's (BUSA) deputy president Martin Kingston was that, while the president repeatedly referred to the "incapacity of the state", the ability "to respond has undoubtedly been compromised by ten lost years" (the Zuma years). The Moody's downgrade "will precipitate a deep structural depression over an extended period of time".

In his assessment of the impact of the dangers of an already weak state, Pieter du Toit wrote that Ramaphosa is "now discovering the convergence of three crises all at once: poor governance and policy choices of the better part of the last decade, colliding with a weakened and brittle economy, being rear-ended by a global health crisis".[188] And government has "little firepower to do anything about it". Despite Ramaphosa's "high emotional intelligence and empathy", and his "tone, approach and demeanour" being what is required of leaders during "times of strife", the inherently weak state led to an inability to launch interventions. There was "little to no latitude to make decisive interventions to cushion the impact on the economy and buttress the healthcare system".

Journalists on the front lines

And, as everywhere else, quality journalism was of the essence. The CPJ sent out a directive on how journalists should protect themselves as "soldiers in the trenches".[189] One of its concerns was protecting media freedom, in relation to which it also used war-like metaphors: as journalists scramble to safely cover the news, the CPJ interacts with "journalists on the front line" to document press freedom violations. It added a special site on its home page, featuring "updated physical, digital, and psychosocial safety advice from CPJ Emergencies for journalists covering the crisis". This was available in more than 15 languages.

Everywhere in the world, the call went out to protect quality journalism in a time of viral fake news versus a real-life fatal virus. In the *Columbia Journalism Review*, Craig Aaron wrote how Covid-19 has "upended" everything, also news models already under severe stress because of the digital revolution.[190]

It was not only the tragedy of an unprecedented human toll and a medical infrastructure that could not meet demands, but also of the economy that received "a death blow". As after the end of the Second World War, the planet would have to take a deep breath, starting all over again at what the Germans called "Stunde Null", when everything that was known no longer existed, and the world stood at a new beginning.[191] Nothing would be the same again – also not journalism and news work.

Besides the human and economic costs and "recovery projects", the media and policymakers were not "talking enough about how recovery and stimulus bills could help journalism".[192] Free Press,[193] an independent, non-profit advocacy organisation headed by Aaron, "champions structural solutions to the news business's dire financial problems" and, along with the viral pandemic, even more complex challenges. Aaron wrote that in the USA they have "long campaigned for more federal and state support for public media, opposed media consolidation, and argued that journalism is too important to democracy to be left to the whims of the market".

Especially in the face of the pandemic, "the public needs good, economically secure journalists more than ever". Journalists are "out there tracking the spread" of the virus, "separating fact from fiction, and holding politicians and powerful institutions accountable". And "[c]rucially, we need local reporters delivering information on how to stay safe and healthy, who is saving lives, [and] what institutional failures are making matters worse". In the USA, federal funds were needed for public media to be doubled to ensure that "trustworthy news and information" are not "hidden behind a paywall". And the money should not be "for *Downton Abbey* reruns", but earmarked specifically for, amongst others, "local journalism".

In South Africa, with a media sector already on its knees, there were no such calls for funding. Rob Rose, editor of the *Financial Mail*, wrote in an email to readers on 2 April that it is clear that quality journalism is needed more than ever before.[194] His magazine was forced to publish only digitally under lockdown, as magazines at the time were considered a "non-essential service" and could not be sold – although, ironically, his was one of the few magazines registered as a newspaper. He said that Covid-19 had "upended the economy, destroyed small business and created unprecedented anxiety", and that the crisis especially underscored "how vital quality, insightful journalism really is". In fact, "quality news and insight have become increasingly rare amid the cacophony".

RSF also emphasised that it would document state censorship and deliberate disinformation and their impact on the right to reliable news and information. Calling its project Tracker19, in reference not only to Covid-19 but also Article 19 of the Universal Declaration of Human Rights, it aimed to evaluate the pandemic's impacts on journalism.[195]

Locally, the crisis had an immediate effect on independent media outlets, such as the *Mail & Guardian*.[196] Khadija Patel, editor-in-chief, had to issue a call for assistance from her readers to help pay salaries. The same happened years ago when the title, "founded in 1985 as an up-yours against the establishment mass media which had been found morally wanting in its often-cosy relationship with the apartheid state", needed financial assistance. On 27 March, the first day of lockdown, Patel had to tweet: "This has been a hard time for independent media around the world. Right now, the @mail&guardian faces a crisis. With advertising revenue going up in smoke and events cancelled, we may not be able to pay salaries next month. Please help us."

Haffajee wrote it was "a shocker and it drove home the rapid domino effect of Covid-19. The conundrum for the M&G of getting readers to pay for online news was the same that media the world over experienced and "where only a few companies have made a success of it". Near Patel's office was the poster put up in 1988 when editors Anton Harber and Irwin Manoim ran a campaign called "Save the Wail". Thirty-two years later, the editor again had to ask readers: "Carry on reading us. Carry on subscribing. Make a fuss." Patel worked out that they needed 7,000 to 8,000 digital subscribers at R100 a month.

"What happened next gave Patel and her team a boost." They were overwhelmed by the response. Even a competitor called: DM's Branko Brkic said he was sending on her tweet. As Haffajee wrote: To run an independent media title "is a labour of love these days", but in what has been called an "infodemic", readers needed "rational and fact-based information". The pandemic underlined the fact that "newsrooms have been decimated and that newsroom sizes are down by half over the decade", with some journalists not getting increases "and the pressure to take scissors to already tough budgets ... common".

This, indeed, was a case of *a luta continua*.

Journalism as a public good

The M&G might have been saved for the moment, but the "double whammy" of the virus and South Africa's economic downgrade meant they "were not out of the woods". Patel, also deputy president of the IPI, said big business and government "have a responsibility to journalism as a public good" and need to support the media by placing their advertisements on news websites instead of social media. In Patel's words: "Businesses who claim a social imperative ought to make more conscious decisions about how their digital advertising is distributed." They route their online advertising through Google, Facebook and other social media platforms, thereby "decimating media around the world".

Just a few days later, the "wail" continued when SANEF joined "fellow Africans in expressing deep concern at the devastating impact" Covid-19 was having on lives and economies across the continent, "leading to the temporary closure of some media houses".[197]

But it was not only temporary closures. Associated Media Publishing announced on 30 April, just a few days before World Press Freedom Day on 3 May, that it would be its last day and that it "[wa]s closing its doors permanently".[198] The company had been publishers of iconic titles such as *Cosmopolitan* since 1982 – but this was the reality the media industry had to deal with. The Covid-19 onslaught was the final nail in the company's coffin.

Yet, the crisis demanded "more and not less media outlets – both print and digital – to inform, educate and provide news about one of the biggest pandemics in our lifetime".[199]

Also, the Centre for Investigative Journalism, amaBhungane, warned about privacy rights concerns regarding Covid-19 tracking.[200] A "substantial rewrite" of the government's controversial digital tracking proposals was an improvement, as new rules, putting "basic transparency" in place with oversight by a judge, also ensured that "most of the data collected" would be deleted within six weeks and, most importantly, that "the emergency measures don't outlast the emergency". It was also reported that it was a relief that "the security agencies who have sought to expand their spying powers in the past – the police and state security agency – are definitively cut out of this process". SANEF also issued the Information Regulator's "Guidance Note" regarding the processing of personal information, as this could, if used wrongly, have an impact on media freedom.[201]

But meanwhile, journalism and the newsroom had to survive the coronavirus. The US Free Press and Free Press Action advocated for direct support for daily and weekly newsrooms[202] where, over thirty years, "tens of thousands of daily and weekly newspaper jobs have disappeared". The severe post-Covid-19 economic downturn "threatens to make a dire situation even worse". Another issue was "new investments" in the news business. Regarding the situation in the US: "We are long overdue for a major investment in services that provide community information." In the US there was a call for Covid-19 to be an opportunity "to revive and reimagine journalism's future." A "First Amendment Fund" should be seeded "to support new positions, outlets, and approaches to newsgathering".

One could make a bigger case for Africa and South Africa and that actions to save the media were in much, much higher need.

A virus as a constitutional threat

Amid fears that the coronavirus could threaten the fragile South African economy even more after it was downgraded by Moody's to junk status, after many threats to do so,[203] ex-editor, ex-SANEF chair and political commentator, Mpumelelo Mkhabela, wrote that the virus also implied a threat to South Africa's Constitution.[204] Even in terms of anarchic racketeering, "[w]hat the constitutional and legal provisions sought to prevent – rampant collusion, excessive pricing, corruption and general rogue market conduct among private sector players" – could not be prevented. Ramaphosa's "otherwise noble national lockdown" suspended "some rights and governance systems enshrined in the Constitution and other laws", which meant "a free for all for some" while it was supposed to trump only one issue, and that was "the right to life of all South Africans". Important provisions in various acts, such as in the Public Finance Management Act for the solicitation of competitive bids for the provision of goods and services, were now suspended to deal with the negative repercussions of a national lockdown. But there were "huge risks" in the "inherent … suspension of some constitution and legislative prescripts". The "already squeezed" public "might end up being fleeced by unethical corporate players". As Mkhabela wrote: "If fruitless and irregular expenditure was already part of the norm while the law was supposedly in full force, what more now that parts of the law are suspended?"

The lockdown, meant as "a necessary step to save the nation from ruin", could "open the doors for unscrupulous elements to literally milk the nation". Although the president had "sternly warned" against this, the department of trade and industry had already begun investigating companies involved in excessive pricing. But there were also "other risks". The country was already being run by the National Command Council, "a semi-dictatorial structure that authorises and enforces regulations spanning all government departments". Mkhabela warned that "abuse of power cannot be ruled out". Still, "public comfort" lay in the fact that the National Disaster Act "invoked by the president in his declaration of the national lockdown [did] not suspend the rule of law or the courts". Mkhabela stressed that the Constitution, the courts, and the rule of law were not on suspension during a state of national disaster or emergency, and emphasised that "we all have to be vigilant not to allow the coronavirus to lead us towards compromising our constitutional order. We'll need it intact post-Covid-19."

The virus as threat to media freedom

The executive director of the CPJ, Joel Simon, said Covid-19 was "spawning" a global crackdown on media freedom.[205] While the WHO's director-general, Tedros Adhanom Ghebreyesus, regularly emphasised "that accurate, timely information is essential to fighting" the pandemic, "around the world, governments [were] cracking down on journalists and implementing sweeping restrictions under the guise of combating misinformation and 'fake news'". Naming many examples, he specifically referred to the law enacted in South Africa that makes it a crime to publish "disinformation" about the pandemic. Again, Simon emphasised that, in "normal times", groups like the CPJ would respond to the expanding global crackdown "by systematically documenting the violations, generating global and domestic media coverage, and leaning on sympathetic governments and international institutions to stand up for press freedom and the rights of journalists". Although they were still doing it, their approach "[wa]s less likely to yield results" at a time when curtailing the spread of the disease had become a "global imperative". There was "a growing acceptance of the false view that the dramatic measures required may come at the expense of civil liberties and democratic rights". The CPJ's focus was "on creating a systematic record of the growing violations" and providing journalists with "comprehensive and up-to-date safety information needed to cover the pandemic". Their extensive safety protocol[206] was translated into 23 languages. They were also already advocating for the release of more than 250 journalists who had been jailed worldwide for their work and "whose lives could be in danger as Covid-19 spreads through the world's prisons".[207]

It was clear. In a new, post-Covid-19 world, media freedom would never be more important. In South Africa, with her still so young and so fragile democracy, only a quarter of a century old after 350 years of colonialism and apartheid, media freedom would be imperative in a post-Covid-19 narrative.

Entering a decisive decade

The RSF's 2020 Word Press Freedom Index identified the next decade as "a decisive decade for journalism, exacerbated by the coronavirus".[208] The crisis "highlighted and amplified" the many crises that threaten "the right to freely reported, independent, diverse and reliable information". The 2020 index indicated that safety for journalists continued to decrease, with only 26% of the 180 countries on the index reflecting a "good" or "satisfactory" situation regarding media freedom. South Africa ranked in the same position as in 2019, namely 31, above the UK at 35 and the US at 45.[209] The RSF report said that the next decade would be[210]

> pivotal for press freedom because of converging crises affecting the future of journalism: a geopolitical crisis (due to the aggressiveness of authoritarian regimes); a technological crisis (due to a lack of democratic guarantees); a democratic crisis (due to polarisation and repressive policies); a crisis of trust (due to suspicion and even hatred of the media); and an economic crisis (impoverishing quality journalism).

These five "areas of crisis" were now compounded by a never foreseen global public health crisis. RSF secretary-general, Christophe Deloire, rhetorically asked: "What will freedom of information, pluralism and reliability look like in 2030?"

He answered: "The answer to that question is being determined today." The index already saw a "clear correlation between suppression of media freedom in response to the coronavirus pandemic, and a country's ranking in the Index". He also said that the crisis provided authoritarian governments with an opportunity to implement the notorious "shock doctrine" – to take advantage of the fact that politics are on hold, the public is stunned, and protests are out of the question – in order to impose measures that would be impossible in normal times. He also said that, for "this decisive decade to not be a disastrous one, people of goodwill, whoever they are, must campaign for journalists to be able to fulfil their role as society's trusted third parties".

World Press Freedom Day 2020

On World Press Freedom Day, 3 May, one year before its 30th commemoration in 2021, SANEF honoured the day with a webinar under Level 4 Coronavirus lockdown, stating that the news media have never been more important – and yet are under severe threat.[211]

Historically, the day has been marked as a day on which citizens, journalists and journalist organisations around the globe "celebrate the fundamental principles of press freedom and its benefits to society". But, while journalism plays a critical role locally, it "simultaneously

… has also been under severe financial threat as the lockdown has prompted advertisers to rein in spending and made it difficult to circulate newspapers and magazines". Two major magazine publishers announced closing their businesses within days: Associated Media Publishers[212] closed its doors, while Caxton[213] closed almost all its magazine titles. Others announced plans to cut salaries by up to 40% and to stop commissioning freelance journalists. Also, community journalists were facing "some of the greatest threats". Not only were jobs at stake, but so were media diversity and the production of quality news to provide verifiable information in the public interest should newsrooms, already under pressure, shrink or news organisations be forced to close. The threats to media freedom were immense, and SANEF on 3 May 2020 "sounded the alarm", despite seeing "audiences soar as citizens seek information on health issues and the economy".[214]

But, while a luta continua … a well-deserved Salut

Maybe it is fitting to end this reconstruction of South Africa's fight for press freedom, media freedom and freedom of expression in the shadow of a never-foreseen threat to media freedom, namely a global viral pandemic, with a salutation to those who were the fighters in the trenches right from the beginning of our media history. And therefore it might just be poignantly appropriate to end this tale, spanning more than 350 years, with the brief, but well-chosen, words of veteran journalist Martie Retief Meiring's message to South African journalists during Covid-19. Her words provide an apt summary of a history of courage and bravery in the face of unimaginable resistance, whether from governmental or, in this case, viral foe:[215]

> Infinite respect to the editorial staffs and technicians who manage to continue, in the face of all the challenges, to collect news from closed-off areas, publish it, and to still print papers and deliver them. It is an era in journalism that will go down in the books. *Salut*.

No doubt, after 300 years of colonialism, almost 50 years of apartheid, and 25 years of ANC rule, it will be a case of *a luta continua*.

ADDENDUM

The Press Code of Ethics and Conduct for South African Print and Online Media (Effective from 1 January 2020) Copyright: 2020 PCSA

The Press Council of South Africa and the Interactive Advertising Bureau South Africa adopt the following Code for print and online media (together referred to as "the media).

Preamble

The media exist to serve society. Their freedom provides for independent scrutiny of the forces that shape society, and is essential to realising the promise of democracy. It enables citizens to make informed judgments on the issues of the day, a role whose centrality is recognised in the South African Constitution.

Section 16 of the Bill of Rights sets out that:

Everyone has the right to freedom of expression, which includes:

a) Freedom of the press and other media;

b) Freedom to receive and impart information or ideas;

c) Freedom of artistic creativity; and

d) Academic freedom and freedom of scientific research.

The right in subsection (1) does not extend to:

a) Propaganda for war;

b) Incitement of imminent violence; or

c) Advocacy of hatred that is based on race, ethnicity, gender or religion, and that constitutes incitement to cause harm.

The media strive to hold these rights in trust for the country's citizens; and they are subject to the same rights and duties as the individual. Everyone has the duty to defend and further these rights, in recognition of the struggles that created them: the media, the public and government, who all make up the democratic state.

The media's work is guided at all times by the public interest, understood to describe information of legitimate interest or importance to citizens.

As journalists we commit ourselves to the highest standards, to maintain credibility and keep the trust of the public. This means always striving for truth, avoiding unnecessary harm, reflecting a multiplicity of voices in our coverage of events, showing a special concern for children and other vulnerable groups, and exhibiting sensitivity to the cultural customs of their readers and the subjects of their reportage, and acting independently.

Application of the Press Code

1. This Code applies to the following content published by members:

- all content that is published in a printed edition;
- all content that is published on a website operated by a member;
- all content that is published on a social media account operated by a member; and
- all content that is created by a member and published on any platform that is available on the world wide web (i.e. online) or in digital format.

2. All content published by a member through one or more of the platforms mentioned in 1 must comply with the Code, regardless of whether the content is in written, video, audio, pictorial or any other form.

3. Members must ensure that when they share content created by a third party through their social media accounts (for example by retweeting) they do so in a manner that is compliant with this Code.

4. Members must develop their own social media policies, guided by this Code.

CHAPTER 1: Media-Generated Content and Activities

1. Gathering and reporting of news

The media shall:

1.1 take care to report news truthfully, accurately and fairly;

1.2 present news in context and in a balanced manner, without any intentional or negligent departure from the facts whether by distortion, exaggeration or misrepresentation, material omissions, or summarization;

1.3 present only what may reasonably be true as fact; opinions, allegations, rumours or suppositions shall be presented clearly as such;

1.4 obtain news legally, honestly and fairly, unless public interest dictates otherwise;

1.5 use personal information for journalistic purposes only;

1.6 identify themselves as such, unless public interest or their safety dictates otherwise;

1.7 verify the accuracy of doubtful information, if practicable; if not, this shall be stated;

1.8 seek, if practicable, the views of the subject of critical reportage in advance of publication, except when they might be prevented from reporting, or evidence destroyed, or sources intimidated. Such a subject should be afforded reasonable time to respond; if unable to obtain comment, this shall be stated;

1.9 state where a report is based on limited information, and supplement it once new information becomes available;

1.10 make amends for presenting inaccurate information or comment by publishing promptly and with appropriate prominence a retraction, correction, explanation or an apology on every platform where the original content was published, such as the member's website, social media accounts or any other online platform; and ensure that every journalist or freelancer employed by them who shared content on their personal social media accounts also shares any retraction, correction, explanation or apology relating to that content on their personal social media accounts;

1.11 prominently indicate when content that was published online has been amended or an apology or retraction published. The original content may continue to remain online but a link to the amendment, retraction or apology must be included in every version of the content which remains available online;

1.12 not be obliged to remove any content which is not unlawfully defamatory; and

1.13 not plagiarise.

2. Independence and Conflicts of Interest

The media shall:

2.1 not allow commercial, political, personal or other non-professional considerations to influence reporting, and avoid conflicts of interest as well as practices that could lead readers to doubt the media's independence and professionalism;

2.2 not accept any benefit which may influence coverage;

2.3 indicate clearly when an outside organization has contributed to the cost of newsgathering; and

2.4 keep editorial material clearly distinct from advertising and sponsored events.

3. Privacy, Dignity and Reputation

The media shall:

3.1 exercise care and consideration in matters involving the private lives of individuals. The right to privacy may be overridden by public interest;

3.2 afford special weight to South African cultural customs concerning the protection of privacy and dignity of people who are bereaved and their respect for those who have passed away, as well as concerning children, the aged and the physically and mentally disabled;

3.3 exercise care and consideration in matters involving dignity and reputation, which may be overridden only if it is in the public interest and if:

3.3.1. the facts reported are true or substantially true; or

3.3.2. the reportage amounts to protected comment based on facts that are adequately referred to and that are either true or reasonably true; or

3.3.3. the reportage amounts to a fair and accurate report of court proceedings, Parliamentary proceedings or the proceedings of any quasi-judicial tribunal or forum; or

3.3.4. it was reasonable for the information to be communicated because it was prepared in accordance with acceptable principles of journalistic conduct; or

3.3.5. the content was, or formed part of, an accurate and impartial account of a dispute to which the complainant was a party;

3.4 not identify rape survivors, survivors of sexual violence which includes sexual intimidation and harassment* or disclose the HIV / AIDS status of people without their consent and, in the case of children, from their legal guardian or a similarly responsible adult as well as from the child (taking into consideration the evolving capacity of the child), and a public interest is evident, and it is in the best interests of the child.

* The World Health Organisation inter alia defines sexual violence as follows: "Sexual violence encompasses acts that range from verbal harassment to forced penetration, and an array of types of coercion, from social pressure and intimidation to physical force…"

4. Protection of Personal Information*

The media shall:

4.1 take reasonable steps to ensure that the personal information under their control is protected from misuse, loss, and unauthorized access;

4.2 ensure that the personal information they gather is accurate, reasonably complete and up to date;

4.3 take steps to verify the accuracy of their information and, if necessary, amend it where a person requests a correction to be made to his or her personal information;

4.4 only disclose sufficient personal information to identify the person being reported on as some information, such as addresses, may enable others to intrude on their privacy and safety; and

4.5 inform the affected person(s) and take reasonable steps to mitigate any prejudicial effects where it is reasonably suspected that an unauthorized person may have obtained access to personal information held by the media.

* "Personal information" is defined as follows in Section 1 of the Protection of Personal Information Act 4 of 2013: "Personal information" means information relating to an identifiable, living, natural person, and where it is applicable, an identifiable, existing juristic person, including, but not limited to (a) information relating to the race, gender, sex, pregnancy, marital status, national, ethnic or social origin, colour, sexual orientation, age, physical or mental health, well-being, disability, religion, conscience, belief, culture, language and birth of the person; (b) information relating to the education or the medical, financial, criminal or employment history of the person; (c) any identifying number, symbol, e-mail address, physical address, telephone number, location information, online identifier or other particular assignment to the person; (d) the biometric information of the person; (e) the personal opinions, views or preferences of the person; (f) correspondence sent by the person that is implicitly or explicitly of a private or confidential nature or further correspondence that would reveal the contents of the original correspondence; (g) the views or opinions of another individual about the person; and (h) the name of the person if it appears with other personal information relating to the person or if the disclosure of the name itself would reveal information about the person.

5. Discrimination and Hate Speech

The media shall:

5.1. avoid discriminatory or denigratory references to people's race, gender, sex, pregnancy, marital status, ethnic or social origin, colour, sexual orientation, age, disability, religion, conscience, belief, culture, language and birth or other status, and not refer to such status in a prejudicial or pejorative context – and shall refer to the above only where it is strictly relevant to the matter reported, and if it is in the public interest; and

5.2 balance their right and duty to report and comment on all matters of legitimate public interest against the obligation not to publish material that amounts to propaganda for war, incitement of imminent violence or hate speech – that is, advocacy of hatred that is based on race, ethnicity, gender or religion, and that constitutes incitement to cause harm.

6. Advocacy

The media may strongly advocate their own views on controversial topics, provided that they clearly distinguish between fact and opinion, and not misrepresent or suppress or distort relevant facts.

7. Protected Comment

7.1 The media shall be entitled to comment upon or criticise any actions or events of public interest; and

7.2 Comment or criticism is protected even if it is extreme, unjust, unbalanced, exaggerated and prejudiced, as long as it is without malice, is on a matter of public interest, has taken fair account of all material facts that are either true or reasonably true, and is presented in a manner that it appears clearly to be comment.

8. Children

In the spirit of Section 28.2 of the Bill of Rights* the media shall:

8.1 exercise exceptional care and consideration when reporting about children**. If there is any chance that coverage might cause harm of any kind to a child, he or she shall not be interviewed, photographed or identified without the consent of a legal guardian or of a similarly responsible adult and the child (taking into consideration the evolving capacity of the child); and a public interest is evident;

8.2 not publish child pornography***; and

8.3 not identify children who have been victims of abuse or exploitation, or who have been charged with or convicted of a crime, without the consent of their legal guardians (or a similarly responsible adult) and the child (taking into consideration the evolving capacity of the child), a public interest is evident and it is in the best interests of the child.

* Section 28.2 of the Bill of Rights in the South African Constitution says: "A child's best interests are of paramount importance in every matter concerning the child."

** A "child" is a person under the age of 18 years.

*** Child Pornography is defined in the Film and Publications Act as: "Any visual image or any description of a person, real or simulated, however created, who is or who is depicted or described as being, under the age of 18 years, explicitly depicting such a person who is or who is being depicted as engaged or participating in sexual conduct; engaged in an explicit display of genitals; participating in or assisting another person to participate in sexual conduct which, judged within context, has as its predominant objective purpose, the stimulation of sexual arousal in its target audience or showing or describing the body or parts of the body of the person in a manner or circumstance which, in context, amounts to sexual exploitation."

9. Violence, Graphic Content

The media shall:

9.1 exercise due care and responsibility when presenting brutality, violence and suffering;

9.2 not sanction, promote or glamorise violence or unlawful conduct; and

9.3 avoid content which depicts violent crime or other violence or explicit sex, unless the public interest dictates otherwise – in which case a prominently displayed warning must indicate that such content is graphic and inappropriate for certain audiences such as children

10. Headlines, Captions, Posters, Pictures and Video / Audio Content

10.1 Headlines, captions to pictures and posters shall not mislead the public and shall give a reasonable reflection of the contents of the report or picture in question; and

10.2 Pictures and video / audio content shall not misrepresent or mislead nor be manipulated to do so.

11. Confidential and Anonymous Sources

The media shall:

11.1 protect confidential sources of information – the protection of sources is a basic principle in a democratic and free society;

11.2 avoid the use of anonymous sources unless there is no other way to deal with a story, and shall take care to corroborate such information; and

11.3 not publish information that constitutes a breach of confidence, unless the public interest dictates otherwise.

12. Payment for Information

The media shall avoid shady journalism in which informants are paid to induce them to give the information, particularly when they are criminals – except where the material concerned ought to be published in the public interest and the payment is necessary for this to be done.

CHAPTER 2: User-Generated Content and Activities*

13. Principles

The media:

13.1 are not obliged to moderate all user-generated content (UGC) in advance;

13.2 shall have a UGC Policy, consistent with the Constitution of the Republic of South Africa, governing moderation and/or removal of UGC or user profiles posted;

13.3 may remove any UGC or user profile in accordance with their policy;

13.4 must make their policy publicly available and set out clearly the:

13.4.1 authorisation process, if any, which would-be users must follow, as well as any terms, conditions and indemnity clauses during such registration process;

13.4.2 content which shall be prohibited; and

13.4.3 manner in which the public may inform them of prohibited content;

13.5 should, where practicable, place a notice on the platforms to discourage the posting of prohibited content;

13.6 should inform the public that UGC is posted directly by users, and does not necessarily reflect their views;

13.7 shall encourage users to report content which may violate the provisions of their policy; and

13.8 shall particularly carefully monitor online forums directed at children.

14. Prohibited Content

Material constitutes prohibited content if it is expressly not allowed in a member's UGC Policy, and in Section 5.2 of this Code (which refers to Section 16 of the Bill of Rights, and overrules anything to the contrary contained in a UGC policy).

15. Defence

15.1 It is a defence for the media to show that they did not author or edit the content complained of;

15.2 However, where a complainant has sent a written notice to the particular media, identifying the content concerned, specifying where it was posted, and motivating why it is prohibited (see Clause 14); the media must then either:

15.2.1 remove the relevant UGC as soon as possible and notify the complainant accordingly; or

15.2.2 decide not to remove the UGC and notify the complainant accordingly. In the latter case, the complainant may complain to the Press Ombud, who will treat it as if the UGC was posted by the member itself.

* This section applies where a complaint is brought against a member in respect of comments and content posted by users on all platforms in controls and on which it distributes its content.

ENDNOTES

Preface

1. L Rabe, *Quote Unquote. Quotations on Freedom of Speech, Journalism, the News Media and a World of Words* (Stellenbosch: Rapid Access Publishers/Sun Media, 2016), 40. https://doi.org/10.18820/9781928314103
2. Ibid., 26.
3. Code of Ethics and Conduct for South African Print and Online Media, http://www.presscouncil.org.za/ContentPage?code=PRESSCODE, accessed 28.11.2018.
4. W. de Kock, *A Manner of Speaking* (Cape Town: Saayman & Weber, 1982), n.p.
5. Ibid., n.p.
6. P.J. Nienaber, *'n Beknopte Geskiedenis van die Hollands-Afrikaanse Drukpers in Suid-Afrika (A Brief History of the Dutch Afrikaans Press in South Africa)* (Bloemfontein, Cape Town & Port Elizabeth: Nasionale Pers Beperk, 1947), 10.
7. T. Pringle, *Narrative of a Residence in South Africa* (Cape Town: Struik, 1966), 174.
8. F.C.L. Bosman, *Hollandse Joernalistiek in Suid-Afrika gedurende die 19de Eeu (Dutch Journalism in South Africa during the 19th Century)* (Reprints from *Ons Land*, 1930).
9. Nienaber, *'n Beknopte Geskiedenis*.
10. J.H.O. du Plessis, "Die Afrikaanse Pers. 'n Studie van die Ontstaan, Ontwikkeling en Rol van die Hollands-Afrikaanse Pers as Sosiale Instelling" ("The Afrikaans Press. A Study of the Origin, Development and Role of the Dutch Afrikaans Press as Social Institution") (Ph.D. diss., Stellenbosch University, 1943).
11. H.L. Smith, *Behind the Press in South Africa* (Cape Town: Stewart, 1945).
12. A. Hepple, *Censorship and Press Control in South Africa* (Johannesburg: Published by author, 1960).
13. A.M. Lewin Robinson, *None Daring to Make Us Afraid. A Study of English Periodical Literature in the Cape Colony from its Beginnings in 1824 to 1835* (Cape Town: Maskew Miller, 1962).
14. R. Ainslie, *The Press in Africa: Communications Past and Present* (New York: Walker, 1966).
15. W. Hachten, *Muffled Drums: The News Media in Africa* (Ames: Iowa State University Press, 1971).
16. A. Hepple, *Press under Apartheid* (London: International Defence Aid, 1974).
17. E. Potter, *The Press as Opposition: The Political Role of South African Newspapers* (Totowa, NJ: Rowman and Littlefield, 1975).
18. R. Pollack, *Up Against Apartheid: The Role and the Plight of the Press in South Africa* (Carbondale, Ill: Southern Illinois University Press, 1981).
19. W.A. Hachten and C.A. Giffard, *Total Onslaught. The South African Press under Attack* (Johannesburg: Macmillan, 1984).
20. K. Tomaselli, R. Tomaselli and J. Muller, *Narrating the Crisis: Hegemony and the South African Press* (Johannesburg: Richard Lyon & Co, 1987).
21. L. Switzer, ed., *South Africa's Alternative Press. Voices of Protest and Resistance 1880–1960* (Cambridge: Cambridge University Press, 1997).
22. L. Switzer and M. Adhikari, eds., *South Africa's Resistance Press. Alternative Voices in the Last Generation under Apartheid* (Athens: Ohio University Press, 2000).
23. De Kock, *A Manner of Speaking*.
24. G.S. Jackson, *Breaking Story. The South African Press* (Boulder, San Francisco, Oxford: Westview Press, 1993).
25. J. Reid and T. Isaacs, *Press Regulation in South Africa: An Analysis of the Press Council of South Africa, the Press Freedom Commission and related discourses* (Johannesburg: Media Policy and Democracy Project, 2015).

26. R. Teer-Tomaselli and D. McCracken, eds., *Media and the Empire* (London and New York: Routledge, 2016).

27. W. Harmse, *SABC 1936 – 1995. Still a Key Player … or an Endangered Species?* (Naledi, 2018).

28. L. Kalane, *The Chapter We Wrote. The City Press Story* (Johannesburg and Cape Town: Jonathan Ball, 2018).

29. A. Dasnois and C. Whitfield, *Paper Tiger. Iqbal Survé and the Downfall of Independent Newspapers* (Cape Town: Tafelberg, 2019).

Chapter 1

1. D. Wigston, "History of the South African Media," in P.J. Fourie, ed., *Media Studies Volume 1: Media History, Media and Society* (Wetton: Juta, 2007), 6.

2. F. Banda, "The Media in Africa," in P.J. Fourie, ed., *Media Studies Volume 1: Media History, Media and Society*, (Wetton: Juta, 2007), 60–63.

3. History of the World, UNESCO, http://www.unesco.org/new/en/communication-and-information/memory-of-the-world/register/full-list-of-registered-heritage/registered-heritage-page-8/the-bleek-collection/#c183643, accessed 20.11.2019.

4. H. Mayell, "'Out of Africa' Phrase in Use Since Ancient Greece," *National Geographic*, 2003, http://news.nationalgeographic.com/news/2003/02/0219_030219_outofafrica.html, accessed 10.02.2015.

5. C.F.J. Muller, *Sonop in die Suide. Geboorte en Groei van die Nasionale Pers 1915–1948 (Sunrise in the South. The Birth and Growth of the Nasionale Pers 1915–1948)* (Cape Town: Nasionale Boekhandel, 1990), 27.

6. D.J. Hattingh, "'n Wysgerige Ondersoek na die Probleem van Persvryheid" ("A Philosophical Investigation into the Problem of Press Freedom") (Ph.D. diss., Potchefstroom University for Christian Higher Education, 1969).

7. D.C. Hallin and P. Mancini, *Comparing Media Systems: Three Models of Media and Politics* (Cambridge: Cambridge University Press, 2004), 26. https://doi.org/10.1017/CBO9780511790867

8. According to Professor Sampie Terreblanche, the current political dispensation is not a democracy, but a political economical system based on a proportional electoral majority system.

9. J. Crwys-Williams, *South African Despatches. Two Centuries of the Best in South African Journalism* (Johannesburg: Ashanti, 1989), vii.

10. Ted Turner, born in 1938, founded CNN in 1980 and is regarded as one of the modern-day media magnates. His company later merged with Time Warner. In 2001, Time Warner merged with AOL to create AOL Time Warner; the company later changed its name back to Time Warner, http://www.tedturner.com/turner-family/ted-turner/, accessed 3.05.2015.

11. W. de Kock, *A Manner of Speaking* (Cape Town: Saayman & Weber, 1982), 6.

12. H.G. Rudolph, "Freedom of the Press or the Right to Know," *South African Law Journal* 81,1 (1981): 85.

13. See reports, e.g., News24, Netwerk24, *Die Burger, The Cape Times* and others from the evening of 12 February 2015 onwards.

14. "SANEF Condemns Thuggish Behaviour by Police at Parliament," statement, 11.03.2015.

15. "Sanef: Zuma Attack on Media Unacceptable," EWN, http://ewn.co.za/2017/12/17/watch-sanef-zuma-attack-on-media-unacceptable, accessed 28.12.2017; "Journalist Assaulted and Ejected from #ANC54," EWN, http://ewn.co.za/2017/12/19/journalist-assaulted-and-ejected-from-anc54, accessed 28.12.2017.

16. See, e.g., F. Verster, "A Critique of the Rape of Justice, With Emphasis on Seven Cartoons by Zapiro (2008–2010)" (Master's thesis, Stellenbosch University, 2010).

17. De Kock, *A Manner of Speaking*, 15.

18. Ibid., 16.

19. J. Sochen, *Movers and Shakers. American Women Thinkers and Activists 1900–1970* (New York: Quadrangle/The New York Times Book Co, 1973), ix.
20. Wigston, "A History of South African Media," 5.
21. S. Sonderling, "Historical Research in Communication," in G.M. du Plooy, ed., *Introduction to Communication* (Cape Town: Juta, 1995), 87.
22. R. Teer-Tomaselli, "Media and Empire in the 20th Century," *Critical Arts* 28,6 (2014): 875. https://doi.org/10.1080/02560046.2014.990608
23. D. McCracken, "In Pursuit of Media History Bunk," in K. Tomaselli, ed., *Making Sense of Research* (Pretoria, Van Schaik, 2018), 45–46.
24. D. Woolf, *A Global History of History* (Cambridge: Cambridge University Press, 2011), 2–5.
25. J. de Villiers, "Geskiedeniswetenskap en die Nuwe Suid-Afrika – Moet die Suid-Afrikaanse Geskiedenis Herskryf word?" ("Historical Science and the New South Africa – Should the South African History be Rewritten?") *Tydskrif vir Geesteswetenskappe (Journal for the Humanities)* 52,2 (2012): 198.
26. Woolf, *A Global History of History*, 75.
27. S. Lamble, "Documenting the Methodology of Journalism," *Australian Journalism Review* 26,1 (2004): 90.
28. M. Wilkerson, "History and Journalism Research," in R. Nafziger and M. Wilkerson, eds., *An Introduction to Journalistic Research* (New York: Greenwood Press, 1949; 1968-reprint), 11.
29. Lamble, "Documenting the Methodology of Journalism," 94.
30. De Villiers, "Geskiedeniswetenskap en die Nuwe Suid-Afrika," 199.
31. Woolf, *A Global History of History*, 35.
32. S.D. Reece, "The Progressive Potential of Journalism Education: Recasting the Academic Professional Debate," *The Harvard International Journal of Press Politics* 4,4 (1999): 72. https://doi.org/10.1177/1081180X9900400405
33. B. Medsger, "Getting Journalism Education Out of the Way," *Essays* (2002), http://journalism.nyu.edu/publishing/archives/debate/forum.1.essay.medsger.html, accessed 10.01.2014: 2.
34. Woolf, *A Global History of History*, 35.
35. De Villiers, "Geskiedeniswetenskap en die Nuwe Suid-Afrika," 198.
36. Sonderling, "Historical Research in Communication," 91.
37. P. Gardner, "Historical Analysis," in V. Jupp, ed., *The Sage Dictionary of Social Research Methods* (London: Sage, 2006), 136.
38. Woolf, *A Global History of History*, 319.
39. A.A. Berger, *Media Research Techniques* (London: Sage, 1991), 167.
40. Sonderling, "Historical Research in Communication," 90.
41. C. Geertz, "Thick Description: Toward an Interpretive Theory of Culture," in C. Geertz, ed., *The Interpretation of Cultures: Selected Essays* (London: Fontana Press, 1993), 5.
42. The phrase, "Journalism is the first rough draft of history", was coined by Phil Graham (1915-1963), publisher of *The Washington Post*. Although the quote is credited to Graham, it was not the first time it had been formulated. The phrase was used repeatedly in his newspaper from the 1940s, with the earliest citation in 1943, by Alan Barth, who wrote, "News is only the first rough draft of history". There were also earlier formulations in the 1900s. Another journalist and *Times* editor, Thomas Griffith (1915-2002), used it in his phrasing, "Journalism is in fact history on the run. It is history written in time to be acted upon: thereby not only recording events but at times influencing them. Journalism is also the recording of history while the facts are not al in."
43. E.R. Babbie, *The Basics of Social Research* (6th ed.) (Belmont: Wadsworth, 2016), 357.
44. P. Nänny, "History of Censorship in South Africa," (Master's assignment, Stellenbosch University, 2004), 1.
45. Address of the President of South Africa, Thabo Mbeki, at the European Parliament, Strasbourg, 17.11.2004, http://www.dfa.gov.za/docs/speeches/2004/mbek1118.htm, accessed 6.04.2015.

46. K. Roelofse, "The History of the South African Press," in L.M. Oosthuizen, ed., *Introduction to Communication – Course Book 5: Journalism, Press and Radio Studies* (Kenwyn: Juta, 1996), 70–71.
47. W.A. Hachten and C.A. Giffard, *Total Onslaught. The South African Press under Attack* (Johannesburg: Macmillan, 1984), viii.

Chapter 2

1. UN Declaration on Human Rights, https://www.un.org/en/universal-declaration-human-rights/, accessed 7.05.2020.
2. RSF, "Who are We?" https://rsf.org/en/our-values, accessed 15.01.2018.
3. Freedom of the Press, Definition, Meaning, Explanation and Information, www.free-definition. com/Freedom-of-the-press.html, cited in L. Rabe, "Ten Years into Democracy – Media Freedom in South Africa," seminar series, Department of Media and Communication, University of Oslo & Freedom of Speech Foundation Fritt Ord, 13.10.2004, 3.10.2004.
4. James Madison, https://www.history.com/topics/us-presidents/james-madison, accessed 13.03.2018.
5. A. Hadland and K. Thorne, *The People's Voice: The Development and Current State of the South African Small Media Sector* (Commissioned by the MDDA, HSRC, 2004), 20.
6. The Universal Declaration of Human Rights, http://www.un.org/en/universal-declaration-human-rights/, accessed 28.12.2017.
7. Freedom of the Press, Definition, Meaning, Explanation and Information.
8. Declaration of Principles on Freedom of Expression in Africa, http://hrlibrary.umn.edu/achpr/expressionfreedomdec.html, accessed 1.02.2018.
9. M.M. Breytenbach, "The Manipulation of Public Opinion by State Censorship of the Media in South Africa (1974–1994)" (D.Phil. diss., Stellenbosch University, 1997), 14–15.
10. Ibid., 16–17.
11. Ibid., 1.
12. A. Mathews, *The Darker Reaches of Government* (Johannesburg: Juta, 1979), 16–17.
13. Breytenbach, "The Manipulation of Public Opinion," 4.
14. A. Hadland, "The South African Print Media, 1994–2004: An application and critique of comparative media systems theory" (D.Phil. diss., University of Cape Town, 2007), 100–101.
15. The ICASA Act of 2000 dissolved the IBA as well as the South African Telecommunications Regulatory Authority, but absorbed substantive parts of the Telecommunications Act of 1996, the IBA Act of 1993 and the Broadcasting Act of 1999. The ICASA Act combined functions of the IBA and SATRA into ICASA as one independent regulatory authority.
16. Hadland, "The South African Print Media," 102.
17. W.A. Hachten and C.A. Giffard, *Total Onslaught. The South African Press under Attack* (Johannesburg: Macmillan, 1984), 229. https://doi.org/10.1007/978-1-349-07685-7_10
18. Hadland, "The South African Print Media," 102–103.
19. J. Duncan, "Another Journalism is Possible: Critical Challenges for the Media in South Africa," Harold Wolpe Memorial Lecture, University of KwaZulu-Natal, Durban, 2003.
20. RSF, "Who are We?"
21. Measuring Press Freedom, Research and Library Services Division, Provisional Legislative Council Secretariat, http://www.legco.gov.hk/yr97-98/english/sec/library/in3_plc.pdf, accessed 3.10.2004.
22. As defined by Professor R.L. Stevenson, Measuring Press Freedom, http://www.legco.gov.hk/yr97-98/english/sec/library/in3_plc.pdf, accessed 3.10.2004.
23. FXI, https://www.fxi.org.za/, accessed 1.02.2018.
24. R2K, http://www.r2k.org.za/about/mission-vision-and-principles/, accessed 1.02.2018.
25. F. Siebert, T. Peterson and W. Schramm, *The Four Theories of the Press* (Urbana-Champaign: University of Illinois Press, 1956).
26. P.J. Fourie, "The Role and Functions of the Media: Functionalism," in P.J. Fourie, ed., *Media Studies. Volume 1: Institutions, Theories and Issues* (Lansdowne: Juta, 2001), 265–269.

27. D. McQuail, *Theories of Mass Communication* (2nd ed.) (London: Sage, 1987).

28. Ibid., 114–115.

29. Ibid., 116–118.

30. Fourie, "The Role and Functions of the Media: Functionalism," 271.

31. Ibid., 192–193.

32. McQuail, *Theories of Mass Communication*, 115–118.

33. J.H.O. du Plessis, "Die Afrikaanse Pers. 'n Studie van die Ontstaan, Ontwikkeling en Rol van die Hollands-Afrikaanse Pers as Sosiale Instelling" ("The Afrikaans Press. A Study of the Origin, Development and Role of the Dutch Afrikaans Press as Social Institution") (Ph.D. diss., Stellenbosch University, 1943), 1.

34. F. Nel, *Writing for the Media in Southern Africa* (Cape Town: Oxford University Press, 2001), 53.

35. A Free and Responsible Press, Commission on Freedom of the Press, http://www.archive.org/details/freeandresponsib029216mbp, 1947, accessed 1.02.2018, 126.

36. A.S. de Beer, "Mass Communication in Society. Pervasive Messages and Images of our Time," in A.S. de Beer, ed., *Mass Media towards the Millennium* (Pretoria: Van Schaik, 1998), 18–20.

37. D. Yutar, *Freedom of the Press in a Post-apartheid South Africa* (Green College, Oxford, Reuter Foundation, Hilary Term, 1995), 2.

38. Hachten and Giffard, *Total Onslaught*, xvi.

39. Ibid., 3.

40. Declaration, Africa Editors' Forum, SANEF (Johannesburg, Eskom Convention Centre, 13 April 2003).

41. Windhoek Declaration, https://en.unesco.org/wpfd, accessed 1.02.2018.

42. G. Berger, "Key Documents for African Media: A Briefing for Sanef," March 2003.

43. Hadland, "The South African Print Media," 101.

44. J.M. Barker, "Is No Policy a Policy Goal?" in K. Tomaselli and H. Dunn, eds., *Media, Democracy and Renewal in Southern Africa* (Colorado Springs: International Academic Publishers, 2001), 15–16.

45. African Charter on Broadcasting, https://crm.misa.org/upload/web/african_charter_on_broadcasting.pdf, accessed 11.06.2020..

46. SADC Protocol on Culture, Information and Sport, https://www.sadc.int/documents-publications/show/797, accessed 11.06.2020.

47. SADC Protocol on Information and Technology, , accessed 1.02.2018.

48. Charter on African Media and the Digital Divide, https://www.pambazuka.org/security-icts/charter-african-media-and-digital-divide, accessed 1.02.2018.

49. African Platform on Access to Information, http://africanplatform.org/, accessed 1.02.2018.

50. African Declaration on Internet Rights and Freedoms, http://africaninternetrights.org/.../3-IGF2014-Workshop-Report-No.-91-Launch-of-an-Afric, accessed 1.02.2018.

51. Hachten and Giffard, *Total Onslaught*, 18.

52. K. Voltmer, "The Mass Media and the Dynamics of Political Communication in Processes of Democratization," in K. Voltmer, ed., *Mass Media and Political Communication in New Democracies* (London: Routledge, 2006), 4.

53. M. Gurevitch and J.G. Blumler, "State of the Art of Comparative Political Communication Research: Poised for Maturity?" in F. Esser and B. Pfetsch, eds., *Comparing Political Communication* (Cambridge: Cambridge University Press, 2004), 338 https://doi.org/10.1017/CBO9780511606991.015; D. McQuail, *McQuail's Mass Communication Theory* (London: Sage, 2005), 178. https://doi.org/10.4135/9780857024374

54. C. Christians and K. Nordenstreng, "Social Responsibility Worldwide," *Journal of Mass Media Ethics* 19,1 (2004): 3–28. https://doi.org/10.1207/s15327728jmme1901_2

55. H. Wasserman, "Freedom's Just Another Word? Perspectives on Media Freedom and Responsibility in South Africa and Namibia," in *International Communication Gazette* 72,7 (2010): 569. https://doi.org/10.1177/1748048510378145

56. I.A. Blankson, "Media Independence and Pluralism in Africa: Opportunities and Challenges of Democratization and Liberalization," in I.A. Blankson and P.D. Murphy, eds., *Negotiating Democracy: Media Transformation in Emerging Democracies* (Albany: SUNY Press, 2007), 24.

57. "Measuring Press Freedom", 2.

58. P. Diederichs and A.S. de Beer, "Newspapers. The Fourth Estate: A Cornerstone of Democracy," in A.S. de Beer, ed., *Mass Communication Towards the Millennium* (Pretoria: Van Schaik, 1998), 04.

59. M. Tsedu, "One Story Can Make All the Difference," *Media Tenor South Africa*, 5,2 (2001): 3.

60. Hachten and Giffard, *Total Onslaught*, 105.

Chapter 3

1. Vasco da Gama, http://www.sahistory.org.za/topic/vasco-da-gamas-voyage-discovery-1497, accessed 3.05.2015.

2. H. Giliomee and B. Mbenga, *New History of South Africa* (Cape Town: Tafelberg, 2007).

3. Pedro Álvares de Cabral, Portuguese navigator, 1467 or 1468–1520, http://www.britannica.com/EBchecked/topic/87709/Pedro-Alvares-Cabral, accessed 3.05.2015.

4. Post Office Tree, Dias Museum, http://www.diasmuseum.co.za/index.php/attractions/post-office-tree, accessed 16.03.2015.

5. Mossel Bay, http://www.capetownmagazine.com/things-to-do-cape-town/mossel-bays-one-and-only-post-office-tree/15_52_866, accessed 16.03.2015.

6. Post Office Tree, Dias Museum.

7. South Africa's First Post Office, http://www.travelground.com/attractions/old-post-office-tree; http://www.capetownmagazine.com/things-to-do-cape-town/mossel-bays-one-and-only-post-office-tree/15_52_866, accessed 16.03.2015.

8. C.F.J. Muller, *Sonop in die Suide (Sunrise in the South)* (Cape Town: Tafelberg, 1990), 1.

9. H. Büttner and G. Claassen, *Goed om te Weet (Good to Know)* (Cape Town: Tafelberg, 2010), 368–369. There are also others claimants of this honour, such as the Dutchman Coster and the Englishman Caxton.

10. Muller, *Sonop*, 1-2.

11. B. Maclennan, *The Wind Makes Dust. Four Centuries of Travel in Southern Africa* (Cape Town: Tafelberg, 2003).

12. The following is based on a review of the book by the author in *Ecquid Novi* 25, 1 (2004).

13. Maclennan, *The Wind Makes Dust*, n.p.

14. Ibid., 3.

15. Giliomee and Mbenga, *New History,* 20.

16. Muller, *Sonop*, 1.

17. J.H.O. du Plessis, "Die Afrikaanse Pers. 'n Studie van die Ontstaan, Ontwikkeling en Rol van die Hollands-Afrikaanse Pers as Sosiale Instelling" ("The Afrikaans Press. A Study of the Origin, Development and Role of the Dutch Afrikaans Press as Social Institution") (Ph.D. diss., Stellenbosch University, 1943), 1–2.

18. Giliomee and Mbenga, *New History*, 71.

19. Ibid., 53.

20. H.B. Thom, "Nasionalisme in ons Geskiedenis" ("Nationalism in our History"), *Die Stellenbosche Oud-Student* (September 1937): 13.

21. L. Rabe, "'n Kultuurhistoriese Studie van die Duitse Nedersetting Philippi op die Kaapse Vlakte" ("A Cultural Historical Study of the German Settlement Philippi on the Cape Flats") (D.Phil. diss., Stellenbosch University, 1994).

22. Claassen, "Magazines. Life's Own Story," in A.S. de Beer, ed., *Mass Media Towards the Millennium* (Pretoria: Van Schaik, 1998), 119.

23. P. Diederichs and A.S. de Beer, "Newspapers. The Fourth Estate: A Cornerstone of Democracy," in A.S. de Beer, ed., *Mass Media Towards the Millennium* (Pretoria: Van Schaik, 1998), 87.

24. "Simon van der Stel, commander and governor at the Cape," http://www.sahistory.org.za/dated-event/simon-van-der-stel-commander-and-governor-cape-born, accessed 3.05.2015.
25. Giliomee and Mbenga, *New History*, 61.
26. Du Plessis, "Die Afrikaanse Pers," 3-4.
27. D.B. Bosman, *Oor die Ontstaan van Afrikaans (On the Origins of Afrikaans)*, (Publisher unknown, 1923), 18–41.
28. Muller, *Sonop*, 1.
29. Giliomee and Mbenga, *New History*, 71.
30. A. Coetzee, *Die Opkoms van die Afrikaanse Kultuurgedagte aan die Rand (The Rise of Afrikaans Cultural Thinking on the Rand)* (Publisher unknown, 1938), 16–17.
31. P.J. Nienaber, *'n Beknopte Geskiedenis van die Hollands-Afrikaanse Drukpers in Suid-Afrika (A Short History of the Dutch-Afrikaans Press in South Africa)*, Tweede Trek-series, no. XXV (Bloemfontein, Cape Town and Port Elizabeth: Nasionale Pers, 1943), 3.
32. Muller, *Sonop*, 2.
33. P.J. Fourie, "Nederlandstalige en Afrikaanstalige Media," Internationale Colloquium Nederlands in de Wereld ("Dutch and Afrikaans Language Media," International Colloquium Dutch in the World) (Brussels: Vrije Universiteit Brussel Press, 1994), 291.
34. Muller, *Sonop*, 2.
35. Du Plessis, "Die Afrikaanse Pers," 8.
36. Muller, *Sonop*, 2.
37. J.H. Altschull, *From Milton to McLuhan* (New York and London: Longman, 1990), 36.
38. D. Yutar, *Freedom of the Press in a Post-Apartheid South Africa* (Green College, Oxford, Reuter Foundation, Hilary Term, 1995), 2.
39. C. Buchinger, "History of Censorship in South Africa" (M.Phil. assignment, Stellenbosch University, 2004), 3.
40. Nienaber, *'n Beknopte Geskiedenis*, 3; Muller, *Sonop*, 2.
41. Fourie, "Nederlandstalige en Afrikaanstalige Media," 291.
42. Du Plessis, "Die Afrikaanse Pers," 8.
43. Nienaber, *'n Beknopte Geskiedenis*, 3.
44. Muller, *Sonop*, 2.
45. W. de Kock, *A Manner of Speaking* (Cape Town: Saayman & Weber, 1982), 17–18.
46. Du Plessis, "Die Afrikaanse Pers," 8.
47. W. Visser, "Die Ontwikkeling van Vakbonde en Georganiseerde Arbeid" ("The Development of Unions and Organised Labour") in F. Pretorius, ed., *Geskiedenis van Suid-Afrika (History of South Africa)* (Cape Town: Tafelberg, 2012), 482.
48. Muller, *Sonop*, 2.
49. J.H.O. du Plessis, "The Rise of the Press in South Africa," *Cape Times*, May 9, 1919.
50. Timeline, History of the SA Print & Advertising Industry, PMSA, 2006.

Chapter 4

1. J.H.O. du Plessis, "Die Afrikaanse Pers. 'n Studie van die Ontstaan, Ontwikkeling en Rol van die Hollands-Afrikaanse Pers as Sosiale Instelling" ("The Afrikaans Press. A Study of the Origin, Development and Role of the Dutch Afrikaans Press as Social Institution"), (Ph.D. diss., Stellenbosch University, 1943), 19.
2. "Magna Carta," https://www.dictionary.com/browse/magna-carta, accessed 21.08.2020.
3. W. de Kock, *A Manner of Speaking* (Cape Town: Saayman & Weber, 1982), 5.
4. P.J. Fourie, "Afrikaans en die Media" ("Afrikaans and the Media"), *Ecquid Novi* 15,2 (1994): 256-283. https://doi.org/10.1080/02560054.1994.9653123
5. P.J. Nienaber, *'n Beknopte Geskiedenis van die Hollands-Afrikaanse Drukpers in Suid-Afrika (A Short History of the Dutch-Afrikaans Press in South Africa)*, Tweede Trek-series, no. XXV (Bloemfontein, Cape Town and Port Elizabeth: Nasionale Pers, 1943), 10.
6. Du Plessis, "Die Afrikaanse Pers," 6.

7. J. de Villiers, "Die Kaapse Samelewing onder Britse Bestuur, 1806-1834" ("Cape Society under British Government, 1806-1834"), in F. Pretorius, ed., *Geskiedenis van Suid-Afrika. Van Voortye tot Vandag (History of South Africa. From Early Years to Today)*, (Cape Town: Tafelberg, 2012), 73.
8. J. Matisonn, *God, Spies and Lies* (Vlaeberg: Missing Ink, 2015), 36.
9. Du Plessis, "Die Afrikaanse Pers", 308.
10. W.A. Hachten and C.A. Giffard, *Total Onslaught. The South African Press under Attack* (Johannesburg: Macmillan, 1984), ix–xi.
11. G.N. Claassen, "Magazines. Life's Own Story," in A.S. de Beer, ed., *Mass Media towards the Millennium* (Pretoria: Van Schaik, 1998), 122.
12. Hachten and Giffard, *Total Onslaught*, 21.
13. C.F.J. Muller, *Sonop in die Suide (Sunrise in the South)* (Cape Town: Tafelberg, 1990), 5.
14. Claassen, Magazines," 122.
15. Hachten and Giffard, *Total Onslaught*, xi–xiii.
16. Ibid., 21–22.
17. E. Potter, *The Press as Opposition. The Political Role of South African Newspapers* (Totowa, NJ: Rowman and Littlefield, 1975), 30–33.
18. Nienaber, *'n Beknopte Geskiedenis*, 6.
19. Hachten and Giffard, *Total Onslaught*, 22.
20. The Cape Town Gazette and African Advertiser, http://www.sahistory.org.za/dated-event/cape-town-gazette-and-african-advertiser-bilingual-newspaper-and-first-publish-news-and-, accessed 6.02.2018.
21. Matisonn, *God, Spies and Lies*, 35–36.
22. Muller, *Sonop,* 4.
23. De Kock, *A Manner of Speaking*, 19–20.
24. Muller, *Sonop*, 3.
25. Muller, *Sonop*, 3 & 5; P. Diederichs and A.S. de Beer, "Newspapers. The Fourth Estate: A Cornerstone of Democracy," in A.S. de Beer, ed., *Mass Communication Towards the Millennium* (Pretoria: Van Schaik, 1998), 87–88.
26. De Kock, *A Manner of Speaking*, 66.
27. Muller, *Sonop*, 5.
28. Hachten and Giffard, *Total Onslaught*, 23.
29. Muller, *Sonop*, 4–5.
30. Du Plessis, "Die Afrikaanse Pers," 9.
31. De Kock, *A Manner of Speaking*, 22.
32. Hachten and Giffard, *Total Onslaught*, 23.
33. Muller, *Sonop*, 6.
34. Diederichs and De Beer, "Newspapers," 88.
35. Hachten and Giffard, *Total Onslaught*, 23.
36. Muller, *Sonop,* 7.
37. Ibid., 5.
38. Du Plessis, "Die Afrikaanse Pers," 306.
39. J. de Villiers, "Die Kaapse Samelewing," 82–85.
40. Muller, *Sonop*, 7.
41. Claassen, Magazines," 122.
42. P.E. Louw, "The Growth of Monopoly Control in the South Africa Press," in P.E. Louw, ed., *South African Media Policy: Debates of the 1990s* (Bellville: Anthropos, 1993), 159.
43. Hachten and Giffard, *Total Onslaught*, 23.
44. D. Wigston, "History of the South African Media," in P.J. Fourie, ed., *Media Studies Volume 1: Media History, Media and Society* (Wetton: Juta, 2007), 30.
45. De Kock, *A Manner of Speaking*, 30.
46. Wigston, "History of the South African Media," 30.

47. P. Diederichs, "Newspapers: The Fourth Estate: A Cornerstone of Democracy," in A.S. de Beer, ed., *Mass Media for the Nineties: The South African Handbook of Mass Communication* (Pretoria: Van Schaik, 1993), 74.
48. Wigston, "History of the South African Media," 30.
49. Hachten and Giffard, *Total Onslaught*, 23–24.
50. Ibid., 25.
51. Du Plessis, "Die Afrikaanse Pers," 10–11.
52. T. Pringle, *Narrative of a Residence in South Africa* (Cape Town: Struik, 1966), 174.
53. De Kock, *A Manner of Speaking*, 2.
54. Du Plessis, "Die Afrikaanse Pers," 12.
55. De Kock, *A Manner of Speaking*, 2.
56. Hachten and Giffard, *Total Onslaught*, 24–25.
57. De Kock, *A Manner of Speaking*, 34.
58. Hachten and Giffard, *Total Onslaught*, 25.
59. P.J. Fourie, "Nederlandstalige en Afrikaanstalige media" ("Dutch and Afrikaans media"), Internationale Colloquium Nederlands in de Wereld (International Colloquium Dutch in the World), (Brussels: Vrije Universiteit Brussel Press, 1994), 291.
60. De Kock, *A Manner of Speaking*, 27–28.
61. Ibid., 29.
62. Ibid., 22–23.
63. Hachten and Giffard, *Total Onslaught*, 145.
64. De Kock, *A Manner of Speaking*, 24.
65. Du Plessis, "Die Afrikaanse Pers," 7.
66. Ibid., 10.
67. De Kock, *A Manner of Speaking*, 1–2.
68. Potter, *The Press as Opposition*, 32.
69. Du Plessis, "Die Afrikaanse Pers," 12.
70. De Kock, *A Manner of Speaking*, 33.
71. L.H. Meurant, *Sixty Years Ago, or Reminiscences of the Struggle for the Freedom of the Press in South Africa and the Establishment of the First Newspaper in the Eastern Provinces*, Facsimile Edition (Cape Town: Africana Connoisseurs Press, 1963; Original: Cape Town: Saul Solomon & Co, 1885), 13.
72. Ibid., 14–17.
73. Du Plessis, "Die Afrikaanse Pers," 11.
74. Meurant, *Sixty Years Ago*, 5.
75. Du Plessis, "Die Afrikaanse Pers," 13–14.
76. De Kock, *A Manner of Speaking*, 51.
77. Hachten and Giffard, *Total Onslaught*, 25.
78. Pringle, *Narrative of a Residence*, 180.
79. Hachten and Giffard, *Total Onslaught*, 26.
80. Potter, *The Press as Opposition*, 32.
81. Louw, "The Growth of Monopoly Control," 159.
82. Hachten and Giffard, *Total Onslaught*, 26.
83. Meurant, *Sixty Years Ago*, 19.
84. De Kock, *A Manner of Speaking*, 41–43.
85. Ibid., 39–40.
86. Diederichs and De Beer, "Newspapers," 88.
87. Du Plessis, "Die Afrikaanse Pers," 15.
88. Nienaber, *'n Beknopte Geskiedenis*, 10.
89. Ibid., 10.
90. Diederichs and De Beer, "Newspapers," 88.
91. Claassen, "Magazines," 122.
92. Wigston, "History of the South African Media," 29.

93. De Kock, *A Manner of Speaking*, 33.
94. Ibid., 35.
95. Diederichs and De Beer, "Newspapers," 88.
96. Potter, *The Press as Opposition*, 32–33.
97. Hachten and Giffard, *Total Onslaught*, 26.
98. Nienaber, *'n Beknopte Geskiedenis*, 15.
99. Wigston, "History of the South African Media," 29.
100. De Kock, *A Manner of Speaking*, 53.
101. Ibid., 44–45.
102. Meurant, *Sixty Years Ago*, 52.
103. Claassen, "Magazines," 122.
104. De Kock, *A Manner of Speaking,* 46–47.
105. Meurant, *Sixty Years Ago*, 63.
106. Ibid., 65.
107. Nienaber, *'n Beknopte Geskiedenis*, 10.
108. De Kock, *A Manner of Speaking,* 48.
109. Du Plessis, "Die Afrikaanse Pers," 17.
110. Meurant, *Sixty Years Ago,* 24.
111. Claassen, "Magazines," 122.
112. De Kock, *A Manner of Speaking,* 48–50.
113. Hachten and Giffard, *Total Onslaught*, 27.
114. Diederichs and De Beer, "Newspapers," 88.
115. De Kock, *A Manner of Speaking*, 2.
116. T. Pringle, *Narrative of a Residence in South Africa* (London: Edward Moxon, 1835; BiblioLife 2008), 88.
117. Hachten and Giffard, *Total Onslaught*, 26.
118. Nienaber, *'n Beknopte Geskiedenis*, 10.
119. Du Plessis, "Die Afrikaanse Pers," 12.
120. De Kock, *A Manner of Speaking*, 3–4.
121. Ibid., 52–53.
122. Ibid., 4.
123. Ibid., 54–55.
124. Wigston, "History of the South African Media," 29.
125. Potter, *The Press as Opposition*, 33.
126. De Kock, *A Manner of Speaking*, 33.
127. Ibid., 57–62.
128. Ibid., 66–68.
129. Ibid., 72.
130. Ibid., 68.
131. Ibid., 69–70.
132. Ibid., 72–74.
133. Ibid., 76.
134. Ibid., 75.
135. Ibid., 75–76.
136. Nienaber, *'n Beknopte geskiedenis*, 15.
137. Du Plessis, "Die Afrikaanse Pers," 17–18.
138. Nienaber, *'n Beknopte geskiedenis*, 15.
139. Hachten and Giffard, *Total Onslaught*, 27.
140. Claassen, "Magazines," 122.
141. W. de Kock, *'n Wyse van Spreke: Die Ontstaan van die Pers in Suid-Afrika* (Cape Town: Saayman & Weber, 1983), 71; Diederichs and De Beer, "Newspapers," 88.
142. De Kock, *A Manner of Speaking,* 65.

143. Ibid., 65–66.
144. Wigston, "History of the South African Media," 29.
145. K. Roelofse, "The History of the South African Press," in L.M. Oosthuizen, ed., *Introduction to Communication – Course Book 5: Journalism, press and Radio Studies* (Kenwyn: Juta, 1996), 72.
146. Potter, *The Press as Opposition*, 33.
147. Meurant, *Sixty Years Ago*, 64.
148. Du Plessis, "Die Afrikaanse Pers," 15–18.
149. Meurant, *Sixty Years Ago*, 64.
150. Diederichs and De Beer, "Newspapers," 88.
151. J.H.O. du Plessis, "Lord Charles Somerset and the Press," *Cape Times*, May 10, 1929.
152. Muller, *Sonop*, 7.
153. Du Plessis, "Die Afrikaanse Pers," 19.
154. De Kock, *A Manner of Speaking*, 5.
155. Potter, *The Press as Opposition*, 33.
156. Claassen, Magazines," 122.
157. Muller, *Sonop*, 9.
158. Claassen, "Magazines," 122.
159. Muller, *Sonop*, 10.
160. Diederichs and De Beer, "Newspapers," 88.
161. Wigston, "History of the South African Media," 34.
162. R.W. Murray, Snr., *South African Reminiscences* (Cape Town: Juta, 1894), 94.
163. De Kock, *A Manner of Speaking*, 86–88.
164. Murray, *South African Reminiscences*, 94.
165. De Kock, *A Manner of Speaking*, 88–89.
166. Ibid., 89.
167. J. du P. Scholtz, *Die Afrikaner en Sy Taal (The Afrikaner and His Language)* (Cape Town: Nasou, n.d.), 41–42.
168. De Kock, *A Manner of Speaking*, 94–95.
169. H. Giliomee and B. Mbenga, *Nuwe Geskiedenis van Suid-Afrika (New History of South Africa)*, (Cape Town: Tafelberg, 2007), 122.
170. De Kock, *A Manner of Speaking*, 95.
171. Ibid., 96.
172. Natal Witness, https://www.media24.com/newspapers/the-witness/, accessed 12.11.2018.
173. De Kock, *A Manner of Speaking*, 96.
174. Ibid., 97.
175. Ibid., 96–98.
176. Hachten and Giffard, *Total Onslaught*, 27.
177. Diederichs and De Beer, "Newspapers," 90.
178. De Kock, *A Manner of Speaking*, 78–83.
179. Hachten and Giffard, *Total Onslaught*, 27.
180. De Kock, *A Manner of Speaking*, 83–85.
181. Du Plessis, "Die Afrikaanse Pers," 17–18.
182. De Kock, *A Manner of Speaking*, 36–38.
183. Du Plessis, "Die Afrikaanse Pers," 7.
184. Ibid., 75.
185. Ibid., 78.
186. Ibid., 8.
187. J.H. Hofmeyr, *Het Leven van Jan Hendrik Hofmeyr* (Publisher unknown, 1913), 44.
188. Du Plessis, "Die Afrikaanse Pers," 19–20.
189. Wigston, "History of the South African Media," 31.
190. Giliomee and Mbenga, *Nuwe Geskiedenis*, 122.
191. Diederichs and De Beer, "Newspapers," 88.

192. T.E.G. Cutten, *A History of the Press in South Africa* (Cape Town: NUSAS, 1935), 40.
193. Hachten and Giffard, *Total Onslaught*, 39.
194. Giliomee and Mbenga, *Nuwe Geskiedenis*, 122.
195. Hachten and Giffard, *Total Onslaught*, 143.
196. S. Johnson, "An Historical Overview of the Black Press," in K. Tomaselli and P.E. Louw, eds., *The Iternative Press in South Africa* (Bellville: Anthropos, 1991), 15.
197. Diederichs and De Beer, "Newspapers," 90.
198. L. Switzer and D. Switzer, *The Black Press in South Africa and Lesotho* (Boston: G.K. Hall, 1979).
199. Diederichs and De Beer, "Newspapers," 90.
200. Roelofse, "The History of the South African Press," 82.
201. Wigston, "History of the South African Media," 36.
202. Hachten and Giffard, *Total Onslaught*, 145–146.
203. Diederichs and De Beer, "Newspapers," 90.
204. Wigston, "History of the South African Media," 37.
205. M. Geertsema, "'n Historiese Oorsig oor die Ontstaan en Ontwikkeling van die Swart Pers in Suid-Afrika" ("An Historical Overview of the Founding and Development of the Black Press in South Africa"), (M.A. thesis, NWU, 1993), 10.
206. De Kock, *A Manner of Speaking*, 98.
207. Ibid., 100–101.
208. Switzer and Switzer, *The Black Press in South Africa and Lesotho*, vii.
209. Hachten and Giffard, *Total Onslaught*, 144–145.
210. T.J. Couzens, "A Short History of the *World* and Other Black South African Newspapers" (Paper, University of the Witwatersrand, Johannesburg, 1977), 2.
211. Hachten and Giffard, *Total Onslaught*, 144.

Chapter 5

1. W. de Kock, *A Manner of Speaking* (Cape Town: Saayman & Weber, 1982), 8–10.
2. H. Giliomee, "Afrikanernasionalisme, 1875–1899," in F. Pretorius, ed., *Geskiedenis van Suid-Afrika. Van Voortye tot Vandag* (*History of South Africa. From Prehistoric Times to Today*), (Cape Town: Tafelberg 2012), 222.
3. J. Grobler, "Staatsvorming en Stryd, 1850–1900" ("Forming of states and struggles, 1850-1900"), in F. Pretorius, ed., *Geskiedenis van Suid-Afrika. Van Voortye tot Vandag* (*History of South Africa. From Prehistoric Times to Today*), (Cape Town: Tafelberg, 2012), 166.
4. De Kock, *A Manner of Speaking*, 79.
5. A. Delius, "Journalism and the Press," paper, 60th anniversary celebrations of Rhodes University (Grahamstown, 1964).
6. Grobler, "Staatsvorming," 153–154.
7. W.A. Hachten and C.A. Giffard, *Total Onslaught: The South African Press Under Attack* (Johannesburg: McMillan, 1984), 29–30.
8. J. Mervis, *The Fourth Estate, A Newspaper Story* (Johannesburg: Jonathan Ball Publishers, 1989), 364.
9. E. Potter, *The Press as Opposition. The Political Role of South African Newspapers* (Totowa, NJ: Rowman and Littlefield, 1975), 37.
10. Hachten and Giffard, *Total Onslaught*, 29–30.
11. De Kock, *A Manner of Speaking*, 6–8.
12. Ibid., 105–106.
13. Ibid., 104.
14. Ibid., 104–105.
15. Ibid., 106–107.
16. W. Visser, "Die Ontwikkeling van Vakbonde en Georganiseerde Arbeid" ("The Development of Unions and Organised Labour"), in F. Pretorius, ed., *Geskiedenis van Suid-Afrika. Van Voortye tot*

Vandag (*History of South Africa. From Prehistoric Times to Today*), (Cape Town: Tafelberg, 2012), 482.

17. De Kock, *A Manner of Speaking*, 100–101.
18. Potter, *The Press as Opposition*, 38.
19. Ibid., 37.
20. Hachten and Giffard, *Total Onslaught*, 31.
21. Potter, *The Press as Opposition*, 37–38.
22. Hachten and Giffard, *Total Onslaught*, 31–32.
23. Delius, "Journalism and the Press."
24. De Kock, *A Manner of Speaking*, 98.
25. EPH, https://www.eggsa.org/newspapers/index.php/eph, accessed 12.11.2018.
26. De Kock, *A Manner of Speaking*, 99.
27. T.E.G. Cutten, *A History of the Press in South Africa* (Cape Town: NUSAS, 1935), 41–42.
28. De Kock, *A Manner of Speaking*, 7.
29. Hachten and Giffard, *Total Onslaught*, 30–31.
30. De Kock, *A Manner of Speaking*, 93.
31. Potter, *The Press as Opposition*, 35.
32. Hachten and Giffard, *Total Onslaught*, 31.
33. Potter, *The Press as Opposition*, 35.
34. P. Diederichs and A.S. de Beer, "Newspapers. The Fourth Estate: A cornerstone of Democracy," in A.S. de Beer, ed., *Mass Media Towards the Millennium* (Pretoria: Van Schaik, 1998), 90; Cutten, *A History of the Press,* 50.
35. Cutten, *A History of the Press,* 50.
36. Potter, *The Press as Opposition,* 36; C. Muller, *Sonop in die Suide* (*Sunrise in the South*), (Cape Town: Tafelberg, 1990), 15; D. Wigston, "A History of the South African Media," in P.J. Fourie, ed., *Media Studies/Media History, Media and Society* (Lansdowne: Juta, 2007), 32.
37. Potter, *The Press as Opposition*, 36.
38. Ibid., 39–41.
39. De Kock, *A Manner of Speaking*, 11.
40. Potter, *The Press as Opposition*, 41.
41. S. Swart, "'An Irritating Pebble in Kruger's Shoe' – Eugène Marais and *Land en Volk* in the ZAR, 1891–1896," *Historia*, 48,2 (2003): 66–68.
42. Ibid., 71.
43. Ibid., 73.
44. Potter, *The Press as Opposition*, 34.
45. Wigston, "History of the South African Media," 35.
46. De Kock, *A Manner of Speaking*, 86.
47. Wigston, "History of the South African Media," 35.
48. De Kock, *A Manner of Speaking*, 89–91.
49. Hachten and Giffard, *Total Onslaught*, 146.
50. De Kock, *A Manner of Speaking*, 23–24.
51. SA History, http://www.sahistory.org.za/dated-event/first-black-sa-newspaper-imvo-zabantsundu-black-opinion-published-king-williams-town-ten, accessed 22.01.2018.
52. Imvo Zabantsundu, http://nhmsa.co.za/news/imvo-zabantsundu-a-brief-history/, accessed 22.01.2018.
53. Hachten and Giffard, *Total Onslaught*, 146.
54. G. Moodie, "New isiXhosa Newspaper Launches Today," http://www.journalism.co.za/blog/isixhosa-newspaper-launches-today/, accessed 22.01.2018.
55. Imvo Zabantsundu.
56. Cutten, *A History of the Press*, 81.
57. S. Johnson, "An Historical Overview of the Black Press," in K. Tomaselli and P.E. Louw, eds., *The Alternative Press in South Africa* (Bellville: Anthropos, 1991), 17.

58. Wigston, "History of the South African Media," 38.
59. Johnson, "An Historical Overview," 19.
60. Wigston, "History of the South African Media," 38.
61. L. Switzer and M. Adhikari, "Preface," in L. Switzer and M. Adhikari, eds., *South Africa's Resistance Press. Alternative Voices in the Last Generation under Apartheid* (Ohio: Ohio University Center for International Studies, 2000), xv.
62. P. Limb, "Representing the Labouring Classes. African Workers in the African Nationalist Press, 1900–1960," in L. Switzer and M. Adhikari, eds., *South Africa's Resistance Press. Alternative Voices in the Last Generation Under Apartheid* (Ohio: Ohio University Center for International Studies, 2000), 80–87.
63. Hachten and Giffard, *Total Onslaught*, 32–33.
64. Ibid., 35–38.
65. H.G. Rudolph, "Freedom of the Press or the Right to Know," *The South African Law Journal*, 81 (1981): 85.
66. Giliomee, "Afrikanernasionalisme," 224.
67. Diederichs and De Beer, "Newspapers," 88
68. Muller, *Sonop*, 13.
69. Diederichs and De Beer, "Newspapers," 88.
70. Grobler, "Staatsvorming," 166.
71. Giliomee, "Afrikanernasionalisme," 226.
72. De Kock, *A Manner of Speaking*, 106.
73. G.N. Claassen, "Magazines. Life's Own Story," in A.S. de Beer, ed., *Mass Media towards the Millennium* (Pretoria: Van Schaik, 1998), 123.
74. Grobler, "Staatsvorming," 167.
75. Giliomee, "Afrikanernasionalisme," 230.
76. Diederichs and De Beer, "Newspapers," 90.
77. Wigston, "History of the South African Media," 30.
78. De Kock, *'n Wyse van Spreke: Die Ontstaan van die Pers in Suid-Afrika (A Manner of Speaking: The Origins of the Press in South Africa)*, (Cape Town: Saayman & Weber, 1983), 108–109.
79. Wigston, "A History of the South African Media," 30–31.
80. De Kock, *A Manner of Speaking*, 10.
81. Ibid., 108–109.
82. Ibid., 10.
83. Ibid., 110–111.
84. H. Giliomee and B. Mbenge, Nuwe Geskiedenis van Suid-Afrika (New History of South Africa), (Cape Town: Tafelberg, 2007), 184, 195.
85. De Kock, A Manner of Speaking, 11.
86. Wigston, "A History of the South African Media," 30.
87. Diederichs and De Beer, "Newspapers," 91.
88. De Kock, *A Manner of Speaking*, 85.
89. Ibid., 112–113.
90. Ibid., 111.
91. Hachten and Giffard, *Total Onslaught*, 22.
92. Diederichs and De Beer, "Newspapers," 90.
93. Hachten and Giffard, *Total Onslaught*, 33.
94. J. Mervis, *The Fourth Estate*, 9–10.
95. Diederichs and De Beer, "Newspapers," 90.
96. Hachten and Giffard, *Total Onslaught*, 33–34.
97. Mervis, *The Fourth Estate*, 11.
98. Swart, "An Irritating Pebble," 67.
99. Hachten and Giffard, *Total Onslaught*, xiii.

100. D. Yutar, *Freedom of the Press in a Post-Apartheid South Africa* (Green College, Oxford: Reuter Foundation, 1995), 4.
101. Swart, "An Irritating Pebble," 69.
102. Ibid., 67.
103. Ibid., 75.
104. Ibid., 67–68.
105. Ibid., 77–78.
106. Ibid, 88–89.
107. Ibid., 90–92.
108. Ibid., 93–96.
109. Yutar, *Freedom of the Press,* 4.
110. Hachten and Giffard, *Total Onslaught,* xiii.
111. Mervis, *The Fourth Estate,* 11–13.
112. Ibid., 15–16.
113. Ibid., 20–22.
114. Ibid., 36.
115. Ibid., 24–25.
116. Ibid., 30–31.
117. Ibid., 33–34.
118. Ibid., 38.
119. Ibid., 44–45.
120. J. Matisonn, *God, Lies and Spies* (Vlaeberg: Missing Ink, 2015).
121. Mervis, *The Fourth Estate,* 45.
122. http://www.marklives.com/2018/05/abc-analysis-q1-2018-the-biggest-circulating-newspapers-in-sa/, accessed 19.12.2018.
123. Mervis, *The Fourth Estate,* 45.
124. L Rabe, "Twintig dae in Desember – Naspers, *Die Burger*, Cillié en Verwoerd" ("Twenty days in December – Naspers, *Die Burger*, Cillié and Verwoerd"), in L. Rabe, ed., *'n Konstante Revolusie. Naspers, Media24 en Oorgange* (A Constant Revolution. Naspers, Media24 and Transitions), (Cape Town: Tafelberg, 2015), 47.
125. Mervis, *The Fourth Estate,* 48–49.
126. Ibid., 80–84.
127. Potter, *The Press as Opposition,* 41–42.
128. De Kock, *A Manner of Speaking,* 108.
129. Ibid., 109–115.
130. Ibid., 115.
131. Ibid., 115.
132. Ibid., 16.
133. Ibid., 117.
134. Ibid., 118.
135. Ibid., 101.
136. Ibid., 103.
137. Ibid., 93.
138. Ibid., 94.
139. Ibid., 98.
140. L.H. Meurant, *Sixty Years Ago, or Reminiscences of the Struggle for the Freedom of the Press in South Africa and the Establishment of the First Newspaper in the Eastern Provinces,* Facsimile Ed. (Africana Connoisseurs Press, 1963; Original: Saul Solomon & Co, Cape Town, 1885), 64.
141. Claassen, "Magazines," 122.
142. J.H.O. du Plessis, "Lord Charles Somerset and the Press," *Cape Times,* May 10, 1929.
143. Muller, *Sonop,* 7.
144. Du Plessis, *Die Afrikaanse Pers,* 19.

145. C. Merrett, *A Culture of Censorship. Secrecy and Intellectual Repression in South Africa* (Cape Town: David Phillip, 1994), 9.

146. Hepple, as quoted in P. Nänny, "History of Censorship in South Africa" (M.Phil. assignment, Stellenbosch University, 2004), 2.

147. Yutar, *Freedom of the Press*, 4.

148. Merrett, *A Culture of Censorship*, 21.

149. Diederichs and De Beer, "Newspapers," 90.

150. D. McCracken, "The Imperial British Newspaper, with Special Reference to South Africa, India and the 'Irish Model'," *Critical Arts*, 29,1 (2015): 10. https://doi.org/10.1080/02560046.2015.1009675

151. Diederichs and De Beer, "Newspapers," 90.

Chapter 6

1. W.A. Hachten and C.A. Giffard, *Total Onslaught. The South African Press under Attack* (Johannesburg: McMillan, 1984), 10.

2. The National Party, http://www.sahistory.org.za/topic/national-party-np, accessed 8.02.2018.

3. N.J. le Roux, *WA Hofmeyr. Sy Werk en Waarde* (*WA Hofmeyr. His Work and Value*) (Cape Town, Bloemfontein, Johannesburg: Nasionale Boekhandel, 1953), 89–97.

4. Hachten and Giffard, *Total Onslaught*, 42.

5. C. Merrett, *A Culture of Censorship. Secrecy and Intellectual Repression in South Africa* (Cape Town: David Phillip, 1994), 9.

6. A. Hadland, "The South African Print Media, 1994–2004: An Application and Critique of Comparative Media Systems Theory" (D.Phil. diss., University of Cape Town, 2007), 186.

7. P. Diederichs and A.S. de Beer, "Newspapers. The Fourth Estate: A Cornerstone of Democracy," in A.S. de Beer, ed., *Mass Media towards the Millennium* (Pretoria: Van Schaik, 1998), 91.

8. A. Wessels. 2013. Email. 13.03.2013.

9. W. Visser, "Die Minerale Revolusie" ("The Mineral Revolution"), in F. Pretorius, ed., *Geskiedenis van Suid-Afrika* (*History of South Africa*) (Cape Town: Tafelberg, 2012), 183.

10. J. Grobler, "Staatsvorming en Stryd, 1850–1900" ("State Formation and Struggle, 1850–1900"), in F. Pretorius, ed., *Geskiedenis van Suid-Afrika Vandag* (*History of South Africa Today*) (Cape Town: Tafelberg, 2012), 153–154.

11. M. Morris, *Apartheid. An Illustrated History* (Jeppestown: Jonathan Ball, 2012), 13.

12. J. Lambert, "Engelssprekende Suid-Afrikaners: Onseker van hul Identiteit" ("English Speaking South Africans: Unsure of their Identity"), in F. Pretorius, ed., *Geskiedenis van Suid-Afrika* (*History of South Africa*) (Cape Town: Tafelberg, 2012), 532–535.

13. E. Potter, *The Press as Opposition. The Political Role of South African Newspapers* (Totowa, NJ: Rowman and Littlefield, 1975), 17–19.

14. Lambert, "Engelssprekende Suid-Afrikaners," 532–535.

15. L. Rabe, "Inleiding" ("Introduction"), in L. Rabe, ed., *'n Konstante Revolusie. Naspers, Media24 en Oorgange* (*Constant Revolution. Naspers, Media24 and Transitions*) (Cape Town: Tafelberg, 2015).

16. H. Wasserman, "Prosus: New Naspers Internet Company Starts with a Bang in Amsterdam", https://www.fin24.com/Companies/ICT/naspers-share-price-loses-32-in-one-go-as-its-new-internet-company-starts-with-a-bang-in-amsterdam-20190911, accessed 11.09.2019.

17. Morris, *Apartheid*, 12.

18. Hachten and Giffard, *Total Onslaught*, 38–39.

19. A. Hadland, "The Political Economy of the South African Press, 1920–50," (M.A. thesis, Oxford University, 1991), 19.

20. Hachten and Giffard, *Total Onslaught*, 40–41.

21. Diederichs and De Beer, "Newspapers," 103.

22. Hachten and Giffard, *Total Onslaught*, 42.

23. W. de Kock, *A Manner of Speaking* (Cape Town: Saayman & Weber, 1982), 11.

24. Ibid., 118–119.

25. J. Mervis, *The Fourth Estate, A Newspaper Story* (Johannesburg: Jonathan Ball, 1989), 122.
26. Ibid., 134–135.
27. Rabe, "Inleiding".
28. Hachten and Giffard, *Total Onslaught*, 41–42.
29. Ibid., 44.
30. Potter, *The Press as Opposition*, 44–45.
31. L. Rabe, Mediahistoriographical Research Project (Unpublished, Stellenbosch, 2014), 56–61.
32. Potter, *The Press as Opposition*, 46–47.
33. W. Wepener, "The Role of the Afrikaans Press," in *Survival of the Press* (Grahamstown: Rhodes University, 1979).
34. Hachten and Giffard, *Total Onslaught*, 179.
35. D. Wigston, "History of the South African Media," in P.J. Fourie, ed., *Media Studies Volume 1: Media History, Media and Society* (Wetton: Juta, 2007), 35–36.
36. Rabe, Mediahistoriographical Research Project, 44.
37. Hachten and Giffard, *Total Onslaught,* 44.
38. Rabe, Mediahistoriographical Research Project, 50.
39. Hachten and Giffard, *Total Onslaught*, 44.
40. Rabe, Mediahistoriographical Research Project, 91.
41. Hachten and Giffard, *Total Onslaught*, 44.
42. Rabe, Mediahistoriographical Research Project, 84–100.
43. Ibid., 60.
44. Ibid., 99.
45. C.F.J. Muller, *Sonop in die Suide (Sunrise in the South)* (Cape Town: Tafelberg, 1990), 296.
46. "Die Afrikaner was Naspers se Eerste in Natal" ("The Afrikaner was Naspers' First in Natal"), *Naspersnuus* (11), 1982, 2.
47. Mervis, *The Fourth Estate*, 149–150.
48. Ibid., 153.
49. Ibid., 184–185.
50. Hachten and Giffard, *Total Onslaught*, 204.
51. Rabe, Mediahistoriographical Research Project, 91–94.
52. Hachten and Giffard, *Total Onslaught*, 204.
53. Rabe, Mediahistoriographical Research Project, 138–140.
54. Mervis, *The Fourth Estate*, 111.
55. Hachten and Giffard, *Total Onslaught*, 146.
56. P. Limb, "Representing the Labouring Classes. African Workers in the African Nationalist Press, 1900–1960," in L. Switzer and M. Adhikari, eds., *South Africa's Resistance Press. Alternative Voices in the Last Generation Under Apartheid* (Ohio: Ohio University Center for International Studies, 2000), 92–94.
57. Limb, "Representing the Labouring Classes," 96–97.
58. Ibid., 100–103.
59. P.E. Louw, "The Growth of Monopoly Control in the South Africa Press," in P.E. Louw, ed., *South African Media Policy: Debates of the 1990s* (Bellville: Anthropos, 1993), 159–162.
60. Ibid., 166–168.
61. Ibid., 169.
62. Rabe, "Inleiding".
63. Louw, "The Growth of Monopoly Control," 170.
64. Potter, *The Press as Opposition*, 66–69.
65. Louw, "The Growth of Monopoly Control," 171–172.
66. Potter, *The Press as Opposition,* 67–69.
67. Louw, "The Growth of Monopoly Control," 173.
68. Potter, *The Press as Opposition*, 72–73.
69. Ibid., 70–71.

70. Ibid., 74.
71. Ibid., 43–44.
72. Ibid., 50–54.
73. Ibid., 55.
74. Ibid., 59–60.
75. Ibid., 61–63.
76. Ibid., 77–78.
77. Diederichs and De Beer, "Newspapers," 91.
78. Hachten and Giffard, *Total Onslaught*, 147.
79. Potter, *The Press as Opposition*, 48.
80. S. Johnson, "An Historical Overview of the Black Press," in K. Tomaselli and P.E. Louw, eds., *The Alternative Press in South Africa* (Johannesburg: Anthropos, 1991), 21.
81. Hachten and Giffard, *Total Onslaught*, 147.
82. L. Switzer and D. Switzer, *The Black Press in South Africa and Lesotho* (Boston: G.K. Hall, 1979), 8.
83. Hachten and Giffard, *Total Onslaught*, 147.
84. Potter, *The Press as Opposition*, 48.
85. Wigston, "History of the South African Media," 38.
86. Limb, "Representing the Labouring Classes," 104.
87. Ibid., 106–109.
88. Ibid., 114.
89. Diederichs and De Beer, "Newspapers," 91.
90. M. Geertsema, "'n Historiese Oorsig oor die Ontstaan en Ontwikkeling van die Swart Pers in Suid-Afrika" ("An historical overview of the founding and development of the black press in South Africa"), (M.A. thesis, NWU, 1993), 15.
91. Sol Plaatje Institute for Media Leadership, https://www.ru.ac.za/spi/about/, accessed 23.03.2018.
92. Limb, "Representing the Labouring Classes," 88.
93. Ibid., 90.
94. Potter, *The Press as Opposition*, 48.
95. Hachten and Giffard, *Total Onslaught*, 146.
96. Diederichs and De Beer, "Newspapers," 91.
97. Hachten and Giffard, *Total Onslaught*, 146; M. Adhikari, *Straatpraatjes (Street Talk)* (Cape Town: Van Schaik, 1996).
98. Mervis, *The Fourth Estate*, 224–226.
99. Hachten and Giffard, *Total Onslaught*, 41.
100. Ibid., 46–48.
101. A.H. Heard, *The Cape of Storms. A Personal History of the Crisis in South Africa* (Fayetteville: University of Arkansas Press, 1990), 160.
102. Hachten and Giffard, *Total Onslaught*, ix.
103. Wigston, "History of the South African Media," 6.
104. Ibid., 9–10.
105. R. Teer-Tomaselli and C. de Villiers, "Radio. Theatre of the Mind," in A.S. de Beer, ed., *Mass Media Towards the Millennium* (Pretoria: Van Schaik, 1998), 153.
106. Hachten and Giffard, *Total Onslaught*, 202.
107. Teer-Tomaselli and De Villiers, "Radio," 153–154.
108. Hachten and Giffard, *Total Onslaught*, 202.
109. Wigston, "History of the South African Media," 11–12.
110. Hachten and Giffard, *Total Onslaught*, 200.

Chapter 7

1. "F.W. de Klerk's speech to Parliament, 2 February 1990," SA History Online, http://www.sahistory.org.za/archive/fw-de-klerk%E2%80%99s-speech-parliament-2-february-1990, accessed 8.01.2018.
2. P.E Louw, "Preface," *South African Media Policy: Debates of the 1990s* (Bellville: Anthropos, 1993), 4.
3. W.A. Hachten and C.A. Giffard, *Total Onslaught. The South African Press under Attack* (Johannesburg: McMillan, 1984), vii.
4. L. Rabe, Mediahistoriographical Research Project (Unpublished, Stellenbosch, 2014), 210–211.
5. J. McClurg, "The Afrikaans Press: From Lapdog to Watchdog," *Ecquid Novi*, 8,1 (1987): 53–61.
6. Hachten and Giffard, *Total Onslaught*, vii–viii.
7. Ibid., xiii.
8. Ibid., 51.
9. Immorality Act, http://www.sahistory.org.za/dated-event/commencement-immorality-act, accessed 12.02.2018.
10. M.M. Breytenbach, "The Manipulation of Public Opinion by State Censorship of the Media in South Africa (1974–1994)," (D.Phil. diss., Stellenbosch University, 1997), 42.
11. K. Roelofse, "The History of the South African Press," in L.M. Oosthuizen, ed., *Introduction to Communication – Course Book 5: Journalism, Press and Radio Studies* (Kenwyn: Juta, 1996), 85.
12. D. Wigston, "History of the South African Media," in P.J. Fourie, ed., *Media Studies Volume 1: Media History, Media and Society* (Wetton: Juta, 2007), 44–45.
13. Roelofse, "The History of the South African Press," 87.
14. C. Merrett, *A Culture of Censorship. Secrecy and Intellectual Repression in South Africa* (Cape Town: David Phillip, 1994), 21.
15. Hepple, as quoted in P. Nänny, "History of Censorship in South Africa" (M.Phil. assignment, Stellenbosch University, 2004), 2.
16. D. Yutar, *Freedom of the Press in a Post-Apartheid South Africa* (Green College, Oxford, Reuter Foundation, 1995), 4.
17. Hachten and Giffard, *Total Onslaught*, 67.
18. L. Rabe, *Quote Unquote* (Stellenbosch: SunMedia, 2015), 25.
19. Ibid., 28.
20. E. Potter, *The Press as Opposition. The Political Role of South African Newspapers* (Totowa, NJ: Rowman and Littlefield, 1975), 7–8.
21. Ibid., 9, 11.
22. Ibid., 15.
23. Ibid., 21.
24. Ibid., 23–24.
25. Ibid., 27.
26. J. Mervis, *The Fourth Estate, A Newspaper Story* (Johannesburg: Jonathan Ball, 1989), 269–270.
27. Ibid., 296.
28. Breytenbach, "The Manipulation of Public Opinion," v–vi.
29. Mervis, *The Fourth Estate*, 279.
30. P. Diederichs and A.S. de Beer, "Newspapers. The Fourth Estate: A Cornerstone of Democracy," in A.S. de Beer, ed., *Mass Media Towards the Millennium* (Pretoria: Van Schaik, 1998), 106.
31. V. Aldaheff, *A Newspaper History of South Africa* (Cape Town: Don Nelson, 1990), 131.
32. J.C. Steyn, *Penvegter* (Cape Town: Tafelberg, 2002), 50–51.
33. Hachten and Giffard, *Total Onslaught*, 52–54.
34. Potter, *The Press as Opposition*, 102–107.
35. Ibid., 109.
36. Hachten and Giffard, *Total Onslaught*, 54–55.
37. Potter, *The Press as Opposition*, 108.
38. Hachten and Giffard, *Total Onslaught*, 63–65.

39. J. Zug, *The Guardian: The History of South Africa's Extraordinary Anti-Apartheid Newspaper* (Pretoria: UNISA Press, 2007), 101.
40. Ibid., 113.
41. G.S. Jackson, *Breaking Story: The South African Press* (Colorado: Westview Press, 1993), 109.
42. Ibid., 107.
43. Zug, *The Guardian*, 113–115.
44. Ibid., 117–118.
45. Ibid., 137–138.
46. M. Morris, *Apartheid: An Illustrated History* (Jeppestown: Jonathan Ball, 2012), 46–51.
47. Hachten and Giffard, *Total Onslaught*, 55.
48. Extension of University Education Act, http://www.sahistory.org.za/dated-event/extension-university-education-act-no-45-commences, accessed 12.02.2018.
49. Hachten and Giffard, *Total Onslaught*, 55–56.
50. Mervis, *The Fourth Estate*, 327–330.
51. Ibid., 332.
52. Ibid., 336.
53. Hachten and Giffard, *Total Onslaught*, 93–94.
54. F. Siebert, T. Peterson & W. Schramm, *Four Theories of the Press* (Illinois: University of Illinois Press, 1956).
55. Hachten and Giffard, *Total Onslaught*, 95.
56. Ibid., 98–99.
57. Ibid., ix.
58. Potter, *The Press as Opposition*, 113–114.
59. R. Tomaselli and K. Tomaselli, "The Political Economy of the South African Pres Press," in K. Tomaselli, R. Tomaselli and J Muller, eds., *Narrating the Crisis: Hegemony and the South African Press* (Johannesburg: Richard Lyon & Co, 1987), 99–100.
60. Potter, *The Press as Opposition*, 114–117.
61. Ibid., 120.
62. Ibid., 122, 123, 126.
63. Tomaselli and Tomaselli, "The Political Economy," 99–100.
64. Potter, *The Press as Opposition*, 127–129.
65. Tomaselli and Tomaselli, "The Political Economy," 99–100.
66. Hachten and Giffard, *Total Onslaught*, 56–57.
67. L. Switzer, "South Africa's Resistance Press in Perspective," in L. Switzer and M. Adhikari, eds., *South Africa's Resistance Press. Alternative Voices in the Last Generation Under Apartheid* (Ohio: Ohio University Center for International Studies, 2000), 1–4.
68. Zug, *The Guardian*, 187.
69. Ibid., 189–190.
70. Ibid., 192.
71. Ibid., 211–213.
72. Ibid., 215–216.
73. Ibid., 219–221.
74. J. Zug, "'Far from Dead.' The Final Years of the *Guardian*, 1960–1963," in L. Switzer and M. Adhikari, eds., *South Africa's Resistance Press. Alternative Voices in the Last Generation Under Apartheid* (Ohio: Ohio University Center for International Studies, 2000), 132–135.
75. Zug, "Far from Dead," 137–138.
76. Zug, "Far from Dead," 141–145.
77. Zug, "Far from Dead", 152–156.
78. Zug, "Far from Dead", 160–163.
79. Hachten and Giffard, *Total Onslaught*, 58–60.

80. L. Switzer and M. Adhikari, "Preface," in L. Switzer and M. Adhikari, eds., *South Africa's Resistance Press. Alternative Voices in the Last Generation Under Apartheid* (Ohio: Ohio University Center for International Studies, 2000), xvi.
81. Hachten and Giffard, *Total Onslaught*, 148.
82. G.N. Claassen, "Magazines. Life's Own Story," in A.S. de Beer, ed., *Mass Media Towards the Millennium* (Pretoria: Van Schaik, 1998), 127.
83. G. Addison, *Review of "Mass Media for the 1990s," Communicare* 12,1: 70.
84. M. Coburn and T. Tserema, "Media Monopolies and the Black Press," *Stellenbosch Journalism Insight,* 1,1: 28–29.
85. Claassen, "Magazines," 127.
86. Hachten and Giffard, *Total Onslaught*, 148–149.
87. Rabe, *Quote Unquote,* 29.
88. Ibid., 159.
89. Hachten and Giffard, *Total Onslaught*, 149.
90. Rabe, *Quote Unquote,* 29.
91. Hachten and Giffard, *Total Onslaught*, 149.
92. L. Rabe, "Twintig Dae in Desember – Naspers, *Die Burger,* Cillié en Verwoerd" (Twenty Days in December – Naspers, *Die Burger*, Cillié and Verwoerd"), in L. Rabe, ed., *'n Konstante Revolusie. Naspers, Media24 en Oorgange (A Constant Revolution. Naspers, Media24 and Transitions)* (Cape Town: Tafelberg, 2015), 11–13.
93. Diederichs and De Beer, "Newspapers," 91.
94. Hachten and Giffard, *Total Onslaught*, 149.
95. Rabe, *Quote Unquote*, 41.
96. Hachten and Giffard, *Total Onslaught*, 149–150.
97. Rabe, Mediahistoriographical Research Project, 281–284.
98. T du Plessis, "Theunissen Super Vee," in L. Rabe, ed., *'n Ton van 'n Man (A Tonne of a Man),* (Cape Town: Tafelberg, 2007), 66.
99. Hachten and Giffard, *Total Onslaught*, 202.
100. Ibid., 200.
101. Ibid., 201–203.
102. R. Teer-Tomaselli and C. de Villiers, "Radio. Theatre of the Mind", in A.S. de Beer, ed., *Mass Media Towards the Millennium* (Pretoria: Van Schaik, 1998), 155–157.
103. Hachten and Giffard, *Total Onslaught*, 203.
104. I. Wilkins and H. Strydom, *The Super Afrikaners* (2nd Ed.) (Johannesburg: Jonathan Ball, 1980), 1.
105. Breytenbach, "The Manipulation of Public Opinion," 38.
106. Hachten and Giffard, *Total Onslaught*, 204.
107. Wilkins and Strydom, *Super Afrikaners*, 11–12.
108. Hachten and Giffard, *Total Onslaught*, xiv.
109. Ibid., 61–62.
110. Ibid., xiv.
111. Ibid., 50–51.
112. Ibid, xiv.
113. N. Gordimer, "New Forms of Strategy – No Change of Heart," *Critical Arts,* 1 (1980): 27.
114. D. Driver, "Control of the Black Mind is the Main Aim of Censorship," *South African Outlook* (June 1980): 10.
115. Hachten and Giffard, *Total Onslaught*, 155.
116. A.H. Heard, *The Cape of Storms. A Personal History of the Crisis in South Africa* (Fayetteville: University of Arkansas Press, 1990), 160–161.
117. Potter, *The Press as Opposition*, 101.
118. Hachten and Giffard, *Total Onslaught*, 65–66.
119. Potter, *The Press as Opposition*, 109–112.
120. Mervis, *The Fourth Estate,* 489.

121. Hachten and Giffard, *Total Onslaught*, 16.
122. L. Rabe, "Die Belang van Mediavryheid in Suid-Afrika: Tweehonderd Jaar, Twee Gevallestudies, van die Magna Carta tot die Muilbandwet" ("The Importance of Media Freedom in South Africa: Two Centuries, two Case Studies, from the Magna Carta to the Secrecy Bill"), *Tydskrif vir Geesteswetenskappe* 56,3 (2016): 869.
123. Hachten and Giffard, *Total Onslaught*, 159–160.
124. Rabe, *Quote Unquote*, 38.
125. Hachten and Giffard, *Total Onslaught*, 159.
126. Ibid., 16–17.
127. Mervis, *The Fourth Estate*, 391–394.
128. Hachten and Giffard, *Total Onslaught*, 67–72.
129. Heard, *The Cape of Storms*, 134, 136–137.
130. Diederichs and De Beer, "Newspapers," 108–109.
131. Hachten and Giffard, *Total Onslaught*, xv.
132. A. Hadland, "The South African Print Media, 1994–2004: An Application and Critique of Comparative Media Systems Theory" (D.Phil. diss., University of Cape Town, 2007), 96.
133. R.E. Teer Tomaselli, "The Politics of Discourse and the Discourse of Politics: Images of Violence and Reform on the South African Broadcasting Corporation's Television News Bulletins – June 1985 – November 1986" (D.Phil. diss., University of Natal, 1992).
134. J. Muller, "Press Houses at War: A Brief History of Nasionale Pers and Perskor," in K. Tomaselli, R. Tomaselli and J. Muller, eds., *Narrating the Crisis: Hegemony and the South African Press* (Johannesburg: Richard Lyon & Co, 1987), 130–138.
135. Hachten and Giffard, *Total Onslaught*, 263–264.
136. Ibid., 267.
137. Ibid., 269.
138. Ibid., 273–274.
139. Ibid., 281–283.
140. P.E. Louw, "The Growth of Monopoly Control in the South Africa Press," in P.E. Louw, ed., *South African Media Policy: Debates of the 1990s* (Bellville: Anthropos, 1993), 172.
141. L. Switzer, "South Africa's Resistance Press," 6, 8–9.
142. Ibid., 11–12.
143. Hachten and Giffard, *Total Onslaught*, 283–284.
144. Ibid., 286–287.
145. Ibid., 156–157.
146. J. Dugard, "Human Rights and the South African Legal Order," (Princeton NJ: Princeton University Press, 1978), 181–192.
147. Rabe, *Quote Unquote*, 29.
148. Hachten and Giffard, *Total Onslaught*, 158.
149. Steyn, J.C., "Die Sensuurstryd" ("The Struggle Against Censorship"), in W.D. Beukes, ed., *Boekewêreld (Book World)* (Cape Town: Tafelberg, 1992), 357–376.
150. Rabe, *Quote Unquote*, 28.
151. Hachten and Giffard, *Total Onslaught*, 161–162.
152. Rabe, Mediahistoriographical Research Project, 250.
153. Hachten and Giffard, *Total Onslaught*, 164–167.
154. Ibid., 171.
155. Ibid., 175.
156. Potter, *The Press as Opposition*, 130–136.
157. Ibid., 146–147.
158. Rabe, "Twintig Dae in Desember," 53–64.
159. Potter, *The Press as Opposition*, 146–147.
160. Ibid., 189.
161. Ibid., 147.

162. Ibid., 149.
163. Ibid., 151.
164. Ibid., 155.
165. Ibid., 162.
166. Ibid., 189–190.
167. Ibid., 194.
168. Ibid., 205.
169. Ibid., 210.
170. T. Vosloo, "*Beeld* – 21 Jaar" ("*Beeld* – 21 Years"), *Ecquid Novi*, 17,1 (1996): 112–116.
171. Order of Ikhamanga Silver, http://www.thepresidency.gov.za/national-orders/recipient/schalk-pienaar-1916-1978, accessed 12.02.2018.
172. S. Pienaar, *Getuie van Groot Tye* (*Witness to Great Times*) (Cape Town: Tafelberg, 1979), 129.
173. Hachten and Giffard, *Total Onslaught*, 182.
174. Breytenbach, "The Manipulation of Public Opinion," 105.
175. Hachten and Giffard, *Total Onslaught*, 184–185.
176. S. Pienaar, "Afrikaners en Hul Koerante: Vriendskap in Spanning" ("Afrikaners and Their Newspapers – Friendship Under Stress"), *Die Burger,* September 15, 1973.
177. Hachten and Giffard, *Total Onslaught,* 182.
178. Ibid., 186.
179. Rabe, *Quote Unquote,* 85.
180. Hachten and Giffard, *Total Onslaught*, 186.
181. Ibid., 182.
182. Rabe, "Twintig Dae in Desember," 53–64.
183. Hachten and Giffard, *Total Onslaught*, 83.
184. P.J. Cillié, "Kruisvaarders vir 'n Idee" ("Crusaders for an Idea"), *Jaar van die Koerant 1988,* supplement to Naspers dailies, August 31, 1988, p. 2.
185. Muller, "Press Houses at War," 118–120.
186. Wigston, "History of the South African Media," 44–45.
187. Roelofse, "The History of the South African Press," 87–88.
188. Wigston, "History of the South African Media," 46.
189. Potter, *The Press as Opposition*, 48–49.
190. G. Mersham, "Television, a Fascinating Window on an Unfolding World," in A.S. de Beer, ed., *Mass Media Towards the Millennium* (Pretoria: Van Schaik, 1998), 211–212.
191. Hachten and Giffard, *Total Onslaught*, 206.
192. P. Orlik, "South Africa: How Long Without TV?" *Journal of Broadcasting* (Spring, 1970): 246.
193. Hachten and Giffard, *Total Onslaught*, 207–209.
194. P.J. Meyer, "Report of the Commission of Enquiry into Matters Relating to Television", RP37/1971 (Pretoria, Government Printer, 1971), 17.
195. Mersham, "Television," 212.
196. Teer-Tomaselli and Tomaselli, "Transformation, Nation-building and the South African Media 1993–1999," in K. Tomaselli and H. Dunn, eds., *Media, Democracy and Renewal in Southern Africa* (Colorado Springs: International Academic Publishers, 2001), 129.
197. Wigston, "History of the South African Media," 15.
198. Hachten and Giffard, *Total Onslaught*, 210–214.
199. Ibid., 217
200. L. Switzer, "South Africa's Resistance Press," 18.
201. Hachten and Giffard, *Total Onslaught*, 4; L. Kalane, *The Chapter We Wrote* (Jonathan Ball, Cape Town, 2018).
202. Rabe, Mediahistoriographical Research Project, 242.
203. Morris, *Apartheid*, 107.
204. J.J.J. Scholtz and J.C. Steyn, "Stryders vir Afrikaans" ("Fighters for Afrikaans"), in W.D. Beukes, ed., *Oor Grense Heen (Across Boundaries)* (Cape Town: Nasionale Boekhandel, 1992), 451–452.

205. W. Wepener, "Rapport is Twee Maande ná sy Geboorte Gemáák" ("Rapport is Made Two Months After its Birth"), *Rapport 25 Jaar Gedenkuitgawe (Rapport 25 Year Commemorative Publication)*, November 6, 1995, p. 5.
206. Scholtz and Steyn, "Stryders vir Afrikaans," 451–452.
207. Hachten and Giffard, *Total Onslaught*, 4.
208. Hachten and Giffard, *Total Onslaught*, 4–5.
209. Hector Pieterson Museum and Memorial, http://www.sahistory.org.za/places/hector-pieterson-museum-heritage-site, accessed 20.02.2018.
210. K. Sibiya, "He Makes Everything Look Simple", in L. Rabe, ed., *Ton van 'n Man (Tonne of a Man)* (Cape Town: Tafelberg, 2007), 63.
211. Breytenbach, "The Manipulation of Public Opinion," 46.
212. Ibid., 51–52.
213. Hachten and Giffard, *Total Onslaught*, 143.
214. C. Merrett, "A Tale of Two Paradoxes: Media Censorship in South Africa, Pre-Liberation and Post-Apartheid," *Critical Arts,* 15,1&2: 51.
215. Switzer, "South Africa's Resistance Press in Perspective," 14–16.
216. Hachten and Giffard, *Total Onslaught*, 135.
217. B. Naudé, *My Land van Hoop (My Land of Hope)* (Cape Town: Human & Rousseau, 1995), 113-114.
218. Ibid., 107–108.
219. Hachten and Giffard, *Total Onslaught*, 6.
220. Ibid., 137.
221. Hadland, "The South African Print Media," 88.
222. Hachten and Giffard, *Total Onslaught*, 136.
223. Ibid., 138–139.
224. Ibid., 142–143.
225. Ibid., 195–196.
226. *Beeld,* March 5, 1980.
227. Hachten and Giffard, *Total Onslaught*, 196.
228. Tomaselli and Tomaselli, "The Political Economy," 73.
229. K. du Pisani, "BJ Vorster en Afsonderlike Ontwikkeling" ("BJ Vorster and Separate Development"), in F. Pretorius, ed., *Geskiedenis van Suid-Afrika (History of South Africa)* (Cape Town: Tafelberg, 2012), 355.
230. Steyn, *Penvegter*, 285.
231. Morris, *Apartheid*, 108.
232. Hachten and Giffard, *Total Onslaught*, 150.
233. M. Shaikh, "On Civic Journalism, Journalistic Inflation and Credential Creep," in L. Rabe, ed., *#Journalism4.0 @ Stellenbosch* (Stellenbosch: AfricanSunMedia, 2018), 163–166.
234. Hachten and Giffard, *Total Onslaught*, 150–152.
235. School for Journalism and Media Studies, https://www.ru.ac.za/jms/about/, accessed 22.01.2018.
236. L. Rabe, ed., *#Journalism4.0 @ Stellenbosch* (Stellenbosch: AfricanSunMedia, 2018).
237. Hachten and Giffard, *Total Onslaught*, 214–215.
238. http://nuwegeskiedenis.co.za/deel-4-hoofstuk-14-die-totale-aanslag/, accessed 27.03.2012.
239. L. Scholtz, email, 24.02.2013.
240. Muller, "Press houses at war," 132–133.
241. Hachten and Giffard, *Total Onslaught*, 72–73.
242. Steyn, *Penvegter*, 291.
243. Rabe, Mediahistoriographical Research Project, 244–245.
244. Steyn, *Penvegter*, 293.
245. Hachten and Giffard, *Total Onslaught*, 191–193.
246. Ibid., 74.

247. M. Oosthuizen, "Persverantwoordelikheid en Rekenskap" (Press Responsibility and Accountability"), *Ecquid Novi* 3,2 (1982): 40–48.
248. Steyn, *Penvegter*, 294.
249. M. Viljoen, "Die Suid-Afrikaanse Pers: 'n Magtige Instelling" ("The South African Press: A Powerful Institution"), *Ecquid Novi* 3,2 (1982): 4–8.
250. Steyn, *Penvegter*, 295.
251. Hachten and Giffard, *Total Onslaught*, 74–75.
252. Wigston, History of the South African Media, 46.
253. Hachten and Giffard, *Total Onslaught*, 230.
254. Wigston, History of the South African Media, 47.
255. K. Roelofse, "The History of the South African Press," 60.
256. Hachten and Giffard, *Total Onslaught*, 229–237.
257. Ibid., 239–242.
258. Ibid., 259–260.
259. Aldaheff, *A Newspaper History of South Africa*, 131.
260. P. Diederichs and A.S. de Beer, "Newspapers," 106.
261. L. Rabe, *Rykie. 'n Lewe met Woorde* (*Rykie. A Life with Words*), (Cape Town: Tafelberg, 2011), 112.
262. Hachten and Giffard, *Total Onslaught*, 6–7.
263. Ibid., 9–10.
264. Heard, *The Cape of Storms*, 134, 139, 143.
265. Hachten and Giffard, *Total Onslaught*, 188.
266. Mervis, *The Fourth Estate*, 434.
267. Ibid., 437.
268. Ibid., 439.
269. Ibid., 443.
270. Hachten and Giffard, *Total Onslaught*, 245–249.
271. Mervis, *The Fourth Estate*, 446.
272. Hachten and Giffard, *Total Onslaught*, 257.
273. Ibid., 243–244.
274. Ibid., 215–216.
275. Ibid., 218.
276. Heard, *The Cape of Storms*, 145–151.
277. Ibid., 154–155.
278. H. Tyson, *Editors Under Fire* (Sandton: Random House, 1987), 175–177.
279. S. du Preez, *Avonture in Angola. Die Verhaal van Suid-Afrika se Soldate in Angola 1975–1976* (*Adventures in Angola. The Story of South Africa's Soldiers in Angola 1976–1976*) (Pretoria: Van Schaik, 1989), 16.
280. Wigston, "History of the South African Media," 47–48.
281. G.S. Jackson, *Breaking Story: The South African Press* (Boulder, Colorado: Westview, 1993), 23.
282. Hachten and Giffard, *Total Onslaught*, 83–84.
283. Wigston, "History of the South African Media," 48–49.
284. Hachten and Giffard, *Total Onslaught*, 85.
285. Wigston, "History of the South African Media," 49.
286. W. de Kock, *A Manner of Speaking* (Cape Town, Saayman & Weber, 1982), 11.
287. Tomaselli and Tomaselli, "The Political Economy," 100–102.
288. Hachten and Giffard, *Total Onslaught*, 76.
289. N. Temko, "Patrick Laurence Obituary," https://www.theguardian.com/media/2011/jul/14/patrick-laurence-obituary, accessed 22.02.2018.
290. Rabe, *Quote Unquote*, 31.
291. Hachten and Giffard, *Total Onslaught*, 76.
292. Ibid., 18–19.
293. Ibid., 77.

294. Wigston, "History of the South African Media," 17; Diederichs and De Beer, "Newspapers," 106.
295. Hachten and Giffard, *Total Onslaught*, 80–83.
296. Diederichs and De Beer, "Newspapers," 106.
297. Hachten and Giffard, *Total Onslaught*, 89.
298. Ibid., 83–84.
299. Ibid., 18–20.
300. P.J. Fourie, "'n Terugkeer na die Onderdrukking van Vryheid van Spraak? Ooreenkomste Tussen die Apartheidsregering(s) en die ANC se Optrede teen die Media" ("A Return to the Repression of Freedom of Speech? Similarities Between the Apartheid Government(s) and the ANC's Actions Against the Media"), *Suid-Afrikaanse Tydskrif vir Geesteswetenskappe (South African Journal of Humanities)* 49,1 (2009): 80.
301. Diederichs and De Beer, "Newspapers," 106.
302. Hachten and Giffard, *Total Onslaught*, 83–85.
303. Ibid., 196–197.
304. E. Barratt, "Choosing to be Part of the Story: The Participation of the South African National Editors' Forum in the Democratisation Process" (M.Phil. thesis, Stellenbosch University, 2006).
305. Hachten and Giffard, *Total Onslaught*, 84–86.
306. Ibid., 99–101.
307. Heard, *The Cape of Storms*, 162–163.
308. Ibid., 191–194.
309. H. Adam, "The Political Sociology of South Africa: A Pragmatic Race Oligarchy," in I. Robertson and P. Whitten, eds., *Race and Politics in South Africa* (New Brunswick: Transaction Books, 1978), 47.
310. Hachten and Giffard, *Total Onslaught*, 220–223.
311. Ibid., 225–228.
312. Ibid., 187.
313. Ibid., 189.
314. Ibid., 188.
315. J.J.J. Scholtz, "Sirkulasiestryd" ("Circulation Struggle"), in W.D. Beukes, ed., *Oor Grense Heen (Across Boundaries)* (Cape Town: Tafelberg, 1992), 290.
316. G. Keyser, "En die Jare Daarna," ("The Years Therafter"), Supplement, *Jaar van die Koerant*, August 31, 1988, p. 13.
317. Muller, "Press Houses at War," 135.
318. Scholtz, "Sirkulasiestryd," 291–292.
319. Muller, "Press Houses at War," 135–137.
320. J. Froneman, "Sluiting van Koerante geen Doodsklok vir Afrikaanse Joernalistiek" ("Closure of Newspapers no Death-knell for Afrikaans Journalism"), *Ecquid Novi* 14,1 (1993): 84–93.
321. Hachten and Giffard, *Total Onslaught*, 178.
322. L. Rabe, "Kroniek van 'n Mondigwording? 'n Mediageskiedkundige Herevaluering van die WVK, Naspers en Afrikaanse Joernalistiek" ("Chronicle of a Coming of Age? A Media-historiographical Re-evaluation of the TRC, Naspers and Afrikaans Journalism"), *Litnet Akademies* 14,3 (2018).
323. Hachten and Giffard, *Total Onslaught*, 178–179.
324. Ibid., 189–191.
325. Ibid., 198–199.
326. Diederichs and De Beer, "Newspapers," 105–106.
327. Tomaselli and Tomaselli, "The Political Economy," 87.
328. Ibid., 87, 90.
329. Ibid., 92–95.

330. J. Grobler, "Swart Verset teen Apartheid, 1950's–1980's" ("Black Opposition Against Apartheid, 1950s–1980s"), in F. Pretorius, ed., *Geskiedenis van Suid-Afrika* (*History of South* Africa) (Cape Town: Tafelberg, 2012), 379–380.
331. W. Esterhuyse, *Eindstryd* (*Endgame*) (Cape Town: Tafelberg, 2012), 59.
332. J.C. Steyn, "Die Sensuurstryd" (Struggle Against Sensorship"), in W.D. Beukes, ed., *Boekewêreld* (Cape Town: Tafelberg, 1992), 376.
333. Steyn, "Die Sensuurstryd," 354.
334. Hachten and Giffard, *Total Onslaught*, 230.
335. Ibid., 276–277.
336. Ibid., 279–280.
337. H.G. Rudolph, "Freedom of the Press or the Right to Know," *The South African Law Journal,* 81 (1981): 81–88.
338. R. Pollak, *Up Against Apartheid: The Role and Plight of the Press in South Africa* (Carbondale: Southern Illinois Press, 1981), 2.
339. Hadland, "The South African Print Media," 140.
340. C.C. Chimutengwende, *South Africa: The Press and Politics of Liberation* (London: Barbican Books, 1978), 48.
341. Hachten and Giffard, *Total Onslaught*, 97.
342. Tomaselli and Teer-Tomaselli, "The Political Economy," 33.
343. S. Jacobs, "Public Sphere, Power and Democratic Politics: Media and Policy Debates in Post-apartheid South Africa (Ph.D. diss., Birkbeck College, University of London, 2004), 4.
344. Tomaselli and Tomaselli, "The Political Economy," 60–61.
345. Ibid., 66.
346. Ibid., 71.
347. Ibid., 74.
348. M. Gevisser, "Ken Owen: SA's Last Great White Editor," M&G, June 28, 1996, https://mg.co.za/article/1996-06-28-ken-owen-outgoing-editor-of-the-sunday-times-in, accessed 20.02.2018.
349. Rabe, *Quote Unquote,* 29.
350. Merrett, "A Tale of Two Paradoxes," 52–53.
351. Rabe, *Quote Unquote,* 31–31.
352. Ibid., 31.
353. Heard, *The Cape of Storms*.
354. Ibid., 218.
355. Ibid., 223–224.
356. Hachten and Giffard, *Total Onslaught*, x.
357. Tomaselli and Tomaselli, "The Political Economy," 75.
358. Hachten and Giffard, *Total Onslaught*, x.
359. L. Rabe, "Inleiding" ("Introduction"), in L. Rabe, ed., *'n Konstante Revolusie. Naspers, Media24 en Oorgange* (*A Constant Revolution. Naspers, Media24 and Transitions*) (Cape Town: Tafelberg, 2015), 11–13.
360. M. Gvaza, "Naspers to List Unit Prosus in Amsterdam on Wednesday", https://www.businesslive.co.za/bd/companies/telecoms-and-technology/2019-09-10-naspers-to-list-unit-prosus-in-amsterdam-on-wednesday/, accessed 24.10.2019.
361. Rabe, "Inleiding", *Konstante Revolusie,* 10.
362. Louw, "The Growth of Monopoly Control," 171.
363. Ibid., 175.
364. Hachten and Giffard, *Total Onslaught*, xi.
365. Ibid., ix.
366. Ibid., ix–x.
367. Mersham, "Television," 221.
368. Ibid., 219.
369. Tomaselli and Tomaselli, "The Political Economy," 78–79.

370. Mersham, "Television," 219–220.
371. Teer-Tomaselli and Tomaselli, "Transformation, Nation-building and the South African Media," 129–130.
372. Wigston, "History of the South African Media," 17–18.
373. Hachten and Giffard, *Total Onslaught*, 102
374. Ibid., xiii.
375. Ibid., 11–13.
376. Ibid., 261.
377. Ibid., 14–16.
378. http://www.rtsa.ro/en/274,the-functioning-of-ombudsman-(public-protector)-in-south-africa-redress-and-checks-and-balances-.html, accessed 20.02.2018.
379. Mervis, *The Fourth Estate*, 473.
380. Ibid., 522.
381. Diederichs and De Beer, "Newspapers," 104–105.
382. D.M. Tutu, "Foreword," in A.H. Heard, *The Cape of Storms. A Personal History of the Crisis in South Africa* (Fayetteville: University of Arkansas Press, 1990), xv–xvii.
383. Heard, *The Cape of Storms*, 113.
384. Ibid., 111.
385. Hachten and Giffard, *Total Onslaught*, 103.
386. M. du Preez, email 22 February 2018.
387. Hachten and Giffard, *Total Onslaught*, 103–105.
388. Ibid., 111–112.
389. Ibid., 113–124.
390. A.S. Mathews, *Freedom, State Security and the Rule of Law. Dilemmas of the Apartheid Society* (Cape Town: Juta, 1986), 117–122.
391. Ibid., 124.
392. Ibid., 148–150.
393. Ibid., 172.
394. Ibid., 194–195.
395. Ibid., 269–270.
396. Hachten and Giffard, *Total Onslaught*, 106–110.
397. Mathews, *Freedom, State Security and the Rule of Law*, 276–277.
398. Ibid., 286.
399. Breytenbach, "The Manipulation of Public Opinion," 337–342.
400. Ibid., 344.
401. Tomaselli and Tomaselli, "The Political Economy," 43; also see Kalane, *The Chapter We Wrote*.
402. A. Hadland, "The South African Print Media," 178.
403. S. Johnson, "An Historical Overview of the Black Press," in K. Tomaselli and P.E. Louw, eds., *The Alternative Press in South Africa* (Johannesburg: Anthropos, 1991), 21.
404. Ibid., 20.
405. Hadland, "The South African Print Media", 179.
406. Tomaselli and Tomaselli, "The Political Economy," 46–57.
407. Hachten and Giffard, *Total Onslaught*, 130.
408. Ibid., 133.
409. Ibid., 130–131.
410. C.A. Giffard, "Media Trends in South Africa", paper presented at the "Road Ahead Conference" (Grahamstown: Rhodes University, 1978), 14.
411. Hachten and Giffard, *Total Onslaught*, 131.
412. Rabe, Mediahistoriographical Research Project, 227.
413. Hachten and Giffard, *Total Onslaught*, 132–135.
414. Rabe, *Quote Unquote*, 32.
415. Hachten and Giffard, *Total Onslaught*, 135.

416. "Peter Magubane," http://www.sahistory.org.za/people/peter-sexford-magubane, accessed 22.02.2018.
417. Hachten and Giffard, *Total Onslaught*, 135.
418. Mervis, *The Fourth Estate,* 455–456.
419. Rabe, Mediahistoriographical Research Project, 133.
420. Ibid., 105.
421. Ibid., 210–211. check
422. L.F. Oosthuysen, "City Press," in W.D. Beukes, (ed.). *Oor Grense Heen (Across Boundaries)* (Cape Town: Tafelberg, 1992), 342; J.J.J. Spies, "Oor die kleurgrens" ("Across the Colour Bar") in W.D. Beukes, ed., *Oor Grense Heen* (Cape Town: Tafelberg, 1992), 430, 434.
423. "Pers Koop Eerste Swart Publikasies" ("Press Buys First Black Publications"), in *Feesbylae. Nasionale Pers 1915–1990*, 1990, p. 16.
424. Oosthuysen, "City Press," 342.
425. Mervis, *The Fourth Estate,* 244.
426. "Uitwaarts na Swart Pers" ("Outward to Black Press"), *Feesbylae. Nasionale Pers 1915–1990*, 1990, p. 52.
427. Spies, "Oor die Kleurgrens," 427.
428. J. van Wyk, J.D. Prins and J.J.J. Spies, "Die Burger-Ekstra en Metro-Burger" ("Die Burger Extra and Metro-Burger") in W.D. Beukes, ed., *Oor grense heen (Across Boundaries)* (Cape Town: Tafelberg, 1992), 340.
429. "Pers Koop Eerste Swart Publikasies," 16.
430. Sibiya, "He Makes Everything Look Simple," 63.
431. J. Mervis, *The Fourth Estate*, 153.
432. Wigston, "History of the South African Media," 40.
433. Ibid., 49–51.
434. P.E. Louw, "The Emergence of a Progressive-alternative Press in South Africa with Specific Reference to *Grassroots*," in *Communicatio* 15,2: 26–27.
435. Johnson, "An Historical Overview of the Black Press," 124.
436. Wigston, "History of the South African Media," 41.
437. Johnson, "An Historical Overview of the Black Press," 27.
438. Wigston, "History of the South African Media," 41–42.
439. Hachten and Giffard, *Total Onslaught*, 3.
440. P.E. Louw and K.G. Tomaselli, "Developments in the Conventional and Alternate Presses, 1980–1989," in K.G. Tomaselli and P.E. Louw, eds., *The Alternative Press in South Africa* (Bellville: Anthropos, 1991), 7–13.
441. C. Faure, "Ondersoekende Joernalistiek en Sosiale Verandering: 'n Ontleding en Evaluering van die Agendastellingsrol van *Vrye Weekblad*" (D.Litt. et Phil. Diss., UNISA, Pretoria), 127.
442. Hachten and Giffard, *Total Onslaught*, 152–154.
443. Heard, *The Cape of Storms*, 54.
444. G. Berger, "Foreword," in L. Switzer and M. Adhikari, eds., *South Africa's Resistance Press. Alternative Voices in the Last Generation Under Apartheid* (Ohio: Ohio University Center for International Studies, 2000), xii–xiii.
445. Switzer, "South Africa's Resistance Press," 38–44.
446. Ibid., 49.
447. F. Krüger, "East Cape News Agencies Reporting on a Black Hole," in L. Switzer and M. Adhikari, eds., *South Africa's Resistance Press. Alternative Voices in the Last Generation Under Apartheid* (Ohio: Ohio University Center for International Studies, 2000), 260–261.
448. J. Seekings, "The Media of the United Democratic Front, 1983–1991," in L. Switzer and M. Adhikari, eds., *South Africa's Resistance Press. Alternative Voices in the Last Generation Under Apartheid* (Ohio: Ohio University Center for International Studies, 2000), 240–251.
449. Switzer, "South Africa's Resistance Press," 50–51.
450. Ibid., 42–53.

451. M. Adhikari, "You Have the Right to Know. *South* 1987–1994," in L. Switzer and M. Adhikari, eds., *South Africa's Resistance Press. Alternative Voices in the Last Generation Under Apartheid* (Ohio: Ohio University Center for International Studies, 2000), 327–329.
452. Ibid., 333, 335.
453. Ibid., 343–348.
454. Ibid., 355–356.
455. Ibid., 359.
456. Ibid., 361–365.
457. I. van Kessel, "Grassroots From Washing Lines to Utopia," in L. Switzer and M. Adhikari, eds., *South Africa's Resistance Press. Alternative Voices in the Last Generation Under Apartheid* (Ohio: Ohio University Center for International Studies, 2000), 283–284.
458. Ibid., 311–312.
459. Ibid., 316–318.
460. Ibid., 322.
461. Switzer, "South Africa's Resistance Press," 54–56.
462. K.G. Tomaselli, "Ambiguities in Alternative Discourse. *New Nation* and the *Sowetan* in the 1980s," in L. Switzer and M. Adhikari, eds., *South Africa's Resistance Press. Alternative Voices in the Last Generation Under Apartheid* (Ohio: Ohio University Center for International Studies, 2000), 397-398.
463. Switzer, "South Africa's Resistance Press," 56.
464. G. Claassen, "Breaking the Mold of Political Subservience. *Vrye Weekblad* and the Afrikaans Alternative Press," in L. Switzer and M. Adhikari, eds., *South Africa's Resistance Press. Alternative Voices in the Last Generation Under Apartheid* (Ohio: Ohio University Center for International Studies, 2000), 404–411.
465. Tomaselli and Louw, 1991, 79.
466. Claassen, "Breaking the Mold," 423–429.
467. Ibid., 435–437.
468. Ibid., 447.
469. "Meer Oor Ons" ("More About Us"), https://www.vryeweekblad.com/meer-oor-ons/, accessed 31.12.2019.
470. Claassen, "Breaking the Mold," 411, 421.
471. Ibid., 442–447.
472. Switzer, "South Africa's Resistance Press," 60.
473. Ibid., 65.
474. C. Merrett and C. Saunders, "The Weekly Mail, 1985–1994," in L. Switzer and M. Adhikari, eds., *South Africa's Resistance Press. Alternative Voices in the Last Generation Under Apartheid* (Ohio: Ohio University Center for International Studies, 2000), 458–466.
475. Ibid., 469–474.
476. Ibid., 476–479.
477. "About us," https://mg.co.za/page/about-us/, accessed 31.12.2019.
478. K. Tomaselli, R. Tomaselli and J. Muller, "The Construction of News in the South African Mediam" in K. Tomaselli, R. Tomaselli and J. Muller, eds., *Narrating the Crisis: Hegemony and the South African Press* (Johannesburg: Richard Lyon & Co, 1987), 32–33.
479. Adhikari, "You Have the Right to Know," 331.
480. T. Mazwai, "The Black Press in South Africa: Censorship From All Sides," *Ecquid Novi: African Journalism Studies*, 11,2 (1990): 202–214.
481. S. Kelsey, *The Newspaperman's Guide to the Law* (London: Butterworth & Co, 1982).
482. Hachten and Giffard, *Total Onslaught*, 126.
483. Rabe, *Quote Unquote*, 27.
484. B. Booyens, "Om nie Blindelings aan te Neuk na Selfvernietiging nie" ("Not to Blindly Stumble to Self-destruction"), in L. Rabe, ed., *#Journalism4.0 @ Stellenbosch* (Stellenbosch: AfricanSunMedia, 2018), 64.

485. B. Booyens, email 22.02.2018.
486. Hachten and Giffard, *Total Onslaught*, 127.
487. L. Switzer, "South Africa's Resistance Press," 30–31.
488. Ibid., 33.
489. Switzer, "South Africa's Resistance Press," 35–38.
490. A. de Beer and E. Steyn, "The National Party and the Media: A Special Kind of Symbiosis," in P.E. Louw. ed., *South African Media Policy: Debates of the 1990s* (Bellville: Anthropos, 1993), 210–211.
491. Weekend Argus, June 1, 1990, p. 4.
492. De Beer and Steyn, "The National Party and the Media," 212.
493. Ibid., 215.
494. W. Currie, "The People Shall Broadcast: The Battle for the Airwaves," in P.E. Louw, ed., *South African Media Policy: Debates of the 1990s* (Bellville: Anthropos, 1993), 40.
495. R. Louw, "Foreword," in P.E Louw, ed., *South African Media Policy: Debates of the 1990s* (Bellville: Anthropos, 1993), 1–2.
496. P.E Louw, "Introduction," in PE Louw, ed., *South African Media Policy: Debates of the 1990s* (Bellville: Anthropos, 1993), 10–11.
497. Teer-Tomaselli and De Villiers, "Radio," 160–161.
498. Ibid., 163.
499. Ibid., 165–166.
500. R. Amner, "Getting Radio Active," *Leading Edge*, 7 (Cape Town: Independent Development Trust), 5.
501. Teer-Tomaselli and De Villiers, "Radio," 161.
502. P.E. Louw, "Restructuring the Media: Can Socialist and Libertarian Principles be Combined?" in P.E. Louw, ed., *South African Media Policy: Debates of the 1990s* (Bellville: Anthropos, 1993), 101.
503. H. Tyson, "Truth, Tolerance, Fairness and Freedom are the Values We Should be Striving For," in P.E. Louw, ed., *South African Media Policy: Debates of the 1990s* (Bellville: Anthropos, 1993), 111.
504. Ibid., 114.
505. Ibid., 115.
506. Ibid., 116–119.
507. Ibid., 120–121.
508. Hachten and Giffard, *Total Onslaught*, 228.
509. I.A. Blankson, "Media Independence and Pluralism in Africa: Opportunities and Challenges of Democratization and Liberalization," in I.A. Blankson and P.D. Murphy, eds., *Negotiating Democracy: Media Transformation in Emerging Democracies* (Albany: SUNY Press, 2007), 19.
510. Heard, *The Cape of Storms*, Preface (np).

Chapter 8

1. P.J. Fourie, "'n Terugkeer na die Onderdrukking van Vryheid van Spraak? Ooreenkomste Tussen die Apartheidsregering(s) en die ANC se Optrede teen die Media" ("A Return to the Repression of Freedom of Speech? Similarities Between the Apartheid Government(s) and the ANC's Actions Against the Media"), *Suid-Afrikaanse Tydskrif vir Geesteswetenskappe (South African Journal of Humanities)* 49,1 (2007): 62–84.
2. G. Berger, "De-racialization, Democracy and Development: Transformation of the South African Media 1994–2000," in K. Tomaselli and H. Dunn, eds., *Media, Democracy and Renewal in Southern Africa* (Colorado Springs: International Academic Publishers, 2001), 151.
3. A. Hadland, "The Enemy Without: How the State Will Shape the Future of Journalism" (Cardiff: Unpublished paper presented at the Future of Journalism conference, 2009).
4. *Free, Fair and Open. South African Media in the Transition to Democracy. Papers, Recommendations and Resolutions: Part 1* (Johannesburg: ANC Campaign for Open Media, 1992).
5. Fourie, "'n Terugkeer na die Onderdrukking van Vryheid van Spraak?" 64–65.

6. J. Duncan, "Talk Left, Act Right: What Constitutes Transformation in Southern African Media?" in K. Tomaselli and H. Dunn, eds., *Media, Democracy and Renewal in Southern Africa* (Colorado Springs: International Academic Publishers, 2001), 25.
7. R. Teer-Tomaselli and K.G. Tomaselli, "Transformation, Nation-building and the South African Media 1993–1999," in K. Tomaselli and H. Dunn, eds., *Media, Democracy and Renewal in Southern Africa* (Colorado Springs: International Academic Publishers, 2001), 123.
8. E. Barratt, "Choosing to be Part of the Story: The Participation of the South African National Editors' Forum in the democratising Process" (M.A. thesis, Stellenbosch University, 2006).
9. P. Diederichs and A.S. de Beer, "Newspapers. The Fourth Estate," in A.S. de Beer, ed., *Mass Media Towards the Millennium* (Pretoria: Van Schaik, 1998), 103–104.
10. Berger, "De-racialization, Democracy and Development," 166.
11. L. Rabe, *Quote Unquote* (Stellenbosch: Sun Media, 2016), 97.
12. Diederichs and De Beer, "Newspapers," 92–93.
13. Ibid., 95.
14. Ibid., 96.
15. Ibid., 95–96.
16. *Finansies en Tegniek*, August 16, 1991, p. 23.
17. Diederichs and De Beer, "Newspapers," 96–97.
18. B. von Lieres, "Culture and the Limits of Liberalism," in S.L. Robins, ed., *Limits to Liberation after Apartheid: Citizenship, Governance and Culture* (Oxford: James Currey, 2005), 22.
19. Teer-Tomaselli and Tomaselli, "Transformation, Nation-building," 123.
20. H. Wasserman, "Freedom's Just Another Word? Perspectives on Media Freedom and Responsibility in South Africa and Namibia," *International Communication Gazette* 72,7 (2010): 568–569.
21. K. Voltmer, "The Mass Media and the Dynamics of Political Communication in Processes of Democratization," in K. Voltmer, ed., *Mass Media and Political Communication in New Democracies* (London: Routledge, 2006), 1–20; H. Wasserman and A.S. de Beer, "Which Public? Whose Interest? The South African Media and its Role During the First Ten Years of Democracy," *Critical Arts* 19,1&2 (2005): 36–51; H. Wasserman and A.S. de Beer, "Conflicts of Interest? Debating the Media's Role in Post-apartheid South Africa," in K. Voltmer, ed., *Mass Media and Political Communication in New Democracies* (London: Routledge, 2006), 59–75.
22. R. Calland, *The First Five Years: A Review of South Africa's Democratic Parliament* (Cape Town: Idasa, 1999), 100.
23. Ibid., 5.
24. Berger, "De-racialization, Democracy and Development," 161.
25. Diederichs and De Beer, "Newspapers," 100.
26. M.M. Breytenbach, "The Manipulation of Public Opinion by State Censorship of the Media in South Africa (1974–1994)" (D.Phil. diss., Stellenbosch University, 1997), 58.
27. A. Hadland, "The South African Print media, 1994–2004: An Application and Critique of Comparative Media Systems Theory" (D.Phil. diss., University of Cape Town, 2007), 93–95.
28. E. Barratt, "Part of the Story," 6.
29. Hadland, "The South African Print Media," 92.
30. Ibid., 121.
31. K. Tomaselli, "Ownership and Control in the South African Print Media: Black Economic Empowerment after Apartheid, 1990–97," *Ecquid Novi* 18,1 (1997): 37.
32. Hadland, "The South African Print Media," 122.
33. R. Horwitz, *Communication and Democratic Reform in South Africa* (Cambridge: Cambridge University Press, 2001).
34. Hadland, "The South African Print Media," 95–96.
35. G. Berger, "Towards an Analysis of the SA Media and Transformation, 1994–99," *Transformation* 38 (1999).
36. Hadland, "The South African Print Media," 97–98.

37. G. Mersham, "Television, A Fascinating Window on an Unfolding World," in A.S. de Beer, ed., *Mass Media Towards the Millennium* (Pretoria: Van Schaik, 1998), 213.
38. Mersham, "Television," 218.
39. Hadland, "The South African Print Media," 97–100.
40. Diederichs and De Beer, "Newspapers," 100–101.
41. Rabe, *Quote Unquote,* 97.
42. Diederichs and De Beer, "Newspapers," 101–102.
43. Berger, "De-racialization, Democracy and Development," 151.
44. Teer-Tomaselli and Tomaselli, "Transformation, Nation-building," 124–126.
45. Duncan, "Talk Left, Act Right," 25.
46. Ibid., 27.
47. D Wigston, "History of the South African Media," in P.J. Fourie, ed., *Media Studies Volume 1: Media History, Media and Society* (Wetton: Juta, 2007), 19.
48. Ibid., 23.
49. Ibid., 26.
50. A. Harber, "SABC Should Encourage Openness, Not Obeisance to Political Will," *Cape Argus,* August 3, 1999, p. 18.
51. Diederichs and De Beer, "Newspapers," 102.
52. K. Tomaselli, R. Tomaselli and J. Muller, eds., *The Press in South Africa* (Johannesburg: Richard Lyon & Co, 1987), 39–42.
53. Hadland, "The South African Print Media," 34–35.
54. J. Mervis, *The Fourth Estate* (Johannesburg: Jonathan Ball, 1989).
55. H.L. Smith, *Behind the Press in South Africa* (Cape Town: Stewart Press, 1945).
56. L. Neame, *Today's News Today: A History of the Argus Company* (Johannesburg: Argus Printing and Publishing Company, 1956).
57. A. Hepple, *Censorship and Press Control in South Africa* (Johannesburg: published by author, 1960).
58. R. Pollak, *Up against Apartheid: The Role and Plight of the Press in South Africa* (Carbondale: Southern Illinois Press, 1981).
59. C. Chimutengwende, *South Africa: The Press and Politics of Liberation* (London: Barbican Books, 1978), 48.
60. W.A. Hachten and C.A. Giffard, *Total Onslaught. The South African Press under Attack* (Johannesburg: McMillan, 1984), 97.
61. Hadland, "The South African Print Media," 33.
62. Ibid., 106.
63. Duncan, "Talk Left, Act Right," 25.
64. Ibid., 31.
65. Ibid., 33–34.
66. Hadland, "The South African Print Media," 149.
67. Ibid., 205.
68. Diederichs and De Beer, "Newspapers," 91–92.
69. Hadland, "The South African Print Media," 150.
70. Ibid., 10.
71. Ibid., 150.
72. Ibid., 11.
73. E. Steyn and A.S. de Beer, "South African National Skills Audit" (Unpublished report, prepared for SANEF, 2002).
74. Hadland, "The South African Print Media," 13.
75. Barratt, "Part of the Story".
76. Hadland, "The South African Print Media", 13–15.
77. C. Milne and A. Taylor, *South Africa: Research Findings and Conclusions* (London: African Media Development Initiative, BBC World Service Trust, 2006).

78. A. Hadland and K. Thorne, *The People's Voice: The Development and Current State of the South African Small Media Sector* (Cape Town: HSRC Press, 2004).
79. Hadland, "The South African Print Media," 15.
80. G. Berger, "More Media for Southern Africa? The Place of Politics, Economics and Convergence in Developing Media Density," *Critical Arts* 18,1 (2004): 59.
81. Wigston, "History of the South African Media," 52–53.
82. Hadland, "The South African Print Media," 16–17.
83. Milne and Taylor, *South Africa: Research Findings and Conclusions.*
84. Naspers Annual Report (2003), 10.
85. Hadland, "The South African Print Media," 152–154.
86. Mersham, "Television," 221.
87. Teer-Tomaselli and Tomaselli, "Transformation, Nation-building," 130.
88. Hadland, "The South African Print Media," 165.
89. I. Manoim, "Print is Dead. The Digital Revolution Continues", *Mail & Guardian: 20 Years* anniversary supplement, *Mail & Guardian*, November 25 to December 1, 2005, p. 4.
90. Hadland, "The South African Print Media," 165–166.
91. R. Greenslade, *Press Gang: How Newspapers Make Profits from Propaganda* (London: Pan Books, 2004).
92. Hadland, "The South African Print Media," 166.
93. Teer-Tomaselli and Tomaselli, "Transformation, Nation-building," 131–134.
94. *Die Burger*, May 11, 1996, p. 12.
95. Berger, "De-racialization, Democracy and Development," 151.
96. Ibid., 153.
97. Ibid., 160.
98. S. Jacobs, "Tensions of a Free Press: South Africa After Apartheid" (Harvard: Research Paper R-22, Joan Shorenstein Center on the Press, Politics and Public Policy, 1999).
99. P.J. Fourie, "Rethinking the Role of the Media in South Africa," *Communicare* 21,1 (2002).
100. A. Hadland, "State-media Relations in Post-apartheid South Africa: An Application of Comparative Media Systems Theory," *Communicare* 26,2 (2007).
101. R. Louw, "National Overview: South Africa," in *So This is Democracy? Report on the State of Media Freedom and Freedom of Expression in Southern Africa* (Windhoek: MISA, 2007).
102. G. Berger, "For Media, SABC is the Frontline for Preventing Political Creep," *Mail & Guardian Online*, www.mg.co.za/article/2009-05-14-for-media-sabc-is-the-frontline-preventing-political-creep, 2009, accessed 28.02.2018.
103. Hadland, "The South African Print Media," 18.
104. A. Johnston, "The African National Congress, The Print Media and the Development of Mediated Politics in South Africa," *Critical Arts* 19,1&2 (2005): 13.
105. Hadland, "The South African Print Media," 18.
106. Ibid., 110.
107. Barratt, "Part of the Story," 32–33.
108. Ibid., 35.
109. Johnston, "The African National Congress," 13.
110. Ibid., 19.
111. Hadland, "The South African Print Media," 111.
112. Milne and Taylor, *South Africa: Research Findings and Conclusions*, 53.
113. Hadland, "The South African Print Media," 111.
114. Vuk'unzenzele, https://www.vukuzenzele.gov.za/general, accessed 27.02.2020.
115. ANC Today, http://anctoday.org.za/, accessed 13.03.2018.
116. S. Nogonyama, *ANC Today* 1(15), May 2001, cited by Hadland, "The South African print media," 112.
117. Diederichs and De Beer, "Newspapers," 85.
118. Hadland, "The South African Print Media," 113–115.

119. W.M. Gumede, *Thabo Mbeki and the Battle for the Soul of the ANC* (Cape Town: Zebra Press, 2005), 306.
120. G.J. Retief, *Media Ethics: An Introduction to Responsible Journalism* (Cape Town: Oxford University Press, 2002), ix.
121. Hadland, "The South African Print Media," 86.
122. K. Owen, "Liberal Institutions Under Pressure: The Press," in R.W. Johnson, D. Welsh and L. Husemeyer, eds., *Ironic Victory: Liberalism in Post-liberation South Africa* (Cape Town: Oxford University Press, 1998), 177.
123. K. Tomaselli, "Ownership and Control," 8.
124. Barratt, "Part of the Story," 22.
125. Hadland, "The South African Print Media," 87.
126. Diederichs and De Beer, "Newspapers," 103.
127. Barratt, "Part of the Story," 23.
128. L. Rabe, "Kroniek van 'n Mondigwording? 'n Mediageskiedkundige Herevaluering van die WVK, Naspers en die Afrikaanse Joernalistiek" ("Chronicle of a Coming of Age? A Media Historiographical Re-evaluation of the TRC, Naspers and Afrikaans Journalism"), *Litnet Akademies* 14,3 (2017); Diederichs and De Beer, "Newspapers," 106.
129. Diederichs and De Beer, "Newspapers," 107–108.
130. Barratt, "Part of the Story," 24.
131. Hadland, "The South African Print Media," 88.
132. Barratt, "Part of the Story," 24.
133. *Cape Times*, January 18, 2007, p. 3.
134. Hadland, "The South African Print Media," 89.
135. C. Merrett, "A Tale of Two Paradoxes: Media Censorship in South Africa, Pre-Liberation and Post-Apartheid," *Critical Arts*, 15,1&2 (2001): 50–64.
136. P.J. Fourie, "Rethinking the Role of the Media in South Africa," 17–41.
137. Hadland, "The South African Print Media," 99.
138. MDDA Act, 2002, http://www.mdda.org.za/mdda-act, accessed 13.03.2018.
139. Hadland, "The South African Print Media," 99–100.
140. MDDA, *Annual Report 2005/6* (Johannesburg: Vulindlela Communications), 9.
141. J. Gerber, "Liphoko no Longer Acting CEO at Media Diversity Agency," News24, September 29, 2017, https://www.news24.com/SouthAfrica/News/liphoko-no-longer-acting-ceo-at-media-diversity-agency-20170929, accessed 13.03.2018.
142. J. Gerber, "Dodgy Contracts at 'Rotten' Media Agency," News24, September 14, 2017, https://www.news24.com/SouthAfrica/News/dodgy-contracts-at-rotten-media-agency-20170914, accessed 13.03.2018.
143. J. Gerber, "New Acting CEO for Media Development and Diversity Agency," News24, December 22, 2017, https://www.news24.com/SouthAfrica/News/new-acting-ceo-for-media-development-and-diversity-agency-20171222, accessed 13.03.2018.
144. Hadland, "The South African Print Media," 192–193.
145. Diederichs and De Beer, "Newspapers," 113–114.
146. Hadland, "The South African Print Media," 196.
147. Ibid., 195.
148. Barratt, "Part of the Story," 55.
149. Hadland, "The South African Print Media," 197.
150. M. Motloung, "Press Complaints Peak," *The Media*, February (2007): 14.
151. SA Press Council, http://www.presscouncil.org.za/, accessed 14.03.2018.
152. Hadland, "The South African Print Media," 198.
153. Barratt," Part of the Story," 56.
154. Motloung, "Press Complaints Peak," 14.
155. Hadland, "The South African Print Media," 198–199.
156. K.G. Tomaselli, "Transformation of the South African Media", *Critical Arts*, 18,1 (2004).

157. Review. Press Council of South Africa, 11.
158. Ibid., 27.
159. Ibid., 38–39.
160. Ibid., 26–27.
161. "The Press Must Change – Mandela," *Mail & Guardian*, https://mg.co.za/article/1992-05-29-the-press-must-change-mandela/, accessed 21.04.2020.
162. L. Rabe, *Quote Unquote*, 30.
163. T. Mbeki, speech, World Press Freedom Day, 2001.
164. Rabe, *Quote Unquote,* 34.
165. Ibid., 35.
166. Ibid., 35.
167. Ibid., 36.
168. Ibid., 36.
169. Ibid., 40.
170. Hadland, "The South African Print Media," 123.
171. Ibid., 125–126.
172. Ibid., 139.
173. M Boloka, "Diversity Goes Global," *Rhodes Journalism Review*, 24 (2004): 31.
174. Hadland, "The South African Print Media," 145–146.
175. Tomaselli, "Ownership and Control," 49.
176. Hadland, "The South African Print Media," 178–179.
177. R. Amner, "Getting Radio Active," *Leading Edge*, 7 (Cape Town: Independent Development Trust), 2.
178. R. Teer-Tomaselli and C. de Villiers, "Radio Theatre of the Mind," in A.S. de Beer, ed., *Mass Media Towards the Millennium* (Pretoria: Van Schaik, 1998), 151.
179. Hadland, "The South African Print Media," 186.
180. W. Bird, "Learning From Our Mistakes," *Rhodes Journalism Review*, 24 (2004): 58.
181. "Declaration of Table Mountain," *Rhodes Journalism Review*, 27 (2007): 6.
182. Hadland, ""The South African Print Media," 189–190.
183. Louw, "National Overview: South Africa."
184. Fourie, "'n Terugkeer na die Onderdrukking van Vryheid van Spraak?" 62.
185. Ibid., 65–68.
186. "National Editors' Forum Concerned with Developments at the SABC," SANEF statement, 2008.
187. Fourie, "'n Terugkeer na die Onderdrukking van Vryheid van Spraak?" 69–70.
188. J. Duncan, "Executive Overstretch: South African Broadcasting Independence and Accountability Under Thabo Mbeki," *Communicatio*, 34,1 (2008): 21.
189. Fourie, "'n Terugkeer na die Onderdrukking van Vryheid van Spraak?" 72.
190. Ibid., 74.
191. *ANC Today – Online Voice of the African National Congress,* 1,1, January 18–24, 2001, as quoted in Fourie.
192. Fourie, "'n Terugkeer na die Onderdrukking van Vryheid van Spraak?" 76.
193. "Treatment of the Media at the 52nd ANC National Conference," SANEF statement, 2008.
194. Fourie, "'n Terugkeer na die Onderdrukking van Vryheid van Spraak?" 77–80.
195. ANC 52nd National Conference 2007, "Resolutions," http://www.anc.org.za/index.html, accessed 3.04.2018.
196. Fourie, "'n Terugkeer na die Onderdrukking van Vryheid van Spraak?" 80.
197. Ibid., 82.

Chapter 9

1. Mkhabela, Keynote Address, "The Decriminalisation of Freedom of Expression in Africa: How Self-Regulation of the Media can Assist," Seminar, ONO: The Decriminalisation of Freedom of Expression in Africa, STIAS, Stellenbosch, 23.04.2015.
2. J. Pauw, *The President's Keepers: Those Keeping Zuma in Power and Out of Prison* (Cape Town: Tafelberg, 2017).
3. ANC Discussion Document, 2010, 3–19.
4. Review, PCSA, 2011, 12.
5. ANC, Discussion Document: Media Diversity and Ownership, National General Council, Durban, 2010.
6. H. Wasserman, "Freedom's Just Another Word? Perspectives on Media Freedom and Responsibility in South Africa and Namibia," *International Communication Gazette* 72,7 (2010): 584.
7. Ibid., 571–572.
8. Ibid., 585.
9. Ibid., 573.
10. I.A. Blankson, "Media Independence and Pluralism in Africa: Opportunities and Challenges of Democratization and Liberalization," in I.A. Blankson and P.D. Murphy, eds., *Negotiating Democracy: Media Transformation in Emerging Democracies* (Albany: SUNY Press, 2007), 15–34.
11. Wasserman, "Freedom's Just Another Word?" 573.
12. Ibid., 576.
13. A.S. de Beer and E. Steyn, "Sanef's 2002 South African National Journalism Skills Audit: An Introduction and the Sanef Report Regarding the Media Industry," *Ecquid Novi* 23,1 (2002): 11–86.
14. Wasserman, "Freedom's Just Another Word?" 577.
15. "Media May be Under Dire Threat Once More," *M&G*, July 26, 2017.
16. Right2Know, https://www.r2k.org.za/about/, accessed 20.11.2019.
17. Rosa Luxembourg Foundation, http://www.r2k.org.za/wp-content/uploads/R2K-RLF-2013.pdf, accessed 20.11.2019.
18. Review, PCSA, 2011.
19. Ibid., 3.
20. Ibid., 7.
21. Ibid., 4.
22. Ibid., 5.
23. J. Reid and T. Isaacs, "Media Policy and Democracy Project: Press Regulation in South Africa: An Analysis of the Press Council of South Africa, the Press Freedom Commission and Related Discourses," Media Policy and Democracy Project, www.mediaanddemocracy.com, November 2015, 37.
24. Ibid., 38.
25. Ibid., 48.
26. Review, PCSA, 2011, 13–14.
27. Ibid., 6.
28. Ibid., 8.
29. Ibid., 28.
30. "Press Freedom in South Africa," https://www.brandsouthafrica.com/south-africa-fast-facts/media-facts/press-freedom-in-south-africa, accessed 27.02.2018.
31. R. Louw, "Scrap Apartheid-Era Laws!" *The Media*, January (2013): 10.
32. G. Daniels, "The ANC's Hysterical Gaze on the Media," *The Media Online*, January (2013), accessed 28.01.2013.
33. C. Sunter, "When Breaking Futures Become Breaking News," *News24*, https://www.news24.com/Columnists/ClemSunter/When-breaking-futures-become-breaking-news-20140218, accessed 27.02.2018.

34. A. Tilley, "The Secrecy Bill More Dangerous Than Ever," https://www.dailymaverick.co.za/opinionista/2014-03-25-the-secrecy-bill-more-dangerous-than-ever/#.WpVT0WdDvZ4, accessed 27.02.2018.
35. "World Press Freedom at Lowest Level in Decade," http://www.abc.net.au/news/2014-05-02/world-press-freedom-lowest-level-decade-freedom-house-report/5425308, accessed 27.02.2018.
36. "Info Bill Will Harm Press Freedom, Says Sanef," https://www.news24.com/SouthAfrica/News/Info-bill-will-harm-press-freedom-says-Sanef-20140503, accessed 27.02.2018.
37. T. du Plessis, Twenty Years after Democracy (2014) .
38. "Secrecy Bill Closer to Becoming Secrecy Law," *Bizcommunity*, https://www.bizcommunity.com/Article/196/466/85831.html, accessed 22.11.2012.
39. Du Plessis, Twenty Years after Democracy.
40. "Fear in the News: The Difference Between Self-Censorship and Ethical Journalism," https://ethicaljournalismnetwork.org/fear-in-the-news-the-difference-between-self-censorship-and-ethical-journalism, accessed 20.10.2018.
41. ANC Discussion Document, 2015; M. Letsoala, "ANC: The media is ganging up on us," *M&G Online*, https://mg.co.za/article/2015-08-18-anc-the-media-is-ganging-up-on-us/, accessed 20.11.2019.
42. B. Phakathi, "New Press Council System Includes Online Publications," *Bizcommunity*, December 17, 2015.
43. K. Rajuili, "The Decriminalisation of Freedom of Expression in Africa: How Self-Regulation of the Media Can Assist," paper, ONO, Stellenbosch, April 2015.
44. J. Reid, "Op-Ed: World Press Freedom Day 2015, SA Edition," *Daily Maverick*, http://www.dailymaverick.co.za/article/2015-04-28-op-ed-world-press-freedom-day-2015-sa-edition/, accessed 28.04.2015.
45. Reid and Isaacs, "Media Policy and Democracy Project," 6.
46. Review, PCSA, 2011.
47. Review, PCSA, 2012.
48. Reid and Isaacs, "Media Policy and Democracy Project," 7.
49. Ibid., 9.
50. Ibid., 10.
51. Ibid., 15.
52. Ibid., 24–28.
53. Review, PCSA, 2015.
54. Reid and Isaacs, "Media Policy and Democracy Project," 31–32.
55. Ibid., 36.
56. L. Rabe, "Die Belang van Mediavryheid in Suid-Afrika: Tweehonderd Jaar, Twee Gevallestudies, van die Magna Carta tot die Muilbandwet" ("The Importance of Media Freedom in South Africa: Two Centuries, Two Case Studies, from the Magna Carta to the Secrecy Bill"), *Tydskrif vir Geesteswetenskappe (Journal for the Humanities)* 56,3 (2016): 866–867.
57. T. Mazwai, "The Present and Future Role of the Press," in *Mau-Mauing the Media, New Censorship for the New South Africa* (Johannesburg: South African Institute of Race Relations, 1991), 11.
58. Louw, "Scrap Apartheid-Era Laws!" 10.
59. E. Barratt, "History of the South African National Editors' Forum" (Unpublished document, Johannesburg, 2003), n.p.
60. Rabe, "Die Belang van Mediavryheid," 867.
61. Daniels, "The ANC's Hysterical Gaze on the Media."
62. M. Tsedu, "One Story Can Make All the Difference," *Media Tenor South Africa* 5,2 (November 2001): 3.
63. Louw, "Scrap Apartheid-Era Laws!" 10.

64. L. Rabe, "Media Freedom, Black Wednesday and 30 Years On: Realities and Illusions" (Unpublished Media Freedom Day Seminar, Cape Town), 18.10.2007.

65. "Guarding the Guardians: A Media Appeals Tribunal? A Right2Know Campaign Discussion Document," September 2011, http://www.r2k.org.za/wp-content/uploads/2012/12/R2K_Media_Freedom_disDoc.pdf, accessed 7.04.2015.

66. "Media Tribunal Unlikely: Press Council," http://www.bizcommunity.com/Article/196/466/88897.html, accessed 7.02.2013.

67. P. de Vos, "Would Media Appeals Tribunal be Constitutional?" www.constitutionallyspeaking.co.za, 7.04.2015.

68. "Guarding the Guardians: A Media Appeals Tribunal?"

69. J. Gerber, "Reguleer Gedrukte Media, Vra Minister" ("Minister Asks for Print Media to be Regulated"), *Die Burger*, April 22, 2015, p. 2.

70. "Republic of South Africa. Protection of State Information Bill," as presented by the Ad Hoc Committee on Protection of Information Bill (National Assembly) (introduced as Protection of Information Bill [B6-21010]) by the minister of state security. B6B-210), http://www.parliament.gov.za/live/commonrepository/Processed/20111125/384294_1.pdf, accessed 7.04.2015.

71. V. Bhardwaj, "The Good and the Bad of the 'Better' Secrecy Bill," *M&G*, October 25–31, 2013, p. 37.

72. K. van Rooyen, "Is Ons Dan Nog Vry?" ("Are We Still Free?") *Die Burger*, February 20, 2014, p. 17.

73. "Guarding the Guardians: A Media Appeals Tribunal?"

74. F. Krüger, "The Only Guarantee of Freedom is Freedom", *M&G*, November 2–8, 2012, p. 34.

75. K. Rajuili, "The Decriminalisation of Freedom of Expression in Africa."

76. See internet/newspaper reports, e.g. *News24*, *Netwerk24*, *Die Burger*, *The Cape Times* and others from the evening of 12 February 2015 onwards.

77. J. Heard, "'n Uur wat Suid-Afrika in die Skande Steek" ("An Hour that Disgraced South Africa"), *Die Burger*, February 17, 2015, p. 9.

78. M. Lamprecht and J. Breytenbach, "Spioene Woel in Parlement" (Spies Active in Parliament"), *Die Burger*, February 18, 2015, p. 1.

79. "GPL's Joint Statement with SANEF Regarding Challenges Experienced by the Media at the 2015 Opening of the Legislature," SANEF statement, 24.02.2015.

80. "SANEF Condemns Thuggish Behaviour by Police at Parliament," statement, 11.03.2015.

81. Films and Publications Act, http://www.acts.co.za/films-and-publications-act-1996/index.html?films_and_publications_act_1996_act_no_65_of_1996_.php, accessed 1.05.2015.

82. K. Rajuili, "The Decriminalisation of Freedom of Expression in Africa."

83. "Guarding the Guardians: A Media Appeals Tribunal?"

84. K. Rajuili, "The Decriminalisation of Freedom of Expression in Africa."

85. J. Thloloe, Panel Discussion, "The Decriminalisation of Freedom of Expression in Africa: How Self-Regulation of the Media can Assist," Seminar, ONO, Stellenbosch, 23.04.2015.

86. G. Berger, "Best Practice in Media Self-Regulation," *African Journalism Studies* 32,2 (2011): 36–57.

87. F. Krüger, "Media Courts of Honour: Self-Regulatory Councils in Southern Africa and Elsewhere," FES Media Africa Series, 2009.

88. "Guarding the Guardians: A Media Appeals Tribunal?"

89. PCSA, "Home Page," http://www.presscouncil.org.za/, accessed 7.04.2015.

90. J. Gerber, "Gewone Mense Moet Betoog" ("Ordinary People Must Protest"), *Die Burger*, February 18, 2015, p. 4.

91. Mkhabela, "The Decriminalisation of Freedom of Expression in Africa."

92. H. Zille, Keynote Address, Annual Conference of ONO, Cape Town, 20.04.2015.

93. RSA, www.rsf.fr/article.php3?id_article=4116, as cited in Rabe, "Ten Years into Democracy" (Unpublished seminar series, Oslo), 2004.

94. RSF, http://en.rsf.org/, accessed 2.01.2015.

95. "Freedom of the Press 2015", Freedom House, https://freedomhouse.org/report/freedom-press/freedom-press-2015, accessed 1.05.2015.
96. A. October, "Kommer in Amerika Uitgespreek oor Persvryheid in SA" ("Concern Expressed in America Regarding Press Freedom in SA"), *Die Burger*, May 1, 2015, p. 2.
97. N. Mandela, "Address to the IPI Congress," Cape Town, 14 February 1994.
98. M. Hunter, "Securocrats Choke Flow of Information," *M&G*, September 12–18, 2004, p. 27.
99. T. du Plessis, History Symposium, Suid-Afrikaanse Akademie vir Wetenskap en Kuns (South African Academy for Science and the Arts), 2016.
100. Louw, "So This is Democracy 2016," 80–83.
101. Ibid., 84.
102. Independent Media Group, https://www.independentmedia.co.za/our-company/about-us/ https://www.independentmedia.co.za/our-company/about-us/, accessed 17.03.2020.
103. Louw, "So This is Democracy 2016", 84–85.
104. F. Krige, *The SABC 8* (Johannesburg: Penguin Random House South Africa, 2019).
105. Freedom House South Africa, https://freedomhouse.org/country/south-africa, accessed 27.02.2018.
106. Global Report 2017, https://freedomhouse.org/report/freedom-press/freedom-press-2017, accessed 27.02.2018.
107. South Africa Freedom House, https://freedomhouse.org/report/freedom-press/2017/south-africa, accessed 27.02.2018.
108. "Broken Heart Syndrome Kills SABC 8 Journalist Suna Venter," https://www.news24.com/SouthAfrica/News/sabc-8-journalist-suna-venter-dead-20170629, *News24*, accessed 27.02.2017.
109. South Africa Freedom House, https://freedomhouse.org/report/freedom-press/2017/south-africa, accessed 27.02.2018.
110. M. du Preez, "A New Era of Modern Leadership Dawned Under Ramaphosa," https://www.news24.com/Columnists/MaxduPreez/a-new-era-of-modern-leadership-has-dawned-under-ramaphosa-20180116, *News24*, accessed 28.02.2018.
111. M. du Preez, "Zuma's Defiant Exit Signifies 9 of SA's Darkest Years," https://www.news24.com/Columnists/MaxduPreez/zumas-defiant-exit-signifies-end-to-9-of-sas-darkest-years-20180213, *News24*, accessed 28.02.2018.
112. Pauw, *The President's Keepers*.
113. P.-L. Myburgh, *The Republic of Gupta: A Story of State Capture* (Johannesburg, Penguin, 2017).
114. M. du Preez, "ANN7 Does Not Deserve Our Activism," *News24*, https://www.news24.com/Columnists/MaxduPreez/ann7-does-not-deserve-our-activism-20180206, accessed 27.02.2018.
115. R. Firth, Profile, https://www.bizcommunity.com/Profile/RichardFirth, accessed 30.03.2020.
116. R. Firth, "Dear FPB, Free Our Kids," https://techcentral.co.za/dear-fpb-free-kids/79459/, accessed 2.06.2018.
117. D. McCleod, "Telecoms Bill Must be Withdrawn – Research Firm Says," https://techcentral.co.za/telecoms-bill-must-withdrawn-research-firm/79469/, accessed 28.02.2018.
118. RSF World Press Freedom Index, https://rsf.org/en/rsf-index-2018-hatred-journalism-threatens-democracies, accessed 26.04.2018.
119. RSF, https://rsf.org/en/south-africa, accessed 18.03.2020.
120. RSF World Press Freedom Index.
121. RSF, https://rsf.org/en/united-states, accessed 18.03.2020.
122. E. Bell, "Keeping a Free and Fair Press is One of the Defining Political Issues of Our Age", *The Guardian Online*, https://www.theguardian.com/media/commentisfree/2018/may/13/keeping-a-free-and-fair-press-is-one-of-the-defining-political-issues-of-our-age, accessed 13.05.2018.
123. J. Matisonn, *God, Lies and Spies* (Vlaeberg: Missing Ink, 2018).
124. "SANEF Strongly Supports the Promotion of Free Internet Access as a Basic Human Right," Media release, 18.02.2018.
125. "Icasa Launches Consumer Advisory Panel," https://techcentral.co.za/icasa-launches-consumer-advisory-panel/80107/, accessed 12.02.2018.

126. A. Harber, "How Investigative Journalists Helped Turn the Tide Against Corruption in South Africa," The Conversation, https://theconversation.com/how-investigative-journalists-helped-turn-the-tide-against-corruption-in-south-africa-93434, accessed 15.03.2018.

127. "SANEF is Shocked by the Attack of Journalist," statement, 20.03.2018.

128. "SA's 'Censorship Bill' Must be Rewritten, ISP Body Says," https://techcentral.co.za/sas-censorship-bill-must-be-rewritten-isp-body-says/82367/, accessed 13.07.2018.

129. UN/OSCE/OAS/ACHPR, Joint Declaration on Freedom of Expression and "Fake News", Disinformation, Propaganda, https://www.osce.org/fom/302796?download=true, accessed 29.03.2018; J. Posetti and A. Matthews, "A Short Guide to the History of 'Fake News' and Disinformation," https://www.icfj.org/news/short-guide-history-fake-news-and-disinformation-new-icfj-learning-module, accessed 29.03.2018.

130. "The Guptas, Bell Pottinger and the Fake News Propaganda Machine," https://www.timeslive.co.za/news/south-africa/2017-09-04-the-guptas-bell-pottinger-and-the-fake-news-propaganda-machine, accessed 29.03.2018; "Dummy's Guide: Bell Pottinger – Gupta London Agency, Creator of WMC," https://www.biznews.com/global-citizen/2017/08/07/dummys-guide-bell-pottinger-gupta-wmc/; "How Bell Pottinger, P.R. Firm for Despots and Rogues, Met its End in South Africa," New York Times, https://www.nytimes.com/2018/02/04/business/bell-pottinger-guptas-zuma-south-africa.html, accessed 4.02.2018; F. Haffajee, "The Gupta Fake News Factory and Me, HuffPost South Africa," https://www.huffingtonpost.co.za/2017/06/05/ferial-haffajee-the-gupta-fake-news-factory-and-me_a_22126282/, accessed 6.04.2018; J. Posetti, "Combating Online Abuse: When Journalists and Their Sources are Targeted," in C. Ireton and J. Posetti, eds., Journalism, 'Fake News' and Disinformation (UNESCO, 2018).

131. "SANEF to Take Steps After Sunday Times Apologies," statement, 16.10.2018.

132. "SANEF Statement on "Brown Envelope Journalism," statement, 16.10.2018.

133. G. Daniels, "A Reflection On the Media: Consolidation and Convergence – Or Shrivelling and Sinking? Daily Maverick, https://www.dailymaverick.co.za/article/2018-10-17-a-reflection-on-the-media-consolidation-and-convergence-or-shrivelling-and-sinking/#.W8f59StWyWs. email, accessed 17.10.2018.

134. On 12 June 2020 SANEF issued a statement that it "welcomes the news that President Cyril Ramaphosa has taken steps to have the controversial and draconian "Secrecy'Bill" reviewed and aligned with the Constitution". It stated the Protection of State Information Bill "has remained unsigned for seven years after it was passed by Parliament following numerous submissions and acrimonious debate". The body said it "welcomes this opportunity to ensure that all aspects of the Bill that are unconstitutional, or too broadly defined, are redrafted". SANEF Statement, 12.06.2020.

135. "SANEF Condemns Minister Tito Mboweni's Threats Against Journalists," statement, 10.11.2018.

136. M. du Preez, "Time to Stop Aiding and Abetting the EFF's Assault on Democracy," News24, https://www.news24.com/Columnists/MaxduPreez/time-to-stop-aiding-and-abetting-the-effs-assault-on-democracy-20181127, accessed 27.11.2018.

137. R. Mathekga, "A War Against the Media is a War Against Democracy," News24, https://www.news24.com/Columnists/Ralph_Mathekga/a-war-against-the-media-is-a-war-against-democracy-20181126, accessed 26.11.2018.

138. J. Burke, "Cyril Ramaphosa is Cautious, But he Must Waste no Time Reforming South Africa," The Guardian, https://www.theguardian.com/world/2019/may/26/cyril-ramaphosa-must-waste-no-time-reforming-south-africa-election?CMP=Share_iOSApp_Other, accessed 26.05.2019.

139. "SANEF Takes Action as Journalists Continue to Come Under Fire," statement, 29.05.2019.

140. "SANEF AGM Takes Critical Decisions to Support the Media Industry and to Launch an Inquiry Into Media Ethics and Credibility Issues," statement, 24.06.2019.

141. State of the Newsroom 2018, https://journalism.co.za/resources/state-of-the-newsroom/, accessed 22.03.2020.

142. "SANEF AGM Takes Critical Decisions."

143. A. Quintal, "Discredited, Threatened, Attacked: Challenges of Covering South Africa's election in the Digital Age," https://cpj.org/blog/2019/07/south-africa-election-journalists-online-harassment-threats-doxx.php, accessed 1.07.2019.
144. F. Haffajee, "An Army of Trolls Marches on in Mindless Violence – And Nobody is Stopping Them," *Daily Maverick*, https://www.dailymaverick.co.za/article/2019-03-07-an-army-of-trolls-marches-on-in-mindless-violence-and-nobody-is-stopping-them/, accessed 7.03.2019.
145. Quintal, "Discredited, Threatened, Attacked."
146. Q. Hunter, Twitter account, https://twitter.com/QaanitahHunter/status/1134874308210253824, 1.06.2019.
147. Quintal, "Discredited, Threatened, Attacked."
148. "SANEF Condemns Harassment of Journalists," statement, 10.07.2019.
149. "SANEF Condemns Harassment and Arrest of Journalists in Durban," statement, 11.07.2019.
150. "SANEF Condemns Harassment of Journalists," statement, 26.07.2019.
151. M. Thamm, "Top Cop Implicated in the Corruption by Nxasana and Booysen Appointed Acting Head of KZN Hawks Organised Crime Unit," *Daily Maverick*, https://www.dailymaverick.co.za/article/2019-06-18-top-cop-implicated-in-corruption-by-nxasana-and-booysen-appointed-acting-head-of-kzn-hawks-organised-crime-unit/, accessed 23.03.2020.
152. A. Jones, "New Leaked Reports Show Why Train Security has Collapsed," GroundUp, https://www.groundup.org.za/article/new-leaked-reports-show-why-train-security-has-collapsed/, 30.10.2018.
153. "Number of Journalists Killed on the Job Rises in 2018," https://www.aljazeera.com/news/2018/12/number-journalists-killed-job-2018-rises-181231021858196.html, accessed 20.11.2019; *Multi-Stakeholder Consultation on Strengthening the Implementation of the UN Plan of Action on the Safety of Journalists and the Issue of Impunity*, Unesco, https://en.unesco.org/sites/default/files/report_-_multi-stakeholder_consultation.pdf, accessed on 20.11.2019.
154. RSF, https://rsf.org/en/ranking/2019, accessed 26.06.2019.
155. "Freedom in Retreat," https://freedomhouse.org/report/freedom-world/2019/democracy-retreat, accessed 20.03.2020.
156. G. Berger, "UNESCO's Safety of Journalists' Agenda: What Impact?" *Australia Journalism Review* 40,2: 29–39.
157. "Journalists Under Attack," International News Safety Institute, https://newssafety.org/casualties/journalists-under-attack/, accessed 2.07.2019.
158. "Africa Report," http://www.africafex.org/afex/wp-content/uploads/2019/04/Annual-FOE-Situation-in-Africa-Report-2018.pdf, accessed 29.06.2019.
159. F. Haffajee, "Twitter and the Rest of Social Media are a Rising Threat to Media Freedom and I am Part of Their Road-Kill," *Daily Maverick*, https://www.dailymaverick.co.za/article/2019-08-06-twitter-and-the-rest-of-social-media-are-a-rising-threat-to-media-freedom-and-i-am-part-of-their-roadkill, accessed 6.09.2019.
160. P. du Toit, "Malema, the EFF and a History of Violence," https://www.news24.com/Analysis/analysis-malema-the-eff-and-a-history-of-violence-20190805, accessed 6.09.2019.
161. Haffajee, "Twitter and the Rest of Social Media."
162. Du Toit, "Malema, the EFF and a History of Violence."
163. "Press Council of South Africa Annual General Meeting," statement, 6.09.2019.
164. M. Mahlase, "Letter From Our Chairperson, SANEF and Five Others v EFF and Another – Setting the Record Straight," statement, 14.09.2019.
165. The full set of court papers is available on https://sanef.org.za/sanef-vs-eff-court-papers-2/.
166. D. McLeod, "Censored: How the M&G Got Taken Down," https://techcentral.co.za/sa-scores-highly-for-internet-freedom-but-worrying-signs-emerge/93822/, accessed 5.11.2019; © 2019 NewsCentral Media, with additional reporting by Kiley Roache, © 2019 Bloomberg LP.
167. "SANEF Calls for EFF to Include a diversity of Journalists at its Elective Conference," statement, 13.12.2019.

168. B. Brkic, "Statement from Daily Maverick Editor-in-Chief Branko Brkic on EFF Congress and Important Media Freedom Issues," https://sanef.org.za/a-statement-from-daily-maverick-editor-in-chief-branko-brkic-on-eff-congress-and-important-media-freedom-issues/, 14.12.2019.

169. P. Croucamp, "Dié Media Deel in Skuld van Skade wat aan Persvryheid Gedoen is" ("These Media Also Are Guilty regarding Damage Done to Press Freedom"), *Vrye Weekblad*, https://www.vryeweekblad.com/menings-en-debat/2019-12-19-di-media-deel-in-skuld-van-skade-wat-aan-persvryheid-gedoen-is/, 19.12.2019.

170. T. Gqubule-Mbeki and A. Harber, "Statement on Court Victory: Thandeka Gqubule-Mbeki and Anton Harber vs EFF and Others," statement, 24 January 2020.

171. "SANEF Congratulate Professor Anton Harber and Thandeka Gqubule Mbeki For Winning the Defamation Case Against The EFF," statement, 24.01.2020.

172. "SANEF Concerned About the Ongoing Escalation in Death Threats & Harassment of Journalists on Social Media," statement, 28.01.2020.

173. "SANEF Concerned By the Arrest of a Journalist in Paarl," statement, 28.01.2020.

174. G. Nicholson, "Former SARS Executive Slams Press Over Rogue Unit," *Daily Mail*, https://www.dailymaverick.co.za/article/2020-01-31-former-sars-executive-slams-press-over-rogue-unit-stories/, accessed 31.01.2020.

175. M. Merten, "Strong-Arm Security at Parliament: Questions Unanswered After String of Bully-Boy Incidents," *Daily Maverick*, https://www.dailymaverick.co.za/article/2020-03-03-strong-arm-security-at-parliament-questions-unanswered-after-string-of-bully-boy-incidents/, accessed 3.03.2020.

176. R. Davis, "Former SABC CEO Claims Hlaudi Motsoeneng Served MultiChoice's Interests on Digital Migration," *Daily Maverick*, https://www.dailymaverick.co.za/article/2020-02-27-former-sabc-ceo-claims-hlaudi-motsoeneng-served-multichoices-interests-on-digital-migration/, accessed 27.02.2020.

177. "#GuptaLeaks: MultiChoice Paid the Guptas Millions," *News24*, amaBhungane, Scorpio, https://www.dailymaverick.co.za/article/2017-11-24-guptaleaks-multichoice-paid-the-guptas-millions/, accessed 27.03.2020.

178. Davis, "Former SABC CEO Claims Hlaudi Motsoeneng".

179. B. Brkic, Newsletter, *Daily Maverick*, 17.03.2020.

180. M. Mahlale, SANEF/MMA Press Freedom Day Webinar, 3.05.2020.

181. Brkic, Newsletter.

182. W. Jordaan, "*Die Burger* Sal Aanhou Verskyn" ("*Die Burger* Will Continue to be Published"), Die Burger, March 27, 2020, p. 3; H. Loubser, "Bly Op Hoogte Met Netwerk24" ("Stay on Track With Netwerk24"), *Die Burger*, March 27, 2020, p. 3.

183. Brkic, Newsletter.

184. "SANEF Welcomes Inclusion of Media as Emergency Workers But Seeks Clarity on Some Details," statement, 24.03.2020.

185. K. Magrobi, "Solidarity to Women From QW+," statement via SANEF, 24.03.2020.

186. R. Poplak, "#Lockdown: The Long Haul has Kicked Off, and the Virus will Determine the Timeline," *Daily Maverick*, https://www.dailymaverick.co.za/article/2020-03-27-lockdown-the-long-haul-has-kicked-off-and-the-virus-will-determine-the-timeline/, 27.03.2020.

187. F. Haffajee, "South Africa 'Headed Into a Deep Structural Depression' – Busa," *Daily Maverick*, https://www.dailymaverick.co.za/article/2020-03-30-south-africa-headed-into-a-deep-structural-depression-busa/, accessed 30.03.2020.

188. P. du Toit, "Reality Bites as Ramaphosa and Government's Lack of Firepower Becomes Clear," *News24*, https://www.news24.com/Analysis/first-take-reality-bites-as-ramaphosa-and-governments-lack-of-firepower-becomes-clear-20200330, accessed 30.03.2020.

189. SANEF CPJ Statement, https://cpj.org/2020/03/cpj-launches-resources-on-covid-19s-impact-on-jour.php, 7.03.2020.

190. C. Aaron, "Journalism Needs a Stimulus. Here's What it Should Look Like," CJR, https://www.cjr.org/analysis/journalism-stimulus.php?ct=t(Top_Stories_CJR_new_Feb_6_1_25_2017_COPY_01)&mc_cid=80414925bb&mc_eid=7cba813f45, accessed 24.03.2020.
191. Stunde Null, https://www.dw.com/en/stunde-null-zero-hour/av-18438711https://www.dw.com/en/stunde-null-zero-hour/av-18438711; https://www.britannica.com/topic/Stunde-Null, accessed 28.03.2020.
192. Aaron, "Journalism Needs a Stimulus."
193. Free Press, https://www.freepress.net/, accessed 28.03.2020.
194. R. Rose, *Financial Mail*, emailed letter to readers, 2.04.2020.
195. RSF, email, received 2.04.2020.
196. F. Haffajee, "Another Save the Wail for the Mail – 32 Years On," *Daily Maverick*, https://www.dailymaverick.co.za/article/2020-04-03-another-save-the-wail-for-the-mail-32-years-on/, accessed 3.04.2020.
197. SANEF press release, 4.04.2020
198. "Associated Media Publishers: The End of an Era," 30.04.2020.
199. SANEF press release, 4.04.2020.
200. M. Hunter and C. Thakur, "Advocacy: New Privacy Rules for Covid-19 Tracking a Step in the Right Direction, But …," *News24*, https://www.news24.com/Columnists/GuestColumn/advocacy-new-privacy-rules-for-covid-19-tracking-a-step-in-the-right-direction-but-20200404-2, accessed 4.04.2020.
201. SANEF press release, 6.04.2020.
202. Aaron, "Journalism Needs a Stimulus."
203. S. Skenjana, "Moody's downgraded SA. What happens now?," *Fin24*, accessed 28.03.2020.
204. M. Mkhabela, "Beware the Coronavirus Threats to our Constitution," *News24*, https://www.news24.com/Columnists/Mpumelelo_Mkhabela/mpumelelo-mkhabela-beware-the-coronavirus-risks-to-our-constitution-20200326, accessed 26.03.2020.
205. J. Simon, "COVID-19 is Spawning a Global Press-Freedom Crackdown," *CJR*, https://www.cjr.org/analysis/coronavirus-press-freedom-crackdown.php, accessed 25.03.2020.
206. Safety Advisory, CPJ, https://cpj.org/2020/02/cpj-safety-advisory-covering-the-coronavirus-outbr.php, accessed 28.03.2020.
207. Simon, "COVID-19 is Spawning a Global Press-Freedom Crackdown."
208. RSF, 2020 World Press Freedom Index, "Entering a Decisive Decade for Journalism, Exacerbated by Coronavirus," press release, 21.04.2020.
209. Ranking, https://rsf.org/en/ranking, accessed 13.05.2020.
210. RSF, 2020 World Press Freedom Index.
211. SANEF, "Journalism Under Severe Financial Threat," email, 3.05.2020.
212. "Associated Media Publishers: The End of an Era," 30.04.2020.
213. "Caxton Withdraws From Magazine Publishing," *Moneyweb*, https://www.moneyweb.co.za/news/companies-and-deals/caxton-withdraws-from-magazine-publishing/, accessed 5.05.2020.
214. "Coronavirus and Press Freedom: Sanef Sounds the Alarm," *News24*, accessed 3.05.2020.
215. M. Meiring, Joernalistiek in dié Tye Verdien Agting (Journalism in These Times Deserves Respect), *Die Burger*, March 24, 2020, p. 10.

Selected Sources

Aaron, C., "Journalism Needs a Stimulus. Here's What is Should Look Like," CJR, March 24, 2020, https://www.cjr.org/analysis/journalism-stimulus.php?ct=t(Top_Stories_CJR_new_Feb_6_1_25_2017_COPY_01)&mc_cid=80414925bb&mc_eid=7cba813f45.

Adam, H., "The Political Sociology of South Africa: A Pragmatic Race Oligarchy," in ed. I. Robertson and P. Whitten , P., eds., *Race and Politics in South Africa* (New Brunswick: Transaction Books, 1978).

Addison, G., Review of "Mass Media for the 1990s," *Communicare* 12,1.

Adhikari, M., *Straatpraatjes (Street Talk)* (Cape Town: Van Schaik, 1996).

Adhikari, M., "You Have the Right to Know. *South* 1987-1994," in L. Switzer and M. Adhikari, eds., *South Africa's Resistance Press. Alternative Voices in the last Generation under Apartheid* (Ohio: Ohio University Center for International Studies, 2000).

Ainslie, R., *The Press in Africa: Communications Past and Present* (New York: Walker, 1966).

Aldaheff, V., *A Newspaper History of South Africa* (Cape Town: Don Nelson, 1990).

Altschull, J.H., *From Milton to McLuhan* (New York and London: Longman, 1990).

Amner, R., "Getting Radio Active," *Leading Edge*, 7 (Cape Town: Independent Development Trust).

ANC 52nd National Conference 2007, "Resolutions," http://www.anc.org.za/index.html.

ANC, Discussion Document: Media Diversity and Ownership, National General Council, Durban, 2010.

ANC Today, http://anctoday.org.za/.

"Associated Media Publishers: The End of an Era," AMP Media release, 30.04.2020.

Babbie, E.R., *The Basics of Social Research* (6th ed.) (Belmont: Wadsworth, 2016).

Banda, F., "The Media in Africa," in P.J. Fourie, ed., *Media Studies Volume 1: Media History, Media and Society* (Wetton: Juta, 2007).

Barker, J.M., "Is No Policy a Policy Goal?" in K. Tomaselli and H. Dunn eds., *Media, Democracy and Renewal in Southern Africa* (Colorado Springs: International Academic Publishers, 2001).

Barratt, E., "History of the South African National Editors' Forum" (Unpublished document, Johannesburg, 2003).

Barratt, E., "Choosing to be Part of the Story: The Participation of the South African National Editors' Forum in the Democratisation Process" (M.Phil. thesis, Stellenbosch University, 2006).

Bell, E., "Keeping a Free and Fair Press is One of the Defining Political Issues of our Age", *The Guardian Online*, May 13, 2018, https://www.theguardian.com/media/commentisfree/2018/may/13/keeping-a-free-and-fair-press-is-one-of-the-defining-political-issues-of-our-age.

Berger, G., "Towards an Analysis of the SA Media and Transformation, 1994–99," *Transformation* 38 (1999).

Berger, G., "Foreword," in L. Switzer and M. Adhikari, eds., *South Africa's Resistance Press. Alternative Voices in the Last Generation under Apartheid* (Ohio: Ohio University Center for International Studies, 2000).

Berger, G., "Key Documents for African Media: A Briefing for Sanef," March, 2003.

Berger, G., "Best Practice in Media Self-Regulation," *Ecquid Novi* 32,2 (2011). https://doi.org/10.1080/02560054.2011.578876

Berger, G., "UNESCO's Safety of Journalists' Agenda: What Impact?" *Australia Journalism Review* 40,2.

Berger, G., "De-Racialization, Democracy and Development: Transformation of the South African Media 1994–2000," in. K. Tomaselli, and H. Dunn, eds., *Media, Democracy and Renewal in Southern Africa* (Colorado Springs: International Academic Publishers, 2001).

Berger, G., "More Media for Southern Africa? The Place of Politics, Economics and Convergence in Developing Media Density," *Critical Arts* 18,1 (2004). https://doi.org/10.1080/02560240485310041

Berger, G., "For Media, SABC is the Frontline for Preventing Political Creep," *Mail & Guardian Online*, 2009, www.mg.co.za/article/2009-05-14-for-media-sabc-is-the-frontline-preventing-political-creep.

Bhardwaj, V., "The Good and the Bad of the 'Better' Secrecy Bill," *M&G*, October 25–31, 2013.

Bird, W., "Learning From Our Mistakes," *Rhodes Journalism Review*, 24 (2004).

Blankson, I.A., "Media Independence and Pluralism in Africa: Opportunities and Challenges of Democratization and Liberalization," in I.A. Blankson and P.D. Murphy, eds., *Negotiating Democracy: Media Transformation in Emerging Democracies* (Albany: SUNY Press, 2007).

Boloka, M., "Diversity Goes Global," *Rhodes Journalism Review*, 24 (2004). https://doi.org/10.3368/ajs.24.1.55

Booyens, B., "Om nie Blindelings aan te Neuk na Selfvernietiging nie" ("Not to Blindly Stumble on to Self-Destruction"), in L. Rabe, ed., *#Journalism4.0 @ Stellenbosch* (Stellenbosch: AfricanSunMedia, 2018).

Bosman, D.B., *Oor die Ontstaan van Afrikaans* (Publisher unknown, 1923).

Bosman, F.C.L. *Hollandse Joernalistiek in Suid-Afrika gedurende die 19de Eeu* (*Dutch Journalism in South Africa during the 19th Century*) (Reprints from *Ons Land*, 1930).

Breytenbach, M.M., "The Manipulation of Public Opinion by State Censorship of the Media in South Africa (1974–1994)" (D.Phil. diss., Stellenbosch University, 1997).

Brkic, B., "Statement from Daily Maverick Editor-in-Chief Branko Brkic on EFF Congress and Important Media Freedom Issues," December 14, 2019, https://sanef.org.za/a-statement-from-daily-maverick-editor-in-chief-branko-brkic-on-eff-congress-and-important-media-freedom-issues/.

Brkic, B., Newsletter, *Daily Maverick*, March 17, 2020.

Buchinger, C., "History of Censorship in South Africa" (M.Phil. assignment, Stellenbosch University, 2004).

Burke, J., "Cyril Ramaphosa is Cautious, But he Must Waste no Time Reforming South Africa," *The Guardian*, May 26, 2019, https://www.theguardian.com/world/2019/may/26/cyril-ramaphosa-must-waste-no-time-reforming-south-africa-election?CMP=Share_iOSApp_Other.

Büttner, H. and Claassen, G., *Goed om te Weet (Good to Know)* (Cape Town: Tafelberg, 2010).

Calland, R., *The First Five Years: A Review of South Africa's Democratic Parliament* (Cape Town: Idasa, 1999).

"Caxton Withdraws from Magazine Publishing," Moneyweb, https://www.moneyweb.co.za/news/companies-and-deals/caxton-withdraws-from-magazine-publishing/.

Chimutengwende, C.C., *South Africa: The Press and Politics of Liberation* (London, Barbican Books, 1978).

Christians, C. and Nordenstreng, K., "Social Responsibility Worldwide," *Journal of Mass Media Ethics* 19,1 (2004). https://doi.org/10.1207/s15327728jmme1901_2

Cillié, P.J., "Kruisvaarders vir 'n Idee" ("Crusaders for an Idea"), *Jaar van die Koerant 1988* (*Year of the Newspaper 1988*), supplement to Naspers dailies, August 31, 1988.

Claassen, G.N., "Magazines. Life's Own Story," in. A.S. de Beer, ed., *Mass Media Towards the Millennium* (Pretoria: Van Schaik, 1998).

Claassen, G., "Breaking the Mold of Political Subservience. *Vrye Weekblad* and the Afrikaans Alternative Press," in L. Switzer and M. Adhikari, eds., *South Africa's Resistance Press. Alternative Voices in the Last Generation under Apartheid* (Ohio: Ohio University Center for International Studies, 2000).

Coburn, M. and Tserema, T., "Media Monopolies and the Black Press," *Stellenbosch Journalism Insight*, 1,1.

Coetzee, A., *Die Opkoms van die Afrikaanse Kultuurgedagte aan die Rand (The Rise of Afrikaans Cultural Thinking on the Rand)* (Publisher unknown, 1938).

"Coronavirus and Press Freedom: Sanef Sounds the Alarm," *News24*, May 3, 2020.

Couzens, T.J., "A Short History of the *World* and Other Black South African Newspapers" (Paper, University of the Witwatersrand, Johannesburg, 1977).

Croucamp, P., "Dié Media Deel in Skuld van Skade wat aan Persvryheid Gedoen is" ("These Media also are Guilty of What Was Done to Press Freedom"), *Vrye Weekblad*, December 19, 2019, https://www.vryeweekblad.com/menings-en-debat/2019-12-19-di-media-deel-in-skuld-van-skade-wat-aan-persvryheid-gedoen-is/.

Crwys-Williams, J., *South African Despatches. Two Centuries of the Best in South African Journalism* (Johannesburg: Ashanti, 1989).

Currie, W., "The People Shall Broadcast: The Battle for the Airwaves," in P.E. Louw, ed., *South African Media Policy: Debates of the 1990s* (Bellville: Anthropos; 1993).

Cutten, T.E.G., *A History of the Press in South Africa* (Cape Town: NUSAS, 1935).

Daniels, G., "The ANC's Hysterical Gaze on the Media," *The Media Online*, January, 2013.

Daniels, G., A Reflection on the Media: Consolidation and Convergence – or Shrivelling and Sinking? *Daily Maverick*, October 17, 2018, https://www.dailymaverick.co.za/article/2018-10-17-a-reflection-on-the-media-consolidation-and-convergence-or-shrivelling-and-sinking/#.W8f59StWyWs.email.

Dasnois, A., and C. Whitfield, *Paper Tiger. Iqbal Survé and the Downfall of Independent Newspapers* (Cape Town: Tafelberg, 2019).

Davis, R., "Former SABC CEO Claims Hlaudi Motsoeneng Served MultiChoice's Interests on Digital Migration," *Daily Maverick*, February 27, 2020, https://www.dailymaverick.co.za/article/2020-02-27-former-sabc-ceo-claims-hlaudi-motsoeneng-served-multichoices-interests-on-digital-migration/.

De Beer, A.S., "Mass Communication in Society. Pervasive Messages and Images of our Time," in A.S. de Beer, ed., *Mass Media Towards the Millennium* (Pretoria: Van Schaik, 1998).

De Beer A. and Steyn, E., "The National Party and the Media: A Special Kind of Symbiosis," in P.E. Louw, ed., *South African Media Policy: Debates of the 1990s* (Bellville: Anthropos, 1993).

De Beer, A.S. and Steyn, E., "Sanef's South African National Journalism Skills Audit: An Introduction and the Sanef Report regarding the Media Industry," *Ecquid Novi* 23,1 (2002). https://doi.org/10.1080/02560054.2002.10798725

"Declaration of Table Mountain," *Rhodes Journalism Review*, 27 (2007).

De Kock, W., *A Manner of Speaking: The Origins of the Press in South Africa* (Cape Town: Saayman & Weber, 1982).

De Kock, W., *'n Wyse van Spreke: Die Ontstaan van die Pers in Suid-Afrika* (Cape Town: Saayman & Weber, 1983).

De Villiers, J., "Geskiedeniswetenskap en die Nuwe Suid-Afrika – Moet die Suid-Afrikaanse Geskiedenis Herskryf Word?" ("Historical Science and the New South Africa – Should the South African History be Rewritten?") *Tydskrif vir Geesteswetenskappe (Journal for the Humanities)* 52,2 (2012).

De Villiers, J., "Die Kaapse Samelewing Onder Britse Bestuur, 1806–1834" ("Cape Society under British Government, 1806–1834"), in F. Pretorius, ed., *Geskiedenis van Suid-Afrika (History of South Africa)* (Cape Town: Tafelberg, 2012).

De Vos, P., "Would Media Appeals Tribunal be Constitutional?" www.constitutionallyspeaking.co.za, April 7, 2015.

Diederichs, P., "Newspapers. The Fourth Estate: A Cornerstone of Democracy," in A.S. de Beer, ed., *Mass Media for the Nineties: The South African Handbook of Mass Communication* (Pretoria: Van Schaik, 1993).

Diederichs, P. and De Beer, A.S., "Newspapers. The Fourth Estate: A Cornerstone of Democracy," in A.S. de Beer, ed., *Mass Communication Towards the Millennium* (Pretoria: Van Schaik, 1998).

Driver, D., "Control of the Black Mind is the Main Aim of Censorship," *South African Outlook* (June 1980).

Dugard, J., "Human Rights and the South African Legal Order" (Princeton NJ: Princeton University Press, 1978).

Duncan, J., "Talk Left, Act Right: What Constitutes Transformation in Southern African Media?" in K. Tomaselli K. and H. Dunn, eds., *Media, Democracy and Renewal in Southern*

Africa (Colorado Springs: International Academic Publishers, 2001). https://doi.
org/10.1080/02500160008537912

Duncan, J., "Another Journalism is Possible: Critical Challenges for the Media in South Africa,"
Harold Wolpe Memorial Lecture, University of KwaZulu-Natal, Durban, 2003.

Duncan, J., "Executive Overstretch: South African Broadcasting Independence and Accountability
under Thabo Mbeki," *Communicatio*, 34,1 (2008). https://doi.org/10.1080/02500160802144504

Du Pisani, K., "BJ Vorster en Afsonderlike Ontwikkeling" (BJ Vorster and Separate Development), in
F. Pretorius, ed., *Geskiedenis van Suid-Afrika* (*History of South Africa*) (Cape Town: Tafelberg, 2012).

Du Plessis, J.H.O., "The Rise of the Press in South Africa," *Cape Times*, May 9, 1919.

Du Plessis, J.H.O., "Lord Charles Somerset and the Press," *Cape Times*, May 10, 1929.

Du Plessis, J.H.O., "Die Afrikaanse Pers. 'n Studie van die Ontstaan, Ontwikkeling en Rol van die
Hollands-Afrikaanse Pers as Sosiale Instelling" ("The Afrikaans Press. A Study of the Origin,
Development and Role of the Dutch Afrikaans Press as Social Institution") (Ph.D. diss.,
Stellenbosch University, 1943).

Du Plessis, T., "Theunissen Super Vee," in L. Rabe, ed., *'n Ton van 'n Man (A Tonne of a Man)*
(Cape Town: Tafelberg, 2007).

Du Plessis, T., Twenty Years after Democracy (2014).

Du Plessis, T., "History Symposium," Suid-Afrikaanse Akademie vir Wetenskap en Kuns
(South African Academy for Science and the Arts), 2016.

Du Preez, M., "A New Era of Modern Leadership Dawned under Ramaphosa," January 16, 2018,
https://www.news24.com/Columnists/MaxduPreez/a-new-era-of-modern-leadership-has-
dawned-under-ramaphosa-20180116.

Du Preez, M., "ANN7 Does not Deserve our Activism," *News24*, February 6, 2018, https://www.
news24.com/Columnists/MaxduPreez/ann7-does-not-deserve-our-activism-20180206.

Du Preez, M., "Zuma's Defiant Exit Signifies 9 of SA's Darkest Years," *News24*, February 13, 2018,
https://www.news24.com/Columnists/MaxduPreez/zumas-defiant-exit-signifies-end-to-9-of-sas-
darkest-years-20180213.

Du Preez, M., "Time to Stop Aiding and Abetting the EFF's Assault on Democracy," *News24*,
November 27, 2018, https://www.news24.com/Columnists/MaxduPreez/time-to-stop-aiding-
and-abetting-the-effs-assault-on-democracy-20181127.

Du Preez Scholtz, J., *Die Afrikaner en Sy Taal (The Afrikaner and His Language)* (Cape Town:
Nasou, n.d.).

Du Preez, S., *Avonture in Angola. Die Verhaal van Suid-Afrika se Soldate in Angola 1975–1976 (Adventures
in Angola. The Story of South Africa's Soldiers in Angola 1976–1976)* (Pretoria: Van Schaik, 1989).

Du Toit, P., "Malema, the EFF and a History of Violence," *News24*, August 5, 2019, https://www.
news24.com/Analysis/analysis-malema-the-eff-and-a-history-of-violence-20190805.

Du Toit, P., "Reality Bites as Ramaphosa and Government's Lack of Firepower Becomes Clear,"
News24, March 30, 2020, https://www.news24.com/Analysis/first-take-reality-bites-as-
ramaphosa-and-governments-lack-of-firepower-becomes-clear-20200330.

Esterhuyse, W., *Eindstryd (Endgame)* (Cape Town: Tafelberg, 2012).

Faure, C., "Ondersoekende Joernalistiek en Sosiale Verandering: 'n Ontleding en Evaluering van die
Agendastellingsrol van *Vrye Weekblad*" (D.Litt. et Phil. Diss., UNISA, Pretoria, 1995).

Firth, R., "Dear FPB, Free Our Kids," *TechCentral*, February 6, 2018, https://techcentral.co.za/dear-fpb-
free-kids/79459/.

Fourie, P.J., "Nederlandstalige en Afrikaanstalige Media," Internationale Colloquium Nederlands
in de Wereld ("Dutch and Afrikaans Language Media," International Colloquium Dutch in the
World) (Brussels: Vrije Universiteit Brussel Press, 1994).

Fourie, P.J., "Afrikaans en die Media" ("Afrikaans and the Media"), *Ecquid Novi* 15,2 (1994). https://doi.
org/10.1080/02560054.1994.9653123

Fourie, P.J., "The Role and Functions of the Media: Functionalism," in P.J. Fourie, ed., *Media Studies.
Volume 1: Institutions, Theories and Issues* (Lansdowne: Juta, 2001).

Fourie, P.J., "Rethinking the Role of the Media in South Africa," *Communicare* 21,1 (2002).

Fourie, P.J., "'n Terugkeer na die Onderdrukking van Vryheid van Spraak? Ooreenkomste Tussen die Apartheidsregering(s) en die ANC se Optrede teen die Media" ("A Return to the Repression of Freedom of Speech? Similarities Between the Apartheid Government(s) and the ANC's Actions Against the Media"), *Suid-Afrikaanse Tydskrif vir Geesteswetenskappe (South African Journal of Humanities)* 49,1 (2009).

Free, Fair and Open. South African Media in the Transition to Democracy. Papers, Recommendations and Resolutions: Part 1 (Johannesburg: ANC Campaign for Open Media, 1992).

Froneman, J., "Sluiting van Koerante Geen Doodsklok vir Afrikaanse Joernalistiek" ("Closure of Newspaper no Death-Knell for Afrikaans Journalism"), *Ecquid Novi* 14,1 (1993). https://doi.org/10.1080/02560054.1993.9653095

Gardner, P., "Historical Analysis," in V. Jupp, ed., *The Sage Dictionary of Social Research Methods* (London: Sage, 2006).

Geertsema, M., "'n Historiese Oorsig oor die Ontstaan en Ontwikkeling van die Swart Pers in Suid-Afrika" ("An Historical Overview of the Founding and Development of the Black Press in South Africa") (M.A. thesis, NWU, 1993).

Geertz, C., "Thick Description: Toward an Interpretive Theory of Culture," in C. Geertz, ed., *The Interpretation of Cultures: Selected Essays* (London: Fontana Press, 1993).

Gerber, J., "Gewone Mense Moet Betoog" ("Ordinary People Must Protest"), *Die Burger*, February 18, 2015.

Gerber, J., "Reguleer Gedrukte Media, Vra Minister" ("Regulate Print Media, Asks Minister"), *Die Burger*, April 22, 2015.

Gerber, J., "Dodgy Contracts at 'Rotten' Media Agency," *News24*, September 14, 2017, https://www.news24.com/SouthAfrica/News/dodgy-contracts-at-rotten-media-agency-20170914.

Gerber, J., "Liphoko no Longer Acting CEO at Media Diversity Agency," *News24*, September 29, 2017, https://www.news24.com/SouthAfrica/News/liphoko-no-longer-acting-ceo-at-media-diversity-agency-20170929.

Gerber, J., "New Acting CEO for Media Development and Diversity Agency," *News24*, December 22, 2017, https://www.news24.com/SouthAfrica/News/new-acting-ceo-for-media-development-and-diversity-agency-20171222.

Gevisser, M., "Ken Owen: SA's Last Great White Editor," *M&G*, June 28, 1996, https://mg.co.za/article/1996-06-28-ken-owen-outgoing-editor-of-the-sunday-times-in.

Giffard, C.A., "Media Trends in South Africa," paper presented at the "Road Ahead Conference" (Grahamstown: Rhodes University, 1978).

Giliomee H. and Mbenga, B., *New History of South Africa* (Cape Town: Tafelberg, 2007).

Gordimer, N., "New Forms of Strategy – No Change of Heart," *Critical Arts*, 1 (1980). https://doi.org/10.1080/02560048008559033

Gqubule-Mbeki T. and Harber, A., "Statement on Court Victory: Thandeka Gqubule-Mbeki and Anton Harber vs EFF and Others," statement, January 24, 2020.

Greenslade, R., *Press Gang: How Newspapers Make Profits From Propaganda* (London: Pan Books, 2004).

Grobler, G., "Staatsvorming en Stryd, 1850–1900" ("State Formation and Struggle, 1850–1900"), in F. Pretorius, ed., *Geskiedenis van Suid-Afrika Vandag (History of South Africa Today)* (Cape Town: Tafelberg, 2012).

Grobler, J., "Swart Verset Teen Apartheid, 1950's–1980's" ("Black Opposition Against Apartheid, 1950s–1980s"), in F. Pretorius, ed., *Geskiedenis van Suid-Afrika (History of South* Africa) (Cape Town: Tafelberg, 2012).

Gumede, W.M., *Thabo Mbeki and the Battle for the Soul of the ANC* (Cape Town: Zebra Press, 2005).

"#GuptaLeaks: MultiChoice Paid the Guptas Millions," *Daily Maverick*, November 24, 2017, https://www.dailymaverick.co.za/article/2017-11-24-guptaleaks-multichoice-paid-the-guptas-millions/.

Gurevitch, M. and Blumler, J.G., "State of the Art of Comparative Political Communication Research: Poised for Maturity?" in F. Esser and B. Pfetsch, eds., *Comparing Political Communication* (Cambridge: Cambridge University Press, 2004). https://doi.org/10.1017/CBO9780511606991.015

Hachten, W., *Muffled Drums: The News Media in Africa* (Ames: Iowa State University Press, 1971).

Hachten W.A. and Giffard, C.A., *Total Onslaught. The South African Press under Attack* (Johannesburg: Macmillan, 1984).

Hadland, A., "The Political Economy of the South African Press, 1920–50," (M.A. Thesis, Oxford University, 1991).

Hadland, A., "The South African Print Media, 1994–2004: An Application and Critique of Comparative Media Systems Theory" (D.Phil. diss., University of Cape Town, 2007).

Hadland, A., "State-Media Relations in Post-Apartheid South Africa: An Application of Comparative Media Systems Theory," *Communicare* 26,2 (2007).

Hadland, A., "The Enemy Without: How the State will Shape the Future of Journalism" (Cardiff: Unpublished paper presented at the Future of Journalism Conference, 2009).

Hadland A. and Thorne, K., *The People's Voice: The Development and Current State of the South African Small Media Sector* (Commissioned by the MDDA, HSRC, 2004).

Haffajee, F., "The Gupta Fake News Factory and Me," *HuffPost SA*, June 6, 2017, https://www.huffingtonpost.co.uk/2017/06/05/ferial-haffajee-the-gupta-fake-news-factory-and-me_a_22126282/.

Haffajee, F., "An Army of Trolls Marches on in Mindless Violence – and Nobody is Stopping Them," *Daily Maverick*, July 7, 2019, https://www.dailymaverick.co.za/article/2019-03-07-an-army-of-trolls-marches-on-in-mindless-violence-and-nobody-is-stopping-them/.

Haffajee, F., "Twitter and the Rest of Social Media are a Rising Threat to Media Freedom and I am Part of their Road-Kill," *Daily Maverick*, August 6, 2019, https://www.dailymaverick.co.za/article/2019-08-06-twitter-and-the-rest-of-social-media-are-a-rising-threat-to-media-freedom-and-i-am-part-of-their-roadkill.

Haffajee, F., "South Africa 'Headed into a Deep Structural Depression – Busa," *Daily Maverick*, March 30, 2020, https://www.dailymaverick.co.za/article/2020-03-30-south-africa-headed-into-a-deep-structural-depression-busa/.

Haffajee, F., "Another Save the Wail for the Mail – 32 Years On," *Daily Maverick*, April 3, 2020, https://www.dailymaverick.co.za/article/2020-04-03-another-save-the-wail-for-the-mail-32-years-on/.

Hallin D.C. and Mancini, P, *Comparing Media Systems: Three Models of Media and Politics* (Cambridge: Cambridge University Press, 2004). https://doi.org/10.1017/CBO9780511790867

Harber, A., "SABC Should Encourage Openness, Not Obeisance to Political Will," *Cape Argus*, August 3, 1999.

Harber, A., "How Investigative Journalists Helped Turn the Tide Against Corruption in South Africa," The Conversation, March 15, 2018, https://theconversation.com/how-investigative-journalists-helped-turn-the-tide-against-corruption-in-south-africa-93434.

Harmse, W., *SABC 1936 – 1995. Still a Key Player ... or an Endangered Species?* (Naledi, 2018).

Hattingh, D.J., "'n Wysgerige Ondersoek na die Probleem van Persvryheid" ("A Philosophical Investigation into the Problem of Press Freedom") (Ph.D. diss., Potchefstroom University for Christian Higher Education, 1969).

Heard, A.H., *The Cape of Storms. A Personal History of the Crisis in South Africa* (Fayetteville: University of Arkansas Press, 1990).

Heard, J., "'n Uur wat Suid-Afrika in die Skande Steek" ("An Hour that Disgraced South Africa"), *Die Burger*, February 17, 2015.

Hepple, A., *Censorship and Press Control in South Africa* (Johannesburg: Published by author, 1960).

Hepple, A., *Press under Apartheid* (London: International Defence Aid, 1974).

Hofmeyr, J.H., *Het Leven van Jan Hendrik Hofmeyr (The Life of Jan Hendrik Hofmeyr)* (Publisher unknown, 1913).

Horwitz, R., *Communication and Democratic Reform in South Africa* (Cambridge: Cambridge University Press, 2001). https://doi.org/10.1017/CBO9780511510151

Hunter, M., "Securocrats Choke Flow of Information," *M&G*, September 12–18, 2004.

Hunter, Q., Twitter account, 2019, https://twitter.com/QaanitahHunter/status/1134874308210253824.

Jacobs, S., "Tensions of a Free Press: South Africa After Apartheid," (Harvard: Research Paper R-22, Joan Shorenstein Center on the Press, Politics and Public Policy, 1999).

Jacobs, S., "Public Sphere, Power and Democratic Politics: Media and Policy Debates in Post-Apartheid South Africa (Ph.D. diss., Birkbeck College, University of London, 2004).

Jackson, G.S., *Breaking Story: The South African Press* (Colorado: Westview Press, 1993).

Johnson, S., "An Historical Overview of the Black Press," in K. Tomaselli and P.E. Louw, eds., *The Alternative Press in South Africa* (Bellville: Anthropos, 1991).

Johnston, A., "The African National Congress, the Print Media and the Development of Mediated Politics in South Africa," *Critical Arts* 19,1&2 (2005). https://doi.org/10.1080/02560040585310031

Jones, A., "New Leaked Reports Show Why Train Security has Collapsed," GroundUp, October 30 2019, https://www.groundup.org.za/article/new-leaked-reports-show-why-train-security-has-collapsed/.

Jordaan, W. "*Die Burger* Sal Aanhou Verskyn" ("*Die Burger* Will Continue to be Published"), *Die Burger*, March 27, 2020.

Kalane, L., *The Chapter We Wrote* (Johannesburg and Cape Town: Jonathan Ball, 2018).

Kelsey, S., *The Newspaperman's Guide to the Law* (Butterworth & Co, 1982).

Keyser, G., "En die Jare Daarna," ("And the Years Thereafter"), Supplement, *Jaar van die Koerant (Year of the Newspaper)*, August 31, 1988.

Krige, F., *The SABC 8* (Johannesburg: Penguin Random House South Africa, 2019).

Krüger, F., "East Cape News Agencies Reporting on a Black Hole," in L. Switzer and M. Adhikari, eds., *South Africa's Resistance Press. Alternative Voices in the Last Generation under Apartheid* (Ohio: Ohio University Center for International Studies, 2000).

Krüger, F., "Media Courts of Honour: Self-Regulatory Councils in Southern Africa and Elsewhere," (FES Media Africa Series, 2009).

Krüger, F., "The Only Guarantee of Freedom is Freedom", *M&G*, November 2–8, 2012.

Lambert, J., "Engelssprekende Suid-Afrikaners: Onseker van hul Identiteit" ("English-Speaking South Africans: Unsure of their Identity"), in F. Pretorius, ed., *Geskiedenis van Suid-Afrika (History of South Africa)* (Cape Town: Tafelberg, 2012).

Lamble, S., "Documenting the Methodology of Journalism," *Australian Journalism Review* 26,1 (2004).

Lamprecht, M. and Breytenbach, J., "Spioene Woel in Parlement" (Spies Active in Parliament"), *Die Burger*, February 18, 2015.

Le Roux, N.J., *WA Hofmeyr. Sy Werk en Waarde (WA Hofmeyr. His Work and Value)* (Cape Town, Bloemfontein, Johannesburg: Nasionale Boekhandel, 1953).

Letsoala, M., "ANC: The Media is Ganging Up on Us," *M&G*, August 18, 2015, https://mg.co.za/article/2015-08-18-anc-the-media-is-ganging-up-on-us/.

Lewin Robinson, A.M., *None Daring to Make Us Afraid. A Study of English Periodical Literature in the Cape Colony from its Beginnings in 1824 to 1835* (Cape Town: Maskew Miller, 1962).

Limb, P., "Representing the Labouring Classes. African Workers in the African Nationalist Press, 1900–1960," in L. Switzer and M. Adhikari, eds., *South Africa's Resistance Press. Alternative Voices in the Last Generation under Apartheid* (Ohio: Ohio University Center for International Studies, 2000).

Loubser, H., "Bly op Hoogte met Netwerk24" ("Stay on Track with Netwerk24"), *Die Burger*, March 27, 2020.

Louw, P.E., "The Growth of Monopoly Control in the South African Press," in P.E. Louw, ed., *South African Media Policy: Debates of the 1990s* (Bellville: Anthropos, 1993).

Louw, P.E., *South African Media Policy: Debates of the 1990s* (Bellville: Anthropos, 1993).

Louw, P.E., "Restructuring the Media: Can Socialist and Libertarian Principles be Combined?" in P.E. Louw, ed., *South African Media Policy: Debates of the 1990s* (Bellville: Anthropos, 1993).

Louw, P.E. and Tomaselli, K.G., "Developments in the Conventional and Alternate Presses, 1980-1989," in K.G. Tomaselli and P.E. Louw, eds., *The Alternative Press in South Africa* (Bellville: Anthropos, 1991).

Louw, P.E., "The Emergence of a Progressive-Alternative Press in South Africa with Specific Reference to *Grassroots*," in *Communicatio* 15,2 (1989). https://doi.org/10.1080/02500168908537664

Louw, R. "National Overview: South Africa," in *So This is Democracy? Report on the State of Media Freedom and Freedom of Expression in Southern Africa* (Windhoek: MISA, 2007).

Louw, R., "Scrap Apartheid-Era Laws!" *The Media*, January (2013).

MacLennan, B., *The Wind Makes Dust. Four Centuries of Travel in Southern Africa* (Cape Town: Tafelberg, 2003).

Magrobi, K., "Solidarity to Women from QW+," Statement, SANEF, 24 March (2020).

Mahlase, M., "Letter From our Chairperson, SANEF and Five Others v EFF and Another – Setting the Record Straight," statement, SANEF, 14 September (2019).

Mahlase, M., SANEF/MMA Press Freedom Day Webinar, 3 May (2020).

Manoim, I., "Print is Dead. The Digital Revolution Continues," *Mail & Guardian: 20 Years* anniversary supplement, *M&G*, November 25–December 1, 2005.

Mathekga, R., "A War Against the Media is a War Against Democracy," *News24*, November 26, 2018, https://www.news24.com/Columnists/Ralph_Mathekga/a-war-against-the-media-is-a-war-against-democracy-20181126.

Mathews, A., *The Darker Reaches of Government* (Johannesburg: Juta, 1979).

Mathews, A.S., *Freedom, State Security and the Rule of Law. Dilemmas of the Apartheid Society* (Cape Town: Juta, 1986).

Matisonn, J., *God, Spies and Lies* (Vlaeberg: Missing Ink, 2015).

Mazwai, T., "The Black Press in South Africa: Censorship From all Sides," *Ecquid Novi*, 11,2 (1990). https://doi.org/10.1080/02560054.1990.9653040

Mazwai, T., "The Present and Future Role of the Press," in *Mau-Mauing the Media, New Censorship for the New South Africa* (Johannesburg: South African Institute of Race Relations, 1991).

McCleod, D., "Telecoms Bill Must be Withdrawn – Research Firm Says," *TechCentral*, February 6, 2018, https://techcentral.co.za/telecoms-bill-must-withdrawn-research-firm/79469/.

McLeod, D., "SA scores highly for Internet Freedom, but worrying Signs emerge," *TechCentral*, November 5, 2019, https://techcentral.co.za/sa-scores-highly-for-internet-freedom-but-worrying-signs-emerge/93822/.

McClurg, J., "The Afrikaans Press: From Lapdog to Watchdog," *Ecquid Novi*, 8,1 (1987). https://doi.org/10.1080/02560054.1987.9652980

McCracken, D., "The Imperial British Newspaper, with Special Reference to South Africa, India and the 'Irish Model'," *Critical Arts*, 29,1 (2015). https://doi.org/10.1080/02560046.2015.1009672

McCracken, D., "In Pursuit of Media History Bunk," in K. Tomaselli, ed., *Making Sense of Research* (Pretoria: Van Schaik, 2018).

McQuail, D., *Theories of Mass Communication* (2nd ed.) (London: Sage, 1987).

McQuail, D., *McQuail's Mass Communication Theory* (London: Sage, 2005). https://doi.org/10.4135/9780857024374

MDDA Act, 2002, http://www.mdda.org.za/mdda-act.

MDDA, Annual Report 2005/6 (Johannesburg: Vulindlela Communications).

Medsger, B. "Getting Journalism Education Out of the Way," *Essays* (2002), http://journalism.nyu.edu/publishing/archives/debate/forum.1.essay.medsger.html.

Meiring, M., "Joernalistiek in dié Tye Verdien Agting" ("Journalism in These Times Deserves Respect"), *Die Burger*, March 24, 2020.

Merrett, C., *A Culture of Censorship. Secrecy and Intellectual Repression in South Africa* (Cape Town: David Phillip, 1994).

Merrett, C., "A Tale of Two Paradoxes: Media Censorship in South Africa, Pre-Liberation and Post-Apartheid," *Critical Arts*, 15,1&2 (2001). https://doi.org/10.1080/02560240185310071

Merrett, C. and Saunders, C., "The Weekly Mail, 1985–1994," in L. Switzer and M. Adhikari, eds., *South Africa's Resistance Press. Alternative Voices in the Last Generation under Apartheid* (Ohio: Ohio University Center for International Studies, 2000).

Mersham, G., "Television, A Fascinating Window on an Unfolding World," in A.S. de Beer, ed., *Mass Media Towards the Millennium* (Pretoria: Van Schaik, 1998).

Merten, M., "Strong-Arm Security at Parliament: Questions Unanswered after String of Bully-Boy Incidents," *Daily Maverick*, March 3, 2020, https://www.dailymaverick.co.za/article/2020-03-03-strong-arm-security-at-parliament-questions-unanswered-after-string-of-bully-boy-incidents/.

Mervis, J., *The Fourth Estate, A Newspaper Story* (Johannesburg: Jonathan Ball, 1989).

Meurant, L.H., *Sixty Years Ago, or Reminiscences of the Struggle for the Freedom of the Press in South Africa and the Establishment of the First Newspaper in the Eastern Provinces* (facsimile ed.) (Cape Town: Africana Connoisseurs Press, 1963; Original: Cape Town: Saul Solomon & Co, 1885).

Meyer, P.J., "Report of the Commission of Enquiry into Matters Relating to Television", RP37/1971 (Pretoria: Government Printer, 1971).

Mhkabela, M., Keynote Address, "The Decriminalisation of Freedom of Expression in Africa: How Self-Regulation of the Media Can Assist," Seminar, ONO: The Decriminalisation of Freedom of Expression in Africa, STIAS, Stellenbosch, 23 April (2015).

Mkhabela, M., "Beware the Coronavirus Threats to our Constitution," *News24*, March 26, 2020, https://www.news24.com/Columnists/Mpumelelo_Mkhabela/mpumelelo-mkhabela-beware-the-coronavirus-risks-to-our-constitution-20200326.

Milne C. and Taylor, A., *South Africa: Research Findings and Conclusions* (London: African Media Development Initiative, BBC World Service Trust, 2006).

Morris, M., *Apartheid. An Illustrated History* (Jeppestown: Jonathan Ball, 2012).

Motloung, M., "Press Complaints Peak," *The Media*, February (2007).

Muller, C.F.J., *Sonop in die Suide. Geboorte en Groei van die Nasionale Pers 1915–1948 (Sunrise in the South. The Birth and Growth of the Nasionale Pers 1915–1948)* (Cape Town: Nasionale Boekhandel, 1990).

Muller, J., "Press Houses at War: A Brief History of Nasionale Pers and Perskor," in K. Tomaselli, R. Tomaselli and J. Muller, eds., *Narrating the Crisis: Hegemony and the South African Press* (Johannesburg: Richard Lyon & Co, 1987).

Murray, R.W., Snr., *South African Reminiscences* (Cape Town: Juta, 1894).

Myburgh, P.-L., *The Republic of Gupta: A Story of State Capture* (Johannesburg: Penguin, 2017).

Nänny, P., "History of Censorship in South Africa," (Master's assignment, Stellenbosch University, 2004).

Naspers Annual Report (2003).

"National Editors' Forum Concerned with Developments at the SABC," SANEF statement, 2008.

Naudé, B., *My Land van Hoop (My Country of Hope)* (Cape Town: Human & Rousseau, 1995).

Neame, L., *Today's News Today: A History of the Argus Company* (Johannesburg: Argus Printing and Publishing Company, 1956).

Nel, F., *Writing for the Media in Southern Africa* (Cape Town: Oxford University Press, 2001).

Nicholson, G., "Former SARS Executive Slams Press over Rogue Unit," *Daily Maverick*, January 31, 2020, https://www.dailymaverick.co.za/article/2020-01-31-former-sars-executive-slams-press-over-rogue-unit-stories/.

Nienaber, P.J., 'n Beknopte Geskiedenis van die Hollands-Afrikaanse Drukpers in Suid-Afrika (A Brief History of the Dutch Afrikaans Press in South Africa)* (Bloemfontein, Cape Town & Port Elizabeth: Nasionale Pers Beperk, 1947).

October, A., "Kommer in Amerika Uitgespreek oor Persvryheid in SA" ("Concern Expressed in America Regarding Press Freedom in SA"), *Die Burger*, May 1, 2015.

Oosthuysen, L.F., "City Press," in W.D. Beukes, (ed.). *Oor Grense Heen (Across Boundaries)* (Cape Town: Tafelberg 1992), 342; J.J.J. Spies, "Oor die Kleurgrens" ("Across the Colour Bar"), in W.D. Beukes, ed., *Oor Grense Heen (Across Boundaries)* (Cape Town: Tafelberg, 1992).

Oosthuizen, M., "Persverantwoordelikheid en Rekenskap," *Ecquid Novi* 3,2 (1982). https://doi.org/10.1080/02560054.1982.9652910

Orlik, P., "South Africa: How Long Without TV?" *Journal of Broadcasting* (Spring, 1970). https://doi.org/10.1080/08838157009363592

Owen, K., "Liberal Institutions under Pressure: The Press," in R.W. Johnson, D. Welsh and L. Husemeyer, eds., *Ironic Victory: Liberalism in Post-Liberation South Africa* (Cape Town: Oxford University Press, 1998).

Pauw, J., *The President's Keepers: Those Keeping Zuma in Power and out of Prison* (Cape Town: Tafelberg, 2017).

Phakathi, B., "New Press Council System Includes Online Publications," Bizcommunity, December 17, 2015.

Pienaar, S., "Afrikaners en Hul Koerante: Vriendskap in Spanning" ("Afrikaners and Their Newspapers – Friendship under Stress"), *Die Burger*, September 15, 1973.

Pienaar, S., *Getuie van Groot Tye (Witness of Great Times)* (Cape Town: Tafelberg, 1979).

Pollack, R., *Up Against Apartheid: The Role and the Plight of the Press in South Africa* (Carbondale, Ill: Southern Illinois University Press, 1981).

Poplak, R., "#Lockdown: The Long Haul has Kicked Off, and the Virus will Determine the Timeline," *Daily Maverick*, March 27, 2020, https://www.dailymaverick.co.za/article/2020-03-27-lockdown-the-long-haul-has-kicked-off-and-the-virus-will-determine-the-timeline/.

Posetti, J., "Combating Online Abuse: When Journalists and Their Sources are Targeted," in C. Ireton and J. Posetti, eds., *Journalism, 'Fake News' and Disinformation* (UNESCO, 2018).

Posetti, J. and Matthews, A., "A Short Guide to the History of 'Fake News' and Disinformation," *International Center for Journalists*, July 23, 2018, https://www.icfj.org/news/short-guide-history-fake-news-and-disinformation-new-icfj-learning-module.

Potter, E., *The Press as Opposition: The Political Role of South African Newspapers* (Totowa, NJ: Rowman and Littlefield, 1975).

Pringle, T., *Narrative of a Residence in South Africa* (Cape Town: Struik, 1966).

Quintal, A., "Discredited, Threatened, Attacked: Challenges of Covering South Africa's Election in the Digital Age," CPJ, July 1, 2019, https://cpj.org/blog/2019/07/south-africa-election-journalists-online-harassment-threats-doxx.php.

Rabe, L., "'n Kultuurhistoriese Studie van die Duitse Nedersetting Philippi op die Kaapse Vlakte" ("A Cultural Historical Study of the German Settlement Philippi on the Cape Flats") (D.Phil. diss., Stellenbosch University, 1994).

Rabe, L., "Media Freedom, Black Wednesday and 30 Years On: Realities and Illusions," (Unpublished Media Freedom Day Seminar, Cape Town), 18 October (2007).

Rabe, L., *Rykie. 'n Lewe met Woorde (Rykie. A Life With Words)* (Cape Town: Tafelberg, 2011).

Rabe, L., "Inleiding" ("Introduction"), in L. Rabe, ed., *'n Konstante Revolusie. Naspers, Media24 en Oorgange (Constant Revolution. Naspers, Media24 and Transitions)* (Cape Town: Tafelberg, 2015).

Rabe, L., "Twintig Dae in Desember – Naspers, *Die Burger*, Cillié en Verwoerd" ("Twenty Days in December – Naspers, *Die Burger*, Cillié and Verwoerd"), in L. Rabe, ed., *'n Konstante Revolusie. Naspers, Media24 en Oorgange (A Constant Revolution. Naspers, Media24 and Transitions)* (Cape Town: Tafelberg, 2015).

Rabe, L. "Die Belang van Mediavryheid in Suid-Afrika: Tweehonderd Jaar, Twee Gevallestudies, van die Magna Carta tot die Muilbandwet" ("The Importance of Media Freedom in South Africa: Two Centuries, Two Case Studies, from the Magna Carta to the Secrecy Bill"), *Tydskrif vir Geesteswetenskappe (Journal for the Humanities)* 56,3 (2016). https://doi.org/10.17159/2224-7912/2016/v56n3a9

Rabe, L., *Quote Unquote. Quotations on Freedom of Speech, Journalism, the News Media and a World of Words* (Stellenbosch: Rapid Access Publishers/SunMedia, 2016). https://doi.org/10.18820/9781928314103

Rabe, L., ed., *#Journalism4.0 @ Stellenbosch* (Stellenbosch: African Sun Media, 2018).

Rabe, L., "Kroniek van 'n Mondigwording? 'n Mediageskiedkundige Herevaluering van die WVK, Naspers en Afrikaanse Joernalistiek" ("Chronicle of a Coming of Age? A Media-

Historiographical Revisit: The TRC, Naspers and Afrikaans Journalism"), *Litnet Akademies* 14,3 (2018).

Rabe, L., Mediahistoriographical Research Project (Unpublished, Stellenbosch, 2014).

Rajuili, K., "The Decriminalisation of Freedom of Expression in Africa: How Self-Regulation of the Media can Assist," paper, ONO, Stellenbosch, April (2015).

Reece, S.D., "The Progressive Potential of Journalism Education: Recasting the Academic Professional Debate," *The Harvard International Journal of Press Politics* 4,4 (1999). https://doi.org/10.1177/1081180X9900400405

Reid, J., "Op-Ed: World Press Freedom Day 2015, SA Edition," *Daily Maverick*, April 28, 2015, http://www.dailymaverick.co.za/article/2015-04-28-op-ed-world-press-freedom-day-2015-sa-edition/.

Reid J. and Isaacs, T., "Media Policy and Democracy Project: Press Regulation in South Africa: an Analysis of the Press Council of South Africa, the Press Freedom Commission and Related Discourses," Media Policy and Democracy Project, www.mediaanddemocracy.com, November (2015).

Retief, G.J., *Media Ethics: An Introduction to Responsible Journalism* (Cape Town: Oxford University Press, 2002).

Roelofse, K., "The History of the South African Press," in L.M. Oosthuizen, ed., *Introduction to Communication – Course Book 5: Journalism, Press and Radio Studies* (Kenwyn: Juta, 1996).

Rose, R. *Financial Mail,* emailed Letter to Readers, 2 April 2020

Rudolph, H.G., "Freedom of the Press or the Right to Know," *South African Law Journal* 81,1 (1981).

SA Press Council, http://www.presscouncil.org.za/.

Scholtz, J.J.J., "Sirkulasiestryd" ("Circulation Struggle") in W.D. Beukes, ed., *Oor Grense Heen (Across Boundaries)* (Cape Town; Tafelberg, 1992).

Scholtz J.J.J. and Steyn, J.C., "Stryders vir Afrikaans" ("Fighters for Afrikaans") in W.D.. Beukes, ed., *Oor Grense Heen (Across Boundaries)* (Cape Town: Tafelberg, 1992).

Seekings, J., "The Media of the United Democratic Front, 1983–1991," in L. Switzer and M. Adhikari, eds., *South Africa's Resistance Press. Alternative Voices in the Last Generation under Apartheid* (Ohio: Ohio University Center for International Studies, 2000).

Shaikh, M., "On Civic Journalism, Journalistic Inflation and Credential Creep," in L. Rabe, ed., *#Journalism4.0 @ Stellenbosch* (Stellenbosch: African Sun Media, 2018).

Sibiya, K., "He Makes Everything Look Simple", in L. Rabe, ed., *Ton van 'n Man (Tonne of a Man)*, (Cape Town: Tafelberg, 2007).

Siebert, F., Peterson, T. and Schramm, W., *The Four Theories of the Press* (Urbana-Champaign: University of Illinois Press, 1956).

Simon, J., "COVID-19 is Spawning a Global Press-Freedom Crackdown," CJR, March 25, 2020, https://www.cjr.org/analysis/coronavirus-press-freedom-crackdown.php.

Skenjana, S., "Moody's Downgraded SA. What Happens Now?" *Fin24*, March 28, 2020.

Smith, H.L., *Behind the Press in South Africa* (Cape Town: Stewart, 1945).

Sochen, J., *Movers and Shakers. American Women Thinkers and Activists 1900–1970* (New York: Quadrangle/The New York Times Book Co, 1973).

Sonderling, S., "Historical Research in Communication," in G.M. du Plooy, ed., *Introduction to Communication* (Cape Town: Juta, 1995).

Switzer, L. ed., *South Africa's Alternative Press. Voices of Protest and Resistance 1880 – 1960* (Cambridge: Cambridge University Press, 1997).

Switzer, L. and Adhikari, M., eds., *South Africa's Resistance Press. Alternative Voices in the Last Generation under Apartheid* (Athens: Ohio University Press, 2000).

State of the Newsroom 2018, https://journalism.co.za/resources/state-of-the-newsroom/.

Steyn, J.C., "Die Sensuurstryd" ("The Struggle against Censorship"), in W.D. Beukes, ed., *Boekewêreld (Book World)* (Cape Town: Tafelberg, 1992).

Steyn, J.C., *Penvegter* (Cape Town: Tafelberg, 2002).

Steyn E. and De Beer, A.S., "South African National Skills Audit" (Unpublished report, prepared for SANEF, 2002).

Sunter, C., "When Breaking Futures Become Breaking News," *News24*, February 18, 2018, https://www.news24.com/Columnists/ClemSunter/When-breaking-futures-become-breaking-news-20140218.

Switzer L. and Switzer, D., *The Black Press in South Africa and Lesotho* (Boston: G.K. Hall, 1979).

Switzer, L., "South Africa's Resistance Press in Perspective," in L. Switzer and M. Adhikari, eds., *South Africa's Resistance Press. Alternative Voices in the Last Generation under Apartheid* (Ohio: Ohio University Center for International Studies, 2000).

Switzer L. and Adhikari, M., "Preface," in L. Switzer and M. Adhikari, eds., *South Africa's Resistance Press. Alternative Voices in the Last Generation under Apartheid* (Ohio: Ohio University Center for International Studies, 2000).

Teer-Tomaselli, R. and De Villiers, C., "Radio. Theatre of the Mind," in A.S. de Beer, ed., *Mass Media Towards the Millennium* (Pretoria: Van Schaik, 1998).

Teer-Tomaselli, R. and Tomaselli, K., "Transformation, Nation-Building and the South African Media 1993–1999," in K. Tomaselli and H. Dunn, eds., *Media, Democracy and Renewal in Southern Africa* (Colorado Springs: International Academic Publishers, 2001).

Teer Tomaselli, R.E., "The Politics of Discourse and the Discourse of Politics: Images of Violence and Reform on the South African Broadcasting Corporation's Television News Bulletins – June 1985 – November 1986" (D.Phil. diss., University of Natal, 1992).

Teer-Tomaselli, R., "Media and Empire in the 20th Century," *Critical Arts* 28,6 (2014). https://doi.org/10.1080/02560046.2014.990608

Teer-Tomaselli, R. and McCracken, D., eds., *Media and the Empire* (London and New York: Routledge, 2016).

Hunter, M. and Thakur, C., "Advocacy: New Privacy Rules for Covid-19 Tracking a Step in the Right Direction, But …," *News24*, April 4, 2020, https://www.news24.com/Columnists/GuestColumn/advocacy-new-privacy-rules-for-covid-19-tracking-a-step-in-the-right-direction-but-20200404-2.

Thamm, M., "Top Cop Implicated in the Corruption by Nxasana and Booysen Appointed Acting Head of KZN Hawks Organised Crime Unit," *Daily Maverick*, June 18, 2019, https://www.dailymaverick.co.za/article/2019-06-18-top-cop-implicated-in-corruption-by-nxasana-and-booysen-appointed-acting-head-of-kzn-hawks-organised-crime-unit/.

"The Press Must Change – Mandela," *M&G*, May 29, 1992, https://mg.co.za/article/1992-05-29-the-press-must-change-mandela/.

Thloloe, J., Panel Discussion, "The Decriminalisation of Freedom of Expression in Africa: How Self-Regulation of the Media can Assist," Seminar, ONO, Stellenbosch, 23 April (2015).

Tomaselli, K., "Ownership and Control in the South African Print Media: Black Economic Empowerment after Apartheid, 1990–97," *Ecquid Novi* 18,1 (1997). https://doi.org/10.1080/02560054.1997.9653194

Tomaselli, K.G., "Ambiguities in Alternative Discourse. *New Nation* and the *Sowetan* in the 1980s," in L. Switzer and M. Adhikari, eds., *South Africa's Resistance Press. Alternative Voices in the Last Generation under Apartheid* (Ohio: Ohio University Center for International Studies, 2000).

Tomaselli, K.G., "Transformation of the South African Media," *Critical Arts*, 18,1 (2004). https://doi.org/10.1080/02560240485310021

Tomaselli R. and Tomaselli, K., "The Political Economy of the South African Press," in K. Tomaselli, R. Tomaselli and J. Muller, eds., *Narrating the Crisis: Hegemony and the South African Press* (Johannesburg: Richard Lyon & Co, 1987).

Tomaselli, K., Tomaselli, R. and Muller, J., *Narrating the Crisis: Hegemony and the South African Press* (Johannesburg: Richard Lyon & Co, 1987).

Tomaselli, K., Tomaselli R. and Muller, J., eds., *The Press in South Africa* (Johannesburg: Richard Lyon & Co, 1987).

Tomaselli, K., Tomaselli R. and Muller, J., "The Construction of News in the South African Media" in Tomaselli, K., Tomaselli R. and Muller, J., eds., *Narrating the Crisis: Hegemony and the South African Press* (Johannesburg: Richard Lyon & Co, 1987).

Thom, H.B., "Nasionalisme in ons Geskiedenis" ("Nationalism in our History"), *Die Stellenbosche Oud-Student*, September (1937).

Tilley, A., "The Secrecy Bill More Dangerous Than Ever," *Daily Maverick*, March 25, 2014, https://www.dailymaverick.co.za/opinionista/2014-03-25-the-secrecy-bill-more-dangerous-than-ever/#.WpVT0WdDvZ4.

"Treatment of the Media at the 52nd ANC National Conference," SANEF statement, 2008.

Tsedu, M., "One Story Can Make All the Difference," *Media Tenor South Africa*, 5,2,4 (2001).

Tutu, D.M., "Foreword," in Heard, A.H., *The Cape of Storms. A Personal History of the Crisis in South Africa* (Fayetteville: University of Arkansas Press, 1990).

Tyson, H., *Editors under Fire* (Sandton: Random House, 1987).

Tyson, H., "Truth, Tolerance, Fairness and Freedom are the Values We Should be Striving for," in P.E. Louw, ed., *South African Media Policy: Debates of the 1990s* (Bellville: Anthropos, 1993).

Van Kessel, I. "Grassroots from Washing Lines to Utopia," in L. Switzer and M. Adhikari, eds., *South Africa's Resistance Press. Alternative Voices in the Last Generation under Apartheid* (Ohio: Ohio University Center for International Studies, 2000).

Van Rooyen, K., "Is Ons Dan Nog Vry?" ("Are We Still Free?") *Die Burger*, February 20, 2014.

Van Wyk, J., Prins, J.D. and Spies, J.J.J., "Die Burger-Ekstra en Metro-Burger" ("The Burger Extra and Metro Burger"), in W.D. Beukes, ed., *Oor Grense Heen (Across Boundaries)* (Cape Town: Tafelberg, 1992).

Verster, F., "A Critique of the Rape of Justice, with Emphasis on Seven Cartoons by Zapiro (2008-2010)" (Master's thesis, Stellenbosch University, 2010).

Visser, W., "Die Ontwikkeling van Vakbonde en Georganiseerde Arbeid" ("The Development of Unions and Organised Labour"), in F. Pretorius, ed., *Geskiedenis van Suid-Afrika (History of South Africa)* (Cape Town: Tafelberg, 2012).

Visser, W., "Die Minerale Revolusie" ("The Mineral Revolution"), in F. Pretorius, ed., *Geskiedenis van Suid-Afrika (History of South Africa)* (Cape Town: Tafelberg, 2012),

Voltmer, K., "The Mass Media and the Dynamics of political Communication in Processes of Democratization," in K. Voltmer, ed., *Mass Media and Political Communication in New Democracies* (London: Routledge, 2006).

Von Lieres, B., "Culture and the Limits of Liberalism," in S.L. Robins, ed., *Limits to Liberation after Apartheid: Citizenship, Governance and Culture* (Oxford: James Currey, 2005).

Vosloo, T., "*Beeld – 21 Jaar*" ("*Beeld – 21 Years*"), *Ecquid Novi*, 17,1 (1996). https://doi.org/10.1080/02560054.1996.9653169

Vuk'unzenzele, https://www.vukuzenzele.gov.za/general.

Wasserman, H., "Freedom's Just Another Word? Perspectives on Media Freedom and Responsibility in South Africa and Namibia," *International Communication Gazette* 72,7 (2010). https://doi.org/10.1177/1748048510378145

Wasserman, H. and De Beer, A.S., "Which Public? Whose Interest? The South African Media and its Role During the First Ten Years of Democracy," *Critical Arts* 19,1&2 (2005). https://doi.org/10.1080/02560040585310041

Wasserman H. and De Beer, A.S., "Conflicts of Interest? Debating the Media's Role in Post-apartheid South Africa," in K. Voltmer, ed., *Mass Media and Political Communication in New Democracies* (London: Routledge, 2006).

Wepener, W., "The Role of the Afrikaans Press," in *Survival of the Press* (Grahamstown: Rhodes University, 1979).

Wepener, W., "Rapport is Twee Maande ná sy Geboorte Gemáák" ("Rapport was Made Two Months after its Birth"), *Rapport 25 Jaar Gedenkuitgawe (25 Year Commemorative Publication)*, November 6, 1995.

Wigston, D., "History of the South African Media," in P.J. Fourie, ed., *Media Studies Volume 1: Media History, Media and Society* (Wetton: Juta, 2007).

Wilkerson, M., "History and Journalism Research," in R. Nafziger and M. Wilkerson, eds., *An Introduction to Journalistic Research* (New York: Greenwood Press, 1949; 1968 -reprint).

Wilkins I. and Strydom, H., *The Super Afrikaners* (2nd ed.) (Johannesburg: Jonathan Ball, 1980).

Woolf, D., *A Global History of History* (Cambridge: Cambridge University Press, 2011).

Yutar, D., *Freedom of the Press in a Post-Apartheid South Africa* (Oxford, Green College, Oxford, Reuter Foundation, Hilary Term, 1995).

Zille, H., Keynote Address, Annual Conference of ONO, Cape Town, 20 April (2015).

Zug, J., "'Far From Dead.' The Final Years of the *Guardian*, 1960–1963," in L. Switzer and M. Adhikari, eds., *South Africa's Resistance Press. Alternative Voices in the Last Generation under Apartheid* (Ohio: Ohio University Center for International Studies, 2000).

Zug, J., *The Guardian: The History of South Africa's Extraordinary Anti-Apartheid Newspaper* (Pretoria: UNISA Press, 2007).

INDEX

A

Aaron, C. 377
Abantu-Batho 104, 137, 138
Abdurahman, A. 149
ACDP 324
Adam, H. 31, 36, 37, 211, 416, 435
Adamson, G. 116
Adhanom, T. 380
Adhikari, M. x, 391, 404, 407, 408, 410, 411,
    419, 420, 435, 436, 441, 442, 445, 446,
    447, 448
Advance 162, 217
Advertiser, The 47, 49, 55, 56, 57, 58, 59, 60,
    61, 62, 63, 65, 66, 67, 68, 69, 70, 71,
    72, 73, 74, 75, 76, 78, 81, 82, 83, 87,
    92, 93, 96, 97, 109, 112, 113, 124, 143,
    249, 398
Advertising Standards Authority (ASA) 290
Advocate-General Act, 1979 227
Advocate-General Amendment Act 55, 1983
    225
African Broadcasting Corporation 151, 152,
    412, 446
African Communist 217
African Drum 170
Africanist 12, 240
African Leader 138
African Lodestar 240
African Media Barometer 300
African Nationalism 45, 104, 105, 127, 137,
    147, 148, 152, 176, 196, 211, 234
African Political Organisation 149
African Union 4, 16, 275
African World 138
Afrikaanse Patriot, Die 76, 100, 101, 109
Afrikaanse Pers Beperk/(1962) 134, 141, 142,
    163, 179, 212
Afrikaner Bond 107, 129
Afrikaner Broederbond (AB) 173, 174, 176,
    180, 191
Afrikaner, Die/De 23, 39, 45, 46, 53, 65, 74, 75,
    76, 84, 90, 92, 98, 99, 100, 101, 102,
    103, 104, 107, 118, 120, 127, 128, 129,
    130, 131, 133, 134, 135, 136, 137, 140,
    141, 142, 145, 149, 150, 151, 152, 154,
    155, 156, 157, 160, 162, 163, 164, 166,
    171, 172, 173, 174, 176, 179, 180, 181,
    182, 183, 184, 187, 188, 189, 191, 192,
    196, 198, 199, 202, 207, 210, 212, 213,
    214, 218, 219, 222, 228, 229, 234, 237,
    240, 245, 246, 254, 256, 258, 263, 264,
    267, 279, 280, 290, 401, 407, 438
Afrikaner Nationalism 45, 76, 104, 107, 118,
    127, 133, 134, 135, 137, 140, 141, 142,
    152, 154, 162, 187, 188, 196, 199, 213,
    234, 264, 280
AHI 141
Ainslie, R. x, 391, 435
Albany News Agency 241
Al-Qalam 246
amaBhungane 320, 339, 365, 379, 433
AMPS 277, 295, 304
ANC 5, 6, 18, 25, 104, 105, 127, 137, 138, 147,
    148, 166, 167, 168, 170, 181, 182, 192,
    211, 217, 220, 231, 235, 238, 239, 240,
    242, 244, 245, 249, 250, 251, 252, 253,
    254, 255, 256, 257, 261, 262, 264, 266,
    267, 268, 269, 270, 271, 273, 280, 281,
    282, 283, 284, 288, 289, 292, 297, 298,
    299, 300, 301, 303, 304, 305, 306, 307,
    308, 309, 311, 312, 313, 314, 315, 316,
    317, 319, 322, 323, 324, 325, 326, 329,
    330, 332, 333, 334, 335, 338, 345, 352,
    353, 355, 359, 363, 367, 375, 376, 382,
    416, 421, 424, 425, 426, 427, 428, 435,
    437, 439, 441, 447
ANC Today 282, 300, 424, 426, 435
Anglo-American 23, 179, 211, 277, 279, 280
ANN7 331, 334, 335, 368, 430, 438
Anti-Censorship Group 251
Appeal Board 184, 229, 242
(Cape) Argus 91, 93, 96, 109, 120, 122, 123,
    150, 221, 275, 297, 423, 440
Argus Group 97, 98, 99, 108, 119, 120, 128,
    130, 132, 135, 138, 139, 143, 144, 145,
    146, 147, 159, 160, 171, 174, 176, 177,
    178, 182, 195, 197, 221, 223, 231, 234,
    240, 243, 244, 245, 264, 267, 269, 276,
    277, 279, 280, 294, 310
Aristotle 3, 4
Article 16 6, 27, 263, 266, 284, 317, 328, 365
Associated Media Publishing 379
Association of Democratic Journalists 251, 290
Association of Scientific and Technical Services
    151
Atomic Energy Act, 1967 227

Audit Bureau of Circulation (ABC) 151, 152, 180, 198, 212, 276, 290
AVBOB 141
Avusa 303, 304
AZAPO 254

B

Bailey, A. 116, 117, 118, 119, 128, 130, 139, 140, 147, 170, 171, 176, 177, 231, 232, 234, 237, 238
Bailey, J.R. 147
Baloyi, W. 289
Bantu 104, 105, 128, 137, 138, 146, 147, 148, 171, 172, 173, 192, 203, 211, 230, 231
Bantu Education Journal 171
Bantu Press 128, 137, 147, 148, 171, 231
Bantustans 167
Bantu World 137, 138, 146, 147, 148, 230, 231
Barberton Herald and Transvaal Mining Mail 124
Barlow, A. 98
Barnato, B. 99, 139
Basson, A. 357, 368
Bateman, B. 357
Battersby, J. 285
Beaverbrook, Lord 145, 279
Beeld vii, 180, 181, 192, 193, 196, 202, 204, 209, 211, 212, 221, 225, 246, 247, 253, 413, 414, 447
Beeld, Die 135, 142, 145, 179, 180, 185, 186, 187, 198, 214, 222, 245, 263, 264
Beit, A. 139
Beit, O. 139
Bell, C. 96
Bell, E. 435
Bell Pottinger 335, 342, 347, 353, 359, 431
Bell, S. 96
Berger, G. 243, 281, 291, 356, 393, 395, 419, 421, 422, 423, 424, 429, 432, 435, 436
Bertrand, C.-J. 327
Beukes, P. 177, 412, 413, 416, 417, 419, 443, 445, 447
Biebouw, H. 37, 38
Bikitsha, N. 351
Biko, S. 192, 194, 195, 205, 214, 219, 258
Bill of Rights 6, 27, 225, 257, 263, 266, 268, 284, 287, 324, 328, 383, 387, 389
Bird, W. 436
Bird, W.W. 49
Black Consciousness 194, 207
Black Editors' Forum 263, 290
Black Man 138

Black Wednesday 171, 194, 344, 346, 429, 444
Bleek, D. 3
Bleek, W.H.I. 3
Bloemfontein Post 98
Board of Reference 160, 174, 175, 200, 292
Boerestaat Party 324
Bokala, W. 252
Bona 147, 170, 171, 231, 234
Boniface, C.E. 75, 77, 78, 85, 92, 124
Boonzaier, D.C. 118
Booyens, B. 254, 420, 421, 436
Bop-TV 222, 223
Bosman, D.B. x, 38, 41, 391, 397, 436
Botha, F. 199
Botha, L. 129, 130, 131, 133, 136, 139
Botha, P.W. 142, 155, 156, 161, 174, 199, 206, 247, 254
Botha, R.F. (Pik) 18, 204, 247
Botha S. 156, 249, 252
Bourke, R. 68, 73
Brand, C.J. 69
Brando, M. 198
Brand, P.A. 77
Brand, R.H. 4
Braude, C. 291
Brebner, W.J.C. 143
Breytenbach, B. 288, 394, 409, 411, 413, 414, 418, 422, 429, 436, 441
Brink, A.P. 184, 229, 248
Bristow-Bovey, D. 291
Brkic, B. 366, 367, 374, 378, 433, 436
Broad-based black economic empowerment (B-BBEE) 307
Broadcast Complaints Commission of South Africa (BCCSA) 284
Broadcasting Amendment Act No 49, 1960 173
Brown, K. 354, 358
Buchanan, D.D. 79, 97
Bunting, B. 161, 167
Bureau for Information 206
Burger, De/Die 39, 118, 124, 128, 134, 135, 136, 141, 142, 143, 154, 156, 159, 179, 185, 186, 192, 196, 197, 199, 202, 221, 225, 234, 254, 280, 285, 392, 405, 411, 419, 424, 429, 430, 433, 434, 439, 440, 441, 442, 443, 444, 447
Burlesque 112
Business Day 253, 280, 294, 297, 301, 352

C

Cambridge Analytica 358
Campbell, A.G. 82

Cape Frontier Times, The 82
Cape Herald 197, 222, 234
Cape of Good Hope Government Gazette, The 48, 49, 52
Cape Patriots 31, 39, 40
Cape Peninsular Publicity Association 151
Cape Times 79, 93, 95, 96, 108, 109, 118, 119, 123, 130, 134, 135, 139, 144, 176, 185, 203, 205, 220, 221, 226, 280, 297, 392, 397, 401, 405, 425, 429, 438
Cape Town Gazette, and African Advertiser, The/Het Kaapsche Stads Courant, en Afrikaansche Berigter 47, 49
Cape Town Mail and Mirror of Court and Council, The 79
Capital Radio 212
Carrim, Y. 374
Cartoons 106, 114, 118, 157, 249, 331, 332, 341, 350, 353, 373
Caxton(s)/CTP 231, 276, 280, 303, 304, 365, 382, 396, 434, 436
Celliers, J.F.E. 98, 107, 113, 114
Censorship x, 5, 17, 20, 115, 175, 176, 183, 184, 204, 251, 292, 391, 393, 394, 397, 406, 409, 411, 412, 414, 420, 422, 423, 425, 428, 431, 436, 437, 440, 442, 443, 445
Censorship Board 176, 184
Chamberlain, N. 150
Chamber of Mines 146
Churchill, W. 268
Cillié Commission 193
Cillié, P. 141, 142, 154, 159, 186, 188, 193, 197, 199, 200, 236, 237, 264, 265, 405, 411, 413, 436, 444
Citizen, The 165, 202, 203, 204, 212, 231, 247, 280, 355, 364, 369
City Press 171, 172, 193, 232, 234, 236, 237, 238, 252, 265, 270, 271, 273, 275, 280, 290, 317, 359, 370, 392, 419, 443
Clarion 161, 162, 217, 232
Cloete, H. 39
CNA 144, 163, 223, 280
Code of Conduct 21, 160, 174, 176, 199, 200, 207, 209, 213, 327, 352
Codesa 17, 256
Coetsee, K. 247
Cohen, F. 115, 116
Coka, G. 138
Cole, L. 72
Colonial Times, The 82
Columbia Journalism Review 377

Comet, The - A Journal for Men of the World 99, 106, 110
Commission of Inquiry in Regard to Undesirable Publications, 1954 55, 57, 160, 200
Commonwealth 8, 169, 182, 201
Communication and the Battle of Ideas 301
Communications Task Group (Comtask) 268
Communist Party 161, 166, 240, 255
Companion to the Cape of Good Hope Almanac 92
Conference of Editors 210, 263, 266, 284
Congress Alliance 166
Congress of Democrats 166, 169
Congress of the People's Charter 162
Constitution Act, 108 of 1996 225
COPE 324
Corporate Africa 279
Cosatu 255, 256
Covid-19 13, 374, 375, 376, 377, 378, 379, 380, 381, 382, 434, 446
CP 180, 181, 182, 214, 222, 229, 254
Criminal Procedure Act, 1955 165, 195, 285, 287, 288, 355
Critic 106, 112
Cronjé, H. 351
Cross, W. 157
Croucamp, P. 367, 368, 433, 437
Cummings, E.E. 261
Cwele, S. 313

D

DA 324, 326, 371, 372, 376
Dadge (Julia Hyde Stansfield) 118
Da Gama, V. 31, 32
Dagblad, Het 121
Dagbreek 134, 135, 142, 143, 163, 179, 180, 186, 212, 264, 265
Dagbreekpers Beperk 143
Dagbreek Trust 143, 179, 180, 265
Daily Dispatch 96, 195, 196, 219, 223, 234, 301
Daily Express 144
Daily Mail 87, 115, 116, 140, 157, 196, 250, 433
Daily Maverick 332, 339, 341, 350, 354, 355, 366, 373, 428, 431, 432, 433, 434, 436, 437, 439, 440, 443, 444, 445, 446, 447
Daily Mirror 147, 171
Daily News 96, 112, 275
Daily Sun 277
Daily Tribune 94, 144
Daily Voice 277

Daniels, G. 314, 315, 344, 345, 346, 427, 428, 431, 437
Da Nova, J. 32
Darnell, B.H. 93
Dasnois, A. xi, 392, 437
Dawn 148
De Ataide, P. 32
De Cabral, P.A. 32
Declaration of Table Mountain 296, 426, 437
Defence Act, 1957 165, 227
Defiance Campaign 165, 170
De Jong, J.E. 89
De Klerk Dibbetz, R. 48
De Klerk, F.W. 143, 153, 265, 409
De Klerk, J. 143
De Klerk, W. 177, 180, 210, 214
De Kock, A. 340
De Kock, W. ix, 8, 89, 437
De Lille, P. 340
De Lima, J.S. 75, 78
Delius, A. 185, 402, 403
Deloire, C. 337, 381
Democratic Left Front (DLF) 326
Denyssen, D. 60, 61, 62
De Villiers, D. 393, 408, 421, 437, 446
De Villiers, J. 437
De Vos, P. 325, 437
Dhlomo, R. 52, 271
Diamond Fields Advertiser 96, 97, 109
Dickens, C. 87, 95
Diggers' News 106, 112, 115
Diggers' News and Witwatersrand Advertiser 112
Directorate of Media Relations 246, 249
Directorate of Publications 207, 229, 246
Dlamini-Zuma, N. 334
Dlodlo, A. 289
Donkin, R. 49, 82
Dormer, F.J. 94, 95, 96, 98, 99, 108, 109, 110, 111, 112, 119, 120, 121, 122, 139
DP 139, 254, 280
Drum 147, 165, 170, 171, 176, 193, 231, 232, 234, 235, 236, 237
DSA Trust 248
DStv 278, 304, 373
Dube, J. 52, 104, 137, 148
Dugard, J. 183, 216, 217, 228, 412, 437
Duma, E. 193, 235, 252
Duncan, J. 326, 394, 422, 423, 426, 437, 438
Du Plessis, J.H.O. 438
Du Plessis, P.G. 214
Du Plessis, T. 172, 293, 317, 328, 438

Du Preez, M. 247, 248, 333, 335, 347, 348, 438
Durban Corporation 151
Du Toit, A. 184, 248
Du Toit, D.F. 102, 103, 109
Du Toit, P. 438
Du Toit, S.J. 101, 102, 103, 107, 121
Dynamo Investments 271

E

Eastern Province Herald, The 66, 91, 96, 109, 111
Eastern Star, The 96, 98, 109, 112, 120
Echo, The 82, 109
Ecna 241
Economist, The 225
EFF 321, 326, 331, 333, 340, 341, 347, 348, 350, 351, 352, 353, 354, 356, 357, 358, 360, 361, 362, 363, 365, 366, 367, 368, 369, 376, 431, 432, 433, 436, 438, 439, 442
Eletha 147
elnews 241
Emigrant, De 80, 98
Engelenburg, F.V. 100, 107
Engels, F. 94
Erasmus Commission 158, 202
Essex, A. 87
Esterhuyse, W. 192, 214, 417, 438
Ethical Journalism Network (EJN) 318
eTV 304
Evening Post 231
Express, De 86, 103, 108, 144, 157, 162, 163, 202, 203, 238, 248, 264
Extension of University Education Act, 1959 162, 410

F

Facebook 282, 320, 321, 322, 329, 341, 342, 351, 358, 379
Fairbairn, J. ix, 43, 49, 51, 53, 54, 55, 56, 57, 58, 59, 60, 61, 62, 63, 64, 65, 66, 67, 68, 69, 70, 71, 72, 73, 74, 75, 76, 77, 78, 79, 80, 81, 82, 83, 87, 89, 93, 94, 108, 111, 177
fairlady 236
Fake news 345, 348
Faure, A. 53, 54, 55, 56, 57, 58, 59, 62, 65, 75, 83, 84, 95, 101, 419, 438
Federale Mynbou 179
Federation of South African Women 166
Fighting Talk 217, 240

Film and Allied Workers Organisation (FAWO)
    269, 271
Films and Publications Act/Bill/Board (FPB) 320,
    321, 322, 326, 335, 336, 341, 364, 429,
    430, 438
Finance Weekly 271
Financial Mail 253, 271, 280, 294, 301, 378,
    434, 445
First, R. 168
Firth, R. 335, 336, 430, 438
Fischer, A. 98
Foreign Correspondents' Association 215, 290
Forum for Internet Freedom in Africa (FIFAfrica)
    338
Forum of Black Journalists (FBJ) 263
Fourie, J. 134, 135
Fourth Estate 13, 21, 158, 272, 281, 284, 371,
    396, 398, 399, 402, 403, 404, 405, 406,
    407, 408, 409, 410, 411, 412, 415, 418,
    419, 422, 423, 437, 443
Franklin, B. 57
Franklin, J. 82
Freedom Charter 238, 268
Freedom House 300, 316, 328, 332, 356, 363,
    364, 365, 430
Freedom of Expression Institute (FXI) 19, 20,
    262, 308, 329, 394
Free Press 74, 124, 377, 379, 424, 434, 441
Friedman, B. 144
Friedman, D. 369
Friend of the Sovereignty and Bloemfontein
    Gazette, The 80, 98, 106
Friend, The 80, 85, 96, 98, 103, 106, 117, 149
FVB 141

G

Galgut, Judge 216
Gallo 153, 223, 280
Gandar, L. 182, 200, 219
Gandhi, M. 104, 149
Gasa, N. 358
Gencor 141, 179
Genootskap van Regte Afrikaners (GRA) 101,
    102, 107
Gereformeerde Kerkbode, De 58
Gerwel, J. 248
Gibson, R. 285, 310
Giffard, C.A. x, 23, 85, 391, 394, 395, 396, 398,
    399, 400, 401, 402, 403, 404, 405, 406,
    407, 408, 409, 410, 411, 412, 413, 414,
    415, 416, 417, 418, 419, 420, 421, 423,
    439, 440

Giliomee, H. 248, 396, 397, 401, 402, 404, 439
Glass Ceiling Research Project 344
Godlonton, R. 41, 49, 75, 77, 80, 81, 82, 83,
    89, 90, 98, 110, 111
Golden Age 112
Golden City Post 170, 231, 237
Golden City Press 232, 234
Gold Field News 112
Google 351, 358, 379
Gordhan, P. 343, 353, 357, 361, 368, 370
Gouvernements Courant der ZAR 98
Government Communication and Information
    System (GCIS) 268, 282, 286
Government Gazette 48, 49, 52, 67, 98, 161,
    167, 168, 184, 205
Government of National Unity (GNU) 273
Gqubule-Mbeki, T. 368, 433, 439
Graaff-Reinet Herald 87, 95
Grahamstad Register en Boeren-vriend, De 80
Graham's Town Journal 75, 80, 81, 89, 91, 92,
    98, 111, 112
Graphic 197, 234, 240, 388
Grassroots 239, 240, 241, 243, 244, 246, 248,
    263, 419, 420, 442, 447
Great Eastern 93
Greig, G. 51, 52, 53, 54, 55, 56, 57, 60, 61, 62,
    63, 64, 65, 66, 67, 68, 71, 72, 73, 74,
    78, 79, 83, 92, 93
Grocott's Penny Mail 112
Grootboom, M. 248
GroundUp 355, 432, 441
Group Areas Act 154, 155, 235, 255
Guardian 148, 161, 162, 167, 169, 217, 225,
    239, 242, 247, 249, 261, 262, 276, 281,
    282, 294, 378, 410, 424, 426, 430, 431,
    435, 436, 442, 448
Gumede, J. 138
Gumede, W.M. 291
Gupta Family 334, 335, 347, 359, 374, 430,
    431, 440, 443

H

Hachten, W. x, 23, 85, 391, 394, 395, 396, 398,
    399, 400, 401, 402, 403, 404, 405, 406,
    407, 408, 409, 410, 411, 412, 413, 414,
    415, 416, 417, 418, 419, 420, 421, 423,
    440
Haffajee, F. 327, 353, 356, 357, 358, 359, 360,
    377, 378, 431, 432, 433, 434, 440
Hamilton, F. 99
Hamsworth, A. (Lord Northcliffe) 115

Harber, A. 249, 293, 339, 340, 368, 378, 423,
    431, 433, 439, 440
Harmse, W. xi, 392, 440
Hazardous Substances Act, 1973 227
Heard, T. 166, 203, 204, 205, 220, 221, 226,
    326, 408, 411, 412, 415, 416, 417, 418,
    419, 421, 429, 440, 447
Hefer Commission 290
Hepple, A. x, 272, 273, 391, 406, 409, 423, 440
Herodotus 9, 10
Hertzog, A. 180, 190
Hertzog, J.B.M. 98
Heunis, C. 245
Hit 231
HNP 129, 180, 182, 222, 229
Hofmeyr, J.H 440
Hofmeyr, M. 269
Hofmeyr, W. 141, 143
Honigby, De 58
Hoofstad 180, 181, 214, 222
Hope, S. 196
Hosking, T. 235
Houghton, W. 110
Huffington Post 369
Human Rights Commission (HRC) 282, 291, 301
Hunter, Q. 440
Hutchinson, A. 34, 170

I

ICFJ 342
Ikwezi 86, 128, 138
Ikwezi Le Afrika 138
Ilanga 104, 128, 137, 148, 231, 234, 276
Ilanga Lase Natal 104, 137
Immorality Act, 1927 154, 409
Immorality Amendment Act, 1950 154
Impey, G. 109, 111
Imvo Zabantsundu 86, 90, 103, 117, 121, 138,
    231, 234, 265, 403
Indaba 86
Independent Broadcasting Authority (IBA) 18,
    256, 257, 261, 269, 271, 272, 304, 394
Independent Communications Authority
    (ICASA) 18, 261, 298, 299, 304, 307,
    332, 336, 339, 364, 394
Independent Media Diversity Trust 247
Independent Newspapers xi, 264, 267, 270,
    273, 276, 277, 279, 297, 303, 304, 354,
    392, 437
Indian Opinion 104, 149
Indian Views 149

Industrial and Commercial Workers' Union (ICU)
    138
I-Net Bridge 281
Information Scandal/Infogate/Muldergate 155,
    156, 159, 165, 187, 200, 201, 202, 203,
    204, 207, 224, 229, 298, 300
Inkatha (Freedom Party) 232, 234, 255, 273
Inkokeli Ya Bantu 148
Inkundla Ya Bantu 148
Interdepartmental Press Liaison Centre 246
Interim Constitution Act 200, 1993 225
Internal Security Act, 1950 227
International Peace Institute 164
International Press Institute 160
Inyaniso 148, 240
Ipepa lo Hlanga 105
Iphepha laboHlanga 352
Isaacs, T. 391, 427, 428, 445, 454
Isasizo 232
Isigidimi Sama Xosa/ Isigidimi Zamaxhosa 86,
    103
Isizwe 232, 240, 241
Isolezwe 276, 277
Izwe Lase Afrika 148
Izwi la Bantu 104, 105, 230
Izwi La Lentsoe La 148
Izwi Lama Afrika 138

J

Jabavu, A. 138
Jabavu, D.D. 122
Jabavu, J.T. 52, 81, 86, 90, 93, 103, 121, 131,
    241
Jackson, D. x, 96, 248, 289, 314, 391, 410, 415,
    441
Jaffer, M. 248
Jameson, L.S. 90, 99, 106, 107, 115, 130
Jeffreys, H. 293
Jeppe, C. 114
Joel, S. 99, 112, 132, 139, 157, 177, 203, 208,
    266, 272, 286, 380
Johannesburg Consolidated Investments (JCI)
    139, 218, 264, 280
Johannesburg Times 112
Johncom 289, 301
Johnnic 264, 270, 271, 273, 276, 280, 294,
    298, 301
Jooste, M. 134, 142, 143, 179, 180, 181, 212
Jordan, P. 148, 267
Josephs, H. 248
Joubert, P. 114
Judge 112

Juniorisation 275, 295, 308, 309
Juta, H.H. 95
Juta, J.C. 94
Juvenal 22

K

//Kabbo 3
Kafir Express 86
Kagiso Trust 265, 270
Kalane, L. xi, 392, 413, 418, 441
Ka-riega News 96
Kemp, J.C.G. 52, 134
Kerkbode, Die 58, 180
Kganyago, L. 376
Khashoggi, J. 349
Kingston, M. 377
Kingswell, G.H. 117, 118, 122
Kipling, R. 98, 106
Kissoon, C. 339
Klaaren, J. 315
Klaaste, A. 194, 235, 245, 252, 263, 270, 317
Koni Media Holdings 301
Koornhof, P. 182, 199
Koranta 148, 149, 231
Koranta Ea Becoana 149
Krog, A. 291
Krüger, F. 326, 419, 429, 441
Kruger, Jannie 176
Kruger, Jimmy 214
Kruger, P. 113, 114

L

Labour Party 129, 130, 136
La Grange, F. 199
La Guma, A. 170
Land en Volk 100, 108, 113, 114, 403
Landstem 177, 180
Langa, P. 312
Lantern 111
Latakgomo, J. 343
Laurence, P. 182, 196, 200, 208, 219, 415
Leader 112, 115, 116, 117, 119, 134, 138, 148, 149, 197, 234
Lee-Warden, L. 168
Leroux, E. 184, 215
Letsoalo, S. 374
Levy, L. 132, 133
Liberation 240, 286, 414, 417, 422, 423, 425, 436, 442, 444, 447
Linnington, E. 291
Liphoko, D. 289, 425, 439
Lippmann, W. 261

Lloyd, L. 3
Lodestar 148, 240
London Missionary Society (LMS) 52, 55, 65, 66, 67, 79, 86
Lotz, I.W. 94
Loubser, H. 374, 433, 441
Louw, E. 154
Louw, M.S. 141
Louw, R. 178, 206, 232, 235, 286, 296, 311, 313, 329, 442
Lovedale Missionary Institute 86
Luthuli, A. 167, 168, 239
Luyt, L. 165, 202, 203

M

Mabille, A. 103
Mabuza, D. 322
Madikizela-Mandela, W. 267
Madison, J. 15, 394
Mafolo, T. 301
Magazine Publishers' Association of South Africa (MPASA) 266
Magna Carta 43, 69, 71, 72, 74, 75, 79, 81, 85, 86, 87, 90, 92, 97, 124, 397, 412, 428, 444
Magubane, P. 170, 193, 195, 235, 236, 419
Mahlase, M. 339, 361, 362, 432, 442
Mail Extra 196
Mail & Guardian 225, 249, 261, 276, 281, 282, 294, 378, 424, 426, 436, 442
Malan, D.F. 129, 156
Malan, F.S. 77
Malema, J. 347, 348, 351, 354, 356, 357, 358, 360, 361, 362, 363, 366, 367, 368, 376, 432, 438
Mamoepa, R. 301
Mandela, N. ix, 18, 153, 168, 226, 243, 247, 255, 258, 265, 266, 267, 270, 274, 288, 292, 328, 333, 369, 426, 430, 446
Mankahlana, P. 282
Manoim, I. 249, 378, 424, 442
Mantashe, G. 314
Manyi, M. 335
Marais, E. 100, 113, 114, 403
Marcus, G. 266, 268
Marx, K. 94, 95
Mashabela, H. 195
Masilela, M. 354
Matanzima, K. 219
Mathekga, R. 348, 349, 431, 442
Mathews, A. 442
Mathews, J. 170

Matisonn, J. 292, 337, 398, 405, 430, 442
Matsepe-Casaburri, I. 299
Mattera, D. 171
Matthews, J. 331, 431, 444
Mayekiso, L. 196
Mayibuye 148, 283
Mazwai, T. 250, 252, 253, 420, 428, 442
Mazzone, N. 372
Mbeki, G. 148
Mbeki, M. 267
Mbeki, T. 3, 12, 271, 282, 292, 393, 425, 426, 438, 439
Mboweni, T. 346, 376, 431
McCauseland, D. 150
McClurg, J. 245, 409, 442
McCombie, T. 111
McCracken x, 8, 392, 393, 406, 442, 446
McLuhan, M. 123, 397, 435
MDM 239, 244
Media24 85, 153, 276, 290, 294, 303, 304, 317, 326, 333, 340, 368, 405, 406, 411, 417, 444
Media Appeals Tribunal (MAT) 7, 25, 292, 298, 301, 303, 306, 307, 309, 310, 311, 313, 314, 317, 319, 320, 321, 322, 323, 325, 326, 327, 328, 330, 343, 345, 429, 437
Media Charter 256, 262, 269, 271, 297
Media Council 175, 178, 207, 208, 210, 246, 255, 257, 292
Media Development and Diversity Agency (MDDA) 18, 261, 288, 289, 394, 425, 439, 440, 442
Media Monitoring Africa (MMA) 331, 338, 433, 442
Media Monitoring Project (MMP) 276, 291, 295
Merriman, J.X. 122, 129
Merten, M. 371, 372, 433, 443
Mervis, J. 112, 115, 117, 132, 157, 177, 203, 208, 225, 235, 238, 272, 402, 404, 405, 407, 408, 409, 410, 411, 412, 415, 418, 419, 423, 443
Meurant, L., Jnr. 54, 62, 74, 83, 92, 111, 124
Meurant, L., Snr. 54
Meyer Commission 212
Meyer, P. 142
Mfundisi, V. 252
Mhlawuli, V. 244, 252
Mhudi 149
Midi group 272
Miller, H. 224
Mill, J.S. 164
Milner, A. 4, 99, 133, 140, 192

Milton, J. vii, 40, 164, 221, 397, 435
Mindport 281
MISA 286, 300, 424, 442
Mkhabela, M. ix, 293, 303, 316, 327, 380, 427, 429, 434, 443
Mkhondo, R. 351
Mkhwanazi, T. 252
M-Net 221, 223, 271, 278, 279, 280, 294, 373
Mobara, L. 361
Modisane, B. 170
Modise, B. 301
Mogoeng, M. 353
Mokhobo, L. 372, 373, 374
Molema, S. 149
Moll, C.P. 56, 78, 92, 98, 124
Molobi, E. 271
Montesquieu 43
Moon 112
Morning Star 86, 138, 169
Morudu, P. 358
Mostert, A. 202, 204
Mothapo, M. 371
Motlana, N. 245, 266, 270, 271
Motsoeneng, H. 322, 331, 372, 373, 433, 437
Moyane, T. 370
Mphahlele, E. 170
Mthembu, J. 289, 314
Mtimkulu, P. 225
Mtintso, T. 252
MTN 278
M.T. Steyn 208
Mufamadi, S. 285
Mulder, C. 156, 177, 180, 198, 200, 201, 202, 203, 204, 222
Mulholland, S. 221, 224
Muller, J. x, 391, 392, 396, 397, 398, 401, 403, 404, 405, 407, 410, 412, 413, 414, 416, 420, 423, 443, 446
MultiChoice 278, 280, 304, 334, 335, 372, 373, 374, 433, 437, 439
Munusamy, R. 290, 352, 353, 357, 358, 362
Murray, B. 359
Murray, R.W., Jnr. 93, 108, 109
Murray, R.W., Snr. 443
Muslim News 234, 240
Muthambi, F. 322, 374
MWASA 177, 194, 195, 196, 210, 224, 233, 251, 266, 275, 290
M-Web 281
Myburgh, P.-L. 443
Myburgh, T. 118

N

NAIL 243, 244, 245, 266, 270, 271, 273, 279, 280, 294
Nakasa, N. 170, 351, 353
Namaqua Nuus 245, 248
Naspers (Nasionale Pers, Nationale Pers, De) vii, 130, 134, 135, 136, 137, 138, 140, 141, 142, 143, 145, 160, 163, 171, 179, 180, 181, 182, 184, 186, 187, 188, 192, 198, 199, 200, 202, 204, 212, 214, 220, 221, 222, 223, 230, 232, 234, 236, 237, 238, 241, 243, 245, 264, 265, 270, 273, 276, 277, 279, 280, 281, 289, 294, 303, 309, 373, 374, 397, 405, 406, 407, 411, 413, 416, 417, 424, 425, 436, 443, 444, 445
Natal Commercial Advertiser 96
Natalier en Pietermaritzburgsche Trouwe Aantekenaar, De 78, 85
Natal Mercury 85, 96, 109, 130, 139, 144, 201, 280
Natal Post 195
Natal Witness, The 79, 85, 96, 97, 116, 223, 401
Nation 6, 77, 105, 128, 167, 229, 232, 234, 239, 240, 242, 244, 245, 246, 250, 251, 253, 263, 267, 271, 279, 303, 349, 413, 418, 420, 422, 423, 424, 446
National Democratic Revolution 305, 319
National Director of Public Prosecutions 285, 355
National Empowerment Consortium (NEC) 264, 294
National Executive Committee (NEC) 269
National Key Points Act, 1980 (NKPA) 227, 313, 316, 324, 325, 330
National Party (NP) 17, 24, 25, 98, 118, 124, 127, 129, 130, 131, 134, 135, 136, 137, 140, 141, 142, 143, 145, 149, 150, 152, 153, 154, 155, 156, 157, 158, 159, 161, 162, 163, 164, 167, 170, 172, 173, 175, 176, 177, 179, 180, 181, 183, 184, 185, 186, 187, 188, 189, 190, 192, 194, 195, 198, 199, 201, 202, 203, 204, 210, 213, 214, 215, 217, 218, 219, 221, 222, 228, 229, 230, 232, 238, 245, 247, 254, 255, 256, 258, 263, 269, 271, 272, 273, 280, 292, 298, 299, 300, 301, 325, 406, 421, 437
National Security Management System 158, 230, 254
Native Administration Act, 1928 157
Naudé, B. 195, 414, 443

Nchabeleng, G. 301
Ncwana, S.M.B. 138, 148
Ndabeni-Abrahams, S. 352
Ndlovu, D. 193, 235
Nederlandsch Zuid-Afrikaansch Tijdschrift, Het (HNZAT) 53, 75
Neethling, C.N. 76
Neethling, L. 287
Nel, L. 220, 229
Nethold 278
Netshitenzhe, J. 266, 268, 286
Netwerk24 374, 392, 429, 433, 441
Network Holding Group 278
New Africa ii, 239, 243, 266
New Age 147, 162, 167, 168, 169, 217, 239, 331
New Era 244, 246, 430, 438
New Nation 229, 232, 239, 242, 244, 245, 246, 250, 251, 253, 263, 267, 271, 279, 420, 446
New National Party (NNP) 273
News24 339, 368, 392, 425, 427, 429, 430, 431, 433, 434, 436, 438, 439, 442, 443, 446
Newspaperman's Guide to the Law, The 205, 253, 420, 441
Newspaper Press Bill of 1977 199
Newspaper Press Union (NPU) ix, x, 73, 80, 81, 93, 94, 102, 103, 108, 109, 110, 111, 117, 118, 120, 122, 128, 131, 132, 160, 161, 165, 174, 175, 176, 177, 178, 199, 200, 204, 205, 207, 208, 209, 210, 211, 213, 245, 246, 266, 290, 292
Newsweek 225
New York Times 161, 199, 393, 431, 445
NewzroomAfrika 354
Ngcuka, B. 285, 290
Ngonyama, S. 282
Ngubane, J. 148
Nieman Fellowship 170, 213, 232
Nienaber, P.J. x, 391, 397, 398, 399, 400, 443
Nkandla 205, 313, 315, 317, 324, 325
Nkosi, L. 170
Nkosi, W. 193, 235
Nqukula, C. 252
Nugent Commission 351
Nugget 112
NUMSA 251
Nyuka, P. 248
Nzimande, B. 314, 319
Nzima, S. 193

O

Official Secrets and Defence Act, 1965 165,
    205, 207, 226, 227
Oggendblad 180, 222
Oilgate 325
Oliphant, R. 248
Ollemans, D. 117, 160
Omar, D. 285
Ombud 225, 291, 292, 361, 389
Omni Media 264
ONO 320, 427, 428, 429, 443, 445, 446, 448
Ons Klyntji 107
Ons Land 75, 77, 108, 391, 436
Ons Vaderland 128, 137
Oosterbroek, K. 352
Oosterlig, Die 137, 142
Oost, H. 133, 134
Open Society Initiative of Southern Africa
    (Osisa) 262
OpenTV 281
Oppenheimer, H. 190, 218
OPSA 142
Ordinance no 60 of 1829 93
O'Reilly, T. 261, 264, 267, 277, 279, 280, 297
Oude Emigrant, De 98
Our Own Mirror 147
Out of Step 246
Owen, K. 219, 284, 417, 425, 439, 444
Owl, The 118

P

PAC 166, 170, 242, 252, 253, 255, 257
Pace 231
Pakendorf, H. 230
Palazzolo, V. 247
Pannevis 102
Paper, Printing, Wood and Allied Workers'
    Union 294
Patel, K. 378
Patel, Q. 252
Patriot, Die 39, 40, 76, 100, 101, 102, 103,
    107, 108, 109, 110, 134, 181, 210, 249
Patrys 163
Pauling, G. 110
Pauw, J. 303, 334, 340, 365, 427, 430, 444
Paver, B.C. 128, 146, 147
PCSA 25, 200, 202, 209, 210, 213, 216, 217,
    284, 290, 291, 292, 298, 301, 311, 312,
    314, 319, 320, 321, 322, 323, 324, 327,
    331, 343, 346, 347, 355, 361, 369, 371,
    383, 427, 428, 429
PDMSA 324, 327

Pearson Plc 261
PEN South Africa 329
People's World 162
Persbel 265, 270
Perskor 86, 104, 132, 138, 140, 141, 142, 179,
    180, 181, 186, 187, 188, 198, 201, 202,
    203, 212, 214, 221, 222, 223, 232, 253,
    264, 265, 270, 271, 279, 280, 294, 412,
    443
Petroleum Products Amendment Act, 1978 227
PFP 139, 181, 224, 228, 254
Phambili 241
Philip, J. 55, 65, 66, 67, 70, 74, 76, 77, 79, 81,
    86, 93, 96
Pienaar, S. 142, 180, 186, 187, 188, 413, 444
Pieterson, H. 193, 414
Pillay, I. 343, 370
Plaatje, S. 52, 148, 149, 408
Pliny the Elder 3, 4, 12
Pogrund, B. 182, 196, 219
Police Amendment Act, 1978 165, 224, 227
Police Amendment Act, 1979 227
Pollack, R. x, 391, 444
Poplak, R. 375, 376, 433, 444
Population Registration Act, 1950 154
Port Elizabeth News 241
Port Elizabeth Telegraph 109, 122
Post 7, 31, 32, 33, 39, 98, 147, 160, 170, 176,
    194, 195, 196, 215, 217, 222, 224, 231,
    232, 234, 237, 239, 240, 244, 250, 286,
    369, 393, 395, 396, 397, 405, 409, 414,
    417, 422, 424, 425, 440, 441, 442, 444,
    447, 448
Potchefstroom University for Christian Higher
    Education (NWU) 197, 392, 402, 408,
    439, 440
Potter, E. x, 272, 273, 391, 398, 399, 400, 401,
    402, 403, 405, 406, 407, 408, 409, 410,
    411, 412, 413, 444
Powell, E. 99
Presbyterian Glasgow Missionary Society 86
President's Keepers, The 303, 334, 427, 430,
    444
Press Board of Reference 174, 175, 200, 292
Press Code ix, 284, 312, 327, 383, 384
Press Council x, 25, 160, 175, 178, 199, 200,
    245, 292, 311, 320, 361, 383, 391, 425,
    426, 427, 428, 429, 432, 444, 445
Press Freedom Commission x, 311, 322, 391,
    427, 445

Press Freedom Day 13, 24, 195, 283, 285, 296, 316, 318, 350, 374, 379, 381, 426, 428, 433, 442, 445

Pretoria News 253, 280

PricewaterhouseCoopers Media Forecast 320

Primedia 303

Pringle, T. x, 43, 49, 50, 51, 53, 54, 55, 56, 57, 58, 59, 60, 61, 62, 63, 64, 65, 67, 71, 72, 73, 74, 76, 77, 79, 81, 83, 99, 108, 177, 221, 248, 391, 399, 400, 444

Print Media Association of South Africa (PMASA) 266, 290

Prisons Act, 1959 165, 219, 227

Progressive Photographic Society 235

Prohibition of Mixed Marriages Act, 1949 154

Promotion of Access to Information Act (PAIA) 287

Prosus 130, 221, 406, 417

Protection of Information Act, 1982 227

Protection of Information Bill 20, 299, 310, 429

Pro Veritate 217

Provincial Press Association 266

Publications Act, 1974 176, 183, 184, 207, 214, 219, 227, 287, 298, 299, 387, 429

Publications Amendment Act, 1979 215

Publications and Entertainments Act, 1963 161, 175, 215

Publications Board 160, 161

Public Protector 225, 315, 322

Public Protector Act, 1994 225

Public Safety and Criminal Law Amendment Act, 1953 165

Q

Qoboza, P. 171, 172, 194, 195, 196, 225, 232, 233, 237, 238, 249, 252, 253, 317

Queenstown Representative 96, 120

Quintal, A. 351, 352, 353, 354, 432, 444

QW+ 375, 433, 442

Qwelane, J. 193

R

Rabone, W.H. 87

Radebe, J. 282

Radio 5 212

Radio 702 212, 370

Radio Bantu 172, 173, 211

Radio Good Hope 173

Radio Highveld 173

Radio Port Natal 173

Rajuili, K. 320, 321, 428, 429, 445

Ramaphosa, C. 271, 333, 334, 338, 349, 353, 358, 361, 375, 376, 377, 380, 430, 431, 433, 436, 438

Rand Daily Mail/RDM 87, 115, 116, 118, 119, 128, 130, 133, 139, 140, 144, 149, 157, 160, 169, 178, 182, 192, 193, 196, 199, 200, 202, 203, 204, 206, 208, 210, 219, 221, 225, 231, 233, 234, 235, 239, 248, 249, 253, 263, 264, 310

Rapport 180, 188, 192, 196, 197, 202, 264, 280, 365, 414, 447

Reddingsdaadbond 141, 179

Redelinghuijs, J.H. 39

Registration of Newspapers Act, 1982 207

Reid, J. x, 321, 323, 391, 427, 428, 445

Reith, J. 152

Relly, G. 211

Rembrandt 179, 265

Reporters Without Borders 15, 19

Republic of Gupta: A Story of State Capture, The 334, 430, 443

Retief Meiring, M. 248, 382

Rhodes, C.J. 89, 90, 94, 95, 96, 99, 103, 106, 107, 112, 113, 119, 120, 121, 122, 139, 148, 197, 264, 271, 291, 402, 407, 418, 426, 436, 437, 439, 447

Rhodesia Herald, The 120

Rhodes University 148, 197, 271, 402, 407, 418, 439, 447

Rhoodie, E. 201, 202, 203

Right to Know (R2K) 19, 20, 21, 219, 310, 318, 321, 325, 328, 392, 394, 404, 417, 420, 427, 429, 435, 445

Riotous Assembly Act, 1956 227

Ritter, J.C. 6, 40, 41, 42, 46, 52

Robertson, J. 42, 46, 47, 48, 416, 435

Robin, C. 206

Roosevelt, F.D. 268

Rose-Innes, R. 103, 122

Rosenthal, R. 221

Rose, R. 445

Ross, J. 52, 66, 96

Rossouw, A. 285

Rousseau, J.-J. 43, 414, 443

RSF 15, 19, 300, 313, 337, 356, 378, 381, 394, 429, 430, 432, 434

Rudolph, H.G. 171, 215, 216, 217, 392, 404, 417, 445

Rumpff, F. 253

Rutherfoord, H.E. 76

S

Saambou 141
Saamstaan 239, 245, 246, 248, 250, 263
SABC xi, 18, 138, 142, 151, 152, 164, 172, 173,
174, 179, 190, 191, 197, 198, 204, 212,
220, 222, 223, 237, 245, 250, 253, 256,
258, 262, 267, 268, 269, 271, 272, 281,
283, 289, 295, 298, 299, 300, 303, 304,
309, 321, 322, 324, 331, 332, 344, 345,
355, 372, 373, 374, 392, 423, 424, 426,
430, 433, 436, 437, 440, 441, 443
SABC 8 331, 332, 430, 441
Sabotage Act, 1962 227
Sachs, A. 167, 168
SACP 247, 249, 257, 314, 319, 324
Sammons, W.L. 87
Sam Sly's African Journal 87
SANEF ix, 15, 16, 26, 86, 263, 275, 282, 285,
286, 290, 291, 296, 299, 300, 303, 308,
309, 311, 316, 320, 325, 326, 327, 329,
330, 331, 338, 339, 340, 342, 343, 344,
346, 347, 350, 351, 352, 353, 354, 355,
357, 360, 361, 362, 363, 365, 366, 369,
370, 374, 375, 379, 380, 381, 382, 392,
395, 423, 426, 429, 430, 431, 432, 433,
434, 442, 443, 445, 447
Santam/Sanlam 140, 141, 143, 152, 179, 214,
279
SAPA 144, 163, 223
SAPPI 141
Sarafina 288
SASO Newsletter 239
SASPU National 240
Satchwell, K. 351, 370
Sauer, J.W. 122
Schadeberg, J. 235
Schlesinger, L.W. 144, 151
Schoeman, B. 143, 180
Schönberg, V.A. 40
Scorpio 365, 433
Sechaba 148
Section 205 of the Criminal Procedure Act,
1977 195, 287, 288, 355
Sekunjalo 331
Self-censorship 25, 252, 296, 318, 329
Self-regulation 22, 25, 321
Seme, P. 52
Sentech 281
Sentinel 112
Serache, N. 193, 235, 252
Seria, R. 252
Sexwale, T. 283, 293

Shaikh, M. 197, 414, 445
Shariff, A. 352
Sharpeville 154, 166, 168, 170, 187, 231, 236,
254
Sheffield, T. 96, 109, 111, 120
Shepstone, T. 79, 110
Shivambu, F. 340, 347, 367
Sibiya, K. 193, 238, 414, 419, 445
Sidego, C. 234
Simon, J. 445
Sisulu, W. 255
Sisulu, Z. 194, 224, 232, 251, 267
Slabbert, F. v Z. 228
Slater, J. 81, 110
Slovo, J. 247
Smith, H.H. 41, 42
Smith, H.L. 445
Smith, J.S. 78
Smuts, J.C. 4, 127, 133, 139, 151
Smuts, J.J. 94
Snowden's torch 315
Soga, A.K. 104
Solomon, S. 93, 95, 96, 109, 110, 120, 122,
123, 139, 399, 405, 443
Sol Plaatje Institute for Media Leadership 148,
408
Somerset, C. x, 49, 50, 51, 52, 53, 54, 55, 56,
57, 58, 59, 60, 61, 62, 63, 64, 65, 66,
67, 68, 69, 71, 72, 73, 75, 76, 79, 83,
84, 96, 99, 110, 122, 177, 245, 401,
405, 438
SONA 6, 282, 321, 325, 326, 327, 331, 332,
333, 371, 372
Sondagnuus 134, 143, 179, 180
Sondagstem 163
Sonderling, S. 8, 393, 445
South 239, 241, 242, 243, 246, 250, 251, 253
South African Associated Newspapers (SAAN)
119, 130, 132, 138, 139, 140, 144, 146,
160, 165, 174, 176, 177, 178, 197, 201,
202, 203, 207, 212, 218, 221, 223, 232,
234, 237, 253, 264, 277
South African Association of Industrial Editors
290
South African Coloured People's Organisation/
Coloured People's Congress 166
South African Commercial Advertiser, The 49,
55, 56, 60, 62, 92
South African Communication Service (SACS)
268
South African Congress of Democrats 166
South African Congress of Trade Unions 166

South African Indian Congress 166

South African Institute of Race Relations 217, 428, 442

South African Journal, The 50, 53, 57, 58, 62, 416, 421, 439

South African Native National Congress 104, 127

South African Party (SAP) 129, 134, 136

South African Press Freedom Report 311

South African Printing and Allied Industrial Federation 266

South African Society of Journalists (SASJ) 144, 145, 174, 176, 177, 185, 195, 210, 221, 237, 251, 274, 275, 289

South African Typographical Union (SATU) 42, 94, 266, 275, 290

South African Union of Journalists (SAUJ) 275, 289, 290

South African War/SAW 4, 45, 55, 77, 90, 98, 99, 103, 105, 111, 112, 113, 114, 115, 117, 122, 127, 128, 129, 130, 132, 133, 134, 137, 139

Sowetan ix, 225, 231, 232, 234, 235, 240, 241, 243, 244, 245, 250, 251, 252, 253, 264, 270, 271, 273, 279, 280, 298, 301, 317, 321, 352, 420, 446

Spark 167, 169, 217, 231, 239

Sparks, A. 87, 208, 233

Specialist Press Association 266, 290

Spicer, M. 267

Springbok Radio 172

Staats Courant 78, 96, 98

Staffrider 240

Staggie, R. 285

Standard and Diggers' News 106, 112, 115

Standard and Transvaal Mercury Chronicle 112

Stapleton, R.J. 77

Star Africa Edition, The 196

Starrenburg, J. 37

Star, The 74, 86, 96, 98, 99, 106, 109, 112, 113, 114, 115, 120, 121, 124, 128, 138, 139, 169, 195, 196, 202, 203, 221, 230, 251, 252, 253, 263, 264, 269, 274, 275, 277, 310, 352

State Information Office 215

State of Emergency 156, 166, 167, 168, 178, 192, 205, 206, 209, 211, 225, 226, 241, 244, 245, 246, 247, 248, 249, 251, 254, 255, 299

State Security Agency 322, 326

State Security Council Secretariat 230

Steenhuisen, J. 371, 372

Stellenbosch University xi, 149, 184, 197, 214, 391, 392, 393, 394, 395, 396, 397, 406, 409, 416, 422, 435, 436, 438, 443, 444, 447

Steward, D. 229, 230

Steyn Commission, 1980, 1982 200, 207, 208, 209, 233

Steyn, R. 269, 310

Stirk, C.H. ix

St. Leger, F.Y. 93

Stow, G.W. 3

Strategic Communications Branch (Stratcom) 230, 348, 368, 369

Strijdom, J.G. 124, 134, 143, 156, 157, 162, 163, 166, 179, 185, 186, 299

Stringfellow, T. 49, 80, 82

Struggle 167, 172, 239, 241, 242, 244, 248, 254, 255, 256, 258, 331, 347, 359, 399, 405, 406, 412, 416, 417, 439, 443, 445

Subramoney, M. 194, 224

Suid-Afrikaan, Die 245, 248

Sunday Express 144, 157, 162, 202, 203, 238, 248, 264

Sunday Independent, The 285, 370

Sunday Post 194, 196, 215, 217, 224, 232, 234, 240

Sunday Star 196

Sunday Sun 277

Sunday Times 116, 117, 118, 119, 130, 132, 133, 137, 139, 140, 144, 176, 177, 196, 197, 219, 224, 225, 238, 253, 261, 263, 264, 284, 299, 301, 331, 342, 343, 348, 352, 353, 370, 431

Sunday Tribune 144, 196

Sunter, C. 315, 427, 446

Suppression of Communism Act, 1950 154, 164, 178, 217

Survé, I. xi, 331, 392, 437

Sweepslag 263

Swellengrebel, H. 39

Switzer, L. x, 85, 391, 402, 404, 407, 408, 410, 411, 412, 413, 414, 419, 420, 421, 435, 436, 441, 442, 445, 446, 447, 448

Syferfontein 212

T

Taco Kuiper Award 339

Tambo, O. 211, 220, 221, 226, 255

Tas, A. 31, 36, 37

Tatler 112

Telkom 281, 304

Terreblanche, S. 248, 392

Thaele, J. 138
Thamm, M. 220, 355, 432, 446
Theal, G.M. 35, 37
Thema, S. 52, 147
Themba, C. 170
Theron Commission 197
Thloloe, J. 193, 195, 225, 235, 327, 354, 429, 446, 461
Thom, H.B. 36, 396, 447
Thompson, L.M. 216
Thomson, Lord 145, 197
Thucydides 9, 10
Time 225, 278, 346, 392, 395, 431, 436, 437, 438
Times Media Ltd. 138
Times, The 68, 91, 123
Tiso Blackstar 342, 352
Tomaselli, K. x, 446
Tomaselli, R. x, 391, 410, 412, 420, 423, 443, 446
Torch 231, 242
Total Onslaught x, 24, 153, 183, 198, 203, 206, 209, 239, 258, 271, 391, 394, 395, 396, 398, 399, 400, 401, 402, 403, 404, 405, 406, 407, 408, 409, 410, 411, 412, 413, 414, 415, 416, 417, 418, 419, 420, 421, 423, 440
Total Strategy 24, 198, 203, 208
To the Point 201, 202, 203
Township Mail 196
Transcript 123
Transvaal Advertiser 113
Transvaal Critic 106
Transvaal Leader 112, 115, 116, 117, 119, 134, 149
Transvaal Mercury Argus 112
Transvaal Mining Argus 112
Transvaal Truth 112
Treason Trial 168
Treurnicht, A. 180, 181, 182, 192
Tricameral Parliament 182, 228
True Love 171, 232, 234, 236
Trump, D. 337, 347, 348, 349, 357, 358, 368, 375
Truth and Reconciliation Commission 247, 283, 285, 287, 416, 425, 445
Tsala Ea Batho 149
Tsala Ea Becoana 149
Tsedu, M. 26, 224, 225, 275, 282, 325, 396, 428, 447
Tugwana, G. 252
Tugwana, J. 193, 235

Turner, T. 5, 392
Tutu, D. 226, 418, 447
Twitter 282, 320, 322, 329, 341, 354, 356, 357, 358, 359, 360, 367, 432, 440
Tyson, H. 206, 225, 253, 254, 257, 258, 269, 310, 415, 421, 447

U

UBJ 194, 195, 232
UDF 172, 239, 241, 242, 244, 254, 255
Ukhozi Investments 270
UmAfrika 276
Umkhonto we Sizwe/MK 167, 168, 335
Umlindi We Nyanga 138
Umrabulo 283
Umshumayeli Wendaba 86
Umteteli Wa Bantu 146
UN 15, 17, 19, 169, 184, 257, 268, 321, 369, 394, 431, 432
United Party (UP) 129, 134, 136, 139, 144, 146, 150, 151, 157, 161, 190, 218, 228
University of the Western Cape 348
Unlawful Organisations Act, 1960 227
UN Universal Declaration of Human Rights 15, 21, 268, 296, 378, 394

V

Vaderland, Die 128, 134, 137, 143, 163, 179, 180, 181, 198, 212
Vale, L. 344
Van de Graaff, C. 8, 40
Van den Bergh, H. 203
Van der Kemp, J.T. 52
Van der Merwe, N. 199
Van der Merwe, S. 230
Van der Stel, S. 36, 397
Van der Stel, W.A. 37
Van der Vyver, J.D. 216
Van de Sandt, B.J. 41
Van Loggerenberg, J. 370, 371
Van Niekerk, C.A. 141
Van Plettenberg, J. 8, 40
Van Reenen, R. 202
Van Rhyn, A.J.R. 159
Van Riebeeck, J. 8
Van Rooyen, K. 229, 429, 447
Van Wyk, P. 351, 354, 367, 447
VBS Bank 351, 367
Venter, S. 332, 430
Veritas 241
verkramp 180, 185, 212
verlig 180, 181, 185, 212

Verwoerd, H.F. 124, 134, 137, 143, 149, 156,
    157, 166, 169, 171, 179, 180, 185, 186,
    188, 190, 198, 214, 299, 405, 411, 444
Verzamelaar, De 75, 78
Viljoen, C. 256, 269
Viljoen, J.H. 163
Viljoen Task Group 269
Vlakplaas 285
Vlok, A. 220
VOC 7, 8, 31, 32, 33, 35, 36, 37, 39, 40, 45, 78
Voice 98, 104, 138, 148, 152, 172, 173, 179,
    234, 240, 277, 289, 299, 394, 424, 426,
    440
Volk, Het 46, 74, 98, 100, 108, 113, 114, 117,
    127, 129, 133, 134, 157, 180, 198, 403
Volksblad, Die/Het 74, 107, 136, 142
Volksbode, De 107
Volkskas 141, 179
Volkstem, Die 98, 100, 102, 105, 107, 108
Volksvriend, Die 74, 100, 107
Voltaire 43, 221
Vongai, C. 291
Voorbrand Publikasies 248
Vorster, B.J. 153, 168
Vorster, K. 184, 185
Vosloo, T. vii, 171, 172, 180, 209, 210, 211,
    214, 220, 237, 238, 270, 292, 413, 447
Vrye Weekblad 226, 239, 245, 248, 261, 263,
    287, 334, 419, 420, 433, 436, 437, 438
Vuk'uzenzele 282

W

Waddell, G. 218
Walker, A. 42, 46, 47, 48, 391, 435
Wallace, E. 115, 116, 128
Washington Star 202, 203
Wasserman, H. 308, 395, 406, 422, 427, 447
Weaver, T. 221
Weber, M. 11
Weber, P. 159
Week, Die 133
Weekend World 171, 192, 194, 195, 196, 217,
    231, 232, 233, 244, 247, 253
Weekly Mail & Guardian, The 249
Weekly Mail, The 250, 420, 442
Weekly Press 100
Weir, J. 103

Wending Publikasies 247
Wepener, W. 135, 180, 188, 407, 414, 447
Wesleyan Mission Society 86
WhatsApp 341, 354, 356, 358
White, A. 318
White, T.C. 83
Whitfield, C. xi, 392, 437
Wigston, D. 8, 392, 393, 398, 399, 400, 401,
    402, 403, 404, 407, 408, 409, 413, 415,
    416, 418, 419, 423, 424, 447
Wikipedia 342
Williams, M. 243, 252, 392, 437
Windhoek Declaration 17, 24, 25, 296, 395
Witness, The 79, 85, 96, 97, 116, 223, 310,
    401, 413, 444
Witwatersrand Advertiser 112
Woods, D. 195, 219
Woolf, D. 9, 393, 448
Worcester Standard 89
Workers' Herald 138
Workers' Unity 148
Work in Progress 246
World 171, 192, 193, 194, 195, 196, 197, 217,
    225, 231, 233, 235, 238, 240, 244, 247,
    250, 253, 317
World Association of Newspapers (WAN) 296
World Editors' Forum (WEF) 296
World Press Freedom Day 13, 24, 283, 285,
    296, 318, 350, 379, 381, 426, 428, 445
World Press Freedom Index 327, 337, 430, 434
Wright, W.K. 110

Y

Yonge, G. 41, 46, 48, 73
Youth Day 191
YouTube 321
Yutar, D. 23, 395, 397, 405, 406, 409, 448

Z

Zapiro 6, 331, 332, 341, 350, 366, 373, 392,
    447
Zenobius 4
Zille, H. 327, 429, 448
Zondo Commission 347, 357, 362, 365, 372,
    374
Zonk 147, 231
Zug, J. 168, 410, 448
Zuid-Afrikaan, De 51, 76, 77
Zuid-Afrikaansch Tijdschrift, Het 53, 75, 84

Zuma, J. 6, 290, 292, 297, 300, 303, 313, 314, 317, 318, 320, 322, 324, 325, 326, 333, 334, 335, 337, 342, 347, 349, 357, 359, 365, 375, 377, 392, 427, 430, 438, 444

Zungu, M. 252

.